Applied Multivariate Research

Applied
Multivariate
Research

Design and Interpretation

Lawrence S. Meyers
California State University, Sacramento

Glenn Gamst
University of La Verne

A. J. Guarino
Auburn University

SAGE Publications
Thousand Oaks ▪ London ▪ New Delhi

For information:

Sage Publications, Inc.
2455 Teller Road
Thousand Oaks, California 91320
E-mail: order@sagepub.com

Sage Publications Ltd.
1 Oliver's Yard
55 City Road
London EC1Y 1SP
United Kingdom

Sage Publications India Pvt. Ltd.
B-42, Panchsheel Enclave
Post Box 4109
New Delhi 110 017 India

Printed in the United States of America

Library of Congress Cataloging-in-Publication Data

Meyers, Lawrence S.
Applied multivariate research : design and interpretation / Lawrence S. Meyers, Glenn Gamst, A.J. Guarino.
    p. cm.
Includes bibliographical references and index.
ISBN 978-1-4129-0412-4 (cloth)
  1. Multivariate analysis. 2. Social sciences—Statistical methods. I. Gamst, Glenn. II. Guarino, A. J. III. Title.
HA31.3.M487 2006
300'.1'519535—dc22

                                    2005009519

07 08 09 10 9 8 7 6 5 4 3

Acquiring Editor:	Lisa Cuevas Shaw
Editorial Assistant:	Karen Gia Wong
Production Editor:	Kristen Gibson
Copy Editor:	Linda Gray
Typesetter:	C&M Digitals (P) Ltd.
Proofreaders:	Liann Lech and Kathleen Allain
Cover Designer:	Glenn Vogel

Contents

List of Figures

Chapter 3

Chapter 4

Chapter 6

Chapter 7

Chapter 11

Chapter 12

Chapter 13

Chapter 14

Chapter 15

List of Tables

Chapter 5

Chapter 6

Chapter 7

Chapter 8

Chapter 12

Chapter 13

Chapter 15

Preface

Our Intended Readers

A textbook is written with a particular audience in mind. For our audience, this is most likely your first relatively complete introduction to multivariate research design. We assume that readers have had some introductory coursework in statistics covering topics such as the normal curve, standard error, correlation, and univariate tests of statistical significance such as analysis of variance. We also assume that readers have had some instruction in research design, including topics such as nonexperimental (correlational), quasi-experimental, and experimental design.

But our intended audience is a bit narrower than that. Although there is wide variation within each of these categories, multivariate students are going to be, at a global level, either relatively mathematically oriented and mathematically sophisticated or not. Those in the first group are going to feel relatively comfortable working with matrix algebra, following and appreciating the derivation of various formulas, and so on. Those in the second group either do not possess that level of mathematical sophistication or do not wish to apply that level of analysis to understand and use multivariate design in their own work. It is primarily for this latter group of students that we have written this book.

Our intended readers will almost certainly be consumers of research. They will probably be graduate students or advanced undergraduate students who intend to read and digest the empirical research studies published in the journal literature that forms the foundation of their discipline. Increasingly, this literature will contain research results based on multivariate designs, and these students are seeking direct and structured exposure to this domain.

Our audience may also be producers of research. If they are in a graduate program, they may be working as research assistants to or as collaborators with faculty members; alternatively, they may be facing the prospect of conducting a multivariate study for their master's thesis or doctoral dissertation. Or perhaps they are professionals who have completed their formal education and are working in a research or clinical setting. Their training may not have included a course in multivariate design that easily translates into meeting their current needs, and they may wish to gain a conceptual understanding of the designs covered in this book so that they can implement some studies on their own.

We place no limitations on the disciplines represented by our readers. The research designs covered here are transportable across most areas that evaluate or attempt to understand some aspect of human functioning. These designs are almost infinitely customizable to fit a particular subject matter. For example, a multivariate analysis of variance design can be applied to test differences among (a) clinical groups for psychologists, nurses, and other health professionals; (b) school districts or instructional methods for educational researchers; (c) community involvement programs for urban, human development, ecological, or recreational studies researchers; and so on.

Our intended readers may also want or need to know how to carry out the statistical analyses for these procedures. Multivariate statistical analysis is, for the most, part performed these days by computer packages. If you wish to learn the mechanics of executing these analyses, then the companion SPSS chapters associated with the multivariate design chapters are for you and you can consult the companion chapters directly. If running these procedures is not on your current agenda, then you can scan or skip these companion chapters at your discretion.

We also assume that although our readers may not want a mathematical treatment of the multivariate topics that we present, neither do they want a "one-page summary" of each technique. We therefore make an effort to discuss most of the topics a bit beyond what we consider to be the very surface level of coverage.

Our mathematical and statistical treatment of the multivariate topics covered in this book was written intentionally at a rudimentary level. Hence, we do not treat the material at the level of matrix algebra or formula derivation. Does this mean that there are no numbers in this book? No, there are plenty of them—correlation matrixes, factor coefficients, and the like. They are important and illustrate the concepts explained in our accompanying narration. Do we present any equations in this book? Yes, certain equations are either critical to or, in our view, will aid in the understanding of the particular concept we are addressing at the time. Do we cover statistical procedures in this book? Absolutely. The bulk of this book presents the rationales, dynamics, and interpretations of these multivariate statistical procedures—we simply attempt to do so in a narrative and conceptual manner.

At the same time, we do not regard this book as a "dumbed-down" version of a "real" multivariate statistics text even though we do not present the mathematical foundation of the analyses. On the contrary, we attempt to convey a solid conceptual understanding of these designs at a level sufficient to provide some reasonable depth of comprehension to the readers. Thus, we consider the use of plain, straightforward, and readable English to be compatible with the idea that it is still possible to discuss multivariate design topics at some level of depth and sophistication.

The Approach Used in the Book

The title of this book, *Applied Multivariate Research: Design and Interpretation,* identifies what this book attempts to address and, by omission, what the book does not presume to address.

Design and Interpretation

Our focus is on the design and interpretation of research. Our goals include providing the basis for students to (a) choose the proper statistical analysis, (b) interpret the results of their own research, and (c) be competent and informed readers of the research literature where the results of others are presented. Those skills, applied at the completion of the data analysis, complement the ability to carefully and appropriately design the research in the first place; thus, another goal is to provide some guidance in research design. Research design skills, in turn, allow students at least in part to evaluate the adequacy of the studies they are reading in the journal literature. We also try to teach these skills within a more concrete application environment rather than focusing on the abstract designs themselves.

The Issue of Statistics

Notice that the term *statistics* does not appear in our title. We do not claim this primer to be a traditional statistics textbook in the sense that we stay away from a mathematical treatment of the subject matter. That said, it must be recognized that statistics and the design and interpretation of research go together. Very commonly, the research designs that we talk about are either the very names of the statistical procedures we use to analyze the data (e.g., a multiple regression design) or they directly point to the statistical procedure (e.g., a two-way between-subjects design implies that researchers will use analysis of variance to analyze the data).

Our Applied Approach

We focus on applying the information we are conveying in at least two ways. First, we want to give readers the opportunity to see, in a concrete way, how they would go about performing the data analysis. We therefore provide for each of our design chapters a separate companion chapter focusing on running SPSS. These companion chapters allow readers the opportunity to skip the performing element if it is not immediately relevant to their needs. If it is important for them to learn how to run the analysis, having this information in a separate chapter allows them to focus on the statistical analysis once they have already assimilated the conceptual underpinnings of the design, which are covered in the first chapter of the companion set.

As a second application strategy, we provide at the end of each SPSS chapter an example of how to write the results of the analysis. Even if our readers will infrequently need to write such results, it is very possible that they will read such narratives in the research literature. Seeing in a concrete way how to go from a printout to a narrative presentation of the results will facilitate their reading of the journals.

Acknowledgements

There are many people who deserve thanks for helping us putting this book together. Among these are the following.

Students in Glenn Gamst's graduate multivariate research courses provided energetic and useful feedback on versions of some of our early chapters and on near-final versions as well. Viewing the chapters through the eyes of these students was a very enlightening experience.

Five anonymous reviewers spent a great deal of time and patience critiquing the last complete draft of all the chapters. Their kind words and keen insights provided very thoughtful and useful suggestions for improving the presentation of the material. We incorporated virtually all of their feedback in preparing final copy.

The staff at Sage, led by our editor Lisa Cuevas Shaw, joined with us in our vision for this book and provided support to us when it was needed. Karen Wong and Margo Crouppen have been very helpful and supportive as we moved into the Sage production process. Linda Gray did a superb job as our copy editor; we are very grateful for her competence and conscientiousness throughout the work. Finally, Kristen Gibson has been our production editor on this project; she responded to all of our questions quickly and efficiently and worked diligently to make the final stages run as smoothly as possible.

But the most significant person to acknowledge and thank is Elita Burmas, who functioned as research and technical analyst, graphic designer, and archivist in the preparation of our chapters. With a psychology master's degree from California State University, Sacramento emphasizing quantitative methods, Elita was able to bring our SPSS material from three different computer systems seamlessly into a single presentation even if it meant repeating the analyses on her own system. She also drew all of the figures that we created and formatted into APA style all of the tables that are not SPSS output. Further, she continuously formatted the copy manuscript to prepare it for publication. Elita did all of this with high levels of skill, grace, enthusiasm, and warmth throughout this entire process, and we will be forever grateful for her participation in this project.

CHAPTER 1

An Introduction to Multivariate Design

The Univariate and Bivariate Domain

This book is about multivariate designs. Such designs as a class can be distinguished from the univariate and bivariate designs with which readers are likely already familiar. Here is an example of a univariate design. Assume that we designed an experimental study with a single independent variable and one dependent variable. For example, perhaps we wished to study the effect of room color (white vs. light blue) on study effectiveness as measured by the number of correct responses made to a multiple-choice test administered on a computer. This is considered to be a univariate design because, to oversimplify the situation for the moment, there is only one dependent variable.

Next, consider a simple correlation design with only two measures. Sometimes these variables are referred to as the *predictor variable* and the *outcome variable* because there is no experimental treatment under the control of the researchers. However, an equally viable argument can be made to dispense with such labels altogether in correlation designs, simply calling them dependent or measured variables and referring to one as the *X* variable and referring to the other as the *Y* variable (Keppel, Saufley, & Tokunaga, 1992, p. 460).

Here is an example of a bivariate design. By administering standardized paper-and-pencil inventories to a sample of individuals, we can quantitatively assess their current levels of self-esteem and depression. The data can then be analyzed using a Pearson product-moment correlation statistical procedure. This simplified example represents a bivariate analysis because the design consists of exactly two dependent or measured variables.

The Tricky Definition of the Multivariate Domain

Some Alternative Definitions of the Multivariate Domain

To be considered a multivariate research design, the study must have more variables than are contained in either a univariate or bivariate design. Furthermore, some subset of these variables must be analyzed together (combined in some manner). For example, let's revisit our hypothetical study of the effect of room color on study effectiveness. As we described it a moment ago, the dependent variable was the number of correct responses on a multiple-choice test. For the present illustration, let's assume that we had structured the situation with an equal emphasis placed on correct responses and speed of responding. For each participant, we would obtain two measures, number of correct responses and speed of responding. Without worrying about the details of how we would do this, it is possible to consider combining these two measures into a single composite measure that might be interpreted to reflect performance efficiency. This combining of variables (two dependent variables in this case) into a composite would bring us into the realm of a multivariate design.

To qualify for the label *multivariate design*, variables must be combined together. But which kinds of variables are to be combined is far from agreed on. Some authors, such as Stevens (2002), count only dependent variables, as in our example, suggesting that a multivariate study must combine together "several" (i.e., more than two) dependent variables. But such a definition puts Stevens in the awkward situation of excluding certain designs that most authors, himself included, would incorporate in a multivariate statistics book. In his own words,

> Because we define a multivariate study as one with several dependent variables, multiple regression (where there is only one dependent variable) and principal components analysis would not be considered multivariate techniques. However, our distinction is more semantic than substantive. Therefore, because regression and components analysis are so important and frequently used in social science research, we include them in this text. (p. 2)

Other researchers, such as Tabachnick and Fidell (2001b), opt to be rather inclusive in their definition of multivariate designs. But their inclusiveness can also get them into some difficulty. To qualify as a multivariate design, Tabachnick and Fidell require that more than one of each type of variable must be combined: "With multivariate statistics, you simultaneously analyze multiple dependent and multiple independent variables. This capability is important in both nonexperimental . . . and experimental research" (p. 2).

The problem with this definition is analogous to what Stevens (2002) faced: Multiple regression, which has only one dependent variable, and principal components analysis, where the multiple variables are traditionally not thought of as dependent variables, appear to be excluded from this definition. Because Tabachnick and Fidell (2001b) argue that you need to simultaneously analyze multiple dependent and independent variables, they, like Stevens, would ordinarily omit certain multivariate topics from their book. But analogous to Stevens's strategy, Tabachnick and Fidell do not let their definition prevent them from covering topics that are ordinarily treated in multivariate texts.

Our Characterization of the Multivariate Domain

Following the lead of Hair, Anderson, Tatham, and Black (1998) and Grimm and Yarnold (2000), we believe that a good way to think about multivariate research is to maintain that the analysis involves combining together variables to form a composite variable. The most common way to combine variables is by forming a linear composite where each variable is weighted in a manner determined by the analysis.

The general form of such a weighted composite is in the form of an equation or function. Each variable in the composite is symbolized by the letter X with subscripts used to differentiate one variable from another. A weight is assigned to each variable by multiplying the variable by this value; this weight is referred to as a *coefficient* in many multivariate applications. Thus, in the expression $w_2 X_2$, the term w_2 is the weight that X_2 is assigned in the weighted composite; w_2 is called the coefficient associated with X_2. A weighted composite of three variables would take this general form:

$$\text{weighted composite} = w_1 X_1 + w_2 X_2 + w_3 X_3$$

These weighted composites are given a variety of names, including *variates, composite variables,* and *synthetic variables* (Grimm & Yarnold, 2000). Variates are therefore not directly measured by the researchers in the process of data collection but are created or computed as part of or as the result of the multivariate data analysis. We will have quite a bit to say about composite variables (variates) throughout this book.

Variates may be composites of either independent or dependent variables, or they may be composites of variables playing neither role in the analysis. Examples where the analysis creates a variate composed of independent variables are multiple regression and logistic regression designs. In these designs, two or more independent variables are combined together to predict the value of a dependent variable. For example, the number of delinquent acts performed by teenagers might be found to be predictable from the number of hours per week they play violent video games, the number of hours per week they spend doing homework (this would be negatively weighted because more homework time would presumably predict fewer delinquent acts), and the number of hours per week they spend with other teens who have committed at least one delinquent act in the past year.

Multivariate analyses can also create composites of dependent variables. The classic example of this is multivariate analysis of variance. This general type of design can contain one or more independent variables, but there must be at least two dependent variables in the analysis. These dependent variables are combined together into a composite, and an analysis of variance is performed on this computed variate as in the case of combining number of correct responses and speed of responding in the study of room color mentioned above. The statistical significance of group differences on this variate (performance efficiency in this example) is then tested by a multivariate F statistic (in contrast to the univariate F ratio that you have studied in prior coursework).

Sometimes variables do not need to play an explicit role of being either independent or dependent and yet will be absorbed into a weighted linear composite in the statistical analysis. This occurs in principal components and in factor analysis, where we attempt to identify which variables (e.g., items on an inventory) are associated with a particular underlying dimension, component, or factor. These components or factors are linear composites of the variables in the analysis.

The Importance of Multivariate Designs

The importance of multivariate designs is becoming increasingly well recognized. It also appears that the judged utility of these designs seems to be growing as well. Here are some of the advantages of multivariate research designs over univariate research designs as argued by Stevens (2002):

1. Any worthwhile treatment will affect the subjects in more than one way. . . .

2. Through the use of multiple criterion measures we can obtain a more complete and detailed description of the phenomenon under investigation. . . .

3. Treatments can be expensive to implement, while the cost of obtaining data on several dependent variables is relatively small, and maximizes information gain. (p. 2)

A similar argument is made by Harris (2001):

> However, for very excellent reasons, researchers in all of the sciences—behavioral, biological, or physical—have long since abandoned sole reliance on the classic univariate design. It has become abundantly clear that a given experimental manipulation . . . will affect many somewhat different but partially correlated aspects of the organism's behavior. Similarly, many different pieces of information about an applicant . . . may be of value in predicting his or her . . . [behavior], and it is necessary to consider how to combine all of these pieces of information into a single "best" prediction. (p. 11)

In summary, there is general consensus about the value of multivariate designs for two very general reasons. First, we all seem to agree that individuals generate many behaviors and respond in many different although related ways to the situations they encounter in their lives. Univariate analyses are, by definition, able to address this level of complexity in only a piecemeal fashion because they can examine only one aspect at a time.

In the simple univariate experiment we described earlier testing the effect of room color on learning, for example, the dependent measure was exam score. But how fast individuals responded to the questions shown on the computer screen, how many questions they answered correctly, and (to add still another dependent variable) even how confident they were in their answers to those questions could also have been evaluated. This information might have contributed to a more complete understanding of the learning experience of those individuals.

All three of these measures would most likely be correlated with each other to a certain degree and all three would most likely tap into somewhat different but related aspects of the participants' responding. Together, they may have provided a more complete picture of the learners' behavior than any one of them in isolation. This study, originally structured as a univariate design, could thus be transformed into a multivariate study with the addition of other dependent variables.

The second reason why the field appears to have reached consensus on the importance of multivariate design is that we hold the causes of behavior to be complex and multivariate. Thus, predicting behavior is best done with more rather than less information. Most of us believe that several reasons explain why we feel or act as we do. For example, the degree to which we strive to achieve a particular goal, the amount of empathy we exhibit in our relationships, and the likelihood of following a medical regime may depend on a host of factors rather than just a single predictor variable. Only when we take into account a set of relevant variables—that is, when we take a multivariate approach—have we any realistic hope of reasonably accurately predicting the level—or understanding the nature—of a given construct. This, again, is the realm of multivariate design.

The General Organization of the Book

The domain of multivariate research design is quite large, and selecting which topics to include and which to omit is a difficult task for authors. Our choices are shown below. To facilitate presenting this material, we used two organizational tactics. First, we grouped the sets of chapters together based on the nature of the variate—the composite variable—computed in the process of performing the multivariate analysis. Second, we generated introductory univariate or bivariate chapters to lead off the first three chapter groups. This was done partly to serve as a refresher to readers and partly to serve as a way of framing certain concepts treated in the multivariate chapters in that group. We end this chapter with a more detailed description of the various parts of this book.

Part I: Foundations

The chapters in this part of the book introduce readers to the foundations or cornerstones of designing research and analyzing data. Our first chapter—the one that you are reading—discusses the idea of multivariate design and addresses the structure of this book. The second chapter on fundamental research concepts covers both some basics that you have learned about in prior courses and possibly some new concepts and terms that will be explicated in much greater detail throughout this book. The following chapters on data screening are applicable to all the procedures we cover later and so are placed as separate chapters in this beginning part. They cover ways to correct data entry mistakes, how to evaluate assumptions underlying the data analysis, and how to handle missing data and outliers.

Part II: The Independent Variable Variate

Some multivariate research designs form composites of independent variables. These designs typically have to do with predicting a value of a dependent variable. An initial chapter on bivariate correlation and simple linear regression leads this group. This chapter is included to provide readers with an opportunity to review material that they have probably covered in previous coursework so that they have a solid foundation for the multivariate chapters that follow. Multiple regression uses quantitative variables as both predictors and the variable being predicted (the criterion variable), whereas logistic regression can accommodate categorical variables in these roles. Finally, discriminant analysis uses quantitative variables to predict membership in groups specified in the data file. Although one can use logistic regression for this purpose, we cover discriminant analysis here because it is one of the "classic" multivariate methods.

Multiple Regression Analysis

Multiple regression analysis is used to predict a quantitatively measured variable, called the *criterion* or *dependent* variable, by using a set of either quantitatively or dichotomously measured predictor or independent variables. It is an extension of simple linear regression where only one predictor and one criterion variable are involved. Each independent variable in the set is weighted with respect to the other predictors to form a linear composite or variate that maximizes the prediction of the criterion variable. The computed value of the variate is equal to the predicted value of the dependent variable, and the weighted composite can be thought of as a specification of the prediction model for the criterion variable.

The multiple regression procedure can be employed when we can formulate the research problem in terms of predicting a quantitatively measured variable. We might use multiple regression analysis, for example, to predict the degree of success that students experience in the first year of college. Success here is the dependent variable and might be assessed by faculty ratings, grade point average, or some other quantitative measure. Predictors, or independent variables, might include high school grade point average, scores on a standardized college entrance exam, and even some attitude measures or personality characteristics that might have been assessed just prior to the start of the academic year.

Logistic Regression Analysis

Logistic regression is conceptually similar to multiple regression in that we use a set of independent variables in combination to predict the value of a dependent variable. In logistic regression, the variable being predicted is measured on a qualitative or categorical scale; in the majority of instances, this dependent variable is dichotomous; that is, it consists of two possible values. The predictors can comprise any combination of categorical and quantitative variables. Logistic regression is more flexible than multiple regression in that it must conform to fewer statistical assumptions to be appropriately used.

One of the strengths of logistic regression is that the model it produces is not linear but instead is sigmoidal (S-shaped). This multivariate procedure therefore permits the predictors to be related to the dependent variable in a nonlinear manner. In the dichotomous dependent variable situation, the result of the procedure—what is being predicted—is the probability of the cases falling into one of the dependent variable's categories. The outcome is often expressed as an odds ratio where we may say that the odds of a case being in one category were, for example, 5.25 times greater than the chances of its being in another category.

Logistic regression can be used any time we are interested in identifying the variables associated with being in one condition over another. Such conditions, which are candidates to serve as dependent variables, are created by the individuals themselves, may be imposed by the society or culture, and could be based on a personality characteristic of the individuals or whatever. Examples of such variables include students who major in the arts versus those who major in the sciences, candidates who passed versus those who failed a state license examination, and individuals who were and were not at risk for a certain disease. Predictor variables would be chosen according to the research problem and, presumably, based on the theoretical models available at the time as well as the empirical research literature.

Discriminant Analysis

Discriminant analysis (sometimes called discriminant function analysis or multiple discriminant analysis) is a technique designed to predict group membership from a set of quantitatively measured variables. There are two types of discriminant function analysis—predictive and descriptive. In predictive discriminant analysis, the goal is to formulate a rule or model that we use to predict group membership (Huberty, 1994). The other type is descriptive discriminant analysis where the focus is the interpretation of the linear combination(s) of the independent variables to describe the differences between the groups. As we shall see later in the book, this descriptive application of discriminant function analysis is often used as a follow-up analysis to significant multivariate analysis of variance.

Discriminant analysis is similar to logistic regression in that the dependent variable is measured on a categorical scale. This categorical variable ordinarily represents groups of participants in the study. The goal of discriminant analysis is to predict the group membership of the cases using a weighted linear composite of the predictor variables. Discriminant analysis is also intimately related to multiple regression. If the same dichotomous variable is used as the criterion variable in multiple regression and as the "groups" variable in discriminant, and if the same variables are used as the predictors in both analyses, then discriminant and multiple regression analysis yield weights for the predictors that are in the same proportion to each other, thus producing exactly comparable models.

An example of predictive discriminant analysis can be found in the research of a student of one of the authors. The student was working as an intern in a facility that housed male juvenile offenders while they were extensively evaluated by a team to recommend to the court if the wards were or were not amenable to (were likely to improve as a result of undergoing) a therapeutic treatment program. The team, consisting of a cadre of health and social system professionals (e.g., psychologist, psychiatrist, social worker, case worker) administered a battery of tests, conducted numerous interviews, analyzed the history and nature of the ward's criminal behavior, and so on over a 90-day period. Files as thick as 5 or 6 inches were commonly built. At the end of the process, the team would engage in a case conference during which all the information was discussed and a "yea" or "nay" decision on treatment amenability was made.

Our student in the above example believed that there was little likelihood that all the information present in these thick files was of equal value in contributing to the amenability decision. Recognizing a research project when she saw one, the student realized that we could obtain all the information in the files for the past few years, including the decision regarding amenability, and process this data set through predictive discriminant analysis. The dependent variable that she used was the dichotomous amenability decision ("yea" or "nay"), and the predictor variables were all those in the files (intelligence score, MMPI scores, and scores on a host of variables each professional thought that it was important to assess). When the dust of the analysis settled, we identified about half a dozen variables that pretty much correctly classified the wards as well as the objective data permitted. We therefore offered the rather unpopular suggestion to the agency that it could conduct the objective part of its assessment in a couple of days rather than a couple of months. Even though the agency did not implement our suggestion, it did provide us with an interesting example of an application of discriminant analysis.

Part III: The Dependent Variable Variate

The prototypical procedure in which one forms a composite of dependent variables is multivariate analysis of variance (MANOVA). We lead off with a chapter devoted to the univariate domain of comparing means and its companion SPSS chapter. This is followed by three pairs of MANOVA chapters covering the two-group case, the case of three or more groups, and the two-way factorial design. All the latter chapters are based on between-subjects designs.

Multivariate analysis of variance (MANOVA) is an extension of the analysis of variance (ANOVA) procedure with which you are already familiar. ANOVA can involve any number of independent variables, although researchers do not ordinarily use more than three or maybe four. No matter how many independent variables are incorporated, however, an ANOVA design contains exactly one dependent variable. For this reason, ANOVAs are classified as univariate designs.

MANOVA designs differ from ANOVA designs in terms of the number of dependent variables involved in the analysis. That is, it is not unusual in many research projects to collect data on more than one dependent variable. Through the ANOVA procedure, each of these dependent variables would be placed in a separate analysis. This is not usually an appropriate strategy to use because in many cases these dependent variables are correlated. Under these circumstances, the researchers are not really performing independent analyses. In an exaggerated sense, they are repeatedly analyzing the same data under different dependent variable labels.

Using the MANOVA procedure in the above context is considered by most researchers as the more appropriate approach to the data analysis. MANOVA will form a linear composite or variate of the dependent variables, weighting them to best differentiate the groups (as represented by the independent variables). This portion of the MANOVA analysis is a descriptive discriminant analysis akin to what we have already described (although, here, the variables making up the variate play the role of dependent variables). Each case is then assigned a value on the variate, and an analysis is run using the variate as the dependent variable. The result of this analysis is a multivariate F ratio. If it is significant, separate univariate ANOVAs are computed for each of the separate dependent variables, but the error term used to evaluate the univariate F ratios is based on the multivariate analysis.

MANOVAs can be used in most situations where we have collected data on multiple dependent variables, especially if these variables are known or are believed to be related to each other. Consider the situation where an inventory containing numerous subscales has been administered to different samples of individuals in an effort to determine if they differ on these measures. The Minnesota Multiphasic Personality Inventory-2 (MMPI-2), for example, which can be thought of as a way to detect the possibility of psychopathology, contains 10 clinical scales and numerous specialized scales. As another example, the California Personality Inventory (CPI), designed to characterize normal personality, contains about a dozen and a half personality scales. Rather than performing 10 separate ANOVAs on the MMPI-2 scales or 17 separate analyses on the CPI, or 27 separate analyses if both inventories were used in the same study, it is not only more appropriate but also substantially more efficient to run one or two MANOVAs on the entire set of dependent variables.

Part IV: The Emergent Variate

The chapters in this group are all concerned with, informally speaking, factor analysis. We say "informally" because in everyday parlance, the term *factor analysis* is used by many nonstatisticians in a generic manner. Actually, it is worth distinguishing between principal components analysis and factor analysis, which we do in the first and second chapter pairs of this section.

Principal components analysis and factor analysis are often thought of as data reduction techniques. They both tap into the idea that a relatively large set of variables measured in a research study, such as items on some inventory, reflect a smaller number of underlying themes than there are items. Both techniques are used to identify the degree to which the variables are associated with these themes.

Both principal components and factor analysis fall under the auspices of exploratory approaches to the analysis of the data. Confirmatory factor analysis takes a different approach, and this is covered in the second chapter pair of this group. Exploratory factor analysis is run through SPSS, but confirmatory analysis, because it is an application of structural equation modeling, must be performed in an alternative program. We have illustrated this and the other structural equation modeling techniques covered in the next group of chapters by using the AMOS program, but other programs (LISREL, EQS, and even SAS) can run these analyses as well.

Exploratory Factor Analysis

Factor analysis begins the chapters devoted to structural analysis. Exploratory factor analysis attempts to summarize or identify the few themes or dimensions that underlie a relatively larger set of variables. These underlying dimensions are the factors that emerge from the analysis, thus revealing the structure of the set of variables. Each factor is a weighted linear composite on which all the variables in the analysis are represented. Different factors are distinguished based on the different patterns of weights assigned to the variables. The number of factors in the solution that is ultimately accepted depends, within certain limits, on the educated judgment of the researchers. More factors will account for a greater percentage of the variance and thus lose less information in the summarization process, but fewer factors will often offer a more efficient and reasonable interpretation. This tension makes for an interesting dynamic in the interpretation of factor analytic results.

We find exploratory factor analysis extensively used in test development. When researchers perform a content analysis of the domain they are targeting for a test or inventory, they will usually generate a relatively large number of items in an attempt to represent it on paper. But if we generate, say, even 60 items, common sense tells us that we are probably not tapping into 60 separate and independent features of the domain. Rather, it is almost certainly true that one subset of items might be more concerned about one particular dimension, another subset of items might be more focused on another dimension, and so forth. Factor analysis can recognize such differential emphases by examining the relationships between the responses given to the items. These differential relationships are synthesized as factors at the end of the analysis.

Confirmatory Factor Analysis

Exploratory factor analysis is analogous to an inductive approach in that researchers employ a bottom-up strategy by developing a conclusion from specific observations. That is, they determine the interpretation of the factor by examining the variate that emerged from the analysis. Confirmatory factor analysis represents a deductive approach in that researchers are predicting an outcome from a theoretical framework, a strategy that can be thought of as a top-down approach.

Confirmatory factor analysis seeks to determine if the number of factors and their respective measured variables support what is expected from the theoretical framework—that is, if the proposed model fits the data. The measured variables (also known as *indicator* or *observed* variables) are selected on the basis of prior theory, and confirmatory factor analysis is employed to determine if the variables correlate with their respective factor(s). These factors are latent (unobservable) constructs known to us through their indicators or observable variables.

In confirmatory factor analysis, the researchers presumably already know the construct represented by the factor at the start of the analysis (just the opposite of exploratory factor analysis). Based on this knowledge, they can posit which of the indicator variables are associated with each factor. Thus, exploratory analysis is used as a theory-generating procedure, whereas confirmatory procedures are employed as a theory-testing procedure (Stevens, 2002).

As an example of confirmatory factor analysis, consider the situation where a researcher has developed an inventory based on the premise that the construct under study can be represented by three distinguishable aspects and that these have been built into the item creation process. Each item as it was developed was tied back to one of the three aspects of the construct that it represented. The inventory is then administered to a large sample representing a population to which the construct is applicable, and it is now time for the results to be factor analyzed. Without a theoretical framework in place, an exploratory factor analysis would be in order. But here, there is a sufficiently specified theoretical framework to permit the researchers to perform a confirmatory factor analysis. The model would specify one latent variable (factor) that was driving (causing, predicting, tied to) one set of items, a second latent variable causally related to a second set of items, and a third latent variable related to a third set of items. The analysis would then indicate how well the data fit the model.

Part V: Model Fitting

In Part V, we focus on model-fitting techniques. By means of these techniques, researchers hypothesize specific causal relationships between variables and then test them to determine how well they fit the data. If the model contains only measured variables, the model-fitting procedure is labeled as *path analysis;* if the model contains latent variables, the model-fitting procedure is called *structural equation modeling.*

Once a model is proposed (i.e., relationships between the variables have been hypothesized), a correlation-covariance matrix is created. The estimates of the relationships between the variables in the model are calculated using the maximum likelihood estimation procedure. Maximum likelihood estimation attempts to estimate the values of the parameters that would result in the highest likelihood of the actual data to the proposed model. These methods often require iterative solutions.

The first pair of chapters in this section presents causal modeling from a multiple regression, path analysis, and structural equation modeling perspective. Very often, alternative models are proposed and researchers are interested in determining which are better able to represent their data—that is, which hypothesized models are better fits to the observed data. The second and final pair of chapters in this section talks about how to compare the alternative models that have been used in confirmatory factor analysis and causal modeling.

Causal Models

Causal modeling calls for researchers to hypothesize rather specifically about the causal (or predictive) relationships that exist between the variables in their research study. If the set of variables is all measured variables, then researchers develop a path model by drawing a path diagram and performing a path analysis. If the model contains latent constructs, then structural equation modeling is used. In both cases, the object of the analysis is to estimate the strength of the relationships between variables as they are structured or arrayed in the model. It is then possible to gauge how well that model fits the data.

Research using causal modeling begins with an arrangement of the variables in diagram form showing a model in which thus and such variables are thought to produce (cause, predict) others, which, in turn, can be hypothesized as causes of still other variables. These models are then translated into a series of linear equations that allows researchers to assess direct effects and indirect effects on a variable. An indirect effect simply means that a variable influences another variable through a mediating variable. For example, one of our students conducted research on predictors of physical exercise. Her results indicated that body self-esteem did not directly influence the amount of physical exercise in which people engaged on a weekly basis; however, body self-esteem did influence exercise attitude, which in turned influenced amount of physical exercise.

Causal inferences are depicted by arrowed lines, and the intent of the analysis is to compute the various coefficients representing each variable-to-variable relationship. Path analysis, performed when all the variables are measured variables, can be accomplished through multiple regression analyses or from a program designed to do model fitting; when latent constructs are included in the model, the analysis must be done as a structural equation model. In any case, the resulting coefficients indicate the relative strength of the path connecting two variables.

Causal modeling is not a substitute for experimental design; that is, it does not involve an attempt to establish the necessary and sufficient conditions that enable researchers to infer that changes in the independent variable caused corresponding changes in the dependent variable. In fact, these sorts of analyses are typically performed on data that have been collected through a correlation methodology in which the variables covary together in the sample with no active intervention by the researchers. Nonetheless, causal modeling allows us to examine hypothesized causal relationships and evaluate alternative models.

We can apply this general approach to a wide range of research arenas. As an example, consider the construct of life satisfaction. We can hypothesize that the degree to which people feel satisfied with their lives may be a function of the depth of friendships they have made, how much love they feel toward others, the degree to which they have met their life goals, their personal wealth, their level of spirituality, their level of education, and so forth. These variables themselves may be able to be placed into some hypothesized causal hierarchy. For example, how much love they feel toward others may predict the depth of the friendships they have made, which, in turn, may predict higher levels of life satisfaction. Alternative causal models could be constructed and compared with each other through the path analysis procedure.

Comparing Models

Model fitting is a tool that allows researchers to build their models and then test them to determine how well they fit the data. It is also possible and in many instances very reasonable for researchers to have generated a couple of different models, either in the confirmatory factor analysis or in the causal model arena, that they wish to compare. Model-fitting techniques allow the researchers not only to see how well each model fits the data but also to compare the alternative models with each other.

For example, one of us was the principal investigator developing a new instrument to assess multicultural competence of mental health practitioners. The research team reviewed the current literature and available instruments and was confronted with the conflict of whether multicultural competence would best be described as a three- or four-factor ability. Employing confirmatory factor analysis, the three- and four-factor models were compared, and the results supported the four-factor model.

In addition, it may be useful to determine whether a model developed in one context is applicable, generalizable, or exportable to another context. The applicability of a model across contexts is referred to as *model invariance.* For example, researchers might very well be interested in examining such invariance across samples representing different populations (e.g., women and men, younger and older individuals) or in determining if a given theoretical factor structure (e.g., the five-factor model of personality) is as good a fit to data collected under Inventory A as under Inventory B. We cover the topic of comparing models in the last pair of chapters.

Recommended Readings

Aiken, L. S., West, S. G., Sechrest, L., & Reno, R. R. (1990). Graduate training in statistics, methodology, and measurement in psychology: A survey of PhD programs in North America. *American Psychologist, 45,* 721–734.

Grimm, L. G., & Yarnold, P. R. (2000). Introduction to multivariate statistics. In L. G. Grimm & P. R. Yarnold (Eds.), *Reading and understanding more multivariate statistics* (pp. 3-21). Washington, DC: American Psychological Association.

CHAPTER 2

Some Fundamental Research Design Concepts

We start our treatment of multivariate research design with a discussion of some fundamental concepts that will serve as building blocks for the design issues contained in this book. We also introduce in this chapter some advanced concepts because they are intimately related to their more basic cousins. Most of these concepts, especially those more advanced, will be revisited in greater depth in later chapters.

Samples and Populations

A population is composed of all entities fitting the boundary conditions of who or what you are intending to subsume in your research. Populations are typically made up of people meeting certain criteria. In basic behavioral science research, the population of interest is often "all humans." Some applied research may target smaller and more specific populations, such as "all breast cancer survivors" or "all senior citizens in community outreach programs."

In most situations, it is not possible to include all the population members in a research study. Instead, we select a workable number of individuals to represent the population. That set of participants in the study is the sample. Very often, the intention of the researchers is to study some process or phenomenon in the sample so that they can generalize to the population from which the sample was drawn. Generalization is one arena where research design gets interesting.

Generalizing from the sample to the population is a delicate matter, so much so that entire chapters or more in research methods textbooks are devoted to this topic. A couple of issues related to samples and populations are at least indirectly touched on in our discussions throughout this book. These are mentioned here to sensitize you to them.

One issue concerns tests of significance. Most of these tests are based on the data obtained from your sample, but they are really testing a certain hypothesis concerning the population. That hypothesis is the null hypothesis stating (a) that the sample means you are comparing represent the very same population or (b) that there is no relationship between the variables that you are studying. The null hypothesis is almost always different from the research hypothesis, which typically asserts that there will be a significant difference between the treatment conditions or that there will be a significant correlation between two variables.

The second issue that affects the generalization of the sample results to the population is attrition within the sample. Multivariate analyses are more prone to lose cases than are univariate analyses. This is true because most of the statistical procedures require participants to have valid values on all the measures. With multiple measures taken on each participant, however, it is more likely that some of them will have missing data on at least one of the measures. When a particular case has a missing value on just one measure, that case will in many instances be removed from the entire analysis. If many participants are dropped in this manner, the possibility exists that those cases remaining in the analysis will make up a subsample quite different from the sample as a whole. Under such a circumstance, conclusions based on the results of those analyses may not be properly generalized back to the original population.

Variables

It is difficult to read a textbook in research design or statistics without immediately encountering the notion of a variable. It is truly one of our fundamental concepts, and it tends to take on increasingly enriched meaning to students as they progress into more advanced coursework.

As a rather abstract but important characterization, a variable is an entity that can take on different values. These values can be, and very often are, numbers that have quantitative meaning. Examples of quantitative variables include grade point average, which can take on numerical values between 0 and 4; simple reaction time, which may generally vary from about 300 milliseconds to about 700 milliseconds; and a global assessment of functioning score, which can range from 0 to 100.

The different values that entities can take may be numbers with no quantitative meaning, such as the numbers basketball players wear on their uniforms. Values may also be names or labels for entities. Examples of these include names of people (e.g., Erin, Paul); types of animals (e.g., squirrels, skunks); and computer platforms (e.g., Mac OS X, Windows). Finally, values may represent arbitrary numerical codes in data files to stand for categories of a variable (e.g., we might code Macintosh users as 1 and PC users as 2).

All the values for these variables have been assigned through a set of rules defining a measurement operation. These measurement operations represent different scales of measurement.

Scales of Measurement

Although the essentials of measurement scales were known for some time, it was S. S. Stevens who impressed this topic on the consciousness of behavioral scientists. As Stevens (1951) tells us, he initially broached this issue in a 1941 presentation to the International Congress for the Unity of Science. He published a brief article addressing scales of measurement a few years later in *Science* (Stevens, 1946), but it was the prominent treatment of this topic in his lead chapter in the *Handbook of Experimental Psychology,* which he edited (Stevens, 1951), that most writers cite as the primary historical source.

Measurement comprises sets of rules governing the meaning of values assigned to entities. Each such set of rules defines a scale of measurement. Stevens (1951) identified four scales: nominal, ordinal, interval, and ratio in that order. Each scale includes an extra feature or rule over those in the one before it. We will add a fifth scale to Stevens's treatment—summative response scale—placing it between the ordinal and the interval scale. Very briefly, here is the essence of each.

Nominal Scales

A *nominal* scale of measurement, sometimes called a *categorical* scale or a *classification system*, has only one rule underlying its use: Different entities receive different values. There is no quantitative dimension implied here at all, no implication that one entity is in any way "more" than another. Examples of nominal scales include, as mentioned above, numbers on basketball uniforms, types of computer platforms, and arbitrary numerical codes for the categories of a variable.

Numerical coding of categorical variables is regularly done when we are entering data into an SPSS data file. Thus, in a study comparing students who enjoy reading different kinds of books for leisure, we might use a 1 to denote a preference for science fiction, a 2 to indicate a preference for mystery novels, and a 3 to signify a preference for humor. In this situation, the numeric codes do not imply anything quantitative; they are used exclusively to represent different categories of preference.

Ordinal Scales

An *ordinal* scale of measurement uses numbers exclusively. These numbers convey "less than" and "more than" information. This translates most easily to rank ordering of entities. It is possible to rank order elements on any quantitative dimension.

Entities may be ranked in the order in which they align themselves on some quantitative dimension, but it is not possible from the ranking information to determine how far apart they are on the underlying dimension. For example, if we were ranking the height of three people, the one 7 feet tall would be ranked 1, the one 5 feet, 1 inch tall would be ranked 2, and the one 5 feet tall would be ranked 3. From the ranked data, we could not determine that two of the individuals were quite close in height.

Summative Response Scales

A *summative response* scale requires respondents to assign values to entities based on an underlying continuum defined by the anchors on the scale. The numbers are ordered, typically in an ascending way, to reflect more of the property being rated. Most common are 5-point and 7-point scales. These scales originated in the classic work of Louis Thurstone in the late 1920s (1927, 1928, 1929; Thurstone & Chave, 1929) in his pioneering work to develop interval level measurement scales to assess attitudes. Based on Thurstone's time-consuming and resource-intensive scale development techniques, summative response scales were developed by Rensis Likert (pronounced "lick-ert" by the man himself) in the early 1930s to make the process more efficient (Likert, 1932), and his colleagues widely disseminated this scaling process later that decade (Likert, Roslow, & Murphy, 1934; Murphy & Likert, 1937). Derivatives of Likert's scale have become increasingly popular ever since.

An example of instructions to respondents using a summative response scale to complete a small inventory on self-esteem might be something such as this:

> Please use the following 5-point scale to indicate how true the item is for you. If the item refers to something that is *not very true* for you, you might respond with a 1 or a 2. If the item covers something that is *very true* for you, you might respond with a 4 or a 5.

Participants would then go on to rate each of a series of items on this summative response scale.

It is called a summative scale because it is possible to add (sum) the ratings together and divide by a constant (usually in the process of taking a mean) to obtain an individual's score on the inventory. We will address this in a little more detail after introducing all the scales, but we will illustrate here that the average derived from a summative response scale is meaningful. Let's say that we administered a short self-esteem inventory to a class of public policy graduate students and that one item on the inventory read, "I feel that I am a worthwhile person." Assume that items were rated on a 5-point scale with higher values indicating more endorsement of the statement. Let's further say that the mean for this item based on all the students in the class was 4.75. Is that value interpretable? Yes, it indicates that the individuals in the sample on average believed pretty strongly that the content of the item was quite true for them—namely, that they were worthwhile people.

Interval Scales

An *interval* scale of measurement has all the properties of nominal, ordinal, and summative response scales but includes one more important feature. Fixed intervals between the numbers represent equal intervals.

The most common illustration of an equal interval scale is the Fahrenheit or Celsius temperature scale. According to Stevens (1951), "Equal intervals of temperature are scaled off by noting equal volumes of expansion" (p. 27). Interval scales also have arbitrary zero points. Zero degrees does not mean the absence of temperature but is set on the Celsius scale to be the temperature at which water freezes.

As was true for summative response scales, it is meaningful to average data collected on an interval scale of measurement. We may therefore say that the average high temperature in our home town last week was 51.4 degrees Fahrenheit.

Ratio Scales

A *ratio* scale of measurement has all the properties of nominal, ordinal, summative response, and interval scales but includes one more important feature. It has an absolute zero point, where zero means absence of the property. Because of this, it is possible to interpret in a meaningful way ratios of the numbers. We can thus say that 4 hours is twice as long as 2 hours or that 3 miles is half the distance of 6 miles.

Algebraic Properties of the Scales

As we suggested above, the sorts of algebraic operations or manipulations that we can legitimately perform on data obtained from each of the scales of measurement is different and will thus limit the kind of data analysis we are able to appropriately use. For example, it would be inappropriate to use the three nominal codes for reading preference noted above as a dependent variable in, say, an analysis of variance (ANOVA) that requires a quantitatively based dependent variable to yield meaningful results.

We will discuss Stevens's classic set of four scales first. Nominal measurement is not quantitatively based. Because of that, the only operations that can legitimately be performed on the data would be that of determining equality or inequality. For example, if we were going to classify entities in our world as either "organic" and "inorganic," then trees and chipmunks would be classified as organic (and thus defined as being equal or comparable in this measurement or classification system) and sand and DVDs would be classified as inorganic (and thus also defined as being equal). However, milk and pencil sharpeners would be classified differently (and thus defined as being unequal in this measurement system).

Ordinal measurement allows us to compare cases in a quantitative manner but only to the extent of making greater-than or less-than determinations. If students are ranked in terms of their height, we may say that one student is taller than another. But it would not make much sense to identify two students whose ranks were 1 and 7 and to add those ranks together (to say that their total rank was 8 makes no sense) or take an average of the two ranks (to say that their average rank was 4 likewise makes no sense).

Interval measurement, where the quantitative scale is marked in terms of equal intervals, allows us to perform adding (subtracting) and averaging to the operations of equality/inequality and greater-/less-than judgments. Thus, we can legitimately add the daily temperatures for the past 7 days and divide by 7 to arrive at a meaningful value: the average temperature for the week.

Ratio measurement, with its absolute zero point, allows us to divide and multiply values to arrive at meaningful results in addition to doing all the above-mentioned operations. This allows us to say, for example, that 4 is twice as much as 2. We cannot meaningfully interpret ratios on any of the other scales. To use temperature (interval measurement) as an example, we would be incorrect in asserting that 40 degrees is twice as warm as 20 degrees. Why? Because there is no absolute zero point to ground us. If you are not sure about this, just remember that a Celsius temperature scale is a transformation of the Fahrenheit scale. These Fahrenheit temperatures would have different values on the Celsius scale but would represent the same temperatures. And the Celsius ratio would yield a different value. This can be contrasted to the Kelvin scale of temperature where zero really does mean the absence of any heat. Using this latter scale with its absolute or true zero point, one can make ratio assertions about temperatures.

Now consider the scale we added to Stevens's list—summative response scales. It allows more operations than an ordinal scale because we can add (and subtract) its values and obtain, as we noted above, a meaningful average. Despite this feature, however, some authors (e.g., Allen & Yen, 1979) have unequivocally placed these ratings scales within the province of ordinal measures. Historically, however, the scales have been treated more liberally. Likert (1932) himself argued that his scaling technique correlated close to 1 with the results of Thurstone's (1928; Thurston & Chave, 1929) equal-appearing interval method. Guilford (1954), in his book *Psychometric Methods*, allowed summative response scales to at least have more interval-like properties than rank order scales. He states that what he called rating methods "achieve the status of ordinal measurements and only approach that of interval measurements" (p. 297). Edwards (1957) goes a bit further, stating that "if our interest is in comparing the mean attitude scores of two or more groups, this can be done with summated-rating scales as well as with equal-appearing interval scales" (p. 157). Summarizing a study by Spector (1976), Ghiselli, Campbell, and Zedeck (1981) tell us, "Of particular interest with regard to Spector's research results is the finding that a majority of existing attitude scales *do* use categories of approximately equal intervals" (p. 414). Given Ghiselli et al.'s summary, it is thus possible that people might treat summative response scales psychologically (cognitively) as approximating interval measurement.

Although it may be the case that some researchers will question the degree to which the points on a summative response scale are precisely evenly spaced, the vast majority of research published in the behavioral and social sciences over the past half century or more has used summative response scales as though they met interval properties. Researchers have added the scale points, have taken means, and have used these measurements in statistical analyses that ordinarily require interval or ratio measurement to properly interpret the results. In our view, this treatment of summative response scales is acceptable, appropriate, and quite useful.

Qualitative Versus Quantitative Measurement

It is possible to identify two categories in which we can classify subsets of these measurement scales: qualitative and quantitative measurement.

Qualitative measurement characterizes what we obtain from the nominal scale of measurement. There is no implied underlying quantitative dimension here even if the nominal values are numerical codes. Researchers sometimes call qualitative variables by other names, such as the following:

- ▶ Categorical variables
- ▶ Nonmetric variables
- ▶ Dichotomous variables (when there are only two values or categories)
- ▶ Grouped variables
- ▶ Classification variables

It is useful for our purposes to think of quantitative measurement in a somewhat restrictive manner. Although the ordinal scale certainly presumes an underlying quantitative dimension, we would generally propose thinking in terms of those scales for which it is meaningful and informative to compute a mean. With the ability to compute a mean and all that this ability implies, the gateway is open to performing a whole range of parametric statistical procedures, such as Pearson correlation and ANOVA. As we have seen, summative response, interval, and ratio scales meet this standard. Researchers sometimes call quantitative variables by other names, such as the following:

- ▶ Continuous variables (although technically, many quantitative variables can be assessed only in discrete steps even if the steps are very close together)
- ▶ Metric variables
- ▶ Ungrouped variables

Roles Played by Variables

The concept of variable is so central to research design, measurement, and statistical analysis that we find it applied in several different contexts. Especially in multivariate analyses, variables can play different roles in different analyses. Sometimes, variables can even switch roles within a single analysis. We therefore encourage you to think of variables in an analysis in this way—as entities specified by researchers to play their roles in a particular analysis, one role in this analysis, perhaps a second role in another analysis. The following sections present a preview of some groupings of these different roles.

Independent Variables, Dependent Variables, and Covariates

Independent Variables

In the prototypical experimental study, the independent variable represents the manipulation of the researchers. In a simple sense, it represents the treatment effect (what the researchers manipulate, vary, administer, and so on). Some of its features are as follows:

▶ It could have only two levels (e.g., control and experimental), but it could easily have three (e.g., control, placebo, and experimental) or more.

▶ It is only a single entity or continuum no matter how many levels represent it.

▶ It is often, but not always, based on qualitative measurement.

Variables are also specifically identified as independent variables in the analysis of data. In an ANOVA, for example, the independent variable is the "breakdown" variable or "factor"—a mean of the dependent variable is computed for each level of the independent variable. In multiple regression, the independent variables are the predictors.

Dependent Variables

In the prototypical experiment, the dependent variable represents the response or performance of the participants that is measured by the researchers. In a correlation design, all the measures can be thought of as dependent variables because researchers do not actively intervene by manipulating any variables (although we can also just think of them as measured variables). In general, dependent variables may be assessed on any scale of measurement. For the types of designs that we cover in this book, the dependent variables are almost always measured on one of the quantitative scales.

Variables are also specifically identified as dependent variables in the analysis of data. In an ANOVA, for example, it is the variance of the dependent variable that is to be explained by the independent variables in the study. It is the variable representing the behavior of the participants. That is, when we say, "The mean for girls was 3.52," what we are really saying is, "The mean value on the dependent variable for girls was 3.52." As another example, in multiple regression analysis, the criterion variable—the variable being predicted by the independent variables—is known as the dependent variable. When we say, "The mean of the criterion variable was 816," what we are saying is, "The mean of the dependent variable in the analysis was 816."

Covariates

A covariate is a variable that either actually or potentially correlates (covaries) with a dependent variable. It is important to recognize the possible influence of a covariate for at least two reasons.

The first reason it is important to know about covariates is that the relationship we observe between two dependent variables or between a dependent variable and an independent variable may lead us to an incorrect conclusion. That is, we would ordinarily infer from the existence of a relationship between two variables that they are directly associated. But that association may be mediated or caused by a third heretofore anonymous variable—the covariate.

A classic but simplified example is the relatively strong correlation between ice cream sales and crime. Higher crime rates are associated with greater quantities of ice cream being sold. Yes, the two variables are correlated; conceptually, however, they are not directly but only coincidentally associated. What mediates this relationship is the weather or the season of the year. For a variety of reasons, certain types of crimes are more likely to occur—or are facilitated by—the warmer weather during the summer months. Presumably, these crimes would take place whether or not ice cream was selling well that season (assuming that ice cream sales did not index the general economic times and complicate our simplified example).

Temperature, then, appears to mediate the relationship between ice cream sales and crime rate. It is thus a *confound* in the research design in the sense that it, too, correlates with both ice cream sales and with crime rate. If we were to include it in the design and assign it the role of a covariate in the data analysis, we would find that the correlation between ice cream sales and crime rate would be weak at best once we statistically accounted for the influence of temperature.

In the context of a regression analysis, if we were using ice cream sales to predict crime rate, we would first enter temperature as a predictor and then enter ice cream sales numbers. Temperature would function as a covariate in this analysis: It would predict as much as it could of crime rate, and ice cream sales would then be left to predict whatever variance remained.

The effects of a covariate can also be assessed in the context of ANOVA, where the analysis becomes known as an analysis of covariance (ANCOVA).

To provide you with a brief hypothetical example, consider an achievement test battery that we administer to a sample of seventh-grade girls and boys. We perform an ANOVA with gender of student as the independent variable and the score in mathematical problem solving as the dependent variable. Assume that the outcome of that analysis shows us that the girls outperform the boys.

Now we note that this test in mathematical problem solving involves verbally presented problems that the students need to reason their way through. Assume that we also know that the girls have higher scores on the verbal component of the test battery. Could their greater verbal proficiency explain the girls' superior performance on the math test? To address this question, we could perform an ANCOVA. The independent variable would be gender and the dependent variable would be mathematical problem solving, the same as in the original analysis. For the ANCOVA, we would add a third variable, verbal skill, to the analysis. Verbal skill would be assigned the role of the covariate in the analysis. We could then examine the relationship between gender and mathematical problem solving when we have statistically removed from that relationship the effects of verbal ability. Thus, it is possible for researchers to statistically control for a variable that was not controlled for in the actual research procedure.

Fluidity of the Roles

Variables can play one role in one context and another role in another context. The discussion on ANCOVA actually contained an example of this. We indicated that we already knew that the girls scored higher on verbal ability than the boys. This suggests that an ANOVA was run with gender as the independent variable and verbal ability as the dependent variable. Furthermore, gender information was collected in a correlation methodology—a test battery was administered to a sample of children and, as is typical, some demographic and biodata information was asked of them as well. Technically, gender was a dependent variable under the method used for data collection, yet it was assigned the role of an independent variable in both the ANOVA and the ANCOVA.

Between-Subjects and
Within-Subjects Independent Variables

Independent variables in experimental research can represent one of two types of operations corresponding to between- or within-subjects manipulations. You need to know the nature of each of your independent variables in the process of developing your research procedures as well as in structuring the ANOVA of your data.

Between-Subjects Variables

If the levels of the independent variables contain different participants (e.g., girls and boys; schizophrenic, depressed, and normal clients), then it is a between-subjects variable. The levels of the variable thus comprise separate groups of cases. Essentially, the scores in the groups are independent of each other.

Within-Subjects Variables

If the levels of the independent variables contain the same participants, then it is a within-subjects variable. The levels of the variable thus comprise separate conditions under which the individuals are measured. The most obvious example of a within-subjects variable is time-related measurement such as a pretest and a posttest. Here, participants are measured once before the treatment is administered and again afterward. Because individuals are measured more than once, a within-subjects variable is also known as a repeated measures variable. Essentially, the scores in the conditions are related to each other.

Latent Variables, Measured Variables, and Variates

Latent Variables

Latent variables are constructs that we identify in the context of various theories (Raykov & Marcoulides, 2000). They are not directly measured or observed and can therefore be assessed only indirectly (Schumacker & Lomax, 1996). The idea that important determiners of human behavior remain hidden from direct view is not at all new. In his analysis of dreams first published in 1900, Sigmund Freud (1938) spoke of the difference between the manifest or conscious dream content and its latent or unconscious meaning. And Edward Chase Tolman (1932), citing his classic research on latent learning done in collaboration with Honzig, distinguished between the latent or unobservable construct of learning and the manifest or observable maze performance of his laboratory rats.

Examples of latent variables abound. Learning, motivation, job success, mental health, attitude toward life, and ethnic identification are all constructs that play important roles in existent theories. One can frame the argument that understanding and attempting to assess variables such as these are the primary reasons that we try to measure human performance in the first place.

Measured Variables

Measured variables are those for which you have obtained actual data. Responses to individual inventory items, choosing this object over that one in a study of choice behavior, the number of seconds children remain in physical contact with their mothers before exploring a new environment, and an indication of whether the participants are female or male are all examples of measured variables. They are in some sense tangible in that each measured variable is directly tied to data entries in the data file. We often contrast measured variables to latent variables. Partly for that reason, measured variables are also known by other names. These names include the following:

▶ Manifest variables. With the use of the term *latent variables*, it is historically appropriate (e.g., Freud, 1938; Tolman, 1932) to use the term *manifest variables* as a label for those variables that we measure in a study.

▶ Indicator variables. Latent variables cannot be directly assessed but they can be indexed or indicated. Using the term *indicator variables* thus suggests that our measured variables are serving, at least in some sense, as proxies for (partial representations of) the latent variables of interest.

▶ Observed variables. If they are measured, these variables must by definition be observed by the researchers.

Linking Latent Variables to Measured Variables

In many forms of multivariate research design, it is either useful or mandatory to posit the existence of latent variables. That is, discussing latent variables in general would be an exercise in pure theory unless some effort was made to study them in an empirical setting. In this empirical effort, we then identify some variables that cannot be directly measured but that can serve as indicators for the constructs.

As an example, consider the broad construct of achievement applied to the outcome of the years one spends in college obtaining a bachelor's degree. One commonly used indicator variable to represent this student effort is grade point average. This is a quantitative achievement index, and it is safe to say that, over the span of thousands of students, those whose grade point averages are in the 3.7 (A–) range have probably learned more than students whose grade point average is in the 2.0 (C) range.

Many students, however, are quick to suggest that grade point average is far from a perfect indicator of performance. Students could have learned quite a bit during their college years but, for a variety of reasons, were not able to do especially well on the exams that were the bases for assigning grades. This argument is reasonable and implies that, at least up to some point, it may be useful to measure more than one indicator of a latent variable. If we had two or three valid indicators of a construct, it might be possible for us to examine what the indicators had in common in order to estimate how much measurement error we were dealing with.

Variates as Latent Variables

Latent variables can also be based on a weighted combination or composite of multiple measured variables. Such composites are called *variates*. Combining a set of manifest variables in this way yields a variable that, although it may be extremely useful, is not itself directly measured. Hence, variates are by their very nature examples of latent variables.

Even if the terminology used here is new to you, the idea that latent variables can be variates is likely to be familiar. Here is an example. We administer the 25-item Coopersmith Self-Esteem Inventory (Coopersmith, 1981) to a given sample. Items are scored 1 for every answer that affirmatively endorses an element of self-esteem (e.g., saying positive things about oneself) and 0 for every answer in the other direction. To generate an individual's self-esteem score, we add the item scores (and multiply by 4).

The self-esteem score that we obtain from the Coopersmith inventory is a linear composite of the scores on the 25 measured variables—the actual (measured, indicator) items—making up the inventory. But the composite known as self-esteem is really a latent variable or a variate. In an empirical sense, we have not directly measured self-esteem as the composite; rather, we have measured 25 separate aspects (components, facets, portions) of self-esteem and then pieced them together statistically to obtain a single value representing that construct.

Variates can also be composed of quite different measures rather than a set of related items on an inventory. For example, we could be interested in how likely students are to seek counseling from their university health center. This variate, which we might call "willingness to seek counseling" might be a function of both measured variables (e.g., family history variables, psychopathological symptoms, prior semester's grade point average) and latent variables (e.g., personality factors, cultural mores).

Much of the work accomplished by the multivariate procedures we present in this book is done to determine which measured variables will be included in the composite, how they should be weighted (combined), or both. Factor analysis, for example, attempts to identify subsets of variables that share a common theme. The factor is a weighted composite of the variables in the analysis—some receiving more weight than others; thus, the factor can be thought of as a variate or latent variable. As another example, multiple regression analysis attempts to build a model—a composite of independent variables—to best predict a dependent variable. In multiple regression, we try to determine the most effective weights to assign to the independent variables to maximize their combined predictive power. That weighted composite of independent variables is a variate as well.

Endogenous and Exogenous Variables

In the chapters discussing path analysis and structural equation modeling, it is necessary to develop a specific model of how the variables in the study are related to or are explained by one another. In such a model, some variables are hypothesized to be explained or predicted by others. The variables being explained are the *endogenous* variables. Other variables are not presumed to be explained by the model. These are the *exogenous* variables and are present only because they are used to explain the endogenous ones. For example, if we hypothesized that both gender and ethnic identification could at least partially account for how closely patients would follow medication regimens, the exogenous variables would be gender and ethnic identification, and the endogenous variable would be compliance with the regime.

Degrees of Freedom

One of the elements in summary tables for an ANOVA is *degrees of freedom*. As you may recall from a previous statistics course, dividing the sum of squares of an effect by the degrees of freedom for that effect yields the mean square value. This is important because the *F* statistic is a ratio of mean squares.

Degrees of freedom is a count of how many values in a set are free to vary given that certain restrictions are in place. The most common example to illustrate this is a small set of numbers whose mean value we identify in advance. If the set contains five numbers and a predetermined mean value, then we are free to select any four of them at our whim or fancy. However, with four numbers in place (any four numbers, by the way) by our free choice, the fifth number must be the one and only value that will give us our predetermined mean. Thus, we have four degrees of freedom in this set of five numbers.

Pagano (1986) defines degrees of freedom as well as anyone when he says that degrees of freedom "for any statistic is the number of scores that are free to vary in calculating that statistic" (p. 263). In many cases, for the reason given in the previous paragraph, we calculate degrees of freedom by subtracting one from the total count. For example, in ANOVA, the total degrees of freedom equals the number of observations minus one, between-subjects degrees of freedom equals the number of partici-pants minus one, and the degrees of freedom associated with an indepen-dent variable equals its number of levels minus one. We test the significance of the Pearson correlation by setting the degrees of freedom equal to the number of pairs minus two. This is because the Pearson r is the standard-ized regression coefficient (this is explained fully in Chapter 3A) in the straight-line regression equation and any linear function must be defined by two points; that is, two points must be fixed—they are not free to vary—in order to define any straight-line function (Ferguson & Takane, 1989, p. 207).

Statistical Significance

Statistical significance is based on the probability of obtaining a particular statistical outcome (e.g., a Pearson r or an F ratio of a given value) by chance given that there is no true relationship in the population (i.e., that the null hypothesis is true). Let's use the Pearson r to conceptually illustrate this point. We collect data to compute a Pearson correlation by acquiring two measures (X and Y) for each person in the sample. Although the researchers may hypothesize that the two measures are related, the statistical test assumes that they are not. If you recall from a prior statistics course, after computing the value of the correlation, you looked that value up on a table in the back of your statistics text to determine if it was statistically significant. Here is the rationale of how that table was generated.

Sampling Distributions

For testing the significance of the Pearson correlation, sets of X and Y scores are generated randomly and then correlated. Because they are generated randomly, there is, by definition, no relationship between these scores in the population. We therefore know that the value of the correla-tion coefficient in the population is zero; that is, we know that the null hypothesis is true. So when we randomly generate the X and Y scores, will the computed correlation for these samples always compute to zero? No—and therein lies the dilemma.

The reason the randomly generated X and Y scores will not regularly compute to zero is that they are only a sample, a subset, of the population. Because we are drawing the numbers randomly, common sense says that the numbers will not always "balance" each other exactly as they would when we drew all the values in the population. And any "imbalance" will result in a nonzero result.

Because any one random sampling could yield a value far removed from zero, we repeat this sampling over and over again. We do this enough times so that we can determine how often we obtain each value of the correlation. Granted, that's a lot of repetitions, but the result is worth the effort. What we get is a frequency distribution of correlations obtained from each of these random samples. This frequency distribution of calculated Pearson correlations is called the sampling distribution of the Pearson r.

The shape of this sampling distribution, it turns out, is a function of the size of the samples used in calculating the statistic. With relatively large sample sizes (well over 100), the sampling distribution for the Pearson correlation is approximately normal. However, with small sample sizes, its distribution can be described by the sampling distribution for the t statistic using $N - 2$ for the degrees of freedom (Jaccard & Becker, 1990). The sampling distribution for t is *leptokurtic* (somewhat more scores in the tails of the distribution and somewhat fewer toward its center). As one more example, the sampling distribution for the F ratio used in an ANOVA is quite positively skewed.

Sampling distributions show us the range and frequency of possible outcomes in computing the particular statistic when the samples have been drawn randomly from the population. Studying these distributions is very informative. We learn, for example, what the average computed value is. In the case of the Pearson correlation, that value is zero, the value corresponding to the population parameter.

But we also see that not all the computed values are zero. Many of them are pretty small, but there are some that are very large. Larger correlations, of course, indicate stronger relationships between the two variables. That observation, too, teaches us a valuable lesson. Remember, we know for sure that there is no relationship between the X and Y scores in the population. Yet, occasionally, in the process of randomly drawing sample after sample, we do obtain X and Y scores that are strongly correlated. Thus, finding a strong correlation in a data set in and of itself does not guarantee that the variables are truly correlated in the population.

The Role of Sample Size

Although the general shape of the sampling distribution of a statistic can be identified (e.g., an approximately normal distribution for the Pearson correlation based on a large sample size), its precise shape is a function of the sample size on which the statistic is based. Take the Pearson correlation we have been using. We know the true population correlation is zero. Hypothetically, if we were to sample an infinite number of X and Y pairs and calculate the correlation, it would compute to zero.

We may not be able to sample an infinite number of scores, but we could sample a gigantic number of them. Doing this many, many times will give us a sampling distribution based on this sample size. As this sample size approached infinity, the odds of obtaining a large correlation would shrink dramatically because we would be coming increasingly closer to sampling the entire population, whose true correlation value is zero.

The situation is quite different for small sample sizes. If our sample size was 10 pairs of X and Y scores (8 degrees of freedom), for example, and we randomly chose our numbers and correlated them repeatedly, we would eventually wind up with some fairly large correlation values. Because this sample size is so far from that of the entire population, we very often would not obtain a "balancing off" in our samples, and the correlation in those samples would veer off from the true value of zero.

Determination of Significance

The impact of sample size plays itself out when we look at the area under the curve of the sampling distribution. We know that for the normal curve, 95% of its area is contained within ±1.96 standard deviation units and that any score farther away from the mean lies in the 5% region (2.5% on either side of the distribution). By convention, scores in this 5% region are said to be relatively rare occurrences, rare enough for us to use this .05 criterion, or alpha level, as our default indicator of statistical significance.

We apply this alpha level rationale to the sampling distributions of most of the statistics we compute. Consider again the Pearson correlation. Because the sampling distribution is approximately normal when our sample size is large, all we need to do under those conditions is determine the value of the correlation falling 1.96 standard deviation units from the mean of the distribution. However, with smaller samples, the complication of sample size intervenes in this process. The correlation value corresponding to this critical distance is then a function of sample size.

Happily, all the calculations for all these distributions were worked out for us years ago. These days, if you use a table to look up your obtained value, all you need to do is access the proper table (e.g., the one for the Pearson correlation), find the entries for the appropriate sample size (or degrees of freedom in some tables), and determine the "critical value" for your alpha level. With an alpha level of .05, that critical value is the correlation value falling at the 5% demarcation for a sampling distribution with that sample size. A correlation of that value or higher is thus likely to occur by chance only 5% of the time in a population whose true correlation value is zero.

Similar tables have been constructed for a wide range of statistics whose distributions may or may not be normal. For example, the t distribution is leptokurtic and the F distribution is positively skewed. Nonetheless, the critical values for at least the .05 and .01 alpha levels are shown in such tables.

But most of the statistical packages such as SPSS take this process one step further. Rather than just recording the .05 and .01 alpha level critical values, these programs are able to tell you the exact probability of a particular statistical value occurring, on the assumption that the numbers generating that statistic are drawn by chance. Thus, for each statistic you calculate, you will see a corresponding probability value that has already taken into account the sample size on which it was based. If your alpha level is .05, then any probability of that value or lower (e.g., .049, .002, .000) meets your criterion for statistical significance.

Levels of Significance

It is not uncommon for students to think in terms of levels of significance and to verbalize this thinking when reporting the results of their statistical analysis. We have heard students say and write statements such as "highly significant," "very significant," or even "extremely significant." We would like to discourage these expressions.

One establishes an alpha level in advance of performing the statistical analysis because one needs to assert the confidence level for claiming a significant finding in advance of looking at the results. The traditional alpha level of .05 specifies that only statistics occurring less than 5% of the time are considered sufficiently unlikely to occur by chance alone. We thus attribute something else (something nonrandom or statistically significant and therefore worthy of our interpretation) to a statistic that should appear only 5% or less of the time. If we set our alpha level at .01, we would consider an outcome to be significant only if it would ordinarily occur 1% or less of the time.

Within this framework, a statistic either reaches or does not reach our established alpha level. We do not attribute any more "potency" to the effect because it reached the .001 level than if it reached the .05 level. Thus, an effect is either statistically significant or nonsignificant (not *insignificant*, by the way, but *nonsignificant*). What students hope to tap into when they speak of a result as highly significant is, in some sense of the term, the potency, strength, or magnitude of the effect that they have observed. As we will see in subsequent chapters, the instincts of students are right on target: The strength of the observed effect is very important to assess. However, it is assessed not by the level of significance but, rather, by a squared correlation coefficient.

Statistical Significance Versus Confidence Interval Estimation

The traditional framework of statistical significance testing has not been universally supported. An alternative conceptualization emphasizing confidence interval estimation has attracted both supporters and critics. The idea behind using confidence intervals can be illustrated in connection with group means: It is possible to assert something positive and tangible about the means of the groups in an experimental study. Borenstein (1994) provides the following example with respect to a controlled clinical trial by suggesting that it may be more useful to state that "the one-year survival rate was increased by 20 percentage points with a 95% confidence interval of 15 to 24 percentage points" (p. 411) than by simply stating that the difference between the experimental and control groups was statistically significant at the .05 level. Giving the range of values that is likely to be observed at a given level of confidence thus allows readers to appreciate the magnitude of measurement error associated with a particular research result. Armed with that information, readers can determine directly the extent to which the results are potentially useful to their applications of relevance.

One of the reasons for the increased interest in using confidence interval estimation over statistical significance testing is that the former permits researchers to attenuate their conclusions rather than forcing a dichotomous decision of the results being either statistically significant or not. In the case of medical research examining the effects of a particular treatment, for example, if the boundaries of a 95% confidence interval subsume an important potential benefit (perhaps possibly preventing a stroke in 1 of 30 patients) even if the experimental and control groups are not significantly different, then the possibility that the treatment may still be worthwhile may not have been ruled out (Guyatt et al., 1995).

The controversy surrounding this issue (the challenge to the traditional approach) is mounting, and we do not have the space here to provide a detailed account of it. The interested reader can consult Cohen (1994), Kirk (1996), Schmidt (1996), Thompson (1996), and Wilkinson et al. (1999) for further details. Suffice it to say that significance testing, if accepted blindly without understanding its base, can be abused about as badly as any other statistical approach. Furthermore, constructing confidence intervals based on a given level of confidence is not incompatible with the underlying concept of statistical significance. In our view, the two are more akin to two sides of the same coin than they are to two competing, mutually exclusive alternatives. We will keep to the traditional approach of statistical significance testing here for the convenience of exposition but will be careful not to interpret results beyond its limits.

Null Hypothesis

It may now be clear to you why such an emphasis has been placed on the null hypothesis within the tradition of testing for statistical significance. When you evaluate the value of your computed statistic against the critical values or just read from the SPSS printout the exact probability of obtaining that value by chance, those critical values or probabilities make sense (can be interpreted in the way you intend) only if the true value of the statistic in the population is in fact "null" (e.g., zero for the Pearson correlation and t). That is, the whole premise underlying the probability tables is that no true relationship exists in the population. This premise is essentially the null hypothesis.

When you reject the null hypothesis, you are asserting that the value for the statistic you obtained occurs so infrequently by chance alone in a population where the true value is "null" that you are willing to say that something more than chance was at work. The rub is, of course, that large values of these statistics actually do occur by chance, and if your study is one of those rare occurrences, you will be in error when you reject the null hypothesis. This error is known as a Type I error, and the chance of making it is exactly equal to the value of your alpha level. That's because your alpha level indicates how often such large values do occur by chance.

We should also very briefly mention an issue in connection with testing the null hypothesis that has been raised over the years and that continues to be raised even now (Thompson, 1994) concerning the assumption that there is no difference at all between the population means. As Thompson (1994) states:

> There is a very important implication of the realization that the null is not literally true in the population. The most likely sample statistics from samples drawn from populations in which the null is not literally true are sample statistics that do not correspond to the null hypothesis—for example, there are some differences in sample means or r in the sample is not exactly 0. And whenever the null is not exactly true in the sample(s), the null hypothesis will always be rejected at some sample size. (p. 843)

In short, if the population mean difference is almost but not quite zero, which Thompson suggests has been argued many times by a variety of writers, then we need to be very careful about what we are doing in our statistical significance testing.

Even if we take the rejection of the null hypothesis at face value and say that the odds are pretty slim that the results could have occurred by chance assuming a zero difference between the means in the population, we should still ask how useful the result is to researchers. This has to do with the topic of strength of effect, and we discuss it in Chapter 8A.

Statistical Power

When you compare the means of two groups using a t test or you evaluate the correlation of two variables with a Pearson r, the null hypothesis is that the two group means do not differ (that they are drawn from the same population) or that the Pearson r does not differ from zero. Sometimes, the null hypothesis is wrong and should be rejected: The means of the groups may truly differ, or the correlation is truly greater than zero. Being able to detect such a group difference or such a nonzero correlation is thought of as statistical power. More power corresponds with greater ability to detect a true effect. An analogy can be made to the process of magnification. Think of holding a magnifying glass (using a statistical test) to the fine detail of a painting (to examine the data). As you use more powerful magnifiers—going from 2× to 5× to 10×, for example—you can see successively greater detail, distinguishing differences that were not readily apparent to the naked eye or to what was seen under the lower-power magnifier.

The individual who may be most associated with promoting the concept of statistical power is Jacob Cohen (1969, 1977, 1988). The issue is important enough, however, to have been incorporated into a range of textbooks, including those covering research methodology (e.g., Rosenthal & Rosnow, 1991), introductory statistics (e.g., Runyon, Coleman, & Pittenger, 2000), and multivariate statistics (e.g., Stevens, 2002). We will briefly discuss a few of the more important issues concerning power.

Type I and Type II Errors

We have already addressed the Type I error. This occurs when you incorrectly reject the null hypothesis, claiming incorrectly that you have a significant group difference or a significant correlation. That is, you have obtained a large enough value of *t* or *r* with a given number of degrees of freedom to be confident that it probably did not occur by chance alone. But you were wrong this time.

A Type II error is the other side of the coin. This error occurs when you fail to find an effect that truly exists. Here, your *t* or *r* value is not large enough, given your degrees of freedom, to reach the critical value for your alpha level. You conclude that the group means do not differ significantly or that the correlation is not significantly different from zero, but you are incorrect. Greater statistical power reduces the chances of a Type II error occurring.

Definition of Power

If the null hypothesis is wrong and there is truly a difference between the means of two groups or the Pearson correlation does differ from zero, then it follows that an alternative hypothesis is true. Once such an alternative hypothesis is articulated, it is possible to compute the chances of accepting it. That probability is called beta. Power is defined as 1 − beta. Three basic factors contribute to the level of statistical power:

▶ Alpha level
▶ Effect size
▶ Sample size

Alpha Level

The alpha level we select for our research specifies the risk we are willing to run when we reject the null hypothesis. At our traditional alpha level of .05, we are willing to be wrong in rejecting the null hypothesis 5% of the time. Thus, although relatively "large" values of our statistic (e.g., *t, F, r*) can occur, we consider such values occurring 5% or less of the time to be sufficiently rare that we are willing to say that something beyond chance is working. If our alpha level is set at .01, our risk is that much less of being wrong when we reject the null hypothesis; if our alpha level is set at .15, our risk is that much greater. As you already know, alpha is the probability of rejecting the null hypothesis when it is true—that is, of committing a Type I error. More stringent alpha levels (.01 is more stringent than .05) represent lower chances of committing a Type I error.

The irony is, of course, that as we make greater and greater efforts to protect ourselves from making a Type I error, we increasingly expose ourselves to committing a Type II error because they are inexorably linked.

Essentially, one cannot be cautious and risky simultaneously. If researchers want to be extremely sure that there is, say, a significant difference between two groups before they commit to the assertion in print, then they are going to miss more true group differences because those differences do not meet their very strict standards. Thus, the very act of making a Type I error less likely to occur results in a greater likelihood of committing a Type II error.

The reverse is also true. To reduce the chances of committing a Type II error, researchers could make their alpha level less stringent. Say that the alpha level is shifted to .20 from the traditional .05 level. Practically, one needs a smaller value of t or r at a given number of degrees of freedom to meet this revised criterion of statistical significance. Such a change would identify more group differences to be significant and, in doing so, would reduce the chances of committing a Type II error. But by doing so, we have increased the probability of committing a Type I error from .05 to .20.

Stevens (2002) nicely summarizes one scenario involving the trade-off between committing a Type I and Type II error:

> The [alpha] level set by the experimenter is a subjective decision. . . . For example, if making a type I error will not have serious substantive consequences, or if sample size is small, setting [alpha] = .10 or .15 is quite reasonable. Why this is reasonable for small sample size will be made clear shortly. On the other hand, suppose we are in a medical situation where the null hypothesis is equivalent to saying a drug is unsafe, and the alternative is that the drug is safe. Here making a type I error could be quite serious, for we would be declaring the drug safe when it is not safe. This could cause some people to be permanently damaged or perhaps even killed. In this case it would make sense to take [alpha] very small, perhaps .001. (p. 4)

One can imagine an alternative scenario in which the consequences of making a Type I error are not severe but where it would be useful to increase statistical power. For example, researchers might be exploring whether a particular variation of psychotherapy can positively affect levels of depression. Assume that the treatment is otherwise benign and is not resource intensive. It may then be worthwhile in the early stages of the research to moderate one's alpha level so that a smaller difference between a control and treatment group would permit researchers to reject the null hypothesis. Although the risk of making a Type I error under these circumstances is increased, no great harm would be accrued. But the benefit of using a treatment that might be effective could outweigh the minor risks of falsely rejecting the null hypothesis.

Effect Size

A second factor that influences power is effect size. Larger effect sizes are associated with greater levels of statistical power. Stevens (2002) defines effect size as "the extent to which the groups differ in the population on the dependent variable(s)" (p. 6). Effect size in this context can be conceived of as the difference between the two means divided by the assumed common population standard deviation (Stevens, 2002). The result of such a computation is often labeled as *d* (Cohen, 1977). "That is, effect size expresses the difference between the means in standard deviation units" (Stevens, 2002, p. 6). In this sense, it is simply a way of standardizing raw scores and is conceptually the same structure underlying *z* scores or the *t* test.

Some writers have provided guidelines for evaluating the magnitude of effect sizes in certain applications. For example, for single sample *t* ratios, effect sizes of .20, .50, and .80 are considered to be small, medium, and large, respectively (Cohen, 1988). For Pearson *r*, effect sizes of .10, .30, and .50 are considered to be small, medium, and large, respectively (Runyon et al., 2000). For the *F* statistic, effect sizes of .01, .06, and .15 are considered to be small, medium, and large (Cohen, 1988).

If statistical power is the ability to detect true effects, then it might not surprise anyone to learn that larger effect sizes are associated with greater levels of power. Think back to our magnifying glass analogy. A small effect size (e.g., two means differing by a fraction of a standard deviation) may require researchers to use a very strong magnifier (considerable statistical power) to find it. A very large effect (e.g., two means differing by 10 standard deviations) may require relatively little statistical power for researchers to identify it. Effect sizes are, of course, part of the natural world that we study, and therefore cannot be adjusted by researchers. The best we can do is to estimate the magnitude of the effect sizes we are studying so that we may accommodate them as best as possible. Recent discussion concerning the reporting of effect sizes (see Wilkinson et al., 1999) encourages the practice of reporting and interpreting effect sizes in their actual research context.

Sample Size

Generally, we can say that researchers achieve greater power with increases in their sample size. This is the case because larger sample sizes are associated with lower standard errors of the mean and narrower confidence intervals (these factors drive the outcome of our statistical tests of significance). Thus, larger sample sizes result in increasingly more stable and precise estimates of population parameters. From a hands-on perspective, degrees of freedom are a direct function of sample size and, all else equal, smaller values of t, F, and r are needed to reject the null hypothesis with greater degrees of freedom.

We should also sound a small note of caution here. Very large sample sizes, as we will explain in Chapter 3A, can enable us to find a significant effect even when that effect is not especially strong. It is actually possible to have so much power in certain situations that small or trivial effect sizes can be distinguished. As we approach these power regions, we increasingly rely on strength-of-effect indexes to help us keep some perspective on our statistical results.

Recommended Readings

Cohen, J. (1994). The earth is round ($p < .05$). *American Psychologist, 49,* 997–1003.

Kirk, R. E. (1996). Practical significance: A concept whose time has come. *Educational and Psychological Measurement, 56,* 746–759.

Kline, R. B. (2004). *Beyond significance testing.* Washington, DC: American Psychological Association.

Thompson, B. (2002). "Statistical," "practical," and "clinical": How many kinds of significance do counselors need to consider? *Journal of Counseling and Development, 80,* 64–71.

Data Screening

O nce your data—whether derived from survey, experimental, or archival methods—are in hand and have been entered into SPSS, you must resist the temptation to plunge ahead with sophisticated multivariate statistical analyses without first critically examining the quality of the data you have collected. This chapter will focus on some of the most salient issues facing researchers before they embark on their multivariate journey. Just like a summer vacationer proceeds in a purposeful way by stopping the mail and newspaper for a period of time, confirming reservations, and checking to see that sufficient funds are available to pay for all the fun, so too must the researcher take equally crucial precautions before proceeding with the data analysis.

Some of these statistical considerations and precautions take the following form:

> ▶ Do the data accurately reflect the responses made by the participants of my study?
> ▶ Are all the data in place and accounted for, or are some of the data absent or missing?
> ▶ Is there a pattern to the missing data?
> ▶ Are there any unusual or extreme responses present in the data set that may distort my understanding of the phenomena under study?
> ▶ Do these data meet the statistical assumptions that underlie the multivariate technique I will be using?
> ▶ What can I do if some of the statistical assumptions turn out to be violated?

This chapter provides the answers to these questions. Chapter 3B will provide a parallel discussion to show how the procedures discussed here can be performed using SPSS.

Code and Value Cleaning

The data cleaning process ensures that once a given data set is in hand, a verification procedure is followed that checks for the appropriateness of numerical codes for the values of each variable under study. This process can be referred to as code and value cleaning.

The cleaning process begins with a consideration of the research project's unit of analysis. Typically, in behavioral science research the "units of analysis"—that is, the entities to which your data are specifically related—are human respondents (in survey or archival research) and human participants (in experimental research). In such situations, the score for each variable that you have recorded in the data file (e.g., the response to a particular item on one of your inventories) represents the behavior of an individual sampled by your research methodology. Collectively (generally) these units can be referred to as *cases*. Examples of other kinds of cases that can be the source of research data include individual mental health service providers, school districts, census tracts, and cities. Here, the value recorded for a variable in your data file represents one of these larger entities (e.g., the number of hours of individual psychotherapy provided to all clients on site in the month of April for a particular mental health facility, the average reading comprehension score on the statewide achievement test of all students in a particular district).

The challenge in code cleaning is to determine, for every case, whether each variable contains only legitimate numerical codes or values and, secondarily, whether these legitimate codes seem reasonable. For example, respondent gender (a nominal level variable) can be arbitrarily coded as 0 for males and 1 for females. To the extent that all cases on the gender variable are coded as either 0 or 1, we can say that this variable is "clean." Notice that code cleaning does not address the veracity or correctness of an appropriately coded value, only whether or not the variable's code is within the specified range.

Conversely, suppose we had collected data from a sample of 100 community mental health consumers on their global assessment of functioning (GAF) Axis V rating of the *Diagnostic and Statistical Manual of Mental Disorders, IV-TR (DSM-IV-TR;* American Psychiatric Association, 2000). GAF scale values can range from 1 (severe impairment) to 100 (good general functioning). Now, further suppose that our experience with these consumers has shown us that the modal (most frequent) GAF score was about 55 with minimum and maximum scores of approximately 35 and 65, respectively. If during the cleaning process we discover a respondent with a GAF score of 2, a logically legitimate but certainly an unusual score, we would probably want to verify its authenticity through other sources. For example, we might want to take a look at the original questionnaire or the actual computer-based archival record for that individual.

Such a cleaning process leads us to several options for future action. Consider the situation in which we find a very low GAF score for an individual. Under one scenario, we may confirm that the value of 2 is correct and leave it alone for the time being. Or after confirming its veridicality, we might consider that data point to be a candidate for elimination on the proposition that it is an outlier or extreme score because we view the case as not being representative of the target population under study. On the other hand, if our investigation shows the recorded value to be incorrect, we would substitute the correct value (e.g., 42) in its stead. Finally, if we deem the value to be wrong but do not have an appropriate replacement, we can treat it as a missing value (by either coding directly in SPSS the value of 2 as missing or, as is more frequently done, by replacing it with a value that we have already specified in SPSS to stand for a missing value).

Distribution Diagnosis

With small data sets containing a few cases, data cleaning can be accomplished by a simple visual inspection process. However, with the typically large data sets required for most multivariate analyses, using computerized computational packages such as SPSS before you start your statistical analysis provides a more efficient means for screening data.

These procedures provide output that display the way in which the data are distributed. We will discuss six types of output commonly used for this purpose: frequency tables, histograms and bar graphs, bar stem-and-leaf displays, box plots, and scatterplot matrices. In Chapter 3B, we will demonstrate how to use these procedures to conduct these analyses with SPSS.

Frequency Tables

A frequency table is a convenient way to summarize the obtained values for variables that contain a small number of different values or attributes. Demographic variables such as gender (with two codes), ethnicity (with between half a dozen and a dozen codes), and marital status (usually with no more than about six categories), along with other nominal level variables, including questions that require simple, dichotomous "yes"–"no" options, all have a limited number of possible values that are easily summarized in a frequency table.

An example of a demographic variable with five codes is "highest academic degree achieved." Table 3a.1 depicts the raw and unorganized data of 51 community mental health center providers described in a study by Gamst, Dana, Der-Karabetian, and Kramer (2001). Each respondent was assigned an arbitrary number at the time of data entry. To make it fit within

Table 3a.1   Terminal Degree Status of Fifty-One Community Mental Health Center Providers

Respondent	Degree	Respondent	Degree
1	MA	27	HS
2	MA	28	MA
3	HS	29	MA
4	MA	30	HS
5	HS	31	MA
6	DOC	32	BA
7	MA	33	MA
8	DOC	34	BA
9	MA	35	MA
10	MA	36	BA
11	MA	37	MA
12	HS	38	MA
13	DOC	39	DOC
14	MA	40	MA
15	DOC	41	BA
16		42	MA
17	MA	43	MA
18	HS	44	DOC
19	DOC	45	OTH
20	MA	46	MA
21	HS	47	OTH
22	HS	48	MA
23	DOC	49	DOC
24	DOC	50	HS
25	MA	51	MA
26	MA		

SOURCE: Gamst, Dana, Der-Karabetian, and Kramer (2001).

Note: MA = master's degree, HS = high school graduate, DOC = doctorate (PhD or PsyD), BA = bachelor's degree, OTH = other.

Table 3a.2   Frequency Table Showing One Out-of-Range Value

Code	Terminal Degree	n	Percentage
1	High school	9	18
2	Bachelor	4	8
3	Master's	25	49
4	Doctorate	10	20
5	Other	2	4
6	—	1	1
	Total	51	100

a relatively small space, we have structured this table to display the data in two columns. A cursory inspection of the information contained in Table 3a.1 suggests a jumble of degree statuses scattered among 50 of the 51 mental health practitioners. A coherent pattern is hard to discriminate.

A better and more readable way to display these data appears as the frequency distribution or frequency table that can be seen in Table 3a.2. Each row of the table is reserved for a particular value of the variable called "terminal degree." It aggregates the number of cases with a given value and their percentage of representation in the data array. A frequency table such as that illustrated in Table 3a.2 enables researchers to quickly decipher the important information contained within a distribution of values. For example, we can see that 49% of the mental health providers had master's degrees and 20% had doctorates. Thus, a simple summary statement of this table might note that "69% of the mental health providers had graduate-level degrees."

Table 3a.2 also shows how useful a frequency table can be in the data cleaning process. Because the researchers were using only code values 1 through 5, the value of 6 (coded for Respondent 16) represents an anomalous code in that it should not exist at all. It is for that reason that the value of 6 has no label in the table. In all likelihood, this represents a data entry error. To discover which case has this anomalous value if the data file was very large, one could have SPSS list the case number and the terminal degree variable for everyone (or, to make the output easier to read, we could first select for codes on this variable that were greater than 5 and then do the listing).

Histograms and Bar Graphs

Some variables have a large number of possible values (e.g., GAF scores, monthly income in dollars and cents, etc.). Typically, these are variables that are measured on one of the quantitative scales of measurement.

Such variables can also be screened through the same process we used in the previous example.

Table 3a.3 presents a frequency table for GAF scores for a portion of an Asian American community mental health consumers sample. Based on this output, we can see two issues of concern. One individual has a score of 2, suggesting very severe impairment of functioning. As mentioned above, such an extreme value is worth checking the raw data and, if valid, possibly considering that person to be an outlier. Another problem is that there are four cases with a value of 0, an out-of-range value on the GAF. There are some possible causes that might explain this latter problem, including (a) a simple misalignment of the data in the data file for those cases and (b) a data entry mistake. In any case, the researchers should be armed with enough clues at this juncture to discover and correct the problem.

Frequency tables summarizing quantitative variables are also useful as a way to gauge the very general shape of the distribution. For the data shown in Table 3a.3, for example, we can see that the largest concentration of scores is in the 40s and 50s. Based on visual inspection, the distribution appears to be relatively close to normal with perhaps a somewhat negative skew. SPSS can produce a graphic representation of the distribution. When the distribution is based on a frequency count of a categorical variable, we should request a bar graph. Conversely, when the distribution is based on a frequency count of a continuous variable, we should request a histogram. Because the distribution in Table 3a.3 is a continuous variable (GAF scores), we will produce a histogram that provides a visual approximation of the distribution's shape (see Figure 3a.1). One advantage of asking for a histogram is that SPSS can superimpose a drawing of the normal curve on the distribution so that we can visually determine how close our scores are to a normal distribution. We have done this in Figure 3a.1, and we can see that the distribution, although not perfect, is certainly "normal-like." However, the descriptive statistics that can be generated by SPSS, such as skewness and kurtosis, would provide a more precise description of the distribution's shape (values of skewness and kurtosis of 0 indicate a normal distribution).

Descriptive Statistics: Skewness and Kurtosis

A variety of opinions can be found concerning what is an unacceptable level of skewness (the symmetry of a distribution) and kurtosis (the clustering of scores toward the center of a distribution) for a particular variable—that is, how far from zero the value needs to be before it is considered a substantial enough departure from normality to be mentioned (we will discuss those concepts later in this chapter). Some statisticians are more

Table 3a.3   An Abbreviated Frequency Table of Global Assessment of Functioning (GAF) Scores for Asian American Community Mental Health Consumers

GAF Scores	n	Percentage
0	4	2.0
2	1	0.5
15	1	0.5
16	2	1.0
21	3	1.5
25	1	0.5
28	3	1.5
31	4	2.0
33	5	2.5
35	2	1.0
36	6	3.0
37	5	2.5
39	7	3.5
40	6	3.0
41	8	4.0
43	10	5.0
45	9	4.5
46	5	2.5
47	10	5.0
48	8	4.0
49	9	4.5
52	13	6.5
53	12	6.0
54	12	6.0
57	11	5.5
58	8	4.0
59	7	3.5
60	8	4.0
65	5	2.5
66	3	1.5
68	4	2.0
73	3	1.5
75	3	1.5
78	1	0.5
80	1	0.5
Total	200	100.0

SOURCE: Gamst et al. (2003).

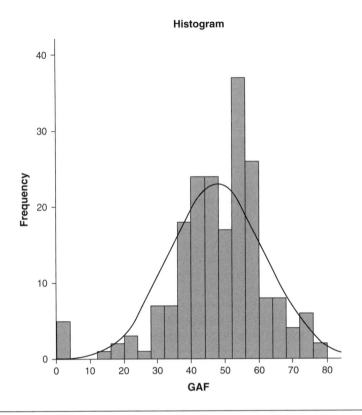

Figure 3a.1 Histogram Showing the Frequency Count of the GAF Scores

comfortable with a conservative threshold of ±0.5 as indicative of departures from normality (e.g., Hair et al., 1998; Runyon et al., 2000), whereas others prefer a more liberal interpretation of ±1.00 for skewness, kurtosis, or both (e.g., George & Mallery, 2003; Morgan, Griego, & Gloeckner, 2001). Tabachnick and Fidell (2001a) suggest a more definitive assessment strategy for detecting normality violations by dividing a skewness or kurtosis value by its respective standard error and evaluating this coefficient with a standard normal table of values (z scores). But such an approach has its own pitfalls, as Tabachnick and Fidell (2001a) note:

> But if the sample is large, it is better to inspect the shape of the distribution instead of using formal inference because the equations for standard error of both skewness and kurtosis contain N, and normality is likely to be rejected with large samples even when the deviation is slight. (p. 44)

Another helpful heuristic, at least regarding skewness, comes from the SPSS help menu, which suggests that any skewness value more than twice its standard error is taken to indicate a departure from symmetry. Unfortunately, no such heuristics are provided for determining normality violations due to extreme kurtosis. The shape of the distribution becomes of interest when researchers are evaluating their data against the assumptions of the statistical procedures they are considering using.

Stem-and-Leaf Plots

Figure 3a.2 provides the "next of kin" to a histogram display called a stem-and-leaf plot. This display, introduced by the statistician John Tukey (1977) in *Exploratory Data Analysis*, represents hypothetical GAF scores that might have been found for a sample of individuals arriving for their first session for mental health counseling. Stem-and-leaf plots provide information about the frequency of a quantitative variable's values by incorporating the actual values of the distribution. These plots are composed of three main components.

On the far left side of Figure 3a.2 is the frequency with which a particular value (the one shown for that row) occurred. In the center of the figure

```
 Frequency     Stem & Leaf

      1.00       1 . 5
      3.00       2 . 001
      3.00       2 . 555
      7.00       3 . 0011222
      9.00       3 . 555555588
     20.00       4 . 00000000000000122344
     26.00       4 . 55555555555555555555555788
     29.00       5 . 00000000000000000000001111113
     28.00       5 . 5555555555555555555555555888
     28.00       6 . 00000000000000000011111222222
     10.00       6 . 5555555558
      9.00       7 . 000000000
      2.00       7 . 55
      3.00       8 . 000

 Stem width:      10
 Each leaf:        1 case(s)
```

Figure 3a.2 Hypothetical Stem-and-Leaf Plot of GAF Scores at Intake

is the "stem" and the far right portion is the "leaf." The stem is the base value that we combine with the leaf portion to derive the full value. For example, for the first row of Figure 3a.2 we note that the lowest GAF score value has a frequency of 1.00. With a stem of 1 and a leaf of 5, we recognize a GAF score value of 15. The next row represents scores in the low 20s. The three scores depicted here are 20, 20, and 21.

Stem-and-leaf plots ordinarily combine a range of individual values under a single stem. In Figure 3a.2, intervals of 5 values are tied to a single stem. Depending on how tightly the scores are grouped, one can have either a finer or more global picture of the distribution.

By observing the distribution of "leaves," researchers can quickly assess the general shape of the distribution; that is, they can form an impression as to whether it is normal, positively skewed (scores are more concentrated toward the low end of the distribution), or negatively skewed (scores are more concentrated toward the high end of the distribution). It is also possible to generally see whether its kurtosis is more positive (a peaked distribution among the middle values) or more negative (a relatively flat distribution) than a normal curve. Again, the skewness and kurtosis statistics that can be obtained through SPSS will sharpen the judgment made on the basis of visual inspection of the stem-and-leaf plot.

Box Plots

Box plots or box and whiskers plots were also introduced by Tukey (1977) to help researchers identify extreme scores. Extreme scores can adversely affect many of the statistics one would ordinarily compute in the course of performing routine statistical analyses. For example, the mean of 2, 4, 5, 6, and 64 is 16. The presence of the extreme score of 64 has resulted in a measure of central tendency that does not really represent the majority of the scores. In this case, the median value of 5 is a more representative value of the central tendency of this small distribution. As we will discuss at length later, extreme scores, known as *outliers,* are often removed or somehow replaced by more acceptable values. Box plots convey a considerable amount of information about the distribution in one fairly condensed display, and it is well worth mastering the terminology associated with box plots so that they become a part of your data screening arsenal. An excellent description of this topic is provided by Cohen (1996), and what we present here is heavily drawn from his treatment.

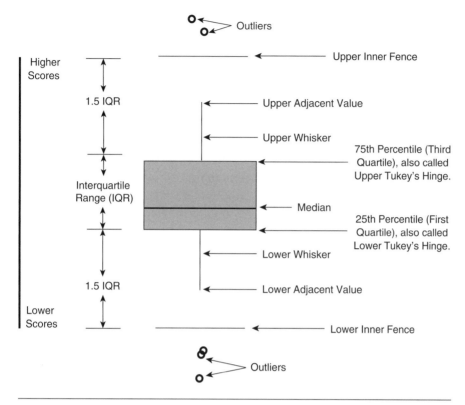

Figure 3a.3 The General Form of a Box and Whiskers Plot Based on Cohen's (1996) Description

The General Form of the Box Plot

The general form of a box and whiskers plot is shown in Figure 3a.3. According to Cohen (1996), the box plot is based on the median rather than the mean because, as we just saw, this former measure is unaffected by extreme scores in the distribution. The "box" part of the box and whiskers plot is drawn in the middle of Figure 3a.3. The median (which is the 50th percentile or second quartile) is shown by the heavy dark line inside the box. In our drawing, the median is not at the center of the box but a bit toward its lower portion. This indicates that the distribution is somewhat negatively skewed (more scores are toward the low end of the scoring continuum).

The borders of the box are set at the 25th percentile (first quartile) and the 75th percentile (third quartile) for the lower and upper border, respectively, because in our box plot, lower scores are toward the bottom and higher scores are toward the top. These quartiles are a little less than ±1 standard deviation unit but nonetheless capture the majority of the cases. As shown in Figure 3a.3, these borders are called Tukey's hinges, and the span of scores between the hinges (the distance between the first and third quartiles) is the interquartile range (IQR).

The two boundary lines appearing above and below it in Figure 3a.3 are called *inner fences.* The one toward the top is the upper inner fence and the one toward the bottom is the lower inner fence. These fences are drawn at the positions corresponding to ±1.5 IQRs. That is, once we know the value for the interquartile range, we just multiply it by 1.5. Scores inside these fences are considered to be within the bounds of the distribution and are therefore not considered extreme.

The "whiskers" portion of the box and whiskers plot are the vertical lines perpendicular to the orientation of the box. The one at the top of the box is the upper whisker, and the one at the bottom of the box is the lower whisker. These whiskers extend only as far as the smallest and largest values that fall within the upper and lower inner fences. The upper whisker ends at the upper adjacent value and the lower whisker ends at the lower adjacent value. Because the whiskers can end before they reach the inner fences, we can tell the "compactness" of the distribution.

The regions beyond the inner fences are considered to be extreme scores by this plotting method. SPSS divides this area into two regions. A data point that is farther than ±1.5 IQRs but less than ±3.0 IQRs is labeled by SPSS as an outlier and is shown in its output as "O." A data point that exceeds this ±3.0 IQR distance is considered to be an extreme score and is given the symbol "E" in its output.

An Example of a Box Plot

Figure 3a.4 provides a SPSS box and whiskers plot of the previous hypothetical GAF score data. As was true for the above example, the median seems to be a little off center and toward the lower end of the box. This suggests a somewhat negative skew to the distribution. In our example, the whiskers here extend all the way to the inner fences. No scores were found in the extreme range (between ±1.5 IQRs and ±3 IQRs) but some scores in the lower portion of the distribution were identified by SPSS as extreme. These are marked as "O"s in Figure 3a.4.

Scatterplot Matrices

We have been discussing various data cleaning and data screening devices that are used to assess one variable at a time; that is, we have assessed

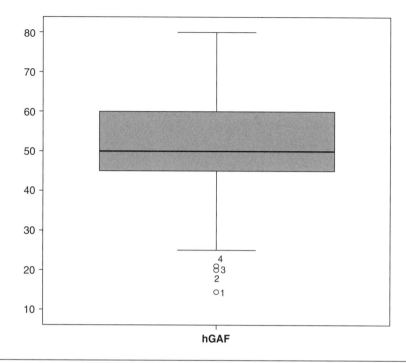

Figure 3a.4 Box Plot of the Hypothetical GAF Scores at Intake

variables in a univariate manner. Because of the complex nature of the statistical analyses we will be employing throughout this book, it is also incumbent on us to screen variables in a bivariate and multivariate manner—that is, to examine the interrelationship of two or more variables for unusual patterns of variability in combination with each other. For example, we can ask about the relationship between GAF intake and GAF termination or between years lived in the United States and GAF intake. These sorts of questions can be routinely addressed with a scatterplot matrix of continuous variables.

We show an example of a scatterplot matrix in Figure 3a.5. In this case, we used four variables and obtained scatterplots for each combination. For ease of viewing, we present only the upper half of the matrix. Each entry represents the scatterplot of two variables. For example, the left-most plot on the first row shows the relationship of Variables A and B. It would appear, from the plot, that they might be related in a curvilinear rather than a linear manner. On the other hand, B and C seem to be related linearly. As we will see later in this chapter, these plots are often used to look for multivariate assumption violations of normality and linearity. An alternative approach to addressing linearity with SPSS, which we will not cover here, is to use the regression curve estimation procedure.

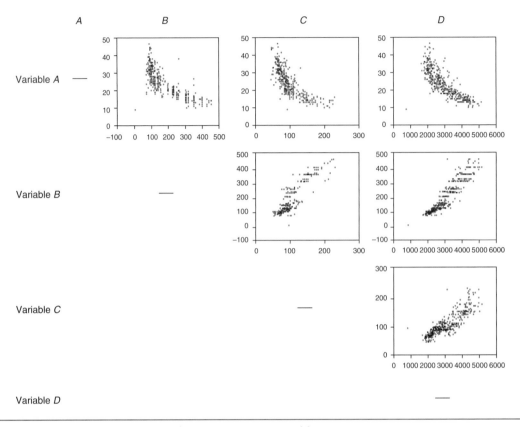

Figure 3a.5 Scatterplot Matrix of Four Continuous Variables

Dealing With Missing Values

During the data screening process, we encounter missing data for a variety of reasons. Respondents may refuse to answer personal questions pertaining to their income, sexual orientation, or current illegal drug use. Conversely, some respondents may not be competent to respond because of a lack of knowledge regarding a particular topic. Participants in an experiment may suffer from fatigue or lack of motivation and simply stop responding. Archival data may be missing because of data entry errors or equipment malfunctions. The paramount question concerning the issue of missing data is whether these missing values are a function of a random or a systematic process.

Missing Values Patterns: Random Patterns of Missing Data

Allison (2002) suggests two broad classes of randomly missing data. Observations are said to be *missing completely at random* (MCAR) if none of the variables in the data set (including all independent and dependent variables) contains missing values related to the values of the variable under scrutiny. For example, missing data for GAF scores at the termination of a treatment program might be considered MCAR if *nonresponse* (another term for missing data) was no more or less likely across major diagnostic classifications.

Although often claimed or implied, the MCAR assumption is seldom achieved (Allison, 2002). A weaker and potentially more achievable version of this assumption is that the missing data are *missing at random* (MAR). This assumption suggests that a variable's missing values are said to be random if, after controlling for other variables, the variable cannot predict the distribution of the missing data. Continuing with our previous example, suppose we found that respondents with missing data on GAF scores at the termination of a treatment program were more likely to be classified in the severe as opposed to the moderate diagnostic categories. These missing GAF scores would then be related to diagnostic category and we would conclude that the GAF score data are not missing at random.

Keeping these missing data assumptions in mind should help guide you in the process of determining the seriousness of your missing data situation. If the data conform to the MCAR or MAR criteria, then perhaps you have what is termed an *ignorable missing data situation* (you probably do not have a problem with the distribution of the missing data but you may still have a problem if you have a great deal of missing data). If the missing data distributions do not meet these criteria, then you are faced with a missing data scenario that you probably cannot ignore. Let's look at several ways of assessing this latter possibility.

Looking for Patterns

Consider the hypothetical clinical outcome study for 15 cases represented in Table 3a.4. The left portion of the table shows the data collected by the agency for four variables. A GAF score is obtained at intake (shown as GAF-T1 for "Time 1") and again 6 months later (GAF-T2 for "Time 2"). Also recorded is the age of the client at intake and the number of counseling sessions for which the client was present. The right portion of Table 3a.4 is a tabulation of the missing data situation; it shows the absolute number of missing data points and their percentage with respect to a complete set of

Table 3a.4   Missing Data Table (Hypothetical Data)

	Variables				Pattern	
Case	GAF-T1	GAF-T2	Age	Sessions	# Missing	% Missing
1	51.0	51.0	30	8	0	0
2	55.0	—	63	4	1	25
3	40.0	—	57	—	2	50
4	38.0	50.0	31	10	0	0
5	80.0	80.0	19	11	0	0
6	40.0	—	50	2	1	25
7	55.0	55.0	19	8	0	0
8	50.0	70.0	20	8	0	0
9	62.0	70.0	20	10	0	0
10	65.0	75.0	19	7	0	0
11	—	—	38	—	3	75
12	50.0	61.0	65	9	0	0
13	40.0	55.0	—	8	1	25
14	40.0	50.0	46	9	0	0
15	32.0	—	44	3	1	25
# Missing in column	1	5	1	2	9	
% Missing in column	6.7	33.3	6.7	13.3	15.0	

NOTE: GAF-T1 = GAF at intake; GAF-T2 = GAF at Time 2; Sessions = number of treatment sessions.

four data points. For example, the third case was missing a second GAF score and a record of the number of therapy sessions he or she attended. Thus, these two missing values made up 50% of the total of four data points that should have been there.

A quick inspection of Table 3a.4 indicates that missing data are scattered across all four of the variables under study. We can also note that 9 of the 15 cases (60%) have no missing data. Because almost all the multivariate procedures we talk about in this book need to be run on a complete data set, the defaults set by the statistical program would select only these 9 cases with full data, excluding all cases with a missing value on one or more variables. This issue of sample size reduction as a function of missing data, especially when this reduction appears to be nonrandom, can threaten the external validity of the research.

Further inspection of Table 3a.4 shows that one third of the sample (5 respondents) had missing data on the GAF-T2 (the 6-month postintake measurement) variable. Normally, such a relatively large proportion of nonresponse for one variable would nominate it as a possible candidate for deletion (by not including that variable in the analysis, more cases would have a complete data set and thus contribute to the analysis). Nonresponse to a postmeasure on a longitudinal (multiply measured) variable is a fairly common occurrence. If this variable is crucial to our analyses, then some form of item imputation (i.e., estimation of what the missing value might have been and replacement of the missing value with that estimate) procedure may be in order.

We should also be attentive to how many missing data are associated with each measure. As a general rule, variables containing missing data on 5% or fewer of the cases can be ignored (Tabachnick & Fidell, 2001b). The second GAF variable, showing a third of its values as missing, has a missing value rate substantially greater than this general rule of thumb; this variable therefore needs a closer look. In the present example, although the remaining three variables exceed this 5% mark as well, the relative frequency of cases with missing data is small enough to ignore.

An important consideration at this juncture, then, is the randomness of the missing data pattern for the GAF-T2 variable. A closer inspection of the missing values for GAF-T2 indicates that they tend to occur among the older respondents. This is probably an indication of a systematic pattern of nonresponse and thus is probably not ignorable.

Finally, we can see from Table 3a.4 that Case 11 is missing data on three of the four variables. Missing such a large proportion of data points would make a strong argument for that case to be deleted from the data analysis.

Methods of Handling Missing Data

Although there are a number of established procedures for dealing with item nonresponse or missing data, experts differ on their personal recommendations for which techniques to use under varying degrees of randomness of the missing data process. For excellent introductory overviews of this topic, see Graham, Cumsille, and Elek-Fisk (2003); Hair et al. (1998); Schafer and Graham (2002); and Tabachnick and Fidell (2001b). More advanced coverage of missing data can be found in Allison (2002), Little and Rubin (2002), and Schafer (1997).

Here are some of the more common approaches used to address missing data situations.

Listwise Deletion

This method involves deleting from the particular statistical analysis all cases that have missing data. We call this method *listwise* because we are deleting cases with missing data on any variable in our list. In this method, a single missing value on just a single variable in the analysis is cause for a case to be excluded from the statistical analysis. As we mentioned previously, this is a standard practice for most computer statistical packages, including SPSS.

A practical advantage of listwise deletion is that this method can be used in a variety of multivariate techniques (e.g., multiple regression, structural equation modeling), and it ordinarily requires no additional commands or computations. One obvious concern about this approach involves the loss of cases that could have been very difficult and expensive (in time or other resources) to obtain. Another concern is that the sample size reduction may increase the estimate of measurement error (standard errors increase with lower sample sizes). Finally, lowering the sample size may drop it below the relatively large N needed for most multivariate procedures.

Allison (2002) gives the listwise deletion method a very strong endorsement when he notes:

> Listwise deletion is not a *bad* method for handling missing data. Although it does not use all of the available information, at least it gives valid inferences when the data are MCAR. . . . whenever the probability of missing data on a particular independent variable depends on the value of that variable (and not the dependent variable), listwise deletion may do better than maximum likelihood or multiple imputation. (p. 7)

Pairwise Deletion

This approach computes summary statistics (e.g., means, standard deviations, correlations) from all available cases that have valid values (it is the SPSS default method of handling missing values for these computations in most of the procedures designed to produce descriptive statistics). Thus, no cases are necessarily completely excluded from the data analysis. Cases with missing values on certain variables would still be included when other variables (on which they had valid values) were involved in the analysis. If we wanted to compute the mean for Variables X, Y, and Z using, for example, the **Frequencies** procedure in SPSS, all cases with valid values on X would be brought into the calculation of X's mean, all cases with valid values on Y would be used for the calculation of Y's mean, and all cases with valid values of Z would be used for the calculation of Z's mean. It is therefore possible that the three means could very well be based on somewhat different cases and somewhat different Ns.

Correlation presents another instance where pairwise deletion is the default. To be included in computing the correlation of X and Y, cases must have valid values on both variables. Assume that Case 73 is missing a value on the Y variable. That case is therefore excluded in the calculation of the correlations between X and Y and between Y and Z. But that case will be included in computing the correlation between X and Z if that case has valid values for those variables. It is therefore not unusual for correlations produced by the **Correlations** procedure in SPSS to be based on somewhat different cases. Note that when correlations are computed in one of the multivariate procedures where listwise deletion is in effect, that method rather than pairwise deletion is used so that the correlations in the resulting correlation matrix are based on exactly the same cases.

Although pairwise deletion can be successfully used with linear regression, factor analysis, and structural equation modeling (see Allison, 2002), this method is clearly most reliable when the data are MCAR. Furthermore, statistical software algorithms for computing standard errors with pairwise deletion show a considerable degree of variability and even bias (Allison, 2002). Our recommendation is not to use pairwise deletion when conducting multiple regression, factor analysis, or structural equation modeling.

Imputation Procedures

The next approaches to missing data that we describe are collectively referred to as imputation procedures. These methods attempt to impute or substitute for a missing value some other value that they deem to be a reasonable guess or estimate. The statistical analysis is then conducted using these imputed values. Although these imputation methods do preserve sample size, we urge caution in the use of these somewhat intoxicating remedies for missing data situations. Permanently altering the raw data in a data set can have potentially catastrophic consequences for the beginning and experienced multivariate researcher alike. For good overviews of these procedures, see Allison (2002), Hair et al. (1998), and Tabachnick and Fidell (2001b).

Mean Substitution

Mean substitution calls for replacing all missing values of a variable with the mean of that variable. The mean to be used as the replacement value, of course, must be based on all the valid cases in the data file. This is both the most common and most conservative of the imputation practices.

The argument for using mean substitution is based on the accepted rubric that the sample mean is the best estimate of the population mean. An analogous argument is used for the mean substitution procedure. The best estimate of what a missing value might be is the mean of the values that we have. Now, we know that not every missing value would fall on this mean—some values would be lower, and some values would be higher. But in the absence of contradictory information, we estimate that the average of these missing values would be equal to the average of the valid values. Based on that reasoning, we then substitute the mean that we have for the values that are missing.

At the same time, it is important to recognize that the true values for these missing cases would almost certainly vary over at least a modest range of scores. By substituting the same single value (the mean of our observed values) for a missing value, even granting that it is a reasonable estimate, we must accept the consequence that this procedure artificially reduces the variability of that variable.

As you might expect from what we have just said, there are at least three drawbacks to the mean substitution strategy. First, the assumption that the missing values are randomly distributed among the cases is an assumption that is not always fully tested. Second, although the mean of a distribution is the best estimate we have of the population parameter, it is still likely to occur within a certain margin of error (e.g., ±1.96 standard error units). Thus, the sample mean, although being our best estimate, may not fall at the true value of the parameter. Third, the variance of the variable having its missing values replaced is necessarily reduced when we remove the missing value and substitute it with the mean of the valid cases. That narrowing of the variance, in turn, can distort the variable's distribution of values (Hair et al., 1998; Tabachnick & Fidell, 2001b) and can therefore bias the statistical analysis.

An offshoot of this approach is to use a subgroup mean rather than a full sample mean in the substitution process. For example, if we know the ethnicity, diagnostic category, or some other information about the cases that is determined to be useful in facilitating prediction, we could calculate the mean of that subgroup and substitute that for the missing value for those individuals in that subgroup. For example, if we had reason to believe that sex was the most relevant variable with respect to Variable K, then we would obtain separate means on K for women and men and substitute the former for any missing K values associated with women and the latter for any missing K values associated with men. This approach may be more attractive than sample-wise mean substitution because it narrows the configuration of cases on which the imputation is based but does require that the researchers articulate their reasoning for selecting the subgroup that they did.

Multiple Regression Imputation

Multiple regression will be discussed in Chapters 5A and 5B. Basically, this approach to item nonresponse builds a multiple regression equation to predict missing values. With multiple regression, we use several independent variables to build a model (i.e., generate a regression equation) that allows us to predict a dependent variable value. When we wish to replace missing values on a particular variable, we use that variable as the dependent variable in a multiple regression procedure. A prediction equation is thus produced based on the cases with complete data. With this equation, we predict (i.e., impute, figure out the particular values to substitute for) the missing values on that variable.

This regression method is a better, more sophisticated approach than many of the previous methods we have reviewed. However, problems can arise when missing values occur on multiple independent variables or on the dependent variable (Allison, 2002). There is also a tendency to "overfit" the missing values because they are predicted from other independent variables (Tabachnick & Fidell, 2001b). Such overfitting produces samples that may not reflect or generalize to the population from which they were drawn. This same theme is echoed by Allison (2002) who notes, "Analyzing imputed data as though it were complete data produces standard errors that are underestimated and test statistics that are overestimated" (p. 12).

Combining Imputation Procedures

Some researchers prefer using combinations of the approaches we have thus far described to address the specific issue that they face in their own data set. Such an approach sometimes overcomes the limitations found in using any one of the imputation methods in isolation. Another way to consolidate the approaches is to make use of expectation maximization.

Expectation Maximization Imputation

Recent software innovations, such as SPSS's optional module **Missing Value Analysis**, has made expectation maximization (EM) imputation an attractive synthesis and extension of some of the approaches that we have described (other statistical software package modules as well as stand-alone programs are also available). The EM imputation approach used by the SPSS **Missing Value Analysis** module uses a maximum likelihood approach for estimating missing values (Little & Rubin, 2002). As we will see in Chapter 14A, maximum likelihood results are very similar to those obtained through least squares linear regression (Allison, 2002).

The EM algorithm is a two-step iterative process. During the E step, regression analyses are used to estimate the missing values. Using maximum likelihood procedures, the M step makes estimates of parameters (e.g., correlations) using the missing data replacements. The SPSS program iterates through E and M steps until convergence or no change occurs between the steps (Allison, 2002; Hair et al., 1998; Tabachnick & Fidell, 2001b).

When comparing EM with regression imputation procedures, Allison (2002) notes some important advantages:

> The EM algorithm avoids one of the difficulties with conventional regression imputations—deciding which variables to use as predictors and coping with the fact that different missing data patterns have different sets of available predictors. Because EM always starts with the full covariance matrix, it is possible to get regression estimates for any set of predictors, no matter how few cases there may be in a particular missing data pattern. Hence, EM always uses all the available variables as predictors for imputing the missing data. (p. 20)

Beyond EM Imputation

A more recently developed approach to estimating missing values is a multiple imputation (MI) procedure (see Allison, 2002; Graham et al., 2003; Schaefer & Graham, 2002; West, Enders, & Taylor, 2005). Although at the time we are writing our book, this MI procedure has been implemented by SAS, SPSS has not yet incorporated it. MI continues where EM stops. Very briefly stated, EM generates an estimate of the missing value. Recognizing that this is not a precise estimate but, rather, has some estimation error associated with it, MI adds to or subtracts from the EM estimate the value of a randomly chosen residual from the regression analysis, thus building some error variance into the estimated value. MI cycles through the prediction and residual selection process in an iterative manner until convergence on estimated values of the parameters of the model is reached.

This whole process is usually performed between 5 and 10 times (West, Enders, & Taylor, 2005), generating many separate parameter estimates. The final values of the estimated parameters of interest are then computed based on the information from these various estimates. Because we are attempting to best predict the missing values, this approach allows us to include in this effort variables that are not necessarily related to the research question but that might enhance our prediction of the missing values themselves, provided that such variables were thoughtfully included in the original data collection process.

Recommendations

We agree with the both sage and tongue-in-cheek advice of Allison (2002) that "the only really good solution to the missing data problem is not to have any" (p. 2). Because the likelihood of such an eventuality is low, we encourage you to explore your missing values situation. As a first step, you could compare cases with and without missing values on variables of interest using independent samples *t* tests. For example, cases with missing gender data could be coded as 1 and cases with complete gender data could be coded as 0. Then you could check to see if any statistically significant differences emerge for this "dummy" coded independent variable on a dependent variable of choice such as respondent's GAF score. Such an analysis may give you confidence that the missing values are or are not related to a given variable under study.

If you elect to use some form of missing value imputation process, it is worthwhile to compare your statistical analysis with cases using only complete data (Tabachnick & Fidell, 2001b). If no differences emerge between "complete" versus "imputed" data sets, then you can have confidence that your missing value interventions reflect statistical reality. If they are different, then further exploration is in order.

We recommend the use of listwise case deletion when you have small numbers of missing values that are MCAR or MAR. Deleting variables that contain high proportions of missing data can also be desirable if those variables are not crucial to your study. Mean substitution and regression imputation procedures can also be profitably employed when missing values are proportionately small (Tabachnick & Fidell, 2001b) but we recommend careful pre-post data set appraisal as outlined above as well as consultation with a statistician as you feel necessary. If you have the SPSS **Missing Values Analysis,** then we suggest using that module to handle your missing values; it will do an adequate job of estimating replacement values. Finally, if you have access to an MI procedure (e.g., SAS) and feel comfortable enough working with it and subsequently importing your data to SPSS to perform the statistical analyses, then we certainly recommend using that procedure.

Outliers

Cases with extreme or unusual values on a single variable (univariate) or on a combination of variables (multivariate) are called outliers. These outliers provide researchers with a mixed opportunity in that their existence may signal a serendipitous presence of new and exciting patterns within a data set, yet they may also signal anomalies within the data that may need to be addressed before proceeding with the statistical analyses. However, extreme splits on dichotomous variables are more the norm than the exception in clinical and applied research. Accordingly, if the sample size is sufficiently large, these extreme bifurcations should not pose a great problem.

Causes of Outliers

Hair et al. (1998) identify four reasons for outliers in a data set.

1. Outliers can be caused by data entry errors or improper attribute coding. These errors are normally caught in the data cleaning stage.

2. Some outliers may be a function of extraordinary events or unusual circumstances. For example, in a human memory experiment, a participant may recall all 80 of the stimulus items correctly, or illness strikes a participant during the middle of a clinical interview, changing the nature of her responses when she returns the following week to finish the interview. Most of the time, the safest course is to eliminate outliers produced by these circumstances—but not always. The fundamental question you should ask yourself is, "Does this outlier represent my sample?" If "yes," then you should include it.

3. There are some outliers for which we have no explanation. These unexplainable outliers are good candidates for deletion.

4. There are multivariate outliers whose uniqueness occurs in their pattern of combination of values on several variables, for example, unusual combined patterns of age, gender, and number of arrests.

Detection of Univariate Outliers

Univariate outliers can be identified by an inspection of the frequency distribution or box plot for each variable. Dichotomous variables (e.g., "yes," "no") with extreme splits (e.g., 90%–10%) between response options should be deleted (Tabachnick & Fidell, 2001b).

For continuous variables, several options exist for determining a threshold for outlier designation. Hair et al. (1998) recommend converting the values of each variable to standard (i.e., z) scores with a mean of 0 and a standard deviation of 1. This can be accomplished easily with SPSS's **Explore** or **Descriptives** programs, where z scores can be computed and saved in the data file for later profiling. As a general heuristic, Hair et al. (1998) recommend considering cases with z scores exceeding ±2.5 to be outliers. These should be carefully considered for possible deletion.

Conversely, Cohen, West, and Aiken (2003) provide this tip on outliers, stating that "if outliers are few (less than 1% or 2% of *n*) and not very extreme, they are probably best left alone" (p. 128).

An alternative approach to univariate detection of outliers involves inspecting histograms, box plots, and normal probability plots (Tabachnick & Fidell, 2001b). Univariate outliers reveal themselves through their visible separation from the bulk of the cases on a particular variable when profiled with these graphical techniques.

Detection of Multivariate Outliers

After inspecting the data set for univariate outliers, an assessment for multivariate outliers is in order. As a first step in looking for outliers on a combination of variables, we recommend running bivariate (i.e., two-variable) scatterplots for combinations of key variables. In these plots (such as we showed earlier in Figure 3a.5), each case is represented as a point on the *X* and *Y* axes. Most cases fall within the elliptical (oval-shaped) swarm or pattern mass. Outliers are those cases that tend to lie outside the oval.

A more objective way of assessing for the presence of multivariate outliers is to compute each case's Mahalanobis distance. The Mahalanobis distance statistic D^2 measures the multivariate "distance" between each case and the group multivariate mean (known as a centroid). Each case is evaluated using the chi-square distribution with a stringent alpha level of .001. Cases that reach this significance threshold can be considered multivariate outliers and possible candidates for elimination.

Multivariate Statistical Assumptions

Statistical assumptions underlie most univariate and multivariate statistical tests. Of special significance to multivariate analyses are the assumptions of normality, linearity, and homoscedasticity. Should one or more of these assumptions be violated, then the statistical results may become biased or distorted (Hair et al., 1998; Keppel, 1991; Tabachnick & Fidell, 2001b).

Normality

The shape of a distribution of continuous variables in a multivariate analysis should correspond to a (univariate) normal distribution. That is, the variable's frequency distribution of values should roughly approximate a bell-shaped curve. Both Stevens (2002) and Tabachnick and Fidell (2001b) indicate that univariate normality violations can be assessed with statistical or graphical approaches.

Statistical Approaches

Statistical approaches that assess univariate normality often begin with measures of skewness and kurtosis. Skewness is a measure of the symmetry of a distribution; positive skewness indicates that a distribution's mean lies on the right side of the distribution, and negative skewness indicates that a distribution's mean lies on the left side of the distribution. Kurtosis is a measure of the general peakedness of a distribution. Positive kurtosis, also called leptokurtosis, indicates an extreme peak in the center of the distribution; negative kurtosis, also called platykurtosis, suggests an extremely flat distribution. A normally distributed variable (one exhibiting mesokurtosis) will generate skewness and kurtosis values that hover around zero. These values can be obtained with SPSS through its **Frequencies**, **Descriptives**, and **Explore** procedures; the latter two procedures also produce significance tests, which are typically evaluated at a stringent alpha level of .01 or .001 (Tabachnick & Fidell, 2001b).

Additional statistical tests include the Kolmogorov-Smirnov test and the Shapiro-Wilk test. Although both tests can be effectively employed, Stevens (2002) recommends the use of the Shapiro-Wilk test because it appears to be "the most powerful in detecting departures from normality" (p. 264). Both tests can be obtained through the SPSS **Explore** procedure. Statistical significance with these measures, ideally with a stringent alpha level ($p < .001$), indicates a possible univariate normality violation.

Graphical Approaches

Graphical approaches that assess univariate normality typically begin with an inspection of histograms or stem-and-leaf plots for each variable. However, such cursory depictions do not provide a definitive indication of a normality violation. A more precise graphical method is to use a normal probability plot, where the values of a variable are rank ordered and plotted against expected normal distribution values (Stevens, 2002). In these plots, a normal distribution produces a straight diagonal line, and the plotted data values are compared with this diagonal. Normality is assumed if the data values follow the diagonal line.

Multivariate Approaches

So far we have been discussing the assumption of univariate normality. The assumption of multivariate normality, although somewhat more complicated, is intimately related to its univariate counterpart. Stevens (2002) cautions researchers that just because one has demonstrated univariate normality on each variable in a data set, the issue of multivariate normality—the observations among all combinations of variables are normally distributed—may not always be satisfied. As Stevens (2002) notes, "Although it is difficult to completely characterize multivariate normality, *normality on each of the variables separately is a necessary, but not sufficient, condition for multivariate normality to hold*" (p. 262). Thus, although univariate normality is an essential ingredient to achieve multivariate normality, Stevens argues that two other conditions must also be met: (a) that linear combinations of the variables (e.g., variates) should be normally distributed and (b) that all pairwise combinations of variables should also be normally distributed.

As we noted previously, SPSS offers a procedure to easily examine whether or not univariate normality is present among the variables with various statistical tests and graphical options. But it does not offer a statistical test for multivariate normality. We therefore recommend a thorough univariate normality examination coupled with a bivariate scatterplot examination of key pairs of variables. If the normality assumption appears to be violated, it may be possible to "repair" this problem through a data transformation process.

Linearity

Many of the multivariate techniques we cover in this text (e.g., multiple regression, multivariate analysis of variance [MANOVA], factor analysis) assume that the variables in the analysis are related to each other in a linear manner; that is, they assume that the best fitting function representing the scatterplot is a straight line. Based on this assumption, these procedures often compute the Pearson correlation coefficient (or a variant of it) as part of the calculations needed for the multivariate statistical analysis. As we will discuss in Chapter 4A, the Pearson r assesses the degree of linear relationship observed between two variables. Nonlinear relationships between two variables cannot be assessed by the Pearson correlation coefficient. To the extent that such nonlinearity is present, the observed Pearson r would be a less representative index of the strength of the association between the two variables—it would identify less relationship strength than existed because it could capture only the linear component of the relationship.

The use of bivariate scatterplots is the most typical way of assessing linearity between two variables. Variables that are both normally distributed and linearly related to each other will produce scatterplots that are oval shaped or elliptical. If one of the variables is not normally distributed, linearity will not be achieved. We can recognize this situation because the resulting scatterplot will be nonelliptical (Tabachnick & Fidell, 2001b). However, there is a downside to running a plethora of bivariate scatterplots, as Tabachnick and Fidell (2001b) aptly note: "Assessing linearity through bivariate scatterplots is reminiscent of reading tea leaves, especially with small samples. And there are many cups of tea if there are several variables and all possible pairs are examined" (p. 78).

Another approach (often used in the context of multiple regression) is to run a regression analysis and examine the residuals plot. Residuals depict the portion (or "left over") of the dependent variable's variance that was not explained by the regression analysis (i.e., the error component). We will see this in Chapter 3B. The "cure" for nonlinearity lies in data transformation.

Homoscedasticity

The assumption of homoscedasticity suggests that quantitative dependent variables have equal levels of variability across a range of (either continuous or categorical) independent variables (Hair et al., 1998). Violation of this assumption results in heteroscedasticity. Heteroscedasticity typically occurs when a variable is not distributed in a normal manner or when a data transformation procedure has produced an unanticipated distribution for a variable (Tabachnick & Fidell, 2001b).

In the univariate analysis of variance (ANOVA) context (with one quantitative dependent variable and one or more categorical independent variables), this homoscedasticity assumption is referred to as *homogeneity of variance*, in which it is assumed that equal variances of the dependent measure are observed across the levels of the independent variables (Keppel, 1991; Keppel et al., 1992).

Several statistical tests can be used to detect homogeneity of variance violations, including Fmax and Levene's test. The Fmax test is computed by working with the variance of each group and dividing the largest variance by the smallest variance. Keppel et al. (1992) note that any Fmax value of 3.0 or greater is indicative of an assumption violation, and they recommend the use of the more stringent alpha level of $p < .025$ when evaluating an F ratio. Alternatively, Levene's test assesses the statistical hypothesis of equal variances across the levels of the independent variable. Rejection of the null hypothesis (at $p < .05$) indicates an assumption violation or unequal variability. Stevens (2002) cautions about the use of the Fmax test because of its extreme sensitivity to violations of normality. The Fmax statistic can be produced through the **ANOVA** procedure, and the Levene test can be produced with the SPSS **Explore** and **Oneway** procedures.

When more than one quantitative dependent variable is being assessed (as in the case of MANOVA), then Box's M test for equality of variance-covariance matrices is used to test for homoscedasticity. Akin to its univariate counterpart, Levene's test, Box's M tests the statistical hypothesis that the variance-covariance matrices are equal. A statistically significant ($p < .05$) Box's M test indicates a homoscedasticity assumption violation, but it is very sensitive to any departures of normality among the variables under scrutiny (Stevens, 2002).

Typically, problems related to homoscedasticity violations can be attributed to issues of normality violations for one or more of the variables under scrutiny. Hence, it is probably best to first assess and possibly remediate normality violations before addressing the issue of equal variances or variance-covariance matrices (Hair et al., 1998; Tabachnick & Fidell, 2001b). If heteroscedasticity is present, this too can be remedied by means of data transformations. We address this topic next.

Data Transformations

Data transformations are mathematical procedures that can be used to modify variables that violate the statistical assumptions of normality, linearity, and homoscedasticity, or that have unusual outlier patterns (Hair et al., 1998; Tabachnick & Fidell, 2001b). First you determine the extent to which one or more of these assumptions are violated. Then you decide whether or not the situation calls for a data transformation to correct this matter. If so, then you actually instruct SPSS to change every value of the variable or variables you wish to transform. Once the numbers have been changed in this manner, you would then perform the statistical analysis on these changed or transformed data values.

Much of our current understanding of data transformations has been informed by the earlier seminal work of Box and Cox (1964) and Mosteller and Tukey (1977). These data transformations can be easily achieved with SPSS through its **Compute** procedure (see Chapter 3B).

A note of caution should be expressed here. Data transformations are somewhat of a "double-edged sword." On the one hand, their use can significantly improve the precision of a multivariate analysis. At the same time, however, using a transformation can pose a formidable data interpretation problem. For example, a logarithmic transformation of a mental health consumer's GAF score or number of mental health service sessions will produce numbers quite different from the ordinary raw values we are used to seeing and may therefore pose quite a challenge to the average journal reader to properly interpret (Tabachnick & Fidell, 2001b). Because of this apparent dialectical quandary, we wish to point out at the start of our discussion that we recommend judicious use of data transformations.

A variety of data transformations are available. In many fields of study, certain data transformations (e.g., log transformations) are well accepted because of the distribution of the dependent variables (e.g., reaction time studies in psychology or personal income studies in economics). Some of the more popular transformations, generally, are the square root, logarithm, inverse, square of X, reflect and square root, reflect and logarithm, and reflect and inverse. Table 3a.5 provides some illustrations of these various transformations for some hypothetical GAF score data. The main purpose of Table 3a.5 is to remind the reader that although all these transformations were based on the same original set of five GAF scores, the resulting data values can appear quite strange at first glance. For example, a GAF score of 50 has a square root of 7.07, a log of 3.91, an inverse root of .02, and so on. Journal readers familiar with the GAF measure may be quite uncertain about the meaning of group or variable means reported in terms of these transformations.

Table 3a.5 underscores concretely the potential interpretation difficulties with which researchers are faced when they attempt to discuss even simple descriptive statistics (e.g., means and standard deviations) that are based on transformed data. One way to avoid the possibility of making confusing or misleading statements pertaining to transformed data is to provide the reader with the original variable's statistical context (e.g., minimum and max-imum values or means and standard deviations reported in raw score values).

Statisticians appear to be divided on their recommendations as to which transformation to use for a particular circumstance (e.g., compare Hair et al., 1998, with Tabachnick & Fidell, 2001b). Nevertheless, a basic strategy in using transformations can be outlined in which a progression (escalation)

Table 3a.5   Comparison of Common Data Transformations With Hypothetical GAF Scores

			Transformation					
Case	Original Value	Square Root	Logarithm	Inverse	Square	Reflect & Square Root	Reflect & Logarithm	Reflect & Inverse
1	1.00	1.00	0.00	1.00	1.00	10.00	2.00	.01
2	5.00	2.24	1.61	.20	25.00	9.80	1.98	.01
3	25.00	5.00	3.22	.04	625.00	8.72	1.88	.01
4	50.00	7.07	3.91	.02	2,500.00	7.14	1.71	.02
5	100.00	10.00	4.61	.01	10,000.00	1.00	0.00	1.00

of transformation strategies is employed depending on the perceived severity of the statistical assumption violation. For example, Tabachnick and Fidell (2001b) and Mertler and Vannatta (2001) lobby for a data transformation progression from square root (to correct a moderate violation), to logarithm (for a more substantial violation), and then to inverse square root (to handle a severe violation). In addition, arc sine transformations can be profitably employed with proportional data, and squaring one variable in a nonlinear bivariate relationship can effectively alleviate a nonlinearity problem (Hair et al., 1998).

Recommended Readings

Allison, P. D. (2002). *Missing data.* Thousand Oaks, CA: Sage.

Barnett, V., & Lewis, T. (1978). *Outliers in statistical data.* New York: Wiley.

Berry, W. D. (1993). *Understanding regression assumptions.* Newbury Park, CA: Sage.

Box, G. E. P., & Cox, D. R. (1964). An analysis of transformations. *Journal of the Royal Statistical Society, 26*(Series B), 211–243.

Duncan, T. E., Duncan, S. C., & Li, F. (1998). A comparison of model- and multiple imputation-based approaches to longitudinal analyses with partial missingness. *Structural Equation Modeling, 5,* 1–21.

Enders, C. K. (2001a). The impact of nonnormality on full information maximum-likelihood estimation for structural equation models with missing data. *Psychological Methods, 6,* 352–370.

Enders, C. K. (2001b). A primer on maximum likelihood algorithms available for use with missing data. *Structural Equation Modeling, 8,* 128–141.

Fox, J. (1991). *Regression diagnostics.* Newbury Park, CA: Sage.

Gold, M. S., & Bentler, P. M. (2000). Treatments of missing data: A Monte Carlo comparison of RBHDI, iterative stochastic regression imputation, and expectation-maximization. *Structural Equation Modeling, 7,* 319–355.

Roth, P. L. (1994). Missing data: A conceptual review from applied psychologists. *Personnel Psychology, 47,* 537–560.

Rousseeuw, P. J., & van Zomeren, B. C. (1990). Unmasking multivariate outliers and leverage points. *Journal of the American Statistical Association, 85,* 633–639.

Rubin, D. (1996). Multiple imputation after 18+ years. *Journal of the American Statistical Association, 91,* 473–489.

Schafer, J. L., & Graham, J. W. (2002). Missing data: Our view of the state of the art. *Psychological Methods, 7,* 147–177.

Stevens, J. P. (1984). Outliers and influential data points in regression analysis. *Psychological Bulletin, 95,* 334–344.

Tukey, J. W. (1977). *Exploratory data analysis.* Reading, MA: Addison-Wesley.

Data Screening Using SPSS

I n this chapter, we apply some of the lessons and statistical advice offered in Chapter 3A. In particular, SPSS applications pertaining to data cleaning; missing values; outliers; and assumption violations of normality, linearity, and homoscedasticity for categorical (nonmetric) and continuous (metric) variables within the univariate and (where appropriate) multivariate context will be offered. Categorical (grouped) variables are used with univariate and multivariate analysis of variance and discriminant and logistic regression analysis procedures, whereas continuous (ungrouped) variables are used in multiple regression, factor analysis, and structural equation modeling. These examples are meant to be illustrative and not necessarily exhaustive of all possible data screening techniques available.

The Look of SPSS

In this and the other "B" chapters of this book, we show in our figures both dialog boxes and output tables displayed on the screen by SPSS. Several points about these figures should be noted. First, although we will refer to the variables by names, the variables are identified by their variable labels rather than their variable names in the dialog boxes. This is the default for SPSS. Second, although we have used Version 12 for our analyses, those readers with different versions should be able to generalize what we say to the version you are using. Third, even with a single version of the program, different operating systems (e.g., Windows 2000, Windows XP, OS X for Mac) will generate different "looks" for the dialog boxes. In fact, some of our work was performed on different computers with different Windows systems; thus, the dialog boxes may have a somewhat different look to them. Because students often experience this situation (e.g., a computer at the university is very current, but their home computer is a bit older), we decided to keep the different looks rather than standardize everything.

Numerical Example

As a numerical example, consider the following variables taken from a study by Gamst et al. (2003). This example is based on a subsample of the cases in the data file. We selected child and adult Asian American community mental health consumers. This gave us a sample size of 96. The following variables are used in the example:

▶ Matching of the race/ethnicity of the modal (most frequent) mental health provider with that of the mental health consumer. This variable is labeled client-modal therapist ethnic match and is named **ematch**. A match is coded as 1 and a nonmatch is coded as 2.

▶ A composite measure of consumer satisfaction was obtained by summing each consumer's responses to the 8-item Consumer Satisfaction Scale. This scale is typically abbreviated as CSQ-8, and thus we name the variable **csq8**. The scale was developed by Larsen, Attkisson, Hargreaves, and Nguyen (1979); it is scored on a 4-point Likert-type scale (with 4 = *high satisfaction* and 1 = *low satisfaction*).

▶ The global assessment of functioning (GAF) was administered at the start of treatment as a pretest and again at the end of treatment as a posttest. These variables are labeled GAF pretest and GAF posttest, respectively, and are named **gafpre** and **gafpost**, respectively. The values of the **gafpre** and **gafpost** variables can range from 1 (*severe impairment*) to 100 (*good general functioning*).

▶ The age of the consumer at the start of treatment was recorded. This variable is labeled and named **age**.

Because **ematch** is a categorical (nonmetric) variable and **csq8, gafpre**, **gafpost**, and **age** are all continuous (metric) variables, we will need to consider the screening issues for these two types of variables separately.

Data Cleaning: All Variables

As an initial step, we begin by doing a data cleaning run with SPSS **Frequencies**. Enter SPSS for Windows and open your SPSS data file by clicking **File → Open → Data** and select the SPSS data file you wish to analyze.

To begin this analysis, we click **Analyze** → **Descriptive Statistics** → **Frequencies,** which produces the SPSS dialog box: **Frequencies.** Click over the five variables of interest, in this case, **ematch, csq8, gafpre, gafpost,** and **age.** The left panel of this box lists all the variables in our file. The **Display frequency tables** box that produces frequency tables has been checked (this is the default). By successively clicking each targeted variable in the left panel and then clicking the **arrow** button, we move these variables over to the **Variable(s)** list box on the right side, as shown in Figure 3b.1. The pushbuttons at the bottom of the dialog box (i.e., **Statistics**, **Charts**, and **Format**) provide the researcher with a number of output options for each frequency table.

By clicking the **Statistics** pushbutton, the **Frequencies: Statistics** dialog box is produced (see Figure 3b.2). This dialog box is composed of four sections: **Percentile Values, Dispersion, Central Tendency,** and **Distribution.** In the present example, we ask for the **Mean, Median, Standard deviation, Minimum, Maximum, Skewness,** and **Kurtosis** values for each variable. Some of this information will be used in diagnostic decisions beyond data cleaning. Click on the **Continue** pushbutton to return to the **Frequencies: Statistics** dialog box. Next, by clicking the **Charts** pushbutton we produce the **Frequencies: Charts** dialog box (see the second box of Figure 3b.2). Here, we request **Chart Type: Histograms: With normal curve**. This will also help us with future diagnostic decisions. Click on the **Continue** pushbutton to return to the main dialog box. Click on **OK** to obtain the output file with the results.

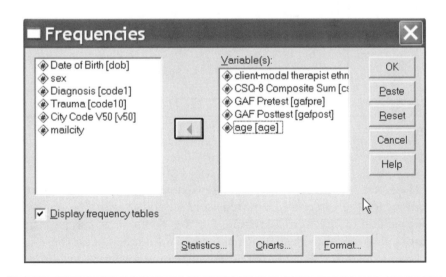

Figure 3b.1   Frequencies Main Dialog Box

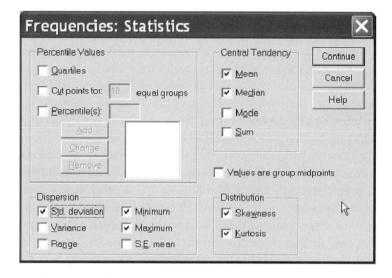

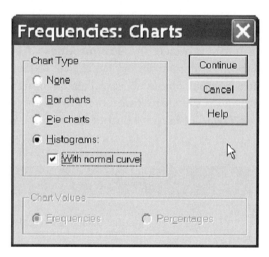

Figure 3b.2   Frequencies: Statistics and Charts Dialog Boxes

Here is a brief summary of what we found. There were no code violations for the categorical **ematch** variable, and no extreme minimum or maximum values were observed for the continuous **csq8**, **gafpre**, **gafpost**, and **age** variables. Means and standard deviations on these continuous variables are all within published ranges and seem reasonable. From this initial assessment, we conclude that these variables are "clean."

Screening Quantitative Variables

Once the plausibility or appropriateness of each continuous variable's range of values has been established (i.e., each variable has been cleaned), we can begin to consider issues of missing values, normality, and univariate outliers with the following SPSS programs: **Frequencies, Descriptives, Explore, and Missing Value Analysis**. Pairwise linearity can be examined with SPSS **Plot,** and assessment for multivariate outliers can be achieved through the SPSS **Regression** procedure. The order in which we discuss these, and the order in which we recommend these procedures be done, is as follows: addressing missing values, dealing with univariate outliers, assessing assumptions, and checking the multivariate outliers.

Missing Values

The **Frequencies: Statistics** table in Figure 3b.3 shows that two of the continuous variables have missing values: **gafpre** has 1 missing value, **gafpost** has 39 missing values, and the other variables contain no missing values. Because the cases with missing values on **gafpre** represent less than 5% of the total cases (actually 1%), which is well below our threshold for

gafpost has 39 missing values

Statistics

		Client-Modal Therapist Ethnic Match	CSQ-8 Composite Sum	GAF Pretest	GAF Posttest	Age
N	Valid	96	96	95	57	96
	Missing	0	0	1	39	0
Mean		1.61	25.9167	50.5158	54.2807	32.7083
Median		2.00	27.5000	50.0000	55.0000	29.0000
Std. Deviation		.489	5.86276	10.99310	16.19607	17.52407
Skewness		−.478	−.938	−.104	−.822	.379
Std. Error of Skewness		.246	.246	.247	.316	.246
Kurtosis		−1.809	.002	−.045	.905	−1.328
Std. Error of Kurtosis		.488	.488	.490	.623	.488
Minimum		1	11.00	20.00	11.00	9.00
Maximum		2	32.00	80.00	83.00	66.00

Figure 3b.3   Frequencies: Statistics Table Output Showing the Missing Number of Cases

possible missing value intervention, we would normally handle this situation with the SPSS default of listwise deletion. However, the large number of missing values for **gafpost** makes it a possible candidate to demonstrate the item imputation process using the **Missing Value Analysis** module (for those of you who have access to this procedure) and the mean substitution facility in SPSS (for those of you who do not have the **Missing Value Analysis** module on your SPSS computer program).

Missing Value Analysis

The missing value analysis (MVA) module is a relatively sophisticated method of addressing various missing data situations. For those of you who have access to this module on your SPSS program, open your data file and click **Analyze → Missing Value Analysis,** which produces the **Missing Value Analysis** dialog box (see Figure 3b.4).

The left panel of this box provides a list of all the variables available for analysis. We are interested in the posttest GAF measure and so we can click over **gafpost** to the **Quantitative Variables** box. On the far right side of the dialog box are the **Patterns** and **Descriptives** pushbuttons. The **Patterns** pushbutton requests various missing data patterns and tabulations. The **Descriptives** pushbutton produces univariate descriptive statistics for each variable and creates a temporary missing indicator variable (missing/nonmissing) that can be assessed with t tests and frequency tables.

Beneath the **Patterns** and **Descriptives** pushbuttons lies the **Estimation** panel that houses four missing value estimation checkboxes: **Listwise, Pairwise, EM,** and **Regression. Listwise** will display statistics (e.g., means) by omitting cases that have missing values on a particular variable (listwise deletion). **Pairwise** produces statistics from all available cases that have valid values (pairwise deletion). Expectation maximization (**EM**) estimates missing values by an iterative (two-step) process. The "**E**" step calculates expected values of parameters, and the "**M**" step calculates maximum likelihood estimates. **Regression** estimates missing values from a regression algorithm. We will checkmark all four boxes for our example. Three additional pushbuttons are available (**Variables, EM,** and **Regression**) that provide special options for the **EM** and **Regression** procedures, including the ability to save the newly imputed missing values in the data file.

By clicking the **Descriptives** pushbutton in the **MVA** dialog box, we produce the **Missing Value Analysis: Descriptives** dialog box, which can also be seen in Figure 3b.4.

One of the options from this dialog box that we have requested is the **Univariate statistics** output displayed in Figure 3b.5. Because of space limitations, other requested output will not be displayed.

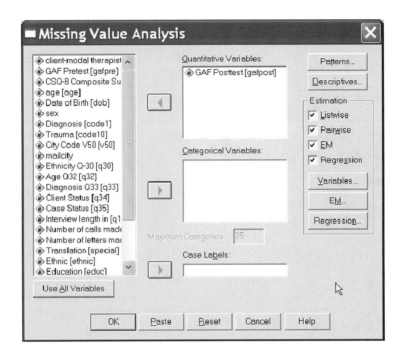

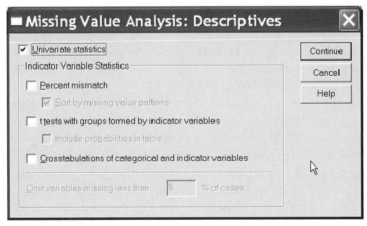

Figure 3b.4 Missing Value Analysis Dialog Boxes

An inspection of the univariate statistics output table shows us that the **gafpost** variable has 39 missing values (we knew this from the frequencies table) that represent 40.6% of the total cases, with 4 cases having extremely low values on this variable. We also note that the **gafpost** mean is 54.28 based on a sample of 57 valid cases.

Univariate Statistics

	N	Mean	Std. Deviation	Missing		No. of Extremes[a]	
				Count	Percent	Low	High
gafpost	57	54.2807	16.19607	39	40.6	4	0

a. Number of cases outside the range (Q1 − 1.5*IQR, Q3 + 1.5*IQR).

Summary if Estimated Means

	gafpost
Listwise	54.2807
All Values	54.2807
EM	54.2807
Regression	53.6042

Figure 3b.5   Univariate Statistics Output and Summary of Estimated Means Output From the Missing Value Analysis Procedure

Because we originally checked all four **Estimation** checkboxes on the **MVA** dialog box (i.e., **Listwise, Pairwise, EM,** and **Regression**) a **Summary of Estimated Means** table is also produced under this **MVA** procedure (see second table of Figure 3b.5).

For **gafpost**, we note that the listwise, pairwise (i.e., **All Values**), and **EM** options produce the same mean value of 54.28. However, we do note a difference between those values and the result of the **Regression** imputation procedure (**gafpost** estimate = 53.60). These estimated missing values parameters can be saved by clicking the **Save completed data** checkbox in the **Missing Value Analysis: Regression** or **EM** dialog box (reached through the **Regression** or **EM** pushbuttons). If data are MCAR (i.e., missing completely at random, as discussed in Chapter 3A), either estimate provides consistent results. If data are MAR (missing at random), we encourage the use of the **EM** procedure (see Hill, 1997). Some authors (e.g., Mertler & Vannatta, 2001) recommend deleting any quantitative variable with more than 15% missing cases. Such a statistically conservative approach seems warranted, in our opinion, if the variable under scrutiny is not of central importance to your study. If you consider the variable to be crucial, then listwise deletion or item imputation appears to be the most parsimonious missing value solution.

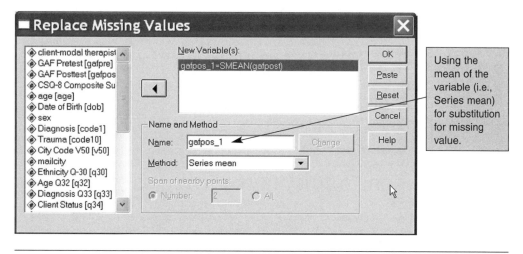

Figure 3b.6 Replace Missing Value Main Dialog Box

Mean Substitution

For those SPSS users without access to the **Missing Value Analysis** module, we will briefly demonstrate the use of the SPSS **Transform** facility for mean substitution of missing values. To begin this analysis, we click **Transform → Replace Missing Values,** which produces the **Replace Missing Values** main dialog box (see Figure 3b.6).

From the variables list panel on the left side, we click over **gafpost**, the variable whose missing values we want to replace, to the **New Variable(s)** panel on the right side of the dialog box. SPSS will automatically designate a new variable and variable name within the **Name and Method** panel (in the present case, **gafpos_1**) that contains the imputed replacement values for those cases that had a missing value on **gafpost**. We have selected **Series mean**, in this case $M = 54.28$ (the mean of the valid values shown in Figure 3b.3) and saved this new configuration as a new variable in our data file. Note that this variable, **gafpos_1**, was created for demonstration purposes only and will not be used in subsequent analyses. Instead, we will continue using **gafpost** with listwise deletion to handle its missing values.

Univariate Outliers

As we noted in Chapter 3A, univariate outliers refer to cases with extreme values on a particular variable. To assess for outliers on our quantitative variables, we begin again by opening our SPSS data file and clicking

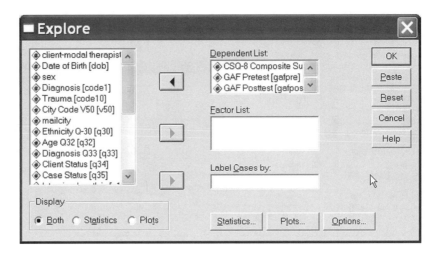

Figure 3b.7 Explore Main Dialog Box

Analyze → Descriptive Statistics → Explore, which opens the **Explore** dialog box (see Figure 3b.7).

The left panel of the dialog box contains a list of all the variables in the analysis. We click over the four quantitative dependent variables (**csq8**, **gafpre**, **gafpost**, **age**) to the **Dependent List** box. The **Factor List** box allows you to click over categorical independent variables that will "break" or profile univariate outliers by each group (or level) of the independent variable. In the present example, we will leave the **Factor List** box blank, because our focus is on the continuous (ungrouped) variables. Below the variable list panel (on the left side) is the **Display** panel, which allows you to toggle between a request for **Statistics** (basic descriptive statistics) or **Plots** (box plots and stem-and-leaf plots) for each variable. The SPSS default is to produce both. Underneath the **Factor List** panel is the **Label Cases by** panel, which allows you to label individual cases by means of a case ID variable instead of the default SPSS-generated case number. On the bottom right-side of the dialog box are three pushbuttons: **Statistics**, **Plots**, and **Options.** These three pushbuttons allow you to request additional descriptive statistics, plots, and ways of overriding the default (listwise) missing values option.

By clicking the **Statistics** pushbutton, the **Explore: Statistics** dialog box is produced (see Figure 3b.8). This dialog box is composed of four checkboxes: **Descriptives** (the default) displays basic descriptive statistics. **M-estimators** apply special maximum-likelihood weights that can be

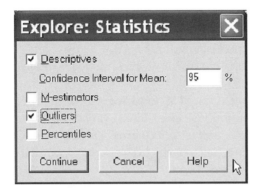

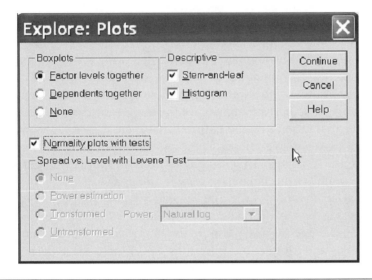

Figure 3b.8 Explore: Statistics and Plots Boxes

applied to cases to estimate central tendency. **Outliers** display cases with the five largest and smallest **Extreme Values** for each dependent variable. **Percentiles** indicate the percentage of cases falling within the 5th, 10th, 25th, 50th, 75th, 90th, and 95th percentiles. For this example, we have clicked on the checkboxes for **Descriptives** and **Outliers.**

A click of the **Plots** pushbutton produces the **Explore: Plots** dialog box (see second box of Figure 3b.8). The **Boxplots** panel produces box plots for each dependent variable for each group or level of the independent variable. If no factor variable (independent variable) is selected (as in the present case), then the box plot represents the total sample. The **Descriptive** panel produces stem-and-leaf and histogram plots of continuous variables through their respective checkboxes. The **Normality plots with tests** checkbox produces normal and detrended probability plots, along with the Kolmogorov-Smirnov statistic and Shapiro-Wilk statistic for testing univariate normality, which we will cover in the next section of this chapter.

Let's take a look at the SPSS **Explore** output as it pertains to univariate outliers for the continuous (ungrouped) variables. Figure 3b.9 lists the five largest and smallest cases with **Extreme Values** on each continuous variable. From this figure, we note the five relatively low values for **gafpost** (i.e., case numbers 64, 65, 66, 72, and 77).

Stem-and-leaf plots for each of the four continuous variables (i.e., **csq8**, **gafpre**, **gafpost**, and **age**) can be seen in Figure 3b.10. These stem-and-leaf plots indicate that **csq8** has no univariate outliers and that **gafpre**, **gafpost**, and **age** had only a few extreme cases.

The stem-and-leaf findings are confirmed with the box plots of the total sample for each continuous variable (see Figure 3b.11). With regard to univariate outliers, however, the box plots provide us with an additional ingredient—the actual case number for the outliers on each variable. Hence, we can see that Case 72 on the **gafpre** variable and Cases 72, 66, 64, and 65 on the **gafpost** variable are possible candidates for deletion. In particular, because Case 72 appears to be an outlier on both **gafpre** and **gafpost**, we would recommend its elimination from future analyses.

Casual examination of the **age** variable box plot suggests that we have five outliers as possible candidates for deletion. However, these univariate outliers on the **age** variable illustrate the importance of being familiar with the variables and sample under scrutiny. Specifically, these particular outliers are simply adult mental health consumers who happen to be greater than or equal to 52 years of age, which can be seen from an inspection. Although they are clearly the oldest respondents in the sample, their age alone would not preclude them from being included in the study. Hence, the lesson is that a software program such as SPSS can *indicate* where the outliers are in your data file, but you must make the final determination of their disposition.

Normality

To address the issue of univariate normality for the quantitative variables, we begin by examining the skewness and kurtosis values for these variables as shown in Figure 3b.3. We note that **gafpre** appears to be normally distributed and that some negative skewness (–.938) is associated with **csq8** and negative skewness (–.822) and positive kurtosis (.905) with **gafpost**. Because these skewness and kurtosis values are within the +1.0 to −1.0 range, we

Extreme Values

			Case Number	Value
CSQ-8 Composite Sum	Highest	1	96	32.00
		2	125	32.00
		3	128	32.00
		4	138	32.00
		5	142	32.00[a]
	Lowest	1	164	11.00
		2	82	11.00
		3	130	13.00
		4	123	13.00
		5	107	13.00
GAF Pretest	Highest	1	177	80.00
		2	117	70.00
		3	173	70.00
		4	174	70.00
		5	179	70.00
	Lowest	1	72	20.00
		2	116	25.00
		3	79	31.00
		4	100	35.00
		5	102	38.00
GAF Posttest	Highest	1	181	83.00
		2	179	82.00
		3	180	82.00
		4	177	80.00
		5	174	73.00
	Lowest	1	64	11.00
		2	65	13.00
		3	66	15.00
		4	72	20.00
		5	77	30.00[b]
age	Highest	1	138	66.00
		2	146	65.00
		3	116	59.00
		4	64	55.00
		5	79	53.00
	Lowest	1	153	9.00
		2	160	10.00
		3	134	11.00
		4	157	12.00
		5	156	12.00[c]

Each case number represents a client in the data file. Clients 64, 65, 66, 72, and 77 have the lowest scores on gafpost.

a. Only a partial list of cases with the value 32.00 are shown in the table of upper extremes.
b. Only a partial list of cases with the value 30.00 are shown in the table of lower extremes.
c. Only a partial list of cases with the value 12.00 are shown in the table of lower extremes.

Figure 3b.9   Extreme Values Output From the Explore Menu

```
CSQ-8 Composite Sum Stem-and-Leaf Plot

Frequency        Stem  &  Leaf

      6.00          1  .  113334
      7.00          1  .  5556777
     14.00          2  .  11123333344444
     16.00          2  .  5555666778888899
     14.00          3  .  00001222222222

Stem width:        10.00
Each leaf:          1 case(s)
```

```
GAF Pretest Stem-and-Leaf Plot

Frequency        Stem  &  Leaf

      1.00  Extremes      (=<20)
      1.00          2  .  5
      3.00          3  .  158
     12.00          4  .  000012555558
     21.00          5  .  000000001555555555588
     14.00          6  .  00000002225558
      4.00          7  .  0000
      1.00          8  .  0

Stem width:        10.00
Each leaf:          1 case(s)
```

```
GAF Posttest Stem-and-Leaf Plot

Frequency        Stem  &  Leaf

      4.00    Extremes      (=<20) ◀
      3.00          3  .  001
      6.00          4  .  001255
     18.00          5  .  000000012355555558
     18.00          6  .  000000001555555588
      4.00          7  .  0003
      4.00          8  .  0223

Stem width:        10.00
Each leaf:          1 case(s)
```

> There are 4 extreme scores of 20 or less.

```
age Stem-and-Leaf Plot

Frequency        Stem  &  Leaf

      1.00          0  .  9
     30.00          1  .  012223455566677777778888999999
      8.00          2  .  00238999
      8.00          3  .  01111347
      3.00          4  .  367
      2.00          5  .  01
      5.00  Extremes      (=<52)

Stem width:        10.00
Each leaf:          1 case(s)
```

Figure 3b.10   Stem-and-Leaf Plots for Csq8, Gafpre, Gafpost, and Age

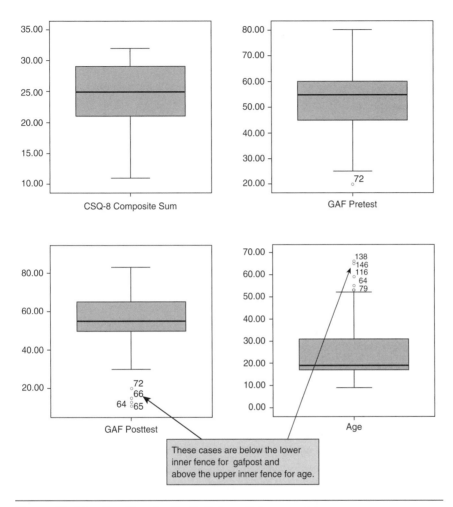

Figure 3b.11 Box Plots for Csq8, Gafpre, Gafpost, and Age

deem them acceptable for our current purposes; alternatively, we could have targeted **csq8** and **gafpost** for transformation. However, the **age** variable shows fairly strong kurtosis (–1.33) and hence is a good candidate for transformation. Following our discussion of variable transformations in Chapter 3A, we choose to transform **age** with a base-10 logarithm.

To accomplish this transformation, we click **Transform → Compute,** which produces the **Compute Variable** dialog box (see Figure 3b.12). In the top left corner is the **Target Variable** box where you enter a name and variable label for the new variable you are creating. We will call this new variable **lage** (for log of age). The top right section of the dialog box contains the **Numeric Expression** box. Below this box is the **Functions** list. Scroll

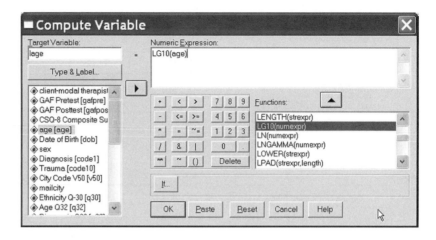

Figure 3b.12   Compute Variable Dialog Box From the Transform Selection

down on the **Functions** list until you reach the **LG10** (log base-10) numeric expression, highlight it, and then click the up arrow button to move it into the **Numeric Expression** box. On the left side of the dialog box (below the **Target Variable** box) is the variable list box. Here, we highlight and click over the original age variable to the **Numeric Expression** box. This replaces the question mark inside the parentheses (**?**) with the original age variable. By clicking **OK** at the bottom of the dialog box, the new variable **lage** is saved to the SPSS data file.

To assess our "handiwork" on our new age variable (**lage**) we again navigate through **Analyze → Descriptive Statistics → Explore**, which produces the **Explore** dialog box (not shown). In this dialog box, we have clicked over to the **Dependent List** box the four continuous variables (**csq8**, **gafpre**, **gafpost**, and **lage**). From the **Statistics** pushbutton, we have elicited the default **Descriptives** (statistics) with listwise deletion. And from the **Plots** pushbutton we requested the **Histogram** and **Normality plots with tests**. Let's take a look at some of the output. Figure 3b.13 displays descriptive statistics on the four continuous variables with listwise deletion.

The transformation of the age variable into **lage** was successful and has reduced considerably this variable's negative kurtosis (e.g., from −1.33 to −.613). Although skewness and kurtosis are still present, they are now within acceptable limits (i.e., between +1.0 and −1.0). These statistical assessments are further confirmed by an examination of the normal probability plots or a **normal Q-Q plot** of each variable (see Figure 3b.14). In these plots, SPSS rank orders the original observations and compares

Descriptives

			Statistic	Std. Error
CSQ-8 Composite Sum	Mean		24.1404	.83450
	95% Confidence	Lower Bound	22.4686	
	Interval for Mean	Upper Bound	25.8121	
	5% Trimmed Mean		24.4006	
	Median		25.0000	
	Variance		39.694	
	Std. Deviation		6.30034	
	Minimum		11.00	
	Maximum		32.00	
	Range		21.00	
	Interquartile Range		8.50	
	Skewness		−.568	.316
	Kurtosis		−.726	.623
GAF Pretest	Mean		52.8246	1.53124
	95% Confidence	Lower Bound	49.7571	
	Interval for Mean	Upper Bound	55.8920	
	5% Trimmed Mean		53.2193	
	Median		55.0000	
	Variance		133.647	
	Std. Deviation		11.56059	
	Minimum		20.00	
	Maximum		80.00	
	Range		60.00	
	Interquartile Range		15.00	
	Skewness		−.428	.316
	Kurtosis		562	.623
GAF Posttest	Mean		54.2807	2.14522
	95% Confidence	Lower Bound	49.9833	
	Interval for Mean	Upper Bound	58.5781	
	5% Trimmed Mean		55.0205	
	Median		55.0000	
	Variance		262.313	
	Std. Deviation		16.19607	
	Minimum		11.00	
	Maximum		83.00	
	Range		72.00	
	Interquartile Range		15.00	
	Skewness		−.822	.316
	Kurtosis		.905	.623
Log Base 10 Age	Mean 95%		1.3578	.02913
	Confidence	Lower Bound	1.2994	
	Interval for Mean	Upper Bound	1.4161	
	5% Trimmed Mean		1.3531	
	Median		1.2788	
	Variance		.048	
	Std. Deviation		.21993	
	Minimum		.95	
	Maximum		1.82	
	Range		.87	
	Interquartile Range		.27	
	Skewness		.497	.316
	Kurtosis		−.613	.623

> Skewness and kurtosis values on this transformed age variable are now acceptable.

Figure 3b.13 Descriptive Statistics Output With Listwise Deletion

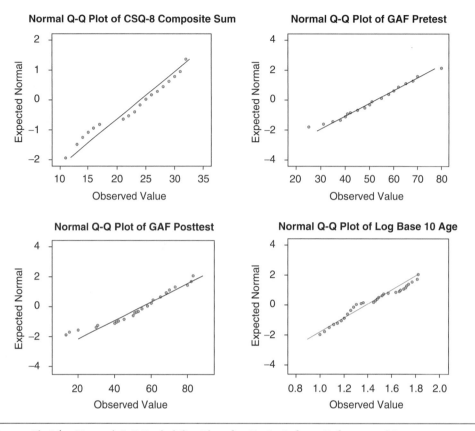

Figure 3b.14   Normal Q-Q Probability Plots for Csq8, Gafpre, Gafpost, and Lage

them with a computed expected normal value. These expected values are standardized scores (*z* scores) that represent each case's rank from lowest to highest (see Tabachnick & Fidell, 2001b). A normal distribution is indicated if the data points fall on or very near the diagonal line. For the most part, this appears to be the case for these continuous variables.

Linearity

To determine if our continuous variables are linearly related to each other, we will run SPSS **Graphs** to examine the shape of the bivariate scatterplots for each combination of variables. As you will recall from our discussion in Chapter 3A, scatterplots that are elliptical or oval shaped are indicative of linearity between two variables. To produce these plots, we

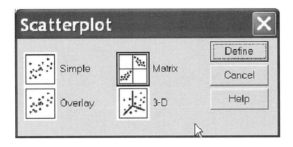

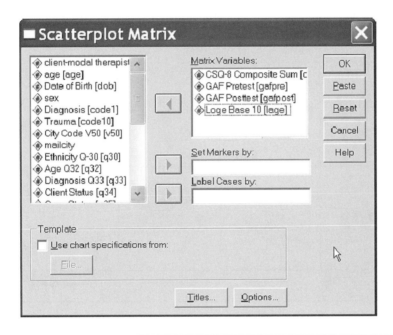

Figure 3b.15 Scatterplot Main Dialog Box and Its Matrix Box

begin by clicking **Graphs → Scatter,** which produces the **Scatterplot** dialog box (see Figure 3b.15). This box provides four scatterplot options: **Simple** plots two variables (*X* and *Y*) on two scale axes for each case. **Overlay** plots two or more *X-Y* variable pairs in the plot frame. **Matrix** plots a matrix of bivariate scatterplots for all possible pairs selected. And **3-D** plots three variables on three axes in a 3-D coordinate system.

In the present example, we highlight the **Matrix** panel and click the **Define** pushbutton, which in turn produces the **Scatterplot Matrix** dialog box (see second box of Figure 3b.15).

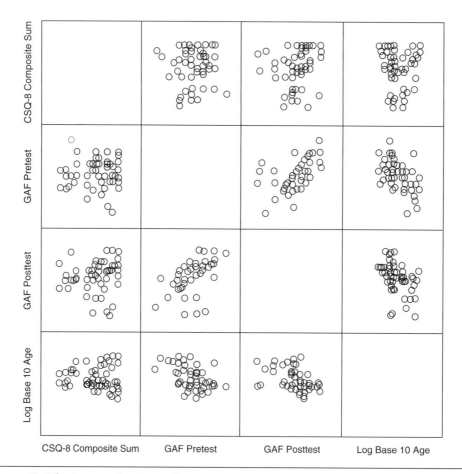

Figure 3b.16 Output of a Scatterplot Matrix

From the variables list panel, we click over the four continuous variables (**csq8**, **gafpre**, **gafpost**, and **lage**) into the **Matrix Variables** box on the right side of the dialog box and then click the **OK** pushbutton. This produces the scatterplot matrix output of the four continuous variables (see Figure 3b.16).

Although certainly not perfect ovals, for present illustrative purposes, these scatterplots appear to depict enough linearity in the relationships of the variables to proceed with the analysis. Alternatively, the researcher could go back and examine univariate normality for each variable and perhaps compute additional variable transformations.

Multivariate Outliers

To check for multivariate outliers among the continuous variables, we need to calculate Mahalanobis distance for each case with the SPSS **Regression** procedure. This is accomplished by clicking **Analyze → Regression → Linear,** which produces the **Linear Regression** dialog box (see Figure 3b.17). The multiple regression technique and the specifics of this box will be elaborated in Chapters 5A and 5B, respectively. For present purposes, we will click over the **caseid** variable (in this example, a unique integer for each case starting with 1 through *N*) to the **Dependent** box and the four continuous variables to the **Independent(s)** box and click the **Save** pushbutton at the bottom of the dialog box. By using **caseid** as our "dependent variable," we can run the procedure without worrying about the bulk of the output.

By clicking the **Save** pushbutton, we produce the **Linear Regression: Save** dialog box (see second box of Figure 3b.17), which will be discussed in more detail in Chapter 5B. For our current purposes, we will click the **Mahalanobis** checkbox in the **Distances** panel and click the **Continue** pushbutton. This brings us back to the **Linear Regression** dialog box, where we click the **OK** pushbutton, which runs a multiple regression whose output we will ignore because it reflects an analysis with **caseid** as the dependent variable.

The result of these steps creates a new variable called **MAH_1**, which is the Mahalanobis distance values for each case on the four continuous variables. This **MAH_1** variable will be automatically saved as a new variable in the data file by SPSS. The Mahalanobis distance values are evaluated with a chi-square (χ^2) distribution, with degrees of freedom equal to the number of variables clicked into the **Independent(s)** area (4 in this case) and evaluated with a *Table of Critical Values* for chi square at a stringent alpha level of $p < .001$ (see Appendix A). In the present example, any case with a Mahalanobis distance value equal to or greater than 18.467 can be considered a multivariate outlier. By running the SPSS **Frequencies** or **Explore** procedures, we can observe the Mahalanobis distance scores. In the present example, we click **Analyze → Descriptive Statistics → Explore,** and in the **Explore** dialog box, we click over the new variable **MAH_1** into the **Dependent List**. Next we click the **Statistics** pushbutton, check the **Outliers** checkbox, click on the **Continue** pushbutton, and then click the **OK** pushbutton. This produces the **Extreme Values** output (i.e., the five highest and lowest cases) for the **MAH_1** variable (see Figure 3b.18). From this output, we note that none of the critical values associated with any of the cases equals or exceeds 18.467; thus we conclude that no multivariate outliers are present among these four continuous variables.

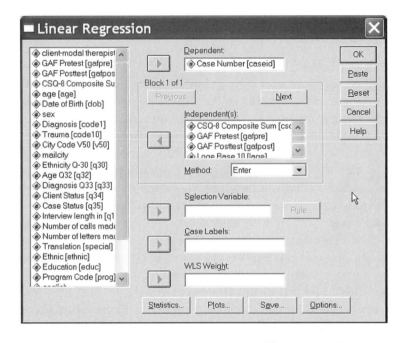

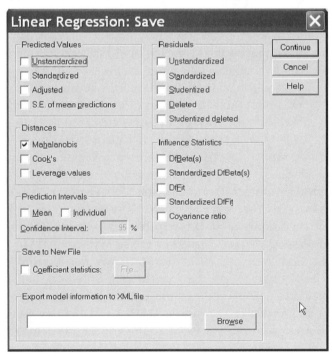

Figure 3b.17 Linear Regression Main Dialog Box and Its Save Box

Extreme Values

			Case Number	Value
Mahalanobis Distance	Highest	1	66	13.94695
		2	65	11.50977
		3	64	10.87904
		4	117	10.07419
		5	72	10.01484
	Lowest	1	126	.08285
		2	122	.18684
		3	131	.35873
		4	141	.40227
		5	143	.49219

Because none of the values exceeds the chi-square criterion, we conclude that there are no multivariate outliers.

Figure 3b.18　Extreme Values Output Table for the Mahalanobis Values

Screening Categorical Variables

When you screen data based on grouped or categorical variables, you need to consider the data for each group or level of the variable in question. For the present purposes, let's assume we are interested in the effects of **ematch** (a categorical variable) on our continuous variable of **gafpost**. Because many of the SPSS procedures we covered for continuous variables are the same for categorical variables, we will dispense with many of the SPSS programming details and examples.

We begin by inspecting the frequency output for **ematch** by clicking **Analyze → Descriptive Statistics → Frequencies.** The output can be seen in Figure 3b.19. The categorical **ematch** variable is disproportionately split: ethnic match = 38.5% and no match = 61.5%; because this is not an extreme or unusual bifurcation (e.g., 90% for one and 10% for the other) we will leave this variable as is and proceed with our screening. We also note that the **ematch** variable contains no apparent code violations (i.e., all the values were 1s and 2s) and there were no missing values (output not shown).

Univariate Outliers

Our goal here will be to check for outliers (cases with extreme values) on **gafpost** within each level (or group) of **ematch**. We accomplish this by clicking **Analyze → Descriptive Statistics → Explore** where we click over **gafpost** into the **Dependent List** and **ematch** into the **Factor**

Client-Modal Therapist Ethnic Match

		Frequency	Percent	Valid Percent	Cumulative Percent
Valid	Match	37	38.5	38.5	38.5
	No Match	59	61.5	61.5	100.0
	Total	96	100.0	100.0	

Figure 3b.19   Frequencies Output for the Ematch Variable

List (see Figure 3b.20). As we have shown previously, by clicking the **Statistics** pushbutton, the **Explore: Statistics** dialog box is produced. Here we click the **Outliers** checkbox, and **Continue**. We can also click the **Plots** pushbutton and its **Stem-and-leaf** and **Normality plots with tests** (which we will consider later).

The outlier output information can be seen in Figure 3b.21. Comparing the two stem-and-leaf plots, it can be determined that the no-match group has two cases with extremely low values. These cases are identified (i.e., case numbers 65 and 66) in the **Extreme Values** and box plot outputs. These two cases would be possible candidates for deletion.

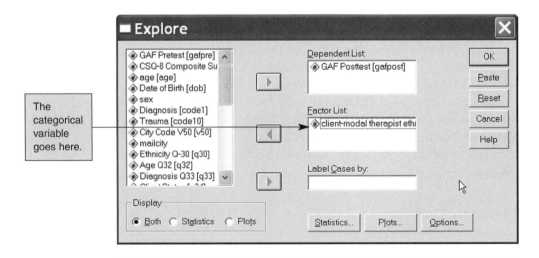

Figure 3b.20   Explore Dialog Box to Look at Gafpost Values Within Each Level of Ematch

```
GAF Posttest Stem-and-Leaf Plot
for ematch= Match

Frequency    Stem & Leaf
      1.00     1 . 1
      1.00     2 . 0
      2.00     3 . 00
      1.00     4 . 5
      4.00     5 . 1235
      5.00     6 . 00055
      1.00     7 . 0

Stem width:     10.00

Each leaf:       1 case(s)
```

```
GAF Posttest Stem-and-Leaf Plot
for ematch= No Match

Frequency      Stem & Leaf
      2.00   Extremes   (=<15)
      1.00       3 . 1
      5.00       4 . 00125
     14.00       5 . 00000005555558
     13.00       6 . 0000015555588
      3.00       7 . 003
      4.00       8 . 0223

Stem width:       10.00

Each leaf:         1 case(s)
```

Extreme Values

Client-Modal				Case Number	Value
GAF Posttest	Match	Highest	1	168	70.00
			2	153	65.00
			3	160	65.00
			4	134	60.00
			5	138	60.00[a]
		Lowest	1	64	11.00
			2	72	20.00
			3	77	30.00
			4	76	30.00
			5	100	45.00
	No Match	Highest	1	181	83.00
			2	179	82.00
			3	180	82.00
			4	177	80.00
			5	174	73.00
		Lowest	1	65	13.00
			2	66	15.00
			3	79	31.00
			4	82	40.00
			5	80	40.00

a. Only a partial list of cases with the value 60.00 are shown in the table of upper extremes

Figure 3b.21 Selected Output for Outlier Information

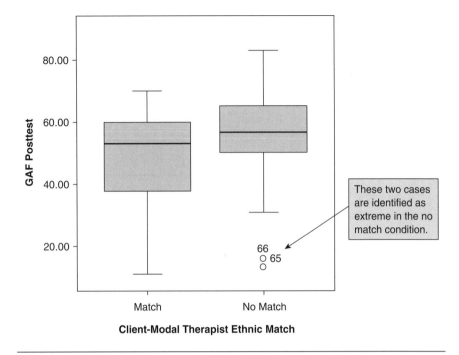

Figure 3b.21   (Continued)

Normality

After missing values and outliers have been addressed, we can check to see if **gafpost** is normally distributed across levels of **ematch**. This has been accomplished within our previous SPSS **Explore** run. Normality can also be assessed with SPSS **Frequencies** procedure. We display the output of the normal probability (Q-Q) plots and tests of normality for **gafpost** at each level (match, no match) of **ematch** (see Figure 3b.22). The **Q-Q plots** indicate some nonnormality for **gafpost** among ethnically matched consumers and normality for the nonmatched consumers.

Analogously, the Kolmogorov-Smirnov and the Shapiro-Wilk tests (see Figure 3b.23) were not significant at the .01 alpha level (which we recommend as a suitably stringent alpha level with these tests because of their sensitivity to any normality departures and particularly with small sample sizes). Should you choose to operate at a less stringent alpha level (i.e., $p < .05$) with these tests of normality, transformation of **gafpost** would then be in order.

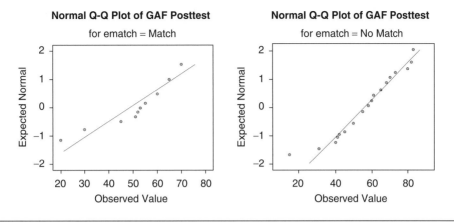

Figure 3b.22   Normal Q-Q Probability Plots for Gafpost When Ematch Is Considered

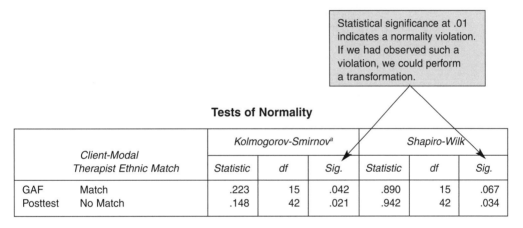

Statistical significance at .01 indicates a normality violation. If we had observed such a violation, we could perform a transformation.

Tests of Normality

	Client-Modal Therapist Ethnic Match	Kolmogorov-Smirnov[a]			Shapiro-Wilk		
		Statistic	df	Sig.	Statistic	df	Sig.
GAF Posttest	Match	.223	15	.042	.890	15	.067
	No Match	.148	42	.021	.942	42	.034

a. Lilliefors Significance Correction.

Figure 3b.23   Output Table Displaying the Tests of Normality

Homoscedasticity

Linearity assumption violations are not assessed when a categorical variable is involved. However, the issue of homoscedasticity or homogeneity of variance (equal variance) of the dependent variable (in this case, **gafpost**) across levels of the independent variable comes into play and can be readily assessed with SPSS (e.g., **One-Way, MANOVA** procedures). To assess homoscedasticity, we

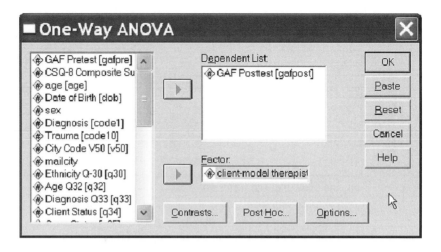

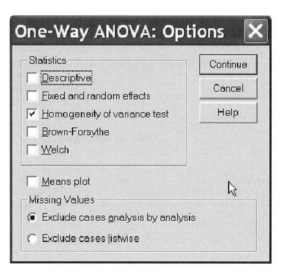

Figure 3b.24 One-Way ANOVA Main Dialog Box and Its Options Box

will run the Levene's Test for Equality of Variances by clicking **Analyze →
Compare Means → One-Way ANOVA,** which produces the **One-Way
ANOVA** dialog box (see Figure 3b.24). As can be seen in Figure 3b.24, from the
variables list panel we have clicked over **gafpost** to the **Dependent List** box
and **ematch** to the **Factor** box. By clicking the **Options** pushbutton, we produce the **One-Way ANOVA: Options** dialog box (see second box of Figure
3b.24) where we check the **Homogeneity of variance test** checkbox.
Clicking **OK** in the original dialog box produces the output that can be seen in

Test of Homogeneity of Variances

GAF Posttest

Levene Statistic	df1	df2	Sig.
.913	1	55	.343

A nonsignificant Levene statistic indicates that we have homogeneity of variance.

ANOVA

GAF Posttest

	Sum of Squares	df	Mean Square	F	Sig.
Between Groups	688.133	1	688.133	2.703	.106
Within Groups	14001.38	55	254.570		
Total	14689.51	56			

Figure 3b.25   One-Way ANOVA Output Results

Figure 3b.25. The Levene statistic is not statistically significant ($p > .05$), telling us that there are equal variances across levels of **ematch** on **gafpost**.

Homogeneity of Variance-Covariance Matrices

The "next of kin" of the homoscedasticity assumption is the multivariate homogeneity of variance-covariance assumption, where the equality of variance-covariance matrices is examined across levels of an independent variable and is evaluated with the SPSS **MANOVA** procedure. Assume that our dependent variables are **gafpre** and **gafpost** and the independent variable remains **ematch**. The test statistic we will use to test this assumption is the **Box's Test of Equality of Covariance Matrices,** which can be produced by clicking **Analyze → General Linear Model → Multivariate**. This produces the **Multivariate** dialog box (see Figure 3b.26). Again, we click over our two dependent variables (**gafpre** and **gafpost**) to the **Dependent Variables** box and the independent variable (**ematch**) to the **Fixed Factor(s)** box. Details on the **MANOVA** procedure will be provided in later chapters.

By clicking the **Options** pushbutton, we produce the **Multivariate: Options** dialog box (see second box of Figure 3b.26), where we check the **Homogeneity tests** checkbox. Clicking the **Continue** pushbutton brings you back to the original dialog box, where we click the **OK** pushbutton that produces the output tables.

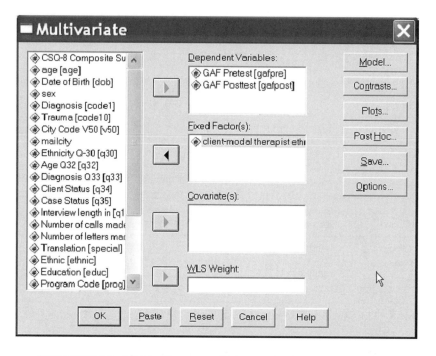

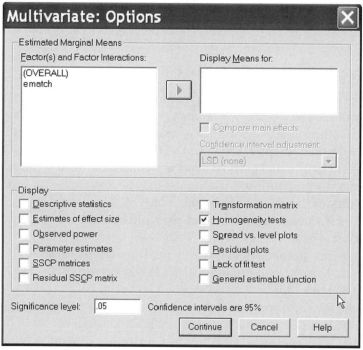

Figure 3b.26 Multivariate Main Dialog Box and Its Options Box

Box's Test of Equality of Covariance Matrices[a]

Box's	
M	4.250
F	1.337
df1	3
df2	11531.67
Sig.	.260

A nonsignificant Box's M Test indicates equal covariance between the dependent variables for the groups composing the independent variables.

Tests the null hypothesis that the observed covariance matrices of the dependent variables are equal across groups.

a. Design: Intercept + ematch.

Figure 3b.27 Multivariate Output Showing Box's Test

One of the output tables we want to see is shown in Figure 3b.27. From that output, we can see that Box's test is not statistically significant ($p > .01$) and thus we can conclude equality of variance-covariance matrices.

Results

Before proceeding with the data analysis, all variables were screened for possible code and statistical assumption violations, as well as for missing values and outliers, with SPSS Frequencies, Explore, Plot, Missing Value Analysis, and Regression procedures. The 96 Asian American mental health consumers were screened for missing values on four continuous variables (csq8, gafpre, gafpost, and age). None was detected for csq8 and age, and 1 missing value was discovered and eliminated through listwise deletion for gafpre. Gafpost had 39 missing values (40.6% of the cases), and these values were replaced with a value based on an expectation-maximization algorithm using SPSS Missing Value Analysis.

Ten univariate outliers (1 for gafpre, 4 for gafpost, and 5 for age) were detected, none of which were considered extreme or unusual enough to require deletion. Because of extreme negative kurtosis, age was transformed with a base-10 logarithm. Pairwise linearity was deemed satisfactory. Multivariate outliers were screened by computing Mahalanobis distance for each case on the four continuous variables, of which none was detected ($p > .001$).

3B Exercises

GAF, Consumer Satisfaction, and Type of Clinical Agency (Public or Private)

This study was conducted to assess if there are differences between GAF and consumer satisfaction between public or private clinical agencies.

Use the SPSS data file for Chapter 3B (located on the Web-based study site—http://www.sagepub.com/amrStudy) to answer the following questions:

1. Identify the independent variable. Identify the dependent variable(s).

2. Are there any missing values for any of the variables? If there are, what do you recommend doing to address this issue?

3. Were there any outliers in this data set? If outliers are present, what is your recommendation?

4. Check the independent and dependent variables for statistical assumptions violations. If there are violations, what do you recommend?

5. Write a sample result section, discussing your data screening activity.

Bivariate Correlation and Simple Linear Regression

The Concept of Relationship

A *correlation* is a way to index the degree to which two or more variables are associated with or related to each other. This concept of relationship is fundamental to understanding research design and statistical analysis, and it is for this reason that we begin our study of multivariate research designs with a discussion of bivariate correlation and simple linear regression.

Perhaps the most basic question that research is designed to answer is whether two variables are related to each other. The attempt to answer this question falls into the domain of bivariate correlation. It is *bivariate* because we are addressing the relationship between two ("bi") variables. Although our focus in this chapter will be on bivariate correlation, we will see in Chapters 5A and 5B that it is possible to deal with relationships involving more than two variables.

Probably the most widely used bivariate correlation statistic is the Pearson product-moment coefficient, commonly called the Pearson correlation. It is abbreviated as r. The Pearson r indexes the extent to which a linear relationship exists between two quantitatively measured variables. A good way to think about a relationship or an association between two variables is in terms of *covariation*. In its most basic form, covariation deals with the patterns exhibited by the two variables being evaluated. For this evaluation to be meaningful, the data must be arranged pairwise—that is, the data must be arranged so that the two pieces of information (one for each variable) derived from the same person are linked to each other. This is shown schematically below. We then wind up with two lists or distributions of scores that are paired with each other.

Person	Variable X	Variable Y
A	A's score on X	A's score on Y
B	B's score on X	B's score on Y
C	C's score on X	C's score on Y

With the data in the form shown above, the amount of covariation that exists between the two variables summarizes how the differences in one variable correspond with the differences in the other. That we have differences is a crucial point. It is difference that creates pattern—it is difference that provides information. Just as a canvas of a single, uniform color would not ordinarily be considered a work of art, a list of identical numbers could have no pattern or no variation, and with no variation, they could not covary with some other set of numbers. With no covariation, there can be no correlation.

We can demonstrate with the use of a series of small data sets how to generally read these covariation patterns. Bear in mind at the outset that what we are looking for is a pattern based on the linked distributions.

Perfect Relationships, Perfect Positive Relationships

Consider the data in Table 4a.1, which have been plotted in the accompanying Figure 4a.1. We have made the pattern more apparent in the table by ordering the list from lowest to highest based on the X score. In Figure 4a.1, individuals' scores on the two variables are shown by a dot indicating where they coincide on the axes. For example, the data point in Figure 4a.1 representing Person A is at the coordinate where X = 10 and Y = 20.

The covariation pattern shown in Table 4a.1 and Figure 4a.1 is as follows: Every Y score is 10 points greater than its corresponding X score. Given this

Table 4a.1 Covariation Pattern Example 1: Perfect Positive Correlation

Person	Variable X	Variable Y
A	10	20
C	25	35
B	30	40
D	50	60

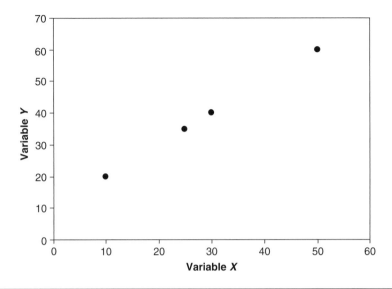

Figure 4a.1 Perfect Positive Relationship

lockstep correspondence, the relationship is as strong as it can be. We can see this in Figure 4a.1 in that each data point is precisely in line with all the others. If we fit a straight line through this lockstep array of data points, that line would intersect all the data points.

When we calculate the Pearson r for this set of data points, we would find it to be +1.00. The positive sign simply means that higher values on X are associated with higher values on Y. A positive correlation thus indicates a direct relationship.

The presence of such a clear covariation pattern makes very accurate prediction possible. Given that these two variables are perfectly correlated, we could precisely predict someone's Y score if we knew how that person had scored on X. For example, someone with an X score of 15 should have a Y score of 25. Prediction is thus founded on correlation; statistically, it is handled through a procedure called *regression*.

Perfect Negative Relationships

To reinforce this idea, consider the data in Table 4a.2, which have been plotted in Figure 4a.2. Again in this table we have ordered the data on the X variable to make the pattern easier to observe, although the pattern becomes quite clear when one examines the figure. As can be seen, higher scores on X are associated with lower scores on Y. This signifies an inverse relationship and results in a negative correlation.

Table 4a.2   Covariation Pattern Example 2: Perfect Negative Correlation

Person	Variable X	Variable Y
E	6	4
F	7	3
G	8	2
H	9	1

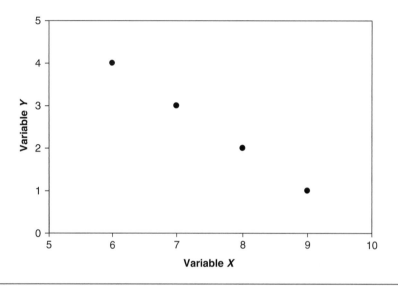

Figure 4a.2   Perfect Negative Relationship

The covariation shown in Table 4a.2 and depicted in Figure 4a.2 is also in lockstep: The Y score is the result of subtracting the X score from 10. In the figure, the data points all fall on a straight line. Thus, we have a perfect relationship. If we calculated the Pearson r, it would turn out to be −1.00. With this perfect correlation, we could again perfectly predict the value of Y from a knowledge of how the person scored on X.

Nonperfect Relationships

Table 4a.3 shows a positive correlation between the two variables, although it is not absolutely perfect. This is perhaps more clearly seen in the plot of these data points as shown in Figure 4a.3. As we can see (a) higher

Table 4a.3   Covariation Pattern Example 3: Strong Positive Correlation

Person	Variable X	Variable Y
E	100	55
F	120	50
G	135	70
H	150	71

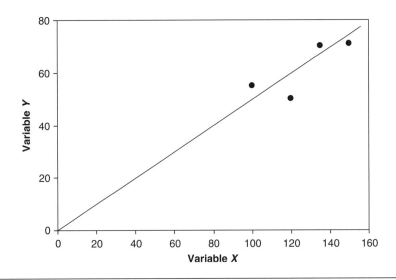

Figure 4a.3   Nonperfect Positive Relationship

scores on *X* are generally, but not absolutely, associated with higher scores on *Y*; (b) even when higher scores on one variable are associated with higher scores on the other variable, there is still some variability in the amount of such differences.

It is possible to draw a straight line that "best fits" the array of points, and this has been done in Figure 4a.3. Because the data points are not in lockstep—that is, because the covariation is not perfect—they do not fall exactly on this line of best fit. But even without perfection, it is possible to see that there is still quite a bit of covariation present. The correlation for these data is .80. In predicting *Y* from a knowledge of *X*, we would do much better than chance, but our prediction could not be perfect because the relationship between the two variables is not perfect.

Absence of Relationship

Table 4a.4 and the accompanying Figure 4a.4 illustrate the situation where there is no relationship at all between the two variables. Lower scores on *X* are not systematically associated with either lower or higher scores on *Y*. That is, *X* scores of 15 and 16 (i.e., lower *X* scores) are linked to *Y* scores of 45 and 10 (i.e., they are linked to both lower and higher *Y* scores). Likewise, higher scores on *X* are not systematically associated with either lower or higher scores on *Y*. That is, *X* scores of 33 and 34 are linked to *Y* scores of 46 and 12.

The lack of any systematic covariation between the two variables can also be seen in Figure 4a.4. The data points appear to be found all over the

Table 4a.4 Covariation Pattern Example 4: Zero Correlation

Person	Variable X	Variable Y
J	15	45
K	16	10
L	33	46
M	34	12

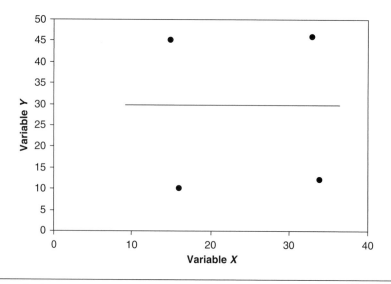

Figure 4a.4 Absence of Relationship

set of axes, and the line of best fit actually turns out to lie in a position that is parallel to the *X* axis. The slope of this line is virtually zero, a mathematical indication that the Pearson *r* would yield a value very close to zero (it's actually –.01).

We stated earlier that there needed to be variation for there to be the possibility of a pattern. Table 4a.5 shows a situation in which there is no variation in the *X* variable. These data are plotted in Figure 4a.5, which shows that the data points are vertically stacked over the *X* value of 50. Every value of *Y* is associated with an *X* value of 50. Without variation on both variables, there can be no possibility of covariation, so the correlation (the covariation) in Figure 4a.5 is zero.

Table 4a.5   Covariation Pattern Example 5: Zero Correlation

Person	Variable X	Variable Y
E	50	75
F	50	80
G	50	85
H	50	90

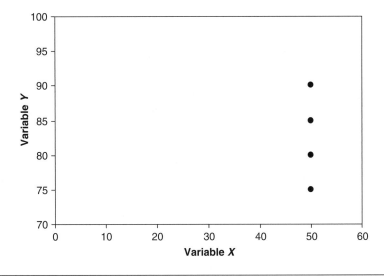

Figure 4a.5   Example of No Variation on the *X* Variable

Notice that with a correlation of zero, there is no predictability. Given such a situation, we could predict the Y value corresponding to a given X value at a rate no better than chance. Another way to think about this lack of predictability is to realize that knowing a person's X score does not improve our ability to predict how he or she would score on Y. Here, our best prediction of Y is the mean of the Y variable itself (which is not terribly helpful).

Strength of Relationship

Statistical Significance and Sample Size

After obtaining the correlation coefficient from a computation or a printout, the first thing that most researchers wish to determine is whether or not the correlation significantly differs from zero. The key element in such a determination is the sample size on which the correlation is based. This is because the sampling distribution of r changes with the size of the sample contributing data to the analysis.

With a sample size as small as 9 (i.e., 7 degrees of freedom, which is determined by subtracting 2 from the number of cases), we need a Pearson r of about .67 or better to achieve statistical significance at the .05 level (two-tailed, where the direction of the effect is not specified in advance). With an N of 27 (degrees of freedom of 25), a Pearson r of about .38 is the threshold value for significance. By the time we reach a sample size around 100, an r value of about .20 is significant at an alpha level of .05, and we need a correlation of only about .10 to be significant if we had about 400 cases. We invite readers to examine for themselves a table of critical values for the Pearson correlation to see a more complete picture of this relationship. Such a table is provided by virtually all introductory statistics texts (e.g., Runyon et al., 2000).

Statistical significance tells us how confident we can be that an obtained correlation is different from zero. If a computed correlation coefficient reaches the .05 alpha level, for example, then we know that correlations of that magnitude or greater occur by chance only 5% or less of the time if the null hypothesis is true. We therefore permit ourselves to assert that in this particular instance our obtained Pearson r differs "significantly" from a value of zero. In that sense, we maintain that a correlation "is significant at the .05 alpha level."

It is important to test the statistical significance of any Pearson r we have computed in our research, especially when we have used small samples. This is the case because we can obtain what appears to be a relatively high value of the correlation coefficient that turns out to be statistically no different from a correlation of zero.

As we work with larger and larger samples, however, we do not need a particularly high value of the correlation to reach significance, so statistical significance testing becomes increasingly less important an issue. With larger sample sizes, the issue of the practical worth of the correlation becomes increasingly relevant. For example, if we have found a correlation between two variables to be .11 based on 400 participants, it may be statistically different from zero, but in very many circumstances that we might study, the magnitude of the relationship may be thought of as quite small. This value of .11 does not represent a strong relationship in many contexts, and predicting one variable from a knowledge of the other may be better than chance but is still pretty error prone. The important point here is that the term *statistically significant* is not the same thing as *substantially*. We learn from the correlation being significant that the relationship exists (it is statistically different from zero) but nothing more.

Strong Versus Weak Correlations

A conventional frame of reference to evaluate the magnitude of a correlation coefficient is provided by Cohen (1988). He suggested that in the absence of context, one might regard correlations of .5, .3, and .1 as large, moderate, and small. But Cohen, as well as many other authors (e.g., Chen & Popovich, 2002), is quick to point out that we almost always have some sort of context within which we can more appropriately judge the size of a correlation. For example, sometimes, in a large correlation table of personality variables, we may not wish to focus on correlations much below the middle .25s. In other contexts, as we will see in Chapters 12A and 12B, some researchers will initially select variables to place on subscales of an inventory only if they are correlated with a factor at .40 or better.

But there are times when even a very small correlation is worth its weight in gold. Chen and Popovich (2002) provide a telling example, stating that "a small correlation can be very impressive, as well as extremely important for various reasons. Recall that Dr. Jonas Salk's experiment only showed a correlation of [−.01] between polio vaccine and paralytic polio" (pp. 42–43).

This very same theme has been emphasized by Thompson (2002) in his discussion of statistical significance, practical significance, and clinical significance. The idea is to capture the utility or practical worth of the relationship for specific applications. As a general strategy, you would want to evaluate the magnitude of the correlation twice—once regarding whether it is statistically different from zero and, if it is, then whether the strength of the relationship is large enough to matter for the application in question.

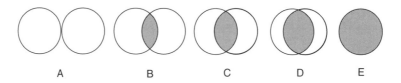

Figure 4a.6 Venn Diagrams Showing a Continuum of Shared Variance From No Shared Variance (A) to Completely Shared Variance (E)

Relationship Strength Is Shared Variance

To say that two variables are correlated or related is to say that they covary. To say that two variables covary is also to say that they share variance. Traditionally, this is depicted pictorially in the form of Venn diagrams. In such drawings, variables are shown as circles, partly to remind us that each variable has a certain amount of variance. If a variable had zero variance (all participants had the same value as shown for variable X in Table 4a.5 above), we would draw it as a vertical line.

Variables can bear different relationships to each other. We show a continuum of these possibilities in Figure 4a.6. In the first picture (Figure 4a.6A), the circles (variables) are next to each other but do not overlap. This represents the fact that they are independent of—not correlated with or related to—each other. The Pearson r is zero. In the last picture (Figure 4a.6E), the circles are fully overlapping. This depicts a correlation of 1.00 (both +1.00 and –1.00), the strongest possible relationship.

In the middle three pictures (Figures 4a.6B, C, and D), the variables partly overlap as highlighted by the shading, and this overlap indicates that they are imperfectly but significantly correlated. The area of overlap is their shared variance. More overlap, showing more shared or common variance, represents a stronger relationship.

It is also possible to quantify the strength of the relationship in a very convenient way: It is the square of the correlation. For the Pearson r, the strength of the relationship is indexed by r^2, which is often called the *coefficient of determination*. The squared correlation value can be translated to a percentage. For example, if we calculated a Pearson correlation of .60, the r^2 would be .36. We could then say that

▶ the two variables shared 36% of each other's variance,

or

▶ the X variable accounted for or explained 36% of the variance of the Y variable.

Interestingly, if the correlation was computed as −.60, we would make the very same statements because r^2 is always positive ($-.60^2 = .36$). Thus, positive and negative correlations of the same absolute value represent the same relationship strength.

If r^2 is the percentage of variance in Y that is explained by X, 36% in this case, then the remaining portion of Y's variance ($1 - r^2$) is $1 - .36$ or .64 and is unexplained. This residual variance, indexed by the expression $1 - r^2$, is called the *coefficient of nondetermination*.

An Alternative Measure of Strength of Relationship

Although we will use r^2 as our index of relationship strength for the Pearson correlation, other indexes have been suggested (Chen & Popovich, 2002). Cohen (1988) has suggested using r itself as the gauge, and Rosenthal (1991) has proposed the ratio of $r^2 / 1 - r^2$. This latter ratio evaluates the amount of explained variance to the amount of unexplained variance and can be interpreted as a way to estimate the signal to noise ratio.

Relation of r and r^2

The squared correlation is assessed on a ratio scale of measurement. We are therefore able to say that an r^2 of .40 represents twice as strong a relationship as does an r^2 of .20. Examples of r values, their associated r^2 values, and the corresponding percentage of shared or explained variance are shown in Table 4a.6.

As can be seen from Table 4a.6, a difference of .10 in terms of r represents rather different jumps in strength of relationship depending on how large the correlation is. For example, when we compare a correlation of .20 with one of .30, we see an increase in explained variance from 4% to 9%, but

Table 4a.6 Values of r, r^2, and Percentage of Shared Variance

r	r^2	%
.10	.01	1
.20	.04	4
.30	.09	9
.40	.16	16
.50	.25	25
.60	.36	36
.70	.49	49
.80	.64	64
.90	.81	81

when we compare a correlation of .80 with a correlation of .90, we see a jump in explained variance from 64% to 81%.

It is also instructive to examine the r and r^2 columns. We would say, for example, that a correlation of .70 (49% shared variance) represents a relationship almost twice as strong as one with a Pearson r of .50 (25% shared variance). These r^2 values help us to gain a bit of perspective, and researchers will ordinarily bear these in mind in the process of interpreting their results. In this book, time after time we will emphasize the squared correlation rather than the correlation itself.

Pearson Correlation for a Quantitative Variable and a Dichotomous Nominal Variable

A general assumption underlying the interpretation of a Pearson r is that the two variables are each measured on a quantitative scale. This is so because the interpretation of the correlation rests on the proposition that larger values on a variable represent more of the assessed quantity than do smaller values. With this assumption in place, the ordering of the numbers is tied to some underlying property of the things that are measured (e.g., five symptoms are more than three symptoms).

The interpretation of a Pearson correlation also can make sense if one of the variables is *dichotomous* (contains only two levels), whereas the other variable is *quantitative*. A convenient way to explain the logic of how a dichotomous variable can appropriately be analyzed with the Pearson r is to use the following hypothetical example. Assume that we have measured the verbal ability of entry-level middle school students and that a portion of the results is shown in Table 4a.7. Further assume that the pattern shown in this small portion of the data is representative of the larger sample.

Table 4a.7 Relationship of a Dichotomous Variable and a Quantitative Variable

			Sex Coding	
Child	Sex	Verbal Score	Alternative A	Alternative B
U	Girl	545	1	2
V	Girl	612	1	2
W	Girl	627	1	2
X	Boy	497	2	1
Y	Boy	534	2	1
Z	Boy	559	2	1

We have organized the rows of Table 4a.7 to make it easier to see what we admit are rather exaggerated results. Looking only at the second and third columns, our results are clear. For this sample and for this measure, the girls appear to have greater verbal ability than the boys. Now the only thing we need to do is achieve the statistical outcome that tells us this very same thing.

To calculate a Pearson correlation, both variables have to be numeric. We therefore need to arbitrarily code sex and decide to use 1 and 2 to represent the different sexes of the children. So far, so good. Now we come to a decision point: Who gets coded as 1, and who gets coded as 2? Assume that we decided to code the girls as 1 and the boys as 2. This is shown as coding Alternative A in Table 4a.7. We now run the Pearson procedure. What are we going to find? We will find that higher verbal scores are associated with 1s and lower verbal scores are associated with 2s—no surprise here because we already know that the girls are the 1s and boys are the 2s.

The value of the Pearson r for the entire sample under this coding scheme must show an inverse relationship under this specific coding scheme. This is so because higher verbal scores are tied to "lower" sex codes (1s) and lower verbal scores are tied to "higher" sex codes (2s). When we perform the calculation on the data shown in Table 4a.7 and round to two decimal places, we obtain a Pearson r of $-.72$. The strength of this relationship is indexed by r^2, giving us .52.

Let's return to our decision point regarding what group was given what code and institute the opposite coding strategy. This is shown in Table 4a.7 as coding Alternative B in which girls are coded as 2 and boys are coded as 1. With only the coding scheme altered, we see that the same higher verbal scores are now associated with 2s and that the same lower verbal scores are now associated with 1s. The reality, however, is still the same—the girls are scoring higher than the boys.

If the reality is unchanged, then the statistical outcome should tell us the same story. And, of course, it does. The Pearson correlation must turn out to be $+.72$ because now the higher verbal scores are linked with "higher" sex codes (2s) and lower verbal scores are linked with "lower" sex codes (1s). And r^2 is the same at .52.

The lesson learned from this example is as follows. When a dichotomous variable is used as one of the variables in computing a Pearson r, the same numeric value will be obtained regardless of which level was coded as 1 and which was coded as 2. The only consequence of using the alternative coding scheme is that the valence of the correlation will be different.

Range (Variance) Restriction

We gave an example earlier in the chapter in which the correlation was zero because we had no variance on the *X* variable. This example can be used to illustrate one additional point. To the extent that one of the variables lacks variation in the sample (but where more variance exists in a broader-based population), the obtained correlation will be too low—the correlation will be lower than it would have been if a broader range of people had been sampled. In the extreme case where there is no variance observed on one of the variables in the sample, the correlation must compute to zero. This situation is called *range restriction,* but it is probably more appropriately called *variance restriction* because variance is a useful framework within which to understand correlation.

Although range or variance restriction applies to the numbers in the data analysis, sometimes the reason we see such restriction in the data can be traced to a weakness in the research design. The key issue on which to focus is that, to the extent that range restriction is present, it will reduce the value of the obtained correlation coefficient. As a result, an obtained statistical result from a certain piece of research may or may not have all that much external validity. We will illustrate this with two simplified examples.

Sample Selection Problem

In the first example, a team of researchers intends to study the relationship between age and self-esteem. They have hypothesized that older individuals will generally have higher self-esteem than younger people. Statistically, they are expecting to obtain a reasonably strong positive correlation. They run their study, however, in a small liberal arts college where the entire freshman class takes the introductory psychology course that makes up their sample. Based on data from 75 participants, the researchers find that their obtained Pearson *r* is not significantly different from zero.

What happened? If we assume that their hypothesis was reasonable and that age and self-esteem are really positively correlated in the general population, then why did they not obtain that result in their study? The answer is likely to be range restriction. Small liberal arts colleges generally attract students directly out of high school who are probably very similar in age. If the youngest participant in their study was 18 years old and their oldest participant was 19 years old, how much of a relationship between age and anything would we expect to find? The answer is, not much. Age simply does not vary enough in the sample to covary with anything. To appropriately test for a relationship involving an age variable, the researchers should have sampled from a much more age-diverse population.

Group Differentiation Problem

In this second example, a different team of researchers wants to test the hypothesis that more preparation time will enhance performance on the Graduate Record Exam (GRE). Their experimental design calls for two groups to be formed; one will prepare for the exam more than the other. They determine that all participants will study for 1 hour each day for 3 days each week. Participants will be randomly assigned to groups, and with each group containing 125 students, the researchers judge that there will be more than sufficient statistical power to identify an experimental effect should it really exist. Preparation time will be the independent variable, and GRE score will be the dependent variable.

The final decision that the researchers need to make is the amount of prep time they will allow for each group. Not wanting to jeopardize anyone's future applications to graduate schools, the researchers operationally define low preparation as studying for 36 weeks (9 months). Being somewhat realistic in how much time they can ask students to prepare for the GRE, they require that the high-preparation participants study for 40 weeks (10 months).

As you might suspect without even seeing the data, the study is bound to reveal that the GRE performance of the two groups was almost identical and certainly not significantly different. Does this mean that study time is not correlated with test performance? No, it just means that these researchers did not find the "right" result. Why? Because of range restriction.

Range restriction is a problem not limited to numbers in data sets. Here, the independent variable was not "strong" enough—did not have sufficient range—to reveal an effect. There is simply not enough difference between preparing for 9 months versus preparing for 10 months to expect it to show up on the GRE. Differences between 1 week and 10 months of study would almost certainly have worked, and differences between 1 month and 10 months would probably have worked, but looking for differences between 9 and 10 months of study was doomed from the start.

The Scatterplot

A common way to visualize the correlation between two variables is to plot the data points on a set of axes. Such a visual display is known as a *scatterplot*. In a correlation analysis, each participant contributes two scores: an *X* score and a *Y* score. Because a standard graph also has *X* and *Y* axes, participants can be depicted by dots placed at the *X,Y* coordinate matching their measured values on the *X* and *Y* variables.

Take the small sample shown in Table 4a.8. Self-esteem and locus of (internal) control (the extent to which people believe that their own actions

Table 4a.8   Two Variables Measured in a Research Study

Case No.	Self-Esteem	Internal Control
1	72	15
2	74	14
3	79	28
4	84	24
5	90	29

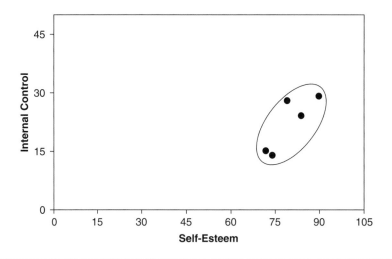

Figure 4a.7   Scatterplot of Self-Esteem Scores and Internal Control Scores

rather than chance or fate are responsible for the life events that happen to them) were two of the measures used in a hypothetical study. Each of the five participants would be represented by a dot in the scatterplot, making a total of five data points to be plotted. For example, the first participant would be located at 72 on the self-esteem axis (we will make this the horizontal or X axis) and 15 on the internal control axis (the vertical or Y axis) of the scatterplot. All five cases have been plotted in Figure 4a.7. We have drawn an oval around these data points to generally describe the overall shape this scatterplot exhibits.

Examining the data in Table 4a.8 and the scatterplot in Figure 4a.7 reveals that the two variables are positively correlated, probably fairly strongly. We know this because higher values of self-esteem are pretty consistently associated with higher values of internal control (and lower values of self-esteem are associated with lower values of internal control). The calculated value of the Pearson *r* turns out to be .86.

The scatterplot in Figure 4a.7 pictures this positive correlation. Even with only five cases in the study, we can detect the general pattern indicative of a relatively strong positive Pearson correlation:

▶ The dots can be described by an oval rather than a square. This tells us that we do observe some relationship between the variables (a square would tell us that the correlation was zero).

▶ The oval slants from the lower left to the upper right. This tells us that the relationship is a direct one (e.g., higher values of one variable are associated with higher values of the other variable) and results in a positive correlation (the oval slanting in the other direction is indicative of an inverse relationship, one that would result in a negative correlation).

▶ The oval does not appear to bend. This is indicative of a linear relationship between the two variables.

▶ The oval is relatively narrow. This corresponds to a relatively strong relationship.

Scatterplots can present us with a very useful picture of how two variables are related. Several example scatterplots based on relatively large samples are shown in Figures 4a.8 through 4a.12. With these larger sample sizes, we have lots of data points and can make a more reliable judgment about the pattern.

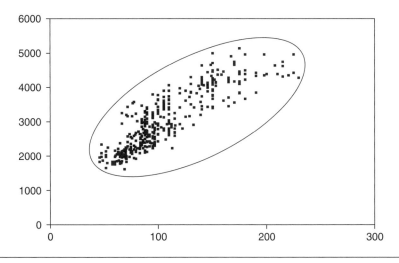

Figure 4a.8   Strong Positive Correlation (*r* = .86)

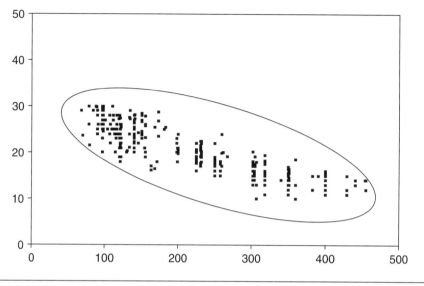

Figure 4a.9   Strong Negative Correlation ($r = -.79$)

Figures 4a.8 and 4a.9 show strong positive and negative correlations, respectively. The Pearson r corresponding to the plot in Figure 4a.8 is .86; the Pearson r corresponding to the plot in Figure 4a.9 is −.79. The relative strength of these relationships is cued by the narrowness of the respective ovals.

Figure 4a.10 shows a more modest degree of a positive relationship, with the value of the Pearson r at .44. The oval slants from the lower left to the upper right, but it is relatively wide.

Figures 4a.11 and 4a.12 are different from those we have covered so far. We have included them to illustrate how important it is to visually examine the scatterplot, especially for large samples where it is difficult to see the patterns in the actual numerical data. These plots are of interest to us because the relationships shown are not linear.

The Pearson correlation coefficient can assess only the degree of linear relationship that exists between two quantitative variables. That is, if a straight line is not the best fit for the data, the Pearson r will be unable to capture the full relationship and may miss the boat entirely under certain circumstances. If we used the Pearson correlation to attempt to assess the relationships pictured in Figures 4a.11 and 4a.12, we might draw an incorrect conclusion from the numerical result.

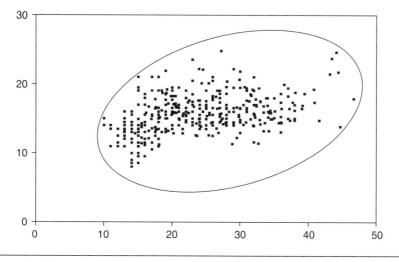

Figure 4a.10   Moderate Positive Correlation (*r* = .44)

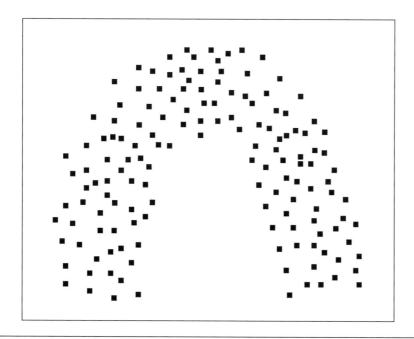

Figure 4a.11   Stylized Curvilinear Relationship

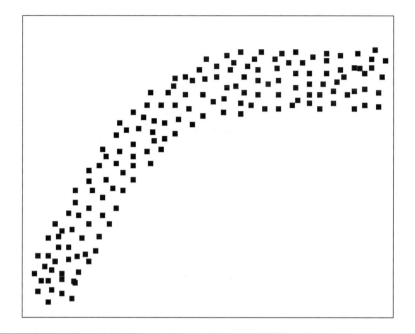

Figure 4a.12   Stylized Curvilinear Relationship

The pattern in Figure 4a.11 can be described as nonmonotonic (it changes direction). Its shape is that of an inverted V—higher values of X are associated with higher values of Y up to a point beyond which increasingly higher values of X are associated with lower values of Y. This is an example of a quadratic function, the equation for which involves Y being computed from the square of X (e.g., $Y = X^2 + 7$). Because there is about as much direct as inverse relationship in the data for Figure 4a.11, the value of the Pearson correlation, if we computed one, would be close to zero. We might then improperly conclude that the two variables were not correlated.

Such nonlinearity could be handled in at least two different ways. First, because an inverted V-shaped relationship can be described by a quadratic rather than a linear function, researchers might opt to examine the correlation between Y and X^2; that is, they would examine the quadratic rather than the linear relationship between the two variables. Second, researchers might be inclined to use an alternative correlation coefficient, such as eta (obtained through analysis of variance), to assess the degree of relationship observed between the variables. The eta correlation coefficient will be discussed in Chapter 8A.

The pattern that can be seen in Figure 4a.12 is another variant of a curvilinear relationship. The function increases linearly up to a certain point and then levels off. A straight line can be fitted to the data, and to that extent the Pearson correlation will return a modest value. But a straight line is not the best fitting function for this relationship, and the curvature that it misses will not be reflected in the Pearson value. Thus, it will underestimate the strength of the covariation between the two variables. Once again, researchers would be better served by applying a nonlinear function to the data or using the eta correlation obtained through analysis of variance instead of the Pearson *r*.

Simple Linear Regression

When we focus on two variables in a research study, computing their correlation gives us most of the information that we ordinarily want. However, as we mentioned earlier, the Pearson correlation between two variables can be used as a basis for the prediction of the values for one variable given a knowledge of the values on the other. When our attention turns to prediction, we are in the realm of regression analysis.

In the situation where we use a single variable to predict another single variable, the particular procedure we use is called *simple linear regression*.

▶ It is simple because only one predictor is involved.
▶ It is linear because we apply a straight-line function to the data and are computing a Pearson correlation.
▶ It is regression because we are predicting something.

An Overview of the Regression Process

The easiest way to conceive of simple linear regression is to imagine a straight line, the regression line, fitted to a scatterplot, something we have talked about briefly earlier in the chapter. This straight regression line would be oriented in the same direction as the oval characterizing the relationship of the variables and would run through the middle of it. The regression line is used as the basis for predicting the variable on the *Y* axis from a knowledge of the variable on the *X* axis.

If we wished to do so at a slight sacrifice of precision, this prediction process could be done pictorially. We would start with a value on the *X* axis, draw a line straight up to the regression line, hang a sharp turn toward the *Y* axis, and continue in a horizontal direction until we reached the *Y* axis. The value at the place where we encountered the *Y* axis would be our predicted value. This procedure is illustrated in Figure 4a.13. Of course, the

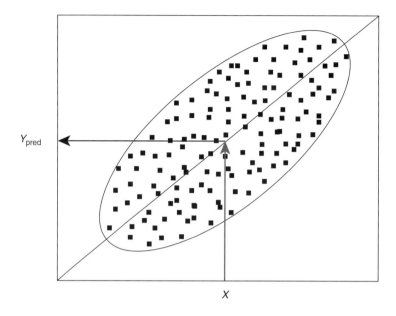

Figure 4a.13   Predicting *Y* From *X* Based on Regression Line

more precise way of predicting *Y* from a knowledge of *X* is to do it algebraically based on the equation for that straight regression line.

The Least Squares Solution

The goal of simple linear regression is to find the proper location (i.e.,
the particular equation) for the regression line. It is found by applying the
least squares procedure.

The least squares solution is a way of fitting a straight line—the regression line in this case—to an array of data. There is only one place in the array
where this solution may be satisfied. The least squares procedure underlying the solution deals with the distances of the data points from the line.

▶ It is a *squares* rule because the distance between each data point and
the line is squared. All these squared distances are then added
together.
▶ It is a *least* squares rule because the regression line is placed at the
position where the sum of the squared distances is minimal.

This least squares solution is sometimes referred to as "ordinary least
squares" to distinguish it from the other, more specialized calculations of

least squares (e.g., generalized, unweighted), which we do not cover in this text. We will use least squares and ordinary least squares interchangeably.

Raw Scores and Standard Scores

We enter raw data into data files. Raw data are literally the data values derived from the measurement operations we were using in our research study. Sometimes the metrics used to measure the two variables differ considerably. In the example shown earlier in Table 4a.8, where we reported the results for self-esteem and internal control, we saw that the scales had rather different magnitudes. Self-esteem scores ranged in the 70s through 90, whereas internal control scores ranged from the teens to the 20s.

As the metrics used to assess the two variables become increasingly more discrepant, it is more difficult to keep track of and deal with the raw values (e.g., how much above or below the sample mean is a participant with an internal control score of 20?). Although we never want to lose or give up raw data, it is often desirable to also convert (transform) the raw scores to standardized scores so that their relative magnitudes can be assessed instantly; in the context of regression, the basic standardized score—the z score—is used.

A z score, as you may recall from previous coursework, indicates how many standard deviation units a particular score lies from the mean of the distribution. For example, a distribution may have a mean of 80 and a standard deviation of 5. Thus, for that set of scores, a raw score of 80 has a z score of zero because it is exactly at the mean, a raw score of 85 has a z score of 1.00 because it lies exactly 1 standard deviation above the mean, and a raw score of 70 has a z score of –2.00 because it lies exactly 2 standard deviation units below the mean.

This transformation from raw scores to z scores is accomplished, as can be seen above, by examining the distance between the score and the mean (by subtracting the mean from the score) and determining how many standard deviations that distance represents (dividing that distance by the standard deviation). The formula for this transformation is therefore as follows:

$$z \text{ score} = \frac{(\text{score} - \text{mean})}{\text{standard deviation}}$$

The value of z scores is found in the fact that the z scale has a mean of 0 and a standard deviation of 1. On the normal curve, 95% of the area is subsumed between ±1.96 z scores. We automatically know that a z score of 1.50 is 1.5 standard deviations above the mean, that a z score of –.75 is .75 standard deviations below the mean, and so on.

One nice thing about using such a standardized scale is that if both variables are transformed to their respective z scales, we can immediately grasp the magnitude of every score in the analysis without trying to remember the details of the raw score measurement. We are also in a much better position to immediately compare variables with each other. Partly because of these benefits of the z scale, most computerized statistical programs, such as SPSS, work in both raw score as well as standardized score mode when they perform a regression analysis. The output of these programs presents us with the regression solution—that is, the equation for the regression line—in both raw score and standard score form.

The Regression Equations

We talk about the regression line in terms of an equation. Although it is really just one function, SPSS displays the components of the equation in two forms—one for the raw scores and another for the standardized scores. This equation serves as the regression model, the representation of the predictive relationship between the two variables.

The Raw Score Equation

The raw score equation for predicting Y based on a knowledge of X is that of a straight line. It is as follows:

$$Y_{pred} = \mathbf{a} + bX$$

The symbols in this equation represent the following:

▶ Y_{pred} is the predicted value of the variable that is being predicted. It is often called the *criterion variable*.
▶ X is the value of the variable used as the basis of the prediction. It is often called the *predictor*.
▶ b is the coefficient of the X variable. It is the amount by which the X variable is weighted or multiplied and so is often called the *b weight* or *b coefficient*. Mathematically, it is the slope of the line. It indicates how much change in Y_{pred} is associated with a change in X.
▶ **a** is the Y intercept of the line. It is the place where the line crosses the Y axis and can be thought of as the value of Y_{pred} when $X = 0$. The Y intercept is a *constant* and is often called that. This value is often not empirically interpretable (e.g., it may not be possible for the predictor to have a value of zero).

A straight line can be drawn on a set of axes once the *Y* intercept and the slope are computed. The object of the work done on the raw scores in simple linear regression is to figure out these two values.

You will note that the term b*X* in the equation is preceded by a plus sign. This is the generic way to represent the additive nature of this term, but it does not require that the term is always positive. It is possible that b*X* could take on a negative value. This will happen when the predictor variable is negatively correlated with the criterion variable. In such a case, we would obtain a negative b value and therefore would need to subtract b*X* from the constant in order to acquire the predicted *Y* value.

We can now also express the ordinary least squares solution in different words. Remember that the dots in the scatterplot mark the actual data points and the regression line indicates the prediction model. The distance between the line and any one of the data points therefore is the distance between the predicted *Y* value and the actual *Y* value. In wording the least squares solution in this alternative way, we can say that we find this difference between every person's predicted and actual *Y* value, square each difference, and then add these squared values together. The regression line may thus be said to occupy the place where the sum of the squared differences between the predicted and actual *Y* scores is at a minimum.

The Standardized Equation

The standardized score equation for predicting *Y* based on a knowledge of *X* is also a straight line function. It is as follows:

$$Y_{z\ pred} = \beta X_z$$

The symbols in this equation represent the following:

▶ $Y_{z\ pred}$ is the *z* score value that is being predicted. As we have seen, it is called the criterion variable in this context.
▶ X_z is the *z* score value of the variable used as the basis of the prediction. As we have also seen, it is called the predictor.
▶ β is the coefficient of the X_z variable. It is the Greek letter beta and is the amount by which the X_z variable is weighted or multiplied and so is often called the beta weight or beta coefficient. In simple linear regression, this beta weight is the Pearson *r* (that's why the symbol *r* is used—it stands for regression).

Note that the constant drops out of the standardized equation. This is because the standardized regression line always passes through the point of origin of the axis set. This is the place where both X and Y are equal to zero. In effect, the constant is still in the equation but its value is zero; thus, there is no sense in writing it in.

Also, as was true for the raw score equation, the expression βX_z could be negative; that is, the Pearson r (or β in the equation) could be negative, indicating an inverse relationship between the predictor and criterion variables.

Interpreting a Regression Coefficient

In simple linear regression, the raw score and beta coefficients represent the slope of the respective regression lines. Larger absolute values indicate greater slopes than smaller values. How we may interpret these coefficients can be illustrated by the regression line shown in Figure 4a.14. Assume that we have determined the raw score regression equation predicting Y from a knowledge of X to be as follows:

$$Y_{pred} = 4 + .50X$$

The b coefficient of .50 informs us that a 1-unit change in X corresponds to an increment of .50 in Y_{pred}. This can be seen both from Figure 4a.14 and from computing the predicted Y scores from X values that are 1 unit apart. For example, if one person had an X value of 4, we would predict that her Y value would be equal to 6, that is, $4 + .50(4) = 4 + 2 = 6$. If a second person had an X value of 5, we would predict that his Y value would be equal to 6.50, that is, $4 + .50(5) = 4 + 2.5 = 6.5$. These two predicted Y values differ by .50, the value of the b coefficient, when the corresponding X values differ by exactly 1 unit.

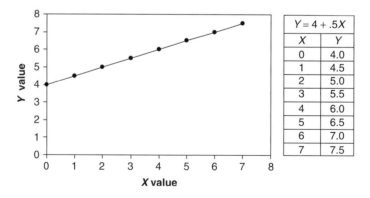

Figure 4a.14 Predicting Values Using a Slope of .50

Statistical Error in Prediction: Why Bother With Regression?

There is an interesting question that some students ask at this point: Using the regression line to predict Y scores of the participants must lead to errors because most of the scores in an actual research study are not really on the regression line. But we know the actual scores of these participants—their data were used to generate the statistical analysis. So why use the regression line to predict the Y value when we can do better (in fact, we would make no errors) by just looking up everyone's score?

The answer is that the regression equation is treated as a model (or "theory") for how one variable in general can be used to predict the other. We collected data on a particular sample only as a way to build this model. We are not necessarily interested in these particular participants per se. Rather, we hope that they are sufficiently representative of the population we wish to characterize so that they can provide us with a solid base on which to build a model. Thus, with the regression function, (a) we can predict how some future individuals who did not participate in the study might perform on Y if we knew how they did on X, and/or (b) we can better understand the general relationship between X and Y.

Prediction Error

Because the regression line is a summary of the data and because the correlation in a real-world data set virtually never reaches the value of 1.00, researchers recognize that some amount of prediction error comes with the territory. This is shown in pictorial form in Figure 4a.15. The Y value we predict is based on the regression line, but scores on the Y variable from Y-low to Y-high are possible in that they are represented in the data set.

Contrast this situation where there is a relatively strong relationship between the two variables with the three other situations pictured in Figures 4a.16 through 4a.18. Figure 4a.16 demonstrates what we never find empirically—a correlation of 1.00. Here, all the data points lie along the regression line. With a perfect correlation, there would be no errors in prediction.

Figure 4a.17 depicts a positive but weak relationship. Notice that for the particular X value from which we are predicting, there is a very wide range of possible Y values associated with it in the data set. Thus, the Y-low to Y-high error band is larger than shown in Figure 4a.15 for the relatively strong relationship.

Figure 4a.18 pictures a situation where there is no correlation between the two variables. The shape of the scatterplot resembles a square (some would call it a circle, but no one calls it an oval). Because

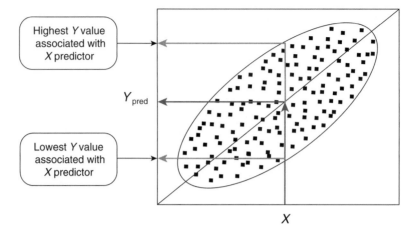

Figure 4a.15 Actual Values of Y Associated With a Given X Can Span a Wide Range

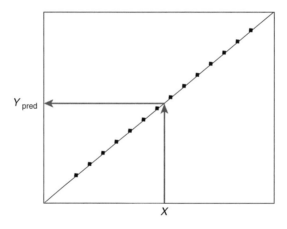

Figure 4a.16 Perfect Correlation With No Prediction Error

there is no relationship between X and Y, knowing the X value does not help us in predicting the corresponding Y value. Our best guess about the Y value—that is, Y_{pred}—in the absence of useful information is therefore the mean of the Y variable. This is reinforced by looking at the regression line: Its slope is zero (the line is horizontal), and its Y intercept is the mean of the Y variable.

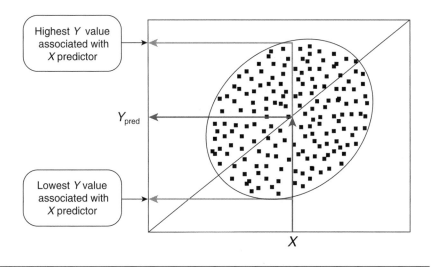

Figure 4a.17   Weak Positive Correlation With Large Prediction Error Band

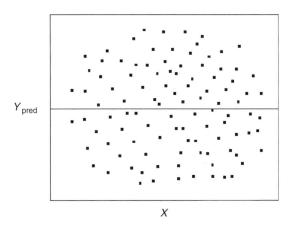

Figure 4a.18   No Relationship, Resulting in a Regression Line With a Slope of Zero

How Simple Linear Regression Is Used

Whereas correlation—especially Pearson correlation—is used extensively, simple linear regression is infrequently used. The reason simple linear regression is used so little is that it is just too simple. Most of us would agree that human behavior is multiply determined. We act the way we act, believe the way we believe, and are the way we are based on many considerations:

our upbringing, our adult histories, our stimulus environment, our current motivational state, and so on. To use just one variable to predict another is neither adequate nor reasonable for most purposes.

So why have we devoted these pages to a topic that is not widely used? Because our treatment of simple linear regression lays a solid foundation for *multiple* linear regression, the attempt to predict Y based on a set of theoretically relevant variables. Multiple regression has a great deal of intuitive appeal for those researchers who believe that much of human behavior is determined by the combination of many factors. We cover the topic of multiple regression in Chapters 5A and 5B.

Recommended Readings

Chambers, W. V. (2000). Causation and corresponding correlations. *Journal of Mind and Behavior, 21,* 437–460.

Cohen, B. H. (1996). *Explaining psychological statistics.* Pacific Grove, CA: Brooks/ Cole.

Cowles, M. (1989). *Statistics in psychology: An historical perspective.* Hillsdale, NJ: Erlbaum.

Galton, F. A. (1886). Regression towards mediocrity in hereditary stature. *Journal of the Anthropological Institute, 15,* 246–263.

Galton, F. A. (1888). Co-relations and their measurement, chiefly from anthro- pometric data. *Proceedings of the Royal Society of London, 40,* 42–73.

Lorenz, F. O. (1987). Teaching about influence in simple regression. *Teaching Sociology, 15,* 173–177.

Salsburg. D. (2001). *The lady tasting tea.* New York: W. H. Freeman.

Stigler, S. M. (1989). Francis Galton's account of the invention of correlation. *Statistical Science, 4,* 73–86.

Stigler, S. M. (1999). *Statistics on the table: The history of statistical concepts and methods.* Cambridge, MA: Harvard University Press.

Bivariate Correlation and Simple Linear Regression Using SPSS

This chapter will briefly demonstrate how to run Pearson product-moment correlations and simple (bivariate) linear regressions with SPSS. For continuity purposes, we will continue our examination of the Asian American mental health consumer data set first discussed in Chapter 3B.

Bivariate Correlation

Main Dialog Box

To produce a bivariate correlation matrix, we begin by clicking **Analyze →
Correlate → Bivariate**. This produces the **Bivariate Correlations** dialog box shown in Figure 4b.1. Variables in this figure are identified by their variable labels. From the variables list panel on the left side, we click over the variables for which we wish to obtain bivariate correlations—in this case, **ematch**, **csq8**, **lage**, **gafpre**, and **gafpost**—to the **Variables** box on the right side.

The variables selected here represent the following: The **ematch** variable is a dichotomous categorical variable indicating whether or not the client and the therapist were of the same ethnicity. A match is coded as 1 and a nonmatch is coded as 2. The **csq8** variable is a measure of client satisfaction, with higher values indicating greater satisfaction with their

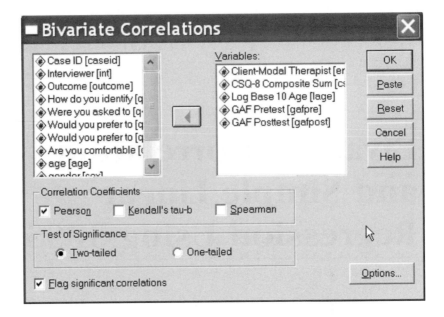

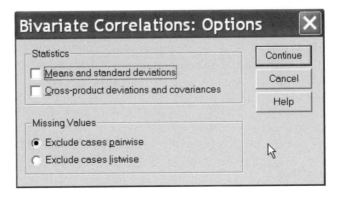

Figure 4b.1 Bivariate Correlations Main Dialog Box and Its Options Box

treatment. The variable **lage** stands for "log age" and represents a log base-10 transformation of the age of the clients as a way to help normalize the distribution. Finally, the last two variables, **gafpre** and **gafpost**, are pretest and posttest scores on the GAF; higher GAF scores represent better general functioning.

In the lower half of the **Bivariate Correlations** dialog box is the **Correlation Coefficients** area with three checkboxes for **Pearson** (the default), **Kendall's tau-b**, and **Spearman.** The Pearson *r* correlation, as we noted in Chapter 4A, is the most common measure of linear association between two variables and is what we have selected to compute. Kendall's *tau-b* is a nonparametric measure of association for ordinal or ranked variables that also takes ties into account. The Spearman *rho,* also based on rank, is a nonparametric version of the Pearson correlation.

Underneath this area lies the **Test of Significance** panel where researchers can specify either a **Two-tailed** (default) significance level, which tests a null hypothesis for which the direction of an effect is not specified in advance, or a **One-tailed** significance level, for which the direction of an effect is specified in advance. We have chosen a two-tailed significance test. At the bottom is the **Flag significant correlations** checkbox, which is checked (default) and identifies significant coefficients at the .05 level with a single asterisk and those significant at the .01 level with two asterisks. This provides an extra visual cue when examining the output and is very often a helpful choice.

Options Pushbutton

By clicking the **Options** pushbutton in the bottom right corner of the main dialog box, the **Bivariate Correlations: Options** dialog box is produced, shown as the second box in Figure 4b.1.

The **Statistics** panel at the top of the **Options** dialog box has two checkboxes for **Means and standard deviations** for each case and **Cross-product deviations and covariances** for each pair of variables. To keep the output simpler, we have chosen not to obtain either set of statistics.

The **Missing Values** panel also has two checkboxes, the **Exclude cases pairwise** (default) allows you to exclude cases with missing values for either or both of the pair of variables involved in the correlation. The **Exclude cases listwise** checkbox eliminates cases that have missing values on any of the variables being correlated. We have chosen to handle missing values by excluding cases pairwise. Thus, respondents who omitted a single response will still be included in the data analysis when SPSS deals with a pair of variables on which respondents had valid values. A click of the **Continue** pushbutton returns you to the original main dialog box where clicking the **OK** pushbutton produces the **Correlations** output seen in Figure 4b.2.

Figure 4b.2 depicts a 5 × 5 (read as "5 by 5") matrix of bivariate Pearson correlations between the five variables in the analysis. Each bivariate Pearson correlation coefficient is depicted along with the probability of that value's occurring by chance and the number of cases on which the correlation is based. For example, for the pairing of **ematch** and **csq8**, the correlation is

Correlations

		Client-Modal Therapist Ethnic Match	CSQ-8 Composite Sum	Log Base 10 Age	GAF Pretest	GAF Posttest
Client-Modal Therapist Ethnic Match	Pearson Correlation	1	−.364**	−.436**	.383**	.216
	Sig. (2-tailed)	.	.000	.000	.000	.106
	N	96	96	96	95	57
CSQ-8 Composite Sum	Pearson Correlation	−.364**	1	.133	−.065	.126
	Sig. (2-tailed)	.000	.	.197	.530	.352
	N	96	96	96	95	57
Log Base 10 Age	Pearson Correlation	−.436**	.133	1	−.497**	−.399**
	Sig. (2-tailed)	.000	.197	.	.000	.002
	N	96	96	96	95	57
GAF Pretest	Pearson Correlation	.383**	−.065	−.497**	1	.552**
	Sig. (2-tailed)	.000	.530	.000	.	.000
	N	95	95	95	95	57
GAF Posttest	Pearson Correlation	.216	.126	−.399**	.552**	1
	Sig. (2-tailed)	.106	.352	.002	.000	.
	N	57	57	57	57	57

**Correlation is significant at the 0.01 level (2-tailed).

The top value in the cell shows the Pearson r.

The middle value shows the significance level.

The bottom shows the sample size on which the correlation is based.

Figure 4b.2 Output Showing the Correlation Matrix of the Five Variables in the Analysis

−.364, indicating that greater satisfaction was expressed when the client was of the same ethnicity as the therapist (the negative valence indicates that higher scores on one measure—say, the **csq8** measure, representing more satisfaction—were associated with lower scores on the other variable—say, ethnic match, using 1 for same ethnicity and 2 for different ethnicity). This correlation had a probability of less than .000 of occurring by chance (the probability is not actually zero but some very small value that rounds to .000 when using three decimal places). This earned the Pearson *r* two asterisks to depict its meeting an alpha level of .01. The correlation computation was based on 96 cases.

As we can see, low to moderate correlations were achieved between all five variables. Interestingly, for these Asian American mental health consumers, service satisfaction (**csq8**) and clinical treatment outcome as measured by the GAF postscores were not related ($r = .126$). The highest correlation, found between the pre- and post-GAF scores, indicates good reliability between these consumers' pre- and posttest clinical assessments.

Simple Linear Regression

The following is an extension of our correlation example. Recall from our discussion in Chapter 4A that simple linear (bivariate) regression is a technique that describes the relationship between a criterion or dependent variable and a predictor or independent variable. This depiction is accomplished by building a regression line or equation that best fits a straight line that can be drawn through data points in a scatterplot. Mathematically, this straight line regression model can be expressed as follows:

$$Y_{pred} = \mathbf{a} + \mathrm{b}X$$

where

Y_{pred} = the predicted value for the dependent variable Y

$\mathbf{a}$ = value of the Y intercept (where the line crosses the Y axis; where $X = 0$)

b = raw score regression coefficient (slope of the line)

X = value of the independent variable X

Because the present focus is on simple linear regression, we will examine the effects of only one independent variable on a dependent variable. In Chapters 5A and 5B, we will expand this discussion in multiple regression, where we examine the effects of two or more continuous independent variables on a dependent variable.

Main Regression Dialog Box

For purposes of illustrating simple linear regression, assume we are interested in predicting our clinical outcome (GAF posttest score) from the age of clients. In the language of regression, age is the predictor or independent variable and the GAF score is the dependent or criterion variable. To begin this analysis, we click **Analyze → Regression → Linear.** This produces the **Linear Regression** main dialog box displayed in Figure 4b.3. From the variables list panel, we click over **gafpost** to the **Dependent** box and **lage** to the **Independent(s)** box. The **Method** box will be left at its default setting of **Enter,** which requests a standard regression analysis. Details about the many other parameters of this dialog box will be covered in our discussion of multiple regression with SPSS in Chapter 5B.

Statistics Tab

By clicking the **Statistics** pushbutton at the bottom of the main regression dialog box, we produce the **Linear Regression: Statistics** dialog box also shown in Figure 4b.3. By default, **Estimates** under the **Regression**

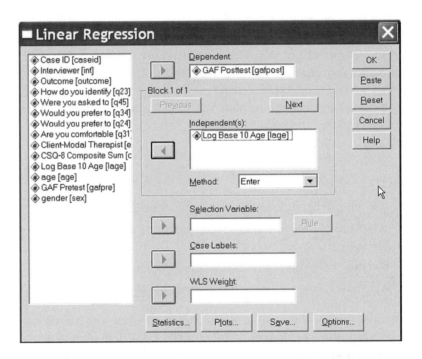

Figure 4b.3   Linear Regression Main Dialog Box and Its Statistics Box

Coefficients panel is checked. This tells SPSS to print the value of the regression coefficient and related measures. We also check **Model fit,** which provides *R*-square, adjusted *R*-square, the standard error, and an ANOVA table.

Clicking the **Continue** pushbutton returns you to the original main dialog box, and again clicking the **OK** pushbutton produces the simple (bivariate) regression output, which can be seen in Figure 4b.4.

Depicted in these three figures is the "bare bones" or minimum information needed to interpret a simple linear regression. The **Model Summary** is shown first in Figure 4b.4. It indicates an adjusted *R*-square (adjusted R^2) value of .144. This suggests that 14% of the variability of consumers' GAF posttest scores can be explained by their age level. Although not large in an absolute sense, it does indicate a relationship between age and general level of functioning. Note that the adjusted R^2 is a little lower than the R^2; this difference represents a correction to the computed R^2 value, which capitalizes to a certain extent on chance. This will be explained in the next chapter.

The nature of the relationship between GAF score and age is also shown in Figure 4b.4 by the value of *R*. This statistic is called the multiple correlation, which we will talk about in Chapter 5A. For now, you should think of it in terms of a Pearson correlation because there are only two variables in the analysis. It is equal to the value of the correlation shown in Figure 4b.2, but here, it is reported by SPSS without its minus sign.

The **ANOVA** table presented next in Figure 4b.4 depicts a significant *F* statistic. This result indicates that our regression equation is statistically significant and justifies examining the results of the regression coefficients shown next.

The **Coefficients** output, the third box of Figure 4b.4, is one of the most important parts of the SPSS regression results. This output consists of three component parts: the unstandardized coefficients, the standardized beta coefficients, and a *t* statistic with its associated significance level. You will recall that our raw score regression equation consists of $Y_{pred} = \mathbf{a} + \mathrm{b}X$ and stands for the following:

predicted DV = intercept constant + regression coefficient(IV)

where DV stands for dependent variable and IV stands for the independent variable.

In the present case, the equation representing the prediction model is this:

GAF posttest = 94.134 − 29.352(lage)

We know this from the left column labeled **B** under the heading **Unstandardized Coefficients**.

Model Summary

Model	R	R-Square	Adjusted R-Square	Std. Error of the Estimate
1	.399ª	.159	.144	14.98847

a. Predictors: (Constant), Log Base 10 Age.

ANOVAb

Model		Sum of Squares	df	Mean Square	F	Sig.
1	Regression	2333.527	1	2333.527	10.387	.002ª
	Residual	12355.981	55	224.654		
	Total	14689.509	56			

a. Predictors: (Constant), Log Base 10 Age.
b. Dependent Variable: GAF Posttest.

Coefficientsa

Model		Unstandardized Coefficients		Standardized Coefficients	t	Sig.
		B	Std. Error	Beta		
1	Constant	94.134	12.524		7.516	.000
	Log Base 10 Age	−29.352	9.107	−.399	−3.223	.002

a. Dependent Variable: GAF Posttest.

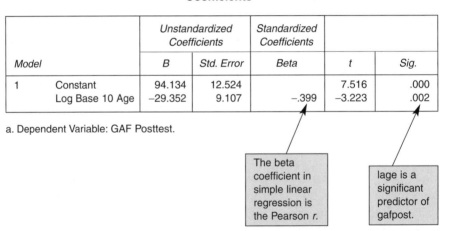

The beta coefficient in simple linear regression is the Pearson *r*.

lage is a significant predictor of gafpost.

Figure 4b.4 Selected Output From the Linear Regression Analysis

Standardized Coefficients

Under the column for the **Standardized Coefficients**, SPSS has printed the beta weight for the age variable. This value is −.399 and is the Pearson correlation (by definition, the beta weight of the predictor in simple linear regression is the Pearson *r*).

The *t* statistic tests whether or not the regression coefficient is statistically significant. In the present case, it is statistically significant, and we conclude that adjusted age level is a significant predictor of GAF posttest.

Results

The Pearson product-moment correlations for the variables used in this study are presented in Table 4b.1. Client match was coded with 1 reflecting a match of ethnicity between the consumer and therapist and 2 indicating that the two were of different ethnicities. As can be seen from Table 4b.1, consumers who were of the same ethnicity as their therapists were more satisfied with the quality of the service they received, were older, and were functioning at a lower level prior to treatment than those consumers whose ethnicity differed from their therapists. It also appears that older consumers were more likely to be matched with a therapist of the same ethnicity and were functioning at a lower overall level than younger consumers.

Of additional interest is the relationship of the GAF pretest and the GAF posttest scores. Although there was mental health treatment intervening between the two, it may still be possible to view the correlation between these two variables as a retest reliability measure. Conceived in this way, the correlation of .55 suggests that the GAF has a relatively good test-retest reliability.

Table 4b.1   Intercorrelations for Asian American Mental Health Consumer Outcome Variables

Variable	1	2	3	4	5
1. Consumer-provider ethnic match[a]	—	−.36*	−.44*	.38*	.22
2. Client satisfaction (CSQ-8)		—	.13	−.07	.13
3. Consumer age (log base-10)			—	−.50*	−.40*
4. Global assessment of functioning (Time 1)				—	.55*
5. Global assessment of functioning (Time 2)					—

a. 1 = consumer and therapist of same ethnicity; 2 = consumer and therapist of different ethnicity.

*$p < .01$.

4B Exercises

Optimism and Longevity

Are there relationships between the following variables?

▶ Socioeconomic status (1–7 rating of occupation; higher ratings indicate higher levels of SES)
▶ Age
▶ Optimism (1–100 rating, higher scores indicate higher levels of optimism)

Using the SPSS data file for Chapter 4B (located on the Web-based study site—http://www.sagepub.com/amrStudy), calculate a correlation matrix for the three variables. Conduct a simple regression between age (the independent variable) and SES (the dependent variable).

1. Which pair of variables achieved the greatest correlation coefficient?

2. As age increases, does optimism increase or decrease?

3. What is the *R* and *R*-square for the simple regression?

4. For every unit increase in age, what is the unit change in optimism?

5. What are *two* interpretations of the correlation coefficient?

6. Compose a results section for this simple regression.

Multiple Regression

General Considerations

Multiple regression is a very useful extension of simple linear regression in that we use several variables rather than just one to predict a value on a quantitatively measured criterion variable. It has become a very popular technique to employ in behavioral research. Many researchers believe that using more than one predictor can paint a more complete picture of how the world works than is permitted by simple linear regression because constructs in the behavioral sciences are believed to be multiply determined. Using only a single variable as a predictor will at best capture only one of those sources. In the words of one author (Thompson, 1991), multivariate methods such as multiple regression have accrued greater support in part because they "best honor the reality to which the researcher is purportedly trying to generalize" (p. 80).

Based on what we have already discussed regarding simple linear regression, it may be clear that multiple regression can be used for predictive purposes, such as estimating from a series of entrance tests how successful various job applicants might be. But the regression technique can also guide researchers toward explicating or explaining the dynamics underlying a particular construct by indicating which variables in combination might be more strongly associated with it. In this sense, the model that emerges from the analysis can serve an explanatory purpose as well as a predictive purpose.

As was true for simple linear regression, multiple regression generates two variations of the prediction equation, one in raw score form and the other in standardized form. These equations are extensions of the simple linear regression models and thus still represent linear regression. We will contrast some differences between linear and nonlinear regression later in the chapter.

The Variables in a Multiple Regression Analysis

The variables in a multiple regression analysis fall into one of two categories: One of them is the variable being predicted; the others are used as the basis of prediction. We discuss each in turn.

The Variable Being Predicted

The variable that is the focus of a multiple regression design is the one being predicted. In the regression equation, as we have already seen for simple linear regression, it is designated as an upper case Y_{pred}. This variable is known as the *criterion variable* but is often referred to as the *dependent variable* in the analysis. It needs to have been assessed on one of the quantitative scales of measurement.

The Variables Used as Predictors

The variables used as predictors comprise a set of measures designated with upper case Xs and are known as the *predictor variables* or the *independent variables* in the analysis.

You are probably aware that in many research design courses, the term *independent variable* is reserved for a variable in the context of an experimental study. Some of the differences in the typical nature of independent variables in experimental and regression studies are listed in Table 5a.1.

Multiple Regression Research

If the research problem is expressed in a form that either specifies or implies prediction, multiple regression becomes a viable candidate for the design. Here are some examples of research objectives that imply a regression design:

▶ Wanting to predict one variable from a combined knowledge of several others
▶ Wanting to determine which variables of a larger set are better predictors of some criterion variable than others
▶ Wanting to know how much better we can predict a variable if we add one or more predictor variables to the mix

Table 5a.1　Some Differences in How Independent Variables are Treated in Experimental and Regression Studies

Independent Variables in Experimental Study	*Independent Variables in Regression Study*
Often actively manipulated but can also be an enduring (e.g., personality) characteristic of research participants.	Usually an enduring (e.g., personality) characteristic of research participants.
Uncorrelated so long as cells in the design have equal sample sizes; as cells contain increasingly unequal sample sizes, the independent variables become more correlated.	All else equal, we would like them to be uncorrelated, but they should be correlated to some extent if that more appropriately reflects the relationships in the population.
Usually nominal (qualitatively measured) variables.	Usually quantitatively measured variables.
Usually coded into a relatively few levels or categories.	Usually fully continuous if possible.

▶ Wanting to examine the relationship of one variable with a set of other variables

▶ Wanting to statistically explain or account for the variance of one variable using a set of other variables

The goal of multiple regression is to produce a model in the form of a linear equation that identifies the best weighted combination of independent variables in the study to optimally predict the criterion variable. Its computational procedure conforms to the ordinary least squares solution; the solution or model describes a line for which the sum of the squared differences between the predicted and actual values of the criterion variable is minimal. These differences between the predictions we make with the model and the actual observed values are the prediction errors. The model thus can be thought of as representing the function that minimizes the sum of the squared errors. When we say that the model is fitted to the data to "best" predict the dependent variable, what we technically mean is that the sum of squared errors has been minimized.

Because the model configures the predictors together to maximize prediction accuracy, the specific weight (contribution) assigned to each independent variable in the model is relative to the other independent variables in the analysis. Thus, we can say only that considering this particular set of variables, this one variable is able to predict the criterion to such and such an extent. In conjunction with a different set of independent variables, the predictive prowess of that variable may turn out to be quite different.

It is possible that variables not included in the research design could have made a substantial difference in the results. Some variables that could potentially be good predictors may have been overlooked in the literature review, measuring others may have demanded too many resources, and still others may not have been amenable to the measurement instrumentation available to researchers at the time of the study. To the extent that potentially important variables were omitted from the research, the model is said to be incompletely specified and may therefore have less external validity than is desirable.

Because of these concerns, we want to select the variables for inclusion in the analysis based on as much theoretical and empirical rationale as we can bring to bear on the task. It is often a waste of research effort to realize after the fact that a couple of very important candidate predictors were omitted from the study. Their inclusion would have produced a very different dynamic and likely would have resulted in a very different model than we have just obtained.

The Regression Equations

Just as was the case for simple linear regression, the multiple regression equation is produced in both raw score and standardized score form. We discuss each in turn.

The Raw Score Equation

The multiple regression raw score equation is an expansion of the raw score equation for simple linear regression. It is as follows:

$$Y_{\text{pred}} = \mathbf{a} + b_1 X_1 + b_2 X_2 + \cdots + b_n X_n$$

In this equation, Y_{pred} is the predicted score on the criterion variable, the Xs are the predictor variables in the equation, and the bs are the weights or coefficients associated with the predictors. These b weights are also referred to as *partial regression coefficients* (Kachigan, 1986) because each reflects the relative contribution of its independent variable when we are statistically controlling for the effects of all the other predictors. Because this is a raw score equation, it also contains a constant, shown as **a** in the equation (representing the Y intercept).

All the variables are in raw score form in the equation even though the metrics on which they are measured could vary widely. If we were predicting early success in a graduate program, for example, one predictor may very well be average GRE performance (the mean of the verbal and quantitative subscores), and the scores on this variable are probably going to be in the 500 to 700 range. Another variable may be grade point average, and this variable will have values someplace in the middle to high 3s on a 4-point grading scale. We will say that success is evaluated at the end of the first year of the program and is measured on a scale ranging from the low 50s to the middle 70s (just to give us three rather different metrics for our illustration here).

The b weights computed for the regression equation are going to reflect the raw score values we have for each variable (the criterion and the predictor variables). Assume that the results of this hypothetical study show the b weight for grade point average to be about 5 and for GRE to be about .01 with a Y intercept value of 46.50. Putting these values into the equation would give us the following prediction model:

$$Y_{pred} = 46.50 + (5)(gpa) + (.01)(GRE)$$

Suppose that we wished to predict the success score of one participant, Erin, based on her grade point average of 3.80 and her GRE score of 650. To arrive at her predicted score, we place her values into the variable slots in the equation. Here is the prediction:

$$Y_{pred} = 46.50 + (5)(gpa) + (.01)(GRE)$$

$$Y_{pred\ Erin} = 46.50 + (5)(gpa_{Erin}) + (.01)(GRE_{Erin})$$

$$Y_{pred\ Erin} = 46.50 + (5)(3.80) + (.01)(650)$$

$$Y_{pred\ Erin} = 46.50 + (19) + (6.50)$$

$$Y_{pred\ Erin} = 72$$

This computation allows you to see, to some extent, how the b weights and the constant came to achieve their respective magnitudes. Although they are all interdependent, we will arbitrarily start with the constant of 46.50 as a given. Analogous to simple linear regression, this value would be Erin's predicted success score if her GRE and grade point average were both zero, a situation, obviously, that would not exist empirically. This value of 46.50 is in the regression equation simply to make the predicted value work out properly.

Now, recall that success, the Y variable, ranges between the low 50s and middle 70s. So how do you obtain Erin's predicted score in the low 70s given a constant of 46.5? Well, grade point average must be in the high 3s, so the b weight for it will have to be high enough for the result of the multiplication to add a decent number to 46.50. On the other hand, Erin's GRE score is mid-600. To predict a 72 in combination with grade point average, the GRE value has to be substantially stepped down, and you need a multiplier considerably less than 1 to make that happen.

Because the variables are assessed on different metrics, it follows that you cannot see from the b weights which independent variable is the stronger predictor in this model. Some of the ways by which you can evaluate the relative contribution of the predictors to the model will be discussed shortly.

The Standardized Equation

The multiple regression standardized score equation is an expansion of the standardized score equation for simple linear regression. It is as follows:

$$Y_{z\,pred} = \beta_1 X_{z1} + \beta_2 X_{z2} + \cdots + \beta_n X_{zn}$$

Everything in this equation is in standardized score form. Unlike the situation for the raw score equation, all the variables are now measured on the same metric—the mean and standard deviation for all the variables (the criterion and the predictor variables) are 0 and 1, respectively.

In the standardized equation, $Y_{z\,pred}$ is the predicted z score of the criterion variable. Each predictor variable (each X in the equation) is associated with its own weighting coefficient symbolized by β and called a beta weight, standardized regression coefficient, or beta coefficient, and just as was true for the b weights in the raw score equation, they are also referred to as partial regression coefficients. These coefficients usually compute to a decimal value, but they can exceed the range of ±1 if the predictors are correlated enough between themselves.

Each βX combination represents the z score of a predictor and its associated beta weight. With the equation in standardized form, the Y intercept is zero and is therefore not shown.

We can now revisit the example used above where we predicted success in graduate school based on grade point average and GRE score. Here is that final equation but this time in standard score form:

$$Y_{z\,pred} = \beta_1 X_{z1} + \beta_2 X_{z2} + \cdots + \beta_n X_{zn}$$

$$Y_{z\,pred} = (.48)(gpa_z) + (.22)(GRE_z)$$

We can also apply this standardized regression equation to individuals in the sample—for example, Erin. Within the sample used for this study, assume that Erin's grade point average of 3.80 represents a z score of 1.80 and that her GRE score of 650 represents a z score of 1.70. We can thus solve the equation as follows:

$$Y_{z\ \text{pred}} = \beta_1 X_{z1} + \beta_2 X_{z2} + \cdots + \beta_n X_{zn}$$

$$Y_{z\ \text{pred}} = (.48)\ (\text{gpa}_z) + (.22)\ (\text{GRE}_z)$$

$$Y_{z\ \text{pred Erin}} = (.48)\ (\text{gpa}_{z\ \text{Erin}}) + (.22)\ (\text{GRE}_{z\ \text{Erin}})$$

$$Y_{z\ \text{pred Erin}} = (.48)\ (1.80) + (.22)\ (1.70)$$

$$Y_{z\ \text{pred Erin}} = (.864) + (.374)$$

$$Y_{z\ \text{pred Erin}} = 1.24$$

The Variate in Multiple Regression

As was discussed in the overview at the very start of the book, multivariate procedures typically involve building, developing, or solving for a weighted combination of variables. This combination is called a *variate*. In the case of multiple regression, we are dealing with a variate made up of a weighted combination of the predictors or independent variables in the analysis. The variate in this instance is the entity on the right side of the multiple regression equation.

Although the variate may not be a measured variable, it is still important in the context of multiple regression. It is often possible to view this variate as representing some underlying dimension or construct (i.e., a latent variable). In the preceding example where we were predicting success in graduate school, the variate might be interpreted as "academic aptitude" indexed by the linear combination of grade point average and GRE score. From this perspective, indicators of academic aptitude were selected by the researchers to be used in the study. They then used the regression technique to shape the most effective academic aptitude variate to predict success in graduate school.

Based on the previous example, the academic aptitude variate is built to do the best job possible to predict a value on a variable. That variable is the predicted success score. Note that the result of applying the multiple regression equation—the result of invoking the linear composite of the predictor variables, the variate—is the predicted success score and not the actual success score. For most of the cases in the data file, the predicted and the actual success scores of the students will be different. The model minimizes these differences; it does not eliminate them. Thus, the variable "predicted success score" and the variable "actual success score" are different variables, although we certainly hope that they are reasonably related to each other. The variate that we have called academic aptitude generates the predicted rather than the actual value of the success score.

A Range of Regression Methods

The main work done in multiple regression is to build the prediction equation. This involves generating the weighting coefficients—the b weights for the raw score equation and the beta coefficients for the standardized equation—as well as the Y intercept for the raw score equation.

Several different methods are available to researchers to build the variate or linear function; these can be organized into two groups or classes. One subset of methods relies exclusively on statistical decision-making criteria built into the computer programs to decide at which point in the process which predictors are to be entered into the equation. These are ordinarily called, as a class, *statistical* methods. The most popular of these statistical methods include the standard, forward, backward, and stepwise methods, although others (not covered here), such as max R-squared and min R-squared, have been developed as well. In using these methods, researchers permit the computer program to autonomously carry out the analyses.

The other subset of methods calls for the researchers to determine which predictors are to be entered into the regression equation at each stage of the analysis. Thus, the researcher rather than the computer program assumes control of the regression procedure. These researcher-based decisions regarding order of entry are typically derived from the theoretical model with which the researchers are working.

The Standard (Simultaneous) Regression Method

The *standard regression method*, also called the *simultaneous* or the *direct method,* is what most authors refer to if they leave the method unspecified. It is the most widely used statistical method. Under this method, all the predictors are entered into the equation in a single "step" (stage in the analysis). The standard method provides a full model solution in that all the predictors are part of it.

The idea that these variables are entered into the equation simultaneously is true only in the sense that the variables are entered in a single step. But that single step is not at all simple and unitary; when we look inside this step, we will find that the process of determining the weights for independent variables is governed by a complex strategy.

The Example to Be Used

Rather than referring to abstract predictors and some amorphous dependent variable to broach this topic, we will present the standard regression method by using an example with variables that have names and meaning. To keep our drawings and explication manageable, we will work with a smaller set of variables than would ordinarily be used in a study conceived from the beginning as a regression design. Whereas an actual regression design might typically have from half a dozen to as many as two dozen or more variables as potential predictors, we will use a simplified example of just three predictors for our presentation purposes.

We have taken our variables from a larger study in which we collected data from 420 college students. The dependent variable we use for this illustration is self-esteem as assessed by Coopersmith's (1981) Self-Esteem Inventory. Two of the predictors we use for this illustration are Tellegen's (1982) measures of the number of positive and negative affective behaviors a person ordinarily exhibits. The third independent variable represents scores on the Openness scale of the NEO Five-Factor Personality Inventory (Costa & McCrae, 1992). Openness generally assesses the degree to which respondents appear to have greater aesthetic sensitivity, seek out new experiences, and are aware of their internal states.

It is always desirable to initially examine the correlation matrix of the variables participating in a regression analysis. This gives researchers an opportunity to examine the interrelationships of the variables, not only between the dependent variable and the independent variables but also between the independent variables themselves.

Table 5a.2 displays the correlation matrix of the variables in our example. We have presented it in "square" form where the diagonal from upper left to lower right (containing the value 1.000 for each entry) separates the matrix into two redundant halves. As can be seen, the dependent variable of self-esteem is moderately correlated with both positive and negative affect but is only modestly correlated with openness. It can also be seen that

Table 5a.2   Correlation Matrix of the Variables in the Regression Analysis

	Esteem	*PosAfect*	*NegAfect*	*NeoOpen*
Esteem	1.000	.555	−.572	.221
PosAfect	.555	1.000	−.324	.221
NegAfect	−.572	−.324	1.000	−.168
NeoOpen	.221	.221	−.168	1.000

positive and negative affect correlate more strongly with each other than either does with openness.

Building the Regression Equation

The goal of any regression procedure is to predict or account for the variance of the criterion variable. In this example, that variable is self-esteem. At the beginning of the process, before the predictors are entered into the equation, 100% of the variance of self-esteem is unaccounted for. This is shown in Figure 5a.1. The dependent variable of self-esteem is in place, and the predictors are ready to be evaluated by the regression procedure.

On the first and only step of the standard regression procedure, all the predictors are entered as a set into the equation. But to compute the weighting coefficients (b weights for the raw score equation and beta weights for the standardized equation), the predictors must be individually evaluated. To accomplish this, and this is the essence of standard regression, each predictor's weight is computed as though it had entered the equation last.

The idea of treating each predictor as if it was the last to enter the model is to determine what predictive work it can do over and above the prediction attributable to the rest of the predictors. In this manner, standard regression focuses on the unique contribution that each independent variable makes to the prediction when combined with all the other predictors.

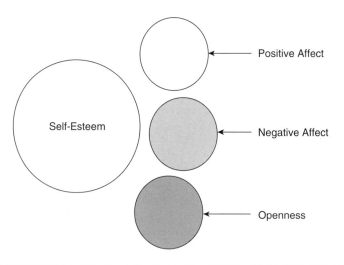

Figure 5a.1   Self-Esteem Dependent Variable Prior to Regression Analysis

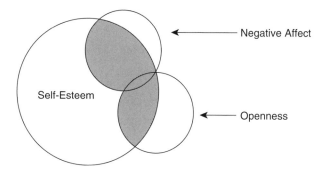

Figure 5a.2   Self-Esteem Variance Accounted for by Simultaneous Entering of Negative Affect and Openness Predictors

The way in which standard regression assesses the unique contribution of each independent variable is the key to understanding the standard method, and we will go through the process here.

The Squared Multiple Correlation

We can demonstrate the dynamics of assessing the unique contribution of each independent variable by focusing on how one of these predictors—say, positive affect—is evaluated. In determining the weight that positive affect will receive in the regression equation, the program momentarily places the other predictors (negative affect and openness) in the equation. This is illustrated by the diagram in Figure 5a.2.

Negative affect and openness are both entered into the equation simultaneously. Their relationship to the dependent variable, self-esteem, is shown in the Venn diagram in Figure 5a.2. Two features of this depiction are important to note at this point.

First, this diagram still represents a correlation. If the criterion variable was shown with just a single predictor, you would immediately recognize a representation of the Pearson (or any bivariate) correlation. The shaded area would show the strength of the correlation, and its magnitude would be indexed by r^2.

The relationship shown in Figure 5a.2 is more complex than that. Three variables, not two, are involved in the relationship. Specifically, we are looking at the relationship of the criterion (self-esteem) to two predictors (negative affect and openness). When we have three or more variables involved in the relationship, we can no longer use the Pearson correlation coefficient to quantify the magnitude of that relationship—the Pearson r can index the degree of relationship only when two variables are being considered. The correlation coefficient we need to call on to quantify the degree of a more complex relationship is known as the *multiple correlation*. It is symbolized as an uppercase italic *R*.

A multiple correlation coefficient indexes the association of one variable with a set of other variables, and the *squared multiple correlation* (R^2), sometimes called the *coefficient of multiple determination*, tells us the strength of this complex relationship.

In Figure 5a.2, the shaded area—the overlap of negative affect and openness with self-esteem—represents the R^2 for that relationship. This R^2 value can be thought of in a way analogous to r^2; that is, it can be thought of in terms of explained or accounted-for variance. In this case, we are explaining the variance of self-esteem.

The R^2 value represents one way to evaluate the model. Larger values mean that the model has accounted for greater amounts of the variance of the dependent variable. How large an R^2 it takes to say that you have accounted for a "large" percentage of the variance depends on the theoretical context within which the research has been done as well as prior research in the topic area.

The second feature important to note in Figure 5a.2 is that negative affect and openness overlap with each other. In Venn diagram format, an overlap of the variables indicates a correlation between them. Here, the two predictors do overlap but not by all that much (they correlate –.17). The degree to which they correlate affects the beta weights these variables are assigned in the regression equation, so the correlations of the predictors become a matter of some interest to researchers using a regression design.

The Partial Correlation and Covariance

With these two other variables in the equation for the moment, we are ready to evaluate the contribution of positive affect. The criterion variable or dependent variable is the focus of the multiple regression design. It is therefore the variance of the dependent variable that we want to account for or predict, and our goal is to account for as much of it as possible with our set of independent variables. We face an interesting but subtle feature of multiple regression in its efforts to maximize the amount of dependent variable variance that we can account for. In the context of multiple regression, our predictors must account for separate portions— rather than the same portion—of the dependent variable's variance. This is the key to understanding the regression process.

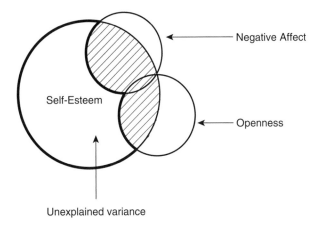

Figure 5a.3   Outlined Area of Unexplained Residual Variance for Self-Esteem Known as $(1 - R^2)$

With negative affect and openness already in the model, and thus already accounting for variance the amount of which is indexed by R^2, positive affect, as the last variable to enter, must target the variance that remains—the *residual* variance—in self-esteem. This is shown in Figure 5a.3, which is the same diagram that was shown in Figure 5a.2 except that we have added a couple of features to it. The shaded area in Figure 5a.3 is the variance of the dependent variable (self-esteem) explained by the two independent variables. It is indexed by R^2. The remaining portion of the dependent variable variance is, by definition, not accounted for by these two predictors. It is shown in the diagram as the blank space in the circle representing self-esteem, and its value must be $1 - R^2$. That is, it is the residual variance of self-esteem after negative affect and openness have performed their predictive (correlational) work.

We have outlined that scallop-like shape showing the unexplained variance of self-esteem with negative affect and openness in the equation by using a heavy line to make it easier to see and have labeled it as "unexplained variance" in Figure 5a.3. In evaluating the contribution of positive affect, the predictor currently under consideration, it is this residual variance of self-esteem that positive affect must target. The question becomes how much of this residual variance can positive affect correlate with on its own.

However strange this sounds, we are talking about the correlation between positive affect and the residual variance of self-esteem when the effects of negative affect and openness have been statistically removed, controlled, or "partialled out." Such a correlation is called a *partial correlation.*

A partial correlation addresses the relationship between two variables when the effects of other variables have been statistically removed from one of them. In this sense, the variables already in the model are conceived of as *covariates* in that their effects are statistically accounted for prior to evaluating the relationship of positive affect and self-esteem.

Once the regression procedure has determined how much positive affect can contribute to the set of predictors already in the model (how much of the residual variance of self-esteem it can explain), the computer starts the process of computing the weight that positive affect will receive in the model. We will not get into that computational process here. Instead, we have presented the situation depicting the results of those computations in Figure 5a.4. In this figure, we have added the positive affect variable into the predictor set. The "prediction work" that it does is shown in a lighter screen. Note that some of the prediction supplied by positive affect is not accomplished by any other variable and that "other" of what positive affect predicts for self-esteem is also predicted by negative affect.

Repeating the Process for the Other Predictors

After the computation of the b and beta weights for positive affect have been made, it is necessary to evaluate another one of the predictors. Thus, positive affect and another predictor are entered into the equation, and the strategy we have just outlined is repeated for the remaining predictor. Each

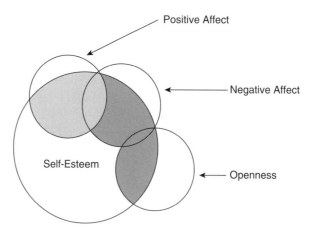

Figure 5a.4 Additional Self-Esteem Variance Accounted for After Entering Positive Affect

independent variable is put through this same process until the weights for all have been determined. At the end of this complex process, the final weights are locked in and the results of the analysis are printed.

We also know the value of R^2 with all the variables in the equation. This final R^2 tells us how much variance of the dependent variable is accounted for by the full regression model. By subtracting that value from 1 $(1 - R^2)$, we can also ascertain how much of the dependent variable's variance remains unexplained; this is the residual variance of the dependent variable after the regression model has accomplished its predictive work. Obviously, adding the value of the coefficient of multiple determination (R^2) to the residual variance $(1 - R^2)$ results in a value of 1.00; this subsumes 100% of the variance of the dependent variable.

The Squared Semipartial Correlation

A Venn diagram suggesting the final solution is shown in Figure 5a.5. We say "suggesting" because even with as small a set as three independent variables, it is difficult to draw all the relationships between them in only two dimensions (we have not captured the correlation between positive affect and openness). As a result, such a pictorial representation is at best an approximation to the full mathematical solution, which we will present in the next section of this chapter.

Despite the shortcoming of using the Venn diagram here, we can still point out an important element of the solution. Note that we have used two different types of shading in the figure. The total filled-in area, combining across all fill portions, represents the total amount of self-esteem variance explained by the regression model, a quantity indexed by R^2.

In Figure 5a.5, the darker cross-hatched areas are associated with explained variance resulting from the overlapping of predictors. Positive and negative affect, for example, explain a common portion of self-esteem variance, which is shown by the dark cross-hatched area between them.

The slanted-line areas are components of explained variance unique to a single predictor; that is, there is no overlap with the other predictors in those regions. This uniquely explained variance is indexed by another correlation statistic known as the *squared semipartial correlation*. It represents the extent to which variables do independent predictive work when combined with the other predictors in the model. Such correlations are, therefore, strongly tied to the specific regression model and may not necessarily generalize if any of these predictors are combined with a different set of predictors in a subsequent study.

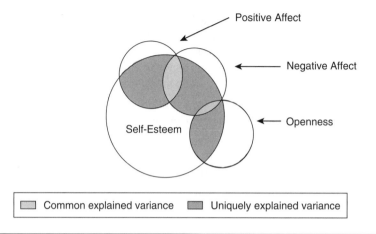

Figure 5a.5   Depiction of Both Common and Uniquely Explained Variance

We can also evaluate how well the model works by examining the squared semipartial correlations (Tabachnick & Fidell, 2001b). With the squared semipartial correlations, you are looking directly at the unique contribution of each predictor within the context of the model, and clearly, independent variables with larger squared semipartial correlations are making a larger unique contribution.

There are some limitations in using this statistic to compare the contributions of the predictors. The unique contribution of each variable in multiple regression is very much a function of the correlations of the variables used in the analysis. It is quite likely, as we stated earlier, that within the context of a different set of predictors, the unique contributions of these variables would change, perhaps substantially. Of course, this argument is true for the beta coefficients as well.

Based on this line of reasoning, one could put forward the argument that it would therefore be extremely desirable to select predictors in a multiple regression design that are not at all correlated between themselves but are highly correlated with the criterion variable. In such a fantasy scenario, the predictors would account for different portions of the dependent variable's variance, the squared semipartial correlations would be substantial, and the overlap of the predictors in Venn diagram format would be minimal.

This argument may have a certain appeal at first glance, but it is not a viable strategy for both practical and theoretical reasons. On the practical side, it would be difficult or perhaps even impossible to find predictors in many research arenas that are related to the criterion variable but at the same time are not themselves at least moderately correlated. On the theoretical side, it is desirable that the correlations between the predictors in a research study are representative of those relationships in the population. All else equal, to the extent that variables are related in the study as they are in the outside world, the research results may be said to have a certain degree of external validity.

The consequence of moderate or greater correlation between the predictors is that the unique contribution of each independent variable may be relatively small in comparison with the total amount of explained variance of the prediction model, because the predictors in such cases may overlap considerably with each other. Comparing one very small semipartial value with another even smaller semipartial value is often not a productive use of your time and runs the risk of yielding distorted or inaccurate conclusions.

Structure Coefficients

In our discussion of the variate, we emphasized that there was a difference between the predicted value and the actual score that individuals obtained on the dependent variable. Our focus here is on the predicted score, which is the value of the variate for the particular values of the independent variables substituted in the model. The *structure coefficient* is the bivariate correlation between a particular independent variable and the predicted (not the actual) score (Dunlap & Landis, 1998). Each predictor is associated with its own structure coefficient.

The numerical value of the structure coefficient is not contained in the output of SPSS but is easy to compute with a hand calculator using the following information available in the printout:

$$\text{Structure Coefficient} = \frac{r_{\text{IV} \times \text{DV}}}{R}$$

where $r_{\text{IV} \times \text{DV}}$ is the Pearson correlation between the given predictor and the actual (measured) dependent variable and R is the multiple correlation. The structure coefficient indexes the correlation between the predictor and the variate; stronger correlations indicate that the predictor is a stronger reflection of the construct underlying the variate.

Summary of the Solution for the Standard Regression Method Example

The results of the regression procedure for our simplified example are displayed in Table 5a.3. For each predictor, we have shown its Pearson correlation (r) with the dependent variable, its raw (b) and standardized (beta) regression weighting coefficients, the amount of self-esteem variance it has

Table 5a.3   Summary of the Example for Multiple Regression

Variable	r	b	beta	Squared Semipartial Correlation	Structure Coefficients	t
Positive affect	.55	2.89	.40	.14	.80	10.61*
Negative affect	−.57	−2.42	−.43	.16	−.82	−11.50*
Openness	.22	.11	.06	.00	.32	1.64
Constant (Y intercept)		56.66				

*$p < .01$.

uniquely explained (squared semipartial correlation), its structure coefficient, and the t value associated with each regression weight. We will discuss each in turn. The constant (the Y intercept) is shown in the last line of the table.

The Regression Equations

Using the raw and standardized regression weights and the Y intercept shown in Table 5a.3, we have the elements of the two regression equations. We produce them below.

The raw score equation is as follows:

$$\text{Self-esteem}_{\text{pred}} = 56.66 + (2.89)(\text{pos affect}) - (2.42)(\text{neg affect}) + (.11)(\text{open})$$

The standardized equation is as follows:

$$\text{Self-esteemz}_{\text{pred}} = (.40)(\text{pos affect}_z) - (.43)(\text{neg affect}_z) + (.06)(\text{open}_z)$$

Variables in the Equation

The predictor variables are shown in the first column of the table. This represents a complete solution in the sense that all the independent variables are included in the final equation regardless of how much they contribute to the prediction model. Such a solution is considered *atheoretical* because all the variables that were originally assessed are included in the final solution.

R^2 and Adjusted R^2

The shaded areas in Figure 5a.5 represent the total amount of variance accounted for by the prediction model. The computer printout shows the actual value for R^2. In the present case, this turned out to be .48 rounded to two decimal places. Thus, the three predictors in this particular weighted linear combination were able to explain about 48% of the variance of self-esteem.

SPSS also prints an adjusted R^2 value, which essentially tries to take into account a bit of error inflation in the regular R^2 value. Because it is a human endeavor, there is always some error of measurement associated with anything we assess. If this error is random, as we assume it to be, then some of that measurement error will actually be in the direction of enhanced prediction. Multiple regression, however, is unable to distinguish between this chance enhancement (i.e., blind luck from the standpoint of trying to achieve the best possible R^2) and the real predictive power of the variables. So it uses everything it can to maximize prediction—it generates the b and beta weights from both true and error sources combined.

The problem for us is that in another sample the random dictates of error will operate differently, and if the old weighting coefficients are applied to the new sample, they will be less effective than they were in the original sample. This overprediction is more of a problem when we have relatively small sample sizes and relatively more variables in the analysis. As sample size reaches more acceptable proportions (20 or more cases per predictor), the inflation of R^2 becomes that much less of an issue. Nonetheless, virtually every statistical program computes an adjusted value for R^2. These programs attempt to extract from the computed R^2 value some portion of it to which we can ascribe error and then subtract that out. We recommend that you report the adjusted R^2 value in addition to the uncorrected value.

The adjusted R^2 is a statistical estimate of the *shrinkage* we would observe if we were to apply the model to another sample. We can instead approach the issue from an empirical perspective through the processes of either *cross-validation* or *double cross-validation*. To perform a cross-validation, we ordinarily divide a large sample in half (into two subsamples) by randomly selecting the cases to be assigned to each. We then compute our regression analysis on one subsample and use those regression weights to predict the criterion variable of the second "hold-back" sample. The R^2 difference tells us the degree of predictive loss we have observed. We can also correlate the predicted scores of the hold-back sample with their actual scores; this can be thought of as the *cross-validation coefficient*.

Double cross-validation can be done by performing the cross-validation process in both directions—that is, performing the regression analysis on each subsample and applying the results to the other. In a sense, you obtain two estimates of shrinkage rather than one. If the shrinkage is not excessive, and there are few guidelines as to how to judge this, you can then perform an analysis on the combined sample and report the double cross-validation results to let readers know how generalizable your model is.

In the present example, the adjusted R^2 value for this analysis is rounded to .48, giving us virtually the same value as the unadjusted R^2 (the actual R^2 was .48257 and the adjusted R^2 was .47883). That such little adjustment was made is probably a function of the sample size to number of variables ratio we used and the fact that we used a very small predictor set.

By virtue of our sample size ($N = 420$), the R^2 of .48 obtained here is clearly statistically significant. However, SPSS tests the efficacy of the model by an analysis of variance. In this case, we can say that these three independent variables in combination significantly predicted self-esteem, $F(3, 416) = 129.32$, $p < .05$, $R^2 = .48$, adjusted $R^2 = .48$. This information is part of the printout, as we will see in Chapter 5B.

We should also consider the magnitude of the R^2 obtained here. One would ordinarily think of .48 as reasonably substantial, and you should not be terribly disappointed with R^2s considerably less than this in your own study. In the early stages of a research project or when studying a variable that may be complexly determined (e.g., rate of spread of an epidemic, recovery from a certain disease), very small but statistically significant R^2s may be cause for celebration by a research team.

Pearson Correlations With the Criterion Variable

The second numerical column in Table 5a.3 shows the simple Pearson correlations between self-esteem and each of the predictors. We have briefly described the correlations earlier. For present purposes, you can see that the correlations between self-esteem and positive affect and openness are positive. This was the case because each of these variables is scored in the positive direction—higher scores mean that respondents exhibit more positive affective behaviors and that they are more open to new or interesting experiences, respectively. Because higher scores on the self-esteem scale indicate greater positive feelings about oneself, it is not surprising that these two predictors are positively correlated with it. On the other hand, negative affect is negatively correlated with self-esteem. This is also not surprising in that individuals who exhibit more negative affective behaviors are typically those who have lower levels of self-esteem.

b and Beta Coefficients

The b and beta coefficients in Table 5a.3 show us the weights that the variables have been assigned at the end of the equation-building process. The b weights are tied to the metrics on which the variables are measured and are therefore difficult to compare with one another. But with respect to their own metric, they are quite interpretable. The b weight for positive affect, for example, is 2.89. We may take it to mean that when the other variables are controlled for, an increase of 2.89 points on the positive affect measure is, on average, associated with a 1-point gain in self-esteem.

Table 5a.3 also shows the Y intercept for the linear function. This value of 56.66 would need to be added to the weighted combination of variables in the raw score equation to obtain the predicted value of self-esteem for any given research participant.

The beta weights for the independent variables are also shown in Table 5a.3. Here, all the variables are in z-score form and thus their beta weights, within limits, can be compared with each other. We can see from Table 5a.3 that positive and negative affect have beta weights of similar magnitudes and that openness has a very low beta value. Thus, in achieving the goal of predicting self-esteem to the greatest possible extent (to minimize the sum of the squared prediction errors), positive and negative affect are given much more weight than openness.

The Case for Using Beta Coefficients to Evaluate Predictors

Some authors (e.g., Cohen et al., 2003; Pedhazur, 1982, 1997; Pedhazur & Schmelkin, 1991) have cautiously argued that at least under some circumstances, we may be able to compare the beta coefficients with each other. That is, on the basis of visual examination of the equation, it may be possible to say that predictors with larger beta weights contribute more to the prediction of the dependent variable than those with smaller weights.

It is possible to quantify the relative contribution of predictors using beta weights as the basis of the comparison. Although Kachigan (1986) has proposed examining the ratio of the squared beta weights to make this comparison, that procedure may be acceptable only in the rare situation when those predictors whose beta weights are being compared are uncorrelated (Pedhazur & Schmelkin, 1991). In the everyday research context, where the independent variables are almost always significantly correlated, we may simply compute the ratio of the actual beta weights (Pedhazur, 1982, 1997; Pedhazur & Schmelkin, 1991), placing the larger beta weight in the numerator of the ratio. This ratio reveals how much more one independent variable contributes to prediction than another within the context of the model.

This comparison could work as follows. If we wanted to compare the efficacy of negative affect (the most strongly weighted variable in the model) with the other (less strongly weighted) predictors, we would ordinarily limit our comparison to only the statistically significant ones. In this case, we would compare negative affect only with positive affect. We would therefore compute the ratio of the beta weights (negative affect / positive affect) without carrying the sign of the beta through the computation. This is shown below:

$$\frac{\text{negative affect}}{\text{positive affect}}$$

$$\frac{-.43}{.40} = 1.075$$

Based on this ratio (although we could certainly see this just by looking at the beta weights themselves), we would say that negative and positive affect make approximately the same degree of contribution to the prediction of self-esteem in the context of this research study with the present set of variables.

Concerns With Using the Beta Coefficients to Evaluate Predictors

We indicated above that even when authors such as Pedhazur (1982, 1997; Pedhazur & Schmelkin, 1991) endorse the use of beta coefficient ratios to evaluate the relative contribution of the independent variables within the model, they usually do so with certain caveats. Take Pedhazur (1997) as a good illustration:

> Broadly speaking, such an interpretation [stating that the effect of one predictor is twice as great as the effect of a second predictor] is legitimate, but it is not free of problems because the Beta[s] are affected, among other things, by the variability of the variable with which they are associated. (p. 110)

Thus, beta weights may not be generalizable across different samples.

Another concern regarding using beta coefficients to evaluate predictors is that beta weight values are partly a function of the correlations between the predictors themselves. That is, a certain independent variable may predict the dependent variable to a great extent in isolation, and one would therefore expect to see a relatively high beta coefficient associated with that predictor. Now place another predictor that is highly correlated with the first predictor into the analysis and all of a sudden the beta coefficients of both predictors can plummet. The first predictor's relationship with the dependent variable has not changed in this scenario, but the presence of the second correlated predictor could seriously affect the magnitude of the beta weight of the first. This "sensitivity" of the beta weights to the correlations between the predictors, reflected in the beta values, places additional limitations on the generality of the betas and thus their use in evaluating or comparing predictive effectiveness of the independent variables.

Recommendations for Using Betas

We do not want to leave you completely hanging at this point in our treatment, so we will answer some obvious questions. Should you use the beta weights to assess the relative strengths of the predictors in your own research? Yes. Should that be the only index you check out? No. The structure coefficients and the squared semipartial correlations should be examined as well.

Positive Versus Negative Weights

The positive and negative regression weights of the predictors reflect the nature of their respective correlations with the dependent variable. This makes sense when you recall that we are predicting self-esteem. The regression model tells us that greater levels of self-esteem will be predicted by the combination of more positive affect and openness and less negative affect. Thus, we should be adding the contribution of positive affect and openness but subtracting the contribution of negative affect in predicting self-esteem.

Squared Semipartial Correlations

The fourth column of Table 5a.3 displays the squared semipartial correlations for each predictor. These correlations are shown in the SPSS printout as "part correlations" and appear in the printout in their non-squared form. This statistic indexes the variance accounted for uniquely by each predictor in the full model. What is interesting here, and this is pretty typical of multiple regression research, is that the sum of these squared semipartial correlations is less than the R^2. That is, .14, .16, and .00 add up to .30 and not to the R^2 of .48.

The reason these squared semipartial correlations do not add to the value of R^2 is that the independent variables overlap (are correlated) with each other. Here, 30% of the variance is accounted for uniquely by the predictors, whereas (by subtraction) 18% of the accounted-for variance is handled by more than one of them. We therefore have some but not a huge amount of redundancy built into our set of predictors.

Using the squared semipartial correlations as a gauge of the relative strength of the predictors results in an evaluation similar to the one we made based on comparing the beta weights. From this perspective, positive and negative affect are approximately tied in their unique contribution to the prediction model under the present research circumstances.

The Structure Coefficients

The next-to-last column in Table 5a.3 shows the structure coefficients. These needed to be hand calculated because SPSS does not provide them. For each independent variable in the table, we divided the Pearson r representing the correlation of the independent variable and the dependent variable (shown in the second numerical column) by the multiple correlation. To illustrate, the square root of .48 (the R^2) is approximately .69. For positive affect's structure coefficient, we divided .55 by .69 to obtain approximately .80.

The structure coefficients indicate that positive and negative affect are reasonably highly correlated with predicted self-esteem and so are very reasonable instances of (they correlate reasonably highly with) the variate. In this example, using the structure coefficients as a basis to compare the contribution of the predictors presents the same picture as those painted by the beta weights and the squared semipartial correlations. Such consistency, however, is not always obtained.

Beta coefficients and structure coefficients differ in at least two important ways.

1. A beta coefficient associated with its predictor reflects the correlations of that predictor with the other predictors in the analysis. A structure coefficient does not take into account the degree to which that predictor correlates with the other predictors.

2. Beta weights can exceed the range of ±1 when the predictors are correlated with each other. Many researchers have a problem interpreting beta weights greater than unity. Structure coefficients are bounded by the range ±1 because they are correlation coefficients, thus making them pretty clearly interpretable.

Our recommendations are consistent with what we offered above for beta weights. We concur with Thompson and Borrello (1985) that the structure coefficients are a useful companion index of relative predictor contribution. Pedhazur (1982) notes that structure coefficients will show the same pattern of relationships as the preregression correlations of the predictors and the criterion. Because of this, Pedhazur is not convinced of the utility of structure coefficients. In our view, by focusing on the correlation between the predictor and the variate, we believe that structure coefficients may add a nuance to the interpretation of the regression analysis that we think is worthwhile.

t Tests

SPSS tests the significance of each predictor in the equation using *t* tests. The null hypothesis is that a predictor's weight is effectively equal to zero when the effects of the other predictors are taken into account. This means that when the other predictors act as covariates and this predictor is targeting the residual variance, according to the null hypothesis the predictor is unable to account for a statistically significant portion of it; that is, the partial correlation between the predictor and the criterion variable is not significantly different from zero. And it is a rare occurrence when every single independent variable turns out to be a significant predictor. The *t* tests shown in the last column of Table 5a.3 inform us that only positive and negative affect are statistically significant predictors in the model; even with our large sample size, openness does not receive a strong enough weight to reach that touchstone.

Step Methods of Building the Model

Step methods of building the regression equation that we briefly cover here are the forward method, the backward method, and the stepwise method. These methods construct the model one variable at a time rather than all at once as the standard method does. The primary goal of these step methods is to build a model with only the "important" predictors in it. The methods differ primarily in how they determine the importance of the predictors.

The Forward Method

In the forward method, rather than placing all the variables in the equation at once, we add independent variables to the equation one variable or step at a time. At each step, we enter the particular variable that adds the most predictive power at that time. If we were working with the set of variables we used to illustrate the standard regression method, negative affect would be entered first. We know this because, with no variables in the model at the start and building the model one variable at a time, the variable correlating most strongly with self-esteem would be entered first.

In the forward method, once a variable is entered into the model, it remains in the model. For the next step, the variable with the highest partial correlation (the correlation between the residual variance of self-esteem and each remaining predictor with negative affect as a covariate) is entered if that partial correlation is statistically significant. In this case, we will assume that positive affect would be entered.

This process is repeated for each remaining predictor with the variables in the model all acting as covariates. We would find, with negative and positive affect in the model, that openness would not be entered; that is, it would not account for a significant amount of the residual variance. Because that is the entire set of predictors, the forward procedure would stop at the end of the second step.

The Backward Method

The backward method works, not by adding significant variables to the equation but, rather, by removing nonsignificant predictors from it one step at a time. The very first action performed by the backward method is the same one used by the standard method; it enters all the predictors into the equation regardless of their worth. But whereas the standard method stops here, the backward method is just getting started.

The model with all the variables in it is now examined, and the significant predictors are marked for retention. Nonsignificant predictors are then evaluated and the most expendable of them—the one whose loss would least significantly decrease the R^2—is removed from the equation. A new model is built in the absence of that one independent variable and the evaluation process is repeated. Once again, the most expendable independent variable is removed. This removal process and equation-reconstruction process continues until there are only significant predictors remaining in the equation. In our example, openness would have been removed at the first opportunity. It is probable that the method would have stopped at that point because both remaining predictors would almost certainly have been significant predictors.

Backward Versus Forward Solutions

Backward regression does not always produce the same model as forward regression even though it probably would have in our simplified example. Here is why: Getting into the equation in the forward method requires predictors to meet a more stringent criterion than variables being retained in the equation in the backward method. This creates a situation in which it is more difficult to get into the equation than to remain in it. Stringency or difficulty is defined statistically by the alpha or probability level associated with entry and removal.

Predictors earn their way into the equation in the forward method by significantly predicting variance of the dependent variable. The alpha level governing this entry decision is usually the traditional .05 level. By most standards, this is a fairly stringent criterion. When we look for predictors to remove under the backward method, the alpha level usually drops to .10 as the default in most programs. This means that a predictor needs to be significant at only .10 (not at .05) to retain its place in the equation. Thus, an independent variable is eligible to be removed from the equation at a particular step in the backward method if its probability level is greater than .10 (e.g., $p = .11$) but it will be retained in the equation if its probability level is equal to or less than .10 (e.g., $p = .09$).

The consequences of using these different criteria for entry and removal affects only those variables whose probabilities are between the entry and removal criteria. To see why this is true, first consider variables that are not within this zone.

▶ If a variable does not meet the standard of $p = .10$, it is removed from the equation. This variable would also by definition not meet the .05 alpha level criterion for entry either, so there is no difference in the outcome for this predictor under either criterion—it is not going to wind up in the equation in either the forward or backward methods.

▶ If a variable does meet the .05 criterion, it will always be allowed entry to the equation and will certainly not be removed by the backward method; again, there is no difference in outcome for such a predictor under either method.

Variables with probability levels between these two criteria are in a more interesting position. Assume that we are well into the backward process and at this juncture the weakest predictor is one whose probability is .08. This variable would not have been allowed into the equation by the forward method if it were considered for entry at this point because to get in, it would have to meet a .05 alpha level to achieve statistical significance.

However, under the backward method, this variable was freely added to the equation at the beginning, and the only issue here is whether it is to be removed. When we examine its current probability level and find it to be .08, we determine that this predictor is "significant" at the .10 alpha level. It therefore remains in the equation. In this case, the model built under the backward model would incorporate this predictor but the model built under the forward method would have excluded it.

The Stepwise Method

The stepwise method of building the multiple regression equation is essentially a composite of the forward and backward methods. The stepwise and forward methods act in the same fashion until we reach the point where a third predictor is added to the equation. The stepwise method therefore begins with an empty equation and builds it one step at a time. Once a third independent variable is in the equation, the stepwise method invokes the right to remove an independent variable if that predictor is not earning its keep.

Predictors are allowed to be included in the equation if they significantly ($p = .05$) add to the predicted variance of the dependent variable. With correlated independent variables, as we have seen, the predictors in the equation admitted under a probability level of .05 can still overlap with each other. This is shown in Figure 5a.6.

In Figure 5a.6, predictor J was entered first, K was entered second, and L was entered third. We are poised at the moment when L joined the equation. Note that between predictors J and L, there is very little work that can be attributed uniquely to K. At this moment, the squared semipartial correlation associated with K (showing its unique contribution to the prediction model) is quite small.

In the forward method, the fact that K's unique contribution has been substantially reduced by L's presence would leave the procedure unfazed because it does not have a removal option available to it. But this is the stepwise method, and it is prepared to remove a predictor if necessary. When the amount of residual variance that K now accounts for is examined, let's presume that it is not significant at the removal criterion of .10 (say its p value is .126). K is thus judged to no longer be contributing effectively to the prediction model, and it is removed from the equation. Of course, as more predictors are entered into the equation, the gestalt could change dramatically, and K might very well be called on to perform predictive duties later in the analysis.

We have just described the reason that the entry criterion is more severe than the removal criterion. It can be summarized as follows. If getting into the equation was easier than getting out, then variables removed at one step

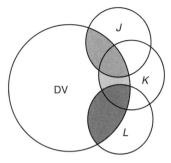

Figure 5a.6 Unique Contribution of Variable *K* Is Reduced by Variable *J* and Variable *L*

might get entered again at the next step because they might still be able to achieve that less stringent level of probability needed for entry. There is then a chance that the stepwise procedure could be caught in an endless loop where the same variable kept being removed on one step and entered again on the next. By making entry more exacting than removal, this conundrum is avoided.

Evaluation of the Statistical Methods

Benefits of the Statistical Methods

The primary advantage of using the standard model is that it presents a complete picture of the regression outcome to researchers. If the variables were important enough to earn a place in the design of the study, then they are given room in the model even if they are not adding very much to the R^2. That is, on the assumption that the variables were selected on the basis of their relevance to theory or at least on the basis of hypotheses based on a comprehensive review of the existing literature on the topic, the standard model provides an opportunity to see how they fare as a set in predicting the dependent variable.

The argument for using the stepwise method is that we end up with a model that is "lean and mean." Each independent variable in it has earned the right to remain in the equation through a hard, competitive struggle. The argument for using the forward and backward methods is similar to one used by those advocating the stepwise method. The forward and backward methods give what their users consider the essence of the solution by excluding variables that add nothing of merit to the prediction.

Criticisms of the Statistical Methods

One criticism of all the statistical methods is that independent variables with good predictive qualities on their own may be awarded very low weight in the model. This can happen because their contribution is being evaluated when the contributions of the other predictors have been partialled out. Such "masking" of potentially good predictors can lead researchers to draw incomplete or improper conclusions from the results of the analysis. One way around this problem is for the researcher to exercise some judgment in which variables are entered at certain points in the analysis, and this is discussed in the section titled "Researcher-Controlled Methods of Building the Model." This issue is also related to multicollinearity, a topic that we discuss later in the chapter.

The step methods have become increasingly less popular over the years as their weaknesses have become better understood and as researcher-controlled methods have gained in popularity. Tabachnick and Fidell (2001b), for example, have expressed serious concerns about this group of methods, especially the stepwise method, and they are not alone. Here is a brief summary of the interrelated drawbacks of using this set of methods.

▶ These methods, particularly the stepwise method, may need better than the 20 to 1 ratio of cases to independent variables because there are serious threats to external validity (Tabachnick & Fidell, 2001b). That is, the model that is built may overfit the sample because a different sample may yield somewhat different relationships (correlations) between the variables in the analysis, and that could completely change which variables were entered into the equation.

▶ The statistical criteria for building the equation identify variables for inclusion if they are better predictors than the other candidates. But "better" could mean "just a tiny bit better" or "a whole lot better." One variable may win the nomination to enter the equation, but the magnitude by which the variable achieved that victory may be too small to matter to researchers.

▶ If the victory of getting into the equation by one variable is within the margin of error in the measurement of another variable, identifying the one variable as a predictor at the expense of the other may obscure viable alternative prediction models.

▶ Variables that can substantially predict the dependent variable may be excluded from the equations built by the step methods because some other variable or combination of variables does the job a little bit better. It is conceivable that several independent variables taken together may predict the criterion variable fairly well, but step procedures consider only one variable at a time.

Balancing the Value of All the Statistical Methods of Building the Model

The standard method works well if you have selected the independent variables based on theory or empirical research findings and wish to examine the combined predictive power of that set of predictors. But because they are functioning in combination, the weights of the predictors in the model are a function of their interrelationships; thus, you are not evaluating them in isolation or in subsets. The standard method will allow you to test hypotheses about the model as a whole; if that is your goal, then that's what you should use.

The stepwise methods are intended to identify which variables should be in the model on purely statistical grounds. Such an atheoretical approach is discouraged by many researchers. On the other hand, there may be certain applications where all you want is to obtain the largest R^2 with the fewest number of predictors, recognizing that the resulting model may have less external validity than desired. Under these conditions, some researchers may consider using a step method.

Before one decides that one of the statistical procedures is to be used, it is very important to consider a researcher-controlled method of performing the regression analysis. Although it does require more thoughtful decision making rather than just entering the variables and selecting a statistical method, the flexibility it affords and the control it offers more than compensate for the effort it takes to run such analyses.

Researcher-Controlled Methods of Building the Model

Researcher-controlled regression methods are really variations on a theme. In all cases, it is the researchers who specify the order of entry of predictors into the equation. The main issue that researchers face is to determine how many variables are instructed to enter the equation at any one time. Several labels are applied to variations of researcher control: *Sequential analysis, covariance analysis, hierarchical analysis,* and *block-entry analysis* are among the most common.

What makes this approach different from the statistical methods described above is that instead of the computer program using statistical criteria to make such entry decisions, the researchers determine which variables they would like to propose as covariates. Selection of covariates should have a solid rational basis in that the decision should be based on a particular theory, or covariate selection should rest on a solid empirical basis in which the research literature has shown the need to take into account the relationship(s) between the criterion variable and one or more of the predictors.

For example, suppose we are interested in predicting performance on the nursing multiple-choice licensing examination. Specifically, suppose that we want to determine the extent to which the time spent in various activities during their internships combines together to predict candidates' exam scores. Further suppose that we believe there is enough variation in the reading skill of licensing candidates to want to statistically control for the effects of reading skill on license exam performance in evaluating those internship experiences.

If we have a measure of reading skill in addition to the time-spent survey results for each individual, we will conduct the regression analysis so that the reading variable is the first to enter the equation and thus we will use this variable as a covariate. That forces the analysis to assign whatever variance in test scores that it can to reading skill. We then enter the internship variables simultaneously to account for whatever variance remains after reading skill does its predictive (covariance) work. Causal hypotheses and mediating variables, which this example is on the borderline of addressing, can be directly examined through the technique of path analysis, described in Chapter 14A.

Other possibilities for order of entry exist because we have now taken control of the process. We can, for example, enter the predictors of our choice into the equation one at a time. Once again, researchers should determine the order of entry on the basis of some theory or at least on some empirical basis, but as long as not too many orders are chosen, it may be possible to test some interesting hypotheses. The main advantage of entering one variable at a time is to give precedence to predictors entered earlier over predictors entered later. As you can imagine, doing such a sequential analysis is a delicate matter. Several independent variables may actually account for the same component of the dependent variable's variance, but only the earlier entered ones will actually get the credit for doing so. This sort of hierarchical analysis works well with more developed theories.

Block-entry analysis, entering subsets of variables in a sequential manner, is a variant of this general researcher-controlled methodology in that one enters a set of variables rather than a single variable at a particular stage of the analysis. For example, if we have variables *K, L, M, N, O, P, Q,* and *R* as predictors of some criterion variable, we might wish to enter variables *L, P,* and *R* together on a single step in the analysis. These variables are therefore entered simultaneously (as described under the standard regression model) where the effects of the other variables (and any variables already in the equation) have been partialled out before the contribution of that variable is computed. One can also enter blocks of variables and single variables at various stages throughout the entire process.

Block-entry analysis can serve at least two research functions. First, as mentioned earlier in a criticism of the step procedures, several variables in combination may predict better than any one of them taken in isolation. Entering variables as a set (block) allows researchers an opportunity to explore that possibility. Second, some variables in a study may either naturally relate to each other or may all pertain to a general area of the content domain and so may lend themselves to be entered as a block. For example, in predicting the strength of certain symptom patterns, one may want to enter physical or medical variables before the more purely psychological variables.

In addition to exploring the theoretical consequences of varying the order of entry of the predictors and in addition to determining the result of using certain variables as covariates, several other issues can be broached by using a sequential form of regression analyses. Here are two examples:

1. A very "expensive" variable achieved substantial weight in the model. To collect data on this predictor might take a great deal of time, trouble, funding, or some combination of these. It may be worthwhile to ask if any variable on the sidelines could do almost as good a job but work for cheaper research wages.

2. A set of variables received negligible weights in the model, but these are easy to measure (e.g., they may be subscales of a single inventory). Similar measures might have been weighted substantially but could be more difficult to work with. It may make sense to investigate the R^2 consequences of replacing the latter with the former.

Outliers

As discussed in Chapter 3A and 3B, outliers are extreme scores on either the criterion or the predictor variables. They are typically thought of as being anomalous values, often three or more standard deviation units from their respective means, that suggest possible problems with the measurement instrument, the way the responses were recorded or transcribed, or the participants' membership in the population that was presumably sampled.

The presence of outliers can adversely affect (distort) the results of the analysis. This distortion takes several different forms (Darlington, 1990). As one example, consider the use of the least squares rule. Because this line-fitting procedure calls for minimizing the squared distance between each data point and the regression line, data points that are extremely far removed from the mainstream have a rather disproportionate influence in determining where the regression line is best placed. That is, because the square of a large distance is extremely large, the regression line is drawn closer to the outlier to keep that squared distance as small as possible. This is done, of course, at a sacrifice—the regression line no longer coincides with the best-fitting location for all the other data points (excluding the outlier). For this reason, most statisticians suggest that outliers should be deleted prior to data analysis.

Researchers should also consider the possibility that the participants whose scores are defined as outliers might actually have something in common. For example, if most of the outliers represent older participants in a sample that contained a good mix of ages, then age may suddenly become an important variable to study.

Collinearity and Multicollinearity

Collinearity is a condition that exists when two predictors correlate very strongly; *multicollinearity* is a condition that exists when more than two predictors correlate very strongly. Note that we are talking about the relationships between the predictor variables only and not about correlations between each of the predictors and the dependent variable.

Regardless of whether we are talking about two predictors or a set of three or more predictors, multicollinearity can distort the interpretation of multiple regression results. For example, if two variables are highly correlated, then they are largely confounded with one another; that is, they are essentially measuring the same characteristic, and it would be impossible to say which of the two was the more relevant. Statistically, because the standard regression procedure controls for all the other predictors when it is evaluating a given independent variable, it is likely that neither predictor variable would receive any substantial weight in the model. This is true because at the time the procedure evaluates one of these two predictors, the other is (momentarily) already in the equation accounting for almost all the variance that would be explained by the first. The irony is that each on its own might very well be a good predictor of the criterion variable. With both variables in the model, the R^2 value will be appropriately high; if the goal of the research is to maximize R^2, then multicollinearity might not be an immediate problem.

When the research goal is to understand the interplay of the predictors and not simply to maximize R^2, multicollinearity can cause several problems in the analysis. One problem caused by the presence of multicollinearity is that the values of the regression coefficients of the highly correlated independent variables are distorted. Often, they are quite low and may even fail to achieve statistical significance. A second problem is that the standard errors of the regression weights of those multicollinear predictors can be inflated, thereby enlarging their confidence intervals, sometimes to the point where they contain the zero value. If that is the case, you could not reliably determine if increases in the predictor are associated with increases or decreases in the criterion variable. A third problem is that if multicollinearity is sufficiently great, certain internal mathematical operations (e.g., matrix inversion) are disrupted and the statistical program comes to a screeching halt.

Identifying collinearity or multicollinearity requires researchers to examine the data in certain ways. A high correlation is easy to spot when considering only two variables. Just examine the Pearson correlations between the variables in the analysis as a prelude to multiple regression. Two variables that are very strongly related should raise a "red flag." As a general rule of thumb, we recommend that two variables correlated in the middle .7s or higher should probably not be used together in a regression or any other multivariate analysis. Allison (1999b) suggests that you "almost certainly have a problem if the correlation is above .8, but there may be difficulties that appear well before that value" (p. 64).

One common cause of multicollinearity is researchers using subscales of an inventory as well as the full inventory score as predictors. Depending on how the subscales have been computed, it is possible for them in combination to correlate almost perfectly with the full inventory score. You should use either the subscales or the full inventory score, but not all of them in the analysis. Another common cause of multicollinearity is including in the analysis variables that assess the same construct. You should either drop all but one of them from the analysis or consider the possibility of combining them in some fashion if it makes sense. For example, you might combine height and weight to form a measure of body mass. As another example, you might average three highly correlated survey items; exploratory factor analysis, discussed in Chapter 12A, can be used to help determine which variables you might productively average together without losing too much information. A less common cause of an analysis failing because of multicollinearity is placing into the analysis two measures that are mathematical transformations of each other (e.g., number of correct and incorrect responses; time and speed of response); researchers should use only one of these measures.

Multicollinearity is much more difficult to detect when it is some (linear) combination of variables that produces a high multiple correlation in some subset of the predictor variables. We would worry if that correlation reached the mid .8s but Allison (1999b, p. 141) gets concerned if those multiple correlations reached into the high .7s (R^2 of about .60). Many statistical programs will allow you to compute multiple correlations for different combinations of variables so that you can examine them. Thus, you can scan these correlations for such high values and take the necessary steps to attempt to fix the problem.

Most regression programs have what is called a *tolerance* parameter that tries to protect the procedure from multicollinearity by rejecting predictor variables that are too highly correlated with other independent variables. Conceptually, tolerance is the amount of a predictor's variance not accounted for by the other predictors ($1 - R^2$ between predictors). Lower tolerance values indicate that there are stronger relationships (increasing the chances of obtaining multicollinearity) between the predictor variables. Allison (1999b) cautions that tolerances in the range of .40 are worthy of concern; tolerance values in the range of .1 are problematic (Myers, 1990; Stevens, 2002).

A related statistic is the *variance inflation factor* (VIF), which is computed as 1 divided by tolerance. A VIF value of 2.50 is associated with a tolerance of .40 and is considered problematic by Allison (1999b); a VIF value of 10 is associated with a tolerance of .1 and is considered problematic by Myers (1990) and Stevens (2002).

Suppressor Variables

Suppressor variables, when included in regression equations, increase R^2, but they accomplish this feat in a somewhat different way from what we have already discussed. Suppressor variables often are not correlated particularly strongly with the criterion variable itself. Rather, they are correlated in a special way with one or more of the other predictor variables, and that is where they do their job.

A suppressor variable works its magic by correlating with what is usually thought of as a source of error in another predictor (Darlington, 1990). Pedhazur (1982) describes it well in saying that by correlating with the error in another predictor, the suppressor variable helps purify that predictor and thereby enhances its predictive power. Often, under these conditions, this suppressor variable will then be given a negative weight in the equation (assuming that the predictor it is partially suppressing is positively correlated with the dependent variable). Tabachnick and Fidell (2001b) have provided the following rubric to help identify a suppressor variable:

▶ The correlation between it and the criterion variable is substantially smaller than its beta weight.

or

▶ Its Pearson correlation with the criterion and its beta weight have different signs (p. 149).

Other signs that you may have a suppressor variable in the equation are offered by Pedhazur (1982):

▶ It may have a near-zero correlation with the criterion variable but yet it is a significant predictor in the regression model.
▶ It may have little or no correlation with the criterion variable but is correlated with one or more of the predictors. (pp. 104–105)

Conceptualizing how a suppressor variable does its work is not an easy matter. Guilford's example (Guilford & Fruchter, 1978) is better than most, and we will present it to you as a way to exemplify this somewhat elusive concept.

J. P. Guilford, one of the great pioneers in measurement and psychometrics, did research for the Air Force during World War II to develop selection procedures for pilots. He speaks of a vocabulary test that slightly negatively correlated with success in pilot training. His research team had also used a reading test in the study (the trainees read passages and answered questions about them), which turned out to correlate positively with success in pilot training.

At first, it must have seemed odd that a vocabulary test slightly negatively correlated with pilot success but that a reading test correlated positively with pilot training success. But Guilford soon realized that the reading test correlated positively with pilot success not because it measured some verbal skill but rather because of the content it presented to the trainees. This content tapped into their experience with mechanical devices and their ability to visualize information contained in the passages.

According to Guilford's appraisal of the situation, the score these trainees received on the reading test was a function of three factors—mechanical experience, visualization, and, of course, verbal comprehension—only two of which (mechanical experience and visualization) were viable predictors of pilot success. The third factor measured by the reading test, verbal comprehension, did not predict success, something he already knew from the results of his vocabulary test. This third factor in the reading test actually represented, from the standpoint of predicting training success, error variance.

Now consider the relationship between the vocabulary test and the reading test. Roughly speaking, the vocabulary test was a measure of verbal comprehension or something that correlated highly with it. From this perspective, the reading test and the vocabulary test share common variance. But not just any variance, mind you. The variance they share is common to what they both measure—verbal comprehension or its kin.

How a suppressor variable works lies, in this example, with what happens when you make use of the correlation between the vocabulary and reading tests. If the vocabulary test was placed in the regression model together with the reading test, even though it could not directly predict pilot success, it would have the opportunity to correlate with that portion of the reading test assessing verbal comprehension. By virtue of that correlation, it would account for (statistically control for or negate) that portion of the reading test's variance attributable to verbal comprehension and thus make the reading test a better predictor than it would be in the absence of the vocabulary test. All that we would need to do is subtract that error variance out.

Based on this reasoning, Guilford (Guilford & Fruchter, 1978) tells us that the "combination of a vocabulary test with the reading test, with a negative weight for the vocabulary test [to subtract out this variance accounted for by the vocabulary test], would have improved predictions [of pilot success] over those possible with the reading test alone" (p. 182). That is, including the vocabulary test would have accounted for and subtracted out the variance due to verbal comprehension in the reading test (which was not contributing to the prediction of success anyhow), freeing up the other components of the reading test (the parts assessing mechanical experience and visualization) to more purely predict success in pilot training. In this context, the vocabulary test would have operated as a suppressor variable.

Linear and Nonlinear Regression: Completely Linear Models

The general regression model that we have been discussing thus far in this chapter is one form of a linear model. For the purposes of this book, we can distinguish between three types of regression models: a form we will call *completely linear,* another form of linear model called *intrinsically linear* (Pedhazur, 1982), and a form of nonlinear model called *intrinsically nonlinear* (Pedhazur, 1982) or *general curve fitting* (Darlington, 1990).

In the completely linear model, both the variables specified by the model (the dependent and the independent variables) as well as the parameters (the coefficients and the intercept) are in their "regular" form. We then multiply each variable by its weight and add the results of that multiplication together (adding the constant in the raw score equation) to obtain the predicted value of the criterion variable.

If there is only one predictor in the model, as is the case in simple linear regression, the equation can be represented geometrically as a straight line in two-dimensional space (in a space defined with X and Y axes). With two predictors in the model, the equation may be represented geometrically as a tilted plane in three-dimensional space (illustrated well by Darlington, 1990). If you think of a room in a house, the two predictor variables cover the floor (the width and the length) of the room and the criterion variable is mapped to the walls (height). Imagine a pitched and tilted ceiling to this room. This ceiling is the plane described by the regression equation. Although it has one more dimension to it than the straight line, it is still a completely linear model composed of flat, straight surfaces. Models with more than two predictors, even though we cannot easily picture them, are also linear in this sense.

Linear and Nonlinear Regression: Intrinsically Linear Models

Another class of linear models has the same basic structure of completely linear models in that (a) each variable has an associated coefficient, (b) we multiply each variable by its coefficient to obtain its weighted value, and (c) we add the results of that multiplication together (adding the constant in the raw score equation) to obtain the predicted value of the criterion variable.

The difference between completely linear models and intrinsically linear models is that in the latter, the variables themselves are not in their "regular" or raw form; rather, they have been "altered" in some manner. In this sense, we can say that the model is linear with respect to its parameters—in that the regression weights are still in "regular" form and we add the weighted variables together to obtain the predicted score—but that the model is nonlinear in its variables. We can think of an intrinsically linear model as one that combines variables that are themselves not linear in the best weighted linear combination to maximally predict the dependent variable.

Variables in an intrinsically linear model can be altered in several different nonlinear ways. We will consider three types of alterations here: transformations of dependent and independent variables, dummy coding of independent variables, and interactions between independent variables.

Transformations

A transformation is used either to bring the data more closely in line with the underlying assumptions of regression or because it makes more sense to frame the relationships between the predictor and criterion variables in terms of a transformed variable. We have already discussed a transformation to a standardized scale (a z-score transformation) that is routinely performed by virtually every statistical program in computing a regression solution, although this type of transformation still keeps the variables in linear form. Other transformations are generally applied to the dependent or criterion variable, and still other transformations are generally applied to the independent or predictor variables that convert them to a nonlinear form.

The most common transformation of the criterion variable (other than standardizing it) is to use its natural logarithm as the value to be predicted (Allison, 1999b). Such a transformation, which we described in Chapter 3A, may help to reduce the degree of heteroscedasticity in the measure.

Another transformation of the dependent variable is a logit transformation, provided that the criterion variable is a proportion (Allison, 1999b). If the criterion variable is symbolized by Y, then this transformation takes the following form:

$$\text{log of the expression } [Y \text{ divided by } (1 - Y)]$$

A common transformation of the predictor variables is to use a polynomial function in which the value of one or more of the independent variables is raised to a power (e.g., X^2). This is called *polynomial* or *curvilinear* regression. A second-order polynomial function, known as a quadratic function, has the predictor raised to the second power. We might use this transformation when we expect the criterion variable to first increase together with the predictor and then to decrease with further increases in values of the predictor variable. For example, using age as a predictor of physical agility, we would expect agility to increase up to some age level but to then show a decrease with further increases in age. A quadratic function has one "bend" in the curve. In contrast, a cubic function (a third-order polynomial in which a predictor X is raised to the power of 3) has two "bends" in the functions and is substantially more complex to interpret. Most researchers would not use a polynomial function in excess of third order.

An additional way to change a predictor variable is to subject it to log transformation. We would tend to use this type of transformation where we expect the criterion and predictor variables to increase together up to some point but then further expect the dependent variable to level off with further increases in the predictor. For example, in predicting income from education, we might expect that higher income levels are associated with increasingly more education up to some point but that more education would not alter income level beyond some point (Allison, 1999b).

Dummy Coding

As we indicated in Chapter 4A, it is appropriate to perform a Pearson correlation analysis with a dichotomously coded categorical variable. In the context of multiple linear regression, we could use such a variable as an independent variable (or we could use it as the criterion variable in either a logistic regression analysis as described in Chapter 6A or in a discriminant function analysis as described in Chapter 7A). To include a dichotomously coded variable as a predictor, we need to assign arbitrary numerical codes to its categories; for example, we could use 1 (for the presence of some property) and 0 (for the absence of some property). This process is called *dummy coding.*

The interpretation of the results of the regression analysis—specifically, the coefficient associated with the dichotomously coded variable—is based on the difference between the two means when adjusted (statistically controlling) for the other predictors in the model. For example, suppose that we were using participation in high-risk sports as one of several predictors of aggressiveness. We code those who have participated in high-risk sports as 1 and those who have not as 0. In the regression analysis, we find that this predictor is significant with a b weight of 12.50. We may then interpret this value to indicate that, when controlling for the other predictors, those who participate in such sports (those coded as 1) have aggression scores on average 12.50 greater than those who have not participated in high-risk sports.

A regression analysis requires that the arbitrary categorical coding yield interpretable results. Thus, we could not legitimately take a categorical variable with three or more levels (e.g., eastern, midwestern, and western regions); code the categories 1, 2, 3 (as examples); and include such a coded variable in the regression analysis. The statistical procedure would treat the values of 1, 2, and 3 as though they represented interval level measurement where 3 designated more of some quality than 2 and 2 designated more of some quality than 1. But because the categories are not quantitatively based (by definition), the results that you obtain will not make any sense. Think of it like this if you are unconvinced: If the categories were coded in all possible ways and you ran separate regression analyses for each coding scheme, you would get widely different regression results. This indicates that none of the coding schemes is appropriate.

At the same time, nominal variables with more than two categories often make interesting and useful predictors. We simply need to dummy code them appropriately to use them in a regression analysis. We do this by creating separate dummy variables to represent portions or levels of the nominal variable. Each dummy variable will be a dichotomous (0, 1) coding of a subcategory (level) of the main variable. Because the dummy variables need to be orthogonal to (independent of) each other, the number of levels of the variable we are allowed to use is one less than the number of categories we have. Thus, with the three geographical regions mentioned above, we can create only two dummy variables (two regions coded 0 and 1) to represent the main variable.

The category excluded from the dummy coding is, in a certain sense, the focal point of the analysis; it is treated as the reference category with which the other categories will be compared. This is because the regression weights of the other categories are interpreted with respect to this reference category. We can illustrate this by selecting for the sake of this example the eastern region as the reference category. We would then dichotomously code the other two categories. If participants lived in the Midwest they would be coded as 1; if they lived elsewhere they would be coded as 0. A similar coding scheme would be used for Westerners: If they lived in the West, they would be coded as 1; if they lived elsewhere, they would be coded as 0.

Every participant receives a value on both of these dummy coded variables. If in the data file, the Midwest variable appeared first and the West variable appeared second, we would know that a case with the combined code 10 lived in the Midwest, a case with the combined code 01 lived in the West, and a case with the code 00 lived in the East. Note that this last code appears as a by-product of our coding scheme because with one less code than we have categories (we use only two dummy variables to handle three categories), we know that someone not falling into one of our two designated codes (someone without a 1 in one of the two fields) must be in the last category. In this way, creating a variable for all but one category is sufficient to classify all the cases in the sample.

In the regression model, residing in the midwestern and western regions are each predictors with their own regression weights. In our interpretation, we use the eastern region, our reference category, as our base. Suppose that we were predicting the number of times individuals changed residences in the prior 5-year period and that region was one of many predictors. Assume that the raw regression weight for the midwestern region was –4.50 and that the raw regression weight for the western region was 9.94. We would then say, when controlling or adjusting for the other variables in the model, that midwestern participants moved on average 4.5 times less than Easterners (the negative b weight tells us that it is less) and that Westerners moved on average almost 10 times more than Easterners.

Selecting the category of the nominal variable to serve as the reference group should be based on statistical or methodological factors. From a statistical perspective, the reference group should be one that, all else equal, has a relatively large sample size (Allison, 1999b). This is because the mean of the reference group will be involved in all the comparisons and should therefore have as small a standard error as possible. From a methodological perspective, the reference group should be the one with which it makes sense to compare the other groups. If there is a "control" or "baseline" group in the nominal variable, that category would present itself as a strong reference group candidate. If there is no such category, as was the case in the example of geographic regions, then the choice is rather arbitrary.

Moderator Variables and Interactions

Consider the case where we have two predictors, X_1 and X_2. At the end of the regression analysis, each predictor is associated with a regression weight. For example, b_1 is the coefficient of X_1. This coefficient is essentially an estimate of the slope of the function for X_1 controlling for X_2. An assumption underlying such an interpretation is that the value of b_1 is the same across the range of X_2; that is, whether or not X_1 and X_2 are correlated, the regression function for X_1 is independent of X_2 (Aiken & West, 1991). This same reasoning can be applied to X_2.

Now suppose that this independence assumption is not true. Instead, the relationship between X_1 and the criterion variable differs for different levels of X_2. With the relationship between X_1 and the criterion depending on the level of X_2, the variable X_2 is thought of as a *moderator variable* in that we need to take into account the level of X_2 in describing the relationship between X_1 and the criterion. When this is the case, we say that X_1 and X_2 interact. Here are two examples of interactions that illustrate how different relationships between one predictor and a criterion variable might be expected at different levels of another predictor:

▶ As predictors of the degree of liberal attitudes held by people, we measure socioeconomic status and age. Let's look at socioeconomic status predicting liberal attitudes at two levels of age. Among younger people, we might find that higher levels of socioeconomic status predict more liberalism; among older people, we might find that higher levels of socioeconomic status predict less liberalism. If this was found, we would say that age and socioeconomic status interact in affecting (predicting) liberalism (Darlington, 1990).

▶ In predicting the self-assurance of managers, we use as independent variables how long participants have been managers as well as their actual managerial ability. Let's focus here on predicting self-assurance from the number of years the managers have held such a position but develop that prediction model separately for high and low ability levels. We might find that high-ability managers become more self-assured with increased time as a manager, but that managers with low ability become less self-assured the longer they have been in the position. Thus, time as manager and managerial ability would interact in predicting self-assurance (Aiken & West, 1991).

In the regression examples we discussed earlier in this chapter, the independent variables always "stood alone" with their regression weights either in their raw form or in some kind of transformed form. That is, we have always dealt with situations where the regression coefficient was the weight assigned to the predictor or some transformation of the predictor to represent one element of the regression model. Interactions involve estimating the coefficient (weight) of the product of two predictors. Usually, these two predictors are also included separately in the model. Thus, at minimum, we would have X_1, X_2, and $X_1 \times X_2$ as three predictors in the models. In this structure, each would be associated with its own regression weight. Our minimal model would then be as follows:

$$Y_{\text{pred}} = \mathbf{a} + b_1 X_1 + b_2 X_2 + b_3 X_1 X_2$$

In the above equation, the term $X_1 X_2$ represents the interaction. The two terms preceding it in the equation containing the stand-alone predictors are known as the *main effects* of the variables; we thus can also address or speak to the main effects of X_1 and X_2.

In the regression solution, if the coefficient associated with the interaction was statistically significant, we must be careful about interpreting the results of the stand-alone variables (the main effects). In the first example above, it would be inappropriate to speak of the slope of socioeconomic status in general (interpret the b coefficient associated with socioeconomic status) because the nature of the relationship would depend on age; in the second example, it would be inappropriate to speak of the overall slope of time as a manager (interpret the b coefficient associated with time in position) because the nature of the relationship depends on ability level.

When there is a significant interaction between predictors, it is necessary to explore its nature in more detail. Essentially, this means that you would examine the *simple slopes,* the slope of a predictor under different levels of the other predictor. To illustrate this for the first example, we would want to predict liberalism with socioeconomic status at different values of age. In some situations, we might have a theoretical or practical reason for selecting certain ages on which to focus. Under such circumstances, we should use those particular ages in the regression model to determine the slope (the regression coefficient) specific to those age levels. If there was no theoretical basis to select particular ages, Aiken and West (1991) appear to endorse the recommendation of Cohen et al. (2003) to use values corresponding to +1 standard deviation, the median, and –1 standard deviation; we would thus estimate the b coefficient at each of these three values in the distribution. In our example, if the mean age was 36 and the standard deviation was 10, then the ages corresponding to these three locations would be 26, 36, and 46. We would then estimate the b coefficient for socioeconomic status at each of these three age levels. You should note that this means generating separate regression models to represent the relationship between the predictor (e.g., socioeconomic status) and criterion (e.g., liberalism) variables at each level (+1, 0, and −1 standard deviation units) of the moderator variable (e.g., age).

With an interaction in the model, we should interpret the main effects with great care. Allison (1999b), using an example of years of schooling and age predicting income, makes this clear:

> What you must always remember is that in models with interactions, the main-effect coefficients have a special (and often not very useful) meaning. The coefficient . . . for age . . . can be interpreted as the effect of age *when schooling is 0.* Similarly, the coefficient . . . for schooling can be interpreted as the effect of schooling *when age is 0.* . . . In general, whenever you have a product term in a regression model, you should not be concerned about the statistical significance (or lack thereof) of the main effects of the two variables in the product. That doesn't mean that you can delete the main effects from the model. Like the intercept in any regression equation, those terms play an essential role in generating correct predictions for the dependent variable. (p. 168)

If the interaction term is significant, then we must focus our attention on simplifying the interaction effect. That means examining the simple slopes. If the interaction is not significant, then you should perform another regression analysis without the interaction term being included. That model will include only the main effects and can be interpreted in the ways described earlier in this chapter.

We described the shape of the function in a two-predictor model to be a plane—the roof of a room serves as a suitable image. In a model that includes the interaction term of these two predictors, the surface can be thought of as "warped" (Darlington, 1990). Imagine a room with walls of different heights; represented geometrically, the roof that would be fitted to such a room would represent the surface of an interaction.

It has been argued (e.g., Aiken & West, 1991; Darlington, 1990) that when interaction terms are included in the model, the predictor and the moderator variables should be *centered;* that is, the mean of the variable should be subtracted from each score on the variable to create a new (transformed) variable representing a deviation score.

Centering can reduce the chances of multicollinearity affecting the analysis. But its primary function is to facilitate the interpretation of the interaction (Aiken, 2005). The regression model that we ordinarily produce showing us a significant interaction represents the situation for the case where the predictor and moderator variables take on a value of zero. Yet it is very often the case that zero is not a possible value for these variables, and it is almost always the case that zero is not a representative value for these variables. For example, scores on a Likert-type summative response scale may have values of 1 through 5, and scores on many national administered standardized exams (e.g., GRE) have scores ranging from 200 to 800. For these measures, no one has achieved a valid score of zero.

To center the scores is to subtract the mean of the variable from each value yielding a deviation score. For example, if the mean GRE verbal score of the sample was 575, then a person whose original score was 600 would have a deviation score of +25. The mean of the predictor will thus have a transformed value of zero. When the predictor and moderator variables are centered in this manner, the ordinary regression solution will still show the prediction model appropriate for zero values of the predictor and moderator variables, but now this centered zero value is the mean of each distribution. The result of centering is that the regression model now represents the case for the typical score in the study.

In generating the regression lines for ±1 standard deviation from the mean, the predictor and moderator variables should be recentered twice— once at the value corresponding to +1 standard deviation and again at the value corresponding to −1 standard deviation. For each recentering operation, a regression analysis should be conducted so that each of these two functions can be obtained and the data points plotted.

Although centering is common practice, some authors have argued that it may not be worthwhile (Kromrey & Foster-Johnson, 1998) for linear regression. Our recommendation is to always center your predictor and moderator variables as Aiken and West (1991) have suggested. The idea here is that centering does not adversely affect the statistical analysis and, in our view, has the added advantage of facilitating your interpretation of the results in many circumstances.

Linear and Nonlinear Regression: Intrinsically Nonlinear Models

There is a whole set of models that do not take a linear form and thus cannot be analyzed through a procedure that uses ordinary least squares. These models are best handled by other curve-fitting techniques. They are represented by equations of different forms. Darlington (1990) gives the following example:

$$Y_{\text{pred}} = \frac{(b_1 X_1 + b_2 X_2)}{(b_3 X_3 + b_4 X_4)}$$

Allison (1999b) gives an example as well:

$$Y_{\text{pred}} = 1 + A_x^B$$

One example of an intrinsically nonlinear model is when the dependent variable is a nominal variable. Such a situation is sufficiently relevant to the research conducted in the behavioral and social sciences that techniques have been developed to deal with such situations. Two analytic approaches to this nonlinear application, logistic regression and discriminant function analysis, will be presented in Chapters 6A and B and 7A and B, respectively.

Canonical Correlation Analysis

In multiple regression, we form a variate of the independent variables to best predict the value of a single criterion measure. However, we are not limited necessarily to using a single dependent variable in our study. It is possible to assemble a set of dependent variables that can also be combined together in some weighted array (variate) whose value can be predicted by a weighted combination of independent variables. This is the realm of canonical correlation (see Sherry & Henson, 2005, for an overview).

Canonical correlation analysis, also referred to as multivariate multiple regression (Lutz & Eckert, 1994), is a statistical test that assesses the relationship between two sets of continuous measured variables. Whereas one set may be considered as the predictor variate, the other set may be deemed the criterion, dependent, or outcome variate. These variates represent the weighted combination of the values on the various predictor variables that will correlate more highly with the criterion variate than any single predictor variable alone.

The advantage of using linear combinations of variables for both the predictor and criterion is that such a design increases the chances of discovering relationships that single-variable designs could not capture. Canonical correlation in that sense is thus a potentially more powerful design than multiple regression, just as a multiple regression design is potentially more powerful than simple linear regression. This gain in power with canonical correlation is noteworthy, of course, to the extent that the variables that are combined in the composite make theoretical sense (Benton, 1991). If the composite dependent variate does make sense—if it is interpretable in the context of the research problem—then it is possible to characterize canonical correlation as Cooley and Lohnes (1976) have done as "the simplest model that can begin to do justice to this difficult problem of scientific generalization" (p. 176).

Canonical correlation analysis is an exploratory statistical method (Tabachnick & Fidell, 2001b) as opposed to a confirmatory statistical procedure. Exploratory analyses are used as theory-generating procedures, whereas confirmatory analyses are treated as theory-testing procedures (Stevens, 2002). We need to be careful when we interpret and attempt to generalize results based on exploratory data analysis. Nunnally (1978) noted that exploratory methods are neither "a royal road to truth, as some apparently feel, nor necessarily an adjunct to shotgun empiricism, as others claim" (p. 371). Exploratory results must be viewed with caution partly because the relationships between the variates may not be replicated in other samples.

There is also the potential difficulty in the interpretation of the canonical function. Mulaik et al. (1989) suggested that one difficulty in interpretation comes about because researchers often lack prior knowledge about the underlying relationships between the variables; they therefore have no basis on which to make an interpretation of the result. It's one matter to predict a single measured variable from a set of independent variables—we do this informally regularly during our daily life in the normal course of social interaction when we take in information from a variety of sources to predict, say, how our friend liked a meal at the new Korean restaurant that just opened near campus. We fully expect that the set of predictor variables in this case is derived from quite different parts of our friend's life: the kind of food she ate as a child, the attitudes of her parents toward new food, her experiences with different types of restaurants when she started to date, how much traveling to different parts of the country (or abroad) she has done, and so on. Generally, the predictor variate, although interpretable, is often and appropriately composed of a diverse set of individual variables.

But it could be quite another matter to predict the value of a composite dependent variable unless that composite really represented a conceptual whole. We do have real-world experience in experiencing composite outcome variables, and it does make sense to us in those contexts. For example, we speak of a friend being "supportive" of us when we experience a difficult time. "Support" is a judgment we make based on several factors relating to our friend's reactions to us, such as willingness to listen to us talk, being physically present, saying certain reassuring things, offering solutions to problems, and maybe giving us a pat on the shoulder or a hug. And these behaviors are probably weighted in our minds (the things we need the most we probably weigh more when we figure out how supportive our friend was). If all the outcome measures that we used in our research were that tightly melded together to form variates that made such intuitive sense, perhaps some of the potential difficulties in interpreting the canonical function would be of less concern. But partly because canonical correlation is an exploratory analysis and is therefore combining variables in the dependent variate that may not have been combined before and that may therefore not produce a variate that is easily assimilated, canonical analysis is often viewed by some "as a last-ditch effort, to be used when all other higher-level techniques have been exhausted" (Hair et al., 1998, p. 444).

Added to this concern about potential interpretation matters, it is also possible that the measured variables employed for the predictor or criterion variables may represent different dimensions. To the extent that this is true, it is possible that more than one linear function relating the predictors and the criterion could emerge. Thus, it is possible that more than one solution to canonical correlation may be put forward, adding an extra layer of complexity to such a design. Although these functions are determined sequentially and are uncorrelated with one another (Stevens, 2002), it is vital that researchers have a reasonably thorough understanding of the content domain they are studying so that they can interpret multiple and independent functional relationships between the independent and dependent variates.

Canonical correlation, although never having been used as frequently as some other techniques such as multiple regression, tends to be used even less often today. In contemporary research, structural equation modeling has gradually replaced canonical correlation analysis (Maruyama, 1998). Structural equation modeling inherently determines statistical significance of the canonical function coefficients and structure coefficients, which is not easily accomplished in conventional canonical analysis (Thompson, 1984). We discuss the topics of structural equation modeling in the last three sets of chapters in this book.

Recommended Readings

Berk, R. A. (2003). *Regression analysis: A constructive critique.* Thousand Oaks, CA: Sage.

Berry, W. D. (1993). *Understanding regression assumptions* (Sage University Papers Series on Quantitative Applications in the Social Sciences, series no. 07-92). Newbury Park, CA: Sage.

Cohen, J. (1968). Multiple regression as a general data analytic system. *Psychological Bulletin, 70,* 426–443.

Conger, A. J., & Jackson, D. N. (1972). Suppressor variables, prediction, and the interpretation of psychological relationships. *Educational and Psychological Measurement, 32,* 579–599.

Draper, N. R., Guttman, I., & Lapczak, L. (1979). Actual rejection levels in a certain stepwise test. *Communications in Statistics, A8,* 99–105.

Green, S. A. (1991). How many subjects does it take to do a multiple regression analysis. *Multivariate Behavioral Research, 26,* 499–510.

Hardy, M. A. (1993). *Regression with dummy variables.* Newbury Park, CA: Sage.

Jaccard, J., & Wan, C. K. (1995). Measurement error in the analysis of interaction effects between continuous predictors using multiple regression: Multiple indicator and structural equation approaches. *Psychological Bulletin, 117,* 348–357.

Kahane, L. H. (2001). *Regression basics.* Thousand Oaks, CA: Sage.

Lorenz, F. O. (1987). Teaching about influence in simple regression. *Teaching Sociology, 15,* 173–177.

McClelland, G. H. (1993). Statistical difficulties of detecting interactions and moderator effects. *Psychological Bulletin, 114,* 376–390.

Park, C., & Dudycha, A. (1974). A cross-validation approach to sample size determination. *Journal of the American Statistical Association, 69,* 214–218.

Schafer, W. D. (1991a). Reporting hierarchical regression results. *Measurement and Evaluation in Counseling and Development, 24,* 98–100.

Schafer, W. D. (1991b). Reporting nonhierarchical regression results. *Measurement and Evaluation in Counseling and Development, 24,* 146–149.

Schroeder, L. D., Sjoquist, D. L., & Stephan, P. E. (1986). *Understanding regression analysis: An introductory guide.* Beverly Hills, CA: Sage.

Sherry, A., & Henson, R. K. (2005). Conducting and interpreting canonical correlation analysis in personality research: A user-friendly primer. *Journal of Personality Assessment, 84*(1), 37–48.

Stevens, J. P. (2002). *Applied multivariate statistics for the social sciences* (4th ed., Chapter 12: Canonical Correlation). Hillsdale, NJ: Erlbaum.

Thompson, B. (1989). Why won't stepwise methods die? *Measurement and Evaluation in Counseling and Development, 21,* 146–148.

Trusty, J., Thompson, B., & Petrocelli, J. V. (2004). Practical guide for reporting effect size in quantitative research in the Journal of Counseling & Development. *Journal of Counseling & Development, 82,* 107–110.

Weiss, D. J. (1972). Canonical correlation analysis in counseling psychology research. *Journal of Counseling Psychology, 19,* 241–252.

Multiple Regression Using SPSS

This chapter focuses on running multiple regression analyses with SPSS. For purposes of continuity, we will continue our analysis of the Asian American consumer mental health data set in the context of both standard and stepwise multiple regression.

As noted in Chapters 3A and 3B, multivariate analyses are typically preceded by data screening activities (i.e., code cleaning and assessing missing values, outliers, and assumption violations) with SPSS programs such as **Frequencies**, **Explore**, **Scatter**, and **Missing Value Analysis (MVA)**. Alternatively, some statistical procedures offer unique diagnostic capabilities germane to the multivariate statistical technique being used: The SPSS **Regression** residuals diagnostics module is an example of this. Although we encourage you to perform your data screening prior to any multivariate work, we also recognize the convenience of doing some of this work "within" the statistical (e.g., **Regression**) procedure. Hence, we will demonstrate some data screening activities using both **Regression** and **Explore**.

Assume that we are again interested in the effects of three continuous independent variables: consumer service satisfaction (**csq8**), consumer age (**lage**), and clinical functioning at intake (**gafpre**) on clinical functioning measured by the GAF posttest (i.e., **gafpost**, the dependent variable). Note that although the present example uses quantitative (metric) independent variables, dichotomous categorical independent variables could have also been included (Tabachnick & Fidell, 2001b).

Data Screening

Previous analyses with this data set indicated no unusual attribute code violations, and with the exception of **gafpost**, missing values were minimal. Because of the importance of **gafpost** and its relatively high proportion of missing values (39 of 96 or 40.6% of cases), we will pursue a conservative course of action by using the SPSS **Regression** default of listwise deletion to avoid attempting to impute 40% of the values of our dependent measure. Note that such a substantial loss of information happens often with archival longitudinal data.

Checking for Multivariate Outliers

Let's begin our analysis by checking for multivariate outliers with Mahalanobis distance through the SPSS **Regression** and **Explore** facilities. Recall from Chapter 3B that we ordinarily run a preliminary regression with **caseid** as the dependent variable and the three continuous variables (**csq8**, **lage**, **gafpre**) as the independent variables. This is accomplished by (a) clicking **Analyze → Regression → Linear** to obtain the **Linear Regression** dialog box; (b) moving the four variables over to the appropriate **Dependent** and **Independent(s)** boxes; (c) clicking the **Save** button at the bottom of this dialog box to produce the **Linear Regression: Save** dialog box; and (d) checking the **Mahalanobis** checkbox to compute and save Mahalanobis distance values for each case in our data file. Remember that none of the other regression output information is of interest to us at this point and should be ignored because we are in data diagnostic mode and not regression modeling mode. Clicking **OK** runs the regression and saves the Mahalanobis distance values for each case as a new variable named **MAH_2**.

Now that we have instructed the regression procedure to calculate a Mahalanobis distance and to save that distance measure for each case in the data file under the variable name **MAH_2**, we can analyze that variable just as we can analyze any other variable in the file. To profile cases with the most extreme distance values, we now run **Explore** (i.e., **Analyze → Descriptive Statistics → Explore**) by clicking over our new variable **MAH_2** into the **Dependent List** box while leaving the **Factor List** box empty. We also click the **Statistics** pushbutton and the subsequent **Outliers** checkbox. This produces the **Extreme Values** output (those cases with the most extreme Mahalanobis distance values) seen in Figure 5b.1.

Recall that we evaluate these distance measures with a chi-square criterion (e.g., degrees of freedom = 3, the number of independent variables) at alpha = $p < .001$. The critical chi-square value in the present case is 16.266

Extreme Values

			Case Number	Value
Mahalanobis Distance	Highest	1	117	10.61565
		2	177	10.40876
		3	72	9.16927
		4	82	8.92797
		5	164	6.81708
	Lowest	1	131	.33155
		2	126	.39237
		3	76	.58689
		4	122	.61010
		5	77	.62213

With 3 degrees of freedom, we would need a chi square value of 16.266 to indicate that these cases were outliers. Here, no outliers are observed.

Figure 5b.1 Output From Explore Showing Extreme Values for Mahalanobis Distance Using the Variable MAH_2 That Was Saved in the **Regression** Procedure

(see Appendix). Because none of our Mahalanobis distance values equals or exceeds this chi-square criterion, we are able to conclude that there are no multivariate outliers. Had we discovered any outliers, we would have deleted those cases at this juncture because multiple regression can be adversely affected by the presence of extreme values.

Testing for Other Assumptions Violations

To test for multiple regression statistical assumption violations, we encounter a choice point. As we noted in Chapter 3B, issues of normality, linearity, and homoscedasticity can be effectively monitored and evaluated with SPSS programs such as **Frequencies**, **Explore**, **Oneway**, and **Scatter**. As we noted previously, we encourage their use prior to beginning your multiple regression runs. An alternative approach to this scenario in the context of multiple regression is to assess for assumption violations by running a preliminary regression analysis and evaluating the residuals scatterplot (Mertler & Vannatta, 2001; Tabachnick & Fidell, 2001b). The residuals scatterplot provides an alternative means of detecting any statistical assumption violations. We now turn to this latter approach.

To produce a preliminary residuals scatterplot that will enable us to check for statistical assumption violations, we click **Analyze → Regression → Linear,** which produces the **Linear Regression** dialog box shown in Figure 5b.2.

In the main dialog box for regression, we have clicked over **gafpost** to the **Dependent** box and the three continuous variables (**csq8**, **lage**,

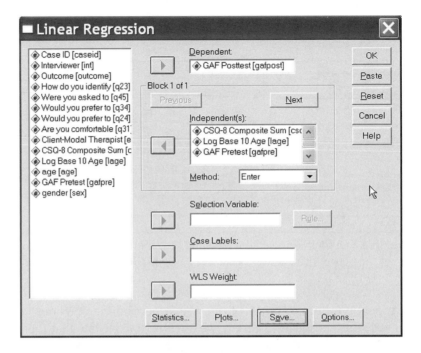

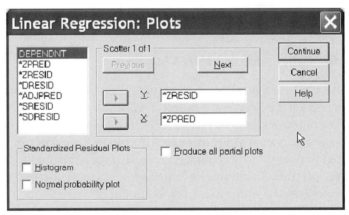

Figure 5b.2   Linear Regression Main Dialog Box Showing the Dependent and Independent Variables Already Specified (Clicked Over) and Its Plots Dialog Box

gafpre) to the **Independent(s)** box. By clicking the **Plots** pushbutton at the bottom of the dialog box, we produce the **Linear Regression: Plots** dialog box (second box of Figure 5b.2). To produce a residuals scatterplot, we click over ***ZRESID** (the standardized residuals, which represent the variance of the criterion variable in z score units remaining after the independent variables have done their predictive work) to the *Y*-axis box and ***ZPRED** (the standardized predicted value, which is the predicted value of the dependent variable in z score units) to the *X*-axis box.

Clicking **Continue** in the **Plots** dialog box brings us back to the original dialog box, where a click of the **OK** tab will produce the output that we present in Figure 5b.3. The rest of the regression output can be ignored at this point in our preliminary analysis.

Figure 5b.3 displays two of the regression output results generated from the commands we issued in the **Plots** dialog box. The first part of this figure displays the **Casewise Diagnostics** table. This table displays residual outliers that depict cases with standardized residuals greater than 3. In the present example, Cases 65 and 66 (with **gafpost** scores of 13 and 15, respectively) have residual outliers in excess of 3 standard deviation units (z scores

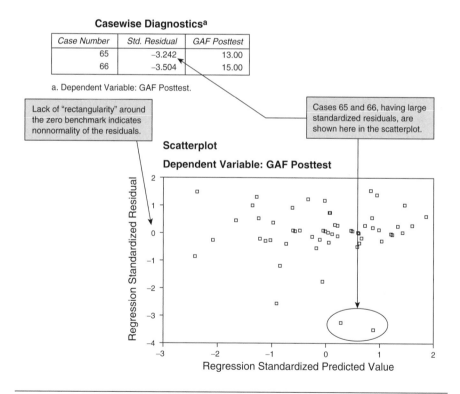

Casewise Diagnostics[a]

Case Number	Std. Residual	GAF Posttest
65	–3.242	13.00
66	–3.504	15.00

a. Dependent Variable: GAF Posttest.

Lack of "rectangularity" around the zero benchmark indicates nonnormality of the residuals.

Cases 65 and 66, having large standardized residuals, are shown here in the scatterplot.

Scatterplot

Dependent Variable: GAF Posttest

Figure 5b.3 Casewise Diagnostic Output Showing Cases With Residual Outliers and Scatterplot of GAF Posttest Showing Standardized Residuals as a Function of Standardized Predicted Values

of –3.242 and –3.504) below the mean (we know that the residuals are below the mean because the z values are negative). Based on this outcome, these two cases should be eliminated from the analysis, and the regression analysis should then be rerun in an iterative fashion until the **Casewise Diagnostics** table does not appear in the output.

The second part of Figure 5b.3 is the accompanying scatterplot that we asked for in the **Plots** dialog box. The residuals (that portion of the dependent variable not predictable from the model) in standardized form are shown by their vertical (Y axis) placement as a function of the value predicted (in standardized form) by the model. Each case is represented by a data point in the scatterplot.

Here's how to read the scatterplot: Let's say a case is predicted to have a z score of 1.27 based on the model; that is, using the standardized regression equation, inserting that particular case's values for the predictor variables, and solving for the predicted value of the criterion variable yields a result of 1.27. Now we examine that case's actual score and determine how close the prediction came to it by subtraction; this is the residual—that is, what "remains" of the actual score once we have done our predictive work. For example, if that case actually had an observed score of 1.27, the difference between predicted and observed scores would be 0; that is, the residual would be 0. Thus, when plotted, this data point would be at a vertical position corresponding to 0 on the Y axis. Overshooting or undershooting the observed value in the process of prediction would lead to a corresponding vertical displacement from the 0 benchmark.

Now it would be unrealistic to expect that all the data points in the scatterplot would line up perfectly along this 0 benchmark. Of course, if they did, we would see a horizontal line of data points at the Y-axis height of 0. This would represent an R^2 of 1.00 where prediction was 100% accurate. Given that our R^2 values will ordinarily be considerably lower than 1.00, what we would hope for is that the scatterplot output was rectangular in shape, centered around the zero value of the residuals.

This "rectangularity" within the residuals (the difference between obtained and predicted dependent variable scores) output indicates that the residuals are normally distributed among the predicted dependent variable scores (Tabachnick & Fidell, 2001b). Residuals output that is *skewed* either to the top (high standardized residual values) or to the bottom (low standardized residual values) of the scatterplot indicates nonnormality among the errors of prediction. Crescent-shaped or curved residuals output indicates nonlinearity between predicted dependent variable scores and errors of prediction. Funnel-shaped residuals output is indicative of a homoscedasticity violation (that the dispersion of errors of prediction are not equal for all predicted dependent variable scores).

Inspection of the residual scatterplot in Figure 5b.3 reveals two observations of note. First, we can see the two outliers toward the bottom right of the figure. These are Cases 65 and 66 that were identified in the **Casewise Diagnostics** output. We also note that there is some skewness in the scatterplot (residuals are more densely concentrated toward the right), indicating a nonnormal distribution. We note in passing (because a complete regression was produced by SPSS even though we are ignoring the rest of the output) that the adjusted R^2 for this initial run was .299.

Remediating Assumptions Violations

We can use one of two strategies as a remedy for statistical assumption violations. One is to perform a transformation of the independent and dependent variables as discussed in Chapters 3A and 3B. Alternatively, eliminating cases with large residual values (those with absolute standardized residual values greater than 3) can produce a better fit by the regression equation and increases the multiple correlation (Tabachnick & Fidell, 2001b). We recommend preliminarily using regression runs to identify and subsequently eliminate residual outliers based on the SPSS **Casewise Diagnostics** output.

Cases can be temporarily eliminated from an analysis by clicking **Data Select Cases.** This produces the **Select Cases** dialog box shown in Figure 5b.4.

By clicking the **If condition is satisfied** checkbox and the **If** pushbutton, we produce another dialog box called the **Select Cases: If** dialog box. This is reproduced also in Figure 5b.4, where we have already clicked over from the variables list panel on the left side the **caseid** variable, followed by a click of the "**~=**" button (which means "not equal to"), and then the value of **caseid** we want eliminated—for example, **65**. By including an ampersand (**&**) in the expression we can also include case **66**.

Clicking **Continue** within the **Select Cases: If** dialog box and then **OK** excludes the cases targeted for elimination.

Because the **Casewise Diagnostics** indicated two cases (Cases 65 and 66) with large residuals, we eliminate them and rerun the analysis looking for other outliers that may emerge in the new analysis. We continue this case elimination process and rerun the analysis in an iterative fashion until the SPSS program does not produce any additional **Casewise Diagnostics** output, which happens when there are no more residual outliers meeting the 3 standard deviation criterion. For this data set, such an iterative process

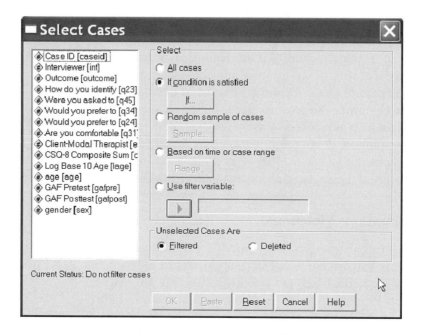

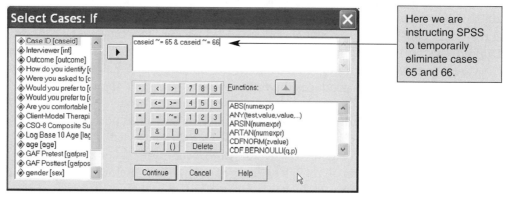

> Here we are instructing SPSS to temporarily eliminate cases 65 and 66.

Figure 5b.4   Select Cases: If Dialog Box

required four regression runs. When the dust settled, we wound up eliminating four cases (Cases 65, 66, 64, and 77). With these cases eliminated from the analysis, adjusted R^2 jumped to .600 (from .299 when these four cases were included in the analysis), and the residuals scatterplot presented in Figure 5b.5, although not perfect, is more rectangular and may be deemed suitable to proceed with the analysis.

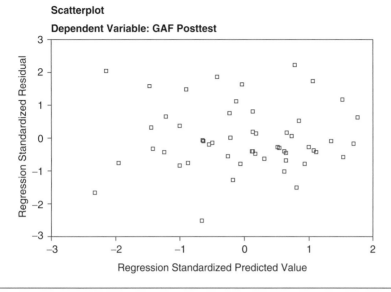

Figure 5b.5   Scatterplot of GAF Posttest Showing Standardized Residuals as a Function of Standardized Predicted Values With the Four Outliers Removed From the Analysis

Setting Up the Standard: Multiple Regression Analysis

Now that we have eliminated the four outliers, we are ready to run the main analysis (and to look at the output, which we have thus far ignored in the data screening process). We begin by running a standard or simultaneous regression analysis. As you will recall from Chapter 5A, a standard multiple regression enters all independent variables into the regression equation simultaneously. Each independent variable is evaluated for its predictive prowess while statistically controlling for all the other predictors in the analysis.

We begin the analysis of our screened data by clicking **Analyze →
Regression → Linear,** which produces the **Linear Regression** dialog box we observed in Figure 5b.2. As you recall, **gafpost** was moved to the **Dependent** box and **csq8, lage,** and **gafpre** were moved to the **Independent(s)** box. Let's discuss in more detail the specifics of the **Linear Regression** dialog box.

The **Method** box, which lies beneath the **Independent(s)** box, provides five different regression methods:

▶ **Enter** (standard regression) enters all independent variables in a single step.

▶ **Stepwise** enters independent variables one at a time and may remove them depending on entry and removal statistical criteria.

▶ **Remove** (one form of researcher-controlled regression) allows you to remove a block of variables in a single step to facilitate standard regression analysis.

▶ **Backward** enters all independent variables into the equation and then sequentially removes them if they do not meet statistical retention criteria.

▶ **Forward** enters independent variables sequentially that have the highest correlation with the dependent variable and meet an entry criterion.

In our present example, we have selected the default **Enter** method to produce a standard multiple regression. Below the **Method** box are the **Selection Variable** and **Case Labels** boxes, which allow you to limit your analysis to a subset of cases having a specific value on a variable. These options are not used very often.

The bottom far-left side of the dialog box contains the **WLS Weight** pushbutton, which allows you to run a weighted least squares regression model. With this method, data are weighted by the reciprocal of their variances. Such an approach may be useful when homoscedasticity assumption violations cannot be remedied. This, too, is not used very often.

The bottom of the dialog box contains four pushbuttons: **Statistics, Plots, Save,** and **Options**, each of which creates its own dialog box, which we will examine. Clicking the **Statistics** pushbutton produces the **Linear Regression: Statistics** dialog box shown in Figure 5b.6.

At the top left of this dialog box is the **Regression Coefficients** box, which contains three checkboxes:

▶ **Estimates** (the default) produces standardized and unstandardized regression coefficients and their respective standard errors, *t* values, and alpha (*p*) levels. Researchers almost always want to obtain these, and we have checked that box to produce them in the output.

▶ **Confidence intervals** produces the 95% confidence intervals for the regression coefficients.

▶ **Covariance matrix** produces variance-covariance and correlation matrices of regression coefficients. Variances are displayed on the diagonal, covariances below, and correlations above the diagonal.

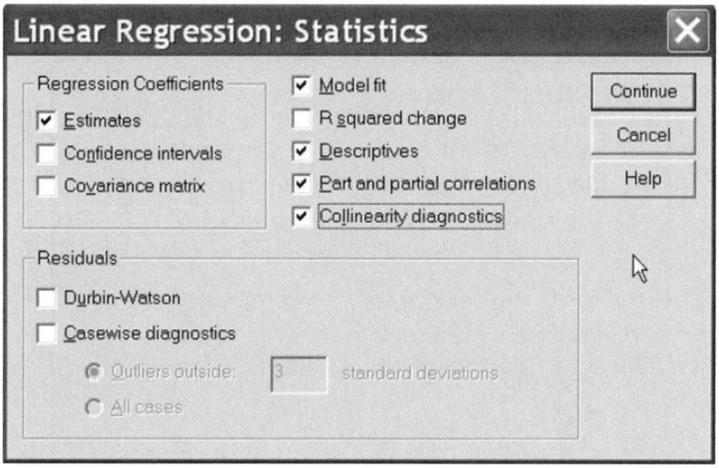

Figure 5b.6 Linear Regression: Statistics, Save, and Options Dialog Boxes

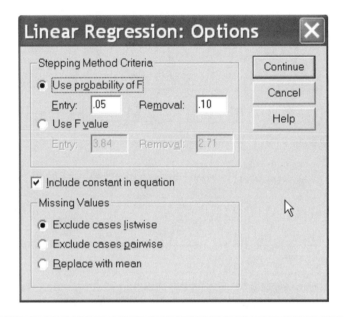

Figure 5b.6 (Continued)

In the present example, we used the **Estimates** option only to produce the regression coefficients but have not requested the b and beta coefficient confidence intervals or the covariance matrix to be printed.

Five other checkboxes are found in the middle of the dialog box (four of which we have checked in the present example).

▶ **Model fit** provides R (the multiple correlation), R^2, adjusted R^2, the standard error, and an analysis of variance (ANOVA) table.

▶ **R-squared change** (not checked in the present example because we are requesting standard multiple regression) is appropriate for the step methods where we are usually interested in seeing the change in R^2 when a variable is entered into or removed from the equation at each step.

▶ **Descriptives** produces variable means, standard deviations, and a correlation matrix.

▶ **Part and partial correlations** produces zero-order, part, and partial correlations.

▶ **Collinearity diagnostics** produces tolerances for each independent variable and diagnostic statistics for assessing multicollinearity between independent variables.

The **Residuals** box at the bottom of this dialog box has two checkboxes, both of which can be used to make detailed assessments of residuals.

▶ **Durbin-Watson** produces the Durbin-Watson statistic for serially correlated residuals.
▶ **Casewise diagnostics** produces case-by-case diagnostics for cases meeting a user-defined selection criterion. Neither of these two checkboxes is activated is the present example.

Clicking the **Plots** pushbutton in the **Linear Regression** dialog box produces the **Linear Regression: Plots** dialog box (see previous Figure 5b.2). This dialog box produces various diagnostic residuals plots. The left side of the dialog box contains the predicted and residual variables list. This list contains the following variables that can be clicked over to the X or Y axis of a subsequent plot: The dependent variable (**DEPENDNT**), standardized predicted values (***ZPRED**), standardized residuals (***ZRESID**), deleted residuals (***DRESID**), adjusted predicted values (***ADJPRED**), studentized residuals (***SRESID**), and studentized deleted residuals (***SDRESID**). In the present example, we requested a scatterplot with the standardized residuals on the Y axis and the standardized predicted values on the X axis—one of the more common residuals plots.

Beneath the Variables list is the **Standardized Residual Plots** box, which contains two checkboxes: **Histogram** and **Normal probability plot**. These plots create either a histogram or a normal probability plot of the standardized residuals. Both are useful when checking for normality violations. The **Produce all partial plots** checkbox generates a residuals plot of the dependent variable and an independent variable when both are regressed on the remaining independent variables. None of these three checkboxes is activated in the present example.

By clicking the **Save** pushbutton at the bottom of the **Linear Regression** dialog box, we produce the **Linear Regression: Save** dialog box, which can also be seen in Figure 5b.6.

This complex dialog box, which is composed of **Predicted Values**, **Residuals**, **Distances**, and **Influence Statistics** boxes, allows the researcher to save various types of residuals, predicted values, and distance measures (such as Mahalanobis distance used for assessing outliers). None of these items was activated in the present example.

The **Options** pushbutton on the **Linear Regression** dialog box produces the **Linear Regression: Options** dialog box that can be seen also in Figure 5b.6.

The main portion of this dialog box is the **Stepping Method Criteria** box, which contains two checkboxes. The **Use probability of F** checkbox

gafpre and csq8 are significant predictors of gafpost, but large is not a significant predictor

Coefficientsa

Model	Unstandardized Coefficients		Standardized Coefficients			Correlations			Collinearity Statistics	
	B	Std. Error	Beta	t	Sig.	Zero-order	Partial	Part	Tolerance	VIF
1 (Constant)	15.476	12.925		1.197	.237					
GAF Pretest	.754	.108	.698	6.984	.000	.753	.706	.613	.771	1.297
CSQ-8 Composite Sum	.411	.175	.207	2.344	.023	.243	.318	.206	.985	1.016
Log Base 10 Age	−5.931	5.879	−.102	−1.010	.317	−.460	−.143	−.089	.761	1.315

a. Dependent Variable: GAF Posttest.

Tolerance values of .01 or less, or VIF values greater than 10, indicate multicollinearity.

Figure 5b.7   Coefficients Output From the Standard Regression Analysis

allows you to adjust the **Entry** value of the significance level of *F* for each variable entered into the equation and its **Removal** criteria. The values of .05 for entry and .10 for removal are the defaults for SPSS. Don't be put off by the labeling of this box. If the forward method is used, SPSS will attend to only the entry criterion; if either the backward or stepwise method is used, SPSS will attend to both the entry and removal criteria; if the standard method is used, SPSS will enter all variables into the equation regardless of their probability levels and will thus disregard these entry and removal criteria. Which method you will apply in the analysis has already been identified on the main dialog box. Beneath this box is the **Include constant in equation** checkbox, which is the default; most multiple regression runs include the constant in the equation.

Interpreting Standard Multiple Regression Output

Output for a standard multiple regression revolves around four component parts: the **Coefficients** output, which is shown in Figure 5b.7, and the **Collinearity Diagnostics**, **Model Summary**, and **ANOVA** output, which can be seen in Figure 5b.8. Although these appear in a different order on the actual output from SPSS, because we initially need to talk about multicollinearity, we will first address information contained in the **Coefficients** and the **Collinearity Diagnostics** outputs.

Collinearity Diagnostics[a]

Model	Dimension	Eigenvalue	Condition Index	Variance Proportions (Constant)	GAF Pretest	CSQ-8 Composite Sum	Log Base 10 Age
1	1	3.885	1.000	.00	.00	.00	.00
	2	.056	8.318	.00	.22	.75	.00
	3	.053	8.529	.00	.23	.13	.19
	4	.005	27.326	.99	.55	.12	.81

a. Dependent Variable: GAF Posttest.

Model Summary[b]

Model	R	R Square	Adjusted R Square	Std. Error of the Estimate
1	.789[a]	.623	.600	8.11971

a. Predictors: (Constant), Log Base 10 Age, CSQ-8 Composite Sum, GAF Pretest.
b. Dependent Variable: GAF Posttest.

ANOVA[b]

Model		Sum of Squares	df	Mean Square	F	Sig.
1	Regression	5335.144	3	1778.381	26.974	.000[a]
	Residual	3230.554	49	65.930		
	Total	8565.698	52			

a. Predictors: (Constant), Log Base 10 Age, CSQ-8 Composite Sum, GAF Pretest.
b. Dependent Variable: GAF Posttest.

Figure 5b.8 Selected Output Tables From the Standard Regression Analysis

Multicollinearity Considerations

The first part of the multiple regression output that researchers should inspect is that portion of the SPSS **Coefficients** table that houses the **Collinearity Statistics** and the **Collinearity Diagnostics** output. The diagnostics found within these SPSS tables address the issue of multicollinearity or high intercorrelation between independent variables. As Stevens (2002) notes, multicollinearity is a problem for multiple regression for at least three reasons: (a) multicollinearity reduces the size of the multiple correlation, (b) the confounding that results from high intercorrelations between the independent variables makes interpretation problematic, and (c) multicollinearity increases regression coefficient variance resulting in a more unstable regression equation.

Although many authors (e.g., Fox, 1991; Stevens, 2002; Tabachnick & Fidell, 2001b) agree that there is no simple solution to diagnosing and remediating multicollinearity, a first step in dealing with this problem would be to examine the intercorrelations between the independent variables. Bivariate correlations of .90 and higher (although we would consider correlations in the mid- or sometimes even in the low .8s to be of concern) are indicative of multicollinearity, and one of these two variables would be a good candidate to delete (Tabachnick & Fidell, 2001b).

SPSS offers several diagnostic multicollinearity assessments beyond a simple inspection of a bivariate correlation matrix for extremely high intercorrelations. One set of diagnostic tools can be found in the **Tolerance** and **Variance Inflation Factor (VIF)** statistics in the **Coefficients** table (as seen in the output table of Figure 5b.7). A variable's tolerance is computed as $1 - R^2$ of an independent variable. To compute tolerance for each independent variable, SPSS runs a separate regression analysis where that predictor plays the role of a criterion variable being predicted by the remaining independent variables in the analysis (Tabachnick & Fidell, 2001b). Tolerance values range from 0 to 1; multicollinearity is indicated for a particular variable if the tolerance value is **.01 or less**. We can see in Figure 5b.7 that the tolerances of all the predictors are far in excess of .01 and therefore suggest that multicollinearity is not a problem.

An alternative to computing a variable's tolerance is to assess the **VIF** for each independent variable. The VIF is the reciprocal of the tolerance (calculated as 1/tolerance) and measures the degree of linear association between a particular independent variable and the remaining independent variables in the analysis. Larger VIF values indicate a greater variance of the regression weight of that predictor (Norusis, 1990). Stevens (2002) recommends a heuristic VIF **greater than 10** as indicative of multicollinearity. Alternatively, Fox (1991) recommends examining the square root of VIF. In our present example, the tolerance and VIF values are well within normal bounds, suggesting that multicollinearity is not present among these independent variables.

Another set of diagnostic tools is found on the SPSS **Collinearity Diagnostics** table in the output shown in Figure 5b.8. We are interested here in the **Condition Index** shown in the third column of the table. This index measures how "dependent" one independent variable is on another. The **Variance Proportions** associated with each variable are shown in the final columns of the output. Belsley, Kuh, and Welsch (1980) and Tabachnick and Fidell (2001b) note that multicollinearity is present if the **Condition**

Index is equal to or greater than **30** and at least two variance proportions for a particular independent variable are greater than **50.** An inspection of these diagnostics indicates that none of these criteria are met. Thus, between the results shown in **Coefficients** and those shown here, we can conclude that multicollinearity is not a problem in this analysis.

Outcome of the Main Analysis

Once the multiple regression diagnostic considerations have been addressed, the "heart" of the multiple regression output can be evaluated. This is contained in the **Model Summary**, **ANOVA**, and **Coefficients** output.

The **Model Summary** table provides a variety of measures assessing the success of the model in predicting the dependent variable. The value of R here is .789. This is a Pearson correlation between predicted values of the dependent variable and the actual values of the dependent variable. The (R^2) coefficient of .623 depicts the amount of variance of the criterion variable accounted for by the combination of the three independent variables. The adjusted R^2 value of .600, a more conservative indicator of the variance accounted for, should be used when samples are small (< 60) and independent variables are numerous (Tabachnick & Fidell, 2001b). We would thus say here that about 60% of the criterion variable's variance is explained by the regression model.

The SPSS **ANOVA** table following **Model Summary** in Figure 5b.8 provides a summary of the analysis of variance for regression. The significant F value, $F(3, 49) = 26.97, p < .001$, indicates that a significant relationship exists between the weighted linear composite of the independent variables as specified by the model and the dependent variable. If this F value was not statistically significant, we would not proceed with further analysis or interpretation of these multiple regression results because it would tell us that our prediction of the criterion variable by using the model is no better than chance.

The SPSS **Coefficients** table (Figure 5b.7) that we have already examined for tolerance and VIF can now be used to obtain the regression weights produced by the analysis. This portion of the output provides the unstandardized b coefficients (shown by SPSS as an uppercase "**B**") and the standardized **Beta** coefficients with their respective *t* tests and significance levels for each independent variable. In addition, three types of correlation coefficients are also reported: **Zero-order**, **Partial**, and **Part** correlations. The **Coefficients** table describes the relative importance of each independent variable in the multiple regression equation or model.

The **Coefficients** output allows us to examine the outcome of the *t* test for each predictor's regression weight. These *t* tests and significance levels allow the researcher to assess each variable's unique contribution to the prediction of the dependent variable. In the present example, both **gafpre** (clinical assessment at intake) and **csq8** (consumer satisfaction) contribute statistically significantly to the prediction of **gafpost** (clinical outcome at Time 2) based on an alpha level of .05. Age (at least in its transformed state), however, makes no significant contribution to that effort.

The **Unstandardized Coefficients** (b) or partial regression coefficients reflect each independent variable in its original unit of measurement and are therefore difficult to compare with each other, because each independent variable can be measured on a unique metric. For example, the b for **lage** (–5.938) is much larger than all the other bs, but that does not necessarily mean that it is the most important variable (in fact, we know that this weight is not significantly different from zero). This problem is at least partly solved with the **Standardized Coefficients** (beta weights). The betas or beta weights allow such comparisons because they are based on z scores with a mean of 0 and a standard deviation of 1. Note that the beta weight for log age is quite low. Remembering our discussion in Chapter 5A warning against using beta weights alone to judge the relative potency of contribution, we can nonetheless suggest here that the pretest GAF score appears to be much more heavily weighted in the model as a predictor of posttest GAF than either of the other two predictors.

The **Zero-order** correlations are simple bivariate correlations between each of the independent variables and the dependent variable (it is zero-order because no variables are being statistically controlled for—used as covariates—in assessing that relationship). As expected, **gafpre** is highly correlated with **gafpost** (.753).

The **Partial** correlation coefficients represent the correlation between the independent and dependent variable after all remaining independent variables have been "partialled out" or controlled for. These are really second-order partial correlations because the other two predictors are used as covariates in these calculations. For example, the partial correlation of **csq8** and the criterion variable (GAF posttest) is .318 and its squared value (not provided by SPSS) is .101. This means that when GAF pretest and log age are first allowed to account for whatever GAF posttest variance they can, then **csq8** can account for 1.01% of the remaining GAF posttest variance.

The **Part** correlation in the table is SPSS' way of labeling the semipartial correlation. When squared, it indicates the unique contribution of the predictor to the model (the variance explained only by the predictor; the explained variance that in Venn diagram form does not overlap with any of the other predictors in the model). By squaring these values ourselves (SPSS does not square them for us) we can tell that the GAF pretest accounts for about 37.6% of the posttest's variance not explained by the other predictors. Corresponding values for the satisfaction and age variables are about 4.2% and 0.8%. These add to about 42.6% of the variance accounted for uniquely by the predictors.

Model Summary[a]

Model	R	R Square	Adjusted R Square	Std. Error of the Estimate	Change Statistics				
					R Square Change	F Change	df1	df2	Sig. F Change
1	.753[a]	.568	.559	8.52212	.568	66.942	1	51	.000
2	.784[b]	.615	.600	8.12134	.047	6.158	1	50	.016

a. Predictors: (Constant), GAF Pretest.

b. Predictors: (Constant), GAF Pretest, CSQ-8 Composite Sum.

c. Dependent Variable: GAF Posttest.

ANOVA[c]

Model		Sum of Squares	df	Mean Square	F	Sig.
1	Regression	4861.745	1	4861.745	66.942	.000[a]
	Residual	3703.953	51	72.627		
	Total	8565.698	52			
2	Regression	5267.892	2	2633.946	39.935	.000[b]
	Residual	3297.806	50	65.956		
	Total	8565.698	52			

a. Predictors: (Constant), GAF Pretest.

b. Predictors: (Constant), GAF Pretest, CSQ-8 Composite Sum.

c. Dependent Variable: GAF Posttest.

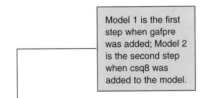

Model 1 is the first step when gafpre was added; Model 2 is the second step when csq8 was added to the model.

Coefficients[a]

Model		Unstandardized Coefficients		Standardized Coefficients	t	Sig.	Correlations			Collinearity Statistics	
		B	Std. Error	Beta			Zero-order	Partial	Part	Tolerance	VIF
1	(Constant)	14.138	5.377		2.630	.011					
	GAF Pretest	.814	.100	.753	8.182	.000	.753	.753	.753	1.000	1.000
2	(Constant)	4.194	6.505	.	.645	.522					
	GAF Pretest	.807	.095	.746	8.498	.000	.753	.769	.746	.999	1.001
	CSQ-8 Composite Sum	.432	.174	.218	2.481	.016	.243	.331	.218	.999	1.001

a. Dependent Variable: GAF Posttest.

Figure 5b.9   Selected Output Tables From the Stepwise Regression Analysis

Excluded Variables[c]

Model		Beta In	t	Sig.	Partial Correlation	Collinearity Statistics		
						Tolerance	VIF	Minimum Tolerance
1	CSQ-8 Composite Sum	.218[a]	2.481	.016	.331	.999	1.001	.999
	Log Base 10 Age	−.130[a]	−1.244	.219	−.173	.772	1.296	.772
2	Log Base 10 Age	−.102[b]	−1.010	.317	−.143	.761	1.315	.761

a. Predictors in the Model: (Constant), GAF Pretest.

b. Predictors in the Model: (Constant), GAF Pretest, CSQ-8 Composite Sum.

c. Dependent Variable: GAF Posttest.

Figure 5b.9 (Continued)

Recall that the R^2 for the model was .623, indicating that 62.3% of the criterion variable's variance was accounted for by the model. We have also just determined that the three predictors uniquely accounted for 42.6% of the variance. The difference between these values is 19.7 percentage points. This represents the total amount of overlapping predictive work that was done by the predictors.

Stepwise Multiple Regression Output

We will now explore stepwise regression output with the previous variables used in the standard regression analysis. Recall that in stepwise multiple regression, independent variables are added to the equation if they make a statistically significant contribution to the regression equation.

To conduct a stepwise multiple regression, we click **Analyze →
Regression → Linear,** which produces the **Linear Regression** dialog box. Again, we click over our dependent variable (**gafpost**) and our independent variables (**csq8, lage, gafpre**). The **Method** box is changed to **Stepwise,** and clicking the **Statistics** pushbutton produces the **Linear Regression: Statistics** dialog box, where we click **R-squared change** in addition to the **Model fit, Descriptives, Part and partial correlations,** and **Collinearity diagnostics** checkboxes used previously. Selected portions of the stepwise multiple regression output can be found in Figure 5b.9. This output is presented in the order generated by SPSS.

The **Variables Entered/Removed** output, which we do not show, simply indicates that **gafpre** and **csq8** met the default SPSS inclusion criteria

($p \leq .05$) for inclusion in the model. By implication, none of the other variables in the predictor set (in this instance, there was only **lage**) found its way into the model. The information here is essentially repeated in the **Coefficients** output. Note that this result is entirely consistent with what we obtained using the standard method.

The **Model Summary** output provides dynamic, step-by-step summary description of the analysis. **Model 1** shown in the first row tells us (perhaps not formatted in the easiest-to-read way) the situation after the first variable was entered into the equation. From the footnote on the R value in the first model, we can see that the predictors are the constant (which is always going to be there) and the first independent variable to be entered, in this case GAF pretest. This model itself accounted for 56.8%, adjusted to 55.9%, of the posttest variance.

The second row of the **Model Summary** table shows what happened at the second step. Because SPSS built a new model, it is called **Model 2**. By virtue of the footnote attached to the R value, we can see that **csq8** was added to the equation. It uniquely added (R^2 change) 4.7% explained variance to the prior model, bringing the adjusted R^2 up to an even .600. Note that although this is exactly the proportion of variance accounted for by the standard model because log age was not significant, you should be aware that the numbers will not necessarily work out to be exactly the same all the time when you compare standard with a step method.

Next, the **ANOVA** summary table and **Coefficients** table indicate that **gafpre** and **csq8** make statistically significant contributions to the prediction of **gafpost**. Finally, the **Excluded Variables** output table shows that **lage** did not make a significant contribution to the multiple regression model. This result confirms the previous standard multiple regression findings.

Results

Standard multiple regression was conducted with global assessment of functioning (GAF at Time 2) as the dependent variable and GAF pretest, Client Satisfaction Questionnaire score (CSQ-8), and consumer age as independent variables. Because of extreme skewness, the age variable was transformed with a log base-10 transformation. Four residual outliers were eliminated using the SPSS casewise diagnostics routine.

As can be seen in Table 5b.1, GAF posttest, as expected, was highly correlated with GAF pretest, indicating good test-retest reliability. Moderate negative correlations were achieved between log of age and the GAF measures. Client satisfaction with services achieved a low positive correlation with GAF posttest.

Regression results are summarized in Table 5b.2. Multiple R for regression was statistically significant, $F(3, 49) = 26.97$, $p < .001$, R^2 $adj = .60$. Two of the three independent variables (GAF pretest and CSQ-8) contributed significantly to the prediction of GAF posttest ($p < .05$). Log base-10 of age, while negatively correlated to GAF posttest, did not make a statistically significant contribution ($p > .05$) to the prediction of GAF posttest.

Table 5b.1 Means, Standard Deviations, and Intercorrelations for Global Assessment of Functioning (Posttest) and Consumer Characteristics Predictor Variables

Variable	M	SD	1	2	3
GAF posttest	57.08	12.84	.75**	.24*	−.46**
Predictor variable					
1. GAF pretest	52.72	11.87	—	.03	−.48**
2. Client satisfaction questionnaire	24.00	6.48		—	−.12
3. Age (log base-10)	1.35	0.22			—

$*p < .05; **p < .01.$

Table 5b.2 Regression Analysis Summary for Consumer Characteristics Variables Predicting Global Assessment of Functioning

Variable	B	SEB	ß
GAF pretest	.75	.11	.70**
Client satisfaction questionnaire	.41	.18	.21*
Age (log base-10)	−5.94	5.88	−.10

Note: $R^2 = .60$ ($N = 53, p < .001$).

$*p < .05; **p < .01.$

5B Exercises

Optimism and Longevity

A cancer specialist from the Los Angeles County General Hospital (LACGH) rated patient optimism in 20- to 40-year-old male patients with incurable cancer in 1970. In 1990, the researcher examined hospital records to gather the following data:

1. Socioeconomic status (1–7 rating of occupation; higher ratings indicate higher levels of SES)

2. Age in 1970

3. Optimism in 1970 (1–100 rating, higher scores indicate higher levels of optimism)

4. Longevity (years lived after the 1970 diagnosis)

Using the SPSS data file for Chapter 5B (located on the CD), calculate a simultaneous multiple regression with SES, age, and optimism as the independent variables and longevity as the dependent variable.

1. Do the independent variables correlate statistically significantly and practically with the dependent variable?

2. Is collinearity between the independent variables a concern?

3. What is the R and adjusted R-square for all independent variables entered simultaneously?

4. What variable(s) provide a significant unique contribution(s)?

5. Compose a results section for this statistical analysis.

Logistic Regression

I n the preceding chapters, we have seen that regression analysis involves a quantitatively measured dependent variable and independent variables that are quantitatively measured, dichotomous, or both. This chapter will address regression analysis where the dependent variable is categorical; the independent variables here may still be quantitative, dichotomous, or both. Although the categorical dependent variable could consist of more than two categories (called a *polytomous* or *multi-nominal* variable under that circumstance), this chapter will address logistic regression designs with a dichotomous (binary) dependent variable. Multinominal logistic regression is beyond the scope of this chapter.

Many research studies in the social and behavioral sciences investigate dependent (outcome) variables of a dichotomous nature. Pedhazur (1997) illustrates these designs:

> The ubiquity of such variables in social and behavioral research is exemplified by a yes or no response to diverse questions about behavior (e.g., voted in a given election), ownership (e.g., of a personal computer), educational attainment (e.g., graduated from college), status (e.g., employed), to name but some. Among other binary response modes are agree-disagree, success-failure, presence-absence, and pro-con. (p. 714)

The use of logistic regression is increasing of late because of the wide availability of sophisticated statistical software and high-speed computers. Hosmer and Lemeshow (2000) report that the use of logistic regression has "exploded during the past decade" (p. ix). Logistic regression analysis has expanded from its origins in biomedical research to fields such as business and finance, criminology, ecology, engineering, health policy, linguistics, and wildlife biology. Logistic regression has become so popular that Huck (2004) predicts, "It may soon overtake multiple regression and become the most frequently used regression tool of all!" (p. 438).

The Variables in Logistic Regression Analysis

In a typical logistic regression analysis, there will always be one dependent variable (dichotomous for our purposes here) and usually a set of independent variables that may be either dichotomous or quantitative or some combination thereof. Furthermore, the dichotomous variables need not be truly binary; for example, researchers may transform a highly skewed quantitative dependent variable into a dichotomous variable with approximately equal numbers of cases in each category. And akin to what we have seen in multiple regression, some of the independent variables in logistic regression analysis may serve as covariates to allow researchers to hold constant or statistically control for these variable(s) to better assess the unique effects of the other independent variables.

Assumptions of Logistic Regression

Although logistic regression makes fewer assumptions than linear regression (e.g., homogeneity of variance and normality of errors are not assumed), logistic regression does require the following:

1. There must be an absence of perfect multicollinearity.

2. There must be no specification errors (i.e., all relevant predictors are included and irrelevant predictors are excluded).

3. The independent variables must be measured at the summative response scale, interval, or ratio level (although dichotomous variables are also allowed).

Logistic regression requires larger samples than does linear regression for valid interpretation of the results. Although statisticians disagree on the precise sample requirements, Pedhazur (1997) suggests using at least 30 times as many cases as parameters being estimated.

In this chapter, three examples of logistic regression will be presented. The first example is the simplest design possible with a single dichotomous independent (predictor) variable (gender) and a dichotomous dependent (criterion or outcome) variable of seeking therapy (yes or no). This example will introduce the basic concepts of logistic regression. The next example will present a single quantitative predictor variable (level of depression) with the same dichotomous dependent variable of seeking therapy. The final example will use two predictors—one dichotomous independent variable (gender) and one quantitative variable (level of depression) to predict the dichotomous dependent variable of seeking therapy. This final analysis will allow us to illustrate how we can assess the unique effects of the independent variables in logistic regression.

Coding of the Dichotomous Variables

In logistic regression, as we discuss it here, the dependent variable will always be dichotomous. Although researchers could use any two arbitrarily selected numbers to label the two categories (e.g., 2 and 3 or 6 and 17), Hosmer and Lemeshow (2000) recommend coding dichotomous variables as 1 for the event occurring and 0 for the event not occurring. It is also possible to use dichotomous variables as predictors; for example, gender (female vs. male) may be predictive of (related to) an event occurring or not (e.g., pass or fail, select one program over another), or having a family history of a certain medical condition (yes vs. no) may be predictive of whether or not individuals are diagnosed with that condition themselves. Such predictors also need to be coded as 1 and 0. Here, those cases who are the focus of the study or who possess some attribute should be coded as 1 and the others coded as 0. In the former example, females (if they were the focus of the study) would be coded as 1 and males would be coded as 0; in the latter example, those having a family history of the condition would be coded as 1 and those with no such history would be coded as 0.

In a very general sense, cases or incidents coded as 1 are referred to (or are thought of) as the *response group, comparison group,* or *target group;* cases or incidents coded as 0 are sometimes called the *referent group, base group,* or *control group.* The ultimate objective of logistic regression is to predict a case's group membership on the dependent variable by calculating the probability that a case will belong to the 1 (event occurring) category.

There are certain advantages to using this 1 and 0 coding scheme. One advantage is that the mean of the distribution is equal to the proportion of 1s in the distribution, thus allowing researchers to immediately know this second piece of information from the first. Consider the situation where there are 100 people in the sample. If 30 of them are coded 1, then the mean of the distribution is .30, which is the proportion of 1s in the data set. The mean of the distribution is also the probability of drawing a person labeled as 1 at random from the sample. Therefore, the indexes of proportion and probability with respect to the value or code of 1 are the same.

So widespread is this type of coding scheme that these indexes have become institutionalized. The mean of a binary distribution coded as 1 and 0 is denoted as P, the proportion of 1s. The proportion of 0s is $(1 - P)$, which is sometimes denoted as Q. The variance of such a distribution is PQ. In the above example where there are thirty 1s in a set of 100 cases, the variance of the distribution is .21 (.3 × .7 = .21) and the standard deviation is the square root of PQ or .458.

Another reason to follow the 1 and 0 coding scheme is that SPSS will automatically recode the lower number assigned to a category to 0 and the higher number of the category to 1 in its logistic regression procedure. For example, if a researcher coded the dichotomous dependent variable as 1 and 2, SPSS will recode the 1 to 0 and the 2 to 1. This automatic recoding can cause no end of confusion, so beginning the procedure in the same way that SPSS finishes it makes keeping track of which group is which a whole lot easier.

The Logistic Regression Model

Conceptually, logistic regression and linear regression are analogous. Both methods produce prediction equations. Recall from Chapter 5A that in multiple regression analysis the ordinary least squares strategy is used to calculate the prediction of a quantitative dependent variable. The regression function is a straight line; that is, the prediction model is a linear combination of the independent variables. Things are a bit different in logistic regression.

Least Squares Is Not Appropriate in Logistic Regression

Because the dependent variable in logistic regression is dichotomous, using the least squares technique to calculate the prediction of a quantitative dependent variable is inappropriate for two reasons.

First, because the dependent variable is dichotomous, the equal variance assumption underlying linear multiple regression is violated. Recall that in multiple regression there is the assumption that the variance of Y is constant across values of X (this is an assumption of homoscedasticity). Equal variances are an unreasonable condition to meet in logistic regression for at least two reasons:

1. The variance is calculated by multiplying the proportion of 1s by the proportion of 0s. Thus, the notion of "equal variances" of presumably the 1s and 0s does not make sense because we have to work with both proportions to compute the variances in the first place.

2. If we take "equal variances" to mean an equal proportion of 1s and 0s (which must be .5 and .5), then we place an unnecessary restriction on the variables that can be used in the analysis. Most variables are probably going to show different numbers of 1s and 0s in the set, and we would certainly be interested in using some of these as dependent variables in a logistic regression analysis.

Second, using the least squares method can produce predicted values greater than 1 and less than 0, values that are theoretically inadmissible. This means that the linear function that we use in multiple regression is inappropriate here. Instead, the shape of the best-fit line in logistic regression is sigmoidal or S-shaped.

We have illustrated in Figure 6a.1 the difference between the S-shaped or sigmoidal logistic function and the linear regression function. Notice that if researchers were to use least squares for a dichotomous outcome, the equation would suggest that a change in one of the predictor variables (labeled generically as X and represented on the X axis) has a constant effect on the probability of the event occurring (shown as Y on the Y axis).

The Logistic Function

If a straight-line function is not workable, what sort of function is better? The answer provided by logistic regression is, perhaps not surprisingly, a logistic function as shown in Figure 6a.1. Variable X is the predictor here and, for the sake of exposition, assume that it is a quantitative variable. Y is the probability of the particular event of interest occurring.

This function is interesting in that it is pretty flat at both the low and high levels of X. Notice in Figure 6a.1 that the corresponding Y values for Xs in the range of 1 through 6 are all around 0. This suggests that differences in this range of X do not make much of a difference in outcome. Let X be

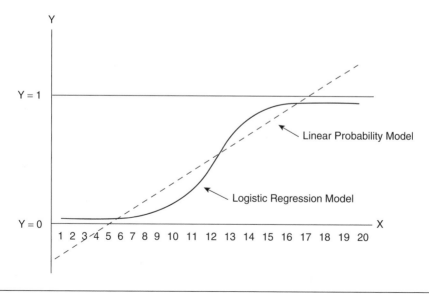

Figure 6a.1 Comparing the Linear Probability and Logistic Regression Models

the amount of distress individuals are experiencing at a given time in their lives, with lower values indicating less distress, and let Y be the probability of seeking therapy. Then the logistic function indicates that people experiencing little stress, whether at levels of 1 or 6 or anyplace in between, are not likely to enter therapy.

An analogous situation is seen at the upper end of the X range where again the function is quite flat. Individuals experiencing lots of distress, whether as low as 15 or as high as 20, are all very likely to seek therapy. Again, distress level within this range does not make much of a difference in prediction.

So where is the "real action" in prediction? It is in the midrange of X where different distress levels are associated with different probabilities of seeking therapy. In fact, the steeper the slope in this range, the more differentiating would be the different distress levels. And it makes sense that prediction of who will seek therapy is more uncertain in this range of distress.

In essence, what we have said is that distress level (X) does not have "a constant effect" on the probability of seeking therapy (Y). And that may make it apparent why least squares multiple regression is less applicable here.

The point is that a linear function defines a situation in which the predictor and the criterion bear a constant relationship to each other; that is, this much difference in the predictor results in that much difference in the criterion over the entire range of the predictor. When a constant relationship is not descriptive of the relationship, least squares, with its fit of a linear function, is not an acceptable strategy to use. This is where the logistic regression model, with its S-shaped function that relates predictors to probabilities of events occurring, takes on a considerable amount of predictive power.

Some Underlying Mathematical Issues

The sigmoidal function represents a nonlinear relationship between the predictor(s) and the binary outcome. Because of this, the mathematical operations underlying logistical regression are a bit more complex than those used in ordinary least squares multiple regression. We will take you through a simplified treatment of these. It is simplified because SPSS does all the mathematical work and our emphasis is not in that domain, but we treat it because what is done mathematically drives the way in which researchers interpret the result of a logistical regression analysis.

The Natural Log (ln) Transformation

Logistic regression requires a mathematical transformation of the original data. The mathematical transformation used in logistic regression is the *natural log* (abbreviated ln) *transformation.* It "bends" the data to fit the sigmoidal curve. The ultimate objective of logistic regression is to predict a case's group membership. This translates to the probability or likelihood of an event occurring for a given value of a predictor variable—more specifically, the probability or likelihood of a case's membership in the response group. Making this prediction requires a sequence of two equations. At first, this set of equations might give you the impression that they are a Rube Goldberg parody (i.e., a structure to accomplish a simple task in the most complicated, elaborate, and ridiculous method). However, these transformations, accomplished over a series of two steps, are necessary to interpret the results of the logistic regression analysis.

Step 1: Forming the Logistic Regression Equation

For calculation purposes in logistic regression, the probability of an event is transformed to odds. Odds are computed by the formula $(P / 1 - P)$, where P is the probability of an event occurring (of the outcome being a 1) and $1 - P$ is the probability of an event not occurring (of the outcome being a 0). It is possible, however, to create a linear relationship between the predictors and odds. Although a number of functions work, one of the most useful is the logit function. It is the ln of the odds that a case belongs to the response group (the group coded as 1).

The logistic regression equation that results is this:

$$\ln [\text{odds}] = a + b_1 X_1 + b_2 X_2 + \cdots + b_n X_n$$

The left side of the equation simply substitutes the ln odds for the predicted dependent variable in linear regression. The b coefficients indicate the change in log odds of membership for any 1-unit change in the independent variables. In this sense, logistic regression is in reality linear regression using the logit as the outcome variable.

Translating the Outcome Variable

To make the above equation more comprehensible, the logistic regression can be rewritten in such a manner that ln, the natural log, is the predicted group membership. We can symbolize predicted group membership as gpred. Thus,

$$g_{\text{pred}} = \ln [\text{odds}] = a + b_1 X_1 + b_2 X_2 + \ldots + b_n X_n.$$

Step 2: Computing the Logit Outcome

Because the logit (i.e., the natural logarithm of an odds ratio) is difficult to interpret, the log odds are transformed into probabilities by taking the antilog (the number corresponding to a logarithm) of the above equation. This is accomplished as follows:

$$e^{gpred} / (1 + e^{gpred}) = \text{predicted probability}$$

That is, the log odds (now represented as g^{pred}) are now inserted into the antilog function where e (the exponential function) $= 2.7182$. This is the antilog equation that transforms the log odds to probabilities. We will talk you through worked numerical examples to show you that this may sound a bit more complicated than it really is.

Deriving the Constant (a) and b Weights

The values for the constant (a) and the b weights are calculated through maximum likelihood estimation (MLE) after transforming the dependent variable into a logit variable. MLE seeks to maximize the log likelihood, which indicates how likely the observed grouping can be predicted from the observed values of the independent variable(s). MLE is an iterative process that starts with an initial arbitrary "guesstimate" and then determines the direction and magnitude of the logit coefficients. SPSS provides the result of that process to you in its output.

Example 1: One Dichotomous Predictor Variable

The research question of interest in our hypothetical study is this: "Is there a gender difference in seeking psychotherapy for depression?" Gender will be the independent (predictor) variable in this study, and seeking psychotherapy will be the dependent (criterion) variable. The occurrence of the event is the outcome (usually positive) in which the researchers are most interested. Based on this reasoning, those individuals seeking therapy will be coded as 1 and those not seeking therapy will be coded as 0. As for gender, assume our focus is on the women in the sample. Because of this focus, females will be coded as 1; we will therefore code the males as 0.

Because the central mathematical concept of logistic regression is the logit, we are going to elaborate on the concepts of (a) probability, (b) odds, and (c) odds ratio. We will use the simple hypothetical study whose results are shown in Table 6a.1 to illustrate these important concepts. Table 6a.1 presents a count of 500 participants seeking psychotherapy by gender.

Table 6a.1 Hypothetical Data Illustrating Gender Differences for Seeking Psychotherapy

	Therapy	*No Therapy*
Female	200	100
Male	50	150
Total	250	250

Overall, there were 300 females and 200 males; of these, 200 females and 50 males sought therapy.

Probability

Probability is the likelihood that an event will occur. It is often expressed as a decimal value. To compute it, take the number of occurrences and divide it by the total number of possibilities. For example, the probability of rolling a 4 on a six-sided die is 1 divided by 6 or .167. One would therefore say that the probability of that event occurring is about .17. Thus, out of 100 attempts, we would expect about 17 of them to result in rolls of 4. Probabilities are constrained to lie between 0 and 1. The constraints at 0 and 1 make it impossible to construct a linear equation for predicting probabilities (ordinary least squares will cause these bounds to be exceeded).

Notice that an equal proportion (50%) of the participants in our example sought psychotherapy (250 sought therapy and 250 did not). Thus, the probability of a study participant seeking therapy is .50. The researchers' interest is, however, in whether this proportion is the same for males and females. The first step would be for the researcher to calculate the odds of seeking therapy for males, and then for females.

Odds

Odds in this example represent the probability of belonging to one group (seeking therapy) divided by the probability of not belonging to that group (not seeking therapy). In this study, the odds of a male seeking psychotherapy are .33 (50 males sought therapy divided by 150 who did not). This means that for every male who sought therapy, three males did not seek psychotherapy. The odds for females seeking psychotherapy are 200 / 100 or 2. This means that a female is twice as likely to seek therapy as not to seek therapy.

Unlike probability, which is bounded by 0 and 1, odds can range from 0 to infinity. If the chances of an event occurring are greater than not occurring, then the odds will be greater than 1. If the chances of an event failing to occur are greater, then the odds will be less than 1. If there is an equal chance of the event occurring or not occurring, then the odds equal 1. Odds of 1 are considered the equivalent of the null hypothesis in logistic regression.

Odds Ratio

Obtaining the odds ratio is one of the important objectives in logistic regression. It is what researchers need to calculate to answer the research question in most logistic regression studies. In this study, the question of whether there is a gender difference in seeking therapy for depression is essentially answered by calculating an odds ratio.

The odds ratio is, as may be obvious from its name, a ratio of the odds for each group. It is a way of comparing whether the probability of a certain event is the same for two groups. The numerator represents the odds of the event occurring (seeking psychotherapy) for the response group (the females) and the denominator represents the odds of the event occurring (seeking psychotherapy) for the referent group (the males).

Analogous to odds, an odds ratio of 1 implies that the event is equally likely in both groups. An odds ratio greater than 1 indicates that the likelihood of an event occurring is more likely in the group coded 1 than in the group coded 0. An odds ratio less than 1 suggests that the event is less likely to occur in the group coded 1 than in the group coded 0. In our hypothetical example, the odds ratio is computed by dividing the odds of females seeking therapy by the odds of males seeking therapy.

Given that the female odds were calculated as 2 and the male odds were calculated as .33, we divide 2 by .33 to obtain 6. We interpret this outcome as follows: Women in this sample were six times more likely than males to seek psychotherapy for depression.

Women were coded as 1 because they were the focus of our study. Had men been our focus, we would have coded the males as 1 and the females as 0. The odds ratio would then have been .33 / 2 = .167, and we would then say that males were one sixth as likely to seek therapy.

The odds ratio just discussed would be considered "crude" or "unadjusted" because no other variables were considered in the analysis. Frequently, logistic regression would employ a set of independent variables to predict or explain the dichotomous dependent variable. When multiple variables are used as predictors in a logistic analysis, the odds ratio is referred to as an *adjusted odds ratio* to indicate the contribution of a particular variable when other variables are controlled or held constant. This controlling for another variable will be illustrated in our third example.

The Logistic Regression Equation

Just as in linear regression, logistic analysis will also produce a single constant (a) and a regression coefficient (b) for each predictor in the model. Recall that the b coefficient in linear regression is derived through the use of ordinary least squares estimation. The least squares strategy seeks to minimize the sum of squared distances of the data points to the regression line, as explained in our preceding chapters. In logistic regression the b coefficients are calculated through MLE after transforming the dependent variable into a logit variable.

MLE seeks to maximize the log likelihood, which reflects how likely it is (the odds) that the observed values of the dependent variable may be predicted from the observed values of the independent variable(s). MLE is an iterative process that starts with an initial arbitrary guesstimate and then determines the direction and magnitude of the logit coefficients. Thus, the b coefficient in logistic regression indicates the change in log odds of membership in the dependent variable code of 1 for any 1-unit change in the independent variable. This increase in log odds is not easily interpreted. The b coefficient will eventually allow the researcher to predict the probability of membership of the response group that is seeking therapy. But remember that the logistic regression equation does not directly predict the probability of an event occurring; rather, it predicts the log odds that an observation will have an outcome (a code) of 1. We therefore need to engage in a two-step process to calculate the probability for a case belonging to the response group.

Computing the Logistic Regression Equation

Recall that determining a case's group membership requires calculating the log odds and then transforming the log odds to probabilities. The first step in calculating the logistic equation for our hypothetical example is based on the linear equation, $g_{pred} = a + b_1X_1$. Note that there is only one predictor (X_1) in the equation because there is only one predictor (gender) in our example study. With more predictors, there would be more terms.

In this example, the values of X_1 will be either 1 for females or 0 for males, and g_{pred} is the ln of the odds of a case in the target group. The logistic regression, through MLE analysis that was performed by SPSS, yielded values of −1.099 for the constant and 1.792 for the b weight. The resulting formula demonstrates the relationship between the regression equations. This is a linear formula. The logistic regression equation to be addressed in the second step is nonlinear.

Thus, for a female,

$$g_{pred} = -1.099 + 1.792(1)$$
$$g_{pred} = 0.693$$

For the second step, the value of .693 is now inserted into the following formula, known as the antilog, to transform the log odds to probabilities:

$$e^{gpred} / (1 + e^{gpred}) = \text{predicted probability}$$

Recall that e is the exponential function and has a value of approximately 2.718. Thus, for a female, the logit equation would be $2.718^{.693}$ / $(1 + 2.718^{.693}) = .667$.

The analogous computations for a male would be as follows:

$$g_{pred} = -1.099 + 1.792(0)$$
$$g_{pred} = -1.099$$
$$\text{predicted probability} = 2.718^{-1.099} / (1 + 2.718^{-1.099}) = .250.$$

Interpreting the Logit Outcome

The calculated probabilities from the logistic analysis can now be used to predict group membership. For this, we need to apply a decision rule for this prediction, a rule based on the predicted probability. The rule used is as follows: If the predicted probability is .5 or greater, then the outcome is to seek therapy (coded as 1; if the probability is less than .5, the case is classified as not seeking therapy (coded as 0).

In this example, females would be classified as seeking therapy because the calculated probability (.667) exceeds .5. Males, however, would be classified as not seeking therapy because their calculated probability (.250) is less than .5. Later, we will compare these predicted group memberships with the actual group memberships as a method to assess the accuracy of the prediction based on the independent variable.

The odds ratio can be calculated directly from e (which has a value of 2.718) and the b coefficient. We simply raise e to the b power. In the present example:

$$e^b = \text{odds ratio}$$
$$e^{1.792} = \text{odds ratio}$$
$$2.718^{1.792} = 6.0$$

As indicated, we interpret the odds ratio here (with females coded as 1) as indicating that women in this sample sought psychotherapy for depression six times more than males.

Example 2: One Quantitative Predictor Variable

This next example presents a single quantitative variable (level of depression) used as a predictor with the dichotomous dependent variable of seeking therapy. For this example, 46 students are assessed by a hypothetical self-report depression inventory. Assume that this inventory validly assesses depression. Further assume that the scores on this inventory can range from a low score of 0, indicating a low level of depression, to a high score of 100, indicating greater levels of depression.

Recall that odds are the probability of belonging to one group (seeking psychotherapy) divided by the probability of not belonging to that group (not seeking psychotherapy). In this example of depression and psychotherapy, the probability of seeking psychotherapy is contingent on depression level. The raw data for a small number of cases in this hypothetical study are shown in Table 6a.2. Those who sought therapy are shown as 1s, and those not seeking therapy are shown as 0s. Depression scores for the cases in the study range from a low of 35 to a high of 80.

Visual inspection of the data contained in Table 6a.2, even though it lists only 46 of the 500 cases in the data file, reveals a pattern we have discussed before in this chapter. In the low regions of depression scores shown in the table, 0s predominate under the therapy outcome, indicating that most of these cases do not seek therapy. In the high regions of depression scores shown in the table, 1s predominate under the therapy outcome, indicating that most of these cases do seek therapy. In the midrange region of depression we find a mixture of 0s and 1s. Although even this limited set of cases would resemble an S-shaped curve if plotted on a set of axes, the entire set of 500 would yield a very clear sigmoidal function.

We can now talk about the data in terms of odds. Assume that in the larger data set, 10 cases had depression scores of 15. Of these 10 individuals, 1 of them (10% or .10) sought therapy and 9 of them (90% or .90) did not. Thus, the odds of seeking psychotherapy for individuals with a low score of 15 are .11 (.10 / .90 = .11). This indicates that for every 1 person with a depression score of 15 who seeks psychotherapy, there are 9 who do not seek therapy.

We can examine the odds of seeking therapy for cases whose depression scores are more in the midrange of the distribution. At a depression score of 55, for example, we find that an equal number of cases did and did not

Table 6a.2   A Set of 46 Cases Drawn From a Larger Sample of 500 Cases
Showing Whether or Not They Sought Psychotherapy and
Their Corresponding Depression Score

Therapy	Depression Score	Therapy	Depression Score
0	35	1	60
0	35	1	60
0	40	1	60
0	40	1	60
1	40	0	65
1	40	0	65
0	45	1	65
0	45	1	65
0	45	1	65
0	45	1	70
0	50	1	70
0	50	1	70
0	50	1	70
0	50	1	70
0	50	1	75
0	50	1	75
1	50	1	75
1	50	1	75
0	55	1	80
0	55	1	80
0	60	1	80
0	60	1	80
1	60	1	80

Note: 0 = No therapy; 1 = therapy.

seek therapy. Therefore, the odds of seeking therapy with a depression score of 55 are 1 (.50 / .50 = 1), indicating that there is an equal chance of seeking and not seeking therapy. Using the same reasoning process, we find that the odds of seeking therapy with a depression score of 85 are 9 (.90 / .10 = 9). At this very high level of depression, for every 9 individuals who seek therapy, there is 1 who does not.

Applying a logistic function makes intuitive sense here. There is little change in the probability of seeking therapy at low or high depression levels. That is, there is little difference between those who are not at all depressed and those who are depressed just a little; these individuals, as a general rule, simply do not seek therapy for depression. At the same time, there is also little difference between those who are very depressed and those who are very, very depressed; these individuals in our database will generally seek therapy. The decision to seek therapy is most volatile or uncertain in the midrange of the depression continuum; increasingly higher depression scores are associated with an increasing likelihood that individuals will seek therapy.

Given such a pattern across the depression range means that the relationship between the predictor and the predicted values is nonlinear. Note also that in our larger hypothetical data set, the odds of seeking therapy with a low depression score was .11 (.10 / .90 = .11), whereas the odds of seeking therapy with a high depression score was 9 (.90 / .10 = 9). These odds reveal an asymmetry (odds of .11 and 9) that may be reconciled through the logit transformation.

The logit transformation resolves both the asymmetrical issue concerning the odds as well as the calculations of different probabilities at different predictor values. Recall that once we calculate the constant (a) and the b coefficient through MLE, a probability can be eventually derived by using the two-step procedure previously described. The formula is this: $g_{pred} = \text{logit} = a + b_1 X_1$, where X_1 is now the depression score. This logistic regression analysis yielded a constant value of -7.734 and a b weight of .139. Thus, for a depression score of, say, 35, the probability of an individual being in the response group is as follows:

$$g_{pred} = -7.734 + .139(35)$$

$$g_{pred} = -2.869$$

This value of -2.869 can now be inserted into the antilog equation to transform the log odds to probabilities, where $e = 2.718$.

$$\text{predicted probability} = 2.718 - 2.869/ (1 + 2.718 - 2.869) = .053.$$

For a depression score of 80, the results would be

$$g_{pred} = -7.734 + .139(80)$$

$$g_{pred} = 3.386$$

$$2.718^{3.386}/ (1 + 2.718^{3.386}) = .966$$

In this example, a depression score of 35 would result in an individual's being classified as someone who is not seeking therapy because the calculated probability (.053) is less than .5. However, a depression score of 80 would result in an individual's being classified as someone who is seeking therapy because that person's calculated probability (.966) exceeds .5.

To calculate the odds ratio in this example, we raise e to the power of b. For this example,

$$e^{.139} = 1.149$$

This tells us that the odds of seeking therapy are 1.149 times greater for a person who had a depression score of, say 35, than for a person with a depression score of 34. For a quantitative variable in general, the odds ratio indicates the odds of the target outcome occurring (the outcome coded as 1) when comparing one level of a predictor with another. For example, when comparing the therapy-seeking behavior of individuals with a depression score of 35 to those of 37, one multiplies the regression coefficient by the size of the difference in quantitative scores before raising e to the power of the coefficient. Thus, the difference between a depression score of 35 and 37 (a 2-unit increase) would be calculated as follows:

$$e^{(2 \times .139)} = e^{.278} = 1.320$$

We would therefore say that those scoring a 37 on depression are 1.32 times greater in seeking psychotherapy than those scoring 35. If there is a 10-point difference on scores, the equation would be

$$e^{(10 \times .139)} = e^{1.39} = 4.01$$

and our interpretation would be that those who scored 70 are 4.01 times greater in seeking psychotherapy than those scoring 60.

The key thing to remember in interpreting an odds ratio is that, by definition, you are comparing one set of cases with another on the outcome coded as 1 in your data file. The odds ratio changes as a function of the "distance" between the two sets. How much of a change is predicted is a function of b, the regression weight, which is the power to which we raise e. The only issue is how many bs we need, which is told to us by the distance between the sets. If the difference is 2 (depression scores of 35 and 37, depression scores of 63 and 65, and so on), then we multiply b by that difference in the power function (e raised to the power of twice b when comparing those who scored 37 with those who scored 35 or when comparing those who scored 65 with those who scored 63).

Example 3: One Continuous and One Dichotomous Variable Predictor

In this final example, the sample of 46 students now has one dichotomous independent variable (gender), with females coded as 1 and males coded as 0, and one continuous variable (level of depression). The dichotomous dependent variable is still the interest in obtaining therapy, coded as 1 for seeking therapy and 0 for not seeking therapy. This third example analysis is presented because logistic regression would generally employ a set of independent variables to predict or explain the dichotomous dependent variable. When more than one predictor variable is used in a logistic analysis, researchers can examine the contribution of one variable when other variables are controlled or held constant. Controlling for another variable (using a variable as a covariate) will be illustrated with this example.

The MLE method yielded a constant (a) of −8.35, a b_{gender} of 2.129, and a $b_{depression}$ score of .131. Thus, for a male (coded as 0) with a depression score of 40, the probability of seeking therapy (target group coded as 1) is

$$g_{pred} = -8.35 + 2.129(0) + .131(40) = -3.11$$

$$\text{predicted probability} = 2.718^{-3.11} / 1 + 2.718^{-3.11} = .042$$

Because the predicted probability of group membership is below .5, this respondent would be predicted not to seek therapy. However, for a female with a depression score of 75, the equation would be

$$g_{pred} = -8.35 + 2.129(1) + .131(75) = 3.604$$

$$\text{predicted probability} = 2.718^{3.604} / (1 + 2.718^{3.604}) = .973$$

Because the predicted probability of group membership is greater than .5, this respondent would be predicted to seek therapy.

Because multiple variables (two in this simple situation) were used as predictors in the logistic analysis, the odds ratio is now referred to as an *adjusted odds ratio* to indicate the contribution of a particular variable when other variables are controlled or held constant. The odds ratio for gender is now $e^{2.129} = 8.404$. This indicates that females (coded as 1) are 8.40 times more likely to seek therapy when we have statistically controlled for depression level. Another way to interpret this result would be to imagine that for the condition in which males and females had identical depression scores, females are about 8.4 times more likely to seek therapy than the males.

Evaluating the Logistic Model

Logistic regression produces a number of tests to assess the validity of the model (i.e., the regression equation). These tests can be characterized as either "absolute measures" (assessing the entire model) or "relative measures" (assessing the unique contribution from the individual independent variable).

Absolute Measures

Likelihood Ratio Test

If a researcher has no information other than the outcome, known as the *constant-only model,* then the researcher's "best guess" of an individual is that he or she will seek therapy because that was the more common outcome with this sample (56.5% in this sample). Thus, without considering any other information (gender or depression level), the likelihood or probability is that an individual will seek therapy.

The first absolute measure of the validity of the model is the likelihood ratio test, which evaluates whether or not the set of the independent variables improves prediction of the dependent variable better than chance. Because each case is independent of the others (one case's decision to seek or not to seek therapy in no way affects the decision of any other case), the probability of seeking therapy can be computed as the percentage of the sample seeking therapy (the percentage of 1s in the sample) raised to the power equal to the number of cases in the sample. For our small data set of 46 cases, 26 sought therapy. That makes up 56.5% of the sample. We thus raise .565 to the 46th power. The result is approximately .00000000000392. This is not an unusual magnitude to obtain because we are raising some decimal value to a power equal to the sample size.

Because these likelihood values are ordinarily very small, the ln of the likelihood is usually reported instead in the output. We calculate this value by multiplying the ln of the above value (the percentage of 1s raised to the power of the sample size) by −2. This outcome (i.e., −2 times the log likelihood) is referred to as −2LL. Taking the ln of the likelihood transforms a typically very small number into a "reasonably large" value that is more familiar to most of us. For example, the ln of .0000000000039 is −26.262. Multiplying this ln by −2 yields a value of 52.52. Why not just leave the ln of the likelihood alone (it's certainly a large enough value for most of us) instead of multiplying it by −2? The answer is that the distribution of −2LL is distributed as chi square, whereas LL by itself is not. Thus, it can be used for assessing the significance of the logistic regression model. Specifically, this test assesses if at least one of the independent variables (covariates) is statistically significantly different from zero.

Omnibus Test of Model Coefficients

The omnibus test of model coefficients is another absolute measure of the validity of the model. The model chi square is a statistical test of the null hypothesis that all the coefficients are zero. It is equivalent to the overall F test in linear regression. The model chi-square value is the difference between the constant-only model and the full model (i.e., with constant and predictors). In this example, the null hypothesis is rejected because the significance is less than .05. The researcher would conclude that the set of independent variables improves prediction of the outcome over the situation where they are not used.

Model Summary

The third absolute measure of the validity of the model is the model summary, which is a goodness-of-fit statistic. This fit statistic is usually not interpreted directly, but is useful when comparing different logistic models.

Pseudo R^2

The Cox and Snell and the Nagelkerke tests are two alternative ways to compute a pseudo R^2 estimate and are thought of as absolute measures of the validity of the model. They are used to determine the percentage of variance in the dependent variable explained by the independent variables in logistic regression and are thus analogous to but not the same as the R^2 generated in multiple regression analysis. Although technically, an R^2 cannot be computed the same way in logistic regression as it is in least squares regression, the two tests are referred to as pseudo R^2. The pseudo R^2 in logistic regression is defined as $(1 - L_{full})/L_{reduced}$, where $L_{reduced}$ represents the log likelihood for the "constant-only" model and L_{full} is the log likelihood for the full model with constant and predictors. Usually, the Nagelkerke pseudo R^2 is preferred because it can achieve a maximum value of 1, unlike the Cox and Snell pseudo R^2.

Hosmer and Lemeshow Test

The Hosmer and Lemeshow test is another absolute measure to assess whether the predicted probabilities match the observed probabilities. A researcher is seeking a nonsignificant p value for this test because the goal of the research is to derive a set of independent variables (covariates) that will accurately predict the actual probabilities. Thus, the researcher does not want to reject the null hypothesis. In this example, the goodness-of-fit statistic is 10.161, distributed as a chi-square value, with the p value of .180 indicating an acceptable match between predicted and observed probabilities.

Relative Measures

Wald Test

The relative measures are used to test the statistical significance of the unique contribution of each coefficient (b) in the model. These coefficients indicate the amount of change expected in the log odds when there is a 1-unit change in the predictor variable with all the other variables in the model held constant. A coefficient close to 0 suggests that there is no change due to the predictor variable. To assess if a coefficient is statistically significantly greater than zero, logistic regression uses the Wald test. This test is analogous to the t test in multiple regression. In this example, gender is statistically significantly associated with seeking psychotherapy exclusive of depression level. Likewise, depression level is statistically significantly associated with seeking psychotherapy exclusive of gender.

However, several authors have identified problems with the use of the Wald statistic. Menard (2002) warns that for large coefficients, standard error is inflated, lowering the Wald statistic (chi square) value. Agresti (1996) states that the likelihood ratio test is more reliable for small sample sizes than the Wald test.

The Issue of Standardized (Beta) Coefficients

Current statistical computer programs do not produce the standardized logit coefficients. However, a researcher could standardize the data first, and the logit coefficients would then be the standardized logit coefficients. Alternatively, researchers could multiply the unstandardized logit coefficients by the standard deviations of the corresponding variables, giving a result that is not the standardized logit coefficient but that can be used to rank the relative importance of the independent variables.

Recommended Readings

Allison, P. D. (1999). Comparing logit and probit coefficients across groups. *Sociological Methods and Research, 28,* 186–208.

Cox, D. R., & Snell, E. J. (1989). *Analysis of binary data* (2nd ed.). London: Chapman & Hall.

DeMaris, A. (1992). *Logit modeling: Practical applications.* Newbury Park, CA: Sage.

Estrella, A. (1998). A new measure of fit for equations with dichotomous dependent variables. *Journal of Business and Economic Statistics, 16,* 198–205.

Fox, J. (2000). *Multiple and generalized nonparametric regression.* Thousand Oaks, CA: Sage.

Hosmer, D. W., Jr., & Lemeshow, S. (2000). *Applied logistic regression* (2nd ed.). New York: Wiley.

Menard, S. (2002). *Applied logistic regression analysis* (2nd ed.). Thousand Oaks, CA: Sage.

Pampel, F. C. (2000). *Logistic regression: A primer.* Thousand Oaks, CA: Sage.

Rice, J. C. (1994). Logistic regression: An introduction. In B. Thompson (Ed.), *Advances in social science methodology* (Vol. 3, pp. 191–245). Greenwich, CT: JAI Press.

Wright, R. E. (1995). Logistic regression. In L. G. Grimm & P. R. Yarnold (Eds.), *Reading and understanding multivariate statistics* (pp. 217–244). Washington, DC: American Psychological Association.

Logistic Regression Using SPSS

I n this chapter, the SPSS binary logistic program will be used to assess if gender (with females coded as 1 and males coded as 0) and level of depression (with scores potentially ranging from 0, indicating no depression, to 100, indicating much depression) can reliably predict which college students will seek psychotherapy (this outcome measure is coded as 1 for yes and 0 for no). Forty-six students (20 males and 26 females) were participants in the study.

Setting Up the Logistic Regression Analysis

From the task bar, select **Analyze → Regression → Binary → Logistic**, which opens up the **Logistic Regression** main dialog box as shown in Figure 6b.1.

To structure the analysis from the **Logistic Regression** dialog box, we click **therapy** over to the **Dependent** box. This is a dichotomously coded variable with 1 representing "seek therapy" and 0 representing "did not seek therapy." The two predictors are **gender** and **depress** and are clicked over to the **Covariates** box. We will enter these two predictors simultaneously, so we leave the default **Method** box at **Enter**. We then click the **Options** pushbutton to continue structuring the analysis.

Logistic Regression

The **Options** dialog box for logistic regression is also shown in Figure 6b.1. In the **Statistics and Plots** box, we have marked only two of the

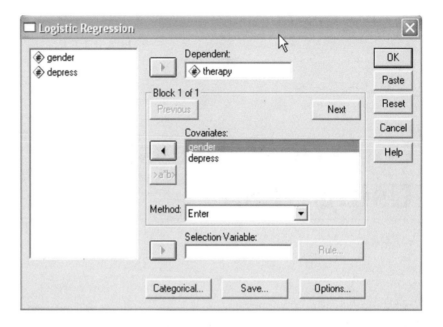

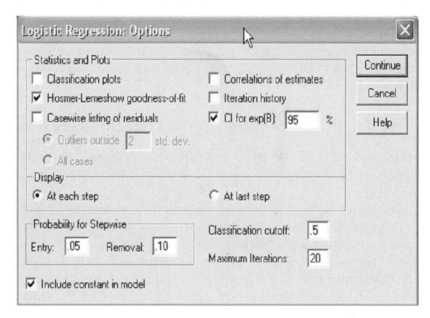

Figure 6b.1 Logistic Regression Main Dialog Box and Its Options
Dialog Box

option checkboxes: the **Hosmer-Lemeshow goodness-of-fit** output and the **CI for exp (B),** which requests the 95% confidence interval for the odds ratio. For **Display,** we have kept the default showing the results **At each step** because under the **Method-Enter,** there is only one step (choosing **At last step** gives us the same output here). The rest of the dialog box incorporates standard SPSS defaults, which we will keep. Clicking the **Continue** pushbutton brings us back to the main **Logistic Regression** dialog box, where we click **OK** to run the analysis and obtain the output.

Output From the Logistic Regression Analysis

Initial Output

The **Case Processing Summary** table seen in Figure 6b.2 is the first piece of output provided by SPSS. It provides information on the number of cases being analyzed. This is useful as a check to make sure that you have the expected number of cases in the analysis. In this instance, all 46 of the cases are included. This table also provides information on missing cases because researchers should be aware of situations where they have unexpectedly lost data.

The next part of the logistic output is the **Dependent Variable Encoding** table also shown in Figure 6b.2. It would indicate whether SPSS had to temporarily recode the outcome variable to conform to the "0" or "1"

Case Processing Summary

Unweighted Cases[a]		N	Percent
Selected cases	Included in analysis	46	100.0
	Missing cases	0	.0
	Total	46	100.0
Unselected cases		0	.0
Total		46	100.0

No missing cases.

a. If weight is in effect, see classification table for the total number of cases.

Dependent Variable Encoding

Original Value	Internal Value
No	0
Yes	1

Figure 6b.2 Case Processing Summary and Dependent Variable Encoding Tables From the Logistic Regression Analysis

coding scheme (not required here because the "seek therapy" variable was already coded in an acceptable way as far as SPSS was concerned). However, for studies where your coding scheme was different from 1 and 0, this information is obviously of critical importance!

Block 0: Beginning Block

The next three tables, the **Classification Table**, the **Variables in the Equation,** tables and the **Variables Not in the Equation** tables, are all displayed under a heading of **Block 0: Beginning Block** (this label is shown as a heading in the SPSS output). These results are computed with only the constant in the equation but without any of the predictor variables included. The **Classification Table** is shown first in Figure 6b.3. It indicates the consequences of having only the constant included in the model. In logistic regression, this situation leads to the prediction of the more common or more frequent outcome. In this example, the more common outcome is that an individual will seek therapy; that is, in this sample, more cases (56.5%) sought therapy than did not. Thus, without considering any other information (gender or stress level), the likelihood or probability is that an individual will seek therapy.

Because each of the cases is independent, the probability of seeking therapy is .56546 = .00000000000392. Because likelihood values are very small, the natural log (ln) of the likelihood is reported in the output. For this example, the ln of .0000000000039 is −26.262. Thus the equation is −26.262 × −2 = 52.52. This statistic is often referred as −2LL (i.e., −2 times the log likelihood). This value, however, does not appear in the SPSS output. Although this model is of no interest, it does provide a baseline for comparison with other models.

The **Variables in the Equation** and the **Variables Not in the Equation** tables simply tell us the state of the model at this juncture—that is, before the variables are entered into the model. With only the constant in the model, there is not sufficient information to significantly predict the outcome variable. Thus, the Wald statistic is not significant.

However, SPSS can anticipate what will happen next, and it shows us this in the **Variables Not in the Equation** table. As you can see, if gender and level of depression were included, these two variables would significantly improve the predictability of the model.

Block 1: Method = Enter

The remaining portion of the output produced by SPSS is listed under the heading **Block 1: Method = Enter** (as was true for Block 0, this

Block 0: Beginning Block

Classification Table[a,b]

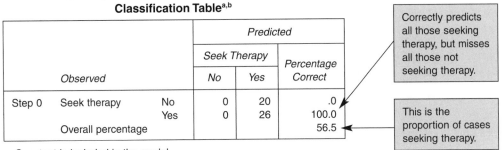

			Predicted		
			Seek Therapy		Percentage Correct
Observed			No	Yes	
Step 0	Seek therapy	No	0	20	.0
		Yes	0	26	100.0
	Overall percentage				56.5

Correctly predicts all those seeking therapy, but misses all those not seeking therapy.

This is the proportion of cases seeking therapy.

a. Constant is included in the model.

b. The cut value is .500.

Variables in the Equation

		B	S.E.	Wald	df	Sig.	Exp(B)
Step 0	Constant	.262	.297	.778	1	.378	1.300

The Wald test is analogous to the *t* test. Here we see that the constant by itself does not significantly improve prediction.

Variables Not in the Equation

			Score	df	Sig.
Step 0	Variables	depress	18.262	1	.000
		gender	10.128	1	.001
	Overall statistics		23.318	2	.000

Figure 6b.3 Selected Output Tables From Block 0 of the Logistic Regression Analysis

label appears in the SPSS printout). Because we have entered our only two independent variables together (as a block), what follows is essentially the results of our analysis. Had we chosen to use some hierarchical strategy with more predictors, we may have had multiple blocks to work through before we reached completion.

The first table SPSS presents is the **Omnibus Tests of Model Coefficients** table that we display in Figure 6b.4. It contains the **model chi square**, a statistical test of the null hypothesis that all the coefficients are zero. It is equivalent to the overall *F* test in linear regression. The **model chi-square** value in this example is 28.240, which is the difference between the "constant-only" model (this value is not displayed in the output) and the full model (with constant and the predictors in it). In this example, the null hypothesis is rejected because the significance is less than .05 (shown by the

Block 1: Method = Enter

Omnibus Tests of Model Coefficients

Step		Chi square	df	Sig.
1	Step	28.240	2	.000
	Block	28.240	2	.000
	Model	28.240	2	.000

Model Summary

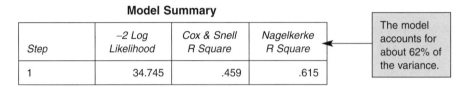

Step	−2 Log Likelihood	Cox & Snell R Square	Nagelkerke R Square
1	34.745	.459	.615

The model accounts for about 62% of the variance.

Hosmer and Lemeshow Test

Step	Chi square	df	Sig.
1	10.161	7	.180

A nonsignificant chi square means that the predicted probabilities match the observed probabilities. This outcome is what most researchers strive to achieve.

Contingency Table for Hosmer and Lemeshow Test

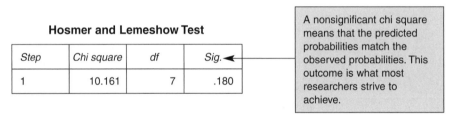

Step		Seek Therapy = No		Seek Therapy = Yes		Total
		Observed	Expected	Observed	Expected	
1	1	6	5.602	0	.398	6
	2	6	5.114	0	.886	6
	3	2	2.980	2	1.020	4
	4	2	3.116	3	1.884	5
	5	2	2.013	4	3.987	6
	6	0	.324	3	2.676	3
	7	2	.464	3	4.536	5
	8	0	.253	5	4.747	5
	9	0	.136	6	5.864	6

This is a more detailed assessment of the Hosmer and Lemeshow Test. Note the close match between the observed and the expected values for each group.

Figure 6b.4   Assessment of Fit of the Logistic Regression Model

.000 under the **Sig.** heading). We would thus conclude that the set of independent variables improves prediction of the outcome. The other two tests, **Block** and **Step**, have the same value as the **Model** statistic because all the variables were entered in one block.

The **Model Summary** table, also shown in Figure 6b.4, presents three measures of how well the logistic regression model fits the data. With all the variables in the model, the goodness-of-fit **–2 Log likelihood** (–2LL) statistic is 34.745. This fit statistic is usually not interpreted directly but is useful when comparing different logistic models.

Technically, R^2 cannot be computed the same way in logistic regression as it is in least squares regression. A pseudo R^2 in logistic regression is defined as $(1 - L_{full}) / L_{reduced}$, where $L_{reduced}$ represents the log likelihood for the "constant-only" model and L_{full} is the log likelihood for the full model with constant and predictors. The **Cox and Snell** pseudo R^2 is .459 and the **Nagelkerke** pseudo R^2 is .615. Usually, the **Nagelkerke** pseudo R^2 is preferred because it can achieve a maximum value of one, unlike the **Cox and Snell** pseudo R^2, which cannot.

The **Hosmer and Lemeshow Test** table, following the **Model Summary** table in Figure 6b.4, provides a formal test assessing whether the predicted probabilities match the observed probabilities. Researchers are seeking a nonsignificant p value for this test because the goal of the research is to derive predictors that will accurately predict the actual probabilities. If the predictions are consonant with the observed values, then there should be little discrepancy between them; that is, there should not be a significant difference between them. Thus, researchers do not want to reject the null hypothesis (the null hypothesis is that the predictions and observed values do not differ). In this example, the goodness-of-fit statistic is 10.161, distributed (and tested) as a chi-square value, and is associated with a p value of .180, indicating an acceptable (close enough) match between predicted and observed probabilities.

The **Contingency Table for Hosmer and Lemeshow Test**, which we also present in Figure 6b.4, demonstrates more details of the Hosmer and Lemeshow test. This output divides the data into approximately 10 equal groups (9 groups for this example) based on the outcome variable. These groups are defined by increasing order of seeking therapy and (unfortunately for a student just learning to read logistic regression output) are called "steps" in the table. The first group (**Step 1**) represents those participants least likely to seek therapy. The observed frequencies were that 6 cases did not seek therapy and 0 cases did. Notice for all the groups how closely the observed and the expected frequencies (based on the prediction model) match. This is a good thing.

The **Classification Table** is shown in Figure 6b.5 and indicates how well the model classifies cases into the two categories of the seeking

Classification Table[a]

			Predicted		
			Seek Therapy		Percentage Correct
Observed			No	Yes	
Step 1	Seek therapy	No	16	4	80.0
		Yes	5	21	80.8
	Overall percentage				80.4

The overall predictive accuracy is 80.4%.

a. Variable(s) entered on Step 1: depress, gender.

Variables in the Equation

		B	S.E.	Wald	df	Sig.	Exp(B)	95.0% CI for EXP(B)	
								Lower	Upper
Step 1[a]	depress	.131	.040	10.782	1	.001	1.140	1.054	1.232
	gender	2.129	.876	5.902	1	.015	8.404	1.509	46.811
	Constant	−8.350	2.368	12.431	1	.000	.000		

a. Variable(s) entered on Step 1: depress, gender.

An increase of 1 on the depression measure increases the odds of seeking therapy by 1.14 times, controlling for gender.

This value of 8.404 is the odds ratio for gender. Females (coded as 1) are 8.404 times more likely to seek therapy than males, controlling for depression.

Figure 6b.5 Classification Table and Variables in the Equation Output

therapy variable. The overall predictive accuracy is 80.4%. Similarly, the model predicted equally well for both those seeking therapy and those not seeking therapy (80.8% and 80.0%, respectively).

Recall from **Block 0** that without considering any other information (participants' gender or stress level), the likelihood or probability of a correct prediction is 56.5% in this sample. A researcher may want to consider how much the prediction has improved over chance. The overall predictive accuracy of 80.4% appears meaningful.

The **Variables in the Equation** table, shown last in Figure 6b.5, presents the b coefficients (written as an uppercase "**B**" by SPSS) and their standard errors (**S.E.**). These coefficients indicate the amount of change expected in the log odds when there is a 1-unit change in the predictor variable with all the other variables in the model held constant. A coefficient close to 0 suggests that there is no change due to the predictor variable. The **Sig.** column represents the *p* value for testing whether a predictor is significantly associated with seeking psychotherapy exclusive of any of the other predictors. The logistic coefficients can be used in a manner similar to linear regression coefficients to generate predicted values. In this example, seeking therapy = –8.350 + .131 (gender) + 2.129 (stress).

The **Exp(B)** column provides the odds ratio (one of the important objectives in logistic regression). The odds ratio for gender is 8.404. This implies that females (because they were coded as 1) are 8.404 times more likely to seek therapy than males in this sample (with a rather large 95% confidence interval of 1.50 to 46.81, suggesting a certain amount of imprecision in our result).

The odds ratio for depression is 1.14 (the 95% confidence interval is 1.054 to 1.23). Because depression is a quantitatively assessed variable, we can interpret this odds ratio of 1.14 to mean that an increase of 1 on the depression measure increases the odds of seeking therapy by 1.14 times. Using a depression score of 35 as a comparison base (it's the lowest score in the example that we have been using, and we need to compare something with something else when talking about an odds ratio), we can say that the odds of seeking therapy are 1.14 times greater for a person who had a depression score of 36 than for a person with a depression score of 35. Any score can serve as a base. To compute the odds ratio for a different depression value, one multiplies the regression coefficient by the size of the increase over a base score before raising *e* to the power of the coefficient. Thus, the difference between a depression score of 35 and 37 (a 2-unit increase would be calculated $e^{(2 \times .139)} = e^{.278}$ = 1.320. Those scoring a 37 on depression are 1.32 times more likely to seek psychotherapy than those scoring 35. If there is a 10-point difference on scores, the equation would be $e^{(10 \times .139)} = e^{1.39}$ = 4.01. For example, those who scored 70 are 4.01 times more likely to seek psychotherapy than those scoring 60. As previously mentioned, these predicted group memberships will be compared with the actual group membership as a method to assess the accuracy of this independent variable (stress level).

Note that SPSS does not produce standardized logit coefficients. However, researchers could standardize the data first. Then the logit coefficients would be the standardized logit coefficients. Alternatively, a researcher could multiply the unstandardized logit coefficients by the standard deviations of the corresponding variables, giving a result that is not the standardized logit coefficient but that can be used to rank the relative importance of the independent variables.

Results

Because the criterion variable is dichotomous (seeking therapy or not), a simultaneous logistic regression was used to model the student's decision to seek psychotherapy. The predictor variables in this study are (a) gender (coded 1 = female, 0 = male) and (b) score on the hypothetical depression scale, with higher scores indicating greater levels of depression. Results of the logistic analysis indicate that the two-predictor model provides a statistically significant improvement over the constant-only model, χ^2 (2, $N = 46$) = 28.24, $p < .001$. The Nagelkerke pseudo R^2 indicated that the model accounted for 62% of the total variance. This suggests that the set of predictors discriminates between those seeking psychotherapy and those not seeking therapy. Prediction success for the cases used in the development of the model was relatively high, with an overall prediction success rate of 80.4% and correct prediction rates of 80.8% for students seeking therapy and 80.0% for those students not seeking therapy. Table 6b.1 presents the regression coefficients (B), the Wald statistics, significance level, odds ratio [Exp(B)], and the 95% confidence intervals (CI) for odds ratios (OR) for each predictor. The Wald test reports that both predictors (gender and depression score) are statistically significant predictors of seeking therapy.

The influence of gender is strong; females are 8.4 times (CI = 1.51, 46.81) more likely to seek psychotherapy than males, adjusting for depression level. For each single point increase in the depression score, there is a 1.14 times greater likelihood of seeking therapy, controlling for gender.

Table 6b.1 Logistic Regression Results for Predicting Whether Psychotherapy Is Sought Using Gender and Depression Scores as Independent Variables

Step	Variable Entered	B	Wald	Significance	Exp(B)	95.0% CI for Exp(B) Lower	Upper
1	Gender	2.129	5.902	.015	8.404	1.509	46.811
	Depress	.131	10.782	.001	1.140	1.054	1.232
	Constant	−8.350	12.431	.000	.000		

6B Exercises

Logistic Regression

The purpose of this study was to predict involuntary psychiatric commitment to a state hospital (0 = No, 1 = Yes). There was one indicator variable: minority status (0 = No, 1 = Yes). In addition, educational level measured in years in school (EDUC) and the M and G Stress Test (STRESS) scored on a 1 to 5 scale, with higher scores indicating higher levels of stress, were included to assess if these variables could reliably predict commitment.

Using the SPSS data file for Chapter 6B (located on the Web-based study site—http://www.sagepub.com/amrStudy), answer the following questions.

1. Do the variables reliably predict commitment to a state hospital? What in the output indicates if the predictors are statistically significant?

2. What are the tests that assess variance explained? Are the results consistent?

3. What is the overall classification rate of the predictors?

4. Which of the variables provide a unique contribution to the prediction?

5. What are the odds that a minority member will be committed to a state hospital compared with a nonminority member?

6. What are the odds of being committed for each increase on the Stress Test?

7. Write a results section on this study.

Discriminant
Function Analysis

Discriminant and Logistic Analysis Compared

The purpose of a discriminant function analysis is similar to logistic regression in that we use it to develop a weighted linear composite to predict membership in two or more groups (Cooley & Lohnes, 1971). In this chapter, we limit ourselves to a discriminant function analysis design that predicts membership in one of two groups.

The Criterion and Predictor Variables

In both discriminant function analysis and logistic regression, the variable being predicted, the *groups* variable as it is sometimes called in discriminant analysis, is a categorical variable. In logistic regression, the predictor variables may be either continuous, dichotomous (categorical variables can be used if they are first dummy coded), or a combination of both. In discriminant function analysis, the predictors are continuous variables (Duarte Silva & Stam, 1995).

The Model Generated

In logistic regression, the model is nonlinear (i.e., sigmoidal or S shape). This means that the changes in the dependent variable (usually dichotomous) are not as great at the low and high ends of the predictors and that the greater changes occur in the middle ranges of the predictors. In discriminant function analysis, the model is linear; thus, the predictors and the criterion have a constant relationship to each other. The weighted combination of the independent variables (known as the discriminant function) is constructed to maximally separate the groups. These weights are calculated to derive a discriminant score for each case. If these scores are used as the dependent variable in a one-way ANOVA with group as the independent variable, the mean discriminant scores for the groups (called *centroids*) would maximally separate the groups. That is, no other derived centroids could separate the groups more.

Discriminant and Regression Analysis Compared

Comparable to multiple regression, discriminant function analysis likewise assumes proper model specification—that is, the inclusion of all important predictor variables and the exclusion of extraneous variables. As is the case for multiple regression, these predictors are considered to be independent variables. Unlike what we have seen for multiple regression, the criterion or dependent variable is a categorical variable representing the groups being differentiated or distinguished. For those who are familiar with experimental design and ANOVA, this may seem a bit reversed because the groups in such research typically represent the independent rather than the dependent variable. Because we are predicting the group membership of the cases in discriminant analysis, however, this categorical variable plays the role of a dependent variable in discriminant analysis.

Assumptions Underlying Discriminant Function Analysis

Unlike the nonlinear nature of logistic regression, discriminant function analysis conforms to the general linear model. Thus, it makes the same rigorous assumptions as multiple regression, including linearity, normality, independence of predictors, homoscedasticity, absence of multicollinearity, and the influence of outliers; it also presumes the use of near interval data (see Chapters 3A and 3B).

Discriminant function analysis, as is true for some of the other general linear model techniques, is fairly robust to violations of most of these assumptions. However, it is highly sensitive to outliers, and these should be resolved as described in Chapter 3A prior to the analysis. If one group contains extreme outliers, these will bias the mean (draw the mean toward it and away from the bulk of the other values) and increase the variance (the squared difference between the outlier and the mean will result in an exceptionally large value in the calculation of the variance). Because overall significance tests are calculated on pooled variances (i.e., the average variance across all groups), these significance tests are prone to a Type I error—that is, reporting statistical significance erroneously in the presence of outliers (McLachlan, 1992).

Because discriminant function analysis assumes that the continuous independent variables are normally distributed, violation of this assumption suggests that we should probably opt for logistic regression. Recall that logistic regression can accommodate both dichotomous and continuous variables, and the predictors do not have to be normally distributed, linearly related, or have demonstrated equal variance within each group (Tabachnick & Fidell, 2001b). Logistic regression is sometimes preferable to discriminant analysis in studies where the variables violate multivariate normal distributions within the criterion groups (Klecka, 1980). However, if the assumption of normality is not violated, logistic regression is less powerful than discriminant analysis (Lachenbruch, 1975; Press & Wilson, 1978).

Sample Size for Discriminant Analysis

Besides the assumptions presented above, there are issues concerning sample size that need to be taken into account. Discriminant analysis permits the groups to be of different sample sizes, but the sample size of the smallest group should exceed the number of predictor variables (by a lot). The maximum number of independent variables should be taken as $N - 2$, where n is the sample size. But although this minimum sample size may allow the analysis to be conducted, it is certainly not recommended (Huberty, 1994). The recommended sample size for the smallest group should be at least 20 times the number of predictors.

Purposes of Discriminant Function Analysis

Whereas logistic regression is used mainly for predictive purposes (i.e., estimating the probability that an event will occur), discriminant function analysis can serve two distinct purposes: (a) prediction, referred to as predictive discriminant analysis, and (b) explanation, referred to as descriptive discriminant analysis (Huberty, 1994).

If the primary purpose of the researcher is to gain understanding of the nature of the variate derived from the linear combination of the predictors, then descriptive discriminant analysis would be performed. Descriptive discriminant analysis is often used as a follow-up analysis to a significant MANOVA to determine the structure of the linear combination of the dependent variables. In fact, discriminant function analysis is computationally identical to MANOVA. Generally, descriptive discriminant function analysis focuses on "revealing major differences among the groups" (Stevens, 2002, p. 285). If, however, the primary purpose of the researcher is to compute a case's membership in one of the groups from the weighted linear combination of the predictors—that is, to classify the cases into the different groups—then predictive discriminant analysis would be performed.

It is true, as students sometimes note, that we already know the predicted values of the quantitative criterion variable in multiple regression and of the group membership in logistic and in discriminant analyses. Students therefore wonder why we engage in the procedure in the first place with the inevitable result that we have prediction error when we can just look at the data file to see these values directly. The answer is linked to the purposes of these analyses. From a descriptive perspective, we are trying to put together a general model—the discriminant function in the present case—to describe the predictive relationship of the independent variables to the dependent variable; our interest is not restricted exclusively to the cases in the sample. From a predictive perspective, we have hopes of using the model to predict the group membership of future samples; again our interest goes well beyond the particular cases in the present sample.

A Two-Group Discriminant Example

To demonstrate a two-group discriminant function analysis, we will use an example in which researchers are trying to determine if successful clinical psychology interns (i.e., those who passed their internship) could be identified by (a) a pre-self-evaluation questionnaire, (b) a preliminary clinical examination score, and (c) an initial committee evaluation rating. The self-evaluation asks the students to project the degree to which they feel they would be successful in their internship. It uses a 5-point response scale, with higher scores indicating greater confidence in clinical ability. The preliminary exam was administered by the internship sites participating in the study and was graded A to F, with A being awarded 5 points and F being awarded 0 points. The initial committee evaluation rating was based on judgments of the entry-level skills exhibited by the new interns. The items on this rating form were scored on a 7-point Likert-type scale, with greater scores indicating a more positive evaluation.

These three continuous variables are the independent variables (or predictors). One year later, the criterion or outcome measure was obtained. This dependent variable was whether or not the student passed the internship. In this study, the outcome variable was dummy coded as 1, representing successful completion, and 0, representing unsuccessful completion (i.e., failure).

Recognizing the Discriminant Design

When we ask if we can project what someone's score on some measure might be or determine with which subset a certain individual or case might be associated, we are dealing in a general way with prediction. That tells us, within the context of the topics covered in this text, that we are in the domain of multiple regression, logistic regression, or discriminant function analysis. In the present example, because the variable we wish to predict (identify) is a categorical and not a quantitative variable, we know that multiple regression is not the technique we should use. The choice between logistic regression and discriminant analysis is decided by the scale of measurement underlying the predictors. In this case, the predictors are all quantitative variables. We have also determined that these variables meet the assumption of normal within-group distributions. With this information, we can then assert that discriminant analysis becomes the procedure of choice.

It is also worthwhile to note two points in connection with the selection of the statistical procedure we would use to analyze the data in this hypothetical study. First, we could use logistic regression with these quantitative predictors even though it is less powerful here. Second, if we did use standard multiple regression with this dichotomous criterion variable, we would actually obtain a mathematically identical solution to the one yielded by standard discriminant function analysis. The unstandardized and standardized discriminant coefficients would be some constant multiple of the b and beta coefficients from the multiple regression equation. Nonetheless, discriminant is the proper choice of procedure to use with the specified variables.

The Discriminant Function

Recall that in multiple regression, the purpose is to develop a linear function (i.e., the best weighted combination of the independent variables) that predicts some quantitative measure (the criterion variable or dependent variable) from a set of other quantitative variables (predictors or independent variables). This linear equation is the prediction model. This prediction model in discriminant analysis is called the discriminant function. The discriminant function in the present example will weight the three predictor variables (pre-self-evaluation, preliminary clinical examination, and initial committee evaluation) such that the two criterion groups (whether or not the student passed the internship) are maximally differentiated. The students will thus be classified based on their score for the discriminant function into a pass or fail group. One of the ways we will evaluate the quality of the solution is by examining how accurately the students were classified into these groups.

In a multiple regression analysis, a predicted score can be calculated from the weighted combination of the independent variables. Similarly, in a discriminant function analysis, one can calculate a discriminant score (designated as D_i) from the weighted combination of the independent variables. The unstandardized discriminant coefficients are used in the formula for making the classifications, much as b coefficients are used in regression in making predictions. For each case, we multiply the score on each predictor by its discriminant coefficient or weight and add the constant. The result of this computation yields the discriminant score. The equation for the discriminant score is as follows:

$$D_i = \mathbf{a} + b_1 X_1 + b_2 X_2 + \cdots + b_n X_n$$

In this equation, D_i is the predicted score on the criterion variable, the Xs are the predictor variables in the equation (i.e., pre-self-evaluation, preliminary clinical examination, and initial committee evaluation), and the bs are the weights or coefficients associated with the predictors. Analogous to multiple regression, these b weights reflect the relative contribution of its independent variable when the effects of all the other predictors are statistically controlled. The equation also contains a constant, shown as $\mathbf{a}$ in the equation (representing the Y intercept).

Unlike the multiple regression equation, which employs the ordinary least squares solution, the weights in the discriminant function are derived through the maximum likelihood method (the same strategy used in logistic regression). The maximum likelihood method is an iterative process that starts with an initial arbitrary "guesstimate" of the weights and then determines the direction and magnitude of the b coefficients to minimize the number of classification errors. This maximum likelihood technique ultimately assigns a case to a group from a specific discriminant cutoff score. The cutoff score is the one that results in the fewest classification errors. When group sizes are equal, the cutoff score is selected between the mean scores (the centroids) of the two groups. If the group sizes are unequal, the cutoff score is calculated from the weighted means. Because the mean discriminant score (centroid) of the unsuccessful interns in this example is $-.782$ and the centroid of the successful interns is $+.782$, the cutoff score is 0. Scores greater than 0 are predicted as belonging to the successful group, and scores equal to or less than 0 are predicted as belonging to the unsuccessful group.

For example, assume that a case has the following scores for the three-predictor variables: 2 (self-evaluation), 3.12 (exam score), 3 (committee evaluation), and 0 (the student was unsuccessful in the internship).

The discriminant function analysis produced the following weights: .703 (self-evaluation), 1.725 (exam score), and .092 (committee evaluation), with −8.043 as the **a** constant. The equation for this case would then be as follows:

$$\mathbf{2}(.703) + \mathbf{3.12}(1.725) + \mathbf{3}(.092) + (−8.043) = \mathbf{−.98}$$

Because this D_i is less than 0, this case is classified as unsuccessful, an accurate classification. Assume that another case had the following scores: 4 (self-evaluation), 4.09 (exam score), 3 (committee evaluation), and 1 (the student was successful). The equation for this case would then be as follows:

$$\mathbf{4}(.703) + \mathbf{4.09}(1.725) + \mathbf{3}(.092) + (\mathbf{−8.043}) = \mathbf{2.11}$$

Because this D_i is greater than 0, this case is classified as successful. Thus, this student also would be correctly classified on the basis of her score on the discriminant function.

Interpreting the Discriminant Function

The predictor variables have been aggregated (with appropriate weights) to create the discriminant function, which is conceptually identical to the variate in multiple regression. To infer the meaning of the discriminant function, we need to review the structure matrix and the standardized canonical discriminant function coefficients.

The structure matrix reports the discriminant loadings of the variables on the discriminant function. These discriminant loadings are the simple Pearson correlations between the predictor variables and the discriminant function. Usually, any predictor with a loading of .30 or more is considered to be central in defining the discriminant dimension. Researchers gain insight into how to label the function by identifying the largest absolute correlation associated with the discriminant function.

The standardized canonical discriminant function coefficients indicate the partial contribution of each variable to the discriminant function controlling for other predictors in the equation. Although the structure coefficients are used to assign meaningful labels to the discriminant function, the standardized discriminant function coefficients are used to assess each independent variable's unique contribution to the discriminant function. These are akin to beta weights in multiple regression and carry with them the same strengths and liabilities. After reviewing the structure matrix and the standardized canonical discriminant function coefficients, researchers may consider eliminating variables that do not significantly contribute to prediction (variables whose coefficients are not statistically significant).

Researchers may also want or need to assess the relative importance of the discriminating variables. Recall that in multiple regression, the relative importance can be assessed by comparing beta weights. In discriminant function analysis, the standardized canonical discriminant function coefficients are used to assess relative importance. Note that the standardized discriminant coefficients will change if variables are added to or deleted from the equation.

Tests of Significance

The null hypothesis for discriminant function analysis is that the means of the two groups on the discriminant function—the centroids—are equal. Several methods are available to test if the discriminant model as a whole is statistically significant, but we present only Wilks's lambda here. Wilks's lambda varies from 0 to 1 and tells us the variance of the categorical groups variable that is not explained by the discriminant function; thus researchers desire lower values.

Wilks's lambda is also used to test for significant differences between the groups on the individual predictor variables. The F test of Wilks's lambda indicates which variables are statistically significant—that is, which variables contribute a significant amount of prediction to help differentiate the groups. Those predictors failing to demonstrate statistically significant differences between the groups could be considered for deletion from the model. If the groups do not differ on the individual predictor variables, then it is unlikely the groups will differ on the discriminant function.

The canonical correlation coefficient is the measure of association between the discriminant function and the outcome variable. The square of the canonical correlation is the percentage of variance explained in the dependent variable.

Accuracy of Classification

The performance of the discriminant function can be evaluated by estimating error rates (probabilities of misclassification). The classification table, also called the prediction matrix, is simply a table in which the rows are the observed categories of the independent variable and the columns are the predicted categories of the independent variable. Such a table is shown in Figure 7a.1.

When prediction is perfect (which is not going to happen in empirical research), all cases will lie on the upper left to lower right diagonal. The

		Predicted Category	
		Group 1	Group 2
Observed Category	Group 1	**Hit**	**Miss**
	Group 2	**Miss**	**Hit**

Figure 7a.1 Classification Table

percentage of cases on the diagonal is the percentage of correct classifications, called the *hit ratio*. This hit ratio is not compared with zero but with the percentage that would have been correctly classified by chance. For our two-group discriminant analysis, the expected hit ratio is 50% (for *n*-way groups with equal splits, the expected percent is $1/n$). Mahalanobis D^2 Rao's *V*, Hotelling's trace, Pillai's trace, and Roy's gcr (see Chapters 10A and 10B) are other indexes of the validity of the discriminant function. Each of these indexes has its own significance tests. Some of these tests are used in stepwise discriminant analysis to determine if adding an independent variable to the model will significantly improve classification of the dependent variable.

Mahalanobis distances are also used in evaluating cases in discriminant analysis. A researcher might wish to analyze a new, unknown set of cases in comparison with an existing set of known cases. Mahalanobis distance is the distance between a case and the centroid for each group. A case will have 1 Mahalanobis distance for each group, and it will be assigned to the group with the smallest Mahalanobis distance. Because Mahalanobis distance is measured in terms of standard deviations from the centroid, a case that is more than 1.96 Mahalanobis distance units from the centroid has less than a .05 chance of belonging to the group represented by the centroid, and a case with 3 distance units would have less than a .01 chance of belonging to that group.

Different Discriminant Function Methods

Just as was true for multiple regression, there are several different methods by which researchers can build the variate or linear function. One important way that these methods differ is the order in which they call for the predictor variables to be entered into the discriminant function. In general, we start with a set of potential predictors of some criterion variable. We finish with either some or all these potential predictors in the discriminant function. The methods differ in how we get from the starting state to the finished state. Here are some of the available strategies:

- ▶ We can enter all the independent variables into the equation at once.
- ▶ We can enter the independent variables one or more at a time.
- ▶ We can sequentially enter only those independent variables that add predictive value to those variables already in the equation.
- ▶ We can first put all the independent variables in the equation and then remove those not contributing to prediction one at a time.

Similar to multiple regression, these different discriminant methods can be organized into two groups: the *statistical* methods (standard and stepwise) and the researcher-controlled methods known as *sequential, hierarchical,* or *covariance* methods. The statistical methods rely exclusively on statistical decision-making criteria built into the computer programs to decide during the development of the equation which predictors are to be entered and which predictors will be removed. In using the statistical methods, researchers allow the computer program to autonomously carry out the analyses.

The standard discriminant method, also known as the simultaneous or the direct method, is what most authors refer to if they leave the method unspecified. Under this method, all the predictors are entered into the equation in a single "step" (stage in the analysis). The standard method provides a full model solution in that all the predictors are part of it. The idea that these variables are entered into the equation simultaneously is true only in the sense that the variables are entered in a single step. But that single "step" is not at all simple and unitary; when we look inside this step, we will find that process of determining the weights for the independent variables is governed by a complex strategy similar to what we described for multiple regression.

The stepwise method of developing the discriminant function is another popular method. The stepwise method begins with an empty equation and builds it one step at a time. Once a third independent variable is in the equation, the stepwise method invokes the right to remove an independent variable if that predictor is not earning its keep. Predictors are allowed to be included in the equation if they significantly add to the predictive function. With correlated predictor variables, as we have seen, the predictors in the equation admitted under a probability level of .05 can still overlap with each other.

With the hierarchical or covariance method, the researchers are the architects of the discriminant function equation. Here, researchers are in full control over the order of entry of variables in the discriminant function. Exactly the same sort of options are available as described for multiple regression, and readers are referred to Chapter 5A for that coverage.

Recommended Readings

Efron, B. (1975). The efficiency of logistic regression compared to normal discriminant analysis. *Journal of the American Statistical Association, 70,* 892–898.

Huberty, C. J. (1984). Issues in the use and interpretation of discriminant analysis. *Psychological Bulletin, 95,* 156–171.

Huberty, C. J., & Barton, R. M. (1989). An introduction to discriminant analysis. *Measurement and Evaluation in Counseling and Development, 22,* 158–168.

Huberty, C. J., Wisenbaker, J. M., & Smith, J. C. (1987). Assessing predictive accuracy in discriminant analysis. *Multivariate Behavioral Research, 22,* 307–329.

Joachimsthaler, E. A., & Stam, A. (1990). Mathematical programming approaches for the classification problem in two-group discriminant analysis. *Multivariate Behavioral Research, 25,* 427–454.

Konishi, S., & Honda, M. (1990). Comparison procedures for estimation of error rates in discriminant analysis under non-normal populations. *Journal of Statistical Computing and Simulation, 36,* 105–115.

McLaughlin, M. L. (1980). Discriminant analysis. In P. Monge & J. Cappella (Eds.), *Multivariate techniques in human communication research* (pp. 175–204). New York: Academic Press.

Panel on discriminant analysis, classification and clustering. (1989). Discriminant analysis and clustering. *Statistical Science, 4,* 34–69.

Press, S. J., & Wilson, S. (1978). Choosing between logistic regression and discriminant analysis. *Journal of the American Statistical Association, 73,* 699–705.

Ragsdale, C. T., & Stam, A. (1992). Introducing discriminant analysis to the business statistics curriculum. *Decision Sciences, 23,* 724–745.

Spicer, J. (2005). *Making sense of multivariate data analysis.* Thousand Oaks, CA: Sage.

Two-Group Discriminant Function Analysis Using SPSS

Overview of the Study

This chapter describes how to conduct a two-group discriminant function analysis using SPSS. Recall that the elements for a two-group discriminant analysis include a dichotomous dependent variable (i.e., two groups) and at least two quantitative conceptually related independent variables. The study presented in Chapter 7A will be the model.

In that study, the researchers were investigating if successful clinical psychology interns (i.e., those who passed their internship) could be identified by (a) a pre-self-evaluation questionnaire using a 5-point response scale, with higher scores indicating greater confidence in clinical ability; (b) a preliminary clinical examination score graded on the typical A to F, with A = 5 points and F = 0 points; and (c) an initial committee evaluation rating scored on a 7-point Likert-type scale, with greater scores indicating a more positive evaluation. These three continuous variables are the independent variables (or predictors), and whether or not the student passed the internship is the dependent variable (or outcome). In this study, the outcome variable was dummy coded as 1, representing successful completion, and 0, representing unsuccessful completion (i.e., failure).

Setting Up the Analysis

To begin our analysis, we select **Analyze → Classify → Discriminant,** which produces the **Discriminant Analysis** main dialog box in Figure 7b.1. We have already moved the dependent variable (**Success**) from the variables list panel to the **Grouping Variable.** Then click on the **Define Range** pushbutton and enter 0 in the **Minimum** box and 1 in the **Maximum** box. This is the range of values for the dependent variable (**Success**). Then enter the three predictor variables into the **Independents** window. Notice that the **Enter independents together** command is the default. This indicates that all the independent variables are entered in a single step (analogous to the simultaneous multiple regression method in chapter 5B). If we selected **Use Stepwise** method, the independent variables are entered one at a time and may be removed depending on a priori statistical criteria. The **Selection Variable** box may be used to select cases from a particular variable. This allows for classifying new cases based on previously existing data or for dividing your data into initial analysis and holdout groups to perform cross-validation.

At the bottom of the dialog box, there are four pushbuttons: **Statistics, Method, Classify,** and **Save,** each of which produces its own dialog box. Clicking the **Statistics** pushbutton produces the **Discriminant Analysis: Statistics** dialog box also presented in Figure 7b.1. Check the **Means** box. This will display the means and standard deviations for all independent variables for both the groups and the entire sample. Select **Univariate ANOVAs.** This command will assess if there are statistically significant differences between the means of the groups (or between the groups if there are three or more in the outcome variable). Click on **Box's M** to test for the equality of the group covariance matrices. This test is sensitive to departures from multivariate normality. Now select **Fisher's Function Coefficients,** which will present the coefficients that can be used for direct classification. Last, select the **Unstandardized Function Coefficients,** which will display the unstandardized discriminant function coefficients. Then select **Continue** to return to the main **Discriminant Analysis** dialog box.

Now select the **Classify** pushbutton, which produces the **Discriminant Analysis: Classification** dialog box also presented in Figure 7b.1. Check the **All groups equal** box (default) under the **Prior Probabilities** area. This indicates that the probabilities of group membership are assumed to be equal. Check the **Summary table** under the **Display** area, which will report the number of cases correctly and incorrectly assigned to each group based on the discriminant analysis. Last, select the **Separate-groups** box under the **Plots** area, which will produce separate-group scatterplots of the discriminant function values. The **Combined-groups** plot is by far the

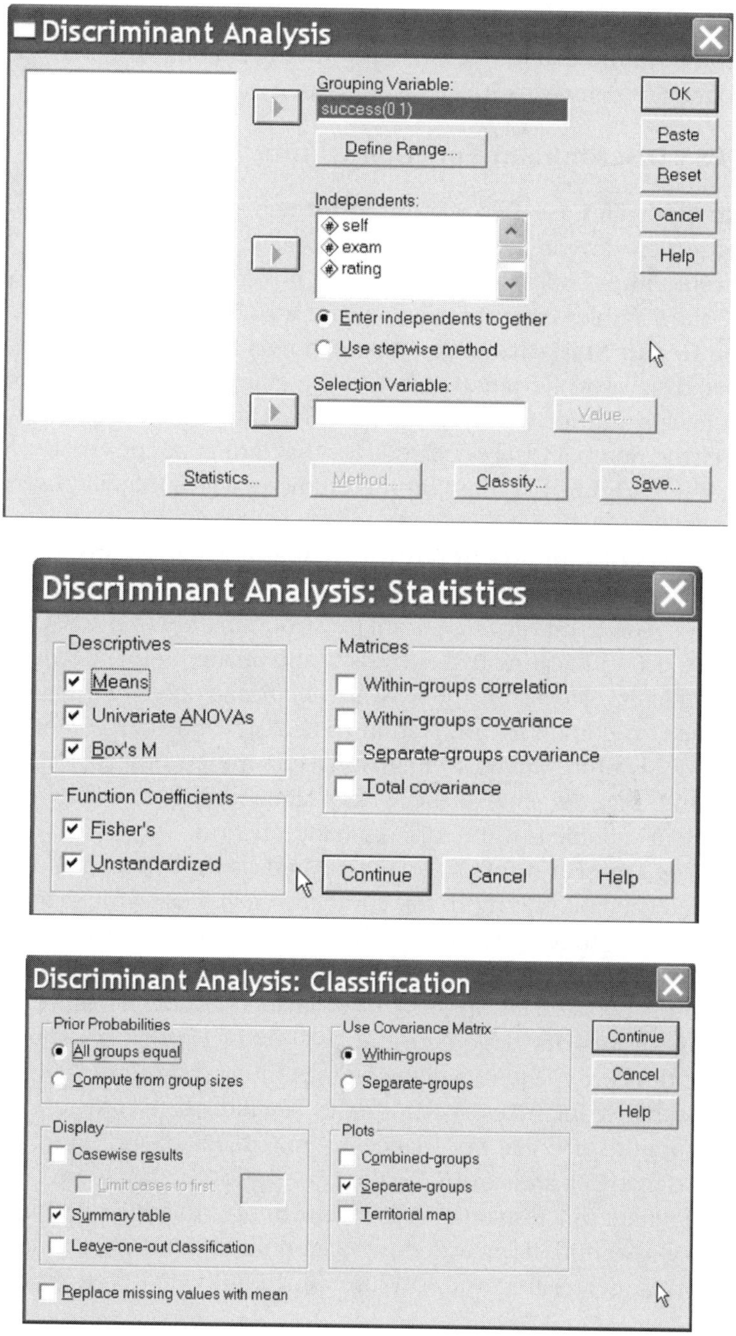

Figure 7b.1 The Discriminant Analysis Main Dialog Box and Its Statistics and Classification Dialog Boxes

most informative, but unfortunately, this choice was disabled by SPSS in the transition from the mainframe version to the personal computer version of the program (if you check it SPSS will ignore it).

The SPSS Discriminant Function Output

The **Analysis Case Processing Summary** table shown in Figure 7b.2 reports if there are any missing or out-of-range group codes (i.e., all the cases were either coded as "0" or "1") or missing discriminating variables (i.e., all the variables have at least one case with data).

The **Group Statistics** table presented next in Figure 7b.2 displays the means and standard deviations of the three independent variables for each of the groups and for the total sample. The **Unweighted** column simply indicates the number of observations for that independent variable for that group. The **Weighted** column, in this study, indicates that all observations are treated equally.

The **Tests of Equality of Group Means** shown in Figure 7b.3 informs us about any significant differences in means of the predictors between the two groups. The F tests are significant for self-evaluation ($p < .019$) and exam score ($p < .000$), indicating that successful and unsuccessful interns differ on these predictors. However, there is no significant difference between the two groups on committee evaluation ($p < .201$), and the researchers may consider in a future analysis eliminating committee evaluation from this model. Note that the smaller the Wilks's lambda, the more important that independent variable is to the discriminant function.

The **Log Determinants** table is presented also in Figure 7b.3. The larger the log determinant, the more the covariance matrices of the groups differ. The "Rank" column provides the number of independent variables (i.e., three in this study). Because discriminant analysis assumes homogeneity of covariance matrices between groups, the determinants should be relatively equal.

The **Test Results** table (see the last box of Figure 7b.3) reports the results of the Box's M test, which assesses the assumption of homogeneity of covariance matrices. Because the significance is greater than .05, the assumption of equal covariances is not rejected, indicating that the covariance matrices are similar for the two groups. It should be noted that the discriminant function analysis is robust to the violation of homogeneity of variance assumption, provided the data do not contain extreme outliers (i.e., z scores greater than the absolute value of 4).

Summary of Canonical Discriminant Functions

Figure 7b.4 presents the **Eigenvalues.** The larger the eigenvalue, the more of the variance of the two-group dependent variable is explained by the

Analysis Case Processing Summary

Unweighted Cases		N	Percent
Valid		50	100.0
Excluded	Missing or out-of-range group codes	0	.0
	At least one missing discriminating variable	0	.0
	Both missing or out-of-range group codes and at least one missing discriminating variable	0	.0
	Total	0	.0
Total		50	100.0

Group Statistics

Successful		Mean	Std. Deviation	Valid N (listwise)	
				Unweighted	Weighted
No	Self Evaluation	2.9200	.81240	25	25.000
	Exam Score	2.8782	.60132	25	25.000
	Committee Evaluation	2.6400	2.34307	25	25.000
Yes	Self Evaluation	3.4800	.82260	25	25.000
	Exam Score	3.5122	.42025	25	25.000
	Committee Evaluation	3.4800	2.23830	25	25.000
Total	Self Evaluation	3.2000	.85714	50	50.000
	Exam Score	3.1952	.60511	50	50.000
	Committee Evaluation	3.0600	2.30713	50	50.000

Figure 7b.2 Output Showing a Count of Cases in the Discriminant Analysis and the Descriptive Statistics for the Groups on the Independent Variables

discriminant function (linear combination of the independent variables). Because the dependent variable in this study has only two categories (successful internship or not successful internship), there is only one discriminant function. However, if there were more categories, the table would have presented multiple discriminant functions listed in descending order of importance. The second column lists the percentage of variance explained by each function. The third column is the cumulative percentage of variance explained. The last column shows the canonical correlation. The canonical correlation of .624 exceeds the criterion of .5 for a strong relationship. Squaring this value provides the percentage of variance explained in the dependent variable (about 39%).

Tests of Equality of Group Means

	Wilks's Lambda	F	df1	df2	Sig.
Self Evaluation	.891	5.865	1	48	.019
Exam Score	.720	18.675	1	48	.000
Committee Evaluation	.966	1.680	1	48	.201

Log Determinants

Successful	Rank	Log Determinant
No	3	.259
Yes	3	−.781
Pooled within-groups	3	−.105

The log determinants are relatively equal, indicating homogeneity of covariance matrices between the groups.

The ranks and natural logarithms of determinants printed are those of the group covariance matrices.

Test Results

Box's M		7.488
F	Approx.	1.163
	df1	6
	df2	16693.132
	Sig.	.323

This indicates equal covariance matrices of the predictors; thus, the assumption of equal covariance is met.

Tests null hypothesis of equal population covariance matrices.

Figure 7b.3   Output Showing the Tests of Equality of the Group Means, Log Determinants, and Test Results From the Discriminant Analysis

Below the **Eigenvalues** table, there is another output called the **Wilks's Lambda** table (see also Figure 7b.4). This table shows another **Wilks's Lambda,** which serves a purpose distinct from the Wilks's lambda in the ANOVA table discussed above. In this table, the Wilks's lambda tests the significance of the eigenvalue for each discriminant function. In this example, there is only one function, and it is significant.

The **Standardized Canonical Discriminant Function Coefficients** table in Figure 7b.5 reports the weights that are analogous to the beta weights (i.e., the standardized weights) in multiple regression, indicating the relative importance of the independent variable in predicting successful or nonsuccessful internship. From this, we note that exam score contributes more to the prediction than self-evaluation, which in turn predicts more than committee evaluation.

Eigenvalues

Function	Eigenvalue	% of Variance	Cumulative %	Canonical Correlation
1	.638[a]	100.0	100.0	.624

> The square canonical correlation (.3898) is the amount of variance accounted for by the discriminant function.

a. First 1 canonical discriminant functions were used in the analysis.

Wilks's Lambda

Test of Function(s)	Wilks's Lambda	Chi square	df	Sig.
1	.611	22.935	3	.000

Figure 7b.4   Eigenvalue Output and Test of the Significance of the Discriminant Function

The **Structure Matrix** shown next in Figure 7b.5 presents the simple (zero-order) correlation of each variable with the discriminant function(s). Recall that there is only one discriminant function in this study. However, if there were more categories in the dependent variable, then there are more discriminant functions (i.e., 1 less than the number of categories or the number of predictors, whichever is less). In that case, there will be additional columns in the table, one for each function. These correlations aid the researcher in labeling the discriminant function(s).

The **Canonical Discriminant Function Coefficients** table (see also Figure 7b.5) contains the unstandardized discriminant function coefficients. These coefficients (or weights) are used in the same way as the unstandardized b coefficients in multiple regression. These unstandardized coefficients can be multiplied by the scores obtained on those corresponding predictors to produce an equation that can predict new cases into the appropriate group.

The **Functions at Group Centroids** table shown in Figure 7b.6 displays the means for the groups. These means are in standardized (z score) form and are based on the variate—that is, the weighted linear composite making up the discriminant function. They can be used to establish a cutting point for classifying cases. If the two groups are of equal size, the best cutting point is halfway between the values of the functions at group centroids (i.e., the average). If the groups are unequal in size, the appropriate cutting point is the weighted average of the two values. Cases with scores on or above the cutting point are classified as "successful with internship," and those cases with scores below the cutting point are assigned as "unsuccessful." SPSS calculates this classification automatically.

**Standardized Canonical
Discriminant Function Coefficients**

	Function
	1
Self Evaluation	.575
Exam Score	.895
Committee Evaluation	.210

These are analogous
to multiple regression
beta weights.

Structure Matrix

	Function
	1
Exam Score	.781
Self Evaluation	.438
Committee Evaluation	.234

Structure coefficients
represent the
correlation between
the variable and the
discriminant function.

Pooled within-groups correlations between discriminating variables and standardized canonical
discriminant functions.
Variables ordered by absolute size of correlation within function.

**Canonical Discriminant
Function Coefficients**

	Function
	1
Self Evaluation	.703
Exam Score	1.725
Committee Evaluation	.092
(Constant)	−8.043

These are analogous
to multiple regression
b weights.

Unstandardized coefficients

Figure 7b.5 Output Showing the Standardized Coefficients, the Structure
Coefficients, and the Unstandardized Coefficients for Variables in the
Discriminant Function

Functions at Group Centroids

	Function
Successful	1
No	−.782
Yes	.782

> Centroids are group averages of the variate in *z*-score form. Note the relative separation between the groups.

Unstandardized canonical discriminant functions evaluated at group means

Classification Function Coefficients

	Successful	
	No	Yes
Self Evaluation	5.657	6.758
Exam Score	12.391	15.090
Committee Evaluation	.401	.544
(Constant)	−27.313	−39.899

Fisher's linear discriminant functions

Figure 7b.6 The Group Centroids and Classification Function Coefficients

Classification Statistics

The **Classification Function Coefficients** table (see also Figure 7b.6) displays the two sets of unstandardized discriminant coefficients (one for each group). These coefficients are multiplied by the obtained score of a participant, which will then predict the group for a case. SPSS calculates this classification automatically.

The **Separate-groups Plots** are shown in Figure 7b.7. They illustrate the number of cases of the standardized scores for each group. We have lined up the zero points on the X axis ($z = 0$) using a dashed vertical line. As can be seen, the two distributions are somewhat displaced from each other, suggesting that they are discriminable.

The **Classification Results** table presented in Figure 7b.8 demonstrates how well the discriminant function was able to classify the cases for each group of the dependent variable. This discriminant function correctly classified 82% of all the cases. The discriminant function was slightly better at predicting the successful interns (88%) than predicting the nonsuccessful interns (76%). On the basis of chance alone, we would predict membership

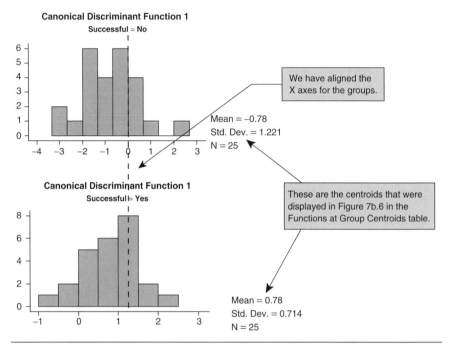

Figure 7b.7   The Separate-Groups Plots for the Discriminant Analysis

Classification Results[a]

		Successful	Predicted Group Membership		Total
			No	Yes	
Original	Count	No	19	6	25
		Yes	3	22	25
	%	No	76.0	24.0	100.0
		Yes	12.0	88.0	100.0

a. 82.0% of original grouped cases correctly classified.

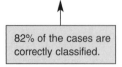

Figure 7b.8   Classification Table From the Discriminant Analysis

in one of two groups to be no better than 50%. The obtained classification accuracy is significantly better than that at 82%, indicating a valid model.

The means of this discriminant function are consistent with this interpretation. The successful interns ($M = .78$) achieved statistically significantly greater scores than did nonsuccessful interns ($M = -.78$). The prediction of internship performance (successful or nonsuccessful) was impressive with an overall classification rate of 82%. There was a slightly greater success rate for the successful interns (88%) than for nonsuccessful interns (76%).

Results

A simultaneous discriminant analysis was conducted to determine whether the three predictors (a) pre-self-evaluation, (b) preliminary clinical examination, and (c) initial committee evaluation could predict internship performance. The overall Wilks's lambda was significant— $\Lambda = .61$, $\chi^2 (3, N = 50) = 22.93$, $p < .001$—indicating that the overall predictors differentiated between the two group internship performance groups (successful and nonsuccessful).

Table 7b.1 presents the within-groups correlations between the predictors and the discriminant function as well as the standardized weights. Based on these coefficients, the preliminary examination score demonstrated the strongest relationship with the discriminant function, whereas self-evaluation demonstrated a moderate relationship, and committee evaluation showed the weakest relationship. This discriminant function was labeled clinical internship aptitude.

Table 7b.1 The Standardized Coefficients and Correlations of Predictor Variables of the Discriminant Function

Predictors	Correlation Coefficients	Standardized Coefficients
Exam score	.78	.90
Self-evaluation	.44	.57
Committee evaluation	.23	.21

7B Exercises

Successful Employment

The following variables were used to predict successful employment (coded 1 = yes, and 0 = no) for patients undergoing rehabilitation at a state agency.

- ▶ Age
- ▶ Years of education
- ▶ Years of previous employment

Using the SPSS data file for Chapter 7B (located on the Web-based study site—http://www.sagepub.com/amrStudy), conduct a discriminant function analysis using the above variables as predictors.

1. Report and interpret the canonical correlation.

2. Are there statistically significant differences between the groups?

3. Report and interpret the Wilks's lambda.

4. Examine the structure matrix. Do all the predictors correlate practically on discriminant function (i.e., > .3)?

5. Report the group centroids.

6. What is the overall classification statistic?

7. Write a results section for this study.

Univariate Comparisons of Means

The Strategy of Comparing Means

In most experimental or quasi-experimental (Cook & Campbell, 1979) studies, and even in many archival research programs, researchers will be faced with participants (cases) measured under two or more different conditions. In such situations, we are typically interested in whether the average performance under one condition differs significantly from that of another condition in the study. Unfortunately, simply looking at the means for each condition will not be particularly informative because in almost all instances, these means will be numerically different. The issue facing researchers is whether the observed mean differences are statistically significant—that is, whether the differences are likely to recur or to be reliable if the study was to be repeatedly done. Statistically, we are asking if it is likely that the two or more conditions represent different populations. To answer this question of statistical significance, it is necessary to subject the data to some statistical treatment.

Your first statistics course or two covered the topics of *t* test and ANOVA, the most commonly used procedures to compare group means. These procedures almost certainly involved analyzing only a single dependent variable and so qualified as *univariate* (one dependent variable) analyses. We use this chapter to briefly review the conceptual base for these univariate procedures before launching into three chapters that address some of their multivariate counterparts.

Measurement Error

The fundamental principle involved in comparing means is this: Any observed mean differences must be evaluated in the context of how much measurement error is present in the research. For example, suppose that we were in the admittedly impossible scenario where we could measure attitude toward life with absolute precision (absolutely no error). Based on such measurement, further suppose that one group of hospitalized patients had a higher attitude score than another. We could then assert without any statistical treatment of the data that the one group was significantly more positive in its outlook than the other. These assertions would be justified because any observed difference in attitude must represent an empirical truth because our measurement operation was entirely error-free.

In reality, such a situation as described above could never occur because measurement always involves some sort of error. By this, of course, we do not mean that researchers are constantly making mistakes (although they can err from time to time). The error to which we are referring emanates from imprecision in elements such as the instruments we use to make the measurements; the fallacy of humans as respondents and as observers; the presence of other cognitive and motor activities in the life of the respondents; and of biological, social, environmental, and cultural processes in the respondents that we do not ordinarily measure or may not even be aware of. This error is always present in any research study. One of the primary goals in teaching students about methodology and design is the hope that they can recognize such error in the research of others and minimize this measurement error in their own research.

The Ratio of Mean Difference to Measurement Error

Measurement Error Is Our Yardstick

The way in which we evaluate the difference between two means is to use an estimate of measurement error as a yardstick in assessing how large the mean difference should be interpreted as being. That is, a given difference between the mean of one condition and the mean of another in and of itself has little meaning. How reliable that difference is—whether it is a "true" difference and indicating that it is likely to reappear most of the time if we take the measurements again, or whether it is just chance that one group scored higher than the other—is assessed with respect to the estimated magnitude of the error surrounding those measurements.

Assume for the sake of an example that we have two groups of respondents to an attitude-toward-life survey. Higher numbers on the 5-point response scale indicate a more positive attitude. Group A averaged 3.5 and Group B averaged 4.0. Both groups are on the positive side of the scale, but Group B has responded with a higher mean rating. The difference is .5 scale points.

Is B's attitude significantly more positive than A's? If there is absolutely no measurement error, then the answer is, as we explained earlier, "yes." If there is measurement error, then the answer depends on the degree to which error is present. Let's quantify such error as plus or minus some amount, much as the media report sampling error based on random probability samples for political polls.

So we have groups with means of 3.5 and 4.0. If the mean of each of the groups could have been ±.1 different from what we observed, then the mean of A could have been between 3.4 and 3.6 and the mean of B could have been between 3.9 and 4.1. Even with this degree of measurement error, we can see that the possible ranges of the two means do not overlap. We can therefore be reasonably confident that the two groups are reliably or significantly different (that the two samples represent different populations).

Now suppose that the mean of each of the groups could have been ±.8 different from what we observed. The mean of A could now be between 2.7 and 4.3 and the mean of B could now be between 3.2 and 4.8. Now the potential ranges of the two means overlap quite a bit, and it is unlikely that they differ significantly. Here, the two samples more likely represent the very same population.

The *t* and *F* Tests

What we have conceptually done in the previous section to evaluate the magnitude of the mean difference is as follows. We have compared the mean difference with an estimate of error by noting the general value of their ratio. Consider the two examples we discussed.

The mean difference was always .5 (4.0 − 3.5 = .5). In the first example, the error was relatively small (±.1), and the ratio of .5 to .1 computed to a value of 5 (which is a fairly large ratio in this context). The ratio indicates that the mean difference is 5 times larger than the error contained in the measurement procedures. Thus, within the framework of this degree of error, a mean difference of .5 would be judged as a relatively large magnitude.

In the second example, the error was much greater (±.8), and the ratio of .5 to .8 resulted in a value less than 1 (which is a fairly small ratio in this context). Here, the ratio indicates that the magnitude of measurement error exceeds the difference between the two mean values. Thus, within the framework of this latter degree of error, the same mean difference of .5 would be judged in this instance as a relatively small magnitude.

$$t = \frac{\text{Mean Difference}}{\text{Standard Error of Mean Difference}}$$

Figure 8a.1 Magnitude of Mean Difference in the Context of the Degree of Measurement Error

On the assumption that we can obtain values for the mean difference and for an estimate of the degree of error, the general rule is as follows: *Larger values of the ratio (mean difference/estimate of error) suggest the greater likelihood that the mean difference is statistically significant.*

What we have just described, the idea of dividing the mean difference by an estimate of error, is actually known to you in a more formalized format. In that more formalized format, the mean difference is obtained by subtracting one mean from the other, and the estimated degree of error is statistically identified as the *standard error of the difference between means.* The ratio, presented in Figure 8a.1, is known as *t* (as in *t* test).

As you may recall from a prior statistics course, the standard error of the difference between means involves theoretically drawing from your population a very large number of sets of random scores for your two samples, computing their mean differences, and generating a frequency distribution of these differences. The standard deviation of this sampling distribution is the standard error of mean differences. It is used as the denominator of the *t* computation.

A *t* test can be used only in situations where the independent variable (the variable on which the conditions are distinguished, such as experimental and control) has two levels—for example, when we are comparing the means of two groups of participants in a study. A one-way ANOVA, which can accommodate any number of levels of the independent variable, is used to generate an *F* ratio. Although the terminology differs somewhat, the conceptual underpinnings of the *t* test and the ANOVA are the same. They are both computed as the ratio of the variability (or differences) of sample means to an estimate of error variance. In fact, in the two-group case, the statistics are essentially variants of each other ($t^2 = F$ or $\sqrt{F} = t$).

Use of *t* and *F*

With only one independent variable having two levels, it is possible to use either a *t* test or one-way ANOVA to compare the means. If the conditions are independent (uncorrelated), then we would use either an independent groups *t* test or a one-way between-subjects ANOVA. If the conditions were correlated (e.g., before-after, a person's score under one condition and his or her score under a second condition), then we would use either a *t* test for correlated scores or a one-way within-subjects (repeated measures) ANOVA. The choice between the *t* test and an ANOVA here reflects the personal preference of the researchers. Once the research design contains three or more groups, no real choice remains. Under this circumstance, researchers must use the ANOVA rather than the *t* test to analyze their results.

One-Way Designs: Effects of One Independent Variable

The designs that we describe here are called experimental designs because the independent variable is often manipulated by or under some degree of control of the researchers. Under these circumstances, researchers ordinarily preselect a small set of conditions that will serve as the levels of their independent variable rather than allow the variable to take on an almost continuous range of values as it does in correlation research. The choice of which levels to use in a particular study is therefore a very important issue and should be decided based on the prevailing theories and the existent research on the topic of interest.

A one-way design derives its name from the fact that there is only one independent variable in the analysis. This variable can have as many levels as is needed to address the question under study or the hypothesis being tested. The purpose of the one-way design is to test for differences between two or three or more levels of the independent variable. These levels define the different groups in a between-subjects design or the different conditions in a within-subjects design.

Researchers must be able to determine which of these designs is being or should be used in a given research study. In the context of describing these designs, we therefore also present some guidelines to help you recognize them in the research literature and to appropriately design your own research.

Between-Subjects Designs

In a between-subjects design, different individuals are assigned to different groups (levels of the independent variable). For example, we might want to compare clients with different diagnoses to see if they differ on a measure of global assessment of functioning (GAF). If the two diagnoses were obsessive-compulsive and depression, then we would have two groups composed

Table 8a.1 ANOVA Summary Table for a One-Way Between-Subjects Design, With Diagnosis as the Independent Variable

Source	Degrees of Freedom	Sum of Squares	Mean Squares	F Ratio
Between Ss	39			
Diagnosis	1			
Error[b]	38			
Total	39			

of different individuals—one group with one diagnosis and another group with the other diagnosis. We would thus have a between-subjects design. The independent variable would be diagnosis (which would have two levels), and the dependent variable would be the measured GAF score.

The data could be analyzed by using either a t test for independent groups (because the independent variable has only two levels) or a one-way between-subjects ANOVA. We will focus on the latter analysis here. The structure of the ANOVA summary table for this design is shown in Table 8a.1. In general, in between-subjects designs, all the variance we have is between-subjects variance and is thus equal to the total variance. In a one-way design, we partition the between-subjects variance into a source representing the independent variable (diagnosis in this study) and unaccounted-for variance within each group that is treated as error variance. We have labeled the error variance with a "b" subscript to reinforce the idea that it is part of the between-subjects variance. There is no within-subjects variance in this study.

Assume that each group in our example contained 20 participants, each of whom was assessed once on the GAF measure. With 40 observations in total, the total degrees of freedom is 39 ($N - 1$), the degrees of freedom associated with diagnosis is 1 (number of levels – 1), and the degrees of freedom for the error term is 38 (the residual). In a between-subjects design, all the variance is between-subjects variance. Thus, the between-subjects source of variance is equal to the total. The degrees of freedom for between subjects is therefore also 39 (number of subjects – 1). Mean squares are computed by dividing the sum of squares for each source of variance by its corresponding degrees of freedom. The F ratio for diagnosis is computed by dividing mean square$_{diagnosis}$ by mean square$_{error\ b}$.

Within-Subjects Designs

In a within-subjects design, all the participants are exposed to each and every condition in the study. For example, we might want to measure the speed of visual search (e.g., locating an object in a complex picture) under different mood conditions (e.g., happy, sad, neutral). In this example, we decide to test the participants on three separate days. On the first day for each person, we randomly decide which mood to instill that day and then test for visual search. On the next day for each person, we randomly decide which of the two remaining moods to induce and test again for visual search. On the third day for each person, we induce the third mood and test for visual search.

This latter design is a within-subjects design. We know this because each person was tested under all three mood conditions. The independent variable here is mood, which has the three levels of happy, sad, and neutral. The dependent variable is the time it took to search for the target.

The structure of the ANOVA summary table for this design is presented in Table 8a.2. In any within-subjects design, the total variance is able to be partitioned into the two global sources of between-subjects variance and within-subjects variance. In within-subjects designs, the only source of between-subjects variance is having multiple participants; it is not further subdividable.

In within-subject designs, the within-subjects variance is partitionable into effects concerned with the independent variables and unaccounted-for or error variance. In a one-way design—we have only one independent variable—the within-subjects variance is composed of the effect of the independent variable and error variance. Because the error variance is part of the within-subjects variance, we have used the letter "w" as a subscript in its designation.

We will assume that there are 15 participants in the study, thus yielding 14 degrees of freedom for the between-subjects source of variance (number of participants – 1). Each participant is measured three times. There is thus a total of 45 observations and therefore total degrees of freedom is equal to 44 (number of observations – 1). Degrees of freedom for the within-subjects

Table 8a.2   ANOVA Summary Table for a One-Way Within-Subjects Design, With Mood as the Independent Variable

Source	Degrees of Freedom	Sum of Squares	Mean Squares	F Ratio
Between Ss	14			
Within Ss	30			
Mood	2			
Error$_w$	28			
Total	44			

source of variance can be taken as a residual ($df_{total} - df_{between\ subjects}$ = 44 – 14 = 30). Given that there are 30 degrees of freedom for within subjects and given that 2 of them (number of levels – 1) are associated with mood, the remaining 28 degrees of freedom must be associated with error$_w$.

The F ratio in which we are primarily interested is the one testing the significance of the independent variable—mood in this case. It is calculated by dividing mean square$_{mood}$ by mean square$_{error\ w}$. If it is significant, we would want to perform a simple effects analysis such as a Tukey test to determine under which moods the participants searched significantly faster and slower.

As a second example of a within-subjects design, we might want to assess the success of a new therapeutic treatment program on mental health. We decide to use a questionnaire asking clients to check all symptoms that apply to them as our measure of mental health. The questionnaire is administered prior to the start of treatment, again at the completion of treatment, and a third time 6 months later. The independent variable is the time of measurement; it has three levels: pretest, posttest, and follow-up. The dependent variable is the number of symptoms endorsed by clients.

The structure of the ANOVA summary table for this design is presented in Table 8a.3. Assume that we have 55 clients who complete our program and participate in the follow-up. We thus have 54 degrees of freedom for between-subjects and 164 degrees of freedom for total variance (55 clients × 3 measures = 165 observations – 1). That leaves 110 degrees of freedom for within subjects (164 for total – 54 for between subjects). Time of measurement uses 2 degrees of freedom, and the remaining 108 degrees of freedom must be associated with error$_w$. The F ratio of interest here is the one associated with time. It is computed by dividing mean square$_{time}$ by mean square$_{error\ w}$.

Table 8a.3 ANOVA Summary Table for a One-Way Within-Subjects Design, With Time of Measurement as the Independent Variable

Source	Degrees of Freedom	Sum of Squares	Mean Squares	F Ratio
Between Ss	54			
Within Ss	110			
Time	2			
Error$_w$	108			
Total	164			

Post Hoc Comparisons, Paired Comparisons

If the *F* ratio for the independent variable is significant, then we are relatively confident that there is a performance difference under the different levels of the independent variable. With only two groups in an analysis, we would immediately know that our two levels are significantly different. In our between-subjects design example above, for example, we would therefore be able to assert that the obsessive-compulsive clients reported higher (or lower) GAF scores than the depressed clients.

If there were three or more levels of the independent variable, then a statistically significant *F* ratio tells us only that there is a relationship between the dependent and independent variable. This relationship essentially says that the scores (values on the dependent variable) are not randomly distributed across the groups (the different codes for levels of the independent variable). That is important to know, but it does not tell us directly which group means actually differ significantly from which others.

To determine which groups differ from which, we must perform a follow-up analysis to the one-way ANOVA. Such an analysis is known as *post hoc comparisons, pairwise comparisons,* or *simultaneous test procedure* (Klockars & Sax, 1986). These analyses assess mean differences between all combinations of pairs of groups while controlling the probability level to avoid alpha inflation. Among the more popular of these comparison procedures are the Duncan, least significant difference, Newman-Keuls, Scheffé, Tukey's honestly significant difference, and Tukey's b procedures. SPSS provides close to two dozen such tests from which to choose. These tests are reviewed in Chapter 10B.

These tests are considered to differ on the degree of stringency that they employ; greater stringency translates to being somewhat less likely to show a significant difference between the means. Duncan's range test, for example, is one of the least stringent and the Scheffé is one of the more stringent. Most researchers have their own favorite post hoc test and use it consistently. In any case, you should decide which test you will use in advance of the data analysis. Do not run all of them and report the one that gave you the most favorable results.

Trend Analysis

In addition to these multiple comparisons tests, there is another analysis that we could perform if the levels of the independent variable approximated at least an interval level of measurement. This is a trend analysis. Such an analysis would be able to assess, at least indirectly, the general shape of the function (of groups represented on the *X* axis with the dependent variable represented on the Y axis). It assumes that the codes used for the independent variable are spaced along the X axis according to interval scale rules. The group means are then plotted to yield a function of a particular shape. A trend analysis basically analyzes the shape of the function.

In a one-way analysis that does not include a trend analysis, you obtain one sum of squares and one F ratio for the effect. A trend analysis partitions this overall effect of the independent variable into linear, quadratic, cubic, and other trends. The number of partitions you are able to ask for is tied to the number of groups. With only two groups, you have only two data points (the two means) and so have only one possible function—a straight line or linear function. No partition is possible. With three groups (three means), you have the possibility of both a linear and a quadratic function and can therefore partition the effect into these two trends. With four groups, you can partition the effect into a linear, a quadratic, and a cubic trend. In general, you have one fewer trend in the partition than you have means. Most researchers, if they test for trends at all, do not push beyond a cubic trend.

Two-Way Factorial Designs: Two Main Effects and One Two-Way Interaction

A factorial combination of two independent variables (a two-way factorial design) satisfies the condition that all combinations of their levels are represented in the design. The simplest factorial design is one with each variable represented by only two levels (it takes at least two levels to have any variance of an independent variable). This is called a 2×2 (two "by" two) design in which the two levels of one variable are factorially combined with the two levels of the other. Such a combination results in the four conditions shown in the cells of Figure 8a.2. Specifically, the four cells are a_1b_1, a_1b_2, a_2b_1, and a_2b_2.

Main Effects

A *main effect* involves comparing the means of the various levels of an independent variable. This is what we did for the one-way designs just discussed. We did not call it a main effect in that section because there was only one effect of interest, and there was little to gain in classifying it. But in connection with designs encompassing more than one independent variable, we regularly talk about main effects.

Each independent variable in a factorial design is associated with its own main effect. The ANOVA that we perform allows us to evaluate the significance of each of them. Because there are two independent variables in a two-way design, two main effects are evaluated.

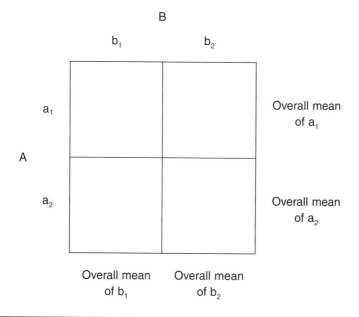

Figure 8a.2 Conditions Represented in a 2 × 2 Factorial Design

We have shown the comparisons associated with the main effects in Figure 8a.2. The main effect of A involves a comparison of the overall mean of a_1 and the overall mean of a_2. This comparison is based on the combined scores across the B variable (b_1 and b_2 are combined for each level of A). This is shown in Figure 8a.2 in the right margin of each row. The statistical question addressed by the ANOVA is whether performance on a_1 (overall) differs on average from performance on a_2 (overall). The focus is entirely on A.

An analogous situation concerns the main effect of B. Here, we focus on the column composites, comparing b_1 overall with b_2 overall. This comparison takes place across all levels of A.

Interaction Effect

In addition to the two main effects, a two-way design allows us to evaluate the *interaction* of the two independent variables. The A × B (A "by" B) interaction reflects the effects associated with the various combinations of the independent variables. It is possible, for example, that the combination a_2b_2 produces quite different effects from any of the other three combinations. Such an outcome would be indicated by a significant interaction effect. Researchers using factorial designs are very often particularly interested in interaction effects. We will discuss this concept in detail later in the chapter.

Three Variations of Factorial Designs

The Number of Variables

Factorial designs call for all the combinations of the levels of the independent variables to be represented by data. Although it is theoretically possible to work with a large number of variables, the complexity of the design increases considerably every time an additional independent variable is added. Keeping each variable to two levels for the sake of illustrating this, a two-way factorial (two independent variables) contains 2×2 or 4 different conditions (combinations), a three-way (three independent variables) contains $2 \times 2 \times 2$ or 8 different conditions, a four-way (four independent variables) contains $2 \times 2 \times 2 \times 2$ or 16 different conditions, a five-way (five independent variables) contains $2 \times 2 \times 2 \times 2 \times 2$ or 32 different conditions, and so on.

In the research literature, the most common factorials are two-way and three-way designs. We will focus here on two-way designs to minimize the complexity of our explication. Analogous to the variations we described for one-way designs, two-way designs can contain between-subjects and within-subjects independent variables. There are three possible combinations, and each represents a different design: between-subjects, within-subjects, and simple mixed designs. We briefly review these three designs here.

Between-Subjects Designs

A between-subjects design requires that all (both in the case of two-way designs) the independent variables are between-subjects variables. What this effectively means is that different individuals are involved in each of the combinations or cells in the design. Each participant contributes only a single score to the overall analysis, representing one combination of the independent variables.

The partitioning of the total variance is analogous to the one-way design, but instead of just one effect, we now have three effects to examine: two main effects (one for each independent variable) and the interaction of the two independent variables. We show this in the general summary table in Table 8a.4.

The degrees of freedom for between subjects is 1 less than the number of participants in the study. Because each person contributes only one score or observation to the analysis, the df_{total} in a between-subjects design is the same as that for the between-subjects source of variance. The degrees of freedom associated with each main effect is computed by subtracting 1 from the number of levels that independent variable has. We compute the degrees of freedom for the interaction by simply multiplying the degrees of freedom for each independent variable involved in it. Degrees of freedom for the error term is taken as the residual.

Table 8a.4   ANOVA Summary Table for a Two-Way Between-Subjects Design, With A and B Representing Between-Subjects Independent Variables

Source	Degrees of Freedom	Sum of Squares	Mean Squares	F Ratio
Between Ss	No. of subjects − 1			
A	No. of levels of A − 1			
B	No. of levels of B − 1			
A × B	$df_A \times df_B$			
Error$_b$	Residual			
Total	No. of observations − 1			

Having three effects to examine means that we are dealing with three *F* ratios, one each for the two main effects and a third for the interaction. Each is computed by dividing its mean square by the error mean square. Thus, the *F* ratio for A is found by dividing mean square$_A$ by mean square$_{error\,b}$, the *F* ratio for B is found by dividing mean square$_B$ by mean square$_{error\,b}$, and the *F* ratio for the A × B interaction is found by dividing mean square$_{A \times B}$ by mean square$_{error\,b}$.

Assuming that we have the same sample size in each cell, these three effects are completely independent of each other. Thus, obtaining a significant *F* ratio for one of them does not affect the potential significance of the other two. Any combination of significance and nonsignificance can be obtained—only the actual data determine the outcome of the analysis.

Within-Subjects Designs

A within-subjects design requires that all (both in the case of a two-way design) the independent variables are within-subjects variables. What this effectively means is that the very same individuals contribute data in each of the combinations or cells in the design. That is, each participant contributes to the overall analysis as many scores as there are cells in the design.

In a within-subjects design, participants are "held constant" across conditions. Because participants essentially act as their own controls, the design is a powerful one. But one must also assume that there are no carryover effects from individuals having been exposed to prior conditions in the design, and this stipulation limits the number and kind of applications for which this design can be used.

The partitioning of the variance of a two-way within-subjects design is presented in Table 8a.5. It represents an expansion of the summary table for a one-way within-subjects design. Again here, the only source of between-subjects variance is due to different participants in the study. The

Table 8a.5 ANOVA Summary Table for a Two-Way Within-Subjects Design, With A and B Representing Within-Subjects Independent Variables

Source	Degrees of Freedom	Sum of Squares	Mean Squares	F Ratio
Between Ss	No. of subjects − 1			
Within Ss	Residual			
A	No. levels of A − 1			
B	No. levels of B − 1			
A × B	$df_A \times df_B$			
Error$_w$	Residual			
Total	No. of observations − 1			

within-subjects source of variance, however, is partitionable into the three effects of interest (the two main effects and the interaction) and the error term. Degrees of freedom for within subjects is computed as $df_{total} - df_{between\ subjects}$. Furthermore, $df_{error\ w}$ is computed as $df_{within\ subjects} - df_A - df_B - df_{A \times B}$. The F ratios for each effect are found by dividing the respective mean square by mean square$_{error\ w}$.

Simple Mixed Designs

A simple mixed design applies precisely to a two-way design. In such a design one of the independent variables (e.g., A) must be a within-subjects variable and the other (e.g., B) must be a between-subjects variable. This is an especially useful design in that it allows us to test different groups of people (e.g., b_1 and b_2) under different conditions (e.g., a_1 and a_2) or to track the different groups over time.

A simple mixed design is limited to two independent variables. Designs containing three or more independent variables with one or more within-subjects variables and one or more between-subjects variables are known as *complex mixed designs.*

Table 8a.6 shows the partitioning of a simple mixed design in which A is a within-subjects variable and B is a between-subjects variable. It is essentially a melding of the one-way between-subjects and the one-way within-subjects designs.

Compared with the previous two designs, the mixed design partitions the variance somewhat more finely. The total variance is first partitioned into between-subjects and within-subjects variance. Thus, $df_{within\ subjects}$ can be obtained by subtracting $df_{between\ subjects}$ from df_{total}.

Each of these two first partitions can itself be further subdivided. Between-subjects variance can be partly explained by variance attributable

Table 8a.6 ANOVA Summary Table for a Simple Mixed Design, With A as a Within-Subjects Variable and B as a Between-Subjects Variable

Source	Degrees of Freedom	Sum of Squares	Mean Squares	F Ratio
Between Ss	No. of subjects − 1			
B	No. of levels of B − 1			
Error$_b$	Residual			
Within Ss	Residual			
A	No. of levels of A − 1			
A × B	$df_A \times df_B$			
Error$_w$	Residual			
Total	No. of observations − 1			

to the main effect of B—that is, attributable to the fact that different participants are exposed to different levels of the B variable. The remaining portion of B's variance is not explained; that is represented by error$_b$. Analogously, within-subjects variance is partitionable into variance due to the main effect of A, the A × B interaction, and error$_w$.

This design allows for something that no design thus far discussed has been able to do. This simple mixed design permits researchers to partition the error variance. Some error variance is due to differences between the participants and is captured by the error$_b$ term. Other variance represents differential individual reactions of the participants to the same experimental conditions and is captured by the error$_w$ term.

The Universals Across Designs

The between-subjects, within-subjects, and mixed designs that we have discussed are based on different procedures for administering the treatment conditions. They also partition the total variance quite differently. Despite these critically important differences, there are two general domains of similarity in these designs.

The first general domain of similarity shared by these designs is that because they are all two-way designs, the same three effects of interest are evaluated. Specifically, there is the main effect of A, the main effect of B, and the A × B interaction. This is true because with only two independent variables in the design, there can be only two main effects and there can be only one interaction.

The second general domain of similarity shared by these designs is that the main effects and the interaction, if significant, are interpreted in the same general manner. In the case of a 2 × 2 design, for example, if the main effect of A is significant, we know that a_1 differs significantly from a_2 in the direction shown by the actual means. This is true regardless of whether A is a between- or a within-subjects variable; it holds because there are only two levels of A, and a significant main effect tells us that the means for these two levels are significantly different.

Furthermore, if there are three or more levels of A, then a significant main effect tells us that there is probably a significant difference between some levels of A. We would then need to perform a post hoc analysis such as a Tukey test to identify where the differences actually lie. This, too, holds regardless of whether A is a between- or a within-subjects variable.

In an analogous fashion, interactions are interpreted in the way driven by the data regardless of whether the two variables are both between-subjects variables, within-subjects variables, or one of each. For all these, one would perform post-ANOVA tests, called *tests of simple effects,* to determine which means were significantly different from which other means. In another section of this chapter, we will briefly discuss some examples of interactions and main effects and in the context of a significant interaction talk about tests of simple effects.

Strength of Effect

Statistical Significance Differs From Strength of Effect

In the discussion of Pearson correlation in Chapter 4A we distinguished between statistical significance and strength of relationship. Statistical significance relates to the likelihood of obtaining a particular statistical outcome (e.g., a Pearson r or an F ratio of a given value) by chance given that there is no true relationship in the population. Strength of effect indexes the amount of dependent variable variance accounted for by the independent variable(s). It is very important to differentiate between these concepts. We will first review some material on significance testing and then broach the issue of strength of effect so that we may distinguish it from significance testing.

Significance Testing

The F ratio in the ANOVA procedure is used to test the significance of the effect to which it is tied, for example, a main effect or an interaction. And just as is true for any such statistic, if it is significant at the .05 alpha level, we are willing to reject the null hypothesis and entertain the notion with 95% confidence that the observed mean differences are not likely due to chance. Thus, if you see the following in a journal article

$$F(2, 45) = 5.27, p < .05$$

you can interpret it to mean that the obtained F ratio of 5.27 or some greater value based on 2 and 45 degrees of freedom would occur by chance less than 5% of the time when the null hypothesis was true or, for short, that the F ratio is statistically significant at the alpha level of .05.

Values of F that occur more rarely than 5.27 if the null hypothesis is true (i.e., larger values) should not be thought of as either "more significant" or as representing a "stronger" effect. Statistical significance is a determination made by researchers based on whether or not a particular result has met or surpassed the alpha level that they had established at the start of the research. That is, a result either meets or does not meet the already established alpha level. Furthermore, the fact that an F ratio is considered by the researchers to have reached the level of statistical significance means that more than zero percent of the variance is explained; it does not necessarily mean that "a lot" of the variance was explained (it does not mean that the effect is "strong"). This is consistent with what we have already discussed in relation to bivariate correlation: Accounting for a statistically significant amount of the variance does not directly tell us the proportion of variance that the effect has explained. Strength of relationship indexes the degree of shared or explained variance that two or more variables have in common. The squared Pearson r is an example of such an index, as is the squared multiple correlation (R^2) in the context of multiple regression.

Commonality of Multiple Regression and ANOVA

As you may already know, the mathematics underlying the computation of multiple regression are also used to calculate the outcome of an ANOVA. Both are surface manifestations of the general linear model. The differences between regression and ANOVA is in the form of the output and not the underlying analysis. Keppel and Zedeck (1989) express the relationship between the two procedures very clearly:

There are many myths about data analysis and its relationship to research. Of particular concern for this book are several myths associated with the differences between analysis of variance (ANOVA) and multiple regression and correlation (MRC). . . . We could easily dispel these myths by showing the equivalence of ANOVA and MRC by algebraic procedures. Both techniques are based on general linear models in which the basic observations (the raw data describing an event) can be decomposed into effects and error components. In fact, it is easy to demonstrate that ANOVA is a special case of MRC. (pp. 6–7)

Thus, at some basic level, the multiple regression and ANOVA procedures are essentially the same. Given that they are comparable, it then stands to reason that the R^2 obtained in a multiple regression analysis must also be available in some form in ANOVA. It also stands to reason that the general interpretation of R^2 in both analyses should be similar even if the terminology differs somewhat. In regression, we speak of the total variance accounted for; in ANOVA, because we look at the separate effects of the independent variables rather than pool them together, we speak of the strength of each of the effects.

For multiple regression, R^2 indexes the amount of dependent variable variance accounted for or explained by the statistically significant regression model that contains the independent variables. In ANOVA we are also interested in accounting for the variance of the dependent variable. We do this by partitioning the total variance of the dependent variable into its component parts—that is, into parts attributable to the main effects and interactions of our independent variables.

With only one statistically significant (main) effect to deal with, such as the case in a one-way between-subjects design, we can think of the independent variable associated with that effect as accounting for a certain amount of variance of the dependent variable. In this instance, the notion of R^2 applies relatively directly.

In more complex designs, using a between-subjects two-way factorial design as an illustration, the dependent variable's variance is partitioned into three different and (assuming equal sample size in the cells) independent sources. In this case, R^2 as we have been characterizing it in multiple regression would apply to the three effects in combination. However, because the whole point of using an ANOVA design is to partition the total variance into separate, stand-alone sources, we actually compute the R^2 value for each separate source, rarely if ever adding them to obtain the overall R^2. In the domain of ANOVA, R^2 is known to most researchers as eta squared (Kirk, 1995).

Two Common Indexes of Strength of Effect

There are many ways to quantify the strength of a particular effect (see Judd, McClelland, & Culhane, 1995; Kirk, 1996; Olejnik & Algina, 2000; Rosenthal, 1994; Snyder & Lawson, 1993). However, in the everyday world of ANOVA, two indexes are commonly used to assess the strength associated with a main effect or an interaction, eta squared, symbolized by η^2, and omega squared, symbolized by ω^2 (Cohen, 1996; Keppel, 1991; Keppel & Wickens, 2004; Kirk, 1995; Maxwell & Delaney, 2000), although Keppel and Wickens (2004) further subdivided the latter into complete omega squared and partial omega squared measures. Both eta squared and omega squared deal with the proportion of the total variance explained by a particular effect. These indexes are ordinarily computed only after we have determined that the F ratio for a given effect is statistically significant. The reason for this is that if an F ratio is not significant, then we know that the effective value for eta squared or omega squared is zero—the effect cannot account for any (significant portion) of the total variance.

Eta Squared

Although it is known by a couple of different names, eta squared is the most common designation given to R^2 in the context of ANOVA (Kirk, 1995). For between-subjects and within-subjects designs, the total sum of squares (SS_{total}) is taken as the measure of total variance and placed in the denominator of a fraction. The sum of squares for the effect (SS_{effect}) is taken as representing the variance attributable to the effect and is placed in the numerator. This effect could be a main effect (e.g., SS_B) or an interaction (e.g., $SS_{A \times B}$). The decimal value of that ratio is eta squared. In general form:

$$\eta^2 = SS_{effect} / SS_{total}$$

Eta is actually a correlation coefficient—one of its other names is the correlation ratio (Guilford & Fruchter, 1978; Keppel & Zedeck, 1989). Because it is based on a correlation, eta squared can take on values between 0 and 1 and is interpreted as the percentage of total variance explained by a given effect. For example, if $SS_{total} = 400$ and $SS_{A \times B} = 40$, the eta squared would equal .10. We would therefore say that the A × B interaction accounted for 10% of the total variance of the dependent variable.

For mixed designs, there is some question about what the denominator of this eta-squared fraction should be. Whereas some argue in favor of the denominator being SS_{total}, others suggest that the between-subjects variance and the within-subjects variance should remain conceptually distinct. Under this latter scenario, the size of the between-subjects effects should be taken with respect to between-subjects variance (i.e., use $SS_{between\ subjects}$ as the denominator) and the size of the within-subjects effects should be taken with respect to within-subjects variance (i.e., use $SS_{within\ subjects}$ as the denominator). Thus, using the shorthand from the simple mixed design shown in Table 8a.6, the scenario we have just described would have you calculate eta squared as follows:

$$\eta^2 = SS_B / SS_{between\ subjects}$$
$$\eta^2 = SS_A / SS_{within\ subjects}$$
$$\eta^2 = SS_{A \times B} / SS_{within\ subjects}$$

It is very important to verbalize the basis for the eta-squared calculation. If one kept the between-subjects and the within-subjects variance distinct, and assuming that the between-subjects variable was gender of child and that the within-subjects variable was time, then we would want to say something like this: *The gender of the child accounted for 35% of the between-subjects variance, and the Gender × Time interaction accounted for 12% of the within-subjects variance.*

It is necessary to verbalize your results in this way because $SS_{\text{between subjects}}$ and $SS_{\text{within subjects}}$ are really subtotals; each represents only some portion of the total variance. Because of this, the calculated percentages (these partition-specific eta-squared values) will be much larger than they would be if you had used SS_{total} as the denominator.

It is also possible to calculate eta squared from the results sections of published articles where you are given the *F* ratio and the degrees of freedom but are not provided with the summary table showing all the sum of squares. In his textbook, Barry Cohen (1996, p. 477) supplies the formula for doing this. Here is the generalized formula based on Cohen's equation:

$$\eta^2 = (df_{\text{effect}})(F_{\text{effect}} \text{ ratio}) / (df_{\text{effect}}) + df_{\text{error}}$$

For the *F* ratio that we presented earlier in this section, the eta-squared value computed to .02. We would thus write:

$$F(2, 45) = 5.27, p < .05, \eta^2 = .02$$

Eta squared is a statistic that is descriptive of the sample, and this is both its strength and its weakness. It is a strength because it tells us exactly how the data have aligned themselves in our research study, and description is always a good thing in science. But because it is so descriptive of the sample, it can overestimate the presumed strength of the effect in the population, and this is considered by some (e.g., Maxwell & Delaney, 2000) to be a weakness of the statistic. As a way to overcome this weakness in eta squared, many researchers prefer to use omega squared.

Omega Squared

Omega squared represents the strength of the effect in the population, and it will always be computed as lower than the value yielded for eta squared. Maxwell and Delaney (2000) explain the reason for this as well as anyone (they prefer the name R^2 to eta squared):

However, even if the population group means were identical, the sample means would almost certainly differ from each other. Thus, although in the population the treatments may account for no variance, R^2 would nonetheless be expected to be greater than zero. . . . This positive bias of R^2, or tendency to systematically overestimate the population proportion, in fact is present whether the population-treatment means are equal or not. It turns out that the extent of positive bias of R^2 can be estimated and is a decreasing function of sample size. (p. 102)

Omega squared is used to offset this positive bias of R^2 (eta squared). But because we almost never know the population parameters as required in the formula to compute omega squared, it is necessary for us to estimate omega squared from the results of our ANOVA. A general formula for estimating omega squared is as follows:

$$\text{est } \omega^2 = [SS_{\text{effect}} - (df_{\text{effect}})(\text{mean square}_{\text{error}})] \, / \, (SS_{\text{total}} + \text{mean square}_{\text{error}})$$

Unlike eta squared, which can range from 0 to 1, the estimated value of omega squared can actually take on negative values when the F ratio is less than 1 (Keppel, 1991). This can happen because the formula for estimating omega squared attempts to statistically correct for the positive bias in eta squared. If you use the estimated omega squared in your own research and obtain a negative value in your calculations, simply convert it to zero (but because F ratios less than 1 will not be statistically significant, the issue should never come up anyway).

Summary

Which one of the strength-of-effect indexes you choose to use is probably not as critical as (a) appreciating the perspective they bring to your research and (b) recognizing some limits to their perspective. Let's briefly discuss each of these points.

Perspective

The value of including a strength-of-effect index in reporting your F ratio is substantial, and some major journal publishers such as the American Psychological Association strongly encourage their authors to report a strength-of-effect statistic. It provides both you and your reader with some grounding in how effectively your independent variables functioned in the study. In some sense, it also gives researchers a dose of humility because in most research studies, the strength of the effects that are found are not ordinarily large.

How high a value of these indexes is considered to be large? It really is relative. Kirk (1996) invoked the notion of *practical significance,* an old idea that Thompson (2002) traces back to Fisher (1925) and Kelley (1935), to incorporate strength-of-effect information in reporting statistical significance. To gauge practical significance, Kirk (1995, p. 178) cited some work by Jacob Cohen suggesting that omega-squared values of .01, .06, and .14 or greater could be described in the behavioral sciences as small, medium, and large. Add about 8 or so points to each (assuming a modest sample size) if you want to think in terms of eta squared. Notice that "large" in the domain of behavioral science is not necessarily large in any absolute sense.

Thompson (2002) added to Kirk's practical significance the idea of *clinical significance.* The question of clinical significance concerns whether or not the relevant groups in a study (e.g., normal vs. clinical, clinical diagnosis *X* vs. clinical diagnosis *Y*) are distinguishable in any meaningful way as a result of some treatment condition.

Some Limitations

The value obtained for either eta squared or omega squared must be viewed in the larger context in which the research is being conducted. Research at the cutting edge of a field that is striking out in new ground may not have yet found the most effective variables to study or may not be in a position to manipulate them in the most effective manner. Thus, one may obtain small values for a given effect but still consider the knowledge gained to be considerable.

Strength of effect can also be affected by the choice of levels one selects for the independent variables. Maxwell and Delaney (2000) point out,

> Including only extreme groups in a study of an individual difference variable would tend to exaggerate the [value of the obtained strength of effect]. On the other hand, failing to include an untreated control group in a clinical study comparing reasonably effective treatments might greatly reduce the [value of the obtained strength of effect] but would not alter the actual powers of the treatments. (p. 104)

Finally, Keppel (1991) gives an illustration in which even small effects can be quite important:

> Now, consider what might happen once [a] researcher has discovered an independent variable that produces a relatively large treatment

effect. Subsequent research will usually not be concerned with the original finding but with a refinement of the discovery into component parts. . . . As theories develop to account for these findings and for the interrelationships among the components, a researcher eventually finds that he or she is no longer working with large effects but with small ones. . . . Under these circumstances, even small differences—as indexed by [omega squared]—may provide a decision between two competing theoretical explanations. (p. 67)

Recommendations

We strongly recommend that you report a strength-of-effect index in your own research and that you ask for it (or compute it yourself) when you encounter the research of others. It is a useful and potentially important piece of information. We tend to report eta squared in our own research, but the estimated omega squared statistic is certainly a viable alternative. At the end of the day, however, as long as you interpret your index in an appropriate way, either one of these should be perfectly acceptable to use.

Some Examples of Main Effects and Interactions: Overview

The final portion of this chapter consists of three general examples of results for main effects and interactions. For the simplified hypothetical examples we use in this section, we have provided only the cell and marginal means. Our focus here is on understanding how the effects and the means representing them allow you to paint a picture of the results. To that end, we have omitted displaying to you the "stuff" of the analysis, such as the raw data, any estimate of the size of the measurement error, the values for the ANOVA summary table, the strength-of-effect index, and the results of simple effects tests. The accompanying SPSS chapter will take you through a variety of complete analyses.

Example 1: Main Effects Not Significant, Significant Interaction

The Results of the Study

In this first hypothetical example, medical students in a particular program take a course in physiology as well as one in bedside manner. To explore the type of teaching method that might be most effective for these courses, students are randomly assigned to either the physiology or the bedside manner course during a given semester and are instructed through either a lecture or a discussion format. This is thus a between-subjects design because the students are in only one of the four conditions. The dependent variable is their performance on a final exam, with the scores standardized so that we can compare them across different courses. The highest possible standardized score is 100.

The mean final exam scores for each condition are shown in Figure 8a.3. Students in the lecture section of the physiology course, for example, averaged a score of 90 on their exam. We also have included the marginal means. For example, the overall mean for all those students exposed to a lecture format (top row) was 75.

A main effect is associated with the marginal means representing the levels of a single independent variable. Looking at teaching method, we find that the overall mean for lecture is 75 and that the overall mean for discussion is 75. Because these means are equivalent, we know that the main effect for teaching method is not significant. The same situation holds for course, where the overall means for physiology and bedside manner are 75 as well. Thus, there is also no significant main effect for course.

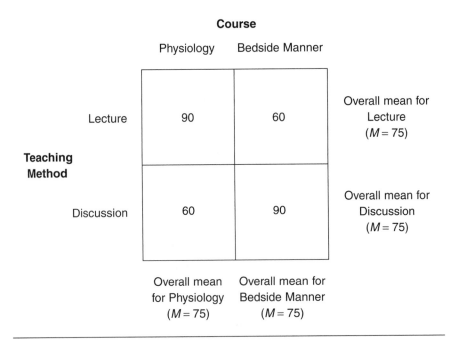

Figure 8a.3 Hypothetical Results From a 2 × 2 Between-Subjects Design

Despite the fact that neither main effect is significant, it is clear from Figure 8a.3 that the conditions in which the students found themselves did make a difference. Their performance is strongly tied to the cells in the design—that is, to the unique combination of conditions they have experienced. And once we tie differential performance to the cells, we have an interaction.

Recognizing an Interaction

It is possible to recognize an interaction by examining the cell means when they are displayed in the matrix-like array shown in Figure 8a.3. Here is what you do:

1. Choose to inspect the array either horizontally by looking at the rows or vertically by looking at the columns. We'll select the horizontal approach here, but you can do the analogous process with respect to the columns. Either way, you will lead to an understanding of the data, the first from the perspective of the independent variable represented by the rows and the second from the perspective of the independent variable represented by the columns.

2. First focus on the top row moving across from left to right and note the pattern that you see in the means. Here, the first row represents the lecture method. The means start high (90) for physiology and drop (to 60) for bedside manner (thus, we can say to ourselves "high"–"low").

3. Next focus on the second row and do the same. For the discussion method, the means start low (60) for physiology and rise (to 90) for bedside manner (conversely, "low"–"high").

4. If the pattern for one row differs from the pattern for another row, and assuming that the error factor is not all that large, then the odds are that you have a significant interaction. If the patterns for all the rows are quite similar (i.e., "low"–"low" or "high"–"high"), then the odds are that the interaction is not significant. In the present instance, the patterns are very different and should be indicative of a significant interaction.

Essentially, an interaction indicates that a different pattern of performance is observed for different levels of an independent variable. This is the same sort of situation that we described in Chapter 5A on multiple regression when we talked about interactions there.

Graphing an Interaction

It is typical to graph an interaction if it is significant, and we have done so in Figure 8a.4. Because both independent variables are measured on a nominal scale of measurement, there is no compelling psychometric reason to select one over the other to be represented on the horizontal (X) axis.

Our choice was to place course on the horizontal axis and to plot the two teaching methods. We suggest that if one variable was emphasized more in the development of the research, that variable might be the one you plot or "line in." We suggest this because you want to draw attention to the more relevant variable (if there is one), and a variable probably receives more attention from readers if it is "plotted" than if it resides on the horizontal axis. Here, teaching method will (in our view) receive a bit more emphasis. The dependent variable is always represented on the vertical (Y) axis.

A couple of details are worthwhile to note about the graph in Figure 8a.4. First, we used different symbols to represent the lecture and discussion methods. Second, we also used different line types to help distinguish the two methods. Explicit and very readable guidelines for how to construct graphs such as these are well worth consulting (American Psychological Association, 2001; Nicol & Pexman, 2003).

Notice from Figure 8a.4 that the two lines drawn in the graph are not parallel. This is another way to recognize an interaction. To say that

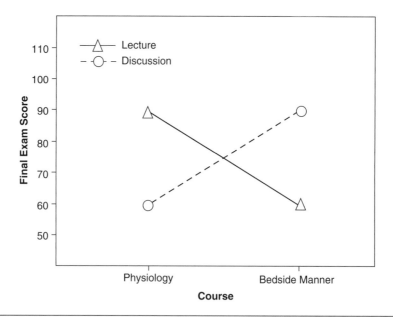

Figure 8a.4 Hypothetical Study Examining How Students Perform on a Final Exam for Physiology and Bedside Manner Courses Following Either Lecture or Discussion Teaching Methods

the lines are not parallel is tantamount to saying that there are different relationships observed for different levels of one of the independent variables. In the present example, the two lines or functions actually cross, but the lines do not need to intersect; the key requirement is only that they are not parallel.

Using Simple Effects to Understand the Interaction

Just as it is necessary to perform a post hoc test after a one-way analysis to determine which pairs of means are significantly different, one should also perform tests of simple effects on interactions that are statistically significant. From the perspective of the rows of Figure 8a.3, saying that a different pattern is seen for the rows tells us that the patterns shown by the means in each row are different—that the simple effects shown in one row differ from the simple effects of the other row. Thus, simple effects focus on the cell means for each level separately for a single independent variable.

The matrix of variables shown in Figure 8a.2 can be used to describe the strategy we use in testing simple effects. For two-way designs, testing simple effects involves isolating (considering separately) the levels of one independent variable and comparing the means of the other. In statistical terms, we test for differences between b_1 and b_2 under the a_1 condition and between b_1 and b_2 under the a_2 condition.

In the context of the variables shown in Figure 8a.4, consider the lecture method (a_1). We have two types of courses, physiology (b_1) and bedside manner (b_2). The means are represented by the open circles in the graph and the question is whether these two groups differ under the lecture method. We would next examine the discussion method (a_2) and again compare the means for the two courses. We are, in a sense, decomposing or simplifying the interaction to be able to explicate it, and this is why it is called a simple effects analysis.

We would then also simplify the other independent variable. Thus, we would isolate the physiology condition (b_1) and compare lecture (a_1) with discussion (a_2). We would repeat this for the bedside manner condition. After running all these simple effects, we would know which means were significantly different from which others. At that point, we could move forward to the interpretation of the interaction.

Critique of Our Strategy for Conducting Simple Effects

The strategy we have just outlined directs you to perform the simple effects analysis on both independent variables. Keppel (1991) tells us that "although there is no compelling reason against such a procedure" (p. 238), most researchers do not ordinarily analyze the simple effects of both the rows and the columns because the row and column means "represent partially redundant information." Researchers ordinarily select the one independent variable for simple effects testing based on reasons that include theoretical relevance, being more categorical in nature (making the split more intuitive), and accounting for more of the total variance (Keppel, 1991). We find it useful many times to examine both independent variables, but the choice is yours to make.

Interpreting an Interaction Based on the Simple Effects Results

Once you obtain a significant interaction and have completed testing all the simple effects, it is necessary for you to interpret—that is, verbalize it. If this is relatively new to you, we suggest the following strategy:

1. Select a variable to narrate.

2. Narrate each level separately.

3. Smoothly and grammatically integrate the sentences.

To illustrate this strategy, we will choose teaching method (because it is plotted) as the variable to narrate here. Now we will narrate the results for lecture and discussion separately:

Under the lecture method, students performed well in physiology but only moderately in bedside manner.

Under the discussion method, students performed moderately in physiology but well in bedside manner.

Putting these sentences together for the final narrative is straightforward in this case. Here is one of many ways to express the interaction:

Under the lecture method, students performed well in physiology but only moderately in bedside manner; under the discussion method, students performed moderately in physiology but well in bedside manner.

Interactions Supersede Main Effects

If a significant interaction is obtained, it means that a different relationship is seen for different levels of an independent variable. For example, we saw one relationship between physiology and bedside manner under the lecture method and a different relationship between physiology and bedside manner under the discussion method.

One implication of obtaining a significant interaction is that a statement of each main effect will not fully capture the results of the study. In this case, for example, to state that the (overall) means of the students taking physiology and bedside manner were equal (this is the main effect of course) is true but really misses the point. A similar argument can be made for the main effect of teaching method.

The general rule is that when an interaction effect is present, the information it supplies is more enriched—more complete—than the information contained in the outcome of the main effects of those variables composing it. Sometimes, as we will see in the next example in this section, a main effect is moderately representative of the results (although it is still not completely adequate to fully explicate the data). Other times, such as is the case here, the main effects paint a nonrepresentative picture of the study's outcome. In the present situation, if we examined only the main effects and ignored the interaction, we would improperly conclude that (a) the method used for teaching the courses did not make a difference, and (b) that students in the two courses performed comparably.

Example 2: Main Effects and the Interaction Are Significant

The second hypothetical example involves a market research study. Volunteer homemakers are given four boxes of detergent containing in total enough soap for a month of laundry. They are also given a daily schedule for using these detergents that randomizes for each participant which box will be used when over that month.

The four boxes given to the homemakers differ in the following ways. Two of the boxes are colored aqua and two of the boxes are colored orange. One of the boxes of each color contains white detergent with small green granules; the other boxes of each color contain white detergent with no granules present. Thus, two independent variables, box color and the presence of granules, are factorially combined into a 2 × 2 design. Order effects are randomized out in that all homemakers keep switching boxes randomly and repeatedly, and each homemaker is on a different random schedule of box use.

The dependent variable is a rating homemakers assign to the detergent's performance using a 7-point response scale. After each use, participants are asked to rate how well they believe the detergent performed. Higher ratings are more positive toward the product. An average representing each box color and granule condition (i.e., four different averages, one for each condition) is taken at the end of the study as the data points for that homemaker. Forty homemakers are involved in this study.

This is a within-subjects design because the same participants are represented in each cell of the study. That is, the preference ratings associated with each condition are supplied by the very same homemakers; each homemaker will have a single preference score for each cell. Unbeknownst to the homemakers (but already suspected by you), the detergents are chemically identical. The manufacturer simply wants to select the packaging and whether or not to color some of the detergent flakes.

Main Effects

The means for this hypothetical study are shown in Figure 8a.5. Each cell mean is based on the same 40 homemakers. These results are plotted in Figure 8a.6. Let's first examine the main effect of box color. The overall mean for aqua is 6.5 and the overall mean for orange is 4.0. It would appear, given modest error variance, that the main effect for box color is likely to be

Granules in Detergent

	Present	Absent	
Aqua	7.0	6.0	Overall mean for Aqua box ($M = 6.5$)
Box Color			
Orange	3.0	5.0	Overall mean for Orange box ($M = 4.0$)
	Overall mean for granules present ($M = 5.0$)	Overall mean for granules absent ($M = 5.5$)	

Figure 8a.5   Hypothetical Results From a 2 × 2 Within-Subjects Design

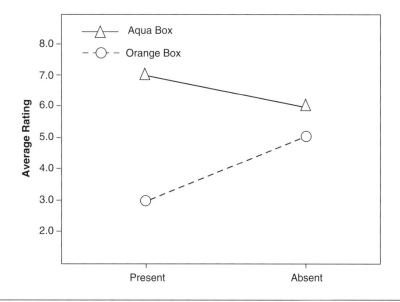

Figure 8a.6 Hypothetical Study Examining How Homemakers Evaluate Two Different Boxes of Laundry Detergent With and Without Granules

significant. Based on this finding in isolation, we would conclude that the homemakers preferred the aqua box over the orange box.

The main effect for granules presents a different picture. Here, the overall mean when granules are present is 5.0 and the overall mean when granules are absent is 5.5. The difference between these two means is less likely to be significant. Assuming that this difference turns out not to be significant, we would conclude, in isolation, that the presence or absence of granules did not make a difference to the homemakers.

Interaction Effect

The issue once again comes down to the interaction effect. We will focus on box color for the sake of explication. The aqua box is shown in the top row of Figure 8a.5 and we can see its pattern: We start high (7.0) and drop somewhat (to 6.0). You can see this drop in the graph in Figure 8a.6. The orange box is shown in the bottom row of Figure 8a.5, and we can see its pattern as well: We start low (3.0) and rise (to 5.0). You can see this rise in the graph; although the functions do not intersect, they are clearly not parallel and are thus strongly suggestive of an interaction of the independent variables.

Based on the above description, it is very likely that the Box Color × Granules interaction is significant, and our interpretation pending completion of the simple effects testing is as follows: Homemakers preferred the aqua box color, somewhat more so if there were granules in the detergent. The orange box color was not preferred but was liked better if there were no granules in the detergent.

Clearly, the interaction paints the most complete picture of the results. One main effect (box color) is to a limited extent somewhat representative of the findings. Homemakers did like the aqua box better than the orange box. Even though that main effect must, of necessity, ignore the issue of the granules, it is still modestly informative.

The other main effect really does not do a good job of summarizing the detailed findings. We might draw the conclusion from the main effect of granules that their presence or absence did not make much of a difference, but the enriched analysis (the interaction) belies that generalization. The presence and absence of granules did make a difference but in opposite directions for the aqua and orange boxes—differences that mostly "canceled each other out" when we looked at the main effect of granules in isolation. This, then, is another example of the interaction effect superseding the generalizations we would make exclusively on the basis of main effects.

Simple Effects Analysis

Once again, with a significant interaction, we would perform our simple effects tests. The strategy is the same as described in the previous example. We would first isolate the levels of box color. That is, we would want to determine if there was a significant difference between the means when the granules are present or absent for the aqua box and whether the means differed when the box was orange. Next, we would want to compare the means for the two box colors under the granules-present condition and then do the same thing for the granules-absent condition. Once these simple effects analyses were completed, we would have sufficient information to interpret the interaction.

Example 3: Significant Main Effects and a Nonsignificant Interaction

The third hypothetical example involves an evaluation of a 4-week program to teach ecological values to first-grade children. A standardized score representing environmental awareness and the practice of environment-enhancing behaviors is developed. Higher scores indicate greater sensitivity; the highest possible score is 250. A baseline measure is first obtained for the children. The instructional program is then administered, and another measure is obtained. To determine if there are any long-term effects of the program, a follow-up measurement is secured 2 months following the end of the program. Boys and girls are tracked separately.

This is an example of a 2 × 3 simple mixed design. The gender of the child is the between-subjects variable. The children are measured three different times in this study; thus, the time that the measurement was taken is the within-subjects variable.

The means for this third hypothetical study are shown in Figure 8a.7 and are plotted in Figure 8a.8. The main effect for gender deals with the comparison of the girls with the boys. Even given a moderate amount of error, from the means it appears that the girls are more environmentally sensitive than the boys. It also appears that the time variable would yield a significant result. It looks as though the program made a substantial impact, and even 2 months later in follow-up, the children seem to be above their baseline, although they may have lost some ground from the time right after the end of the program. Simple effects tests would be needed to know exactly how to interpret these findings.

Time of Measurement

Gender of Child	Baseline	Program End	Follow-up	
Girls	100	200	150	Overall mean for girls ($M = 150$)
Boys	50	150	100	Overall mean for boys ($M = 100$)
	Overall mean for Baseline ($M = 75$)	Overall mean for Program End ($M = 175$)	Overall mean for Follow-up ($M = 125$)	

Figure 8a.7 Hypothetical Results From a 2 × 3 Mixed Design

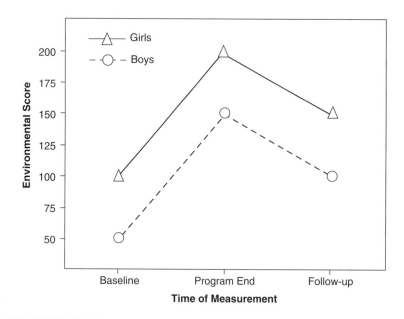

Figure 8a.8 Hypothetical Study Examining How Girls and Boys Score on Environmental Awareness Throughout a 4-Week Program to Teach Ecological Values

We can examine the interaction in the same way as we did for the previous examples. The girls, represented in the top row of Figure 8a.7, start modestly (at 100), gain a full 100 points to end the program at 200, and fall back 50 points at follow-up. The boys start with a dismal 50, also gain 100 points by the end of the program to reach 150, and likewise fall back 50 points by follow-up to finish with a mean of 100.

The pattern for the girls and the boys is exactly the same. This may be seen perhaps more clearly in the graph in Figure 8a.8, where the functions for the two groups are perfectly parallel. Thus, even though each function rises and then falls, it does so in exactly the same way for the girls and boys. We therefore know that the interaction is not statistically significant—the two functions are parallel to each other.

The Transition to Multivariate Design

This chapter has covered *t* tests and ANOVA designs where we used one or more independent variables. We were especially focused toward the end of this chapter on designs involving two independent variables. In all these analyses, however, there was only one dependent variable.

Note that it is conceivable that in any of the studies we described here the researchers could have measured more than one variable in their methodology. In Example 1, where we used lecture and discussion methods of instruction in two different kinds of classes, we assessed performance with a final exam. It is entirely reasonable for the researchers to also have collected student evaluations of the courses to acquire a more personal perspective on how the students felt. Had they done this, there would have been a second dependent variable available to be analyzed.

The key issue for us is that, even if a second (or third or fourth) dependent variable had been included in the research design, the procedures we have described in this chapter would have had to be applied separately to each of them. For example, we would have used a second 2 × 2 ANOVA to analyze student evaluations (assuming that there was a single summary value for these ratings).

The reason for this is that all the analyses we have discussed in this chapter were univariate designs. Univariate *t* tests and ANOVAs can accommodate only one dependent variable at a time. Our attention shifts in the following three chapters to situations where we can simultaneously analyze two or more dependent variables within a single analysis. These designs to be covered next are therefore known as *multivariate designs.*

Recommended Readings

Box, J. F. (1978). *R. A. Fisher, the life of a scientist.* New York: Wiley.

Cowles, M., & Davis, C. (1982). On the origins of the .05 level of statistical significance. *American Psychologist, 37,* 553–558.

Ellis, M. V. (1999). Repeated measures designs. *Counseling Psychologist, 27,* 552–578.

Himmelfarb, S. (1975). What do you do when the control group doesn't fit into the factorial design? *Psychological Bulletin, 82,* 363–368.

Kirk, R. E. (1996). Practical significance: A concept whose time has come. *Educational and Psychological Measurement, 56,* 746–759.

Kline, R. B. (2004). *Beyond significance testing.* Washington, DC: American Psychological Association.

Lovie, A. D. (1979). The analysis of variance in experimental psychology: 1934–1945. *British Journal of Mathematical and Statistical Psychology, 32,* 151–178.

Mittag, K. C., & Thompson, B. (2000). A national survey of AERA members' perceptions of statistical significance tests and other statistical issues. *Educational Researcher, 29,* 14–20.

Snyder, P., & Lawson, S. (1993). Evaluating experimental results using corrected and uncorrected effect size estimates. *Journal of Experimental Education, 61,* 344–349.

Thompson, B. (2002). "Statistical," "practical," and "clinical": How many kinds of significance do counselors need to consider? *Journal of Counseling and Development, 80,* 64–71.

Turner, J. R. (2001). *Introduction to analysis of variance: Design, analysis, and interpretation.* Thousand Oaks, CA: Sage.

Vacha-Haase, T. (2001). Statistical significance should not be considered one of life's guarantees: Effect sizes are needed. *Educational and Psychological Measurement, 61,* 219–244.

Wilkinson, L., & Task Force on Statistical Inference. (1999). Statistical methods in psychology journals: Guidelines and explanations. *American Psychologist, 54,* 594–604.

Univariate Comparisons of Means Using SPSS

This chapter illustrates the use of SPSS when making univariate comparisons of the means on a single dependent measure. In Chapter 8A, we briefly reviewed a variety of experimental design situations that involved the assessment of a single dependent variable with a gallimaufry of independent variable scenarios. These design situations included (a) assessing two independent group means (*t* test for independent samples), (b) assessing two related group means (*t* test for correlated groups), (c) assessing one independent variable with three or more independent groups (one-way between-subjects ANOVA), (d) assessing one independent variable with three or more related (nonindependent) groups (one-way within-subjects ANOVA), (e) assessing one quantitative independent variable with three or more levels (one-way analysis of trend), (f) assessing two independent variables with independent groups (two-way between-subjects ANOVA), and (g) assessing one between- and one within-subjects independent variables (two-way mixed design).

In this chapter, we will provide SPSS applications with a large data set based on clients from an urban community mental health center, and on occasion, several hypothetical (fictitious) data sets will also be used. Assume that issues of missing values, outliers, homogeneity of variance, normality, and independence have been addressed prior to analysis (see Chapters 3A and 3B for more on these topics).

Numerical Example 1: Independent-Samples *t* Test

In this first numerical example, let's assume we are interested in the effects of client gender (the independent variable) on global assessment of functioning (GAF) at the client's initial intake assessment (the dependent variable). In this situation, the independent variable represents two independent groups—namely, males and females.

We begin by clicking **Analyze → Compare Means → Independent-Samples T Test,** which opens the **Independent-Samples T Test** dialog box (see Figure 8b.1). Notice that we have moved our continuous dependent variable **gaft1** to the **Test Variable(s)** panel. If we had additional dependent variables to evaluate, we could move them over as well. Also note that our independent variable **sex** has been moved to the **Grouping Variable** panel. After moving your dichotomous or categorical independent variable over to the **Grouping Variable** box, SPSS prompts you with two question marks inside a set of parentheses **(??)**. After this prompt, you click the **Define Groups** pushbutton, which produces the **Define Groups** dialog box (see second box of Figure 8b.1).

SPSS defaults to the **Use specified values** checkbox. What SPSS requires is for you to indicate what the values are for your grouping or dichotomous independent variable. In the present data set, we have arbitrarily coded males as 1 and females as 2; hence, for **Group 1,** we insert a **1** and for **Group 2** we insert **2.** The **Cut point** checkbox is handy for temporarily creating a dichotomous independent variable from a continuous or metric variable based on a numeric cut point that you provide. For example, the cut point could be the median of a variable's distribution. SPSS will take all codes less than the cut point (or median) to form **Group 1** and all codes greater than or equal to the cut point to form **Group 2.** Creation of such a dichotomous variable is sometimes referred to as a *median split.* Clicking **Continue** brings you back to the original dialog box. Clicking the **Options** pushbutton produces the **Independent-Samples T Test: Options** dialog box (see the third box of Figure 8b.1).

This dialog box consists of three components. The **Confidence Interval** box is set at the SPSS default of 95%. Users can enter a value between 1 and 99 (most typical values are 90, 95, and 99). The **Missing Values** box contains two checkboxes. The **Exclude cases analysis by analysis** checkbox is the default and excludes cases that have missing values for the variable involved in the test. The **Exclude cases listwise** checkbox eliminates cases that have missing values for any of the variables used in any of the analyses. The option to exclude cases analysis by analysis was used in the present example because there was only one variable **(gaft1)** being examined. Clicking **Continue** brings you back to the original

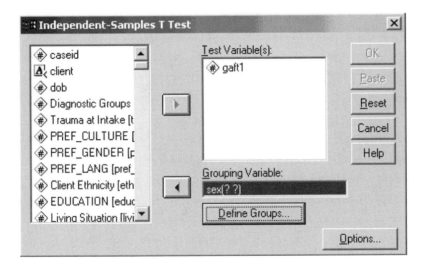

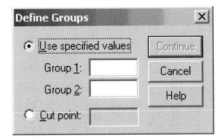

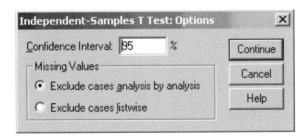

Figure 8b.1 Independent-Samples *t* Test Main Dialog Box and Its Define Groups and Options Dialog Boxes

Independent-Samples T Test dialog box, and clicking **OK** runs the analysis. The output for this procedure can be found in Figure 8b.2.

The first table in Figure 8b.2 depicts the **Group Statistics** table. From this table, we note that the GAF at Time 1 (**gaft1**) variable is disproportionately split on the client gender independent variable. Female clients

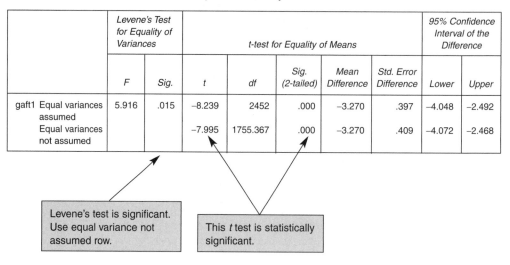

Figure 8b.2 Group Statistics Output and Independent-Samples Test for the Independent-Samples *t* Test

(*M* = 48.22, *SD* = 9.066) had somewhat higher initial clinical assessments than did male clients (*M* = 44.95, *SD* = 10.228).

The second table of Figure 8b.2 is the **Independent Samples Test** output. The left side of this table depicts the results of the **Levene's Test for Equality of Variances,** which is statistically significant. This result indicates that the sample variances are not equal, thus necessitating the use of a separate variance estimate when evaluating the difference between the group means. This is accomplished by using the **Equal variances not assumed** output row. The null hypothesis, that there are no gender differences, is assessed in the middle section of the table labeled **t-test for Equality of Means**. The **Mean Difference** (44.95 − 48.22) of −3.270, produced a *t* value of −7.995, which was evaluated at 1,755 degrees of freedom and was found to be statistically significant. We conclude that female mental health clients at intake were assessed on average as having somewhat better mental health functioning than the men.

Results

An independent-samples *t* test compared the mean GAF intake score for male community mental health clients ($M = 44.95$, $SD = 10.23$) with those of women ($M = 48.22$, $SD = 9.07$). This comparison was found to be statistically significant, $t(755) = −7.99$, $p < .001$. This result indicates that female clients were evaluated as functioning at a slightly higher level than the male clients at initial clinical intake.

Numerical Example 2: Paired-Samples *t* Test

In this second numerical example, assume we are interested in comparing mental health clients' clinical assessment at the initial intake interview (**gaft1**) with their assessment at Time 2, either discharge or annual review (**gaft2**). Our experimental hypothesis is that the average GAF score should improve (increase) over time as a consequence of treatment. This experimental design is considered a within-groups or repeated measures design because the same participants contribute a GAF score at Time 1 and a GAF score at Time 2. Because these two groups contribute a pair of scores, this statistical technique is often called a *paired samples t test* or *correlated t test*. We begin this analysis by clicking **Analyze** → **Compare Means** → **Paired-Samples T Test**, which opens the **Paired-Samples T Test** dialog box (see Figure 8b.3).

From the variables list panel, we have clicked on the two variables of interest—**gaft1** and **gaft2**. These variables appeared in the **Current Selections** box at the bottom of the dialog box (not shown). Clicking the right arrow moves these variables to the **Paired Variables** box (the right-side of the **Paired-Samples T Test** dialog box). The **Options** pushbutton again provides case exclusion analysis by analysis or listwise as was also the case in the **Independent-Samples T Test** example. Clicking **OK** runs the analysis. The output can be seen in Figure 8b.4.

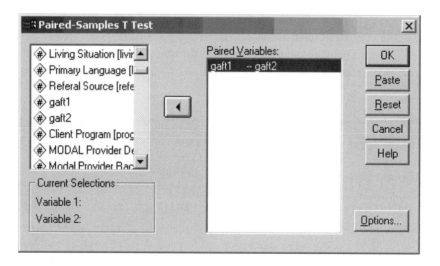

Figure 8b.3   Paired-Samples *t* Test Main Dialog Box

Figure 8b.4 contains three tables. The first one is **Paired Samples Statistics,** which shows the descriptive statistics for our pair of variables. SPSS refers to this as **Pair 1** to differentiate multiple paired analyses in the same run. We note that mental health clients at initial intake averaged GAF assessments of *M* = 46.67, and at Time 2 these scores increased slightly to *M* = 49.09. The sample consisted of 1,504 mental health clients who provided Time 1 and Time 2 assessments. The second table, the **Paired Samples Correlations**, indicates a moderate positive correlation (*r* = .443, *p* < .000) between clients' GAF Time 1 and GAF Time 2 evaluations. The **Paired Samples Test** output appears last in the figure. The mean difference between the pair of means is *M* = −1.42. The paired samples *t* test produced a *t* value of −4.499 and was evaluated at 1,503 degrees of freedom. This result was statistically significant (*p* < .000), indicating improvement in the GAF scores between Time 1 and Time 2.

Results

A paired-samples *t* test compared initial mean intake GAF scores of mental health clients with their GAF assessment at discharge or annual review (Time 2). This test was found to be statistically significant, *t*(503) = −4.50, *p* < .0001, indicating modest improvement between these clients' GAF scores at Time 1 (*M* = 47.67, *SD* = 9.11) and Time 2 (*M* = 49.09, *SD* = 13.15).

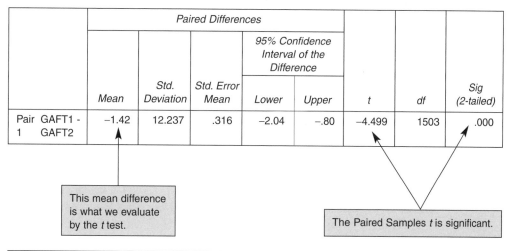

Paired Samples Statistics

		Mean	N	Std. Deviation	Std. Error Mean
Pair 1	GAFT 1	47.67	1504	9.107	.235
	GAFT 2	49.09	1504	13.148	.339

Paired Samples Correlations

		N	Correlation	Sig	
Pair 1	GAFT1 & GAFT2	1504	.443	.000	The two variables are moderately correlated.

Paired Samples Test

		Paired Differences							
					95% Confidence Interval of the Difference				
		Mean	Std. Deviation	Std. Error Mean	Lower	Upper	t	df	Sig (2-tailed)
Pair 1	GAFT1 - GAFT2	−1.42	12.237	.316	−2.04	−.80	−4.499	1503	.000

This mean difference is what we evaluate by the *t* test.

The Paired Samples *t* is significant.

Figure 8b.4 Selected Output From the Paired-Samples *t* Test Analysis

Numerical Example 3: One-Way Between-Subjects ANOVA

In Example 3, we cover the procedures for running a one-way between-subjects ANOVA, where there is one continuous dependent variable and one categorical independent variable with two or more levels. Some statisticians (e.g., Keppel et al., 1992) argue persuasively for using one-way

ANOVAs in lieu of the t test procedures we considered previously. The benefit of a one-way ANOVA is that this single procedure can address situations in which the independent variable has two, three, or more levels or groups.

Running a one-way between-subjects ANOVA can be accomplished in a variety of ways with SPSS (e.g., **One Way**, **Means**, and **General Linear Model-Univariate**). We will focus on the **General Linear Model** approach with SPSS in order to produce consistency between these univariate analyses on which we are currently focusing and the multivariate analyses we will conduct in later chapters. For a syntax-based approach to analysis of variance (ANOVA) procedures using SPSS **MANOVA,** consult Page, Braver, and MacKinnon (2003).

For the present numerical example, suppose we are interested in the effects of type of gender match (male match, female match, no match) between the client and his or her mental health provider (the independent variable) and GAF score at Time 2 (the dependent variable). The null hypothesis predicts that there will be no difference in GAF scores among the groups (H_0: male match = female match = no match). The alternative hypothesis predicts that there will be a difference among the groups (H_1: male match ≠ female match ≠ no match).

We begin our analysis by clicking **General Linear Model** → **Univariate,** which produces the **Univariate** dialog box (see Figure 8b.5). Notice that we have moved the GAF Time 2 (**gaft2**) variable over to the **Dependent Variable** box and the gender match variable (**genmatch**) to the **Fixed Factor(s)** box. For this analysis, we will leave all other SPSS default options in place with the exception of two pushbuttons on the right side of the dialog box. Clicking the **Post Hoc** pushbutton produces the **Univariate: Post Hoc Multiple Comparisons for Observed Means** dialog box (see the second box of Figure 8b.5). This SPSS dialog box provides the investigator with the ability to run 18 separate multiple comparison tests, which we will review in Chapter 10B. Note that we have double-clicked the independent variable **genmatch**, which moves it over to the **Post Hoc Tests for** box and activates the **post hoc test** checkboxes in the bottom half of the dialog box. We have checked the **Tukey** checkbox, requesting that a Tukey HSD (honestly significant difference) post hoc test be performed to compare the three **gaft2** means on the gender match independent variable. Clicking **Continue** moves us back to the **Univariate** dialog box.

Clicking the **Options** pushbutton produces the **Univariate: Options** dialog box (see the third box of Figure 8b.5). Notice that we have double-clicked the independent variable (**genmatch**) in the **Factor(s) and Factor Interactions** box, which automatically moves **genmatch** to the **Display Means for** box, which requests SPSS to display the dependent variable means for each level of the independent variable. We have also clicked three

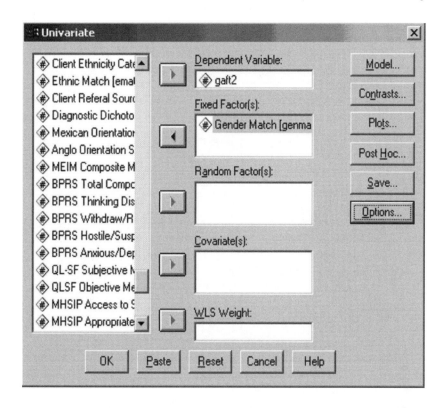

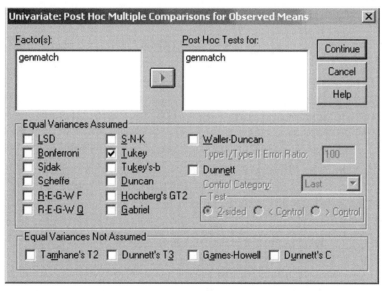

Figure 8b.5 Univariate Main Dialog Box and Its Post Hoc Multiple Comparisons for Observed Means and Options Dialog Boxes

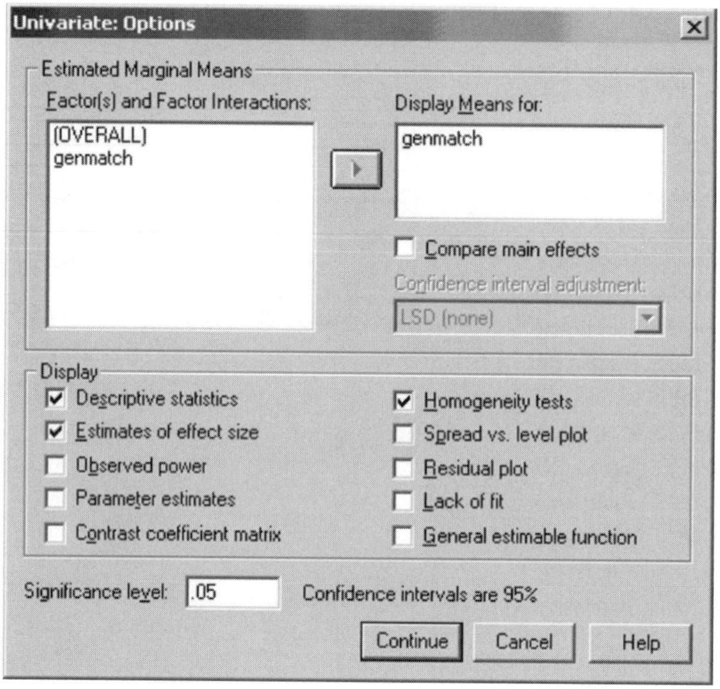

Figure 8b.5 (Continued)

checkboxes in the **Display** box. **Descriptive statistics** provides means, standard deviations, and counts for the dependent variable across levels of the independent variable. **Estimates of effect size** produces the partial eta-squared statistic, which reflects a ratio of the variance accounted for by the independent variable to the total variance. The **Homogeneity tests** produces the **Levene's test for equality of variances** for the dependent variable across the levels of the independent variable. If this test is not statistically significant, then equal variances (homogeneity) can be assumed. Clicking **Continue** brings us back to the **Univariate** dialog box, and clicking **OK** runs the analysis, which can be seen in Figures 8b.6, 8b.7, and 8b.8.

The first output table in Figure 8b.6 displays the **Between-Subjects Factors** information. We note relatively large but disproportionate cell sizes for the gender match independent variable.

The means, standard deviations, and subsample sizes are also displayed in Figure 8b.6. Clinical outcomes were highest for female clients receiving services from a female mental health service provider ($M = 53.08$, $SD = 12.065$) and lowest for male clients receiving services from male

Between-Subjects Factors

		Value Label	N
Gender Match	1	Male Match	276
	2	Female Match	668
	3	No Match	449

Descriptive Statistics

Dependent Variable: gaft2

Gender Match	Mean	Std. Deviation	N
Male Match	43.91	13.397	276
Female Match	53.08	12.065	668
No Match	47.51	12.512	449
Total	49.47	13.008	1393

Levene's Test of Equality of Error Variances[a]

Dependent Variable: gaft2

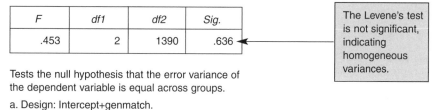

F	df1	df2	Sig.
.453	2	1390	.636

The Levene's test is not significant, indicating homogeneous variances.

Tests the null hypothesis that the error variance of the dependent variable is equal across groups.

a. Design: Intercept+genmatch.

Figure 8b.6 Selected One-Way Between-Subjects ANOVA Outputs

providers ($M = 43.91$, $SD = 13.397$). The next output table displays the **Levene's Test of Equality of Error Variances**, which is not statistically significant, $F(2, 1390) = .453, p > .636$. This result tells us that we have equal variances among the three groups on the **gaft2** dependent variable, and that we can proceed with the analysis with some confidence.

The **Tests of Between-Subjects Effects** output table is seen in Figure 8b.7. The table is composed of seven columns that depict source of variation (**Source**), the sum of squares (**Type III Sum of Squares**), degrees of freedom (**df**), mean squares (**Mean Square**), F values (**F**), significance levels (**Sig**), and effect sizes (**Partial Eta Squared**). The **Corrected Model** and **Intercept** sources of variation relate to the regression used to conduct

Tests of Between-Subjects Effects

Dependent Variable: gaft2

Source	Type III Sum of Squares	df	Mean Square	F	Sig.	Partial Eta Squared
Corrected Model	18960.446[a]	2	9480.223	60.841	.000	.080
Intercept	2842168.873	1	2842168.873	18240.18	.000	.929
genmatch	18960.446	2	9480.223	60.841	.000	.080
Error	216588.567	1390	155.819			
Total	3644640.000	1393				
Corrected Total	235549.014	1392				

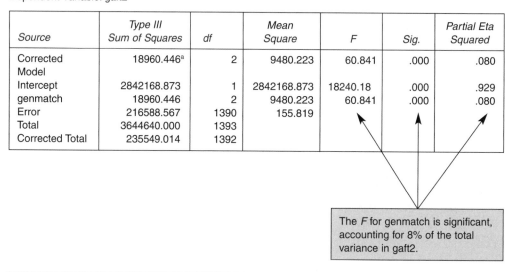

The *F* for genmatch is significant, accounting for 8% of the total variance in gaft2.

Figure 8b.7 Output Showing the Tests of Between-Subjects Effects for One-Way ANOVA

Multiple Comparisons

Dependent Variable: gaft2
Tukey HSD

(I) Gender Match	(J) Gender Match	Mean Differences (I-J)	Std. Error	Sig.	95% Confidence Interval	
					Lower Bound	Upper Bound
Male Match	Female Match	−9.17*	.893	.000	−11.26	−7.07
	No Match	−3.60*	.955	.000	−5.84	−1.36
Female Match	Male Match	9.17*	.893	.000	7.07	11.26
	No Match	5.57*	.762	.000	3.78	7.36
No Match	Male Match	3.60*	.955	.000	1.36	5.84
	Female Match	−5.57*	.762	.000	−7.36	−3.78

Based on observed means.
*The mean difference is significant at the .05 level.

9.17 is the difference between the gaft2 score mean for male match and female match. This difference is significant.

Figure 8b.8 Post Hoc Multiple Comparison Information

the ANOVA (see Chapter 9B for additional details) and can be ignored in the present analysis. The **genmatch** source evaluates the effects of the gender match independent variable. We note that the *F* value is 60.841 and is evaluated with 2 and 1,390 (between and within groups) degrees of freedom. We note the **Sig** value for this effect indicates that the *F* value is statistically significant beyond the .001 level. Note that the denominator or within-groups degrees of freedom comes from the **Error** source portion of the table. The **Partial Eta Squared** statistic (.080) indicates that gender match accounts for 8% of the total variance in GAF Time 2 assessment.

Because the "main effect" of gender match was found to be statistically significant and this independent variable has more than two levels, we can proceed with a post hoc multiple comparison evaluation of the three group means. A Tukey HSD test has been chosen to make this evaluation and can be seen next in the output.

The **Multiple Comparisons** table in Figure 8b.8 is produced by subtracting all possible combinations of the three gender match groups from each other, which produces the **Mean Differences** column (e.g., the male match minus female match = $43.91 - 53.08 = $ **−9.17**). These mean differences are evaluated with a special statistical formula (see Chapter 10B) and evaluated at alpha = .05. An inspection of the **Sig** column indicates that all the groups differ from one another. Female gender matches ($M = 53.08$) produced the highest GAF scores at Time 2, followed by clients who received no gender match ($M = 47.51$), who in turn had significantly higher scores than clients receiving a male match ($M = 43.91$).

Results

A one-way between-subjects ANOVA compared the mean GAF score at annual review or discharge for clients receiving treatment from the following types of gender-matching situations with their mental health provider: female match, male match, no match. This assessment was statistically significant, $F(2, 1{,}390) = 60.84$, $p < .001$, partial $\eta^2 = .08$. A Tukey HSD test ($p < .05$) indicated that the female match GAF score mean ($M = 53.08$, $SD = 12.07$) was significantly higher than the no match ($M = 47.51$, $SD = 12.51$) and the male match means ($M = 43.91$, $SD = 13.40$). The no match condition was also significantly higher than the male match condition.

Numerical Example 4: One-Way Within-Subjects ANOVA

Consider the following hypothetical study and data. The effects of type of psychotherapy (psychoanalytic, cognitive-behavioral, brief) on community mental health clients' perceived service satisfaction was examined with six clients. Assume that all clients had comparable intake diagnoses. A total of six clients were tested ($N = 6$) under three psychotherapy treatment conditions ($a = 3$) in a completely counterbalanced order. Clients were given 10 one-hour psychotherapy sessions of each type by the same therapist. An eight-item service satisfaction questionnaire, on a 4-point Likert-type scale, was completed at the end of each 10-week period. To run this analysis, we begin by clicking **Analyze → General Linear Model → Repeated Measures,** which produces the **Repeated Measures Define Factor(s)** dialog box (see the top portion of Figure 8b.9).

In the **Within-Subject Factor Name** box, SPSS defaults with the variable name: **factor1**. Erase this name and substitute a variable name of your choice. Note that it must be eight characters or less and not duplicate any of your other variable names. In the present example, we will use **treatmnt** as our new within-subject variable name. At the **Number of Levels** box, we type in **3** to indicate the number of levels (psychoanalytic, cognitive-behavioral, brief) we are including in our within-subject factor (**treatmnt**). Remember, each level represents a different observation or measure of service satisfaction for the same client. Clicking **Add** moves our new factor name (**treatmnt**) and number of levels (**3**) to the list box. This is shown in the bottom portion of Figure 8b.9. We will leave the **Measure Name** box blank. This box is used when more than one dependent variable is measured for each participant; for example, each type of treatment (psychoanalytic, cognitive-behavioral, brief) is measured at Time 1 and Time 2.

Next we click the **Define** pushbutton, which opens the **Repeated Measures** dialog box (see Figure 8b.10). In the variables list panel (on the left side of the dialog box) we need to highlight the three variable names involved in the analysis by pointing the cursor at the first variable and depressing the left mouse button and dragging it over all three variable names. Then click the right arrow button to replace the question marks ("**??**") in the **Within-Subjects Variables** box. We will leave the **Between-Subjects Factor(s)** and **Covariates** boxes blank because neither of these variables is used in the present example.

At the bottom of the **Repeated Measures** dialog box are six pushbuttons, and for five of them, we will leave the SPSS defaults in place. Clicking the **Options** pushbutton produces the **Repeated Measures: Options** dialog box, which can also be seen in Figure 8b.10.

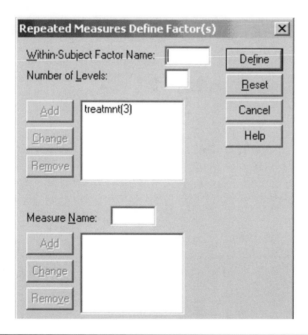

Figure 8b.9 Repeated Measures Define Factor(s) Dialog Box and How It Looks After Making the Necessary Changes to Show "treatmnt" as Our New Within-Subject Variable Name

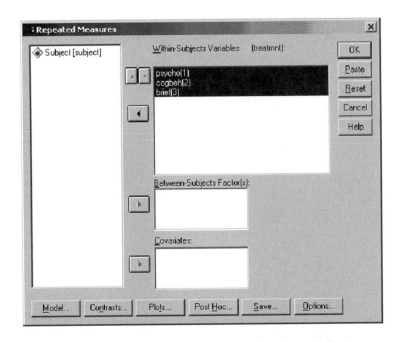

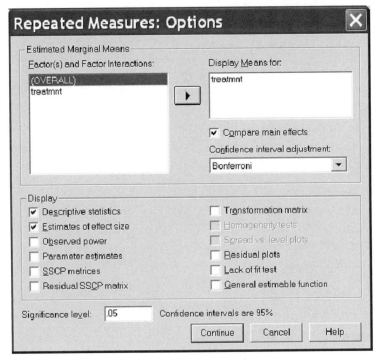

Figure 8b.10 Repeated Measures Main Dialog Box and Its Options Dialog Box

Notice that we have double-clicked the variable name **treatmnt** in the **Factor(s) and Factor Interactions** box, which automatically moves it to the **Display Means for** box. This requests that SPSS display the means for the three within-subjects factors. Note that we have also checked the **Compare main effects** checkbox and selected a **Bonferroni** adjustment (to control for Type I error) in the **Confidence interval adjustment** drop-down list. This selection is comparable to running a series of paired-sample *t* tests among the psychoanalytic, cognitive-behavioral, and brief psychotherapy means, with an adjusted alpha level. Two additional checkboxes have also been activated. The **Descriptive statistics** checkbox requests means, standard deviations, and counts for all dependent variables. The **Estimates of effect size** checkbox produces the partial eta-squared statistic. Clicking **Continue** brings you back to the **Repeated Measures** dialog box, and clicking **OK** runs the analysis. Selected output can be seen in Figures 8b.11 and 8b.12.

The first output table of Figure 8b.11 is the **Within-Subjects Factors** list, which displays the factor name (**treatmnt**) and the three dependent variables that compose it. The **Descriptive Statistics** table (also in Figure 8b.11) indicates that clients receiving brief psychotherapy ($M = 28.983$, $SD = 1.0962$) reported the highest levels of satisfaction. Sample sizes per group were equal but very small. SPSS produces a default **Multivariate Tests** output, which in effect runs a one-way multivariate analysis of variance (MANOVA) on the composite treatment variable. Because this is essentially a univariate chapter, we will skip this portion of the output and consider this topic in Chapters 10A and 10B.

Mauchly's Test of Sphericity (Mauchly, 1940) can be seen also in Figure 8b.11. This is a special test to simultaneously determine whether or not two assumptions are met. First, it tests if the dependent variable variance-covariance matrices are equal or homogeneous (usually referred to as homogeneity of variance) for a within-subjects design. The null hypothesis is that the variances are equal. In testing the equality of variances across the levels of the repeated measure, it is analogous to Levene's test for between-subjects design. Second, it tests whether the correlations between the levels of the within-subjects variable are comparable. The null hypothesis is that these correlations are equal. Because we need more than two levels of the repeated measure to have more than one correlation, the Mauchly test will not produce useful results with a two-level repeated measure.

If this test is not statistically significant, then the sphericity assumption has been met and you can proceed with interpreting a standard *F* statistic (one that is evaluated with unadjusted degrees of freedom) found next in Figure 8b.12 in the row for the **Source treatmnt** labeled **Sphericity**

Within-Subjects Factors

Measure: MEASURE_1

Treatment	Dependent Variable
1	psycho
2	cogbeh
3	brief

Descriptive Statistics

	Mean	Std. Deviation	N
Psychoanalytic	22.317	.8159	6
Cognitive-behavioral	25.133	1.0746	6
Brief	28.983	1.0962	6

Mauchly's test is not significant, indicating equal covariance matrices (sphericity). Evaluate the Sphericity Assumed F value for Tests of Within-Subjects Effects.

Mauchly's Test of Sphericity[b]

Measure: MEASURE_1

Within Subjects Effect	Mauchly's W	Approx. Chi Square	df	Sig.	Epsilon[a]		
					Greenhouse-Geisser	Huynh-Feldt	Lower-bound
Treatment	.963	.149	2	.928	.965	1.000	.500

Tests the null hypothesis that the error covariance matrix of the orthonormalized transformed dependent variables is proportional to an identity matrix.

a. May be used to adjust the degrees of freedom for the averaged tests of significance. Corrected tests are displayed in the Tests of Within-Subjects Effects table.

b. Design: Intercept
   Within Subjects Design: treatment.

Figure 8b.11   Selected Descriptive and Diagnostic Tables of the Within-Subject Procedure

---

Assumed. Conversely, should **Mauchly's Test of Sphericity** be statistically significant ($p < .05$), then heterogeneity of covariance is indicated. In such a situation, SPSS generates three correction options—**Greenhouse-Geisser**, **Huynh-Feldt**, and **Lower-bound**; the **Lower-bound** correction is more conservative than the other two. As Kinnear and Gray (2000) note,

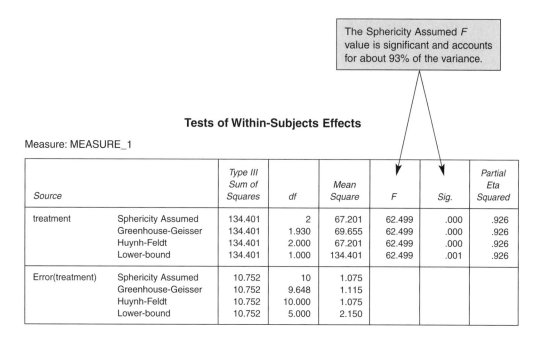

The Sphericity Assumed *F* value is significant and accounts for about 93% of the variance.

Tests of Within-Subjects Effects

Measure: MEASURE_1

Source		Type III Sum of Squares	df	Mean Square	F	Sig.	Partial Eta Squared
treatment	Sphericity Assumed	134.401	2	67.201	62.499	.000	.926
	Greenhouse-Geisser	134.401	1.930	69.655	62.499	.000	.926
	Huynh-Feldt	134.401	2.000	67.201	62.499	.000	.926
	Lower-bound	134.401	1.000	134.401	62.499	.001	.926
Error(treatment)	Sphericity Assumed	10.752	10	1.075			
	Greenhouse-Geisser	10.752	9.648	1.115			
	Huynh-Feldt	10.752	10.000	1.075			
	Lower-bound	10.752	5.000	2.150			

Pairwise Comparisons

Measure: MEASURE_1

(I) treatment	(J) treatment	Mean Difference (I-J)	Std. Error	Sig[a].	95% Confidence Interval for Difference[a] Lower Bound	Upper Bound
1	2	−2.817*	.645	.022	−5.095	−.538
	3	−6.667*	.602	.000	−8.794	−4.539
2	1	2.817*	.645	.022	.538	5.095
	3	−3.850*	.545	.003	−5.777	−1.923
3	1	6.667*	.602	.000	4.539	8.794
	2	3.850*	.545	.003	1.923	5.777

Based on estimated marginal means.

*The mean difference is significant at the .05 level.

a. Adjustment for multiple comparisons: Bonferroni.

Figure 8b.12 Selected Output of the Within-Subject Procedure

these tests produce a more conservative estimate by reducing the numerator and denominator degrees of freedom of the F ratio by a specially computed weighting factor called *epsilon,* which is uniquely derived by each method from the variance-covariance matrix. We multiply the two degrees of freedom associated with the F ratio by the epsilon values of the particular correction and test the significance of F with these corrected degrees of freedom. Notice that the actual F values remain the same, but because the degrees of freedom are lower (epsilon values are less than 1 if Mauchly's W is significant), the power of the statistical evaluation is reduced; this in turn compensates for the violation of the sphericity assumption. In the present example, we note in Figure 8b.11 a Mauchly's W value of .963, which is translated by SPSS into an *approximate chi-square* value of .149 and evaluated with 2 degrees of freedom. This test is not statistically significant ($W(2) = .963, p < .928$), indicating homogeneity of covariance.

Because Mauchly's test of sphericity was not statistically significant, we can proceed with an assessment of the **Sphericity Assumed** F value in the **Tests of Within-Subjects Effects** output (see Figure 8b.12). With 2 and 10 degrees of freedom, the observed F value is 62.499, is significant at the .000 level, and accounts for nearly 93% (.926) of the total variance. The statistically significant F value informs us that we can reject the null hypothesis that the psychotherapy interventions produce the same level of client service satisfaction. Our next task is to determine where the differences lie.

We are also going to omit the SPSS default **Tests of Within-Subjects Contrasts,** which is useful when you are evaluating a quantitative within-subjects variable such as number of trials in a learning study or number of therapy sessions in a clinical study. After a statistically significant omnibus F test, this table evaluates the linear, quadratic, and other sources of variability in the study.

The last output table shown in Figure 8b.12 depicts the table of **Pairwise Comparisons,** which evaluates all possible combinations of service satisfaction means. For example, the first **Mean Difference** comparison involves **treatmnt 1** versus **treatmnt 2** (psychoanalytic minus cognitive-behavioral, $22.317 - 25.133 = -2.817$), which is statistically significant at the Bonferroni adjusted alpha level of .022. From this table, we can see that the brief psychotherapy condition produced statistically significant higher service satisfaction than did the psychoanalytic or cognitive-behavioral conditions (mean difference = 6.667, 3.850, respectively). In addition, the cognitive-behavioral treatment generated significantly higher satisfaction ratings than did the psychoanalytic group (mean difference = 2.817).

Results

A one-way within-subjects ANOVA was conducted relating the type of psychotherapy (psychoanalytic, cognitive-behavioral, brief) to mental health clients' perceived service satisfaction. The observed F value was statistically significant, $F(2, 10) = 62.50$, $p < .001$, partial $\eta^2 = .93$. Bonferroni pairwise comparison tests ($p < .05$) suggested that clients receiving brief psychotherapy ($M = 28.98$, $SD = 1.10$) evidenced greater service satisfaction than did clients receiving psychoanalytic ($M = 22.32$, $SD = .82$) or cognitive-behavioral treatment ($M = 25.13$, $SD = 1.08$). In addition, clients receiving cognitive-behavioral treatment garnered greater satisfaction than did their counterparts in the psychoanalytic condition.

Numerical Example 5: One-Way Trend Analysis

Suppose we have data on the number of therapy sessions (a quantitative independent variable) and clinical outcome as measured by GAF score, the dependent variable. Six clients are given 30 consecutive 1-hour per day psychotherapy sessions over a 30-day period. Therapist GAF evaluations are made at the end of 10, 20, and 30 days. In this situation, we are not particularly interested in group differences (e.g., 10 sessions versus 20 sessions) but, rather, in the functional relationship between the levels of the independent variable and the means of the dependent variable (Keppel & Wickens, 2004).

Rather than examining group differences, we instead focus on plotting the treatment means and considering their shape or trend. In practice, this usually means conducting an omnibus within-subjects ANOVA (as we did in the previous example) followed by an assessment of the type of relationship between the independent variable and the dependent variable. If this relationship can be expressed or described by a straight line, we say that there is a linear trend present. For example, a linear trend with our present independent and dependent variables might show that as the number of therapy sessions increases, GAF scores also increase (this result would make therapists happy). Alternatively, a more complicated picture might occur in which GAF scores increase and then flatten out after 20 sessions (these result might make hospital or clinic administrators happy). When graphed, these data produce an elbow or shift in the line or function, and we say that a quadratic (nonlinear) component is present in our data.

Such polynomial functions can be assessed directly with SPSS by clicking **Analyze → General Linear Model → Repeated Measures,** which opens the **Repeated Measures Define Factor(s)** dialog box. As in the previous numerical example, we delete the SPSS default **Within-Subject Factor Name: Factor1** and replace it with our new factor name: **session**, and for the **Number of Levels** box we type in **3**. Click the **Add** button to register with SPSS the name and number of levels of the within-subjects variable. Clicking the **Define** pushbutton generates the **Repeated Measures** dialog box. We define **sess10**, **sess20**, and **sess30** as the three levels (neither of the above two dialog boxes are shown) and click **Plots**.

Clicking the **Plots** pushbutton produces the **Repeated Measures: Profile Plots** dialog box (see Figure 8b.13). After moving our factor variable (**session**) from the **Factors** panel to the panel for **Horizontal Axis,** we clicked the **Add** button. Figure 8b.13 shows the result of this series of steps. Click **Continue** to return to the **Repeated Measures** main dialog window. We encourage you to plot your results because one of the objectives of a trend analysis is to describe the shape or profile of the dependent variable means across levels of the independent variable.

Clicking the **Options** pushbutton produces the **Repeated Measures: Options** dialog box (not shown) where we have clicked the **Descriptive**

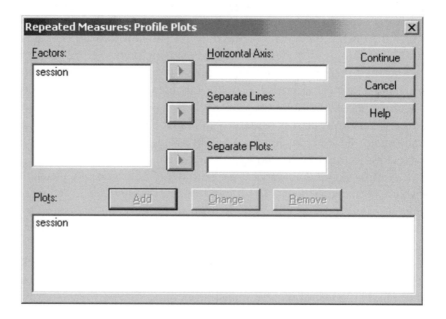

Figure 8b.13   Repeated Measures: Profile Plots Dialog Box

statistics and **Estimates of effect size** checkboxes. Clicking **Continue** brings us back to the **Repeated Measures** dialog box, and clicking **OK** runs the analysis. Selected output can be seen in Figures 8b.14 and 8b.15.

Figure 8b.14 depicts the **Within-Subjects Factors** table, which tells us that our within-subjects independent variable session has three levels.

Within-Subjects Factors

Measure: MEASURE_1

Session	Dependent Variable
1	sess10
2	sess20
3	sess30

Descriptive Statistics

	Mean	Std. Deviation	N
10 Sessions	44.67	2.875	6
20 Sessions	65.50	1.378	6
30 Sessions	65.00	1.673	6

Mauchly's Test of Sphericity[b]

Measure: MEASURE_1

Within Subjects Effect	Mauchly's W	Approx. Chi Square	df	Sig.	Epsilon[a] Greenhouse-Geisser	Huynh-Feldt	Lower-Bound
Session	.783	.979	2	.613	.822	1.000	.500

Tests the null hypothesis that the error covariance matrix of the orthonormalized transformed dependent variables is proportional to an identity matrix.

a. May be used to adjust the degrees of freedom for the averaged tests of significance. Corrected tests are displayed in the Tests of Within-Subjects Effects table.

b. Design: Intercept
   Within Subjects Design: session

Figure 8b.14 Selected Descriptive and Diagnostic Tables From the Within-Subjects Trend Procedure

Descriptive Statistics are displayed next. Client GAF scores average about 44.67 after 10 therapy sessions. These scores jump to 65.50 after 20 sessions and appear to remain fairly constant after 30 sessions.

The **Mauchly's Test of Sphericity** output can be seen in the third output table in Figure 8b.14. This test is not statistically significant (**Mauchly's** $W = .783$, approximate chi square = $.979$, $p > .613$), indicating equality of the dependent variable covariance matrix.

Shown next, in Figure 8b.15, is the **Tests of Within-Subjects Effects** output. Because **Mauchly's test of sphericity** was not statistically significant

Tests of Within-Subjects Effects

Measure: MEASURE_1

Source		Type III Sum of Squares	df	Mean Square	F	Sig.	Partial Eta Squared
session	Sphericity Assumed	1695.444	2	847.722	199.204	.000	.976
	Greenhouse-Geisser	1695.444	1.643	1031.779	199.204	.000	.976
	Huynh-Feldt	1695.444	2.000	847.722	199.204	.000	.976
	Lower-bound	1695.444	1.000	1695.444	199.204	.000	.976
Error (session)	Sphericity Assumed	42.556	10	4.256			
	Greenhouse-Geisser	42.556	8.216	5.180			
	Huynh-Feldt	42.556	10.000	4.256			
	Lower-bound	42.556	5.000	8.511			

Tests of Within-Subjects Contrasts

Measure: MEASURE_1

Source		Type III Sum of Squares	df	Mean Square	F	Sig.	Partial Eta Squared
session	Linear	1240.333	1	1240.333	262.042	.000	.981
	Quadratic	455.111	1	455.111	120.471	.000	.960
Error (session)	Linear	23.667	5	4.733			
	Quadratic	18.889	5	3.778			

Both the linear and the quadratic components of the function are significant.

Figure 8b.15   Selected Output From the Within-Subjects Trend Procedure

($p > .05$), we can interpret the results row labeled **Sphericity Assumed**. Had Mauchly's test of sphericity been statistically significant, indicating heterogeneity of covariance, we would have needed to use one of the progressively more conservative F statistic adjustments (i.e., **Greenhouse-Geisser, Huynh-Feldt,** or **Lower-bound**).

The F value for the within-subjects independent variable (sphericity assumed) is 199.204 and evaluated with 2 and 10 degrees of freedom. This effect is statistically significant ($p < .000$), indicating that the number of therapy sessions affects the clinical outcome measure. The partial eta-squared value of .976 indicates that our independent variable accounts for nearly 98% of the total variance in this hypothetical study.

Last in Figure 8b.15 there is a table for the **Tests of Within-Subjects Contrasts**. Here, we determine the mathematical properties underlying the relationship between the independent variable (number of therapy sessions) and the dependent measure (GAF score). To make this assessment, we first look at the **Source** column labeled "**session**." Here, we can see the separate F tests for the linear and quadratic components of variation. Both F values ($F_{linear} = 262.042$, and $F_{quadratic} = 120.471$) are statistically significant ($p < .000$), indicating both linear and quadratic components to the dependent variable function.

The function relating GAF scores to number of therapy sessions can be better understood by examining a plot of the dependent measure across the three levels of the independent variable (see Figure 8b.16). Clearly, GAF scores are relatively low after 10 sessions but show good improvement by Session 20 (this reflects the linear component of the function). Between Session 20 and Session 30, the function "flattens out" (thus reflecting the quadratic component of this data).

Results

A one-way trend analysis was performed relating the number of therapy sessions mental health clients received (10, 20, or 30 sessions) to their clinical outcome as measured by their GAF score at the end of each 10-session period. The observed F ratio was statistically significant, $F(2, 10) = 199.20$, $p < .001$, partial $\eta^2 = .98$. An analysis of the linear, $F(1, 5) = 262.04$, $p < .001$, partial $\eta^2 = .98$, and quadratic components of trend, $F(1, 5) = 120.47$, $p < .001$, partial $\eta^2 = .96$, indicated that both were statistically significant and accounted for nearly all the total variance in the dependent measure.

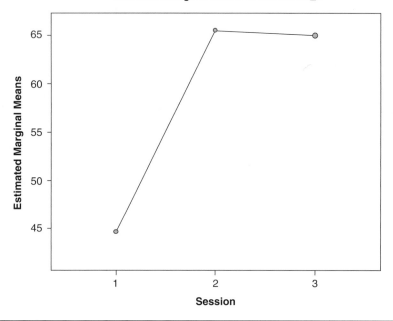

Figure 8b.16   Plot of GAF Scores Across the Three Levels of Therapy Sessions

Numerical Example 6: Two-Way Between-Subjects ANOVA

For our two-way between-subjects ANOVA example, we use data derived from a community mental health center. The independent variables are client gender (male, female) and client ethnicity (White American, Latino American, African American). The dependent variable is client GAF score at Time 2 (annual review or termination).

We begin this analysis by clicking **Analyze → General Linear Model → Univariate,** which opens the **Univariate** dialog box (see Figure 8b.17), where we have clicked over **gaft2** to the **Dependent Variable** box and **sex** and **newethnc** (our independent variables) to the **Fixed Factor(s)** box.

When dealing with two or more independent variables, the researcher encounters multiple choice points in the analytical decision-making process. One important consideration is whether to focus on the main effects or interaction effect(s) within your analysis. We find it helpful, at this juncture, to run the analysis and in effect "take a peek" at the results to determine if the main effects and interaction effect(s) are statistically significant. This knowledge can help guide the type of post hoc and

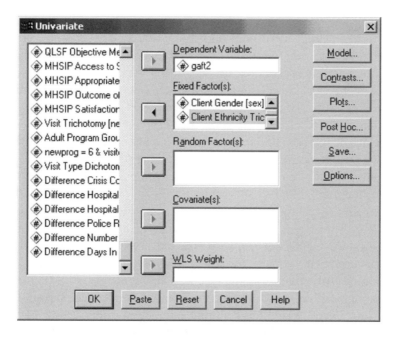

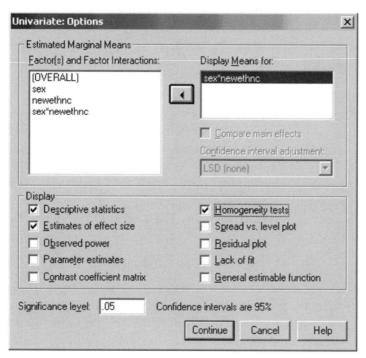

Figure 8b.17   Univariate Main Dialog Box and Its Options Dialog Box

other analyses you might want to request from SPSS. For example, if your interaction is statistically significant, then your focus should be on interpreting the interaction by means of analyzing its simple effects. Conversely, if the interaction is not statistically significant but one or both of the main effects is significant, then your focus will be to assess each significant main effect with multiple or planned comparisons tests.

In the present example, we ran the analysis (by clicking **OK** in the **Univariate** dialog box) and found that both main effects (gender and client ethnicity) and their interaction (Gender × Client Ethnicity) were statistically significant. We can use this knowledge in selecting appropriate options from the SPSS menus.

Because the interaction is statistically significant, we will not focus on any post hoc appraisals of the client ethnicity main effect. Hence, the only pushbutton we will click in the **Univariate** dialog box is **Options**; all other SPSS defaults will remain in place. Clicking **Options** produces the **Univariate: Options** dialog box (see also Figure 8b.17).

Although both main effects and the interaction effect are statistically significant, we have highlighted only the interaction effect in the **Factor(s) and Factor Interactions** box and clicked the right arrow button to paste it into the **Display Means for** box. In the **Display** box at the bottom of the dialog box, we have checked the **Descriptive statistics**, **Estimates of effect size**, and **Homogeneity tests**, as we have described in previous analyses. Clicking **Continue** takes us back to the **Univariate** dialog box, and clicking **OK** runs the analysis. The SPSS output tables can be seen in Figures 8b.18 and 8b.19.

The **Between-Subjects Factors** output can be found first in Figure 8b.18 where we find large but somewhat disproportionate subsample sizes. Next, in the **Descriptive Statistics** output, we observe that White American males ($M = 46.24$, $SD = 12.171$) have the highest GAF scores among the male clients and that Latino American females ($M = 53.65$, $SD = 12.294$) produced the highest GAF score among the female clients. The **Levene's Test of Equality of Error Variances** output is not statistically significant, $F(5, 1411) = 1.862$, $p > .098$, thus indicating homogeneity (equality) of variances among the dependent variable groups. We can proceed with interpreting the ANOVA results.

Another output table, shown in Figure 8b.19, is the **Tests of Between-Subjects Effects**. As we noted previously (from our earlier "peek"), both main effects of **sex** (gender) and **newethnc** (client ethnicity) are statistically significant ($p < .000$). However, the interaction is also statistically significant, with an F value of 6.882 that was evaluated at 2 and 1,411 degrees of freedom and was found to be significant at alpha = .001. The **Partial Eta**

Between-Subjects Factors

		Value Label	N
Client Gender	1	Male	483
	2	Female	934
Client Ethnicity Trichotomy	1	White American	474
	2	Latino American	604
	3	African American	339

Descriptive Statistics

Dependent Variable: gaft2

Client Gender	Client Ethnicity Trichotomy	Mean	Std. Deviation	N
Male	White American	46.24	12.171	184
	Latino American	43.52	12.704	163
	African American	40.74	13.440	136
	Total	43.78	12.885	483
Female	White American	50.53	10.784	290
	Latino American	53.65	12.294	441
	African American	49.68	14.369	203
	Total	51.82	12.454	934
Total	White American	48.87	11.521	474
	Latino American	50.92	13.187	604
	African American	46.10	14.656	339
	Total	49.08	13.163	1417

Levene's Test of Equality of Error Variances[a]

Dependent Variable: gaft2

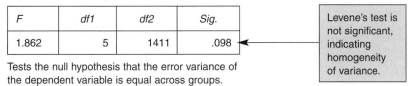

F	df1	df2	Sig.
1.862	5	1411	.098

Levene's test is not significant, indicating homogeneity of variance.

Tests the null hypothesis that the error variance of the dependent variable is equal across groups.

a. Design: Intercept+sex+newethnc+sex* newethnc

Figure 8b.18   Selected Descriptive and Diagnostic Tables From the Between-Subjects Procedure

Tests of Between-Subjects Effects

Dependent Variable: gaft2

Source	Type III Sum of Squares	df	Mean Square	F	Sig.	Partial Eta Squared
Corrected Model	25876.524[a]	5	5175.305	33.274	.000	.105
Intercept	2735380.430	1	2735380.430	17587.01	.000	.926
Sex	18457.723	1	18457.723	118.673	.000	.078
Newethnc	2596.699	2	1298.350	8.348	.000	.012
Sex * newethnc	2140.920	2	1070.460	6.882	.001	.010
Error	219458.624	1411	155.534			
Total	3658537.000	1417				
Corrected Total	245335.147	1416				

a. R Squared = .105 (Adjusted R Squared = .102).

The interaction is significant and supersedes the significant main effects.

Client Gender * Client Ethnicity Trichotomy

Dependent Variable: gaft2

Client Gender	Client Ethnicity Trichotomy	Mean	Std. Error	95% Confidence Interval	
				Lower Bound	Upper Bound
Male	White American	46.245	.919	44.441	48.048
	Latino American	43.521	.977	41.605	45.438
	African American	40.743	1.069	38.645	42.840
Female	White American	50.531	.732	49.094	51.968
	Latino American	53.653	.594	52.488	54.818
	African American	49.685	.875	47.968	51.402

Figure 8b.19 Selected Output Tables From the Between-Subjects Procedure

Squared value of .010 indicates that this statistically significant interaction effect accounts for only about 1% of the total variance. The last output table of Figure 8b.19 displays the means involved in this significant interaction.

Because the interaction is significant, our next step is to conduct simple effects analyses. In the present example, a simple effects analysis is the same as selecting out only the male clients in our data set and conducting a one-way ANOVA among the three client ethnicity means depicted in Figure 8b.19. If this ANOVA is statistically significant (i.e., there are differences between the three male ethnic group means), we can then proceed with a post hoc multiple comparison assessment of these three means. A similar one-way ANOVA for the female clients would also be conducted.

There are at least four different ways of performing a simple effects analysis in SPSS. Here is a very brief outline describing them, assuming that we are running simple effects for the independent variable represented by the rows:

- ▶ We can use a **Select Cases** procedure to capture participants in a_1 and then run a one-way analysis to compare the means of b_1 and b_2. If there were three or more groups, we would invoke a post hoc test such as the Tukey comparison. We would then select the participants in a_2 and perform a similar analysis.
- ▶ We can **Sort Cases** on the *A* independent variable (placing all a_1 cases in front of all the a_2 cases in the data file). We would then do a **Split File** on the A variable and subsequently invoke the same one-way analysis as above. The analysis would be run on each split, producing all the analyses we needed.
- ▶ We can write syntax using the **mwithin** structure on the **MANOVA** procedure (this is not available in the point-and-click mode, instead requiring a syntax window for researchers to write the few lines of required command structure).
- ▶ We can use the **univariate** path of the **General Linear Model (GLM)** to structure the analysis. Some syntax is required to be written, but you can formulate the analysis through point-and-click and then click the **paste** button to give you a syntax window that displayed the syntax for the directions that you selected via point-and-click. All you would have to do is type in the **compare (factor) adj (method)** to instruct SPSS to perform the simple effects analysis. These days, this is probably the preferred procedure to analyze the simple effects of an interaction. Below is a minimal example of what the analysis looks like, with *Y* as the name of the dependent variable and *A* and *B* as the independent variables. This analysis will isolate the levels of *A* and compare the *B* means with each other. Thus, if there were three levels of *B*, the comparisons would be b_1 with b_2, b_1 with b_3, and b_2 with b_3 for each level of A. These comparisons would use a Bonferroni correction or adjustment to control for Type I error inflation.

GLM Y by A B

/emeans = tables (A × B) compare (B) adj (Bonferroni)

/design.

We will demonstrate a procedure in keeping with our menu-driven (nonsyntax) approach to using SPSS. We begin by clicking **Data → Select Cases,** which produces the **Select Cases** dialog box (see Figure 8b.20) where we have activated the **If condition is satisfied** checkbox.

Clicking the **If** pushbutton (below this checkbox) produces the **Select Cases: If** dialog box (see second box of Figure 8b.20), where we pasted our variable name **sex** (for client gender) into the box on the right side of the dialog box. We have also clicked the = button and the **1** button to complete our logical expression **sex = 1**. This instruction tells SPSS to include only those cases where sex = 1 (i.e., only males) in any future analysis. Clicking **Continue** moves us back to the **Select Cases** dialog box, and clicking **OK** activates only cases that meet our stated criteria. If you look at the data file, you will see that all other cases (the females, and any cases with missing values on this variable) have a slash (/) through their **caseid** number, indicating that they are temporarily removed from the analysis. By changing the **Select If** logical expression to **sex = 2**, we can exclude all the male cases in a subsequent analysis.

With only our male cases activated in the data set, we can now proceed to run a one-way ANOVA by clicking **Analyze → General Linear Model → Univariate,** which again produces the **Univariate** dialog box (see Figure 8b.21), where we have pasted **gaft2** into the **Dependent Variable** box and **newethnc** (our independent variable) into the **Fixed Factor(s)** box. Notice that **sex** is not included in the **Fixed Factor(s)** box because this one-way ANOVA is examining client ethnicity "collapsed" across levels of gender. In effect, we are instructing SPSS to perform a one-way ANOVA with client ethnicity as the independent variable and GAF at Time 2 as the dependent variable on only the male clients. We will then conduct the same analysis for the female clients.

Clicking **Post Hoc** in the **Univariate** dialog box produces the **Univariate: Post Hoc Multiple Comparisons for Observed Means** dialog box (see also Figure 8b.21). Notice that we have double-clicked the **newethnc** variable name in the **Factor(s)** box, which pastes this variable name into the **Post Hoc Tests for** box and activates 18 multiple comparisons tests at the bottom of the dialog box. We have checked the **Tukey** checkbox, requesting Tukey HSD multiple comparisons to be made on the **newethnc** group means, pending a statistically significant omnibus one-way

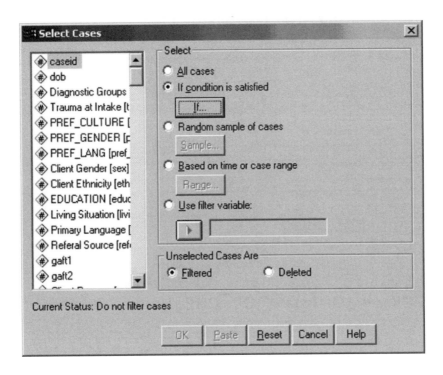

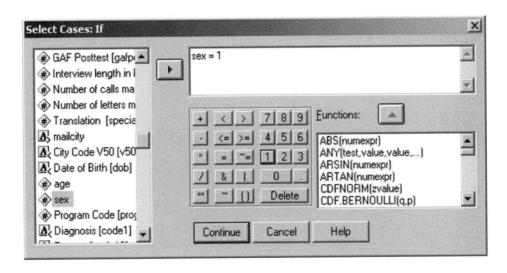

Figure 8b.20   Select Cases Main Dialog Box for Selecting Specific Cases and Its If Condition
Is Satisfied Dialog Box

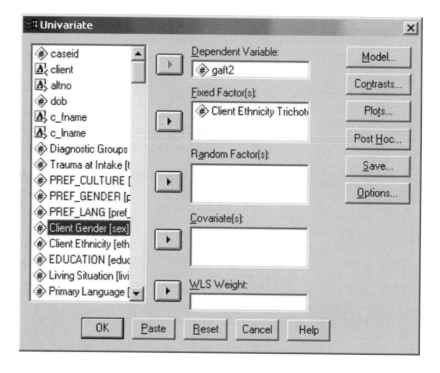

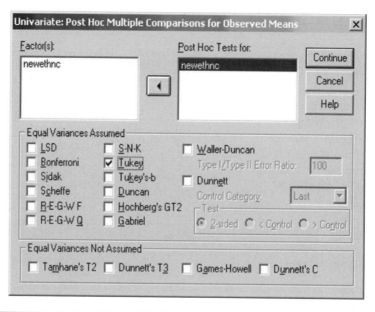

Figure 8b.21 Univariate Main Dialog Box and Its Post Hoc Multiple Comparisons for Observed Means Dialog Box

ANOVA *F* test. Clicking **Continue** brings us back to the **Univariate** dialog box, and clicking **OK** runs the analysis.

The SPSS output can be seen in Figures 8b.22 and 8b.23. Figure 8b.22 first depicts the **Between-Subjects Factors** output table. With female clients eliminated from the analysis, sample sizes are still more than adequate. Next, the **Descriptive Statistics** output suggests that White American male clients ($M = 46.24$, $SD = 12.171$) had somewhat higher GAF

Between-Subjects Factors

		Value Label	N
Client Ethnicity Trichotomy	1	White American	184
	2	Latino American	163
	3	African American	136

Descriptive Statistics

Dependent Variable: gaft2

Client Ethnicity Trichotomy	Mean	Std. Deviation	N
White American	46.24	12.171	184
Latino American	43.52	12.704	163
African American	40.74	13.440	136
Total	43.78	12.885	483

Levene's Test of Equality of Error Variances[a]

Dependent Variable: gaft2

F	df1	df2	Sig.
.258	2	480	.773

Tests the null hypothesis that the error variance of the dependent variable is equal across groups.

a. Design: Intercept+newethnc.

Figure 8b.22 Selected Descriptive and Diagnostic Tables for Between-Subjects Procedure

Tests of Between-Subjects Effects

Dependent Variable: gaft2

Source	Type III Sum of Squares	df	Mean Square	F	Sig.	Partial Eta Squared
Corrected Model	2383.189[a]	2	1191.594	7.367	.001	.030
Intercept	900110.607	1	900110.607	5565.065	.000	.921
Newethnc	2383.189	2	1191.594	7.367	.001	.030
Error	77636.662	480	161.743			
Total	1005628.000	483				
Corrected Total	80019.851	482				

a. R Squared = .030 (Adjusted R Squared = .026).

> This *F* ratio applies only to males.

Multiple Comparisons

Dependent Variable: gaft2
Tukey HSD

(I) Client Ethnicity Trichotomy	(J) Client Ethnicity Trichotomy	Mean Difference (I-J)	Std. Error	Sig.	95% Confidence Interval	
					Lower Bound	Upper Bound
White American	Latino American	2.72	1.368	.116	−.49	5.94
	African American	5.50*	1.438	.000	2.12	8.88
Latino American	White American	−2.72	1.368	.116	−5.94	.49
	African American	2.78	1.477	.145	−.69	6.25
African American	White American	−5.50*	1.438	.000	−8.88	−2.12
	Latino American	−2.78	1.477	.145	−6.25	.69

Based on observed means.
*The mean difference is significant at the .05 level.

Figure 8b.23 Selected Output Tables for Between-Subjects Procedure

Time 2 scores than their Latino and African American counterparts. **Levene's Test of Equality of Error Variances** was not statistically significant, $F(2, 480) = .258, p > .773$. This result tells us that the error variance for the dependent variable (**gaft2**) is equal across all three groups.

Figure 8b.23 displays the **Tests of Between-Subjects Effects**. The **Source** row in which we are most interested is labeled **newethnc** and shows an *F* value of 7.367, which is evaluated at 2 and 480 degrees of freedom and is statistically significant at the .001 alpha level. The **Partial Eta Squared** statistic (.030) indicates that this client ethnicity effect accounts for 3% of the total variance.

Because of the statistically significant *F* ratio, Tukey HSD post hoc tests were computed among all possible comparisons of the male client ethnicity means and are displayed in the **Multiple Comparisons** table (see second table of Figure 8b.23). This output tells us that the statistically significant *F* value was due to a significant difference between the White American (*M* = 46.24) and the African American (*M* = 40.74) male GAF scores at Time 2 (mean difference = 5.50). This was partially responsible for the statistically significant Gender × Client Ethnicity interaction effect we encountered back in the **Tests of Between-Subjects Effects** output.

A second simple effects analysis was run with only the female clients. Because the steps involved are exactly the same as the simple effects analysis with males, we will not detail those analyses here. This simple effect analysis was statistically significant also (*F* = 9.483, *p* < .001, partial eta squared = .020). Tukey HSD post hoc tests (*p* < .01) showed that the female Latino American clients (*M* = 53.65) had significantly higher GAF scores than their White American (*M* = 49.68) or African American (*M* = 50.53) counterparts.

In sum, the statistically significant interaction was a function of the White American male clients achieving higher clinical outcomes at Time 2 than their African American counterparts, whereas female Latino American clients achieved higher GAF scores than did their White and African American counterparts. These results produced the interaction.

Results

GAF at Time 2 scores were analyzed by means of a two-way between-subjects ANOVA with three levels of client ethnicity (White American, Latino American, African American) and two levels of client gender (male, female). All effects were found to be statistically significant. The main effect of client gender showed that female clients (*M* = 51.29, *SE* = .43) achieved higher clinical outcomes (GAF scores) than did male clients: (*M* = 43.50, *SE* = .57), *F*(1, 1411) = 118.67, *p* < .001, partial η^2 = .08.

(Continued)

(Continued)

The main effect of client ethnicity, $F(2, 1,411) = 8.35$, $p < .001$, partial $\eta^2 = .01$, was assessed using the Tukey HSD multiple comparison test. Results showed that African American clients achieved significantly lower GAF scores ($M = 45.21$, $SE = .69$) than did their White American ($M = 48.39$, $SE = .59$) and Latino American ($M = 48.59$, $SE = .57$) counterparts.

The interaction effect, $F(2, 1,411) = 6.88$, $p < .001$, partial $\eta^2 = .01$, was analyzed using simple effects analysis and the Tukey HSD test. The relevant means can be seen in Table 8b.1. The statistically significant interaction was a function of White American male clients achieving higher clinical outcomes than their African American counterparts. Conversely, female Latino American clients achieved higher GAF scores than did their White and African American counterparts. These results, collectively, produced the significant interaction effect.

Table 8b.1 Mean GAF Score at Time 2 as a Function of Client Gender and Client Ethnicity

| | Client Ethnicity | | | | | | | | |
| | White American | | | Latino American | | | African American | | |
Gender	M	SD	N	M	SD	N	M	SD	N
Male	46.25_a	12.17	184	43.52_b	12.70	163	40.74_a	13.44	136
Female	$50.53_{a,b}$	10.78	290	53.65_a	12.29	441	$49.69_{a,b}$	14.37	203

Note: Means in a row sharing subscripts are significantly different. The higher the GAF score, the better the clinical outcome.

Numerical Example 7: Two-Way Mixed Design

In a two-way mixed design (also referred to as a *split-plot* design), one independent variable is a between-subjects factor and the other independent variable is a repeated or within-subjects factor. For the present numerical example, assume that we are interested in the effects of client gender on service satisfaction (CSQ-8 score) with three different types of psychotherapy. Thus, we have chosen to assess each client after 10 sessions each of psychoanalytic, cognitive-behavioral, and brief psychotherapy. Assume that therapy type was properly counterbalanced across all participants. Each client is assessed at each of the three psychotherapeutic interventions—psychoanalytic (b$_1$), cognitive-behavioral (b$_2$), and brief (b$_3$). Participants were also categorized into male (a$_1$) and female (a$_2$) groups. The result was a mixed design, with gender as the between-subjects variable and therapy type as a within-subjects variable. Therapy type was completely counterbalanced, requiring six participants in each gender condition. The dependent variable was a measure of service satisfaction (CSQ-8) at the end of 10 sessions with each type of treatment.

To conduct this analysis, we begin by clicking **Analyze → General Linear Model → Repeated Measures,** which opens the **Repeated Measures Define Factor(s)** dialog box (see Figure 8b.24). In the **Within-Subject Factor Name** box we have erased the SPSS default name (**Factor1)** and typed in **treat** (for treatment) as our new within-subject factor name. In the **Number of Levels** box we have typed in **3** (for the three treatment types). Clicking the **Add** button pastes the factor name and number of levels, **treat(3)**, into the unlabeled box at the top-center of the dialog box as can be seen in the top portion of Figure 8b.24.

Clicking the **Define** pushbutton opens the **Repeated Measures** dialog box (see also Figure 8b.24). From the **Variable List** box (on the left side of the dialog box) we have highlighted the three variable names (**psycho, cogbeh, brief**) that will compose the within-subjects factor, **treat,** and have moved these names to the **Within-Subjects Variables (treat)** box by clicking the right arrow button. We have also clicked over the client gender variable to the **Between-Subjects Factor(s)** box.

Clicking the **Plots** pushbutton on the bottom produces the **Repeated Measures: Profile Plots** dialog box (see Figure 8b.25). To set up the plot, we moved **treat** (the name of the within-subjects factor) from the **Factors** panel to the panel for the **Horizontal Axis** and we have moved **gender** (the between-subjects factor) to the panel for **Separate Lines.** Clicking the **Add** button specifies this plot for SPSS as **treat*gender** in the **Plots** panel in Figure 8b.25. Clicking **Continue** returns us to the **Repeated Measures** dialog box. We will not click the **Post Hoc** tab because our between-subjects variable (gender) has only two levels.

Clicking the **Options** pushbutton produces the **Repeated Measures: Options** dialog box (see also Figure 8b.25). Notice that we have clicked over the main effects and interaction effects (i.e., gender, treat, gender × treat) in the **Factor(s) and Factor Interactions** box to the **Display Means for** box. (Note that we will ignore any output on any effect that is not statistically significant.) We have clicked the **Compare main effects** box and selected **Bonferroni** adjustments to the alpha levels for our multiple comparisons and also activated the **Descriptive statistics, Estimates of effect size,** and **Homogeneity tests** checkboxes. Clicking **Continue** brings us back to the **Repeated Measures** dialog box, and clicking **OK** runs the analysis.

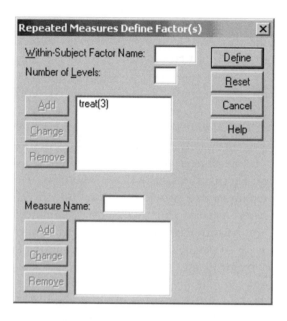

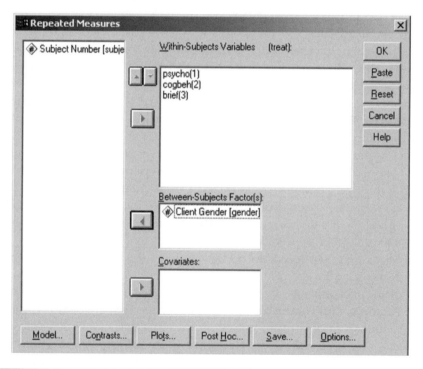

Figure 8b.24 Repeated Measures Define Factor(s) Main Dialog Box and Dialog Box Appearing After Clicking the Define Pushbutton

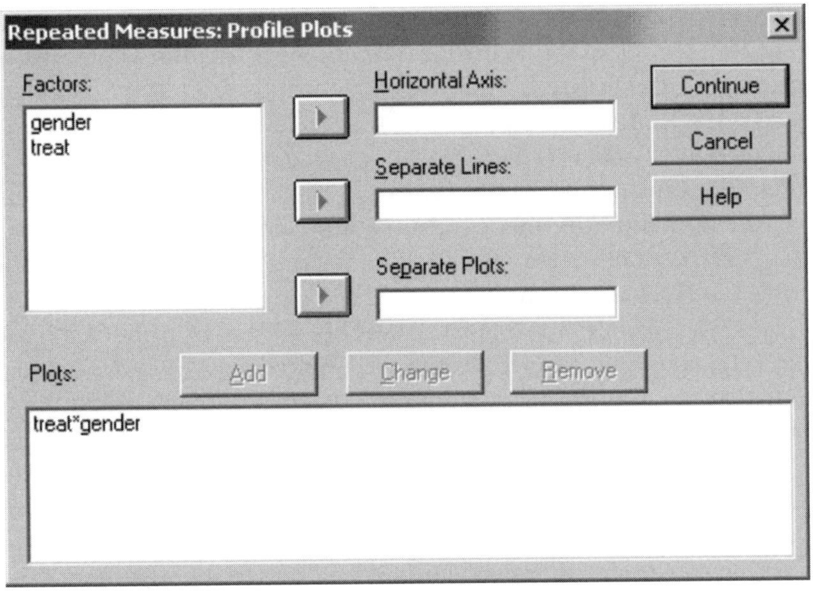

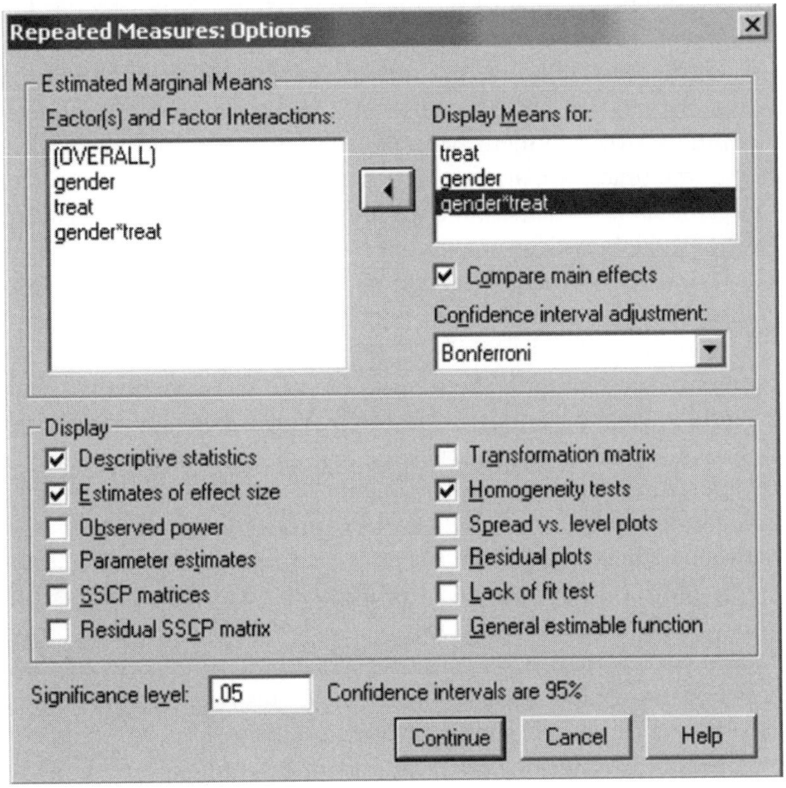

Figure 8b.25   Repeated Measures: Profile Plots Dialog Box and Options Dialog Box

Selected SPSS output can be seen in Figures 8b.26, 8b.27, and 8b.28. Figure 8b.26 depicts the **Within-Subjects Factors**, **Between-Subjects Factors**, and **Descriptive Statistics** tabled output. An inspection of the **Descriptive Statistics** output shows that the **Brief** psychotherapy group mean (see the **Total** row, $M = 29.058$) is somewhat higher than the other treatment group means. Sample sizes are small but equal across groups. **Box's Test of Equality of Covariance Matrices** is not statistically significant ($p > .937$), indicating that the covariance matrices of the dependent variable are equal across groups.

Figure 8b.27 indicates that the **Mauchly's Test of Sphericity** is not statistically significant (**approximate chi square** = .854, $p > .652$), indicating that we do not need to use adjusted degrees of freedom in the interpretation of the within-subjects F tests.

The **Tests of Within-Subjects Effects** are also displayed in Figure 8b.27. Because Mauchly's test of sphericity was not statistically significant, we can use the **Sphericity Assumed** rows when interpreting the F tests for the within-subjects main (**treat**) and interaction (**treat * gender**) effects. Notice that the main effect of treatment type (**treat**) produced an F value of 86.492, which is evaluated at 2 and 20 (error) degrees of freedom (**df**), and is statistically significant at alpha = .000. The **Partial Eta Squared** value was .896, indicating that nearly 90% of the within-subjects variability is accounted for by treatment type. We will follow up this significant main effect with multiple comparisons tests, but first let's examine the remaining sources of variability—namely, the within-subjects interaction effect (**treat * gender**) and the between-subjects effect of **gender**.

The **Treat * Gender** interaction effect is also displayed. This effect is not statistically significant, $F = .012, p < .998$, indicating that treatment type does not interact or vary across levels of client gender.

Before proceeding to the between-subjects effects, we need to examine the **Levene's Test of Equality of Error Variances** also shown next in Figure 8b.27. We note a nonsignificant F test for each within-subjects factor group, indicating homogeneity (equality) of variance of the dependent variable across groups. Thus, we can now proceed with an assessment of the between-subjects effects.

Figure 8b.28 displays the **Tests of Between-Subjects Effects**. Notice that the row labeled **gender** (for the main effect of client gender) produced an F value of .149, which was evaluated at 1 and 10 degrees of freedom and was not statistically significant ($p > .708$). This result tells us that client satisfaction was comparable among males and females.

Because the within-subjects main effect of treatment type was statistically significant, we can now proceed to evaluate the three treatment type

Within-Subjects Factors

Measure: MEASURE_1

Treat	Dependent Variable
1	psycho
2	cogbeh
3	brief

Between-Subjects Factors

		N
Client Gender	1	6
	2	6

Descriptive Statistics

	Client Gender	Mean	Std. Deviation	N
Psychoanalytic	1	22.317	.8159	6
	2	22.500	1.0863	6
	Total	22.408	.9209	12
Cognitive-Behavioral	1	25.133	1.0746	6
	2	25.167	1.1725	6
	Total	25.150	1.0724	12
Brief	1	28.983	1.0962	6
	2	29.133	1.5578	6
	Total	29.058	1.2866	12

Box's Test of Equality of Covariance Matrices[a]

Box's M	2.698
F	.300
df1	6
df2	724.528
Sig.	.937

Tests the null hypothesis that the observed covariance matrices of the dependent variables are equal across groups.

a. Design: Intercept+gender
   Within Subjects Design: treat

Figure 8b.26 Selected Descriptive and Diagnostic Tables From Mixed Design Procedure

Mauchly's Test of Sphericity[b]

Measure: MEASURE_1

Within Subjects Effect	Mauchly's W	Approx. Chi Square	df	Sig.	Epsilon[a]		
					Greenhouse-Geisser	Huynh-Feldt	Lower-bound
treat	.909	.854	2	.652	.917	1.000	.500

Tests the null hypothesis that the error covariance matrix of the orthonormalized transformed dependent variables is proportional to an identity matrix.

a. May be used to adjust the degrees of freedom for the averaged tests of significance. Corrected tests are displayed in the Tests of Within-Subjects Effects table.

b. Design: Intercept+gender
   Within Subjects Design: treat

Tests of Within-Subjects Effects

> The main effect of treat is significant.

Measure: MEASURE_1

Source		Type III Sum of Squares	df	Mean Square	F	Sig.	Partial Eta Squared
treat	Sphericity Assumed	268.057	2	134.029	86.492	.000	.896
	Greenhouse-Geisser	268.057	1.834	146.165	86.492	.000	.896
	Huynh-Feldt	268.057	2.000	134.029	86.492	.000	.896
	Lower-bound	268.057	1.000	268.057	86.492	.000	.896
treat * gender	Sphericity Assumed	.037	2	.019	.012	.988	.001
	Greenhouse-Geisser	.037	1.834	.020	.012	.984	.001
	Huynh-Feldt	.037	2.000	.019	.012	.988	.001
	Lower-bound	.037	1.000	.037	.012	.915	.001
Error(treat)	Sphericity Assumed	30.992	20	1.550			
	Greenhouse-Geisser	30.992	18.339	1.690			
	Huynh-Feldt	30.992	20.000	1.550			
	Lower-bound	30.992	10.000	3.099			

> The Treat × Gender effect is not significant.

Levene's Test of Equality of Error Variances[a]

	F	df1	df2	Sig
Psychoanalytic	.299	1	10	.597
Cognitive-Behavioral	.087	1	10	.775
Brief	.353	1	10	565

Tests the null hypothesis that the error variance of the dependent variable is equal across groups.

a. Design: Intercept + gender
   Within Subjects Design: treat

Figure 8b.27   Selected Output Tables From Mixed Design Procedure

Tests of Between-Subjects Effects

Measure: MEASURE_1
Transformed Variable: Average

Source	Type III Sum of Squares	df	Mean Square	F	Sig.	Partial Eta Squared
Intercept	23480.454	1	23480.454	26018.73	.000	1.000
Gender	.134	1	.134	.149	.708	.015
Error	9.024	10	.902			

Estimates

Measure: MEASURE_1

treat	Mean	Std. Error	95% Confidence Interval	
			Lower Bound	Upper Bound
1	22.408	.277	21.790	23.026
2	25.150	.325	24.427	25.873
3	29.058	.389	28.192	29.925

Pairwise Comparisons

Measure: MEASURE_1

(I) treatment	(J) treatment	Mean Difference (I-J)	Std. Error	Sig.[a]	95% Confidence Interval for Difference[a]	
					Lower Bound	Upper Bound
1	2	−2.742*	.539	.001	−4.289	−1.194
	3	−6.650*	.425	.000	−7.871	−5.429
2	1	2.742*	.539	.001	1.194	4.289
	3	−3.908*	.551	.000	−5.489	−2.328
3	1	6.650*	.425	.000	5.429	7.871
	2	3.908*	.551	.000	2.328	5.489

Based on estimated marginal means.
*The mean difference is significant at the .05 level.

a. Adjustment for multiple comparisons: Bonferroni.

SPSS is comparing the means of the within-subjects variables. These numbers correspond to the names of the levels shown in the Within-Subjects Factors table (see Figure 8b.26).

Figure 8b.28 Additional Selected Output Tables From Mixed Design Procedure

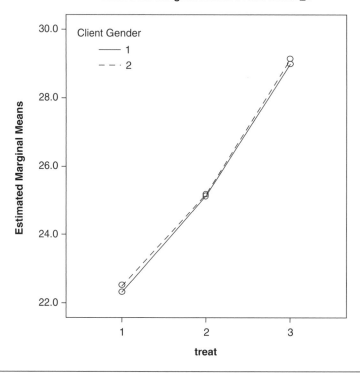

Estimated Marginal Means of MEASURE_1

Figure 8b.29   Plot of the Level of Treatment Means as a Function of Gender

(**treat**) means in the **Estimates** tabled output and evaluate all pairwise comparisons of these means in the **Pairwise Comparisons** table, both of which can also be seen in Figure 8b.28. These **Bonferroni** adjusted multiple comparisons indicate that Group 3 (brief, mean difference = 6.650) is significantly different from Group 1, the psychoanalytic group, and that Group 3 is significantly different from Group 2 (cognitive-behavioral, mean difference = 3.908) and that Group 2 (cognitive-behavioral, mean difference = 2.742) is significantly different from the psychoanalytic group. Thus, the present results indicate that client satisfaction is highest (regardless of gender) for clients receiving brief psychotherapy (M = 29.058), followed by cognitive-behavioral (M = 25.150), and last, psychoanalytic treatment (M = 22.408). The results of an SPSS plot of these means as a function of gender can be seen in Figure 8b.29.

Results

Client service satisfaction scores were analyzed by means of a two-way mixed design ANOVA having two levels of client gender (male, female) as a between-subjects factor and three levels of treatment type (psychoanalytic, cognitive-behavioral, brief) as a within-subjects factor. The interaction effect of Treatment Type × Gender was found to not be statistically significant ($F < 1.0$). The between-subjects main effect of gender was found not to be statistically significant, $F(1, 10) = .149, p > .05$, indicating comparability between the perceived service satisfaction of male ($M = 25.48, SE = .22$) and female ($M = 25.60, SE = .22$) clients.

The within-subjects main effect of treatment type was found to be statistically significant, $F(2, 20) = 86.49, p < .001$, partial $\eta^2 = .90$. The nature of this effect was determined using a Bonferroni adjusted multiple comparison test ($p < .05$). Results showed that the psychoanalytic ($M = 22.41, SD = 92.0$), cognitive-behavioral ($M = 25.15, SD = 1.07$), and brief ($M = 29.06, SD = 1.29$) treatment type means all differed significantly from one another and can be seen in Table 8b.2.

Table 8b.2   Mean GAF Score at Time 2 as a Function of Client Gender and Client Ethnicity

Treatment Type								
Psychoanalytic			Cognitive-Behavioral			Brief		
M	SD	N	M	SD	N	M	SD	N
22.41$_a$	92	12	25.15$_{a,b}$	1.07	12	29.06$_{a,b}$	1.29	12

Note: Means in a row sharing subscripts are significantly different. The higher the service satisfaction score, the greater the perceived satisfaction.

8B Exercises

Independent-Samples *t* Test: Sex Differences in Spelling Ability

A developmental psychologist examines whether females (coded as 2) score statistically significantly greater on spelling tests than males (coded as 1). Using the SPSS *t*-test data file for Chapter 8B (located on the Web-based study site—http://www.sagepub.com/amrStudy), conduct a GLM technique for the *t* test.

1. What are the mean scores in the experimental and control groups?
2. Is the difference one that we would predict? Explain.
3. In this study, how was the homogeneity of variance assumption tested? Was the assumption violated?
4. What was the "observed power" of this study? How is this interpreted? Is it satisfactory?
5. What is the value of eta squared? Does it have practical significance?

One-Way Between-Subjects ANOVA: Reward Structure on Intrinsic Motivation in First Graders

An experiment on the effects of reward structure on intrinsic motivation is conducted. Participants are 48 first graders, each randomly assigned to one of four conditions. The reward structure conditions are (a) individualistic, (b) cooperative, (c) competitive, and (d) no rewards. The task rewarded is success on subtraction exercises. The treatment lasts for 3 weeks. Following the treatment, intrinsic motivation to do subtraction problems is assessed during five nonstructured "free-choice" sessions. The outcome is the number of minutes spent on subtraction problems.

Using the SPSS one-way ANOVA data file for Chapter 8B (located on the Web-based study site—http://www.sagepub.com/amrStudy), answer the following questions.

1. According to the omnibus test, are the *four* means significantly different? What is the exact *p* of the omnibus?
2. What are the mean scores in the four conditions?
3. What is the effect size as measured by eta squared? Is it a small, medium, or large effect?
4. In this study, how was the homogeneity of variance assumption tested? Was the assumption violated?
5. Are the results from the LSD post hoc consistent with the results of the Scheffé post hoc?

One-Way Trend Analysis: Ability to Concentrate (Temporal)

A psychologist assesses the effectiveness of a new technique to learn to concentrate for ADHD elementary school children. Eight children are taught the new technique and are tested three times during the semester. The test is the amount of time on task measured in minutes. The data are provided below. Conduct the proper statistical analysis.

Using the SPSS one-way trend data file for Chapter 8B (located on the Web-based study site—http://www.sagepub.com/amrStudy), answer the following questions.

1. What is the effect size as measured by eta squared? Is it a small, medium, or large effect?

2. What does the Mauchly's test of sphericity tell us?

3. Is the effect of the treatment linear or quadratic? Explain.

4. Write a results section for this research.

2 × 3 Between-Subjects Factorial ANOVA: Study Environments by Gender

This study investigates differences in *three* different study environments. This study also investigates if gender "moderates" (i.e., within each study environment, does one gender attain greater improvement than another?). To answer these questions a factorial ANOVA needs to be conducted.

Variables in study:

▶ Study environments (Envir): 1 = Front of TV; 2 = Library; 3 = Food Court
▶ Sex: 1= Male; 2 = Female
▶ Grade improvement (GPAIMPR): −.25 to +.50

Using the SPSS 2 × 3 ANOVA data file for Chapter 8B (located on the Web-based study site—http://www.sagepub.com/amrStudy), answer the following questions.

1. Are the main effects of sex and environment and their interaction statistically significant?

2. How much variance is accounted for by the statistically significant effects?

3. Would a researcher be interested in the main effects, if interaction effect is statistically significant? Explain.

4. What would be the proper follow-up tests for a statistically significant interaction effect?

5. What is the substantive conclusion of this research?

6. Write a results section for this study.

MANOVA

Comparing Two Groups

A s we saw in Chapters 8A and 8B, ANOVA is applied to designs with single dependent measures and is thus conceived as a univariate procedure. Even if researchers measured more than one dependent variable, as is often the case, they can analyze only one at a time using ANOVA. The next six chapters cross into the domain of multivariate ANOVA in which many dependent variables are simultaneously analyzed within a single ANOVA design. When we make this transition, we find ourselves in the domain of *multivariate analysis of variance,* abbreviated as MANOVA.

This chapter introduces MANOVA by focusing on the two-group between-subjects design. We are thus interested in assessing the effects of one dichotomous (two-group) independent variable on two or more quantitative dependent variables. For example, we might study the effects of gender (male, female) on worker job satisfaction and worker absenteeism, or we might be interested in the effect of treatment type (cognitive-behavioral, psychoanalytic) on global assessment of functioning (GAF) and consumer service satisfaction.

Although these research questions can certainly be addressed with univariate statistical procedures that examine each dependent variable separately (e.g., using *t* tests or one-way ANOVAs), they can also be profitably explored (or properly done) in the multivariate realm by examining the dependent measures *collectively* and *simultaneously* by means of a multivariate generalization of the *t* test called Hotelling's T^2 (or MANOVA for the two-group independent variable context).

The Use of MANOVA

The strategy of taking more than one index of the behavior of participants in a research study has much to be said in its favor. Rarely is one aspect of behavior so isolated from other aspects of the overall response that it can paint a comprehensive picture of how someone responded to a situation. To return to an example that we just mentioned, we would certainly expect that employees who were more satisfied with their job would in general have less absenteeism than those who were less satisfied. In measuring the effects of some sort of workplace intervention program, both satisfaction and absenteeism are likely to be indicators of some more general or latent variable concerning the feelings of employees toward their job. This latent variable might be called "employee contentment" and would represent the composite variable subsuming satisfaction and absenteeism. Focusing on only one aspect of employee contentment, such as job satisfaction, thus provides only part of the issue in which we as researchers are really interested.

MANOVA and Variates

This is similar to the multiple regression situation where the weighted set of predictors can be thought of as forming a variate that is then related to the criterion variable. An analogous situation occurs in MANOVA. The dependent variables in a MANOVA design are combined into a weighted linear composite. In MANOVA, the weights are determined to be those that allow the variate to maximally distinguish (differentiate, discriminate) between the groups (the levels of the independent variable) in the study. Multiple regression yields a single weighted combination of predictors because the criterion variable is quantitatively measured. Because the target of the prediction in MANOVA is the independent variable, which is treated as a categorical variable, the number of variates derived by a MANOVA is the lesser of (a) the number of dependent variables and (b) the number of groups (levels of the independent variable) minus 1. Because this chapter explores differences between two groups, the number of derived variates will always be 1.

MANOVA and Vectors

Single measures are often referred to as scalar measures. We use them as dependent variables in experimental designs because that single measure is considered adequate in assessing a variable of interest to the researchers. Multiple measures are often referred to as *vectors*. Vectors are a set (combination) of numbers that describes a phenomenon and is very useful in those all-too-frequent situations where no single number is sufficient to quantify the phenomenon. Essentially, the variate can be thought of as an example of a vector where the variate value is computed as a weighted sum of its components.

Vectors are fairly commonly used by us in everyday living. An example of a vector from our general experience would be speed. We understand speed in a rather direct sense of how fast we are traveling. But speed is really composed of two separate physical variables: distance and time. Thus, if it takes us half an hour to travel 30 miles, we know that we are traveling at 60 miles per hour. In this case, we have divided distance by time to calculate speed. In the MANOVA designs we will be discussing, it is appropriate to speak of vectors to represent the dependent variable variate. Here, the vectors are computed as a weighted sum of the dependent variables.

When MANOVA Is Appropriate

So what exactly is the benefit of conducting a simultaneous analysis of multiple dependent variables? Seven immediate advantages can be identified (Bray & Maxwell, 1985; Stevens, 2002).

First, single dependent measures seldom capture completely a phenomenon being scrutinized. Multiple measures provide the researcher with a certain amount of useful redundancy (through the correlation of the multiple measures) and the ability to broaden or enhance the conceptual domain under study. For example, job satisfaction could be tapped with a single item: "How satisfied are you with your current job?" Although such a global measure will provide useful information, a better approach would be to explore separate and unique job satisfaction facets (e.g., satisfaction with pay, benefits, coworkers, location, etc.) that can initially be combined into one global job satisfaction vector that can subsequently be decomposed into its separate job satisfaction constituents.

Second, MANOVA provides some control over the overall alpha level or Type I error rate (i.e., the chance of making a false rejection of the null hypothesis). If we were to examine gender differences (the independent variable), for example, with four job satisfaction dependent variables (pay, benefits, coworkers, and location) using four separate univariate t tests or one-way ANOVAs each evaluated at the .05 alpha level, we would expect a statistically significant effect 5% of the time for each dependent measure. In practice, the alpha level we wind up with across these four analyses actually lies someplace between 5% and 18.5% (i.e., $1 - (.95)(.95)(.95)(.95)$). The point is that multiple univariate t tests or ANOVAs can inflate the operational alpha level

(Type I error), a state of affairs often called *probability pyramiding;* using MANOVA avoids this problem (see Hummel & Sligo, 1971).

Third, univariate statistical tests tend to ignore the intercorrelation found between dependent variables. As we will see, MANOVA considers dependent variable intercorrelation by examining the variance-covariance matrices.

Fourth, MANOVA enables researchers to examine relationships between dependent variables at each level of the independent variable.

Fifth, MANOVA provides researchers with statistical guidance to reduce a large set of dependent measures to a smaller assemblage.

Sixth, MANOVA helps to identify dependent variables that produce the most group (independent variable) separation or distinction.

And seventh, MANOVA can "tease out" group differences that may become masked with univariate statistical analyses but are discovered under conditions of increased power in the multivariate situation.

When MANOVA Should Not Be Used

Conversely, there are at least three circumstances under which we would either not want to use MANOVA or approach MANOVA with considerable caution (see Bray & Maxwell, 1985).

First, MANOVA should not be used if the dependent variables are uncorrelated. As we will see, the ideal situation for using MANOVA is when the dependent variables are moderately correlated. Weinfurt (1995), for example, uses an example in which the correlations between three dependent variables ranged between .21 and .36 to illustrate the appropriateness of a MANOVA design.

Second, and this is the other side of what we just talked about, MANOVA should not be used with a set of dependent variables that is very highly correlated. Statistically, such correlations will run the risk of a multicollinearity condition, which could cause the analysis to yield improper results if SPSS allowed the analysis to proceed in the first place. Conceptually, to the extent that variables are highly correlated, they can be said to be measuring the same construct and are therefore redundant.

There are two common situations that we have found where students encounter this problem. One situation occurs when students use the subscales of an inventory together with the total inventory scores as dependent variables. The subscales here are portions of the total score and thus in combination correlate very highly (sometimes almost perfectly) with the total score. The solution to this situation is to run two analyses, one using only the subscales and another using the total score.

A second situation in which the dependent variables are too highly correlated occurs when one of the dependent variables is computed from one or more of the others. For example, if researchers use the time it takes for a response to be made as well as the speed of the response as dependent variables, they will have created multicollinearity because speed is the reciprocal of time and the two are therefore perfectly correlated. As another example, using two variables such as GAF at Time 1 and GAF at Time 2 as well as the difference score (GAF 2 minus GAF 1) would create perfect linear dependence that would produce multicollinearity.

A third situation in which MANOVA should not be used or, perhaps more appropriately, should be used with great caution is when the target user or the recipient of the analysis has limited statistical or technical knowledge. The assumptions underlying MANOVA as well as the output of the analysis is considerably more complex than its univariate cousins, and this poses greater interpretation and communication challenges for the researchers and their audience. Using complicated statistical tools such as MANOVA places the burden squarely on the shoulders of the researchers to explain the output of the analysis in ways that do justice to the results while at the same time help the end user understand what was found.

The Univariate *t* Test

As noted in Chapter 8A, the univariate *t* test addresses the question of whether two population means are equal. For example, the independent variable could be gender (male, female) and the dependent variable global assessment of functioning (GAF). The *t* test is a way of testing the null hypothesis (H_0), which states that in the population there is no difference (for example) on GAF score between men and women.

Symbolically, the null hypothesis can be expressed as follows:

$$H_0: \mu_{Men} = \mu_{Women}$$

To test the null hypothesis, we calculate the following statistic:

$$t = \frac{Mean_{Men} - Mean_{Women}}{\sqrt{SE_{diff}}}$$

Where $Mean_{Men}$ is the mean value on the dependent measure for men, $Mean_{Women}$ is the mean value on the dependent value for women, and SE_{diff} is the standard error of the difference between two means. The *t* statistic is evaluated with $N - 2$ degrees of freedom, where N is the total number of scores.

The top portion of this t ratio is the mean difference between the two genders on a single dependent variable; it can be conceptualized as an index of between-group variability. The term in the denominator of this ratio is the standard error of the difference between means; it can be thought of as an index of within-group variability. This standard error is calculated by following this set of steps: (a) divide the variance of the men's scores by the number of men in the sample, (b) divide the variance of the women's scores by the number of women in the sample, (c) subtract the result of (b) from the result of (a) to achieve a single value, and (d) take the square root of this single value.

The standard error of the difference between means is, as is true for virtually all standard error statistics, an estimated standard deviation of a hypothetical sampling distribution. Here, the sampling distribution is based on mean differences. Hypothetically, if we randomly sampled the same number of men and women and assessed them on our GAF dependent variable, we would obtain a certain mean difference. If we did it again, we would find another mean GAF score difference. If we sampled an infinite number of times, we would obtain a certain amount of variability in these mean differences (greater sample sizes would result in less variability of the sample mean differences). We would also find that these difference values were distributed in a normal manner. The standard error of mean differences is the standard deviation of this normal sampling distribution. Our best estimate of that standard deviation is SE_{diff}.

The t ratio is thus a count of the distance between two means using the SE_{diff} as a metric. That is, we can determine the difference between means in SE_{diff} units. For example, if the mean for men was 60 and the mean for women was 50, the difference would be 10. With a SE_{diff} of 2, the genders can be thought of as differing by 5 SE_{diff} units, which in the context of t is a relatively large value.

The Multivariate Hotelling's T^2

In the previous univariate example, we hypothesized about the relationship between gender (the independent variable) and GAF score (the dependent variable). Suppose we included a second, but related, dependent variable such as service satisfaction to our study. Assume that clients' GAF score and satisfaction with the service they received are moderately correlated. Although separate univariate t tests (one for each dependent variable) are certainly an option, a more acceptable as well as more elegant approach would be to employ *Hotelling's* T^2 (or MANOVA in the two-group case). In this situation, the linear composite or variate might be thought of as "therapy efficacy."

Hotelling's T^2 creates a vector (variate or weighted linear composite) that best separates the levels or categories of the independent variable. Hotelling's T^2 tests a multivariate null hypothesis of the general form:

$$H_0: \begin{bmatrix} \mu_{11} = \mu_{12} \\ \mu_{21} = \mu_{22} \\ \ldots = \ldots \\ \ldots = \ldots \\ \ldots = \ldots \\ \mu_{p1} = \mu_{p2} \end{bmatrix}$$

The above hypothesis indicates that the population mean vectors are equal across the two groups. Note that p is the number of dependent variables and that the two subscripted numbers refer to the dependent variable and the independent variable group or level, respectively. Hence, μ_{21} represents the population mean of Dependent Variable 2 for Group 1. For the present example, where we have just the two dependent variables of GAF score and satisfaction, the null hypothesis simplifies to this:

$$H_0: \mu_{\text{GAF Males}} = \mu_{\text{GAF Females}}$$

$$\mu_{\text{Satis Males}} = \mu_{\text{Satis Females}}$$

As is true for the univariate t, this multivariate version produces a test statistic that can be compared with a critical value to determine statistical significance. The main difference between the two is that the univariate t test compares two population means, whereas Hotelling's T^2 multivariate analogue compares two vectors of means.

Some Mathematical Aspects of T^2

The calculations that produce the T^2 statistic are necessarily complex (and tedious) because of the manipulation of vectors or matrices of numbers and are beyond the scope and rationale of this text. However, some of the conceptual underpinnings of these calculations can be profitably explored.

As we noted previously, the univariate t test is essentially a ratio of between-group variability over within-group variability or error. This ratio produces a coefficient (the t value) that can be subsequently evaluated for statistical significance. Stevens (2002) shows that Hotelling's T^2 can be computed by (a) substituting the dependent variable means with a vector of means for each group and (b) replacing the univariate error term (or denominator) by its matrix analogue S (the estimated population covariance matrix).

Using matrix algebra (see Stevens, 2002), it is possible to mathematically generalize the univariate t to its multivariate counterpart. Similar to its univariate counterpart (t), Hotelling's T^2 creates a ratio of between-group variability (based on the mean vectors) to within-group variability (as represented by the inverse of the covariance matrix). Through matrix algebra, these matrices of numbers are reduced to a single value called a *determinant* that expresses the generalized variance of a matrix. Based on this, we can make the multivariate assessment of between- to within-group variance (Harris, 2001).

When Hotelling provided us with his T^2, he knew that it was related to F. Stevens (2002) notes that Hotelling (1931) was the first to demonstrate that T^2 can be transformed into the F distribution using the following conversion formula:

$$F = \frac{n_1 + n_2 - p - 1}{(n_1 + n_2 - 2)\, p}\, T^2$$

with p and $(N - p - 1)$ degrees of freedom (p equals the number of dependent variables). In the above conversion formula, n_1 and n_2 represent the sample sizes of Groups 1 and 2.

Interpretation of Hotelling's T^2

The Hotelling's T^2 computed value can be compared with a critical value to determine its significance level (Hair et al., 1998). If its probability of occurrence is below a predetermined alpha level (e.g., $p < .05$), then we are able to conclude that gender differences (if that is our independent variable) exist and that there are unequal mean vectors for our dependent variables (Weinfurt, 1995). That is, we can conclude that the two groups differ significantly on the population values of the vector represented by the dependent variables used in the analysis.

In practice, most computer statistical packages do not routinely display a Hotelling's T^2 value and its corresponding degrees of freedom and level of significance. Instead, T^2 is transformed, by means of the previously noted formula (and its facsimiles), into F values with four multivariate statistics commonly found in MANOVA statistical computer programs: Wilks's lambda, Pillai's trace, Hotelling's trace, and Roy's largest root. Each of these tests assesses the multivariate between- and within-group variability and computes a multivariate test coefficient that is in turn converted to an F value, which is evaluated much as any other F statistic. The specifics on each of these four multivariate test statistics will be discussed in greater detail in Chapter 10A when we explore MANOVA with three or more groups. The important point to remember here is that these four tests will produce the same (F test) result when the independent variable has only two levels (Tabachnick & Fidell, 2001b).

A statistically significant effect, as evidenced by the above tests (at the .05 level or less) indicates that group differences on the dependent variate exist. Concretely, if we obtained a significant F ratio for our previous example, we would conclude that gender differences exist on the weighted composite (dependent variate) of respondents' GAF scores and service satisfaction ratings.

What to Do After a Significant Multivariate Effect

Once a statistically significant multivariate effect has been established (i.e., we reject the null hypothesis that our independent variable groupings are equal on the weighted composite dependent variate), researchers need to examine the nature of the variate. There are a number of established procedures, which we will now briefly review. It should be noted at this juncture that if the multivariate test is *not* significant ($p > .05$), we would normally not proceed with any further analysis. Instead, we would conclude that the dichotomous independent variable is not differentially distributed on the dependent measures.

Multiple Univariate t or F Tests

Perhaps the most popular procedure to follow up multivariate significance is to conduct separate t tests or ANOVAs on each dependent variable with an adjusted alpha level (e.g., Hair et al., 1998; Stevens, 2002; Weinfurt, 1995). The adjustment to the alpha level is called a *Bonferroni correction,* which reduces the possibility of operating with an inflated Type I error rate due to the use of multiple univariate tests. The adjustment is made by the formula α/p, where the omnibus alpha level (typically .05) is divided by the number of dependent variables. Based on our previous example, we have the following: .05/2 or .025, which becomes the new (more stringent) alpha level we would then use to evaluate each dependent measure. These univariate tests require no additional post hoc multiple comparison tests because the independent variable has only two treatments or levels. Although we recommend this approach, other commentators (Bray & Maxwell, 1985; Tabachnick & Fidell, 2001b; Weinfurt, 1995) urge caution with this process and recommend some of the following procedures instead.

Roy-Bargmann Step-Down Analysis

Step-down analysis is an alternative procedure for assessing each dependent variable separately following a statistically significant multivariate effect. Here, a univariate F value is computed for each dependent variable after controlling for the effects of the remaining dependent measures in the analysis. This procedure is analogous to hierarchical regression in that we require that the dependent measures have a logical, theoretically based, a priori causal ordering (Tabachnick & Fidell, 2001b; Weinfurt, 1995). The dependent variables would then be evaluated in that order.

Consider an example with the three dependent variables of GAF posttest, satisfaction with the mental health services that were provided, and number of visits clients made to the facility to illustrate this step-down process. Assume that our literature review or clinical experience led us to the understanding that GAF posttest scores, which reflect the general state of health of clients after treatment, are a major determinant of their assessment of service satisfaction. In turn, satisfaction with the services they receive is a major reason or cause for how often clients actually come to the mental health facility. Under these conditions, we would have a reasonable foundation on which to base a step-down analysis.

The first step-down F would examine GAF posttest scores and would be the same as a standard univariate F test. The second step-down F would examine service satisfaction while holding GAF posttest scores constant. Here, GAF posttest scores would essentially be treated as a covariate, and thus all remaining step-down "steps" are really separate analyses of covariance (ANCOVAs). The third step-down F would test mental health visits while holding both GAF posttest scores and service satisfaction constant. From this procedure, the investigator can determine the relative contribution of the dependent measures producing the multivariate effect.

We certainly recommend this approach if you are working with correlated multiple dependent measures *and* if these measures contain some logical hierarchical ordering. However, we will not emphasize this procedure because of issues of pragmatics and continuity. In SPSS, Roy-Bargmann step-down analyses can be produced only through the syntax-based

MANOVA procedure and not through the menu-driven **GLM →**
Multivariate procedure. The interested reader should consult Tabachnick
and Fidell (2001b) regarding SPSS programming details for step-down analysis. We note in passing that step-down analyses can also be achieved through
a series of ANCOVAs. For example, one can perform one ANCOVA using
GAF posttest scores as the dependent variable and satisfaction as a covariate
and then perform a second ANCOVA using GAF posttest scores as the
dependent variable and both satisfaction and number of visits as covariates.

Discriminant Analysis

Recall that the strategy used by Hotelling's T^2 (MANOVA) creates a variate
of dependent variables that maximizes the difference between the two levels
or categories of the independent variable. As we noted in Chapter 7A, MANOVA
is "next of kin" to discriminant analysis. In these two analyses, the same variables take on different roles: The continuous variables are assigned the role of
predictors or independent variables in discriminant analysis. In Hotelling's T^2
or MANOVA, these variables take on the role of dependent variables. In both
analyses, these variables are combined into a linear composite that best differ-
entiates the levels of the categorical variable. The categorical variable takes on
the role of dependent variable in discriminant analysis in that we are predicting membership in one of the two groups. In Hotelling's T^2 or MANOVA, this
variable is the independent variable, and we are evaluating whether the levels
of this variable (the groups) differ from each other on the variate.

Conducting a discriminant analysis following a statistically significant T^2
or MANOVA allows the investigator to better understand the nature of the
variate by providing both the structure coefficients to determine the "structure" of the variate and the weights of the dependent variables (which are
analogous to the beta weights in multiple regression) to demonstrate the
unique contributions of the measured variables (Weinfurt, 1995).

Special Issues Concerning Hotelling's T^2 and MANOVA

Sample Size Requirements

Because of the additional burden of analyzing simultaneously multiple
dependent measures, Hotelling's T^2 or MANOVA requires larger sample sizes
than its univariate ANOVA counterpart. A minimal sample size heuristic is that
the number of cases per cell must exceed the number of dependent variables. Some authors (e.g., Hair et al., 1998) argue for at least 20 cases per cell
to achieve minimal levels of power.

Dependent Variables

Hotelling's T^2 or MANOVA is most efficient with high negative correlation or moderate correlation (.6) among the dependent variables (Tabachnick & Fidell, 2001b). Dependent variables that have high positive correlations are redundant, so using this procedure is considered somewhat wasteful and counterproductive. Two possible solutions to such strong correlation (.8 or .9) would be as follows:

▶ Create a new composite dependent variable. Although there is no particular limit on the number of dependent variables you can use to build the dependent variate, we encourage judicious restraint and recommend no more than 10 dependent conceptually related variables (Bray & Maxwell, 1985).

▶ Delete one (or more) of the dependent variables prior to the analysis so that such a strong correlation is no longer observed.

This multivariate analysis should also not be used if there are very low correlations between the dependent measures. Instead, separate ANOVAs with a Bonferroni adjustment would probably be in order. A significant *Bartlett's test of sphericity* ($p < .001$) is indicative of sufficient correlation between the dependent variables to proceed with the multivariate analysis.

Power of Multivariate Tests

Power concerns the adequacy of your study's statistical test (e.g., one of the four multivariate tests discussed previously) to detect an actual treatment effect. The power of a statistical test is a function of three parameters: the alpha level, sample size, and the effect size (i.e., the extent to which treatment groups differ on the dependent variable). There is an inverse relationship between power and alpha level. Power decreases when alpha levels become more stringent (i.e., move from .05 to .01). Thus, moving to the .01 or .001 alpha level to reduce the possibility of Type I error also reduces your power. The trick is to find a proper balance between alpha and power. This balance is informed by considering the effect size of the variables under study. In the present two-group example, effect size is the difference in the means divided by their standard deviation (Stevens, 1980). In practice, the power of a statistical test (regardless of sample size) will always increase if the effect size increases. Small effect sizes require larger samples to produce adequate statistical power of, for example, .80 (i.e., we have an 80% chance of detecting a significant result if the effect exists). Increasing sample size reduces sampling error and subsequently increases power.

Table 9a.1 Power of Hotelling's T^2 at $\alpha = .05$ for Small Through Very Large
Overall Effect and Group Sizes

Number of Dependent Variables	N_a	Effect Size (D^{2b})			
		Small	Medium	Large	Very Large
2	15	.26	.44	.65	.95
2	25	.33	.66	.86	.97
2	50	.60	.95	1.00	1.00
2	100	.90	1.00	1.00	1.00
3	15	.23	.37	.58	.91
3	25	.28	.58	.80	.95
3	50	.54	.93	1.00	1.00
3	100	.86	1.00	1.00	1.00
5	15	.21	.32	.42	.83
5	25	.26	.42	.72	.96
5	50	.44	.88	1.00	1.00
5	100	.78	1.00	1.00	1.00
7	15	.18	.27	.37	.77
7	25	.22	.38	.64	.94
7	50	.40	.82	.97	1.00
7	100	.72	1.00	1.00	1.00

SOURCE: Adapted from Stevens (1980).

a. $N_s = N_1 = N_2$.

b. D^2 = Mahalanobis distance.

We demonstrate the collaborative role of these three parameters in Table 9a.1, which is adapted from Stevens (1980). From Table 9a.1, we note that small or moderate effect sizes with sample sizes greater than or equal to 25 produce relatively poor power (< .45) and never achieve adequate power (> .70). Conversely, when effect sizes are large, then 15 cases per group is sufficient to yield moderate or greater statistical power.

Statistical Assumptions and Limitations

Outliers and Missing Values

Hotelling's T^2 (MANOVA) and its univariate counterpart (*t* test and ANOVA) are particularly sensitive to outliers or extreme values on the dependent measures. Failure to exclude outliers or transform the data could inflate Type I or II error rates. Likewise, missing values in a multivariate analysis become more problematic because of the complexity of the dependent variate. We encourage the reader to review relevant sections in Chapters 3A and 3B for discussions on how to address these problems.

Independence

The participants, respondents, or cases that compose the levels or groups of an independent variable must be independent of each other when conducting a Hotelling's T^2 or MANOVA. Experimentally, independence of participants is assumed if participants have been randomly assigned to treatments or conditions of the study. Occasionally, problems occur with the use of intact groups (e.g., selecting as participants whole sets of individuals, such as classes in a program or clients of a given facility) where the entire set of individuals is exposed to or placed in one treatment level.

Sometimes dependence occurs with quasi-experimental or archival research where time-ordered effects may occur for respondents who provide information over time (e.g., GAF scores at Time 1 and Time 2). When this occurs, you are probably better off treating the dependent variables as a repeated measure and using the appropriate ANOVA design (one-way within-subjects or mixed design) to analyze the data.

Homogeneity of Variance-Covariance Matrices

The assumption of equivalence or homogeneity of covariance matrices for each dependent variable across groups is the multivariate analogue to the homogeneity of variance assumption in ANOVA and multiple regression. Instead of testing for comparability of variances on a single dependent measure between the levels of the independent variable, all the coefficients in the covariance matrix of dependent variables are examined. Violation of this homogeneity of covariance matrices assumption when sample sizes are fairly equal produces minor consequences.

The standard vehicle for assessing equivalence-of-covariance matrices is the Box's M test, where statistical significance ($p < .001$) is indicative of heterogeneity or inequality. Remedies for this assumption violation include the usual transformations of the dependent variables. If heterogeneity persists despite the best efforts of researchers to use the techniques described in Chapter 3A, then we recommend using Pillai's criterion to evaluate the significance of the multivariate effect (Tabachnick & Fidell, 2001b).

Multivariate Normality

The Mardia's statistic is a way to assess for multivariate normality, but this statistic is not available in SPSS. Because no specific computerized test is readily available in SPSS to test for multivariate normality, most investigators check for univariate normality for each dependent variable, and transformations are used to address any normality departures. Note that Box's M test is highly sensitive to normality violations; thus, normality should probably be addressed before computing Box's M test.

Linearity

Linear relationships are assumed between pairs of dependent variables. If nonlinear (curvilinear) relationships are observed, transformations may be in order.

Numerical Hypothetical 2-Group Example

Because MANOVA can involve a certain amount of complexity, it is useful to discuss an example analysis to show how the material we have presented here fits together. Assume that we are interested in the effects of therapy type (cognitive-behavioral vs. psychoanalytic) as the independent or grouping variable on the dependent variables of community mental health clients' GAF and service satisfaction (Client Satisfaction Questionnaire-8, CSQ-8) scores (see Chapter 3B for details on these measures). Further assume that these severely mentally ill clients were randomly and independently assigned to one of the two treatment conditions. Note that we could have included more than two dependent measures, but we have chosen to keep this Hotelling's T^2 example as simple as possible. The null hypothesis we hope to reject is that the vectors of means for each group are equal (i.e., therapy type has no differential effect on our dependent variate). Condensed summaries of results can be seen in Tables 9a.2 through 9a.7.

Table 9a.2 presents the data for 55 study participants. From Table 9a.2, we note that although the samples are fairly small, sufficient statistical power should be available to detect a real difference in the population if we assume that moderate effect sizes are present for our manipulation. An inspection of the dependent variable means for each group or level of the independent variable (therapy type) shows that the clients receiving cognitive-behavioral treatment had somewhat higher mean scores on GAF and CSQ-8 than did clients who received psychoanalytic intervention. The dependent variable standard deviations for each group are fairly close, suggesting comparable levels of variability for each dependent measure. Pearson rs were computed between the two dependent measures (GAF and CSQ-8) for each group or level of the independent variable. A moderate positive correlation ($r = .426$) was found for the cognitive-behavioral group, and a low zero-order correlation ($r = .086$)

Table 9a.2 Client Global Assessment of Functioning (GAF) and Service Satisfaction (CSQ-8), by Therapy Type (Hypothetical Data for Hotelling's T^2 or Two-Group MANOVA)

			Therapy Type		
Group 1: Cognitive-Behavioral (n = 30)[a]			*Group 2: Psychoanalytic (n = 25)[b]*		
Caseid	*GAF*	*CSQ-8*	*Caseid*	*GAF*	*CSQ-8*
1	65	30.3	31	50	24.3
2	69	27.1	32	55	22.1
3	73	31.0	33	61	25.6
4	60	29.4	34	66	25.0
5	58	27.4	35	58	24.0
6	70	30.1	36	50	26.0
7	71	30.9	37	45	27.0
8	55	27.0	38	53	26.5
9	65	28.5	39	59	25.5
10	60	29.1	40	61	25.0
11	66	27.8	41	70	29.0
12	60	29.2	42	65	26.2
13	70	30.3	43	55	24.8
14	70	31.0	44	50	24.0
15	65	26.5	45	62	23.2
16	65	27.0	46	66	26.0
17	55	26.5	47	69	27.0
18	72	30.0	48	50	25.1
19	70	31.0	49	58	28.1
20	65	28.7	50	55	25.5
21	60	28.0	51	60	23.2
22	55	27.0	52	60	23.0
23	70	30.1	53	65	22.0
24	75	29.2	54	65	24.0
25	65	25.0	55	50	25.0
26	62	24.3			
27	60	30.3			
28	68	26.7			
29	70	28.0			
30	68	25.5			
	M	*SD*		*M*	*SD*
GAF	65.23	5.62		58.32	6.84
CSQ-8	28.43	1.90		25.08	1.73

a. $r = .426$; $p < .01$.

b. $r = .086$; $p > .05$.

was observed for the psychoanalytic group. These correlations suggest some variability in the dependent variable covariance and will be assessed with Box's M test.

Table 9a.3 examines group tests of normality and diagnostics for each dependent variable. Normality tests for each group-dependent variable combination were not statistically significant, indicating no serious normality violations. This was also confirmed with the skewness and kurtosis statistics; all were within the -1 to $+1$ range. Because there are no normality violations observed here, we can proceed with confidence to an assessment of the covariance matrix.

Box's M and Levene's test are shown in Table 9a.4. Here, we observe that the Box's M test of the equality of variance-covariance matrices is not

Table 9a.3 Client Global Assessment of Functioning (GAF) and Service Satisfaction (CSQ-8) Normality Tests and Diagnostics, by Therapy Type

		Group 1: Cognitive-Behavioral		Group 2: Psychoanalytic	
		Statistic	*Significance*	*Statistic*	*Significance*
GAF	Normality test				
	Kolmogorov-Smirnov	.150	.083	.128	.200
	Shapiro-Wilk	.939	.088	.958	.372
	Skewness	.353		.112	
	Kurtosis	.832		.928	
CSQ-8	Normality test				
	Kolmogorov-Smirnov	.129	.200	.081	.200
	Shapiro-Wilk	.946	.131	.982	.918
	Skewness	.362		.220	
	Kurtosis	.782		.033	

Table 9a.4 Tests of Equality of Covariance Metrices and Equality of Error Variances

	Overall		GAF		CSQ-8	
	Statistic	*Significance*	*Statistic*	*Significance*	*Statistic*	*Significance*
Box's M	3.157	.338				
Levene's			1.41	.241	1.16	.286

significant, indicating equality or homogeneity. The separate Levene's tests for each dependent variable were not statistically significant either, which confirms the equal variances we believe to be true in our visual inspection of the data in Table 9a.2.

Bartlett's test of sphericity is shown to be statistically significant in Table 9a.5. This indicates that there is sufficient correlation between the two dependent variables to proceed with the analysis. A moderate positive Pearson correlation ($r = .502$) was observed between GAF and CSQ-8.

We are now ready to review the multivariate test results in Table 9a.6. Instead of a Hotelling's T^2 value, computer statistical programs such as SPSS translate T^2 into four multivariate test statistics that are expressed as F values. In the two-group case, these F values will be identical, so we show only one of them (Roy's largest root). In the present case, this multivariate test shows that Roy's largest root yields an F value of 25.445, which is statistically significant. We may then conclude that the group mean vectors are not equal (therapy type is having an effect on the dependent variate). For the interested reader, the Hotelling's T^2 coefficient can be approximated by multiplying the Hotelling's trace value (in the present example, .979) by $N - g$, where N is the total sample size and g is the number of groups. Thus in the present example we have the following:

$$T^2 = (.979)(55 - 2) = (.979)(53) = 51.887$$

Table 9a.6 also depicts a partial eta-squared value of .495, indicating that nearly 50% of the variance is accounted for by the combined dependent

Table 9a.5 Test of Intercorrelation of Dependent Variables

	Statistic	Significance
Bartlett's test of sphericity	67.510	.000
Pearson correlation:		
GAF by CSQ-8	.502	.000

Table 9a.6 Multivariate Test Results

Effect	Multivariate Test	Value	F	Significance	Partial Eta Squared
Therapy type	Roy's largest root	.979	25.445	.001	.495

Table 9a.7   Univariate Test Results

Dependent Measure	Independent Variable (Group) Means		Pairwise Comparison Difference	*F*	Significance
	Cognitive-Behavioral	Psychoanalytic			
GAF	65.23	58.32	6.91	16.96	.00
CSQ-8	28.43	25.08	3.35	45.95	.00

variables. This partial eta-squared is calculated as 1 minus the adjusted determinant of the error matrix and is considered a more conservative and appropriate index of treatment magnitude with MANOVA (Tabachnick & Fidell, 2001b).

Because a multivariate effect is present, we can proceed to examine separate univariate *F* tests. These are shown in Table 9a.7. To control for alpha inflation, we perform a Bonferroni adjustment to our alpha level ($.05/2 = .025$). Evaluating the *F* tests (one for each dependent variable) against our corrected alpha level indicates that both are statistically significant ($p < .025$). A visual inspection of the means suggests that cognitive-behavioral therapy produces higher clinical outcomes (GAF scores) and greater service satisfaction (CSQ-8) than does psychoanalytic treatment.

Recommended Readings

Bochner, A. P., & Fitzpatrick, M. A. (1980). Multivariate analysis of variance: Techniques, models, and applications in communication research. In P. R. Monge & J. N. Cappella (Eds.), *Multivariate techniques in human communication research* (pp. 143–174). New York: Academic Press.

Everitt, B. S. (1979). A Monte Carlo investigation of the robustness of Hotelling's one and two sample T^2 tests. *Journal of the American Statistical Association, 74,* 48–51.

Hakstian, A. R., Roed, J. C., & Lind, J. C. (1979). Two-sample T^2 procedure and the assumption of homogeneous covariance matrices. *Psychological Bulletin, 56,* 1255–1263.

Holloway, L. N., & Dunn, O. J. (1967). The robustness of Hotelling's T^2. *Journal of the American Statistical Association, 62,* 124–136.

Hotelling, H. (1931). The generalization of Student's ratio. *Annals of Mathematical Statistics, 2,* 360–378.

Hummel, T. J., & Sligo, J. (1971). Empirical comparison of univariate and multivariate analysis of variance procedures. *Psychological Bulletin, 76,* 49–57.

Lauter, J. (1978). Sample size requirements for the T² test of MANOVA (tables for one-way classification). *Biometrical Journal, 20,* 389–406.

Lix, L. M., & Keselman, H. J. (2004). Multivariate tests of means in independent groups designs: Effects of covariance heterogeneity and nonnormality. *Evaluation & the Health Professions, 27,* 45–69.

Stevens, J. P. (1980). Power of the multivariate analysis of variance tests. *Psychological Bulletin, 88,* 728–737.

Zwick, R. (1986). Rank and normal scores alternatives to Hotelling's T². *Multivariate Behavioral Research, 21,* 169–186.

Two-Group
MANOVA Using SPSS

Overview of the Study

This chapter extends our Chapter 9A discussion of two-group MANOVA (Hotelling's T^2) with an application using SPSS. Recall that the ingredients for a two-group MANOVA include a categorical independent variable with two levels or treatment **groups** and at least two quantitative, conceptually related dependent measures.

The present numerical example is derived from a community mental health data set for fiscal year 2002–2003 among 2,455 severely mentally ill (SMI) adult clients (aged 19 years or older) who received mental health services during this time frame. Outcome and other information were collected at initial intake (Time 1) and again at annual review or discharge (Time 2). Because of the special needs and challenges of working with this client population, complete pre-post information on each client was not always captured.

Three variables will be examined in the present example. The independent variable is client gender (male, female); this variable is named "**sex**" in the data file. The dependent variables are derived from the California Quality of Life inventory (CA-QOL; Lehman, 1988; Purvis & Higgins, 1998), a 40-item quality-of-life instrument that can be reduced to two subscales: objective and subjective quality of life. The objective items examine the clients' living situation, activities, family contacts, social contacts, finances, safety, and general health. The subjective items probe satisfaction in arenas such as life, living situation, daily activities, family relationships, finances, safety, and health. All the items are scored on a 7-point Likert-type scale

(1 = *terrible* and 7 = *delighted*). Thus, higher subscale means are associated with better quality of life.

Initial Data Screening

Generating a Case Identification Number

The present large archival data set did not contain a case-identifying variable—that is, a unique integer from 1 to *n* that can be used to identify specific cases. Such a variable is essential to the process of data screening because it is often necessary for researchers to pinpoint particular cases in the data set for careful review. With small data sets, this deficiency can be remedied by creating a new variable and entering a unique value for each case by hand. This becomes quite tedious when there are hundreds or even thousands of cases in the set. Because an identifying variable is so important, we show you how to create a **caseid** variable with SPSS. This procedure will generate the actual values of this new variable for you. We begin by clicking **Transform → Compute,** which produces the **Compute Variable** dialog box seen in Figure 9b.1.

The left side of this dialog box is the **Target Variable** box where we have typed in the name of our new variable **caseid**. By clicking the **Type & Label** pushbutton, you can provide an optional variable label. On the right side of the dialog box is the **Numeric Expression** box, where you type in **$casenum**.

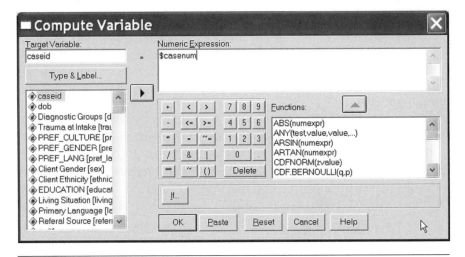

Figure 9b.1   Compute Variable Dialog Box Preparing to Generate Case Identification Numbers

The expression "$casenum" is an SPSS built-in procedure to accomplish exactly what we are doing here. Clicking the **OK** pushbutton then creates a new variable called **caseid** (in this example), which contains a sequential number for each case beginning with 1 through n (in the present example, $n = 2,455$). The new **caseid** variable is appended automatically to the end of your SPSS file and can also be "dragged" to any other location within the file that you desire (the first column is a terrific place for this variable).

Missing Values

Now let's start our data screening assessment by checking for missing values on each of the three variables through the SPSS **Explore** procedure. Because we have reviewed these procedures in detail in Chapter 3B, we will focus on the interpretation of the output itself, because the details of maneuvering through the SPSS dialog boxes remain the same. We begin by clicking **Analyze → Descriptive Statistics → Explore,** which opens the **Explore** dialog box where we would select **subject** and **object** (the subjective and objective quality-of-life subscales, respectively) for the **Dependent List** box and **sex** for the **Factor List** box. In addition, we click the **Statistics** pushbutton and its subsequent **Outliers** checkbox and click the **Plots** pushbutton and its **Normality plots with tests** checkbox.

Figure 9b.2 reports the **Case Processing Summary** results of that analysis. It profiles the number of valid and missing cases for each dependent variable by client gender. A severe missing-values problem is evidenced with about half (54.9% of the males and 53.9% of the females) of the cases with missing values on **subject** and **object**. Although this situation limits our ability to generalize to the entire population of SMI adults, it is a fairly

Case Processing Summary

Client Gender		Cases					
		Valid		Missing		Total	
		N	Percent	N	Percent	N	Percent
QL-SF Subjective Mean	Male	415	45.1%	505	54.9%	920	100.0%
	Female	708	46.1%	827	53.9%	1535	100.0%
QL-SF Objective Mean	Male	415	45.1%	505	54.9%	920	100.0%
	Female	708	46.1%	827	53.9%	1535	100.0%

Figure 9b.2 Case Processing Summary Showing Valid and Missing Values

typical occurrence with real-world archival mental health datasets. Accordingly, we will use the SPSS listwise deletion default option when analyzing these data, because item imputation procedures would be inappropriate for such a large proportion of cases.

Univariate Outliers

Univariate outliers are assessed with box plots for each dependent variable. Figure 9b.3 depicts the box plot for **subject** separated by **gender**. Toward the upper right portion of the output (above the axis point for female) we can see an asterisk indicating a univariate outlier (Case Number 1,964) among the female respondents (with an actual score of 10.44 on this variable). You can now see the necessity of using case numbers to identify clients in the data set. This case will be deleted from all subsequent

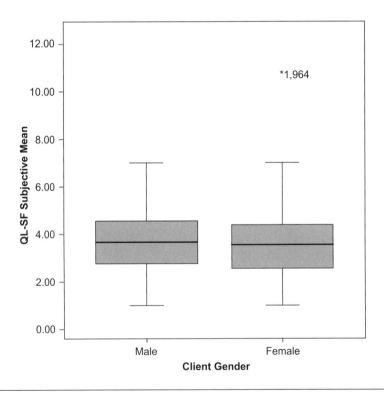

Figure 9b.3 Box and Whiskers Plot for Subjective Subscale Scores of the Quality of Life Inventory

analyses. No such extreme values pattern was evidenced for **object**, the other dependent variable in our analysis.

Multivariate Outliers

A check for multivariate outliers is accomplished by computing a Mahalanobis distance measure for each case with the SPSS **Regression** procedure (see Chapter 3B). We click **Analyze → Regression → Linear** to produce the **Linear Regression** dialog box and its constituent dialog boxes, which we will not repeat here. Remember to click over **caseid** (the variable we created at the beginning of this chapter or some other nonessential variable) into the **Dependent** box and **sex** into the **Independent(s)** box. After clicking **Save**, click the **Mahalanobis** checkbox; this creates and saves Mahalanobis distance measures (**MAH_1**) for each case, which can then be profiled with **Explore** and subsequently evaluated as a chi-square statistic.

Once the distance measures are saved to the file as a new variable called **MAH_1**, we can profile them with SPSS **Explore** by clicking **Analyze → Descriptive Statistics → Explore** where we click over the new variable **MAH_1** to the **Dependent List** box (leave the **Factor List** box blank) and click the **Statistics** pushbutton and check the **Outliers** checkbox before clicking **OK**.

Remember, the most **Extreme Values** of the Mahalanobis distance measure (**MAH_1**) are displayed by SPSS (not shown in the present example) and are evaluated (by the researchers) with a chi-square distribution and a stringent alpha level ($p < .001$) with degrees of freedom equal to the number of variables being examined—in this case, $df = 1$. Based on these criteria, no multivariate outliers were observed.

Normality

We are now poised to explore issues of normality and other assumption violations among our variables. Let's begin by inspecting the frequency output of the gender independent variable (**sex**) by clicking **Analyze → Descriptive Statistics → Frequencies,** which produces the **Frequencies** dialog box (not shown) where we click over the variable **sex**. The resulting output can be seen in Figure 9b.4. The output shows a disproportionate (but not extreme) split between males (37.5% of the cases) and females (62.5% of the cases). Only six cases had missing values.

Client Gender

		Frequency	Percent	Valid Percent	Cumulative Percent
Valid	Male	920	37.4	37.5	37.5
	Female	1534	62.4	62.5	100.0
	Total	2454	99.8	100.0	
Missing	System	6	.2		
Total		2460	100.0		

Figure 9b.4   Frequency Output for Client Gender

Normality for each continuous dependent variable at each level of the independent variable can be assessed through the SPSS **Explore** procedure, which generates the **Descriptives, Tests of Normality,** and **Normal Q-Q Plots** output by clicking **Analyze → Descriptive Statistics → Explore.** We move over our two dependent variables (**subject** and **object**) to the **Dependent List** box and the independent variable (**sex**) to the **Factor List** box (not shown). Remember that descriptive statistics is an SPSS default and will thus be automatically produced. By clicking the **Plots** pushbutton and the **Normality plots with tests** checkbox we will produce the normal Q-Q plots.

Figure 9b.5 provides descriptive statistics for each dependent variable profiled by client gender. We note that skewness and kurtosis are minimal and within the ±1.0 range.

Figure 9b.6 shows us that some of the normality tests (Kolmogorov-Smirnov and Shapiro-Wilk) are statistically significant (even with a stringent alpha level of $p < .001$), indicating that some normality violations are present in both dependent measures. However, the **normal Q-Q plots** in Figure 9b.7 look reasonably normal (i.e., data points are close to the diagonal lines), and hence we judge these data ready for analysis.

Overview of the Two-Group MANOVA Analysis

SPSS provides two separate procedures for conducting a MANOVA. The general linear model or **GLM** procedure is menu driven and is therefore similar in function to all the other SPSS statistical procedures reviewed in this book. It is the one we will emphasize. Besides being relatively easy to use (once you gain some familiarity with it), the **GLM** procedure is the vehicle through which we can conduct a variety of multiple comparisons or post hoc tests

Descriptives

Client Gender				Statistic	Std. Error
QL-SF Subjective Mean	Male	Mean		3.6949	.06436
		95% Confidence	Lower Bound		3.5684
		Interval for Mean	Upper Bound	3.8214	
		5% Trimmed Mean		3.6777	
		Median		3.6667	
		Variance		1.719	
		Std. Deviation		1.31116	
		Minimum		1.00	
		Maximum		7.00	
		Range		6.00	
		Interquartile Range		1.81	
		Skewness		.185	.120
		Kurtosis		−.474	.239
	Female	Mean		3.5048	.04823
		95% Confidence	Lower Bound	3.4101	
		Interval for Mean	Upper Bound	3.5994	
		5% Trimmed Mean		3.4884	
		Median		3.5556	
		Variance		1.644	
		Std. Deviation		1.28230	
		Minimum		1.00	
		Maximum		7.00	
		Range		6.00	
		Interquartile Range		1.78	
		Skewness		.153	.092
		Kurtosis		−.456	.184
QL-SF Objective Mean	Male	Mean		1.3128	.01837
		95% Confidence	Lower Bound	1.2767	
		Interval for Mean	Upper Bound	1.3489	
		5% Trimmed Mean		1.3085	
		Median		1.2857	
		Variance		.140	
		Std. Deviation		.37413	
		Minimum		.43	
		Maximum		2.29	
		Range		1.86	
		Interquartile Range		.57	
		Skewness		.120	
		Kurtosis		−.757	.239
	Female	Mean		1.3222	.01362
		95% Confidence	Lower Bound	1.2955	
		Interval for Mean	Upper Bound	1.3490	
		5% Trimmed Mean		1.3142	
		Median		1.2857	
		Variance		.131	
		Std. Deviation		.36215	
		Minimum		.50	
		Maximum		2.29	
		Range		1.79	
		Interquartile Range		.57	
		Skewness		.304	.092
		Kurtosis		−.613	.184

Figure 9b.5   Descriptive Statistics for the Two Dependent Variables Separated by Gender

Tests of Normality

	Client Gender	Kolmogorov-Smirnov[a]			Shapiro-Wilk		
		Statistic	df	Sig.	Statistic	df	Sig.
QL-SF Subjective Mean	Male	.043	415	.061	.990	415	.006
	Female	.039	707	.013	.990	707	.000
QL-SF Objective Mean	Male	.090	415	.000	.980	415	.000
	Female	.080	707	.000	.980	707	.000

a. Lillefors Significance Correction.

Figure 9b.6   Results From Tests of Normality

on marginal means following a statistically significant multivariate effect and univariate ANOVA.

An alternative way to conduct a MANOVA with SPSS is through the use of the syntax-based **MANOVA** procedure. In the earlier days of SPSS, the only way to perform a multivariate ANOVA was to use the **MANOVA** procedure. Back then, users viewed a blank screen and wrote all the syntax for all their analyses. As SPSS was brought forward to personal computers using graphical user interfaces with mouse, pointer, icons, and windows, some procedures designed for the "point and click" environment were added. The **GLM** procedure was one of those. Rather than remove the **MANOVA** procedure from its repertoire, however, SPSS just expanded with this new procedure that had very similar capabilities.

We describe this history because it may help readers cope with a portion of the terminology here. MANOVA, as we have been using the term, has and continues to be our abbreviation for the research design labeled "multivariate analysis of variance." But there is also a procedure in SPSS carrying the name "MANOVA," which is a syntax-only way to perform a MANOVA analysis. We will go out of our way to make sure to call it "MANOVA procedure" when we are talking about this SPSS analysis.

The MANOVA procedure generates much of the same output that the **GLM** procedure produces, but it can also compute Roy-Bargmann step-down analyses (recall that these analyses test for group mean differences on a single dependent measure while controlling for the other dependent variables). We recommend using the **MANOVA** procedure only after you have become acquainted with SPSS MANOVA output through the **GLM** procedure and when you feel comfortable enough to write the few lines of syntax in an SPSS syntax window.

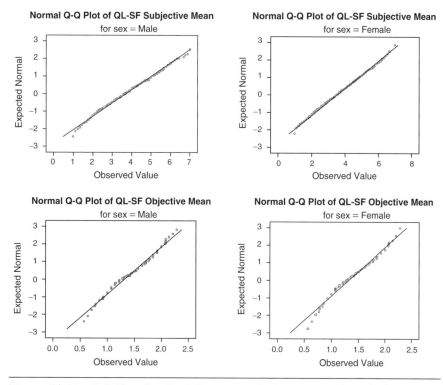

Figure 9b.7   Q-Q Plots for the Subjective and Objective Quality of Life Scale for Male and Female Clients

Setting Up the Analysis

To begin our analysis, we click **Analyze → General Linear Model → Multivariate,** which produces the **Multivariate** main dialog box shown in Figure 9b.8. Notice that we have moved our two dependent variables (**subject** and **object**) from the variables list panel to the **Dependent Variables** box and our independent variable (**sex**) to the **Fixed Factor(s)** box. The **Covariate(s)** box is left blank because there are no covariates in this study. The **WLS Weight** box is also blank. This box provides *weighted least squares* adjustment if heterogeneity of variance persists between the groups.

The right side of the dialog box contains six pushbuttons: **Model, Contrasts, Plots, Post Hoc, Save,** and **Options,** each of which produces its own dialog box that we will briefly review.

The **Model** pushbutton produces the **Multivariate: Model** dialog box (not shown). This dialog box is usually left in its default, **Full factorial,**

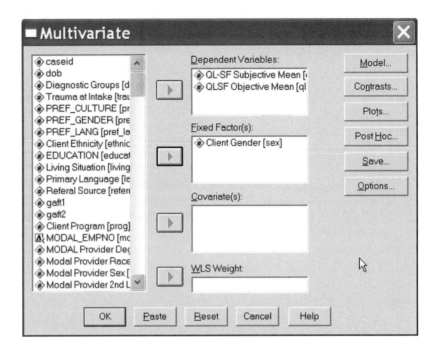

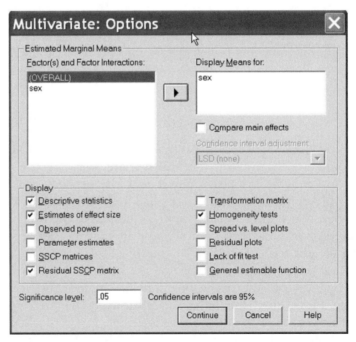

Figure 9b.8   Multivariate Analysis Main Dialog Box and Its Options Dialog Box

setting, which requests that all main effects, interaction effects, and covariates be tested. In the present example, the full model is appropriate and requested.

The **Custom** checkbox under the **Specify Model** box is appropriate to check for statistically significant interaction effects between independent variables and covariates. If this interaction is not statistically significant, then the investigator can proceed with a full factorial analysis. The **Custom** model command can also be used to eliminate higher-order interaction effects not being investigated. The default setting for the **Sum of squares** box is set at **Type III** sum of squares, which requests that each effect be tested after adjusting for all other model effects. This setting is rarely modified. The **Model** dialog box is left unmodified in the present example because we are working with a single independent variable.

If we click the **Contrasts** pushbutton of the **Multivariate** dialog box, the **Multivariate: Contrasts** dialog box will appear (not shown). Contrasts or *planned comparisons* are useful when your independent variable has three or more groups and you have specific a priori comparisons to test. A pull-down menu can be found in the **Change Contrast** box that allows for **Simple** or more complex (**Special**) comparisons. The default requests no contrasts, as in the present example.

The **Plots** pushbutton produces the **Multivariate: Profile Plots** dialog box (not shown). This dialog box generates line graphs that display dependent variable means at each level of the **Factor** or independent variable. The default is to request no plots, as in the present example.

The **Post Hoc** pushbutton produces the rather full-named **Multivariate: Post Hoc Multiple Comparisons for Observed Means** dialog box (not shown). This dialog box allows researchers to perform *post hoc* or *multiple comparisons tests* after a statistically significant omnibus univariate *F* test indicates differences between the (three or more) levels of the independent variable.

Post hoc tests compare every possible pair combination of means on each dependent variable. SPSS offers 18 different post hoc tests, each of which attempts to uniquely control Type I error and power. We will talk more about these tests in Chapter 10B. The default, no post hoc tests, is in place with the current example because our independent variable (sex) has only two levels.

The **Save** pushbutton generates the **Multivariate: Save** dialog box. This dialog box (which is not often used) is segmented into four parts that allow researchers to produce various predicted values, case diagnostics, and residuals; it also provides the opportunity to save certain statistics to the data file. None of these options is requested in the present example.

The last pushbutton, **Options**, produces the **Multivariate: Options** dialog box that is also shown in Figure 9b.8. Double clicking the sex variable in the **Factor(s) and Factor interactions** box will move this variable over to the **Display Means for** box, which will produce *estimated dependent variable* means for each level of the independent variable. These means are the same as the observed means produced with the **Descriptive statistics** checkbox if there are no covariates in the analysis, and a complete model is specified (all main effects and interactions) as in the present case. When covariates are present, estimated means should be reported as well as the observed (unadjusted) means. Directly below the **Display Means for** box is the **Compare main effects** checkbox, which tests for statistically significant differences for every pair of estimated marginal means for each main effect or independent variable. We have not selected this because with just two levels of our independent variable, a significant F ratio for the main effect automatically tells us that the two groups are significantly different.

At the bottom of the **Options** dialog box is the **Display** box with 12 checkboxes. In the present example, we have activated four checkboxes. **Descriptive statistics** produces observed means and standard deviations for all dependent variables at each level of the independent variable. **Estimates of effect size** produces partial eta squared for each effect in the multivariate model. The **Residual SSCP matrix** is the only way you can obtain Bartlett's test of sphericity through the **GLM** procedure. This measure tests whether there is statistically significant correlation between the dependent variables. This checkbox also generates the sum of squares and cross-products of residuals matrix, which can be ignored in most situations. The **Homogeneity tests** provide Levene's test for equality of variances for each dependent variable across all levels of the independent variable.

The other checkboxes (that were not activated) provide the following information:

- ▶ **Observed power** evaluates whether an F test will detect differences between groups. Note that such "after-the-fact" calculations have come under criticism for providing meaningless post hoc diagnostics (Keppel & Wickens, 2004).
- ▶ **Parameter estimates** provides parameter estimates, t tests, confidence intervals, and power for each test.
- ▶ **SSCP matrices** produces sum of squares and cross-products matrices.
- ▶ **Transformation matrix** generates a transformation of the dependent variables.

- ▶ **Spread vs. level plots** displays group variability and is useful in detecting the source of heterogeneity of variance.
- ▶ **Residual plots** produces plots of observed, standardized, and predicted residuals to help identify outliers.
- ▶ **Lack of fit test** tests the adequacy of the multivariate model. If this test is statistically significant, it suggests that the current multivariate model is inadequate.
- ▶ **General estimable function** produces a table of general estimable functions that can be used to test custom hypotheses.

Running the Analysis

We are now ready to run the Hotelling's T^2 or two-group MANOVA by clicking the **OK** button at the bottom of the **Multivariate** dialog box. The two-group MANOVA output can be seen in Figures 9b.9 and 9b.10.

The first output in Figure 9b.9 displays the **Between-Subjects Factors** table, which depicts one factor (independent variable) with two levels containing relatively large but unequal sample size.

The **Descriptive Statistics** table is shown next in Figure 9b.9. This output provides each dependent measure's observed (unadjusted) means, standard deviations, and sample sizes for each level of the independent variable.

Box's Test of Equality of Covariance Matrices presented next in Figure 9b.9 is not statistically significant (Box's $M = 4.887, p > .181$), indicating that the dependent variable covariance matrices are equal across the levels of the independent variable (**sex**).

Bartlett's Test of Sphericity is statistically significant (approximate chi square $= 1598.459, p < .001$), indicating sufficient correlation between the dependent measures to proceed with the analysis.

The "heart" of the MANOVA output lies in the **Multivariate Tests** output shown next in Figure 9b.10. This table is composed of two parts. The top portion of the table (**Intercept**) evaluates whether the overall quality-of-life mean differs from zero. Because of its statistical significance, we conclude that it does differ from zero, indicating that quality of life varies in the population. Of more importance is the evaluation of the effect of the independent variable (**sex**) in the bottom half of the table.

Recall that when we evaluate a univariate t or F statistic, we are assessing a ratio of between-group variability (i.e., treatment effects plus error) to within-group variability (i.e., error or nuisance variation, measurement error). In the multivariate situation, we are no longer dividing a single number that represents between-group variability by a single number that represents within-group variability. Rather, we are dividing (actually inverting) two matrices or vectors (between and within) of numbers. Because the end result of

Between-Subjects Factors

		Value Label	N
Client Gender	1	Male	415
	2	Female	707

Descriptive Statistics

	Client Gender	Mean	Std. Deviation	N
QL-SF Subjective Mean	Male	3.6949	1.31116	415
	Female	3.5048	1.28230	707
	Total	3.5751	1.29572	1122
QL-SF Objective Mean	Male	1.3128	.37413	415
	Female	1.3222	.36215	707
	Total	1.3187	.36649	1122

Box's Test of Equality of Covariance Matrices[a]

Box's M	4.887
F	1.626
df1	3
df2	2.6E + 07
Sig.	.181

The assumption of equal dependent variables covariance matrices is supported.

Tests the null hypothesis that the observed covariance matrices of the dependent variables are equal across groups.

a. Design: Intercept + sex

Bartlett's Test of Sphericity[a]

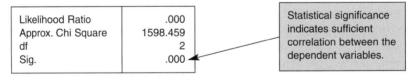

Likelihood Ratio	.000
Approx. Chi Square	1598.459
df	2
Sig.	.000

Statistical significance indicates sufficient correlation between the dependent variables.

Tests the null hypothesis that the residual covariance matrix is proportional to an identity matrix.

a. Design: Intercept + sex.

Figure 9b.9   Selected Descriptive and Diagnostic Tables From the GLM Analysis

this matrix manipulation is not a single number, as in the univariate situation, multivariate tests have been developed that translate these matrix-based ratios into a single value that can be evaluated as an *F* statistic.

Multivariate Tests[b]

Effect		Value	F	Hypothesis df	Error df	Sig.	Partial Eta Squared
Intercept	Pillai's Trace	.935	8078.586[a]	2.000	1119.000	.000	.935
	Wilks's Lambda	.065	8078.586[a]	2.000	1119.000	.000	.935
	Hotelling's Trace	14.439	8078.586[a]	2.000	1119.000	.000	.935
	Roy's Largest Root	14.439	8078.586[a]	2.000	1119.000	.000	.935
Sex	Pillai's Trace	.007	3.760[a]	2.000	1119.000	.024	.007
	Wilks's Lambda	.993	3.760[a]	2.000	1119.000	.024	.007
	Hotelling's Trace	.007	3.760[a]	2.000	1119.000	.024	.007
	Roy's Largest Root	.007	3.760[a]	2.000	1119.000	.024	.007

a. Exact statistic.
b. Design: Intercept + sex.

Using the Wilks's lambda criterion, the multivariate effect of sex on the quality of life variate is significant.

Figure 9b.10   Multivariate Test Output

Four multivariate tests are commonly employed in computerized statistical programs: Pillai's trace, Wilks's lambda, Hotelling's trace, and Roy's largest root. As we noted in Chapter 9A, Wilks's lambda is most typically reported in the literature, followed by Pillai's trace if the Box's *M* test is statistically significant, indicating heterogeneity of variance-covariance matrices. All these tests evaluate the null hypothesis of no independent variable (group) differences in the population on the dependent variate.

An actual value for each multivariate test statistic is displayed in the **Value** column of the table (e.g., Wilks's lambda = .993) and is translated by SPSS into an *F* value that is evaluated with specific hypothesis (between groups) and error (within groups) degrees of freedom. In the present example, $F(2, 1119)$ = 3.760, $p < .04$, *partial* η^2 = .007. Remember that the *F* values will always be the same in a two-group Hotelling's T^2 analysis. This statistically significant multivariate test tells us there are reliable differences between gender groups on the composite dependent quality-of-life variate. We should also note in passing, however, that we are accounting for a very small proportion of the total variance (.007) with this independent variable.

Because the multivariate test is statistically significant, we can proceed with an assessment of each dependent measure. Shown in Figure 9b.11 is the **Levene's Test of Equality of Error Variances**, which tests for homogeneity of variance violations for each dependent variable. The evaluation of each dependent measure is not statistically significant ($p > .05$), indicating equal error variance across levels of gender.

Each dependent variable is evaluated separately in the **Tests of Between-Subjects Effects** (shown next in Figure 9b.11). The F values obtained from these analyses are identical to running separate univariate ANOVAs for each dependent measure. This output summarizes standard ANOVA output (i.e., sum of squares, degrees of freedom, mean squares, F values, significance level, and partial η^2) for each dependent variable.

The left side of the table specifies the **Source** of the particular analysis. The **Corrected Model** source is identical to the **sex** source because it consolidates all model effects, with the exception of the intercept. The **Intercept** source (as we noted previously) tests whether each mean differs significantly from zero and is not of much interest to us.

The **sex** source is where we focus our attention, because this source evaluates the effect of gender (**sex**) for each dependent variable. As we can see, a statistically significant effect of **sex** was evidenced for the quality-of-life subjective subscale but not for the quality-of-life objective mean subscale. Thus, we can conclude that the statistically significant multivariate effect we found was "driven" in part by the impact of gender on the subjective quality-of-life appraisals of these mental health consumers.

To see the specific manner in which client gender affected their judgments regarding the subjective quality of life, we examine the group means for each dependent variable. These are shown in the last table of Figure 9b.11 labeled **Client Gender,** and are the estimated marginal means that we requested in the **Options** dialog window. Separate male and female means are shown for each level of the QL-SF inventory. We may now say that males had statistically significant higher **subject** scores ($M = 3.695$, $SE = .063$) than did females ($M = 3.505$, $SE = .049$). No statistically significant differences were observed for the **object** dependent measure, with males averaging ($M = 1.313$, $SE = .018$) and females averaging ($M = 1.322$, $SE = .014$).

The last portion of the **Source** section contains the **Error** source, which summarizes the within-group variability. The **Total** source consolidates all sources of variability in the analysis. The **Corrected Total** excludes the intercept.

Levene's Test of Equality of Error Variances[a]

	F	df1	df2	Sig.
QL-SF Subjective Mean	.288	1	1120	.592
QL-SF Objective Mean	1.352	1	1120	.245

Tests the null hypothesis that the error variance of the dependent variable is equal across groups.
a. Design: Intercept + sex.

Tests of Between-Subjects Effects

Source	Dependent Variable	Type III Sum of Squares	df	Mean Square	F	Sig.	Partial Eta Squared
Corrected Model	QL-SF Subjective Mean	9.456[a]	1	9.456	5.656	.018	.005
	QL-SF Objective Mean	.024[b]	1	.024	.175	.676	.000
Intercept	QL-SF Subjective Mean	13555.025	1	13555.025	8107.282	.000	.879
	QL-SF Objective Mean	1815.685	1	1815.685	13508.531	.000	.923
Sex	QL-SF Subjective Mean	9.456	1	9.456	5.656	.018	.005
	QL-SF Objective Mean	.024	1	.024	.175	.676	.000
Error	QL-SF Subjective Mean	1872.592	1120	1.672			
	QL-SF Objective Mean	150.540	1120	.134			
Total	QL-SF Subjective Mean	16222.650	1122				
	QL-SF Objective Mean	2101.809	1122				
Corrected Total	QL-SF Subjective Mean	1882.048	1121				
	QL-SF Objective Mean	150.563	1121				

a. R Squared = .005 (Adjusted R Squared = 004)
b. R Squared = .000 (Adjusted R Squared = −.001)

> We have a significant univariate sex effect for subject, but the univariate effect for object is not significant.

Client Gender

Dependent Variable	Client Gender	Mean	Std. Error	95% Confidence Interval	
				Lower Bound	Upper Bound
QL-SF Subjective Mean	Male	3.695	.063	3.570	3.819
	Female	3.505	.049	3.409	3.600
QL-SF Objective Mean	Male	1.313	.018	1.277	1.348
	Female	1.322	.014	1.295	1.349

Figure 9b.11 Univariate Test Output

Results

A Hotelling's T^2 or two-group between-subjects multivariate analysis of variance (MANOVA) was conducted on the two dependent variables: subjective quality of life and objective quality of life. The independent variable was gender of mental health client.

One extreme score or univariate outlier was observed for the subjective quality-of-life dependent measure and was eliminated from the analysis, leaving a total of 1,122 mental health clients. Females consisted of 63.0% of the sample. Evaluation of the properties of the data set (e.g., normality, equality of variance-covariance matrices) determined that these data met the necessary statistical assumptions to support the analyses.

Using Wilks's criterion (see Table 9b.1) the composite dependent variate was significantly affected by gender (Wilks's λ, $F[2, 1120] = 3.76$, $p < .024$, partial $\eta^2 = .007$). Univariate ANOVAs were conducted on each dependent measure separately to determine the locus of the statistically significant multivariate effect. From Table 9b.1 we can see that gender significantly affected subjective quality of life, $F(1, 1120) = 5.66$, $p < .018$, partial $\eta^2 = .005$. Means and standard deviations of the two dependent variables for the two groups are presented in Table 9b.2. It appears that male mental health clients achieved higher subjective quality of life ($M = 3.70$, $SD = 1.31$) than females ($M = 3.51$, $SD = 1.28$). No statistically significant gender effects were observed for objective quality of life, $F(1, 1120) = 0.18$, $p > .05$.

Table 9b.1   Multivariate and Univariate Analysis of Variance for Quality of Life Measure

	Multivariate		Univariate	
Source	df	F^a	Subjective Quality of Life[b]	Objective Quality of Life[b]
F ratios for gender	1	3.76*	5.66**	0.18
MSE			9.46	0.02

Note: Multivariate F ratios were generated from Wilks's criterion.

a. Multivariate $df = 2, 1119$.

b. Univariate $df = 1, 1120$

*$p < .05$; **$p < .01$.

Table 9b.2 Mean Scores and Standard Deviations for Measures of Subjective and Objective Quality of Life as a Function of Gender

Group	Subjective Quality of Life		Objective Quality of Life	
	M	*SD*	*M*	*SD*
Male	3.70	1.31	1.31	1.37
Female	3.51	1.28	1.32	0.36

9B Exercises

Anxiety and Country

This study examined differences in anxiety level between an industrial country and a nonindustrial country. Anxiety is assessed three ways—cognitive, affective, and behavioral—with higher scores indicating higher levels of the anxiety dimensions.

Using the SPSS data file for Chapter 9B (located on the Web-based study site—http://www.sagepub.com/amrStudy), answer the following questions.

1. Is MANOVA an appropriate statistical technique for this research? Explain.

2. Examine the mean scores on the anxiety dimensions between the two countries. Do there appear to be mean differences between the two groups on the three dependent variables?

3. According to the Wilks's lambda test, is there a significant difference between the two countries on the linear combination (the variate) of the dependent variables?

4. What is the effect size? Is it weak, moderate, or strong?

5. Examine the univariate output. Do all the dependent variables demonstrate significant differences?

6. Write a results section for this study.

MANOVA

Comparing Three or More Groups

T his chapter extends our previous two-group MANOVA discussion to the situation where researchers wish to assess the effects of one independent variable with three or more levels or treatment groups on several dependent measures. This approach is sometimes referred to as a *k-group MANOVA* or *one-way MANOVA*. For example, an investigator might be interested in the effects of type of treatment (cognitive-behavioral, psychoanalytic, brief) on global assessment of functioning (clinical outcome) and consumer service satisfaction.

The Hotelling's T^2 (or two-group MANOVA) that we covered previously is a special case or generalization of the k-group or one-way MANOVA. As such, the previous rationale for the use of a two-group MANOVA also remains in place for the k-group or one-way MANOVA. Similarly, statistical assumption violation issues (independence, homogeneity of variance-covariance matrices, and normality) remain the same and can be reviewed in Chapters 9A and 9B.

The Univariate *F* Test

Recall that in a univariate ANOVA, a single quantitative (metric) dependent variable is assessed with one or more categorical (nonmetric) independent variables. The null hypothesis takes the following form:

$$H_0 : \mu_1 = \mu_2 = \cdots \mu_i$$

This null hypothesis can be understood to represent the idea that all the population means are equal). Furthermore, in a univariate one-way ANOVA the total variability of a study (the total sum of squares) is partitioned between two component parts: between-group variance or sum of squares (variability due to treatment effects and error) and within-group variance or sum of squares (variability due to measurement error). Symbolically, these components take the following form:

$$SS_T = SS_b + SS_w$$

These sums of square are then weighted with their respective degrees of freedom to produce variance estimates known as mean squares (MS_b and MS_w). A ratio is formed between these two variance estimates (called the F ratio where $F = MS_b / MS_w$), which is evaluated with an appropriate degrees of freedom.

The Multivariate F

In the multivariate (MANOVA) situation, several continuous (metric) dependent variables are assessed with one or more categorical independent variable(s). The null hypothesis in the multivariate case takes the following form:

$$H_0 : = \mu_1 = \mu_2 = \cdots = \mu_i$$

This multivariate null hypothesis expresses the idea that all the population mean vectors or sets (symbolized by bold μs) are equal.

In MANOVA, the univariate sums of squares are replaced with sum of squares and cross-product (SSCP) matrices. These SSCP matrices consist of dependent variable sum of squares or variances along the diagonal of the matrix and covariances (cross-products) on the off-diagonal elements that represent the common variance shared between two variables (Weinfurt, 1995). Similar to its univariate cousin ANOVA, which partitions the total variability into sum of squares between and within components, so, too, MANOVA produces a similar matrix analogue bifurcation. MANOVA (through its SPSS-**GLM** realization) produces a total SSCP matrix (**T**) that can be separated into a between-group SSCP matrix (**B**) and a within-group SSCP matrix (**W**). Symbolically, these matrix components form the following multivariate analogue to the univariate sum of squares partitioning:

$$T = B + W$$

Total SSCP Matrix = Between SSCP Matrix + Within SSCP Matrix

As we noted in Chapters 9A and 9B, through matrix algebraic manipulations conducted within the SPSS-**GLM** program, these matrices of coefficients are converted into single values called *determinants.* Determinants reflect the generalized variance of each matrix. Thus, **T** (the determinant for the total sum of squares and cross-products matrix) reflects the multivariate generalization of how the cases in each independent variable level or group deviate from the grand mean of each dependent variable. Similarly, **B** (the between-group sum of squares and cross-product matrix) reflects the differential treatment effects on the set of dependent variables and is the multivariate generalization of the univariate between-group sum of squares. Last, **W** (the within-group sum of squares and cross-products matrix) is the multivariate generalization of the univariate within-group sum of squares and represents how the cases in each level or group of the independent variable deviate from the dependent variable means (Stevens, 2002).

As noted in Chapters 9A and 9B, there are four commonly used multivariate test statistics: Pillai's trace, Wilks's lambda, Hotelling's trace, and Roy's largest root. The most prominent of these tests in the research literature is Wilks's lambda (Λ), which is basically a ratio of **W** to (**B** + **W**). In practice, if the independent variable has a statistically significant effect on the dependent variables—that is, if treatment effects are present—then **B** (the treatment variance-covariance) will be relatively large and **W** (the residual or error variance-covariance) will be small. Because Wilks's lambda is an inverse criterion, smaller values provide more evidence of treatment effects (Stevens, 2002). To evaluate any of the multivariate test statistics (including Wilks's lambda) SPSS translates the multivariate test value into a multivariate (Rao's) *F* statistic, which can be evaluated much as any other *F* value.

With three or more levels (groups) of the independent variable, these multivariate *F* values tend to differ slightly (remember, they are all the same in the two-group situation), but all tend to yield the same statistically significant or not significant decision. Although Wilks's lambda is most typically reported in the literature, Pillai's trace should be reported if the dependent variables are plagued by significant heterogeneity of variance-covariance matrices.

Following a Significant Multivariate Effect

A statistically significant multivariate effect tells us that the independent variable is associated with differences between the vectors or sets of means. Thus, we can presume that treatment effects exist. The next step in this process is to discover which specific dependent variables are affected. As we indicated in Chapter 9A, we recommend the use of separate univariate ANOVAs for each dependent measure with a Bonferroni adjustment to the operational alpha level (.05 divided by the number of dependent variables) to reduce the possibility of Type I error. Each statistically significant univariate F statistic can then be further evaluated with a post hoc or multiple comparison test that assesses every pairwise combination of means on each dependent measure. These post hoc tests, from the Type I error-liberal least significant difference (LSD) test to its conservative counterpart, the Scheffé test, will be reviewed in some detail in Chapter 10B.

Hypothetical Three-Group Example

Assume that we are interested in the effects of therapy type (this time with three levels: cognitive-behavioral, psychoanalytic, brief) on clinical outcome (GAF) and service satisfaction (CSQ-8) scores. The null hypothesis is that the set or vector of means (on the dependent variate) for each group (or level of the independent variable) is equal to the others. Condensed summaries of results can be seen in Tables 10a.1 through 10a.7.

In Table 10a.1, we note the addition of a third level or group (brief psychotherapy) to the independent variable example that we used in the previous chapter. Sample size is small but acceptable for purposes of illustration. An inspection of the dependent variable means for each group suggests that the psychoanalytic treatment group generated somewhat lower clinical outcome and service satisfaction scores than did clients receiving cognitive-behavioral or brief psychotherapy.

Pearson r correlations were computed between the two dependent measures at each level (group) of the independent variable. A moderate positive correlation was observed for the cognitive-behavioral ($r = .426$) and brief ($r = .458$) psychotherapy groups, and a low positive correlation ($r = .086$) was found for the psychoanalytic group. The differences between these correlations may suggest variability in the dependent variate covariance and will be addressed with the Box's M test.

Table 10a.2 examines normality and diagnostics for each dependent variable across levels of the independent variable. Nearly all the normality tests are not significant ($p < .05$), indicating no normality violations, with the exception of the GAF scores for the brief psychotherapy group. However, the skewness and kurtosis values for this latter group were deemed adequate; thus, any normality violations were considered minor, allowing us to proceed with the analysis.

Normality Tests and Diagnostics, by Therapy Type

Table 10a.3 depicts a statistically nonsignificant Box's M test, indicating equality of variance-covariance matrices. Separate Levene's tests for each

Table 10a.1 Client Global Assessment of Functioning (GAF) and Service Satisfaction (CSQ-8), by Therapy Type (Hypothetical Data for Three-Group MANOVA)

	Therapy Type							
Group 1: Cognitive-Behavioral[a]			*Group 2: Psychoanalytic[b]*			*Group 3: Brief[c]*		
Caseid	*GAF*	*CSQ-8*	*Caseid*	*GAF*	*CSQ-8*	*Caseid*	*GAF*	*CSQ-8*
1	65	30.3	31	50	24.3	56	69	30.1
2	69	27.1	32	55	22.1	57	55	29.0
3	73	31.0	33	61	25.6	58	70	31.0
4	60	29.4	34	66	25.0	59	68	28.0
5	58	27.4	35	58	24.0	60	72	29.9
6	70	30.1	36	50	26.0	61	68	29.0
7	71	30.9	37	45	27.0	62	65	28.2
8	55	27.0	38	53	26.5	63	67	28.0
9	65	28.5	39	59	25.5	64	66	27.1
10	60	29.1	40	61	25.0	65	56	30.1
11	66	29.2	41	70	29.0	66	72	27.9
12	60	29.2	42	65	26.2	67	70	27.0
13	70	30.3	43	55	24.8	68	61	29.0
14	70	31.0	44	50	24.0	69	65	27.0
15	65	26.5	45	62	23.2	70	55	29.0
16	65	27.0	46	66	26.0	71	69	30.0
17	55	26.5	47	69	27.0	72	66	28.3
18	72	30.0	48	50	25.1	73	70	26.5
19	70	31.0	49	58	28.1	74	70	30.0
20	65	28.7	50	55	25.5	75	66	29.1
21	60	28.0	51	60	23.2	76	68	27.9
22	55	27.0	52	60	23.0	77	69	30.0
23	70	30.1	53	65	22.0	78	70	30.0
24	75	29.2	54	65	24.0	79	65	26.0
25	65	25.0	55	50	25.0	80	66	29.0
26	62	24.3						
27	60	30.3						
28	68	26.7						
29	70	28.0						
30	68	25.5						
	M	*SD*		*M*	*SD*		*M*	*SD*
GAF	65.23	5.62		58.32	6.84		65.92	4.92
CSQ-8	28.43	1.90		25.08	1.73		28.77	1.33

a. $n = 30$, $r = .426$, $p < .01$.

b. $n = 25$, $r = .086$, $p > .05$.

c. $n = 25$, $r = .458$, $p > .05$.

Table 10a.2 Client Global Assessment of Functioning (GAF) and Service Satisfaction (CSQ-8) Normality Tests and Diagnostics, by Therapy Type

		Group 1: Cognitive-Behavioral		Group 2: Psychoanalytic		Group 3: Brief	
		Statistic	Sig.	Statistic	Sig.	Statistic	Sig.
Normality tests							
GAF	Kolmogorov-Smirnov	.150	.083	.128	.200	.226	.002
	Shapiro-Wilk	.939	.088	.958	.372	.858	.003
	Skewness	−.353		−.112		−1.066	
	Kurtosis	−.832		−.928		.602	
CSQ-8	Kolmogorov-Smirnov	.129	.200	.081	.200	.169	.063
	Shapiro-Wilk	.946	.131	.982	.918	.935	.115
	Skewness	−.362		.220		−.449	
	Kurtosis	−.782		.033		−.699	

Table 10a.3 Tests of Equality of Covariance Matrices and Equality of Error Variances

	Overall		GAF		CSQ-8	
	Statistic	Sig.	Statistic	Sig.	Statistic	Sig.
Box's M	7.949	.265				
Levene's test			2.34	.103	2.11	.128

dependent variable were also not statistically significant, indicating equal variances for each dependent measure across the levels of therapy type.

A statistically significant Bartlett's test of sphericity ($p < .001$) as shown in Table 10a.4 indicates sufficient correlation between the dependent variables to proceed with the analysis. A moderate positive correlation ($r = .502$) was observed overall between the two dependent measures.

Table 10a.5 presents the multivariate test results, all of which indicate a statistically significant effect of therapy type on the dependent variate. Because equality of variance-covariance matrices was evidenced with the nonsignificant Box's M test, most researchers would report the Wilks's lambda F value of 17.088, $p < .001$, with a partial eta-squared value of .310. This result tells us we can reject the null hypothesis that the group mean

Table 10a.4 Test of Intercorrelation of Dependent Variables

	Statistic	*Significance*
Bartlett's test of sphericity	100.010	.000
Pearson correlation: GAF by CSQ-8	.502	.000

Table 10a.5 Multivariate Test Results

	Multivariate Test	*Value*	*F*	*Sig.*	*Partial Eta Squared*
Therapy type	Pillai's trace	.524	13.674	.000	.262
	Wilks's lambda	.476	17.088	.000	.310
	Hotelling's trace	1.102	20.654	.000	.355
	Roy's largest root	1.102	42.411	.000	.524

vectors are equal and instead conclude that therapy type influences the dependent variate. We can also note that about 31% of the total dependent variate variance is accounted for by therapy type.

Because we observed a statistically significant multivariate effect, we can proceed to examine separate univariate F tests with Bonferroni adjustments to our operational alpha level (.05/2 = .025). We note in Table 10a.6 that both univariate F statistics are statistically significant ($p < .025$). This result indicates that both dependent variables contribute to the significant multivariate effect.

Because statistically significant univariate Fs were observed and the independent variable contained more than two levels, a Scheffé post hoc multiple comparison test was computed for each dependent measure. The results of the post hoc comparisons are shown in Table 10a.7.

Table 10a.7 summarizes pairwise comparisons between each pair of means for each dependent variable. For example, the GAF dependent measure comparison for cognitive-behavioral and psychoanalytic groups is computed by subtracting one group mean from the other (e.g., 65.23 − 58.32), which produces a difference score of 6.9133. Difference scores are evaluated by means of special multiple comparisons formulas (briefly discussed in Chapter 10B) at an alpha level of .05. These results suggest that cognitive-behavioral and brief psychotherapy produce statistically significantly higher clinical outcome and service satisfaction scores than does psychoanalytic psychotherapy.

Table 10a.6 Univariate Test Results

	Dependent Measures	
	GAF	CSQ-8
Independent variable (group) means		
Cognitive-behavioral	65.23	28.43
Psychoanalytic	58.32	25.08
Brief	65.92	28.77
F statistic	13.29	37.35
Significance	.000	.000
Partial eta squared	.257	.492

Table 10a.7 Multiple Comparison Post Hoc Tests (Scheffé) for GAF and Service Satisfaction

Dependent Variable	(I) Therapy Type	(J) Therapy Type	Mean Difference (I-J)
GAF	Cog-beh	Psychoanalytic	6.9133*
	Cog-beh	Brief	−.6867
	Psychoanalytic	Brief	−7.6000*
Service satisfaction	Cog-beh	Psychoanalytic	3.3460*
	Cog-beh	Brief	−.3380
	Psychoanalytic	Brief	−3.6840*

Note: Cog-beh = Cognitive-behavioral.

*$p < .05$.

Recommended Readings

Huberty, C. J. (1989). Multivariate analysis versus multiple univariate analyses. *Psychological Bulletin, 105,* 302–308.

O'Brien, R. G., & Kaiser, M. K. (1985). MANOVA method for analyzing repeated measures designs: An extensive primer. *Psychological Bulletin, 97,* 316–333.

Olson, C. L. (1974). Comparative robustness of six tests in multivariate analysis of variance. *Journal of the American Statistical Association, 69,* 894–908.

Olson, C. L. (1976). On choosing a test statistic in MANOVA. *Psychological Bulletin, 83,* 579–586.

Olson, C. L. (1979). Practical considerations in choosing a MANOVA test statistic: A rejoinder to Stevens. *Psychological Bulletin, 86,* 1350–1352.

Shaffer, J. P., & Gillo, M. W. (1974). A multivariate extension of the correlation ratio. *Educational and Psychological Measurement, 34,* 521–524.

Stevens, J. P. (1972). Four methods of analyzing between variation for the k group MANOVA problem. *Multivariate Behavioral Research, 7,* 499–522.

Thomas, D. (1992). Interpreting discriminant functions: A data analytic approach. *Multivariate Behavioral Research, 27,* 335–362.

Weinfurt, K. P. (1995). Multivariate analysis of variance. In L. G. Grimm & P. R. Yarnold (Eds.), *Reading and understanding multivariate statistics* (pp. 245–276). Washington, DC: American Psychological Association.

Wilkinson, L. (1975). Response variable hypotheses in the multivariate analysis of variance. *Psychological Bulletin, 82,* 408–412.

MANOVA

Comparing Three or
More Groups Using SPSS

This chapter extends our Chapter 10A discussion of k-group or one-way MANOVA with an application using SPSS. The ingredients for a k-group MANOVA require a categorical (nonmetric) independent variable with three or more levels or groups and at least two quantitative (metric) conceptually related dependent measures.

The present numerical example is an extension of the previous Chapter 9B numerical example of severely mentally ill adult community mental health clients. The dependent variables will remain the same as in the previous analysis: objective and subjective quality of life (see Chapter 9B for details). The independent variable is client ethnicity.

Recoding to Create Our Independent Variable

Because our independent variable, client ethnicity (**ethnic**), is new to our MANOVA example, let's begin by examining its frequency distribution. We do this by clicking **Analyze → Descriptive Statistics → Frequencies**, which produces the **Frequencies** dialog box (shown in Figure 10b.1). We will leave all default options in place by simply clicking the **OK** pushbutton, which produces the output also shown in Figure 10b.1.

The output shows disproportionate numbers of clients by ethnic group. Specifically, White, Latino, and African American clients represent 93.4% of the

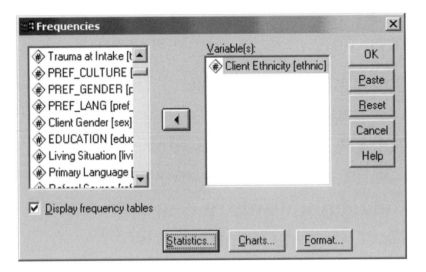

Client Ethnicity

		Frequency	Percent	Valid Percent	Cumulative Percent
Valid	White	856	34.8	34.9	34.9
	Latino	914	37.1	37.2	72.1
	African American	524	21.3	21.3	93.4
	Asian/Pacific	55	2.2	2.2	95.7
	Indian	17	.7	.7	96.4
	South East Asian	11	.4	.4	96.8
	Filipino	28	1.1	1.1	98.0
	Other	48	2.0	2.0	99.9
	Unknown	2	.1	.1	100.0
	Total	2455	99.8	100.0	
Missing	System	6	.2		
Total		2461	100.0		

Figure 10b.1 Frequencies Procedure Dialog Box With the Ethnicity of Clients Selected and Its Output

total ($N = 2{,}455$) clients. To eliminate the severe unequal subsample sizes this disproportionality will produce, we will create a new client ethnicity variable (**newethnc**) that will contain only White, Latino, and African American clients.

We accomplish this recoding by clicking **Transform → Recode → Into Different Variables.** This opens the **Recode into Different Variables** dialog box (see Figure 10b.2). To begin this recoding process, which will create a new variable, we move over the original client ethnicity

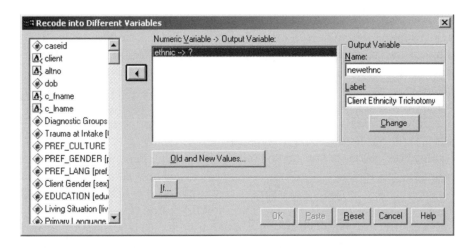

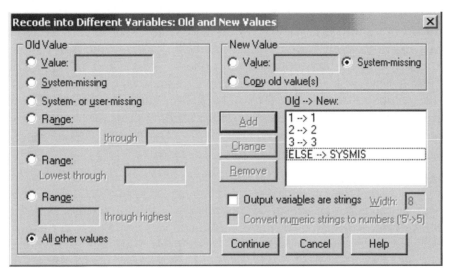

Figure 10b.2 Recode Dialog Boxes to Create a New Client Ethnicity Variable

variable (**ethnic**) to the **Numeric Variable → Output Variable** box in the center of the dialog box. This activates the **Output Variable, Name,** and **Label** boxes where we type in a new variable name. In the present case, we have invented the new name of "**newethnc**" and a short variable label "**Client Ethnicity Trichotomy**." We then click the **Change** pushbutton (underneath the **Label** box) to tell SPSS to prepare the way for the change.

We then click the **Old and New Values** pushbutton to obtain the dialog box depicted next in Figure 10b.2. This box consists of three main sections: the lower right of the dialog box contains the **Old → New** area, which summarizes the result of your recoding efforts. To indicate our recoding, it is necessary to know our original coding scheme on the ethnic variable. As it turns out, our original ethnic variable conveniently coded White, Latino, and African American clients as 1, 2, and 3, respectively. Because we will be working with only three ethnic groups in this example, it is preferable to use Codes 1, 2, and 3. We can therefore continue the same coding scheme for our new variable (**newethnc**).

Because we will not be including the other clients in the present example, the easiest way to meet this goal is to lump all the other codes together under the "system missing values" umbrella that SPSS calls "sysmis." To do this, we begin by typing in **1** in the **Old Value** box (then press tab, tab) and **1** in the **New Value** box, which automatically activates the **Add** button in the **Old → New** box. Clicking **Add** completes this recoding operation. The same procedure is conducted for Codes 2 and 3. Last, we click **All other values** at the bottom of the **Old Value** box and click **System-missing** in the **New Value** box, followed with a click of the **Add** button. This last recoding procedure recodes Codes 4, 5, 6, 7, and 8 to a system missing value, which effectively eliminates these codes from the new variable. Clicking **Continue** moves you back to the **Recode into Different Variables** dialog box, and clicking **OK** creates and saves this new variable to (the end of) your SPSS data file.

Initial Data Screening

Now we can begin preliminary data screening of the three target variables (**newethnc, subject, object**). As explained more completely in Chapter 3B, we begin by clicking **Analyze → Descriptive Statistics → Explore.** This opens the **Explore** dialog box (not shown). Assume, in this dialog box, that we moved our two dependent measures (**subject** and **object**) to the **Dependent List** box and our new independent variable (**newethnc**) to the **Factor List** box. Further assume that (a) **Descriptives** and **Outliers** have been requested from the **Explore: Statistics** dialog box and (b) **Normality plots with tests** and **Stem-and-leaf** plots from the **Explore: Plots** dialog box have also been requested.

Figure 10b.3 depicts the **Case Processing Summary** results, which indicates that roughly half the cases in each ethnic group have missing values on both dependent measures. Although this is unfortunate, it is also not unexpected with archival data on a severely mentally ill (SMI) population. Hence, we will use the SPSS missing values default—listwise deletion—to handle this missing values situation. Recall that listwise deletion will eliminate all cases

Case Processing Summary

	Client Ethnicity Trichotomy	Cases					
		Valid		Missing		Total	
		N	Percent	N	Percent	N	Percent
QL-SF Subjective Mean	White American	397	46.4%	459	53.6%	856	100.0%
	Latino American	422	46.2%	492	53.8%	914	100.0%
	African American	237	45.2%	287	54.8%	524	100.0%
QL-SF Objective Mean	White American	397	46.4%	459	53.6%	856	100.0%
	Latino American	422	46.2%	492	53.8%	914	100.0%
	African American	237	45.2%	287	54.8%	524	100.0%

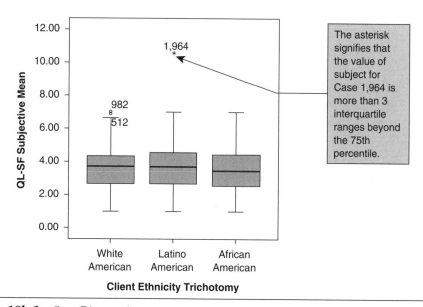

Figure 10b.3 Case Diagnostics

with missing values on the dependent measure from the analysis. This is acceptable because our initial sample size was relatively large despite our working with only a portion of the client data represented in the data file.

Univariate outliers are assessed with box plots for each dependent variable. Figure 10b.3 also depicts the box plot for **subject**, where two extreme scores (the overlapping rounded symbols beyond the upper inner fence) were found for the White American classification (cases 982 and 512) and one extreme score for the Latino American group (case 1,964). These three cases will be eliminated from all subsequent analyses. The box plot for the

object dependent measure (not shown) produced no extreme scores for any of the ethnicity groups. A check for multivariate outliers (not shown) indicated no multivariate outliers were present.

Univariate normality for each dependent variable at each level of the independent variable can be assessed with the SPSS **Explore** procedure. But before proceeding with the **Explore** procedure, we will demonstrate how to temporarily eliminate the three cases with extreme dependent variable scores from subsequent analyses. To eliminate specific cases, we begin by clicking **Data → Select Cases,** which opens the **Select Cases** dialog box displayed in Figure 10b.4. In this box, we click the **If condition is satisfied** circle in the **Select** box. We then click the **If** pushbutton, which produces the **Select Cases: If** dialog box also shown in Figure 10b.4.

In the **Select Cases: If** dialog box we click over (or type in) the following statement:

$$caseid \sim = 512 \ \& \ caseid \sim = 982 \ \& \ caseid \sim = 1964.$$

This logical expression tells SPSS to select or use all cases in the subsequent analyses *except* Cases 512, 982, and 1,964. Clicking **Continue** and then **OK** activates this command.

Univariate normality can next be examined through the SPSS **Explore** procedure by clicking **Analyze → Descriptive Statistics → Explore.** Here, we move our two dependent variables (**subject** and **object**) to the **Dependent List** box and the independent variable (**newethnc**) to the **Factor List** box. As we noted in Chapter 9B, the **Explore** procedure automatically defaults with descriptive statistics, and by clicking **Plots** and checking the **Normality plots with tests** checkbox, normal Q-Q plots and tests of normality will be produced.

Selected output tables are shown in Figures 10b.5 and 10b.6. The first table (Figure 10b.5) provides descriptive statistics for each dependent variable profile by client ethnicity (**newethnc**). All skewness and kurtosis values are fairly minimal and within the ±1.0 range.

The next output table, shown in Figure 10b.6, indicates that most of the normality tests (Kolmogorov-Smirnov and Shapiro-Wilk) are statistically significant, indicating possible normality violations within the distributions of both dependent measures.

However, as we also noted in Chapter 9B, the normal Q-Q plots look reasonably normal (i.e., data points are fairly close to the diagonal lines) and thus we judge these variables ready for analysis (see Figure 10b.7). Alternatively, we could have attempted to transform these dependent measures to try to achieve greater normality by following the procedures outlined in Chapters 3A and 3B.

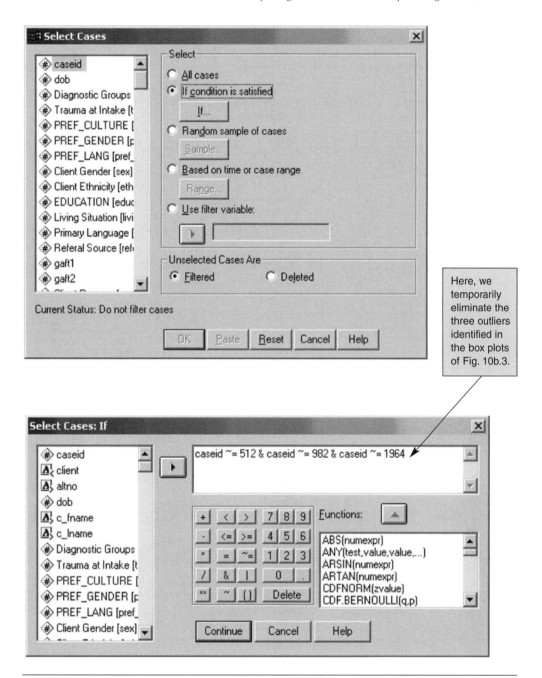

Figure 10b.4 Select Cases Main Dialog Box and Its If Condition Is Satisfied Box

Descriptives

Client Ethnicity				Statistic	Std. Error
QL-SF Subjective Mean	White American	Mean		3.5311	.06023
		95% Confidence	Lower Bound	3.4127	
		Interval for Mean	Upper Bound	3.6495	
		5% Trimmed Mean		3.5247	
		Median		3.5556	
		Variance		1.433	
		Std. Deviation		1.19704	
		Minimum		1.00	
		Maximum		6.67	
		Range		5.67	
		Interquartile Range		1.67	
		Skewness		.093	.123
		Kurtosis		−.447	.245
	Latino American	Mean		3.6133	.06371
		95% Confidence	Lower Bound	3.4881	
		Interval for Mean	Upper Bound	3.7386	
		5% Trimmed Mean		3.6005	
		Median		3.6667	
		Variance		1.709	
		Std. Deviation		1.30716	
		Minimum		1.00	
		Maximum		7.00	
		Range		6.00	
		Interquartile Range		1.94	
		Skewness		.098	.119
		Kurtosis		−.593	.237
	African American	Mean		3.4985	.09075
		95% Confidence	Lower Bound	3.3197	
		Interval for Mean	Upper Bound	3.6773	
		5% Trimmed Mean		3.4657	
		Median		3.4444	
		Variance		1.952	
		Std. Deviation		1.39704	
		Minimum		1.00	
		Maximum		7.00	
		Range		6.00	
		Interquartile Range		1.89	
		Skewness		.302	.158
		Kurtosis		−.341	.315
QL-SF Objective Mean	White American	Mean		1.3838	.01903
		95% Confidence	Lower Bound	1.3464	
		Interval for Mean	Upper Bound	1.4212	
		5% Trimmed Mean		1.3809	
		Median		1.3571	
		Variance		.143	
		Std. Deviation		.37815	
		Minimum		.57	
		Maximum		2.29	
		Range		1.71	
		Interquartile Range		.64	
		Skewness		.124	.123
		Kurtosis		−.882	.245

Client Ethinicity			Statistic	Std. Error
Latino American	Mean		1.2906	.01749
	95% Confidence Interval for Mean	Lower Bound	1.2562	
		Upper Bound	1.3249	
	5% Trimmed Mean		1.2807	
	Median		1.2857	
	Variance		.129	
	Std. Deviation		.35879	
	Minimum		.57	
	Maximum		2.21	
	Range		1.64	
	Interquartile Range		.54	
	Skewness		.371	.119
	Kurtosis		−.505	.237
African American	Mean		1.2691	.02263
	95% Confidence Interval for Mean	Lower Bound	1.2245	
		Upper Bound	1.3137	
	5% Trimmed Mean		1.2635	
	Median		1.2143	
	Variance		.121	
	Std. Deviation		.34840	
	Minimum		.50	
	Maximum		2.21	
	Range		1.71	
	Interquartile Range		.55	
	Skewness		.248	.158
	Kurtosis		−.485	.315

Figure 10b.5 Descriptive Statistics for Each Dependent Variable

Tests of Normality

	Client Ethnicity Trichotomy	Kolmogorov-Smirnov[a]			Shapiro-Wilk		
		Statistic	df	Sig.	Statistic	df	Sig.
QL-SF Subjective Mean	White American	.037	395	.200*	.992	395	.036
	Latino American	.049	421	.018	.998	421	.002
	African American	.051	237	.200*	.982	237	.005
QL-SF Objective Mean	White American	.093	395	.000	.977	395	.000
	Latino American	.087	421	.000	.977	421	.000
	African American	.080	237	.001	.985	327	.016

*This is a lower bound of the true significance.
a. Lillefors significance correction.

Figure 10b.6 Output Table Showing the Results for the Tests of Normality

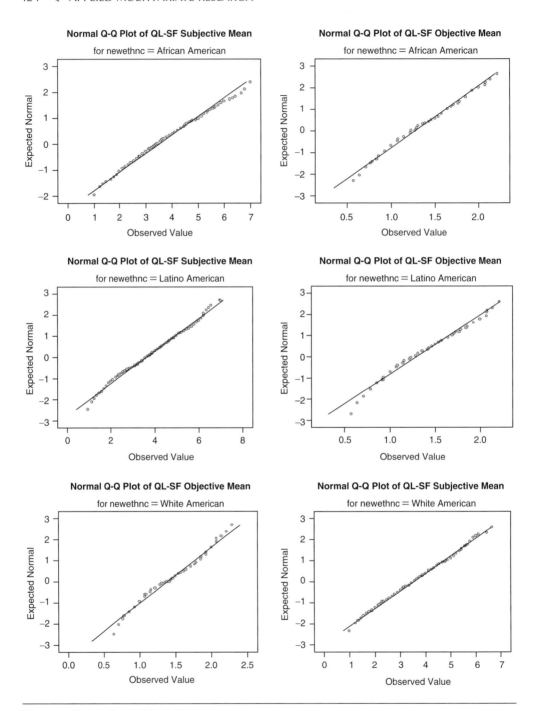

Figure 10b.7 Normal Q-Q Plots

MANOVA Dialog Boxes for the k-Group Case

To begin our analysis, we click **Analyze → General Linear Model → Multivariate,** which opens the **Multivariate** dialog box (not shown). We move over to the **Dependent Variables** box our two dependent measures (**subject** and **object**) and our independent variable (**newethnc**) to the **Fixed Factor(s)** box.

From the **Multivariate** dialog box, clicking the **Options** pushbutton produces the **Multivariate: Options** dialog box (also not shown). We checked in the **Display** box (in the lower half of the dialog box) four useful sets of statistics (see also Chapter 9B). **Descriptive statistics** provides means, standard deviations, and counts for each dependent measure at each level of the independent variable. The **Estimates of effect size** checkbox produces the partial eta squared. The **Residual SSCP matrix** checkbox is the only way to generate Bartlett's test of sphericity (in the SPSS **GLM** procedure). Last, the **Homogeneity tests** checkbox produces the Levene's test of equality of error variances.

Post Hoc Testing

Clicking the **Post Hoc** pushbutton creates the **Multivariate: Post Hoc Multiple Comparisons for Observed Means** dialog box (see Figure 10b.8). Double clicking the independent variable (**newethnc**) in the **Factor(s)** box moves this variable to the **Post Hoc Tests for** box and activates the **Equal Variances Assumed** and **Equal Variances Not Assumed** boxes (at the bottom half of the dialog box). The former contains 14 post hoc comparison checkboxes, and the latter contains 4 additional possibilities. We will briefly review all 18 of these. Note that in the present example, we have checked the **Tamhane's T²** checkbox at the bottom of the dialog box.

Some authors (e.g., Keppel & Wickens, 2004) argue persuasively for the use in many experimental contexts of specified-in-advance planned comparisons (which can be produced by clicking the **Contrasts** pushbutton in the **Multivariate** dialog box). Alternatively, many nonexperimental situations (e.g., archival data analysis) lend themselves to a post hoc testing of all possible pairwise comparisons of between-group means. Metaphorically, planned comparisons are usually driven by specific research hypotheses. It is analogous to visiting a bookstore to purchase *Walden* by Henry David Thoreau and the *Lord of the Rings* trilogy by J. R. R. Tolkien. The researchers are asking the question: "Do you have these specific books in stock?"

Conversely, post hoc analyses typically are only loosely driven by theoretical aims. These are analogous to visiting a bookstore hoping to find

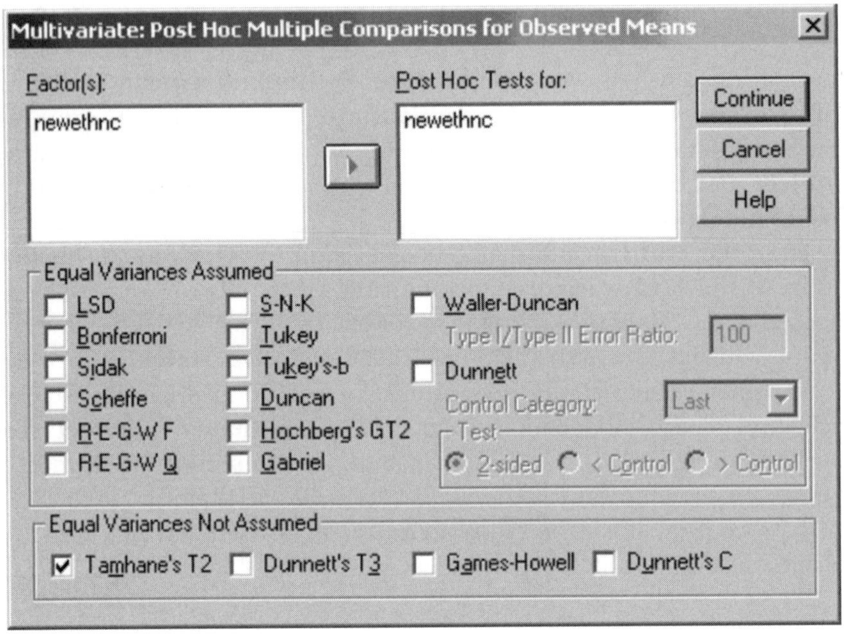

Figure 10b.8 Post Hoc Multiple Comparisons for Observed Means Dialog Box Found by Clicking the Post Hoc Pushbutton on the Multivariate Main Dialog Box

something of interest and purchasing whatever seems to interest you at the moment. The researchers are asking the question: "Do you have anything interesting in stock today?"

Because the post hoc approach involves testing every possible pair of treatment means, the possibility of making a Type I error or of obtaining a false positive conclusion increases as you increase the number of comparisons. For example, if your independent variable has five treatment (levels) groups, then you would need to evaluate $(a \times (a - 1))/2 = 10$ pairwise comparisons (where a is the number of treatment groups). If we multiply our alpha level by the number of comparisons—$(.05 \times 10) = .5$—and round this value upward to a whole number (1), we can expect to generate 1 false positive among our 10 pairwise comparisons. To compensate for this potential exponential increase in Type I error rate, statisticians have developed a gallimaufry of multiple comparison tests that attempt to minimize Type I error and stabilize or increase statistical power in the face of statistical violations (particularly homogeneity of variance).

These multiple comparison tests compare individual pairs of means—that is, they compare each group with every other group (this is called *familywise* comparison) with special algebraically derived formulas that are assessed with a variety of statistical distributions such as *t, F,* studentized range, and so on (Keppel & Wickens, 2004; Seaman, Levin, & Serlin, 1991; Toothaker, 1991). The actual statistical algorithms that make up these post hoc tests vary in complexity and will not concern us here because SPSS makes these computations for us and seamlessly evaluates each pairwise comparison for statistical significance.

We have listed below a brief summary of these multiple comparison post hoc tests as they appear in the **Multivariate: Post Hoc Multiple Comparisons for Observed Means** dialog box.

Tests Listed Under Equal Variance Assumed

LSD

The LSD or least significant difference test uses a *t* test to make all possible pairwise comparisons of group means following a statistically significant omnibus *F* test. This test is the most liberal (i.e., it has relatively high statistical power and a greater likelihood of committing a Type I error). Most authors caution against its use (e.g., Keppel & Wickens, 2004), but there are still advocates who recommend its use (Carmer & Swanson, 1973).

Bonferroni

The Bonferroni procedure (also called the Dunn's test) uses *t* tests to assess all pairs of group means but controls the overall (familywise) error rate by adjusting the operational alpha level by the number of comparisons being made. This procedure is considered a moderately conservative approach. Although often employed in the literature, this procedure tends to overcorrect with a large number of comparisons (Keppel & Wickens, 2004).

Sidak

The Sidak (also called Sidak-Bonferroni; the "S" is pronounced "Sh") also makes all pairwise comparisons based on a *t* test but uses more stringent alpha level adjustment procedures than the Bonferroni test. This too is considered a moderate (neither too liberal nor too conservative) post hoc test.

Scheffé

The Scheffé test conducts simultaneous pairwise comparisons of all means using the *F* distribution. This procedure is the most conservative (i.e., less statistical power and fewer chances of making a Type I error) of the post hoc tests. The Scheffé test may be most useful when moving into "uncharted" theoretical waters where a carefully articulated conservative stance may be most appropriate.

REGWF and REGWQ

REGWF is the Ryan-Enoit-Gabriel-Welsch step-down procedure based on the *F* test, and REGWQ is the Ryan-Enoit-Gabriel-Welsch step-down procedure based on the studentized range. Both of these moderate procedures are modifications of the Newman-Keuls procedure. These procedures are recommended by some authors over the use of the Newman-Keuls procedure (Keppel & Wickens, 2004).

SNK

The SNK (Student-Newman-Keuls) compares all pairwise combinations of means using the studentized range distribution. Using a stepwise procedure, means are ranked in ascending order and extreme differences are successively tested. This moderate procedure has a tendency to inflate Type I error rate and is not recommended by some observers (Keppel & Wickens, 2004).

Tukey

The Tukey procedure (also called the honestly significant difference, or HSD, test) considers all pairwise comparisons by using the standard error of the mean and the studentized range distribution. This procedure controls the experimentwise (overall) error rate at the rate for the entire set of all pairwise comparisons. This moderately conservative procedure is recommended by many commentators (e.g., Keppel & Wickens, 2004).

Tukey's-b

The Tukey's-b test also uses the studentized range distribution to make pairwise comparisons. This procedure uses an average of the Tukey HSD test and the SNK to evaluate each comparison. This test is not highly recommended (Keppel & Wickens, 2004).

Duncan

The Duncan test (like the SNK, REGWF, and REGWQ) is based on stepwise testing. This moderately liberal procedure rank orders the means similar to the SNK test, but uses an experimentwise control for Type I error rather than individual comparison adjustments.

Hochberg's GT2

The GT2 test is similar to the Tukey HSD, but it was specifically designed to address unequal sample sizes.

Gabriel

The Gabriel test is a more liberal version of the Hochberg's GT2.

Waller-Duncan

The Waller-Duncan test employs a Bayesian algorithm that adjusts the assessment criterion on the size of the overall F statistic. This approach also allows researchers to specify the ratio of Type I error to Type II error within the test comparison.

Dunnett

The Dunnett's test is useful when a control group is being compared with a set of experimental groups. The test statistic is the t test.

Tests Listed Under Equal Variance Not Assumed

Tamhane's T2

The Tamhane's T2 test produces pairwise comparisons based on the t test and adjusts for unequal variances. This is considered a conservative test.

Dunnett's T3

The Dunnett's T3 provides pairwise comparisons based on the studentized maximum modulus and can be used with unequal variances.

Games-Howell

The Games-Howell is a liberal pairwise comparison test that can be used with unequal variances.

Dunnett's C

The Dunnett's C is a pairwise comparison test based on the studentized range and can be used with unequal variances.

Recommendations

As far as specific recommendations go, we agree with Keppel and Wickens (2004) that the Tukey HSD is a sound way to control for Type I error rate. If control of Type I error rate is not a major concern but gaining statistical power is a primary goal, then the LSD test is certainly worth considering. If unequal variances are observed among the treatment groups, then the more conservative Tamhane's T2 test may be in order.

MANOVA Output for the k-Group Case

Once we have completed the **Post Hoc** dialog box, we are ready to run the analysis. Clicking **Continue** brings us back to the main dialog box, and clicking **OK** runs the analysis. The k-group or one-way MANOVA output can be seen in Figures 10b.9 and 10b.10.

The first output in Figure 10b.9 displays the **Between-Subjects Factors** table, which depicts the count or sample size for each of the three levels of the independent variable (**newethnc**). We note large but unequal cell sample sizes among the three groups.

The **Descriptive Statistics** table shown next in Figure 10b.9 depicts each dependent measure's observed (unadjusted) means, standard deviations, and sample sizes at each level of the independent variable. Latino American clients have the highest subjective quality-of-life average, and White Americans produced the highest objective quality-of-life mean.

Box's Test of Equality of Covariance Matrices can be seen next in Figure 10b.9. This statistic is significant (Box's $M = 13.651$, $p < .034$), indicating that the dependent variable covariance matrices are not equal across the levels of the independent variable (**newethnc**). The unequal variances may be a function of the unequal group sample sizes noted earlier. In the present example, we elect to proceed with the analysis rather than transform the dependent measures, but we will use Pillai's trace to assess the multivariate effect.

Barlett's Test of Sphericity is statistically significant (approximate chi square = 1495.148, $p < .000$), indicating sufficient correlation between the dependent variables to proceed with the analysis (see last box of Figure 10b.9).

The **Multivariate Tests** output table appears next in Figure 10b.10. Our primary interest is in the bottom half of this table (see previous Chapter 9B discussion of the **Intercept** portion of this table). The section of the table labeled "**newethnc**" followed by four multivariate tests evaluates the multivariate null hypothesis of no independent variable (**newethnc**) differences in the population on the dependent (quality of life) variate.

As we noted in Chapters 9A and 9B, when the Box's M test is statistically significant (as in the present case), heterogeneity of variance-covariance

Between-Subjects Factors

		Value Label	N
Client Ethnicity Trichotomy	1	White American	395
	2	Latino American	421
	3	African American	237

Descriptive Statistics

	Client Ethnicity	Mean	Std. Deviation	N
QL-SF Subjective Mean	White American	3.5311	1.19704	395
	Latino American	3.6133	1.30716	421
	African American	3.4985	1.39704	237
	Total	3.5566	1.28801	1053
QL-SF Objective Mean	White American	1.3838	.37815	395
	Latino American	1.2906	.35879	421
	African American	1.2691	.34840	237
	Total	1.3207	.36693	1053

Box's Test of Equality of Covariance Matrices[a]

Box's M	13.651
F	2.268
df1	6
df2	8484885
Sig.	.034

The significant Box's *M* indicates heterogeneity of covariance. We will therefore evaluate the multivariate *F* using Pillai's trace.

Tests the null hypothesis that the observed covariance matrices of the dependent variables are equal across groups.

a. Design: Intercept+newethnc

Bartlett's Test of Sphericity[a]

Likelihood Ratio	.000
Approx. Chi Square	1495.148
df	2
Sig.	.000

Tests the null hypothesis that the residual covariance matrix is proportional to an identity matrix.

a. Design: Intercept+newethnc

Figure 10b.9   Selected Descriptive and Diagnostic Output From the MANOVA Procedure

Multivariate Tests[c]

Effect		Value	F	Hypothesis df	Error df	Sig.	Partial Eta Squared
Intercept	Pillai's Trace	.936	7678.878[a]	2.000	1049.000	.000	.936
	Wilks' Lambda	.064	7678.878[a]	2.000	1049.000	.000	.936
	Hotelling's Trace	14.640	7678.878[a]	2.000	1049.000	.000	.936
	Roy's Largest Root	14.640	7678.878[a]	2.000	1049.000	.000	.936
newethnc	Pillai's Trace	.023	6.186	4.000	2100.000	.000	.012
	Wilks' Lambda	.977	6.210[a]	4.000	2098.000	.000	.012
	Hotelling's Trace	.024	6.234	4.000	2096.000	.000	.012
	Roy's Largest Root	.023	11.855[b]	2.000	1050.000	.000	.022

a. Exact statistic.
b. The statistic is an upper bound on *F* that yields a lower bound on the significance level.
c. Design: Intercept+newethnc.

> There is a significant multivariate effect of newethnc.

Figure 10b.10 Multivariate Test Results

matrices is present, necessitating the use of the Pillai's trace multivariate test because of its robustness in the presence of unequal dependent variate variance. We note a Pillai's trace value of .023, which is subsequently translated into an *F* statistic of 6.186. This *F* statistic is evaluated at degrees of freedom of 4 and 2100. At these degrees of freedom, the *F* value is statistically significant ($p < .000$). We can determine from the partial eta-squared value of .012 that the independent variable (**newethnc**) accounts for a small amount of the total variance. These results can be summarized as $F(4, 2100) = 6.186$, $p < .001$, partial eta squared = .012.

Because our multivariate test is statistically significant (while admittedly accounting for only 1% of the variance in our dependent variate), we can proceed with a separate assessment of each dependent measure. Figure 10b.11 displays the results of the **Levene's Test of Equality of Error Variances**, which tests for homogeneity of variance violations for each dependent measure. In the present example, both dependent variables have statistically significant Levene's tests, indicating heterogeneity (unequal) variances among the groups on each dependent measure. This is not entirely surprising because the Box's *M* test also indicated heterogeneity (of the variance-covariance matrices) among the combined dependent variate. Again, we will proceed with the (univariate) analyses but suggest interpretive caution in the written results section because of the unequal variability among the treatment groups.

Levene's Test of Equality of Error Variances[a]

	F	df1	df2	Sig.
QL-SF Subjective Mean	3.537	2	1050	.029
QL-SF Objective Mean	3.157	2	1050	.043

Tests the null hypothesis that the error variance of the dependent variable equal across groups

a. Design: Intercept+newethnc.

> There is a significant univariate effect of newethnc for object but there is no significant effect for subject.

Tests of Between-Subjects Effects

Source	Dependent Variable	Type III Sum of Squares	df	Mean Square	F	Sig.	Partial Eta Squared
Corrected Model	QL-SF Subjective Mean	2.411[a]	2	1.206	.726	.484	.001
	QL-SF Objective Mean	2.587[b]	2	1.293	9.766	.000	.018
Intercept	QL-SF Subjective Mean	12411.545	1	12411.545	7477.622	.000	.877
	QL-SF Objective Mean	1703.936	1	1703.936	12866.561	.000	.925
Newethnc	QL-SF Subjective Mean	2.411	2	1.206	.726	.484	.001
	QL-SF Objective Mean	2.587	2	1.293	9.766	.000	.018
Error	QL-SF Subjective Mean	1742.816	1050	1.660			
	QL-SF Objective Mean	139.053	1050	.132			
Total	QL-SF Subjective Mean	15065.353	1053				
	QL-SF Objective Mean	1978.338	1053				
Corrected Total	QL-SF Subjective Mean	1745.228	1052				
	QL-SF Objective Mean	141.640	1052				

a. R Squared = .001 (Adjusted R Squared = .001)
b. R Squared = .018 (Adjusted R Squared = .016)

Multiple Comparisons

Tamhane ◀

> Tamhane's T2 post hoc test is used due to unequal variances.

Dependent Variable	(I) Client Ethnicity Trichotomy	(J) Client Ethnicity Trichotomy	Mean Difference (I-J)	Std. Error	Sig.	95% Confidence Interval Lower Bound	95% Confidence Interval Upper Bound
QL-SF Subjective Mean	White American	Latino American	−.0822	.08767	.724	−.2920	.1275
		African American	.0326	.10892	.987	−.2285	.2936
	Latino American	White American	.0822	.08767	.724	−.1275	.2920
		African American	.1148	.11088	.658	−.1509	.3805
	African American	White American	−.0326	.10892	.987	−.2936	.2285
		Latino American	−.1148	.11088	.658	−.3805	.1509
QL-SF Objective Mean	White American	Latino American	.0932[*]	.02584	.001	.0314	.1551
		African American	.1147[*]	.02957	.000	.0439	.1855
	Latino American	White American	−.0932[*]	.02584	.001	−.1551	−.0314
		African American	.0215	.02860	.836	−.0470	.0900
	African American	White American	−.1147[*]	.02957	.000	−.1855	−.0439
		Latino American	−.0215	.02860	.836	−.0900	.0470

Based on observed means.
*The mean difference is significant at the .05 level.

> Because object was the only significant dependent variable we should restrict our examination of the pairwise comparisons to this variable.

Figure 10b.11   Additional Selected Output From the MANOVA Procedure

The **Tests of Between-Subjects Effects** evaluates each dependent variable separately and can also be seen in Figure 10b.11. Of particular interest is the middle portion of the table labeled **newethnc** that depicts the separate univariate ANOVAs for each dependent variable (see Chapter 9B for a discussion of the other components of this table). From this table, we note a "split decision"; the subjective quality-of-life (**subject**) dependent measure was not statistically significant, $F(2, 1050) = .726, p > .484$, partial eta squared $= .001$, indicating comparable subjective quality-of-life scores among the three ethnic groups. However, the univariate ANOVA for objective quality of life (**object**) was statistically significant, $F(2, 1050) = 9.766, p < .001$, partial eta squared $= .018$. Apparently, differences between the three ethnic groups on objective quality of life contributed to the multivariate effect.

To determine specifically which groups differ significantly on the objective quality-of-life dependent measure, pairwise comparisons are assessed with the Tamhane test, using the SPSS default of alpha = .05. The results of the post hoc tests are also presented in Figure 10b.11.

Note that the post hoc tests were performed for both dependent variables despite having achieved statistical significance for only one of them. The reason for this is that SPSS does not know what alpha level the researchers have adopted for the study and in some sense does not care. It was told to run the Tamhane procedure within the multivariate context and so it did. It is therefore the responsibility of the researchers to know how to properly extract and interpret the relevant information from the printout rather than just automatically accepting everything that they see on the screen. Because the omnibus (overall) F test for the subjective quality of life was not statistically significant ($p > .05$), we therefore understand that we must ignore those pairwise comparisons in the top portion of the table.

The lower portion of the table depicts the objective quality-of-life pairwise comparisons. For example, we can see that the **Mean Difference** between White American and Latino American clients was .0932 and was statistically significant at the $p < .001$ level. Similarly, White American clients achieved a **Mean Difference** between African American clients of .1147, which was also statistically significant. By referring back to the earlier **Descriptive Statistics** table (Figure 10b.9), we can see more clearly what these pairwise comparison results are telling us. Specifically, White American clients had significantly higher objective quality-of-life scores ($M = 1.29$, $SD = .39$) than did Latino American clients ($M = 1.29$, $SD = .36$). Similarly, White American clients also had higher objective quality-of-life scores than did African American clients ($M = 1.27$, $SD = .35$). This differential effect in favor of the White American clients on the objective quality-of-life dependent measure was responsible for the statistically significant multivariate effect.

Results

A k-group or one-way between-subjects multivariate analysis of variance (MANOVA) was conducted on two dependent variables: subjective quality of life and objective quality of life. The independent variable was client ethnicity (White American, Latino American, African American).

Three extreme scores or univariate outliers were observed for the subjective quality-of-life dependent measure and were eliminated from the analysis, leaving a total N of 1,053 mental health clients. Client ethnicity was distributed as Latino American (40.0%), White American (37.5%), and African American (22.5%). A statistically significant Box's M test ($p < .034$) indicated unequal variance-covariance matrices of the dependent variables across levels of client ethnicity and thus necessitated the use of Pillai's trace in assessing the multivariate effect.

Using Pillai's trace (see Table 10b.1), the dependent variate was significantly affected by client ethnicity, Pillai's trace = .023, $F(4, 2100) = 6.19$, $p < .0001$, partial $\eta^2 = .012$. Univariate ANOVAs were conducted on each dependent measure separately to determine the locus of the statistically significant multivariate effect. From Table 10b.1, we can see that client ethnicity significantly affected objective quality of life, $F(2, 1050) = 9.77$, $p < .0001$, partial $\eta^2 = .018$.

Tamhane post hoc tests, appropriate when heterogeneity of variance is present (see Table 10b.2), suggested that White American clients ($M = 1.38$, $SD = 0.38$) had significantly higher objective quality-of-life scores than did their Latino American ($M = 1.29$, $SD = 0.36$) and African American ($M = 1.27$, $SD = 0.35$) counterparts. No statistically significant client ethnicity effects were observed for subjective quality of life, $F(2, 1050) = 0.73$, $p > .05$. Caution should be exercised when interpreting these results because of the heterogeneity of variance-covariance matrices observed in the present study.

Table 10b.1 Multivariate and Univariate Analyses of Variance for Quality-of-Life Measure

| | Multivariate | Univariate | |
| | | | |
Source	F^a	Subjective Quality of Life[b]	Objective Quality of Life[b]
Client ethnicity	6.19*	0.73	9.77*
MSE		1.66	0.13

Note: Multivariate F ratios were generated from Pillai's trace.

a. Multivariate $df = 4, 2100$.

b. Univariate $df = 2, 1050$.

*$p < .01$.

Table 10b.2 Mean Scores and Standard Deviations for Measures of Subjective and Objective Quality of Life as a Function of Gender

| | Subjective Quality of Life | | Objective Quality of Life | |
| | | | | |
Group	M	SD	M	SD
White American	3.53	1.20	1.38[a]	0.38
Latino American	3.61	1.31	1.29[b]	0.36
African American	3.50	1.40	1.27[b]	0.36

Note: Means with different superscripted letters differed significantly at the .05 level by means of Tamhane post hoc test.

10B Exercises

Father Perceived Parenting Competence

This research examined 60 fathers on their perceived parenting competence. The fathers were selected from three groups: (a) fathers with a child with no disabilities, (b) fathers with a physically disabled child, and (c) fathers with a mentally retarded child. All the fathers responded to the Perceived Parenting Competence Scale (PPCS), which has three subscales: (a) caretaking responsibilities, (b) emotional support provided to the child, and (c) recreational time spent with the child. The researcher is investigating if there are any differences among the three groups of fathers.

Using the SPSS data file for Chapter 10B (located on the Web-based study site—http://www.sagepub.com/amrStudy), answer the following questions:

1. What is the formula to determine the maximum number of variants possible for this problem?
2. Are there statistically significant differences among the groups on the linear combination of the dependent variables?
3. What is the effect size as determined by the Wilks's lambda?
4. Was the assumption of equality of covariance matrices *seriously* violated?
5. Which of the dependent variables achieved statistically significant differences between the groups?
6. Identify the proper post hoc for the "caretaking responsibilities" variable. Explain your answer.
7. What is a possible explanation on why "emotional support" failed to achieve statistical significance?
8. What is the effect size for the "recreational time" variable?

Three-Group MANOVA

This research examined the effects of homeless status (chronic, acute, and currently not homeless) on people's perceived life satisfaction as measured by quality of life and general health status.

Using the SPSS data file for Chapter 10B (located on the Web-based study site—http://www.sagepub.com/amrStudy), answer the following questions:

1. Is there sufficient correlation between the dependent variables to justify the use of MANOVA?
2. Was the assumption of equality of covariance matrices violated? Explain.
3. Is there a statistically significant multivariate effect of homeless status on the dependent variate?
4. Which of the dependent variables achieved statistically significant differences among the groups?
5. Identify the proper post hoc analyses for any statistically significant univariate effects. Explain your answer.
6. Why would a researcher conduct a MANOVA instead of several ANOVAs?
7. Write a results section for this research.

MANOVA

Two-Way Factorial

This chapter extends our previous discussions of two-group MANOVA (Chapters 9A and 9B) and k-group MANOVA (Chapters 10A and 10B) to the two-way (two independent variables) MANOVA situation, sometimes referred to as a factorial or two-way MANOVA, where the effects of two independent variables are examined simultaneously on two or more conceptually related dependent variables. For example, an investigator might be interested in the effects of gender (male, female) and type of treatment (psychoanalytic, cognitive-behavioral, brief) on global assessment of functioning (clinical outcome) and consumer service satisfaction.

The rationale we outlined previously (Chapters 9A and 10A) for using MANOVA is also appropriate when two (or more) independent variables are considered. Likewise, the issues relating to statistical assumption violations of independence, homogeneity of variance-covariance matrices, and normality are comparable and can be reviewed in Chapters 9A and 9B.

The Univariate and Multivariate Factorial Design

The previous MANOVA chapters shared an important commonality: They each addressed the multivariate analysis of a single independent variable. In the univariate statistical domain, where we examine one dependent variable at a time, these single-factor analyses can provide very useful information. This is also true in the multivariate domain as well, where two or more dependent measures are profitably assessed by means of a single (categorical) independent variable.

Challenges arise when researchers work with multiple independent variables (in the univariate or multivariate context) in a study. If they opt to analyze one independent variable at a time, they will drive up Type I (false positive) error rates. Furthermore, single-factor independent variable assessments (either univariate or multivariate) do not allow researchers to determine how independent variables jointly affect the dependent measure(s).

Advantages of Univariate and Multivariate Factorial Designs

Keppel et al. (1992) note several distinct advantages that univariate factorial designs have over single-factor approaches, although these advantages are also recognized by most researchers in the field. Our discussion is based on their thoughts, but we have extended the arguments to subsume the multivariate domain as well.

Simultaneous Manipulation of Independent Variables

A univariate factorial design is defined as the joint or simultaneous manipulation of two or more independent variables to determine their unique and joint effect on a single dependent variable. Likewise, a multivariate factorial design examines the unique and joint effects of two or more independent variables on two or more dependent variables—both collectively (the dependent variate) and separately (as in the univariate case). Accordingly, factorial designs provide researchers with a richer context within which they may explore the phenomena under study. Adding an additional independent variable to the use of a single one can potentially increase the *ecological validity* or real-world meaningfulness of the study. This is true for at least two general reasons: First, most phenomena we wish to study in the social and behavioral sciences are observed in the presence of a host of conditions. Up to a point, the more of these conditions we can treat or manipulate as independent variables in a study, the more we are able to reproduce the real-world conditions and thus explain the operations of these variables. Second, as outlined in our discussion of multiple regression in an earlier chapter, we tend to believe that most of the phenomena we study are multiply determined. For the same reason that we would include multiple potential predictors in a regression study, we would want to include more than one independent variable in an experimental design.

Main Effect and Interactions

A second advantage of univariate and multivariate factorial designs is found by examining the concepts of main effects and interaction effects.

In the univariate situation, main effects reflect the separate treatment effects of one independent variable averaged (or collapsed) over the levels of the other independent variable(s) on a single dependent measure. Similarly, main effects in the multivariate context refer to the separate effects of one independent variable collapsed over the levels of the other independent variable(s) on a set or vector of dependent variable means. Each independent variable is considered to be a single main effect. For example, Factor A might be type of treatment and Factor B could be gender of client. Assessing the main effects of each independent variable (Factor A and Factor B) is analogous to conducting single-factor analyses in the univariate and multivariate contexts.

But factorial designs also provide us with a new ingredient that is not present in the single-factor case. This new component is the interaction effect, which assesses the joint influence of two or more independent variables. In the univariate two-factor case, an interaction depicts how the variables combine to influence the dependent measure. This combinatory effect occurs when one independent variable changes at the different levels of the second independent variable. Similarly, an interaction effect in the multivariate context depicts how two (or more) independent variables combine to influence the composite dependent variate. Thus, a second advantage of factorial designs lies in their ability to show how independent variables combine or interact to influence the dependent measure(s).

Numerical Hypothetical Two-Way Factorial Example

To extend our previous hypothetical example, assume that we are interested in the effects of therapy type (psychoanalytic, cognitive-behavioral, brief) and client gender (male, female) on clinical outcome (GAF) and service satisfaction (CSQ-8) scores.

Table 11a.1 depicts the raw data matrix for a 3 × 2 (read 3 by 2) between-subjects factorial design with Factor A consisting of three levels of therapy type (psychoanalytic, cognitive-behavioral, brief) and Factor B consisting of two levels of gender (male, female). The first part of the table shows the data for males, and the second part of the table shows the data for females. Sample size is small but deemed adequate by meeting the minimum cell size of 20 recommended by Hair et al. (1998). An inspection of the dependent variable means (GAF and CSQ-8) for each of the six treatment combinations suggests a consistent ascending ordering of dependent variable means (for both men and women) for clients receiving psychoanalytic, cognitive-behavioral, and brief psychotherapy services. Pearson r correlations were computed between the two dependent measures for each of the six

Table 11a.1 Client Global Assessment of Functioning (GAF) and Service Satisfaction (CSQ-8), by Therapy Type and Gender (Hypothetical Data for 3 × 2 Factorial MANOVA)

			Male (b_1)					
Psychoanalytic (a_1)			Cognitive-Behavioral (a_2)			Brief (a_3)		
Case ID	GAF	CSQ-8	Case ID	GAF	CSQ-8	Case ID	GAF	CSQ-8
1	33	22.1	21	41	25.6	41	65	30.1
2	35	23.3	22	45	25.8	42	66	29.8
3	41	21.5	23	55	26.9	43	69	27.1
4	38	22.4	24	59	27.1	44	50	26.4
5	45	22.9	25	58	27.0	45	55	27.0
6	46	24.9	26	50	24.0	46	64	30.3
7	37	20.1	27	57	25.0	47	66	30.4
8	37	25.6	28	55	24.9	48	68	29.0
9	40	21.7	29	55	26.7	49	59	28.7
10	49	25.1	30	59	27.1	50	51	27.1
11	41	22.1	31	52	22.7	51	55	26.1
12	45	23.7	32	53	23.1	52	57	28.1
13	45	25.0	33	55	25.0	53	62	30.7
14	40	25.0	34	56	26.1	54	60	30.1
15	36	21.1	35	55	26.2	55	63	29.8
16	35	22.2	36	58	28.1	56	64	28.9
17	40	23.4	37	50	23.4	57	50	26.1
18	45	24.1	38	51	24.5	58	66	28.1
19	39	20.1	39	55	25.5	59	68	29.9
20	35	21.0	40	55	26.6	60	69	30.0
$M =$	40.10	22.87	$M =$	53.70	25.57	$M =$	61.35	28.69
$SD =$	4.48	1.71	$SD =$	4.57	1.48	$SD =$	6.38	1.57
$n = 20$	$r = .537$	$p < .01$	$n = 20$	$r = .445$	$p < .05$	$n = 20$	$r = .691$	$p < .001$

treatment combinations. As can be seen in Table 11a.1, moderate positive correlations (ranging between .368 and .691) were observed between the dependent measures across conditions.

Table 11a.2 depicts normality tests and diagnostics for each dependent variable across the levels of the independent variables. Just over half of the normality tests were found to be statistically significant ($p < .05$), indicating a dependent variable distribution departure from normality for some of the treatment combinations. These normality violations may be due in part to the skewness and kurtosis observed among the GAF scores in the

	Female (b_2)							
Psychoanalytic (a_1)			*Cognitive-Behavioral (a_2)*			*Brief (a_3)*		
Case ID	GAF	CSQ-8	Case ID	GAF	CSQ-8	Case ID	GAF	CSQ-8
61	33	21.1	81	51	25.5	101	66	30.3
62	34	21.7	82	48	24.6	102	64	30.5
63	35	22.6	83	47	26.7	103	65	31.1
64	42	23.0	84	55	28.1	104	51	29.5
65	47	22.1	85	58	25.4	105	55	28.1
66	46	23.7	86	57	26.1	106	58	27.1
67	39	22.4	87	57	27.2	107	60	30.3
68	37	22.4	88	55	27.0	108	61	30.8
69	41	23.1	89	55	28.1	109	62	31.0
70	40	24.4	90	44	25.0	110	65	30.0
71	45	22.0	91	59	26.1	111	66	31.7
72	45	20.0	92	57	27.3	112	55	29.6
73	44	23.3	93	58	28.9	113	55	29.0
74	38	23.1	94	58	28.9	114	50	28.1
75	39	22.8	95	56	26.5	115	52	28.9
76	40	24.5	96	57	26.0	116	66	29.0
77	45	22.1	97	58	25.5	117	69	30.1
78	42	23.6	98	55	25.0	118	68	30.3
79	40	23.5	99	56	26.1	119	65	29.1
80	37	21.7	100	50	27.0	120	62	28.0
M =	40.45	22.66	*M =*	54.55	26.55	*M =*	60.75	29.63
SD =	4.07	1.90	*SD =*	4.24	1.26	*SD =*	5.92	1.20
n = 20	*r* = .676	*p* > .05	*n* = 20	*r* = .368	*p* > .05	*n* = 20	*r* = .527	*p* < .01

cognitive-behavioral conditions. Normally, transformations of these GAF scores would probably be recommended here. However, to expedite our presentation, we will deem these normality tests adequate and proceed with the analysis.

Table 11a.3 depicts a statistically nonsignificant Box's M test ($p < .499$), indicating equality of variance-covariance matrices. Separate Levene's tests for each dependent variable found a marginally statistically significant ($p < .047$) effect for the GAF dependent measure and a statistically non-significant ($p > .05$) test for the service satisfaction dependent measure. These results indicate that relatively equal variances are in place for each dependent variable.

Table 11a.2 Client Global Assessment of Functioning (GAF) and Service Satisfaction (CSQ-8) Normality Tests and Diagnostics, by Therapy Type and Gender

| | Therapy Type | | | | | |
| | Psychoanalytic | | Cognitive-Behavioral | | Brief | |
Normality Test	Statistic	Significance	Statistic	Significance	Statistic	Significance
GAF						
Kolmogorov-Smirnov	.143	.038	.279	.000	.161	.010
Shapiro-Wilk	.958	.143	.856	.000	.906	.003
CSQ-8						
Kolmogorov-Smirnov	.075	.200	.070	.200	.146	.032
Shapiro-Wilk	.978	.619	.980	.703	.941	.036
GAF						
Skewness	.104		−1.32		−.535	
Kurtosis	−.930		1.32		−.998	
CSQ-8						
Skewness	.025		−.215		−.582	
Kurtosis	−.437		.034		−.526	

| | Gender | | | |
| | Male | | Female | |
Normality Test	Statistic	Significance	Statistic	Significance
GAF				
Kolmogorov-Smirnov	.126	.019	.157	.001
Shapiro-Wilk	.956	.032	.958	.036
CSQ-8				
Kolmogorov-Smirnov	.074	.200	.101	.200
Shapiro-Wilk	.970	.149	.958	.040
GAF				
Skewness	−.107		−.190	
Kurtosis	−1.03		−1.03	
CSQ-8				
Skewness	−.038		−.087	
Kurtosis	−.822		−1.16	

Table 11a.3 Tests of Equality of Covariance Matrices and Equality of Error Variances

	Overall		GAF		CSQ-8	
	Statistic	*Significance*	*Statistic*	*Significance*	*Statistic*	*Significance*
Box's *M*	15.026	.499				
Levene's Test			2.33	.047	1.86	.106

    The Bartlett's test of sphericity in Table 11a.4 was statistically significant ($p < .001$), indicating sufficient correlation between the dependent variables to proceed with the analysis. The correlation between the two dependent measures was a high positive one ($r = .861$), which may indicate that these two dependent variables measure a common construct and may profitably be combined into a single measure and examined with a univariate analysis of variance procedure. Again, for present purposes, we judge this high positive correlation between our dependent variables to be acceptable and proceed with the multivariate analysis.

    Table 11a.5 presents the multivariate test results for each independent variable separately (main effects) and their interaction. Because the Box's *M* test was not statistically significant, we report only the Wilks's lambda test results. From Table 11a.5, we can see that both main effects were statistically significant. We note in passing that the main effect of gender was marginally significant ($p < .057$) and accounted for less than 5% of the total variance.

Table 11a.4 Test of Intercorrelation of Dependent Variables

	Statistic	Significance
Bartlett's test of sphericity	177.900	.000
Pearson correlation:		
GAF by CSQ-8	.861	.000

Table 11a.5 Multivariate Test Results

	Multivariate Test	Value	F	Significance	Partial Eta Squared
Therapy type	Wilks's lambda	.164	82.89	.000	.595
Gender	Wilks's lambda	.951	2.94	.057	.049
Therapy Type × Gender	Wilks's lambda	.943	1.68	.155	.029

The statistically significant main effect of therapy type ($p < .000$) accounted for nearly 60% of the total variance. The interaction of Therapy Type × Gender was not statistically significant. These two statistically significant main effects together with the lack of a significant interaction allow us to reject the null hypotheses that the therapy type and gender group mean vectors are equal and, instead, conclude that both therapy type and gender uniquely influence the dependent variate.

Because we observed statistically significant multivariate main effects of therapy type and gender, we can proceed to examine the two separate univariate F tests, with a Bonferroni adjustment to our alpha level, giving us an adjusted alpha level of .025 (.05 divided by the two univariate effects = .025). We note in Table 11a.6 that for the main effect of therapy type, both univariate F statistics were statistically significant ($p < .000$), with each accounting for more than 75% of the total variance. However, after Bonferroni adjustment, the main effect of gender was not statistically significant ($p > .025$) for either

Table 11a.6 Univariate Test Results

	Dependent Measure	
	GAF	CSQ-8
Independent variable (group) means		
Therapy type		
Psychoanalytic	40.28	22.76
Cognitive-behavioral	54.12	26.06
Brief	61.05	29.16
F statistic	177.65	208.13
Significance	.000	.000
Partial eta squared	.757	.785
Independent variable (group) means		
Gender		
Male	51.72	25.71
Female	51.92	26.28
F statistic	.048	4.988
Significance	.828	.027
Partial eta squared	.000	.042
Therapy Type × Gender		
F statistic	.215	2.334
Significance	.807	.102
Partial eta squared	.004	.039

Table 11a.7 Multiple Comparison Post Hoc Tests (Tukey) for GAF and Service Satisfaction, by Therapy Type

Dependent Variable	(I) Therapy Type	(J) Therapy Type	Mean Difference (I-J)
GAF	Brief	Psychoanalytic	20.77*
	Brief	Cognitive-behavioral	6.93*
	Cognitive-behavioral	Psychoanalytic	13.85*
Service satisfaction	Brief	Psychoanalytic	6.40*
	Brief	Cognitive-behavioral	3.10*
	Cognitive-behavioral	Psychoanalytic	3.30*

*$p < .05$.

of the dependent measures, indicating comparable levels of clinical outcome (GAF) and service satisfaction (CSQ-8) among men and women respondents. The univariate interaction analyses can be ignored because their multivariate counterpart was not statistically significant.

Because we observed statistically significant univariate Fs for the main effect of therapy type for both dependent variables, and because therapy type has more than two levels, we can proceed with Tukey HSD (honestly significant difference) post hoc multiple comparison tests to compare each dependent variable's group means. Table 11a.7 summarizes pairwise comparisons between each pair of means for each dependent variable.

Table 11a.7 shows the difference between pairs of means for each group on each of the dependent measures. An asterisk indicates that the difference is significant. For example, the GAF dependent measure comparison with the brief and psychoanalytic groups (see Table 11a.6 for respective means) is computed by subtracting one group mean from the other (e.g., 61.05 − 40.28), which produces a difference score of 20.77. These difference scores are evaluated by means of special multiple comparisons formulas that were briefly reviewed in Chapter 10B. With all mean differences showing as statistically significant, the results suggest that the highest levels of clinical outcome and service satisfaction were achieved by clients receiving brief psychotherapy followed by cognitive-behavioral and then psychoanalytic intervention.

The Time Dimension in Multivariate Data Analysis

Most of the statistical designs covered in this book are cross-sectional in nature. That is, the statistical analysis is employed on a set of observations (cases) that represents a single point in time. Cross-sectional data sets run the gamut of a self-report questionnaire completed by a random sample of college freshmen on their first day of class, school districts reporting averages of standardized test scores, or exit interview data gleaned from interviews of a sample of voters exiting their precinct polling station. Such designs capture behavior, attitudes, opinions, and feelings at one moment in time, much like a photographic snapshot.

The construct of time has historically been studied by means of univariate and multivariate analysis of variance procedures. In the univariate situation, participants or cases are measured more than once on a dependent variable. For example, clients could be given a mental health evaluation at initial intake, at 6 months into their treatment, and again at the end of their first treatment year. These three longitudinal snapshots of client functioning (sometimes referred to as trend analysis) can be used to track treatment progress over time. To evaluate change, we would use a within-subjects design in which the three periodic assessments would constitute the repeated measure. Alternatively, we could incorporate a second dependent variable (e.g., client satisfaction) into this same experimental design scenario and use MANOVA to analyze the effects of these multiple dependent measures over time (e.g., Keppel & Wickens, 2004; Tabachnick & Fidell, 2001a).

A variety of longitudinal data analysis designs are gaining considerable momentum in the multivariate literature (Diggle, Heagerty, Liang, & Zeger, 2002; Hand & Crowder, 1996) that represent more complex and sophisticated approaches to the study of time-related effects. These methods include panel data analysis, cohort analysis, hierarchical linear models (HLM), and survival analysis. Although each technique is certainly unique, they also share some fundamental commonalities, such as focusing on responses or behavior over time and using methods related to multiple regression analysis (see Allison, 1990). We will briefly note each in passing.

Panel Data Analysis

Panel studies (or linear panel analyses) are based on repeatedly measuring the same set of participants over time. For example, a metropolitan newspaper might locate a small group of undecided registered Republican and Democrat voters ($N = 20$) via a telephone interview 1 year prior to a presidential election. These individuals become the panel, and their political attitudes and preferences can be assessed on a monthly basis, right up to the November election. For overviews of this method, see Cronbach and Furby (1970), Finkel (1995), Kessler and Greenberg (1981), and Menard (1991).

Cohort Data Analysis

Cohort analysis compares one or more groups of individuals, usually within a defined age range, at different points in time. Different participants are selected from the same cohort at each test point. Cohorts are assumed to consist of individuals who have experienced similar significant life events and personal contexts; in some sense, they have entered some sort of system at the same time. Here are two examples:

▶ Individuals in a large corporation are selected to start a 6-month management training program. Although they may differ on many characteristics (age, geographic region of origin) they make up a cohort based on training. We could study their success in the training program and follow up every year to determine their effectiveness as managers.

▶ Individuals born between 1946 and 1964 are known as the "baby boomer" generation and make up a cohort based on age. A sample of these persons could be surveyed at 5- or 10-year intervals to examine their attitudes about world political events or views about domestic social policy.

A number of methodological issues affect the proper assessment of cohort data, including participant age effects, cohort status effects, and the time period, all of which influence the variability within the study and must be accounted for. These issues can be addressed in part by means of dummy coding and interaction analysis (Glenn, 2004; Mason & Fineberg, 1985; Mason & Wolfinger, 2001; Rodgers, 1982).

Hierarchical Linear Models (HLM)

Hierarchical linear models were originally developed to study nested data (levels of variables are specific to one level of another variable)—for example, mental health clients nested within specific therapeutic programs, who are in turn nested within mental health agencies. One assumption underlying the analysis of this sort of structure is that clients within a cluster will share certain commonalities because of their shared context. The HLM approach is also referred to as multilevel models, linear mixed models, random coefficient models, or random effects models. The dependent variables in HLM can be either continuous or categorical (see Kenny, Bolger, & Kashy, 2002; Raudenbush & Bryk, 2002, for useful overviews).

HLM has also been extended to the analysis of longitudinal data where the research goal is to examine change and the factors that affect both intra- and inter-individual change (e.g., Hox, 2000; MacCallum, Kim, Malarkey, & Kiecolt-Glaser, 1997; Raudenbush, 2001; Singer & Willett, 2003; Weinfurt, 2000). At least three major approaches to HLM can be identified (see Diggle et al., 2002; Singer & Willett, 2003). One approach is called *marginal analysis* where the investigator builds a model that focuses on the dependent variable average and how this mean changes over time. A second approach is to develop transition models that focus on how the dependent variable is a function of or depends on previous values of the dependent measure and other variables. A third HLM longitudinal approach is to construct a random effects model where the focus becomes how regression coefficients vary among participants. Several recent and readable applications of HLM to longitudinal data can be found in O'Connell and McCoach (2004) and Lane and Zelinski (2003).

Survival Analysis

Survival analysis, also called event history analysis, encompasses a number of methods (e.g., life table analysis, Kaplan-Meier method, Cox regression model) that predict the survival time between two events for one or more groups of participants or cases (see, e.g., Hosmer & Lemeshow, 2002; Lee & Wang, 2003; Singer & Willett, 1991; Wright, 2000). These methods were first developed in the medical, epidemiological, and biological fields to examine the survival times of patients undergoing various types of medical treatment and hence suggested the name of the procedure.

Survival analysis has been successfully extended to other fields, including the social and behavioral sciences as well as business and marketing. For example, Gamst (1985) used this approach to determine the length of time individuals would continue to subscribe to a newspaper under different financial incentive scenarios. But survival analysis can be applied to a host of interesting and very important topics (e.g., how long adolescents will remain in high school before dropping out, how long patients are likely to follow a medication regime before putting their medicine aside). Generally, we are interested in the length of time that cases in a target group remain "active" or "alive" (in either a literal or figurative sense).

The challenge in survival analysis is that the original number of participants can be quite variable between two points in time. Participants may continue to survive, or they may quit, drop out, or become lost to follow-up. These latter situations are called censored events and must be taken into account to produce accurate survival curve estimates. Several descriptive methods (e.g., life tables and Kaplan-Meier survival functions) are available for estimating survival times for a sample or comparing the survival of two or more groups. Regression models (e.g., Cox, 1972) are also available to examine the contribution of continuous (metric) independent variables to survival time.

Recommended Readings

Bird, K. D., & Hadzi-Pavlovic, D. (1983). Simultaneous test procedures and the choice of a test statistic in MANOVA. *Psychological Bulletin, 93,* 167–178.

Box, G. E. P., Hunter, W. P., & Hunter, J. S. (1978). *Statistics for experimenters.* New York: Wiley.

Cole, D. A., Maxwell, S. E., Avery, R., & Salas, E. (1994). How the power of MANOVA can both increase and decrease as a function of the intercorrelations among dependent variables. *Psychological Bulletin, 115,* 465–474.

Gabriel, K. R. (1969). A comparison of some methods of simultaneous inference in Manova. In P. R. Krishnaiah (Ed.), *Multivariate analysis-II* (pp. 67–86). New York: Academic Press.

Hand, D. J., & Taylor, C. C. (1987). *Multivariate analysis of variance and repeated measures.* London: Chapman & Hall.

Harris, R. J. (1993). Multivariate analysis of variance. In L. K. Edwards (Ed.), *Applied analysis of variance in behavioral science* (pp. 255–296). New York: Marcel Dekker.

Huberty, C. J., & Morris, J. D. (1989). Multivariate analysis versus multiple univariate analyses. *Psychological Bulletin, 105,* 302–308.

McDonald, R. A., Seifert, C. F., Lorenzet, S. J., Givens, S., & Jaccard, J. (2002). The effectiveness of methods for analyzing multivariate factorial data. *Organizational Research Methods, 5,* 255–274.

Mudholkar, G. S., & Subbaiah, P. (1980). MANOVA multiple comparisons associated with finite intersection tests. In P. R. Krishnaiah (Ed.), *Multivariate analysis V* (pp. 467–482). Amsterdam: North-Holland.

Spector, P. E. (1977). What to do with significant multivariate effects in multivariate analyses of variance. *Journal of Applied Psychology, 62,* 158–163.

MANOVA

Two-Way Factorial Using SPSS

This chapter is the last in our "trilogy" on MANOVA applications. The focus of the present chapter will be on using SPSS to analyze a factorial design where the investigator has two categorical independent variables and two (or more) quantitative measured and conceptually related dependent variables.

The present numerical example is an extension of our previous examples found in Chapters 9B and 10B that focus on severely mentally ill adult community mental health clients. The dependent variables are objective and subjective quality of life (see Chapter 9B); the independent variables are client ethnicity (which we used in the previous chapter) and client gender. To avoid redundancy, we will abbreviate our data screening presentation for the present example. Assume that pertinent issues relating to missing values, outliers, linearity, normality, and homogeneity of variance-covariance matrices were addressed.

MANOVA Dialog Boxes and Output for the Two-Way Factorial

To begin our analysis, we click **Analyze → General Linear Model → Multivariate.** This opens the **Multivariate** dialog box (not shown). We move our two dependent variables over to the **Dependent Variables** box and our two independent variables to the **Fixed Factor(s)** box.

Clicking the **Post Hoc** pushbutton produces the **Multivariate: Post Hoc Multiple Comparisons for Observed Means** dialog box (not shown). Because our client ethnicity independent variable (**newethnc**) has more than two levels, it becomes a possible candidate for post hoc evaluation, pending a statistically significant multivariate main effect of client ethnicity. We double-clicked the **newethnc** variable in the **Factor(s)** box, which simultaneously moves this variable to the **Post Hoc Tests for** box and activates the 18 multiple comparison tests at the bottom half of the dialog box. We selected the **Tukey HSD** multiple comparison test.

The **Options** pushbutton produces the **Multivariate: Options** dialog box (also not shown). The box on the far-left side of the dialog box is the **Factor(s) and Factor Interactions** box. The effects of each independent variable and the interaction of the two independent variables are displayed here. Double-clicking any of these main or interaction effects moves the variable to the **Display Means for** box and produces estimated marginal means for that effect in the output. When no covariates are used in the analysis (we are not using covariates here), these estimated marginal means are the same as the observed means. We asked for the marginal or main effect means for the **newethnc** variable.

We also selected four checkboxes in the **Display** box of this dialog box. **Descriptive statistics** provides means, standard deviations, and counts for each treatment combination. **Estimates of effect size** produces partial eta squared for each main and interaction effect. The **Residual SSCP matrix** computes the Bartlett's test of sphericity. Last, the **Homogeneity tests** checkbox generates the Levene's test for the homogeneity of variance assumption.

Figure 11b.1 displays the **Between-Subjects Factors** tabled output, which provides counts or sample size for each independent variable broken by treatment or level. We note large and unequal sample sizes among the various treatment conditions.

Figure 11b.1 also displays the **Descriptive Statistics** output. It presents each dependent variable's observed mean, standard deviation, and sample size for each treatment combination. A casual scanning of the various dependent variable means suggests that White American male clients report the highest levels of subjective quality of life ($M = 3.7319$) and objective quality of life ($M = 1.3863$).

Box's Test of Equality of Covariance Matrices, shown in Figure 11b.2, is not statistically significant (Box's $M = 20.220$, $p < .168$), which indicates that the dependent variable covariance matrices are equal across the levels of the independent variables. This observed homogeneity or equality of covariance matrices will allow us to use Wilks's lambda to assess our multivariate effects.

Bartlett's Test of Sphericity, presented also in Figure 11b.2, is statistically significant (approximate chi square = 1527.139, $p < .000$). This

Between-Subjects Factors

		Value Label	N
Client Ethnicity Trichotomy	1	White American	397
	2	Latino American	422
	3	African American	237
Client Gender	1	Male	391
	2	Female	665

Descriptive Statistics

	Client Ethnicity Trichotomy	Client Gender	Mean	Std. Deviation	N
QL-SF Subjective Mean	White American	Male	3.7319	1.23854	164
		Female	3.4190	1.18956	233
		Total	3.5483	1.21829	397
	Latino American	Male	3.6871	1.34460	127
		Female	3.6047	1.34997	295
		Total	3.6295	1.34729	422
	African American	Male	3.6775	1.41260	100
		Female	3.3679	1.37605	137
		Total	3.4985	1.39704	237
	Total	Male	3.7035	1.31620	391
		Female	3.4909	1.30378	665
		Total	3.5696	1.31180	1056
QL-SF Objective Mean	White American	Male	1.3863	.38239	164
		Female	1.3846	.37545	233
		Total	1.3853	.37785	397
	Latino American	Male	1.2933	.37305	127
		Female	1.2918	.35491	295
		Total	1.2922	.36002	422
	African American	Male	1.2384	.34809	100
		Female	1.2915	.34818	137
		Total	1.2691	.34840	237
	Total	Male	1.3183	.37499	391
		Female	1.3242	.36307	665
		Total	1.3220	.36736	1056

Figure 11b.1 Between-Subjects Factors Output Showing Cell Sample Sizes and the Descriptive Statistics for Each Cell

Box's Test of Equality of Covariance Matrices[a]

Box's M	20.220
F	1.341
df1	15
df2	2252449
Sig.	.168

Tests the null hypothesis that the observed covariance matrices of the dependent variables are equal across groups.

a. Design: Intercept+newethnc+sex+newethnc * sex.

Bartlett's Test of Sphericity[a]

Likelihood Ratio	.000
Approx. Chi Square	1527.139
df	2
Sig.	.000

Tests the null hypothesis that the residual covariance matrix is proportional to an identity matrix.

a. Design: Intercept+newethnc+sex+newethnc * sex.

Figure 11b.2　Output Showing Box's Test of Equality of Covariance Matrices and Bartlett's Test of Sphericity

indicates sufficient correlation between the dependent variables to proceed with the analysis.

The **Multivariate Tests** output table appears in Figure 11b.3. We will focus on the bottom three fourths of the table, which includes the **newethnc, sex**, and **newethnc * sex**. These correspond to the multivariate main effects and interaction results (see Chapter 9B for a discussion of the **Intercept** portion of this table).

Because the Box's M test was not statistically significant, indicating equality of covariance matrices, we are free to use any of the multivariate tests to evaluate our main effects and interaction. Wilks's lambda is the most commonly used multivariate test statistic and the one we will use. Typically, if statistical significance is or is not found with one of the four multivariate tests, the other three tests will also reflect a similar result.

We begin by examining the multivariate main effect of client ethnicity (**newethnc**). The Wilks's lambda value = .978, which is subsequently translated into a F value of 5.995 and evaluated at hypothesis (between groups) and error (within groups) degrees of freedom of 4 and 2098. This F value is

Multivariate Tests[c]

Effect		Value	F	Hypothesis df	Error df	Sig.	Partial Eta Squared
Intercept	Pillai's trace	.931	7106.800[a]	2.000	1049.000	.000	.931
	Wilks's lambda	.069	7106.800[a]	2.000	1049.000	.000	.931
	Hotelling's trace	13.550	7106.800[a]	2.000	1049.000	.000	.931
	Roy's largest root	13.550	7106.800[a]	2.000	1049.000	.000	.931
Newethnc	Pillai's trace	.022	5.973	4.000	2100.000	.000	.011
	Wilks's lambda	.978	5.995[a]	4.000	2098.000	.000	.011
	Hotelling's trace	.023	6.016	4.000	2096.000	.000	.011
	Roy's largest root	.022	11.410[b]	2.000	1050.000	.000	.021
Sex	Pillai's trace	.010	5.325[a]	2.000	1049.000	.005	.010
	Wilks's lambda	.990	5.325[a]	2.000	1049.000	.005	.010
	Hotelling's trace	.010	5.325[a]	2.000	1049.000	.005	.010
	Roy's largest root	.010	5.325[a]	2.000	1049.000	.005	.010
Newethnc * Sex	Pillai's trace	.003	.891	4.000	2100.000	.469	.002
	Wilks's lambda	.997	.890[a]	4.000	2098.000	.469	.002
	Hotelling's trace	.003	.890	4.000	2096.000	.469	.002
	Roy's largest root	.003	1.511[b]	2.000	1050.000	.221	.003

a. Exact statistic.
b. The statistic is an upper bound on F that yields a lower bound on the significance level.
c. Design: Intercept+newethnc+sex+newethnc * sex.

> The multivariate main effects are significant, but the interaction is not.

Figure 11b.3 Multivariate Tests of Statistical Significance

statistically significant ($p < .000$), indicating differences between the three client ethnic groups on the dependent variate. As indicated in the last column of the output, the partial eta-squared value tells us that this main effect accounts for only about 1% of the total variance.

Next, we look at the multivariate main effect of client gender. The Wilks's lambda value of .990 is translated into an F value of 5.325 and evaluated at 2 and 1049 (between- and within-groups degrees of freedom, respectively). This F is also statistically significant ($p < .005$) and indicates gender differences on the dependent variate. Again, this multivariate main effect is accounting for only 1% of the variance.

Last, the multivariate interaction effect produced a Wilks's lambda value of .997, which is translated into an F value of .890 and evaluated with degrees of freedom of 4 and 2098. This F is not statistically significant

($p < .469$), indicating that the multivariate interaction effect of Client Ethnicity × Gender does not account for a significant proportion of the variance.

Because both multivariate main effects were found to be statistically significant, we can proceed with a separate assessment of each dependent variable for each main effect. This process is begun with an inspection of

Levene's Test of Equality of Error Variances[a]

	F	df1	df2	Sig.
QL-SF Subjective Mean	1.343	5	1050	.244
QL-SF Objective Mean	1.755	5	1050	.119

Tests the null hypothesis that the error variance of the dependent variable is equal across groups.

a. Design: Intercept+newethnc+sex+newethnc * sex.

Tests of Between-Subjects Effects

Source	Dependent Variable	Type III Sum of Squares	df	Mean Square	F	Sig.	Partial Eta Squared
Corrected Model	QL-SF Subjective Mean	18.464[a]	5	3.693	2.158	.057	.010
	QL-SF Objective Mean	2.791[b]	5	.558	4.199	.001	.020
Intercept	QL-SF Subjective Mean	11853.977	1	11853.977	6926.403	.000	.868
	QL-SF Objective Mean	1596.460	1	1596.460	12008.86	.000	.920
Newethnc	QL-SF Subjective Mean	2.238	2	1.119	.654	.520	.001
	QL-SF Objective Mean	2.610	2	1.305	9.817	.000	.018
Sex	QL-SF Subjective Mean	12.760	1	12.760	7.456	.006	.007
	QL-SF Objective Mean	.064	1	.064	.480	.488	.000
Newethnc* Sex	QL-SF Subjective Mean	2.960	2	1.480	.865	.421	.002
	QL-SF Objective Mean	.132	2	.064	.481	.488	.001
Error	QL-SF Subjective Mean	1796.990	1050	1.711			
	QL-SF Objective Mean	139.587	1050	.133			
Total	QL-SF Subjective Mean	1796.990	1056				
	QL-SF Objective Mean	1987.996	1056				
Corrected Total	QL-SF Subjective Mean	1815.454	1055				
	QL-SF Objective Mean	142.378	1055				

a. R Squared = .010 (Adjusted R Squared = .005).
b. R Squared = .020 (Adjusted R Squared = .015).

> Only object showed a significant univariate effect for newethnc.

> Only subject showed a significant univariate effect for sex.

Figure 11b.4 Levene's Test of Equality of Error Variances and Univariate Tests of Significance

the **Levene's Test of Equality of Error Variances** output in Figure 11b.4. For both dependent measures, the test is not statistically significant ($p > .05$), indicating homogeneity or equality of variances among the groups on each dependent measure. We can now proceed with univariate ANOVAs for both main effects on each dependent variable with a Bonferroni adjusted alpha level of $.05/2 = .025$.

These univariate F tests can be found in the **Tests of Between-Subjects Effects** tabled output also in Figure 11b.4. Of particular interest is the upper-middle portion of the table labeled **newethnc** and **sex** that depict separate univariate ANOVAs for each dependent variable on each main effect (see Chapter 9B for a discussion of the other components of this table).

We note a "split decision" for both main effects. For the client ethnicity (**newethnc**) main effect, we find that subjective quality of life was statistically not significant, $F(2, 1050) = .654$, $p < .520$, whereas objective quality of life was statistically significant, $F(2, 1050) = 9.817$, $p < .000$, partial eta squared = .018. Hence, differences between the three ethnic groups on objective quality of life produced the statistically significant multivariate main effect of client ethnicity.

Conversely, for the client gender main effect we find that the subjective quality-of-life dependent measure was statistically significant, $F(1, 1050) = 12.760$, $p < .006$, partial eta squared = .007. With only two levels of this variable, we know that males and females differ significantly on subject. An inspection of the **Descriptive Statistics** means (Figure 11b.1) collapsed across client ethnicity shows that male clients had significantly higher subjective quality of life ($M = 3.70$) than did the female clients ($M = 3.46$). This difference produced the statistically significant multivariate effect of gender.

Because the main effect of client ethnicity was statistically significant for the objective quality-of-life dependent measure, we can examine exactly where the significant difference lies with a post hoc examination of the three treatment means. These **Estimated Marginal Means** are displayed next in Figure 11b.5, where we note that White American clients garnered the highest objective quality-of-life mean of 1.385.

Tukey HSD comparisons for the objective quality-of-life dependent measure (ignore the subjective quality-of-life results because this dependent variable was not associated with a significant effect here) can also be seen in Figure 11b.5. From this table, we can observe that White American clients evaluated their objective quality of life significantly higher than did Latino American (the mean difference was .0930) and African American clients (the mean difference was .0232). These differences produced the multivariate main effect of client ethnicity.

Client Ethnicity Trichotomy

Dependent Variable	Client Ethnicity Trichotomy	Mean	Std. Error	95% Confidence Interval	
				Lower Bound	Upper Bound
QL-SF Subjective Mean	White American	3.575	.067	3.445	3.706
	Latino American	3.646	.069	3.510	3.782
	African American	3.523	.086	3.354	3.691
QL-SF Objective Mean	White American	1.385	.019	1.349	1.422
	Latino American	1.293	.019	1.255	1.331
	African American	1.265	.024	1.218	1.312

Multiple Comparisons

Tukey HSD

Dependent Variable	(I) Client Ethnicity Trichotomy	(J) Client Ethnicity Trichotomy	Mean Difference (I-J)	Std. Error	Sig.	95% Confidence Interval	
						Lower Bound	Upper Bound
QL-SF Subjective Mean	White American	Latino American	−.0812	.09147	.648	−.2959	.1335
		African American	.0498	.10739	.888	−.2023	.3018
	Latino American	White American	.0812	.09147	.648	−.1335	.2959
		African American	.1310	.10619	.434	−.1182	.3802
	African American	White American	−.0498	.10739	.888	−.3018	.2023
		Latino American	−.1310	.10619	.434	−.3802	.1182
QL-SF Objective Mean	White American	Latino American	.0930	.02549	.001	.0332	.1529
		African American	.1162	.02993	.000	.0460	.1865
	Latino American	White American	−.0930	.02549	.001	−.1529	−.0332
		African American	.0232	.02960	.714	−.0463	.0926
	African American	White American	−.1162	.02993	.000	−.1865	−.0460
		Latino American	−.0232	.02960	.714	−.0926	.0463

Based on observed means.
*The mean difference is significant at the .05 level.

Figure 11b.5 The Estimated Marginal Means Output for the Three Ethnicity Groups for Each Dependent Variable and Post Hoc Multiple Comparison Tests Among the Ethnicity Groups

Results

A two-way between-subjects multivariate analysis of variance (MANOVA) was conducted on two dependent variables: subjective quality of life and objective quality of life. The independent variables were client ethnicity (White American, Latino American, African American) and client gender (male, female).

No extreme scores, outliers, or statistical assumption violations were noted in the present data. A statistically nonsignificant Box's M test ($p > .05$) indicated equality of variance-covariance matrices of the dependent variables across levels of the independent variables.

Using Wilks's lambda (see Table 11b.1), the dependent variate was significantly affected by the main effects of client ethnicity, Wilks's lambda = .978, $F(4, 2098) = 5.97$, $p < .000$, partial $\eta^2 = .011$, and client gender, Wilks's lambda = .990, $F(2, 1049) = 5.33$, $p < .005$, partial $\eta^2 = .010$. An inspection of gender group means showed that male clients had significantly higher subjective quality of life ($M = 3.70$) than did the female clients ($M = 3.46$). This difference produced the statistically significant multivariate effect of gender. The multivariate interaction effect of Ethnicity × Gender was not statistically significant, $F < 1.0$.

Univariate ANOVAs were conducted on each dependent measure separately to determine the locus of the statistically significant multivariate main effect of client ethnicity. From Table 11b.1 we can see that client ethnicity significantly affected objective quality of life, $F(2, 1050) = 9.82$, $p < .000$, partial $\eta^2 = .018$. Tukey HSD post hoc tests (see Table 11b.2) suggested that White American clients ($M = 1.39$, $SE = .02$) had significantly higher objective quality of life than did their Latino American ($M = 1.29$, $SE = .02$) and African American ($M = 1.27$, $SE = .02$) counterparts. No statistically significant client ethnicity effects were observed for subjective quality of life, $F < 1.0$. Caution should be exercised in interpreting these results because of the small amount of variance accounted for with the present independent variables.

Table 11b.1 Multivariate and Univariate Analyses of Variance for Quality-of-Life Measure

	Multivariate	Univariate	
Source	F^a	Subjective Quality of Life[b]	Objective Quality of Life[b]
Client ethnicity	5.995*	.654	9.817*
Client gender	5.325*	7.456*	.048
Ethnicity × gender	.890	.865	.497
MSE		1.711	.133

Note: Multivariate f-ratios were generated from Wilks's lambda.

a. Multivariate df = 4, 2098 (client ethnicity), 2, 1049 (client gender).

b. Univariate df = 2, 1050 (client ethnicity), 1, 1050 (client gender).

*$p < .01$.

Table 11b.2 Mean Scores and Standard Deviations for Measures of Subjective and Objective Quality of Life as a Function of Client Ethnicity

	Subjective Quality of Life		Objective Quality of Life	
Group	M	SE	M	SE
White American	3.575	.067	1.385[a]	.019
Latino American	3.646	.069	1.293[b]	.019
African American	3.523	.086	1.265[b]	.024

Note: Means with different superscripted letters were significantly different at the .05 level by means of a Tukey HSD post hoc test.

11B Exercises

Factorial (2 × 3) MANOVA

This study investigates the symptomatic improvement (measured by indexes of both worry and general emotion) of three different anxiety treatments for females and males. We are therefore interested not only in gender differences and treatment differences but also in whether or not gender moderates the effectiveness of the treatments (i.e., whether gender significantly interacts with treatment). To address these issues we use a factorial MANOVA design.

Variables in study:

▶ Treatment: 1 = medication; 2 = psychotherapy; 3 = placebo
▶ Sex: 1 = male; 0 = female
▶ Worry scale
▶ Emotion scale

Using the SPSS data file for Chapter 11B (located on the Web-based study site—http://www.sagepub.com/amrStudy), answer the following questions:

1. Is there a sufficient correlation between the dependent variables to justify the use of MANOVA?

2. Was the assumption of equality of covariance matrices violated? Explain.

3. Is there a statistically significant multivariate interaction effect? Identify the dependent variable(s) of this interaction effect.

4. What would be the proper follow-up tests for a statistically significant interaction effect?

5. Identify the proper post hoc analyses for any statistically significant univariate effects. Explain your answer.

6. Is there a statistically significant multivariate gender effect on the dependent variate?

7. Why would a researcher conduct a MANOVA instead of several ANOVAs?

8. Write a results section for this research.

Principal Components and Factor Analysis

How Factor Analysis Is Used in Psychological Research

The term *data crunching* generally refers to a process in which a considerable quantity of data is reduced down to a more manageable or consolidated whole. Principal components analysis and factor analysis are the quintessential data-crunching procedures. Their general purpose is to identify a relatively small number of themes, dimensions, components, or factors underlying a relatively large set of variables. The way they do this is by distinguishing sets of variables that have more in common with each other than with the other variables in the analysis. What the subsets of variables have in common are the underlying components or factors.

Principal components analysis and factor analysis are very closely related data reduction techniques differing at both the statistical and the conceptual levels. Because many researchers use the term *factor analysis* in a generic way whether they are referring to principal components analysis or to one of the variations of factor analysis (Gorsuch, 1983), we will adopt this generic language in the beginning of this chapter just for introductory purposes, but we will address the differences between component and factor analysis both later on in this chapter as well as in Chapter 13A because it is important to distinguish between these techniques.

One of the most common applications of this data-crunching procedure is in test development, and the examples we present here are drawn from this domain. Using factor analysis in this context, researchers analyze the responses of participants to a relatively large number of test items. Their

▶ 465

goals are to choose the items that will appear on the final version of the survey and to determine if the construct assessed by the inventory can best be measured by reasonable and viable subscales. The factors will indicate which items should be assigned to which subscale.

Another potential application of factor analysis might be to help researchers organize or conceptualize a set of measures that they have obtained in the context of a research program. For example, researchers may have administered a large battery of cognitive tests to a sample of participants to determine which ones might be assessing a similar mental process. Here, each factor will represent a set of measures that are relatively strongly related to each other. Further analyses can then be conducted based on the factors rather than on the individual measures themselves; for example, we can examine group differences in a MANOVA using the factors as dependent variables, we can predict group membership through logistic regression or discriminant analysis using the factors as predictors, or we can predict the value of a quantitative variable in multiple regression with the factors as the independent variables.

In the prior sections of this book, we have talked about independent variable and dependent variable variates (weighted linear combinations of variables). Factor analysis still involves the construction of variates, but we do not ordinarily need to distinguish between independent variables and dependent variables in this context. The key requirement is that we have a set of quantitatively measured variables whose underlying structure we wish to explore. Factors resulting from the analysis are the variates, the weighted combinations of variables. The statistical procedure is designed, in part, to produce the weights of those variables in the linear combination.

Origins of Factor Analysis

A very readable and informative history of the development of factor analysis is provided in the beginning of Harry Harmon's (1960, 1967) classic text. Harmon tells us that the origins of this statistical technique can be traced to Charles Spearman (1904), who is considered to be the father of factor analysis, although Anastasi (Anastasi & Urbana, 1997) suggests that an earlier paper by Karl Pearson (1901) might have established a beginning on which Spearman could build. In any case, Spearman proposed a two-factor theory of intelligence by identifying a general intelligence factor (which came to be symbolized as *g*) underlying all cognitive abilities as well as factors specific to particular abilities (e.g., memory for number sequences, ability to perceive spatial relations).

Harmon (1960) goes on to say that

> it had become quite apparent that Spearman's Two-Factor Theory was not always adequate to describe a battery of psychological tests. So group factors found their way into factor analysis; although the experimenters, at first, were very reluctant to admit such deviation from the base theory and restricted the group factors to as small a number as possible. What actually happened was that the *theory* of a general and specific factors in Spearman's original form was superseded by theories of many group factors, but the early *method* [of Spearman] continued to be employed to determine these many factors. Then it naturally followed that some workers explored the possibility of extracting several factors directly from a matrix of correlations among tests, and thus arose the concept of multiple-factor analysis in the work of Garnett [1919]. (pp. 3–4)

Garnett (1919) had given us the freedom to extract more than two factors directly from the correlation matrix, and Harmon (1960) talks about a surge of interest in these kinds of techniques in the mid-1920s and 1930s leading to the continued advancement of factor analysis. As we will see later in this chapter, another extremely productive flurry of activity in the late 1940s and early 1950s resulted in the development of factor rotation.

Sample Size Issues

Factor analysis is one of the large-sample statistical procedures that we discuss in this book. Guidelines for judging the adequacy of the sample size for such an analysis are available from several sources (e.g., Bryant & Yarnold, 1995; Comrey & Lee, 1992; Gorsuch, 1983; Hutcheson & Sofroniou, 1999). Comrey and Lee (1992), for example, have provided the following very general evaluations of the adequacy of various sample sizes for factor analysis:

50	very poor
100	poor
200	fair
300	good
500	very good
1,000	excellent

It is useful to think about the sample size for your analysis not only in general but also in terms of the ratio of participants to variables in the analysis (e.g., number of survey items). Our general recommendation is this: *Do not drop below an N of 200. Start with a target ratio of 10 participants for every variable. With a larger number of variables, you can back off in this sample-size-to-number-of-variables ratio.*

Here are some examples that may help to illustrate our recommendations. If you are analyzing a 10-item inventory, plan to collect data on about 200 participants. If you are analyzing a 25-item inventory, run about 250 participants. If you are analyzing a 90-item inventory, run about 400 participants. If you are analyzing a 500-item inventory, you can probably run between 700 and 1,000 participants and expect to find a stable solution.

A Simplified Example: Correlations Near 1 and 0

Factor analysis attempts to summarize and synthesize the relationships between the variables contained in the analysis. It starts at the same place that many of the other multivariate procedures begin—with the correlation matrix showing the Pearson rs between pairs of variables. Bivariate correlations assess the degree to which the variables are associated or related. A correlation matrix contains these pairwise correlations for all the variables. To make the relationships of the variables that much easier to see, in the following discussion, we will talk about correlations that are either extremely high or extremely low.

A Three-Variable Example

As a prelude to our discussion of factor analysis, consider the very small correlation matrix of the three hypothetical survey items labeled as A, B, and C shown in Table 12a.1. These are correlations of the responses to particular questions on a hypothetical survey or inventory. That is, for the A-B correlation, respondents' answers to Item A are evaluated with respect to their responses to Item B; for the A-C correlation, respondents' answers to Item

Table 12a.1 Correlation Matrix for Variables A Through C

	B	C
Variable A	.87	.12
Variable B		.07

A are evaluated with respect to their responses to Item C; and for the B-C correlation, respondents' answers to Item B are evaluated with respect to their responses to Item C. With only three variables in the matrix it is relatively easy to see, without any elaborate statistical procedure such as factor analysis, that Items A and B are very strongly correlated but that neither is related much to Item C.

The obtained Pearson r value of .87 assesses the association between A and B. From this value, we know that responses to Item B are very predictable from a knowledge of the responses to Item A. For Pearson r values of .12 and .07 to be found between C and A and C and B, respectively, we know that responses to Item C are not at all predictable from the responses participants gave to either Item A or Item B.

Translated into the language of the test developer, these correlations suggest to us that the content addressed in Item A is presumably related to the content addressed in Item B because the two questions tend to evoke corresponding (i.e., correlated, covarying) responses; stronger endorsement of A matches up with stronger endorsement of B, and weaker endorsement of A matches up with weaker endorsement of B. By the same reasoning, these correlations also tell us that the content of Item C is presumably not related to that of Items A and B because the responses of the questionnaire respondents to C are, by and large, independent of their responses to A and B. We can thus go on to say that Variables A and B have quite a bit in common with each other (i.e., they exhibit quite a bit of shared variance) but do not have very much in common with Variable C.

A Four-Variable Example

Now consider a slightly larger set of variables in an expansion of the preceding example, which we will use to broach the topic of factor analysis. In this somewhat larger study, we have added Item D to the original three survey questions. The correlation matrix that includes this newly added variable is displayed in Table 12a.2. Here, we see that D is pretty strongly related to C but is not related to A and B. At this juncture, we can then draw the

Table 12a.2 Correlation Matrix for Variables A Through D

	B	C	D
Variable A	.87	.12	.11
Variable B		.07	.17
Variable C			.86

inference that A and B have much in common, that C and D have much in common, and that A and B have little in common with C and D.

Another way to verbalize what we can infer from the relationships between the survey questions is to say that the set of four variables shown in Table 12a.2 really represents two sets of two variables each. Because factors distinguish sets of variables that have more in common with each other than with the other variables in the analysis, we may then also say that the four variables represent two underlying factors. From the correlations of these variables, Items A and B appear to be the primary indicators of one factor, and Items C and D appear to be the primary indicators of the other factor. In essence, what we have just done from our examination of the correlation matrix is to perform a conceptually based factor analysis.

These factors that we have identified are not themselves directly measured variables. Instead, they are latent variables (*variates* or *weighted linear composites* as we have called them in the prior chapters). Each factor is composed of the four variables in the analysis, but the variables have different weights in the two factors. In one variate or factor, A and B should be weighted quite highly, whereas C and D should have negligible weights. We therefore say that A and B are strong indicators of that factor (and that C and D are weak indicators of that factor). The situation is reversed in the other variate. There, C and D should be weighted quite highly, whereas A and B should have negligible weights. In this case, C and D would be the strong indicators of that factor (and A and B would be weak indicators).

As we have seen in other multivariate designs (e.g., regression analysis, discriminant analysis), it is also useful to examine the relationship (correlation) between each of the variables contained in the linear composite and the variate as a whole. You probably recall that such correlations are called *structure coefficients.* The weights assigned to the variables in the linear composite and the structure coefficients both provide us with a perspective for interpreting the variate or factor.

The weights of the variables as well as the structure coefficients associated with the variables are ordinarily shown in a table called a *factor matrix.* Such tables are a standard feature in the computer output of a factor analysis procedure. We show such a factor matrix in Table 12a.3 for Variables A through D. In this table, the variables in the analysis occupy the rows and the factors occupy the columns. These factors were obtained from the results of the rotation phase of the analysis (we will talk about rotation in detail later); we therefore refer to this factor matrix as a *rotated factor matrix.*

Because an orthogonal strategy was used for the rotation (we will explain this in our discussion of rotation), the numerical entries in the table represent at the same time the weights of the variables in the linear composite as

Table 12a.3 Two-Factor Rotated Matrix for Variables A Through D

	Factor 1	Factor 2
B	.96563	.06356
A	.96439	.05828
C	.03566	.96422
D	.08635	.96065

well as the structure coefficients. Either way of viewing these values is acceptable in the process of interpreting the results of the factor analysis. For ease of presentation, we have organized the results in Table 12a.3 in a fashion that groups or sorts the correlations (the weights) by factor and orders them within each factor. All statistical programs such as SPSS are capable of generating this kind of output format.

The rotated factor matrix is one of the main ingredients composing a statistical solution to the factor analysis procedure. A convenient way to examine the rotated factor matrix is to first focus on the rows of the table to understand how the variables are behaving. Once we have digested this information, we can then concentrate on the columns in an effort to interpret the factors.

Using this strategy, we first examine the rows of Table 12a.3. Remember that we can view the table entries as structure coefficients. From this perspective, the top two rows of this rotated factor matrix show the correlations of Variables A and B with each of the two factors. Variable B is (slightly) more strongly correlated with Factor 1 than is Variable A and so is listed first in the top grouping. Reading across these first two rows reveals a consistent story: A and B are both strongly correlated with Factor 1 and are not correlated with Factor 2. The last two rows of Table 12a.3 show the correlations of C and D with each of the two factors. Reading across these rows, we can see that Variables C and D are not correlated with Factor 1 but are strongly correlated with Factor 2.

We can now focus on the columns (the factors) of this rotated factor matrix. In this matrix, each factor is composed of a weighted combination of the four variables, and we can view the numbers in the table as representing those weights. The key to dealing with the information contained in the rotated factor matrix is to notice the difference in the pattern of the weights in the two factors. Looking first at Factor 1, we find that it is strongly exemplified by Variables A and B and weakly represented by C and D. That is, A and B have been weighted quite strongly, and C and D have been weighted quite weakly in the establishment of Factor 1. An analogous finding is obtained for Factor 2 in which C and D have received the very substantial weights, whereas the weights assigned to A and B are negligible.

Table 12a.4 Correlation Matrix for Variables A Through F

	B	C	D	E	F
Variable A	.87	.12	.11	.92	.08
Variable B		.07	.17	.89	.13
Variable C			.86	.10	.88
Variable D				.14	.91
Variable E					.06

The process of examining the columns or factors of the rotated factor matrix is the way that the factors are "interpreted" by researchers—knowing the content of Items A and B in effect unveils the essence of Factor 1 because these variables are the primary indicators of this factor, and knowing the content of Items C and D discloses the essence of Factor 2 because they are the primary indicators of that factor.

A Six-Variable Example

Let's expand the example further by adding two additional variables, E and F, to the correlation matrix. This is shown in Table 12a.4. There are many more relationships to deal with now given the inclusion of these two additional variables. But because we are building on what we presented in the previous table and because we are still working with correlations that are relatively near 1 and 0, it is still possible to discern the interrelationships between the six variables contained in Table 12a.4. Because we have constructed this example with unambiguous interpretation in mind, we have made E strongly related to A and B, whereas we have made F strongly related to C and D. Given this pattern, it is not surprising that we have built this example such that E and F have no substantial relationship.

Although there is more information in Table 12a.4 than in the prior correlation matrices, we can still identify two factors based on the correlations between the pairs of variables; that is, we can still identify two relatively distinct sets of survey items. One set of variables (one factor) is composed of Inventory Questions A, B, and E, and the other set of questions is composed of C, D, and F. Analogous to what we stated above, we can say here that A, B, and E have a great deal in common and that C, D, and F, likewise, have a great deal in common. That is, it appears that the variables within each set share a great deal of variance and that there is not much shared variance (not much of a relationship) between the two sets.

Just as in the prior example, what we have essentially done here for this more complex correlation matrix is to again perform a conceptually based

Table 12a.5 Two-Factor Rotated Matrix for Variables A Through F

	Factor 1	*Factor 2*
E	.97136	.04630
A	.96344	.05026
B	.95153	.07340
F	.03577	.96865
D	.09035	.95795
C	.04405	.94933

factor analysis of the Variables A, B, C, D, E, and F. We have determined that there are two factors underlying this set of variables. One of the factors was represented by A, B, and E, and the other factor was represented by C, D, and F. Each set of variables shares a great deal of variance. The factor is, at a conceptual level, that shared variance, and the factor would ordinarily be labeled as whatever it is that the items in the set have in common.

Our conceptually based factor analysis coincides very well with the results of the statistical analysis that we performed on these correlations. We show in Table 12a.5 the rotated factor matrix from that analysis. In looking at the rows of this matrix, we can see a very general pattern—variables are pretty strongly correlated with one of the factors while showing no substantial correlation with the other factor. Note that even though the pattern is quite similar, the values of these correlations are different from those shown in the prior rotated factor matrix for Variables A through D. This is to be expected because the two variates (factors) represented in Table 12a.5 are linear composites of six rather than four variables and therefore depict entities that are at least partially different from those in Table 12a.3.

Examining the columns (the factors) in Table 12a.5 reaffirms and extends the story that emerged in the previous example. Factor 1 here is best indicated by Survey Questions A, B, and E (with C, D, and F playing little role in that composite variate). In contrast, Factor 2 is best signified by Questions C, D, and F (with A, B, and E playing little role in that composite variate).

Introducing a Little Fuzziness Into the Example: Modest Relationship Strengths

We will now expand our example one final time to illustrate another point. We have added Items G and H to our set of variables, and we show the entire correlation matrix in Table 12a.6. We acknowledge that the table is beginning to get very cluttered, but stay with us for just a little longer.

Table 12a.6   Correlation Matrix for Variables A Through H

	B	C	D	E	F	G	H
Variable A	.87	.12	.11	.92	.08	.61	.08
Variable B		.07	.17	.89	.13	.57	.15
Variable C			.86	.10	.88	.14	.56
Variable D				.14	.91	.09	.60
Variable E					.06	.55	.07
Variable F						.08	.58
Variable G							.07

We have written in correlations for G that tie it to A, B, and E, but not to the other variables. Similarly, we have written in correlations for H that tie it to C, D, and F, but not to the other variables. Thus, we still have two factors represented by the variables in this matrix—A, B, E, and G on the one hand and C, D, F, and H on the other hand. And we can still say that the variables within each factor have a great deal more in common with each other than they have with those in the other factor.

But here we have much more diversity in the strengths of the relationships of the variables within each factor. Consider the factor represented by A, B, E, and G. If you look at the correlations for these variables, you will see that the first three of them are tied together quite strongly. Given that the correlation for A-B is .87, for A-E is .92, and for B-E is .89, we understand that there is a large amount of shared variance among this trio. Although G is related to these three, the ties are not nearly that strong. The correlations for G-A, G-B, and G-E are .61, .57, and .55, respectively. A similar situation exists for the second factor.

When we think in terms of factors, we would say that one factor is represented by variables A, B, E, and G and another factor is indexed by variables C, D, F, and H. But given the ties that bind them together, we hope you can see that G is less related to its factor than are A, B, and E, and H is less related to its factor than are C, D, and F.

This conceptual treatment is reinforced by the statistical outcome of the analysis. We present the rotated factor matrix for this two-factor solution in Table 12a.7. Once again, the results are unambiguous in that variables correlate substantially with one factor and do not correlate with the other factor. Variables G and H, because they are less related to the other variables in their respective factors as we have described above, show a relatively lower (but still substantial) correlation with their respective variate.

Examining the columns of the rotated factor matrix in Table 12a.7, we see that the factors are clearly differentiated. Factor 1 is best represented by

Table 12a.7 Two-Factor Rotated Matrix for Variables A Through H

	Factor 1	Factor 2
A	.95558	.04616
E	.94828	.04119
B	.93463	.08318
G	.73099	.06213
F	.03521	.95125
D	.08330	.94641
C	.05697	.92905
H	.05845	.73754

A, E, B, and G and Factor 2 is best represented by F, D, C, and H. Yet in these two sets of variables, G and H are less potent indicators of their respective variate than the other three variables in the set. When we discuss how you would interpret a factor, we will have you focus on the content of those variables that are more strongly related to the factor. Here, for example, we would focus on A, E, and B to interpret Factor 1 and on F, D, and C to interpret Factor 2.

In the research you perform, you can expect that the fuzziness we introduced into this last correlation matrix will be closer to what you will obtain than the exaggerated examples we used earlier. That is, you may find that although a number of variables are correlated with a factor to a certain extent, not all will be strongly correlated with it. Some variables will have a stronger relationship with (overlap more with, be better indicators of) the factor than other variables. Generally, we expect the variables to have different weights when we obtain the linear function that defines the factor. In the process of choosing a name for (interpreting) a factor, something that the researcher almost always has to (and wants to) do, we should allow ourselves to be more influenced by variables that are more strongly related to (correlated with) the factor than those that are more weakly related to it.

Acquiring Perspective on Factor Analysis

This final example with Variables A through H is really an oversimplified, almost-best-case illustration of the factor analysis process. We started with a set of eight variables—it would be unlikely that we would have such a small number of items if we were actually developing a test, survey, or inventory—and reduced them down to two pretty clear factors. Because this was a contrived example, it worked out to be a wonderfully clean solution. That is, we lost very little information in the process of this data crunching. Even given the simplicity of our example, however, looking at some of the issues and implications of what went on will provide a good foundation for appreciating what factor analysis is all about.

The Importance of Individual Variables

The importance of the individual variables in a factor analysis presents us with one of the great ironies of behavioral research. It can be best illustrated in the context of test development. As you have no doubt already learned, developing good-quality items that assess the proper content of a construct is an absolute requirement of proper test development. The presence of poorly written items and items that are not germane to the topic can adversely affect the assessment process by substantially lowering the validity and reliability of the instrument.

Faced with a well-understood and well-documented content domain, the number of different items that can be generated is, if not infinite, then very, very large. Yet of the zillions of items that can potentially be written to measure a construct, only four or five dozen are likely to ever be produced, and only about two or three dozen may ever be included on the preliminary versions of the inventory. These few dozen items will be used to represent a content domain that could be composed of thousands and thousands of potential items.

We do not write thousands of items for a very good reason. There would be too much redundancy in the set to justify the effort—it is just too much work for no real gain. But it is naive to believe that the two or three dozen items we did write are completely independent of each other. By virtue of the fact that the items are all related to the same global construct, we would expect that they bear some relation to each other. Now, common sense tells us that for many of the constructs we wish to assess, there are going to be sets of items that are more related to each other than to other items in the inventory, something that we have already illustrated and that occurs time and time again.

For the sake of this illustration, assume that A through H completely represent the content domain that the inventory is designed to measure (pretend that it is a small domain). But these are eight of thousands of potential items that could have been written. Based on the content domain, Item A could just as easily have been written as AA, B as BB, and so on, where AA is a variation of A, BB is a variation of B, and so forth.

Assume that the relationships of these items are represented in Table 12a.6. If that is true, and if we had written AA instead of A, BB instead of B, and so on through HH instead of H, then it would be reasonable to expect that AA, BB, EE, and GG would form one factor and that CC, DD, FF, and HH would form a second factor.

We could carry out this example further using AAA through HHH, AAAA through HHHH, and so on for hundreds of variations. And in each case, we would expect the same sort of factor structure to emerge. As long as all these items were of good quality, it should not matter if we used A or AA or AAA or AAAA in our inventory. As long as that part of the content domain was covered, and written well, we should be happy.

So here is the irony. Although we sweat to carefully write specific test items that are clear, unambiguous, and unitary, and although test takers are responding to these specific items, in a larger sense, the items are not important in and of themselves but are important only insofar as they represent a particular part of the content domain. Whether we had used A or AA or AAA or AAAA in combination with B or BB or BBB or BBBB and C or CC . . . , we should still find that the As, Bs, Es, and Gs would emerge as one factor and that the Cs, Ds, Fs, and Hs would emerge as a second factor.

What is important at the level of interpreting what the inventory is measuring is not the individual items (most of the time) but, rather, the fewer number of factors that underlie these items. For although we could envision writing thousands or millions or zillions of items for this content domain, they would still represent only the two general factors that describe this construct. In some sense, then, although the items are the concrete entities of the measurement enterprise, what are more "real," or certainly more useful, are the more abstract (latent) factors underlying these items.

How Much Information Is Lost in the Crunch

One of the hopes of researchers using factor analysis is that not much information is lost in the process of reducing a large number of variables down to a few number of factors. The outcome of this hope will be reflected in the quality of the solution. To the extent that variables are strongly related to their factors and not strongly related to the other factors, we say that the factor solution is a good one where not much information is lost. To the extent that the results depart from this ideal, we say that the solution is less good. We will show you how to make this assessment after covering the basics of factor analysis.

When Visual Inspection No Longer Works

We have used contrived and simplified small examples to illustrate the essence of factor analysis. If everything was always this easy, we would have very limited use for the actual statistical procedures available on SPSS and other statistical programs. But the real world of research often uses more than eight variables, and it is always the case that the interrelationships of the variables are more complicated than presented even in our most extended example. And so it happens that we can rarely rely exclusively on visual inspection of the correlation matrix to tell us what our factors are. Fortunately, we can direct a computerized statistical package such as SPSS to process the correlations by performing mathematical routines in place of our visual inspection. We must always bear in mind, however, that at the end of this mathematical processing, we still need to interpret the results as researchers; that is, we need to interpret the results at the human level.

Factor Analysis as an Umbrella Label

A Hint of Complexity

We have been using the term *factor analysis* as a generic label to stand for a process that allows us to identify a few components, factors, or dimensions that underlie a larger set of variables. As was true for some of the other procedures that we have covered in earlier chapters, such as multiple regression and discriminant analysis, factor analysis subsumes a set of related statistical techniques; therefore, some distinctions (decisions in some of the procedures to be used) must be made when actually running such an analysis.

We need to make certain distinctions here because factor analysis is ordinarily conducted in two successive phases—the extraction phase is done first and is then followed by the rotation phase. Each phase can be accomplished using different analytic methods. In the extraction phase, one can "extract" factors via several alternative processes, or one can extract components (a simpler kind of factor that we will actually use to illustrate the extraction process). From a technical perspective, we would call what we were doing either a factor analysis or a principal components analysis depending on the analytic technique used in the extraction phase. Once components or factors have been extracted, most researchers rotate them before interpreting the results. Not surprisingly, different rotation procedures may be applied as well.

Our Approach

The most straightforward way we have found to describe the extraction process is to focus on a principal components analysis because it is a bit simpler to explicate than a factor analysis (simpler does not imply better—many researchers prefer one of the factor analysis procedures over principal components). In this discussion, we will use the term *component* rather than *factor* as a label for the variate. Following that, we will conceptually distinguish between principal components and factor analysis, and we will briefly characterize some of the extraction methods that fall under the category of factor analysis. We will then address the rotation process, discussing both orthogonal and oblique strategies.

The First Phase: Component Extraction

The Concept of Extraction

As has been true for the other multivariate procedures that we have covered, the goal of the extraction process is to account for variance. At the start of the extraction process, all the variance is unaccounted for; when it finishes, it will have accounted for all the variance. A solution will be selected by researchers someplace between these extremes but presumably with more rather than less variance accounted for.

What is being "extracted" is variance. Think of the notion of extraction as accounting for variance. Each successively identified component will account for (extract) a certain amount of the total original variance. For this process to make sense, two questions need to be answered: (a) What is a component? (b) From what is variance being extracted?

What Is a Component?

A component is a weighted linear combination of the variables being analyzed—a variate. The mathematical function describing this straight line contains all the variables in the analysis. Each variable is weighted based on its contribution or relationship to the principal component in much the same way as is done in multiple regression. This variate is analogous to the dependent variable in a multiple regression analysis (Pedhazur & Schmelkin, 1991).

From What Is Variance Being Extracted?

Variance is being extracted from the total variance of the variables in the analysis. In principal components analysis (unlike the other multivariate procedures we have described), each variable can be thought of as contributing one unit of variance. If there are eight variables in the analysis, for example, then the total amount of variance is equal to eight.

In addition to equaling the total variance, the number of variables also equals the total number of components that it is possible to extract from the set. When all eight components are extracted from a set of eight variables, we say that the analysis has gone to completion in the sense that it has accounted for all the variance. Although SPSS will take the analysis to completion, we will wish to stop far short of that in identifying a principal components solution that we wish to interpret.

The Extraction Process

Although the extraction process is done at a mathematical level by the computer, we will explain what is happening with a pictorial illustration. This picture that we construct is, admittedly, oversimplified. Despite that limitation, however, it can capture the important features of the first few steps in component extraction. We will first put the picture with all its props in place, then tell you the rules of extraction, and finally describe the process itself.

A Pictorial Illustration

Imagine a miniature cuboid galaxy hanging in the air in front of you punctuated by a few bright "stars" here and there as drawn in Figure 12a.1. The "stars" in the picture are the variables in the analysis. The cuboid galaxy represents at least the visible part of the factor or multidimensional space defined by the positions of the variables. We have asked you to imagine a three-dimensional universe (a cube) because that is a shape that people can see in their mind's eye and a shape that we can draw. There are actually more than three dimensions in this space. In fact, there are as many dimensions as there are variables in the analysis. This multidimensional space (sometimes referred to as hyperspace) is the site of the component extraction process.

In this image of a cuboid factor space, the positions of the variables (representing the variables) relative to each other are determined by their correlations. Variables that are more strongly correlated are closer to each other. We depict this in Figure 12a.2, where the two data points relatively close to each other are shown as being moderately correlated, whereas the data points at opposite sides of the space are shown as being very weakly related to each other. This idea that correlation is a gauge of distance is important and will be elaborated upon later in our discussion.

Now include in this image a set of laser beams, each a little bit longer than our little factor space. You have complete control over where you place these lasers. These laser beams are straight lines, and they will be the components once they are positioned in this space. You have as many of these components as there are variables in this multidimensional space because the extraction process will run to completion.

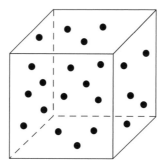

Figure 12a.1   Three-Dimensional View of Multidimensional Space

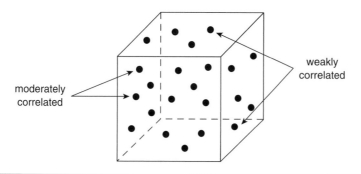

Figure 12a.2   Variables Located Closer Together Are More Correlated Than
Those Located Farther Apart

The Rules of Component Extraction

Here are the rules governing the extraction of components from this
multidimensional space:

1. Extraction, the fitting of lines into this multidimensional space in our
   pictorial illustration, is done one component at a time.

2. Every component must be thrust through the gravitational center of
   that space.

3. Once the first component has been thrust into the space, all suc-
   ceeding components must intersect the one or ones already in the
   space at right (90°) angles.

4. When a component is inserted into this multidimensional space, it must account for all the variance that it is possible for it to account for, that is, it must occupy the one orientation that meets the criterion for best fit.

5. If there are already components in the space, a newly extracted component must account for variance not already accounted for by the ones already there.

Extracting Components

Do not let the terminology get in the way of your understanding of the extraction process. Principal components are fitted into the multidimensional space and represent the lines of best fit. Best fit is defined in terms of accounting for the most variance and, as we will see shortly, meets the least squares rule for fitting straight lines to data arrays.

The term *extraction* is used to convey the idea that these components, these fitted straight lines or variates, are accounting for or extracting variance from the system. Thus, we start with all the variance unaccounted for. When we fit the first component to the variables, we will account for a certain amount of variance. It is in this sense that we have extracted variance. Ultimately, when all the components have been fitted, all the variance will have been extracted—that is, accounted for.

Let's extract our first component. Using our pictorial illustration, you must position one of the components through the center of this factor space at any angle such that you come as close as possible to *all* the variables. The position that your beam should occupy is solvable once you identify the rule governing the choice of this position—namely, that there is only one place (i.e., only one linear function) where the sum of squares of the distances of the variables from the line are a minimum—all you need to do is apply the least squares rule (or permit the computer to do it for you). We have illustrated this in Figure 12a.3. Thus successful, you now have a factor space with a laser beam through its gravitational center.

This is the first extracted component and will have accounted for a certain amount of variance. In fact, because this is the very first component, it will have been positioned in the best place in the entire space. This is given to us in Rule 4 above. It will thus have accounted for (extracted) more variance than any subsequently fitted line.

We will next extract (fit) the second component (Rule 1 states that we must do this process one component at a time). Extracted components are to intersect each other at 90° according to Rule 3 above. This means that the components during this extraction phase are orthogonal to each other; that

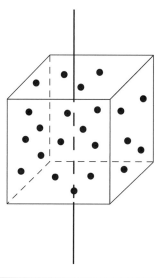

Figure 12a.3 The First Component Is Placed at the Optimal Location as Defined by the Least Squares Rule

is, they are independent of (uncorrelated with) each other. In our imaginary factor space, we will take a second laser beam and position it perpendicular to the one already in place (Rule 3) as shown in Figure 12a.4. It, too, must intersect the factor space's center (Rule 2), and it, too, must occupy the best place left to it given that the first component has the very best absolute place (Rule 4). Applying the least squares rule will yield the information necessary to place this second component appropriately.

The third component to be extracted must also intersect the factor space's center and must be perpendicular to the components (two thus far) that have been identified to this point. This component, too, must occupy the best place left to it given that the first and second components have taken the very best and next best absolute places already. This is pictured in Figure 12a.5. With the third component extracted from this component space, our imaginary factor space now has three components sticking out of it.

Unfortunately, it is impossible for us to provide you with a visual representation of the imaginary factor space once we extract more than three components because we will have run out of tangible dimensions for the universe in which we live. Through the wonders of mathematics, however, any number of dimensions beyond three can be put in place, but if the image with three straight lines made sense to you, it is not necessary to stretch your visual imaging beyond that.

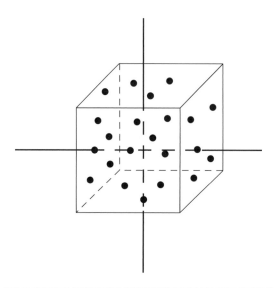

Figure 12a.4 The Second Component Is Placed in the Next Most Optimal
Location Orthogonal to the First

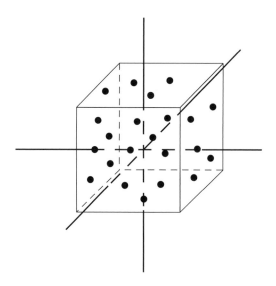

Figure 12a.5 The Third Component Is Placed in the Third Most Optimal
Location Orthogonal to the First Two

Point of Diminishing Returns

One can continue on in the manner just described, extracting as many components as there are variables. But it will also be true that once the first few components have been fit, there will not be any decent places for the other components to be positioned (i.e., they will not account for very much variance), and their existence will be superfluous. Thus, a *complete solution* as it is called is not very interesting; the real issue in principal components analysis is to stop the process when "enough" components have been extracted.

Distances of Variables From a
Component Correlation as a Distance Measure

We have already indicated that correlation can be used as a measure of distance between variables. It is time to more fully discuss this idea. When we say that two variables are highly correlated, we are also saying that they are strongly related to or are associated with each other. So important is this idea that researchers have gone so far as to quantify this strength of association. As discussed in an earlier chapter, for the Pearson r, the strength of relationship is indexed by examining the r^2.

Picturing the correlation between two variables as overlapping circles as was done in Chapter 4A, the area common to them (the overlap) is r^2. The stronger the relationship, the more overlap we would draw. If we were able to take two variables and continuously make them more and more related, we would see the two circles start off with little overlap and gradually move toward each other as the strength of relation increased. In this diagrammatic way, it can be seen that the variables are indeed getting physically closer as they become increasingly more related. Thus, it is that correlation (actually the correlation squared) can be used as a measure of distance, although the verbalization of it may at first sound backward (it's not):

- ▶ Weaker correlations represent more distance between the variables (they are farther apart).
- ▶ Stronger correlations represent less distance between the variables (they are closer together).

Component-Variable Distances

Components are variates—linear combinations of the variables in the analysis, very much analogous to what we have already seen in multiple regression. We could compute a component score for each participant on each component if we so wished. This would be done by taking the person's score on the first variable and multiplying by its coefficient, taking the person's score on the second variable and multiplying that by its coefficient, and so on, and then adding all those values together to achieve a single value for the component.

Once we had the numeric value of each component for each participant, we could then correlate the component score with the score for each variable. To compute a correlation, all we need are two quantitative values. In this situation, one value would be the score on the component (variate), and the other would be the score on the variable under consideration. Listing these pairs of numbers for each participant gives us the setup to compute a Pearson r and thereby allows us to generate the r^2 for each component-variable pair. These correlations, which we have talked about earlier, are structure coefficients.

The squared correlations—these r^2 values—are directly translatable into distance indexes. Keeping with our pictorial illustration, we have these components passing near some variables and farther from other variables. We can use the r^2 values to let us know how close each variable is to the beam (component). A large r^2 tells us that the two entities—here, the component and the variable—are quite close to each other, whereas a small r^2 tells us that they are relatively far apart.

This idea is schematized in Figure 12a.6. For simplicity, we show five data points at different distances from the component or variate (assume for this example that we have pictured the situation after the rotation phase has been completed). These distances are measured in terms of the strength of association (correlation) between the variate and the variable. As can be seen, the smallest distances represent the strongest correlations between the component and the variable, the middle distance represents a more moderate correlation, and the largest distance represents a relatively weak correlation.

Eigenvalue

Distances of the variables to the component, measured in terms of r^2, are quite important. We (well, the computer) can use these correlations to apply the least squares rule, and thus determine the proper location of the component. That is, the sum of squares of the distances of the variables to the line is minimal at the position of the component. If distance is measured in terms of r^2, then we can simply add all the r^2 values to obtain the sum of these squares for each component. The sum of these squared correlations for each component over the full set of variables is called an *eigenvalue*. In terms of the least squares rule, this optimal position where the squared distances are minimal represents the best or closest fit of the line to the data points. Thus, this position represents the place where the eigenvalue of the component is maximal.

We have illustrated the computation of an eigenvalue in Figure 12a.7, where we show again the distances between the five variables and a component

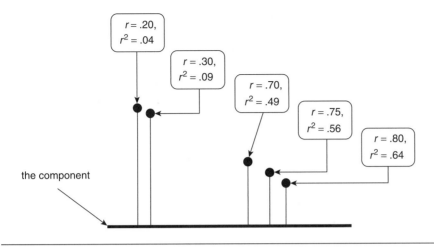

Figure 12a.6 The Squared Variable-Component Correlation Coefficient Is an Indicator of the Distance Between the Variable and the Factor

from the prior figure. In this situation, the eigenvalue of the component is equal to 1.82 and is obtained from determining the sum of the r^2 values (distances from the variate) of the variables.

Each component has an associated eigenvalue. This makes sense in that it is possible to assess the distance (again measured in terms of correlation) between any given data point and any given component. We have illustrated this in Table 12a.8, which shows the two-factor rotated factor matrix for the analysis pictured in Figure 12a.7. Assume that we have determined that there are two factors underlying these five variables. Further assume that the distances of the variables we provided to you earlier were between the variables and Factor 1 and are reproduced in the first numerical column of Table 12a.8. But because there is a second factor in the solution (intersecting the first at 90°), one can also examine the distances of the variables from that second factor as well.

The positioning of the variables on these factors is shown in Figure 12a.8. Each variable occupies a coordinate coinciding to the distance it lies from each factor. For example, Variable V correlates .80 with Factor 1 and thus lies relatively close to it, but it correlates only .05 with Factor 2 and so lies quite far from that factor. In Figure 12a.8, Variable V is placed at the (Factor 1, Factor 2) coordinate of (.80, .05).

The eigenvalue for each factor is the sum of the squared correlations of the variables in the analysis. As we have seen, the eigenvalue for Factor 1 is 1.82. Because we have supplied the correlations of the variables with the second factor in Table 12a.7, it is now possible to also calculate the

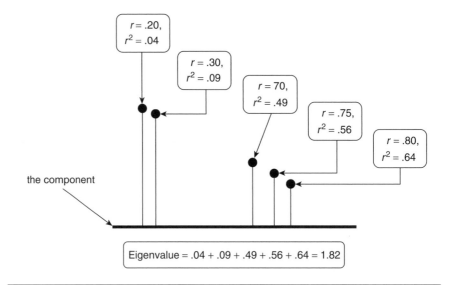

the component

Eigenvalue = .04 + .09 + .49 + .56 + .64 = 1.82

Figure 12a.7   The Sum of the Squared Correlations Is the Eigenvalue of the Component

Table 12a.8   Two-Factor Rotated Matrix for Variables V Through Z

	Factor 1	Factor 2
V	.80	.05
W	.75	.10
X	.70	.20
Y	.20	.85
Z	.30	.70

eigenvalue for this factor. The r^2 values for Variables V, W, X, Y, and Z are .0025, .01, .04, .72, and .49, and the sum of these values is 1.26; this is the eigenvalue of the second factor.

Principal Components Versus Factor Analysis

Causal Flow

We have indicated that the component is analogous to the dependent variable in a multiple regression analysis. This is because principal components are latent or composites descriptive of the information contained in the measured variables (the variables in the analysis). In some sense, the

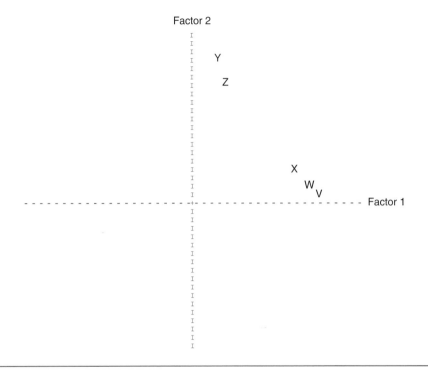

Figure 12a.8 Factor Loadings of Five Variables on Two Factors Shown in Graphic Form

components "arise from" the measured variables. From a causal modeling perspective, the causal flow is from the measured variables to the latent components. Because we think of independent variables as causes of dependent variables, the measured variables are analogous to independent variables and the components are analogous to dependent variables. Factor analysis shifts this conception around. The measured variables are taken as "indicators" of the factors. Here, the causal flow is from the factor (still a latent variable) to the measured indicator variables. Thus, the factors are analogous to the independent variables, and the measured variables are analogous to the dependent variables. This whole conception is discussed in much greater detail in Chapter 13A.

Variance Explained

Another difference between principal components and factor analysis is how each identifies the target variance that is to be explained. Principal components analysis, as we have seen, deals with the total amount of variance in the data set. We thus measured the magnitudes of the first few components by how much of the total variance they can account for. The total variance on which we focus in principal components analysis is partitioned in factor analysis.

In factor analysis, the total variance of each variable is partitioned into two segments. One segment is common or shared (overlapping) variance—variance that is shared with the other variables in the analysis. The other segment is variance unique to the variable itself. Only the common variance is used in factor analysis. This approach is adopted because it is argued that if the point of factor analysis is to describe the structure of the set of variables in the analysis, then we should really be looking only at the shared or common variance of the variables. That is, the factor structure should be descriptive of what the variables have in common rather than including what is idiosyncratic (unique) about them. Factor analysis therefore deals only with the shared variance—the covariance—of the variables in the analysis. The magnitudes of the factors are thus measured by how much of the common variance (the covariance) they can account for.

These two perspectives partly play themselves out in how the correlation matrix is prepared for the component or factor extraction process. As we have already seen, the extraction process begins with the correlation matrix, examples of which are shown in the tables near the beginning of this chapter. The main issue at hand is the value that is to be used on the diagonal of the matrix, the place representing the correlation of each variable to itself. In those tables, we did not actually place values on the diagonal. This was done to enable the tables to be more easily read by having fewer numbers in them but also to avoid raising the issue of what to place on the diagonal before we were ready to discuss it more fully.

Students are taught in their early statistics course that a variable correlated with itself should yield a value of 1.00. This value of 1.00, however, represents all the variance (the total variance) of the variable. It is therefore an acceptable value to be used in principal components analysis because this procedure analyzes the total variance.

But using 1s on the diagonal of the correlation matrix is not appropriate in factor analysis. Rather, factor analysis will use some estimate of a variable's *communality* on the diagonal. Communality estimates are intended to represent how much a variable has in common with the remaining variables in the analysis. For example, if Variable J shares 83% of its variance with the other variables (with the remaining variance being unique to that variable), then the value that would be used for the diagonal element for Variable J in many variations of factor analyses would be .83 instead of 1.00.

Each variable in the analysis is associated with its own communality. It is the squared multiple correlation resulting from the multiple regression prediction model in which the variable is being predicted by the other variables.

It is also the sum of the squared correlations between the variable and the other variables (we square the correlations in the factor matrix and add across the rows). Communalities thus give an indication of the degree to which a variable was represented in the factor solution.

We can briefly illustrate the idea of communality, symbolized in texts as h^2, by contrasting principal components analysis with principal axis factor analysis. In the full principal components solution, each variable's communality will be equal to 1 because all its variance will have been accounted for in the solution. For a less than full solution, say a three-component solution, a variable's communality will be less than that; it will be the sum of the squared correlations in the three-component factor matrix.

In the full principal axis solution, each variable's initial communality will be less than 1 because only the common variance and not the unique variance will be considered. It is these values that are originally placed on the diagonal of the correlation matrix; it will be estimated in an iterative fashion in the extraction process until a stabilized (and somewhat lower) value is reached. Finally, in a less than full solution, a variable's communality will be computed in the same manner as was done for principal components (sum the squared correlations across the row of the factor matrix), but again because only the common variance is analyzed, these communalities will be less than those corresponding communalities computed for a principal components analysis.

Different Extraction Methods

Partitioning the variance of the variables into common and unique variance and then deciding on how to perform the extraction process have given rise to several alternative procedures developed under the aegis of factor analysis. We summarize some of the more popular ones here and mention principal components analysis as well.

- ▶ *Principal components analysis* uses 1s on the diagonal of the correlation matrix in the process of extraction and is the method described above.
- ▶ *Principal axis factoring* (also called *principal factors*) differs from principal components analysis mainly by using estimates of communalities (a measure of shared variance) on the diagonal in the extraction process. SPSS does this by starting with squared multiple correlations (a measure of the relationship between a particular variable and the set of remaining variables in the analysis—hence the term *communality*), but alternative methods (e.g., choosing the largest correlation in the row of the correlation matrix) can be used instead. Many programs such as SPSS then reestimate these

communality values via an iterative process to achieve a "better" estimate of this shared variance. Once stable estimates have been achieved, a factor analysis is performed in the manner already described above for principal components analysis.

▶ *Generalized least squares* factoring and *unweighted least squares* factoring both attempt to minimize the off-diagonal differences between the observed and reproduced correlation matrices (because factors are meant to represent the relationships between the variables, one should be able to perform a "back-to-the-future" operation of "reproducing" [guessing] what the original correlation matrix must have been like to begin with). Communalities are derived from the solution rather than estimated from it. The two procedures differ in that generalized least squares factoring gives greater weight to variables more strongly related to other variables in the set (those with higher communality values) whereas unweighted least squares weights all variables equally.

▶ *Maximum likelihood* factor extraction is related to the generalized least squares method in that it, too, uses weights proportional to the relatedness of the variables. However, maximum likelihood calculates weights for the variables on the factors that maximize the probability of having sampled the correlation matrix from a multivariate normally distributed population. Thompson (2004) contrasts the ordinary least squares approach with maximum likelihood theory by noting that rather than trying to reproduce the sample data, the maximum likelihood procedure attempts to use the sample data to directly estimate the population covariance matrix. He does go on to say that "estimating population parameters with a statistical theory that optimizes the estimation . . . is very appealing. Better estimation of population parameters should yield more replicable results" (p. 127). Maximum likelihood, as we will see in the following chapters, is extensively used in confirmatory factor analysis, path analysis, and structural equation modeling.

▶ *Alpha* factoring also starts with communality estimates on the diagonal. Its extraction strategy is designed to maximize the reliability (defined by Cronbach's coefficient alpha) of the factors.

▶ In *image factoring*, the common (shared) factor variance is estimated via multiple regression to predict the value of the variable. This predicted value is known as the "image" of the variable. The "anti-image" of the variable is the difference between the actual and predicted values. Factor extraction is performed on the image covariance matrix containing the squared images on the diagonal.

Recommendations Concerning Extraction

Based on the preceding discussion, it may seem that principal components analysis and the various forms of factor analysis might each yield vastly different results in this extraction phase. One of the pleasant surprises experienced by students when they actually perform these various procedures on the same data set is that the extraction results are quite often remarkably similar given a relatively large sample size and reasonable reliability of the measurements. The primary difference between the output of these two general approaches is that principal components analysis will account for more variance than the factor analyses. This discrepancy occurs because factor analysis targets only the common variance, which is always less than the total variance dealt with by principal components.

So what extraction procedure should you use in your own research? Some researchers (e.g., Kazelskis, 1978) have argued that principal components analysis, by focusing on the total variance, can provide a somewhat inflated solution (e.g., it will account for more variance and will show higher correlations between the variables and the factors) than the data really warrant, and the argument can be made to either correct the component correlations or to use one of the factor analysis methods. At the same time, a look through the research journals suggests that principal components analysis is an increasingly popular extraction technique (Bryant & Yarnold, 1995). Traditional wisdom, however, suggests that there is probably not going to be much difference in the interpretation based on either principal components or factor analysis, especially when you are analyzing more than two dozen or so variables that each are reasonably related to the dimensions tapped into by the components or factors (Gorsuch, 1983; Stevens, 2002).

Theoretically, principal components analysis is conceptually simpler than factor analysis. Principal components analysis attempts to summarize or aggregate sets of correlated variables and in that sense is relatively empirical (inductive). From the same standpoint, factor analysis is more complex in that factors are thought of more as causes that underlie or drive the correlations between the variables. Although both procedures are considered "exploratory," factor analysis is more related to theory development (Tabachnick & Fidell, 2001b). We will discuss the tie between factor analysis and theory more explicitly in our treatment of confirmatory factor analysis (see Chapter 13A).

Here is our general recommendation. For many applications that you are likely to encounter, principal components analysis should probably be sufficient to meet your needs. If you opt for factor analysis, our tastes run toward either generalized least squares, maximum likelihood, or principal axis solutions.

In discussing the next phase of the analysis, the rotation phase, there is little value for us to distinguish between principal components and factors. We will therefore talk in terms of factor analysis to keep our language simple, but please note that what we say is applicable to principal components analysis as well.

The Second Phase: Factor Rotation

By virtue of the mathematical procedure underlying the extraction process, the first extracted factor accounts for the most variance, the second extracted factor accounts for the next largest portion of the variance, and so on. Researchers and statisticians have argued that the mathematically based placement of these factors does not optimize the interpretability of the solution. Hence, once the number of factors to be interpreted is selected, the factors are then rotated. We mean by *rotation* the pivoting of the first *n* number of extracted factors around their point of intersection. The outcome of this rotation phase is what researchers ordinarily interpret.

Factor rotation is designed to achieve simple structure (we will discuss this in a moment). From the histories presented by Harmon (1960) and Harris (2001), we learn that Thurstone (1947) was the first person to explicate the concept of rotation to achieve his standards for simple structure. However, Thurstone's stringent criteria for realizing this state were unable to be satisfied by most data sets, prompting several statisticians in the early 1950s (Carroll, 1953; Ferguson, 1954; Neuhaus & Wrigley, 1954; Tucker, 1955) to develop an alternative rotational procedure known as *quartimax*.

Although quartimax was an improvement over Thurstone's method, it did not generally meet the needs of most researchers. Quartimax tended to identify one general factor that correlated with most of the variables in the analysis. This outcome was problematic to many investigators in that some of the variables captured by this general factor were not necessarily related to each other. Thus, the quartimax rotation strategy did not really distinguish subsets of related variables (i.e., separate factors) that would be of use to researchers. This problem was finally solved in 1958 when Kaiser published the results of his dissertation on another alternative strategy to factor rotation. Kaiser's publication introduced to the field the rotation strategy known as *varimax* that most researchers currently prefer.

The Goal of Simple Structure: The Least Squares Rule in Operation

The least squares rule, as used in the factor extraction process, has an awful lot to be said in favor of its use, but at least one of its properties

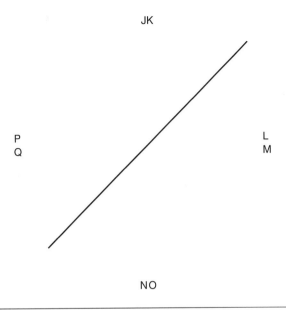

Figure 12a.9   The First Factor Fit to the Factor Space

becomes something of a liability here. This rule really represents moderation, compromise, and a lack of commitment. It is the "one solution fits all" approach that does not work in many situations. To minimize the squared distance from all the variables taken together, the line (factor) cannot afford to come too close to some variables because it would have to then be terribly far from others. In the world of squared distances, large distances become magnified in importance. Positioning of the factor thus becomes a very delicate matter.

The result of this strategy of compromise is shown in Figure 12a.9. It is a very simplified picture of the first extracted factor fitted to a set of eight variables, J through Q, before any rotation process has been accomplished. As you can see, the line of best fit is not all that far from the eight variables, but neither does it come all that near any of them.

In Figure 12a.10, we have added the second extracted factor to the mix (we are still in the extraction phase here). This second factor is also subject to the least squares rule, and it is positioned as conservatively as the first. This situation is a bit at odds with the goal of simple structure.

Achieving Simple Structure

Rotation of the extracted factor structure does not change the amount of variance accounted for but simply redistributes the variance across the

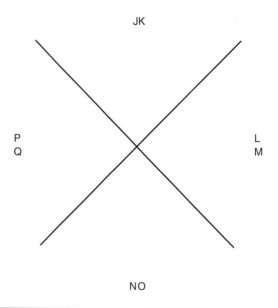

Figure 12a.10   The First Two Factors Fit to the Factor Space

factors to facilitate interpretation by trying to achieve "simple structure." Simple structure is obtained when the correlations of the variables with the factors would be either very high (values near 1) or very low (values near 0). Rotation is an iterative process of "twisting" or "pivoting" the factor structure in the multidimensional space until a satisfactory "fit" is established.

To be moved closer to some variables in this rotation process (to achieve correlations closer to 1), each factor must actually move farther away from other variables (and thus reduce those correlations closer to the target of 0). Because the factors are being rotated together, we care less about newly computed eigenvalues but more about how clear the simple structure becomes. Most researchers do not even compute the new eigenvalues of the factors once rotation has been done. In fact, we do not ordinarily keep track of which rotated factor was originally which extracted factor.

Figure 12a.10 showed the outcome after extracting the second factor from the data. For this example, assume that we have made the decision to stop the extraction process at this point and to rotate these first two factors. We show the results of this rotation in Figure 12a.11.

In the rotation process that we are using (a varimax rotation—we will describe this shortly), the factors are kept at a 90° angle of intersection with each other and so will remain orthogonal to each other after the rotation is completed (we will explain this in the following section of this chapter).

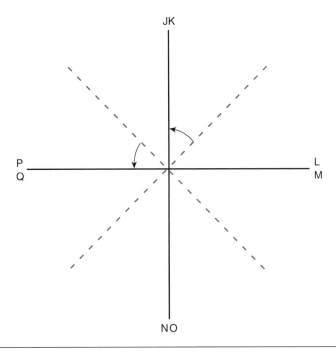

Figure 12a.11   Rotating the Two Factors to Achieve Simple Structure

In your mind's eye when you imagine this rotation process, also imagine putting some super glue on the intersection point of the factors so that when they are rotated or pivoted, they will move as a single structure.

We have used lighter dashed lines in Figure 12a.11 to show the original position of the factors and have used a solid black line to show the position of the factors following this rotation process. Each factor has been repositioned closer to four of the variables at the expense of moving away from the other four. We have not changed the total amount of variance accounted for, but that total variance has been redistributed in the process of striving to achieve simple structure. If we were interpreting the two-factor solution, it is this rotated solution with which we would be working.

We can illustrate this process numerically as well by drawing on one of our previous examples. We presented toward the beginning of this chapter (in Table 12a.3) the rotated factor matrix for the four-variable example of Items A through D, which demonstrated a two-factor structure in a numerical manner. Here, in Table 12a.9, we reproduce that information again, but this time we also show you the factor matrix prior to rotation (the factor matrix resulting from the extraction process).

Table 12a.9 Extracted (Pre-Rotated) and Rotated Factor Matrix for Variables A Through D

		Factor 1	Factor 2
Extraction	B	.73530	−.62913
(Pre-Rotated)	D	.73292	.62701
Factor Matrix	A	.73073	−.63204
	C	.69914	.66497
	B	.96563	.06356
	A	.96439	.05828
Rotated Factor Matrix			
	C	.03566	.96422
	D	.08635	.96065

As we can see from the top portion of Table 12a.9, the least squares solution shown for the pre-rotation result (the factor matrix resulting from the extraction phase) was truly a compromise. Variable B, for example, correlated about .74 with Factor 1 and about −.63 with Factor 2. And Variable C, as another example, correlated almost equally with both factors.

The extraction process placed the two factors such that they were moderately close to all the variables. As a consequence, although the factors were not all that far from the variables, neither were they especially close to at least some of them. Thus, all four variables are correlated with both factors, with correlations ranging from the low .6s to the low .7s.

It is now possible to appreciate why we prefer to work with the results of the rotation process. Recall the correlation matrix, the place where the factor analysis all started. In our discussion of that matrix, it was very clear that there were two viable factors represented by the four variables—one factor composed primarily of A and B and another composed primarily of C and D. But that structure is not apparent from the factor matrix following the extraction phase. Even though Variables A and B are not related to Variables C and D, all four are substantially correlated to each of the factors. The extraction process, driven by the least squares rule, has succeeded in having all the variables as related as possible to all the factors but has not differentiated sets of variables for us.

The rotation phase picks up from where the extraction process leaves off. Once we identify the number of factors with which we want to work, we abandon the least squares rule. Instead, we allow the rotation process to be driven by the goal of simple structure so that the relationships between the variables can reemerge from the blandness of ordinary least squares.

You can see in the bottom portion of Table 12a.9 the dramatic structural change as a result of the rotation process. The factors were given an opportunity to make a commitment—to achieve simple structure. Factor 1 was thus placed quite close to (it was allowed to correlate quite strongly with) A and B, and Factor 2 was thus placed quite close to C and D. Of course, in the process of committing to A and B, Factor 1 wound up much farther away from C and D. That turned out to be acceptable, however, because the position of Factor 2 worked out well to complement that of Factor 1. Thus, the rotation process accomplished the goal of achieving simple structure and our effort to interpret the factor analysis results was thus facilitated.

Although the factors were repositioned in the factor space, the total amount of variance accounted for in this two-factor solution remained unchanged. This can be easily verified by simply computing the sum of all the squared pre-rotated correlations and comparing them with the sum of all the squared rotated correlations. If you do the math, both sets of squared correlations sum to the value of 3.73669.

Orthogonal Factor Rotation

The term *orthogonal* is a statistical concept indicating that two or more entities are independent of (not correlated with) one another. An orthogonal rotation strategy keeps the factors independent of each other during the rotation process. Geometrically, factors are orthogonal if they cross each other at 90°. In Figure 12a.11, we retained the 90° angle between the factors when we rotated them, and in all the previous examples of rotated factor matrices involving Variables A through H, the results were based on the orthogonal rotation strategy known as varimax.

Three methods of orthogonal rotation are available in most statistical packages:

▶ *Varimax* rotation, introduced by Kaiser (1958) as an alternative to the quartimax strategy, simplifies the correlations within each factor (the columns of the factor matrix) by striving toward 1s and 0s. It simplifies the factors (the columns of the factor matrix). Varimax rotation works toward having some factors correlate quite strongly with some variables (correlations nearer to 1) but more weakly with the other variables (correlations nearer to 0). Because it is focused on the factors (as are the researchers most of the time), this method is the most frequently used orthogonal rotation strategy.

▶ *Quartimax* rotation, resulting from the work done in the early 1950s, simplifies the variables (the rows of the factor matrix). It does this by having a variable correlate more strongly (nearer to 1) to one factor and more weakly (nearer to 0) to all other factors. As we have already described, this strategy tends to drive the rotated solution toward a single general factor. Quartimax rotation is infrequently used today not only because it is variable- rather than factor-oriented but also because researchers do not often prefer one dominant factor.

▶ *Equimax* rotation attempts to effect a compromise between varimax and quartimax rotational strategies; it, too, has failed to electrify the interests of most researchers.

Oblique Factor Rotation

The key difference between orthogonal and oblique rotation is that oblique rotation does not require the rotation process to keep the factors uncorrelated. In geometric terms, the mandate that the factors remain at 90° is no longer in effect. Instead of super gluing the factors together as we had you imagine for orthogonal rotation, here we suggest that you form an image of the factors connected to a hinge at their point of intersection. This would allow the factors to be pivoted if need be to form an oblique angle (hence the term *oblique rotation*) rather than being forced to remain perpendicular to each other.

There are two oblique rotation methods available in SPSS: *Direct Oblimin* and *Promax*. The former is the more processor-intensive procedure and is the one that you should probably use in your own research if you are doing an oblique solution; it is the one we focus on in this text. Promax is a simpler and faster method to obtain an oblique solution and should probably be considered for use if you need to save processing time when you have a very large data set.

In the Direct Oblimin rotation, the amount of correlation permitted between factors is under the control of the researcher, although most computer programs such as SPSS have default values that are usually pretty acceptable (SPSS uses the term "delta value") for how much correlation is permitted if the researchers do not specify a value (SPSS's default is a delta value of zero).

To permit a particular degree of correlation to exist between factors is not to require that the factors achieve that much correlation. Rather, the correlation value is a ceiling or maximum that is permitted should the factors exhibit that much relationship. The idea here is to permit the factors some leeway so that if they do correlate somewhat, the factor structure would be allowed to incorporate that in the solution.

So why set a limit at all? Because the situation is similar to the hands of an analogue clock where the minute hand can come closer and closer to the hour hand and at some point overlap it. If two factors are allowed to be placed extremely close to each other, perhaps intersecting each other at 5° or 10°, one can question whether the two factors are all that different from each other. It is therefore useful to set some sort of limit, then, to prevent the factors from being located too close to each other.

We have provided an illustration of an oblique rotation in Figures 12a.12 and 12a.13. Figure 12a.12 shows variables labeled as A through H arrayed in the factor space, which we have divided into quadrants to help you see the pattern. Take the two lines as factors that are being obliquely rotated to achieve the best simple structure they can.

As shown in Figure 12a.13, in this simplified example, the best fit of these two factors to the eight variables in the analysis is obtained when the factors intersect at about 135° if you look at the oblique angle of intersection (or 45° if you look at the acute angle of intersection) rather than 90°. For those of you who remember geometry, in a right triangle, the cosine of angle X is the ratio of A to B where A is the side that is adjacent to angle X and B is the hypotenuse. It turns out that the correlation of the factors is equal to the cosine of the angle formed by the two factors. In the case of the factors crossing at 90°, we have learned that these factors are orthogonal (independent, uncorrelated). Well, the cosine of 90° is zero (which it has to be because the factors are uncorrelated in this configuration, i.e., $r = 0$).

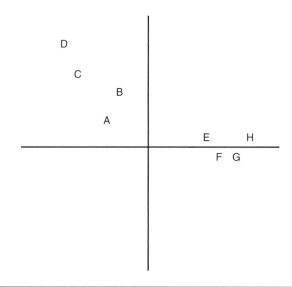

Figure 12a.12　An Array of Variables Shown in Two Dimensions

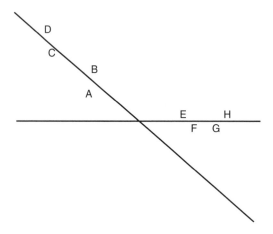

Figure 12a.13   Oblique Rotation of Factors Can Sometimes Achieve Simple
Structure Better Than Orthogonal Rotation

Choosing Between Orthogonal and Oblique Strategies

In most studies, researchers present the results of just one of the factor rotation strategies. Very often, the decision as to which one is more appropriate is made on the basis of the theory or model from which the study was generated. That is, ideally, the model has indicated whether the factors should be correlated or not, and that direction may well be sufficient for researchers to commit to one or the other strategy.

In the absence of any solid expectations, it is not uncommon for researchers to initially perform an oblique rotation solution. This allows them to examine the factor correlations that are provided as part of the oblique rotation output. Based on these computed factor correlations, researchers determine whether an oblique or orthogonal rotation strategy is more appropriate for their analysis.

We can supply you with a very general rule of thumb to start your decision-making process if you need to decide between oblique and orthogonal rotations based on the statistical analysis: With factor correlations generally in the range of the high .3s or better, most researchers would probably opt to work with an oblique rotation; with factor correlations in the teens or less, many researchers would probably opt to work with an orthogonal (most likely varimax) solution; with factor correlations between these two ranges, the decision is less clear cut and may vary substantially among researchers.

Reading Features of the Factor Analysis Printout

Although we will cover this in a more hands-on way in our worked example in Chapter 12B, there are certain parts of the printout that have immediate use helping researchers accept a particular solution to the factor analysis. We will briefly cover these features here by returning to the context of our simplified and hypothetical eight-variable example with the Variables A through H.

Variance Accounted For

As we have seen, eigenvalues indicate the amount of variance each component has accounted for. For the extraction phase, the first component will have the largest eigenvalue, the second component the next largest eigenvalue, and so on. This is one of the first portions of the output that researchers will examine. You will find a table in any printout that you examine that looks similar to what we have presented in Table 12a.10. The example used in this table shows the factor analysis solution of Variables A through H from an earlier example in this chapter. The correlation matrix for these variables, which you may wish to review, was presented in Table 12a.6.

Because there are eight variables in the analysis, the total amount of variance is equal to 8. After the first factor is in place, we can compute the correlation between each variable and the factor. We then square these correlations and sum them to achieve the eigenvalue of the factor. Eigenvalues are directly interpretable in terms of variance accounted for.

In Table 12a.10 we see that the first factor has an eigenvalue of 3.64341; that is, the first factor has accounted for about 3.64 units of variance. Because the total amount of variance is 8, dividing 3.64 by 8 tells us the proportion of the total variance extracted by the first factor. That turns out to be 45.5%, and this is shown in the next column of Table 12a.10. By the same reasoning, the second factor accounts for 35.2% of the total variance. Together, as shown in the last column of the table, the first two factors have accounted for almost 81% of the variance.

As shown in Table 12a.10, the extraction process has gone to completion in the sense that all eight factors have been extracted. Together, these eight factors have cumulatively accounted for all the variance. Because the usual goal in such an analysis is to account for the most variance with the fewest number of factors, we certainly want to work with fewer than all the eight factors extracted here.

Although this solution is a bit exaggerated, it does demonstrate some valid and important points.

Table 12a.10 Eigenvalues and Variance Accounted for in the Eight-Variable Factor Analysis of Variables A Through H

Factor	Eigenvalue	% Variance Accounted For	% Cumulative Variance
1	3.64341	45.5	45.5
2	2.81393	35.2	80.7
3	.58015	7.3	88.0
4	.53570	6.7	94.7
5	.19279	2.4	97.1
6	.10758	1.3	98.4
7	.07462	.9	99.4
8	.05181	.7	100.0

▶ The first factor always accounts for the most variance, the second factor for the next most variance, and so forth.

▶ Our focus is almost always on the cumulative percentage of variance accounted for. Here, the first two factors accounted for an incredible 80.7% of the variance.

▶ It is not an issue here, but factors that cannot muster enough strength to achieve an eigenvalue of 1 are ordinarily not going to be part of the solution. That is, researchers are not usually going to go that far down the list of possible factors to select.

▶ Researchers have the desire to work with factor solutions that appear to capture enough of the variance to provide confidence that they did not lose too much information in the data crunching process. A very rough rule of thumb proposed by some authors (e.g., Tabachnick & Fidell, 2001b) is that the solution should account for at least 50% of the variance.

▶ The factor solution is cumulative starting with the first factor. When we select a factor solution, what we are really saying is that we select the first n number of factors.

▶ In the example, we would select the two-factor solution as most viable. We saw this in the correlation matrix shown earlier in this chapter. As you can see from Table 12a.10, we gain a chunk of variance by reaching down to the second factor. The third factor is not contributing an awful lot of explained variance and its eigenvalue is below the value of 1.

Eigenvalue Plot

Another part of the printout that we would want to examine is the plot of eigenvalues. It is a visual depiction of the first two columns of the table illustrated in Table 12a.10. In real-world data sets where the solution is not oversimplified by textbook writers, researchers can sometimes see the pattern more clearly than in the table. The idea behind this graphical way to determine the number of factors in a solution was introduced by Raymond B. Cattell in 1966.

In an eigenvalue plot, eigenvalues are represented on the *Y* axis and the factors are represented on the *X* axis. An idealized curve might look like a negatively decelerating curve (similar to Ebbinghaus's forgetting curve). This plot of eigenvalues is known as a *scree distribution* or *scree plot*. Generally, as one part of the decision process aimed at determining the number of factors there should be in the solution, one looks for where the scree plot is still reasonably dropping (factors are still contributing to variance accounted for in potentially meaningful ways) and where it starts to straighten out (the point of diminishing returns where no gain is made by choosing additional factors).

The scree plot for our eight-variable example is presented in Figure 12a.14. As can be seen in Figure 12a.14, by the time we reach the third factor the function is pretty much attenuated, visually suggesting that the two-factor solution is probably the most viable.

An example of a somewhat more complex scree plot is shown in Figure 12a.15. We clearly make gains from the first to the second factor and from the second to the third factor. There may some gain by incorporating the fourth factor and a bit more with the fifth factor, but it is not clear from the scree plot if these gains are both worthwhile. The sixth and later factors are probably not strong enough to warrant inclusion in the final solution.

In this example, we would thus be inclined to nominate the two-factor through five-factor solutions as candidates for solution, with the most likely number of factors in the final decision probably being either three or four based on this scree plot. We would therefore want to examine the rotated factor matrix for each alternative solution, determine which variables were associated with which factors, and generate a label for each factor in each analysis. Based on several considerations discussed later, we would single out one of these sets as our solution.

The Rotated Factor Matrix

Varimax Rotated Factor Matrix

What is finally interpreted by researchers is the rotated factor matrix. Using our simplified eight-variable example, this matrix, originally shown in Table 12a.7, is once again reproduced in Table 12a.11. These results represent the varimax rotation of the two factors.

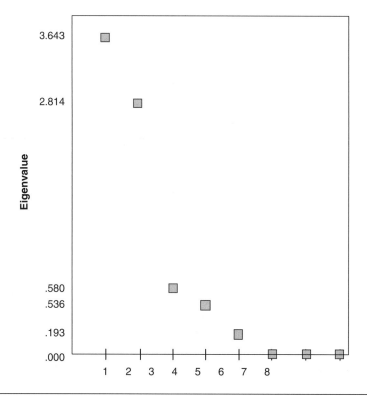

Figure 12a.14   A Scree Plot of Eigenvalues

Looking down the columns, we can see that varimax rotation has done a good job in achieving simple structure (of course, we constructed this example to exaggerate this point). With a couple of exceptions as we note below, the correlations of the variables to the factors are either relatively high or relatively low.

The Magnitude of the Variable Weights

In the context of a rotated factor matrix, the attention of researchers is focused on the magnitude of the structure and/or pattern coefficients (these are the correlations in an orthogonal rotation and are at the same time the structure and pattern coefficients; as we will see, in an oblique rotation these coefficients are different). Many researchers call these values by the colloquial and generic label of *loadings*. The key question here is how large a coefficient or "loading" should be before we accept it as sufficiently relating to the factor to commit ourselves to that interpretation. Comrey and Lee

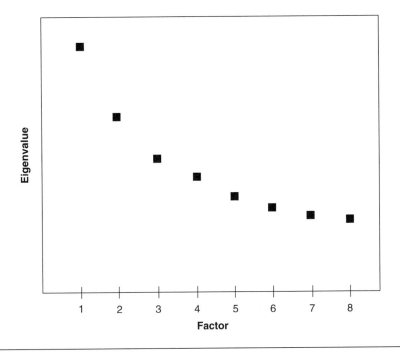

Figure 12a.15   Another Somewhat More Complex Scree Plot

(1992) have characterized coefficients of .7 as excellent, .63 as very good, .55 as good, .45 as fair, and .32 as close to minimal. Few if any authors recommend going below about .3. Tabachnick and Fidell (2001b) have argued for .32 as rock bottom, Gorsuch (1983) has suggested that .3 may be too small, especially if there are many variables in the analysis, and Stevens (2002) has recommended .40 in order to achieve practical worth.

Table 12a.11   Varimax Rotated Factor Matrix for the Two-Factor Solution of Variables A Through H

	Factor 1	*Factor 2*
A	.95558	.04616
E	.94828	.04119
B	.93463	.08318
G	.73099	.06213
F	.03521	.95125
D	.08330	.94641
C	.05697	.92905
H	.05845	.73754

Our recommendation is to base your decision in part on your sample size. With less than about 200 cases, think in terms of values in the .40 to .45 range as minimal. With larger samples, we suggest using about .40 as your rough guide, but variables with coefficients or loadings in the high .3s might be captured as well with a clear factor structure.

These recommendations address the interpretation of a rotated factor solution but may be too lenient if you wish to build a composite subscale based only on the subset of variables that you define as loading on the factor. At least under certain circumstances, variables with coefficients much below .5 can actually reduce the reliability of scales, especially those built from a combination of close to a dozen variables.

Interpreting Factors

For the purposes of this example, we will accept a variable as related to a factor if it has produced a structure or pattern coefficient of .4 or better. The interpretation process starts by examining the variables in Table 12a.11 row by row. For each row where we get a relatively high coefficient, we mark the result. Thus, we would say that A and B both "load" on Factor 1, C and D load on Factor 2, E loads on Factor 1, and F loads on Factor 2. Variables G and H are not associated with such extraordinary high coefficients but certainly correlate strongly enough on their respective factors to be included in the interpretation of the solution.

Interpretation of the solution is now possible to make by examining the columns. Recall two points: (a) A factor or component is what the variables correlated with it have in common; (b) variables more highly correlated with the factor or component share more in common with it. Thus, Factor 1 can be identified by emphasizing the content of A, E, and B, and Factor 2 can be identified by emphasizing the content of F, D, and C.

To illustrate this idea, assume that A, E, and B were the following items on an inventory:

I try to avoid being in a crowd.

I tend to stay away from parties.

I don't enjoy social events.

These three variables all correlate relatively strongly with the factor. What is the factor? One way to approach this is to think of the game show where you are given specific instances and must come up with the general category. In this case, the instances are as follows: avoid crowds, stay away from parties, and dislike social events. So what is the category? It is something like social avoidance, and thus "social avoidance" is the interpretation of the factor.

Negative Factor Coefficients

This illustration, by the way, is based on Scale 0, Social Introversion, of the MMPI-2. Although we have given the essence of the items rather than reproducing the items verbatim, it is worth noting that the second and third items are reverse worded on the inventory. The items would thus be something like the following:

I try to avoid being in a crowd.

I like parties.

I enjoy social events.

If the factor is truly social avoidance, then the last two items would be negatively correlated with the factor. That is, those who were more socially avoidant would try harder to avoid crowds (positive correlation) but would be less enthused with parties (negative correlation) and would enjoy social events to a lesser extent (negative correlation). The variable weights on the factor would look like the following:

Variable	Factor 1
A	.95558
E	−.94828
B	−.93463

The negative values would simply indicate that the relationship between the variable and the factor is an inverse one. Remember that a correlation of .94 represents the same strength of relationship as −.94 because r^2 is always positive. Positive and negative structure or pattern coefficients simply reflect the way the variable is measured (e.g., the way an item is worded); stronger relationships, whether direct or inverse, still reflect more association on the factor.

Obliquely Rotated Factor Matrix

In an orthogonal rotation, the values in the rotated factor matrix represent both the correlations (structure coefficients) of the variables with the factors and the weights of the variables (pattern coefficients) in the linear function defining the variate (factor). The structure coefficients are equal to the weights in an orthogonal rotation precisely because the factors are independent of each other.

In an oblique rotation strategy, the factors are permitted to be correlated (and virtually always are, at least a little). Because the factors are no longer independent of (orthogonal to) each other, the weights of the variables in the linear function (variate, factor) no longer must be equal to the structure coefficients. Therefore, instead of the single rotated factor matrix produced by an orthogonal rotation strategy, an oblique rotation strategy generates two somewhat different rotated factor matrices, one presenting the weights of the variables in the linear function (pattern matrix) and one presenting the correlations of the variables with the factors (structure matrix).

▶ The *pattern matrix* presents what are called pattern coefficients. Pattern coefficients are the weights that have been assigned to variables in the linear functions (variates, factors). This is analogous to what is done in regression, and pattern coefficients are essentially multiple regression beta weights. To the extent that the factors are relatively strongly correlated these coefficients can (and occasionally do) go beyond the range of ±1.

▶ The *structure matrix* presents the structure coefficients. Structure coefficients depict the correlations between the variables and the factors (variates). They are true correlations and are therefore bounded by the range of ±1. Generally, these values tend to be just a bit higher than those of the pattern coefficients (except when the factors are very highly correlated), but using these coefficients in interpreting the factor solution should often result in the same characterization of the factors.

Recommendations

It may not surprise you to learn that different authors have offered alternative viewpoints on which obliquely rotated factor matrix researchers should use for their interpretation and hence which they should report to readers. Hair et al. (1998), Mertler and Vannatta (2001), and Tabachnick and Fidell (2001b) have proposed that the pattern matrix be used. On the other hand, Thompson (1984, 1991) has stressed the importance of the structure coefficients in interpreting classical parametric analyses, and Courville and Thompson (2001) have argued that the structure coefficients are important in factor analysis as well as in regression. In addition, Diekhoff (1992), Gorsuch (1983), and Pedhazur and Schmelkin (1991) urge that both structure and pattern coefficients be considered in interpreting factors.

Although it is possible that the pattern and structure matrices would provide somewhat different impressions about the nature of the underlying factor structure, it is frequently the case that the two pictures are relatively consonant with one another. That is, although the pattern coefficients may be somewhat larger if the factors are highly correlated and the structure coefficients may be somewhat higher if the factors are not highly correlated, they will very often result in a very similar interpretation. Thus, variables easily meeting your criterion for being accepted as relatively strongly representing a factor (e.g., variables loading in the range of .70 where your loading criterion is .40) are likely to emerge on the same factor in both the pattern and structure matrices. We do urge you to examine both matrices to determine if this sort of an outcome holds for your particular data analysis.

For the purposes of this discussion, we will assume that both the pattern and structure matrices yield similar interpretations. Because both ways of viewing the results are viable and useful, the choice as to which rotated factor matrix to present probably comes down to the language used in articulating the framework from which the research was derived. That is, if the theoretical framework conceptualized the factor loadings in terms of weights or in terms of correlations to the variate, then that is very likely the language you would want to maintain and that, in turn, tells you which of the two matrices you would present in communicating your results.

If that framework is neutral on which viewpoint is more reasonable to take, then your choice of which matrix to present may be driven by how comfortable you are in talking about weights versus structure coefficients. It seems to us that somewhat more researchers report the pattern matrix, and that alternative is a perfectly reasonable reporting strategy to follow. But the structure matrix presenting the variable-factor correlations may sometimes turn out to be a little clearer and a little easier to discuss and might therefore be considered for reporting on those occasions.

Selecting the Factor Solution

As you can deduce from our discussions in this chapter, there is no agreement on a single factor extraction method to use. And unless the factors are substantially correlated, in which case you should really use an oblique rotation, it is often a close call as to whether to report a varimax or an oblique rotation. Thus, you cannot follow a prescribed formula to achieve your factor analytic solution. In one of the editions of his classic testing textbook, Lee Cronbach (1970) said it very plainly: "There is no one 'right' way to do a factor analysis any more than there is a 'right' way to photograph Waikiki Beach" (p. 315). Cronbach's words are still true today.

The solution finally accepted by researchers is an informed but ultimately a subjective choice. Tabachnick and Fidell (2001b) suggested that at least for analyses containing up to about 40 variables, the number of factors whose eigenvalue is above 1.00 can be estimated in advance by dividing the number of variables by 3 to 5. In the majority of analyses, however, researchers are unlikely to accept that many components or factors in their final decision.

The choice of the factor solution is based on multiple features of the results, including the following:

▶ *The theoretical and empirical milieu.* Research is carried out in a context that allows researchers to speculate in advance of data collection what some of the themes underlying the data might be. Thus, although the guidelines here may appear quite data driven, they must always be taken with respect to what the researchers already know about the content domain under study.

▶ *The plot of the eigenvalues.* You do not want to get into the region of diminishing returns and will most likely select a solution before you reach that point.

▶ *The amount of variance accounted for by different solutions.* Accepting more factors will allow you to account for more of the variance, but at some point you may be identifying more factors than is reasonable for the construct. You can begin to see this when you find that the content of and the labels for a couple of the factors are difficult to tell apart. At that point, the increased amount of accounted-for variance is probably doing more harm than good.

▶ *The number of variables used to represent factors.* It is appropriate to have a decent number of variables taken as illustrating the factor. This is true for at least two reasons: (a) You want to be clear what the factor is, and more variables loading on the factor give you more information on which to base your interpretation, and (b) if you plan to create subscales based on the factor structure, you need enough variables that are highly correlated to the factor to achieve an acceptable level of reliability. Although it is difficult to provide an exact number of variables that will always meet these criteria, generally we can say that four or five items per factor is usually as small a count as you would ordinarily want to have.

▶ *The strength of the coefficients.* Even if you use a lenient loading criterion of .40, variables correlated with the factor near this lower limit are clearly not strongly related to the factor. Ideally, you should have enough variables in the .7 range or higher to not worry about bringing in variables that are in the .4s.

▶ *The reasonableness of the interpretation.* If you have to articulate a bottom line for characterizing what researchers finally select, this feature is it. As characterized by Johnson and Wichern (1998), ultimately, the selection of a factor structure is not judged on any single quantitative basis but rather on what they call a "Wow" criterion: "If, while scrutinizing the factor analysis, the investigator can shout 'Wow, I understand these factors,' the application is deemed successful" (p. 565). As it turns out, reasonableness emerges from the other considerations already mentioned. That is, solutions accounting for relatively small percentages of the variance (e.g., less than 40%) will tend not to have many variables with strong loadings showing up on the factors and are unlikely to be conducive to clear and forthright interpretation.

One strategy that we have found to be helpful in selecting the factor structure that is most reasonably interpreted is trying out a small range of factor solutions based on the scree plot and the amount of variance accounted for. Our intent in this process is to try to "surround" the solution that is most likely to be accepted (e.g., if we guess that either the three- or four-factor solution is going to be eventually selected, we would run the two-, three-, four-, and five-factor solutions). This process can be thought of as laying out the evolution of the factor structure, and it very often helps researchers with factor interpretation by making them aware of which variables have formed stable groupings over the multiple solution set. The bottom line, however, always rests squarely on the sensibility of the interpretation of the factor structure as formulated by the researchers.

Recommended Readings

Conway, J. M., & Huffcutt, A. I. (2004). A review and evaluation of exploratory factor analysis practices in organizational research. *Organizational Research Methods, 6,* 147–168.

Eysenck, H. J. (1952). The uses and abuses of factor analysis. *Applied Statistics, 1,* 45–49.

Fabrigar, L. R., Wegener, D. T., MacCallum, R. C., & Strahan, E. J. (1999). Evaluating the use of exploratory factor analysis in psychological research. *Psychological Methods, 4,* 272–299.

Gorsuch, R. L. (1990). Common factor analysis versus component analysis: Some well and little known facts. *Multivariate Behavioral Research, 25,* 33–39.

Hayton, J. C., Allen, D. G., & Scarpello, V. (2004). Factor retention decisions in exploratory factor analysis: A tutorial on parallel analysis. *Organizational Research Methods, 7,* 191–205.

Kline, P. (1994). *An easy guide to factor analysis.* New York: Routledge.

Pett, M. A., Lackey, N. R., & Sullivan, J. L. (2003). *Making sense of factor analysis: The use of factor analysis for instrument development in health care research.* Thousand Oaks, CA: Sage.

Spearman, C. (1904). "General intelligence," objectively determined and measured. *American Journal of Psychology, 15,* 201–293.

Thompson, B. (2004). *Exploratory and confirmatory factor analysis: Understanding concepts and applications.* Washington, DC: American Psychological Association.

Wood, J. M., Tataryn, D. J., & Gorsuch, R. L. (1996). Effects of under- and overextraction on principal axis factor analysis with varimax rotation. *Psychological Methods, 1,* 254–365.

Zwick, W. R., & Velicer, W. F. (1986). Comparison of five rules for determining the number of components to retain. *Psychological Bulletin, 99,* 432–442.

Principal Components and Factor Analysis Using SPSS

W e begin our SPSS example using a principal components extraction analysis paired with a varimax rotation, one of the most popular factor analytic approaches. A second example using principal axis factoring and an oblique (direct oblimin) rotation follows. Both are described in some detail.

Preparing to Run a Principal Components Analysis With a Varimax Rotation

The present example is adapted from a larger study by Gamst et al. (2004) that explored the cultural competence of 1,244 mental health providers in California. Participants completed a number of instruments, including four self-report cultural competence questionnaires: the Multicultural Awareness, Knowledge, Skills Survey (MAKSS; D'Andrea, Daniels, & Heck, 1991), the Multicultural Counseling Awareness Scale (MCAS-B; Ponterotto & Alexander, 1996), the Cross-Cultural Counseling Inventory–Revised (CCCI–R; LaFromboise, Coleman, & Hernandez, 1991), and the Multicultural Competency and Training Survey (MCCTS; Holcomb-McCoy, 2000). The 157 items making up these four instruments were measured on a 4-point summative response scale ranging from *strongly disagree* (1) to *strongly agree* (4).

Begin by entering SPSS and open your SPSS save file by clicking **File** → **Open** → **Data** and selecting the SPSS data file you wish to analyze.

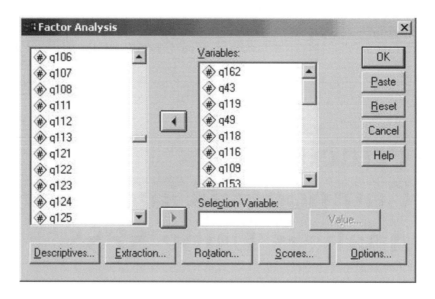

Figure 12b.1 Factor Analysis Main Dialog Box

Getting to Factor Analysis

To begin our analyses we click **Analyze → Data Reduction → Factor.** This action produces our first SPSS dialog box: **Factor Analysis,** and we show this dialog box in Figure 12b.1.

The left panel of this box lists all the variables in our file. By successively clicking variables in the left panel and then clicking the right arrow, we can move the target variables (in the present example, individual cultural competence items) over to the variables list panel on the right side. For the present example, the 21 items we plan to factor analyze have been moved over. We did not select the variables in numerical order because we wanted to keep items from the same source together in our variable list; thus, our listing starts with **Q162**, then **Q43**, and so on. Variables can be selected in any order, and usually one selects variables from the first to the last as they appear in the data file.

The pushbuttons at the bottom of the dialog box (**Descriptives**, **Extraction**, **Rotation**, **Scores**, and **Options**) provide the researcher with a variety of procedural choices to which we will now turn our attention.

By clicking the **Descriptives** pushbutton, the **Factor Analysis**: **Descriptives** dialog box is produced. We reproduce this box in Figure 12b.2. This dialog box is composed of two sections: **Statistics** and **Correlation Matrix.**

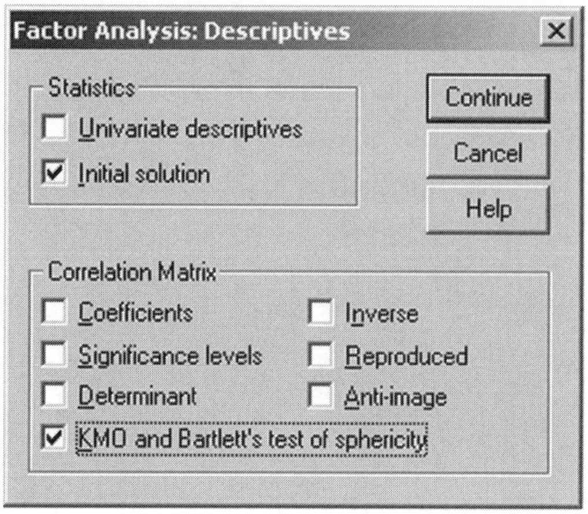

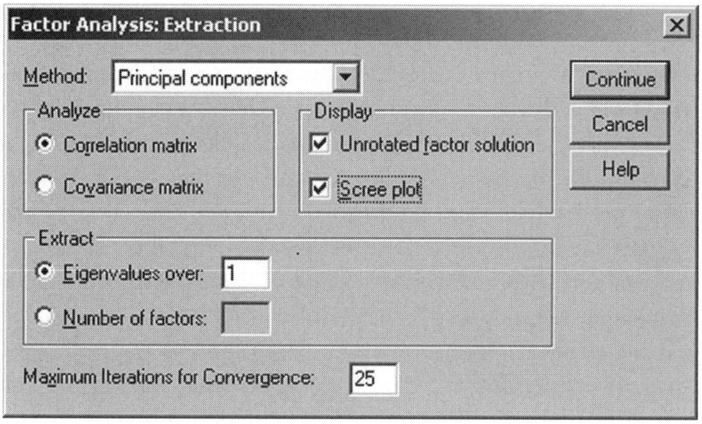

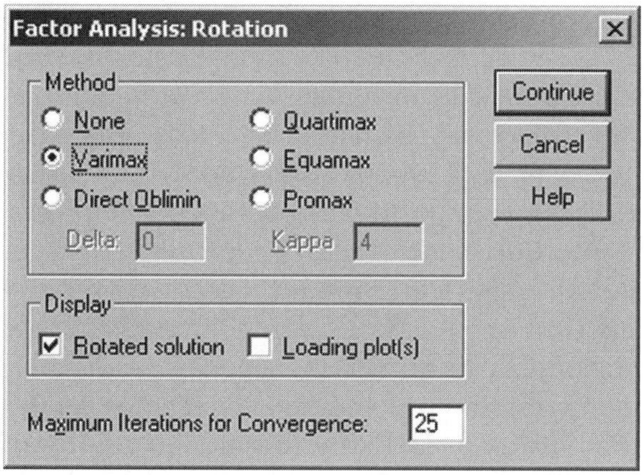

Figure 12b.2 Dialog Boxes for Descriptives, Extraction, Rotation, and Options From the Factor Analysis Main Dialog Box

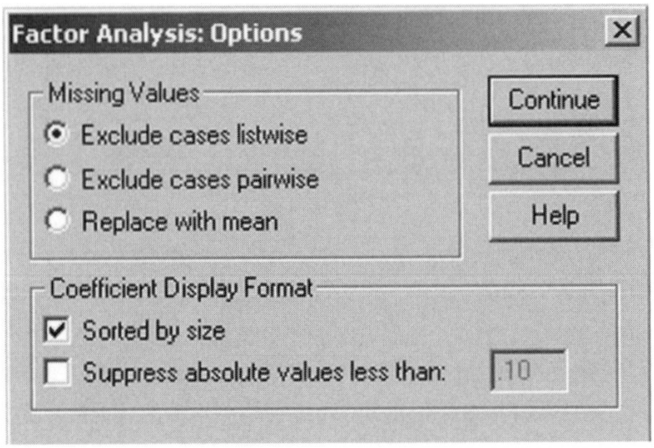

Figure 12b.2 (Continued)

The **Statistics** section provides two options. Clicking **Univariate descriptives** will provide the number of valid cases, mean, and standard deviation for each variable. The **Initial solution** checkbox will produce an initial (unrotated) solution, including communalities, eigenvalues, and percentage of variance explained, which can be compared with the final (rotated) solution.

The **Correlation Matrix** section produces eight separate options, including a Pearson correlation matrix (**Coefficients**) with significance levels for all variables in the analysis. These Pearson coefficients should be scanned to check for consistent patterns of variability or relationships between variables. We recommend this inspection be conducted during the initial data screening and univariate/multivariate assumption violation check discussed in Chapters 3A and 3B. Clicking on the **KMO and Bartlett's test of sphericity** checkbox produces the Kaiser-Meyer-Olkin (KMO) measure of sampling adequacy, which is a rough indicator of how adequate the correlations are for factor analysis. As a general heuristic (see Kaiser, 1970, 1974), a value of .70 or above is considered adequate. Bartlett's test of sphericity provides the investigator with a test of the null hypothesis that none of the variables are significantly correlated. This test should be significant before proceeding with the factor analysis. The **Correlation Matrix** section can also generate several other items, including the **Determinant**, and the **Inverse**, **Reproduced**, and **Anti-image** correlation matrices, which are useful for specialized diagnostic considerations but are beyond the scope of our discussion.

Clicking the **Extraction** pushbutton of the **Factor Analysis** dialog box produces the **Factor Analysis: Extraction** dialog box shown also in Figure 12b.2. This box is composed of five sections: **Method**, **Analyze**, **Display**, **Extract**, and **Maximum Iterations for Convergence**.

The **Method** box allows the investigator to choose from one of seven methods of factor (or component) extraction. We have chosen to use the **Principal components** method (the default option) in this example.

The **Analyze** panel enables the investigator to produce either the **Correlation** or the **Covariance matrix**. We have chosen the correlation matrix here.

The **Display** panel allows the researcher to obtain an **Unrotated factor solution** and a **Scree plot**. The unrotated solution, although certainly optional, can be helpful to the investigator when it is compared with the final rotated solution. The **Scree plot** provides one source of information researchers generally use to determine the number of factors or components they will accept in the final solution.

The **Extract** panel defaults to selecting factors or components whose eigenvalues exceed 1. We encourage use of this default as well as the scree plot to help guide your decision making. Should theoretical or pragmatic circumstances dictate, investigators can override this constraint and provide their own selection criteria. Because we have a working familiarity with this data set, we can say in advance that the solution emerging from this analysis is the most viable one.

Last, the **Maximum Iterations for Convergence** section defaults at 25 iterations or algorithmic passes to achieve a solution. We have kept the default here.

The **Factor Analysis**: **Rotation** dialog box can be produced by clicking the **Rotation** pushbutton of the **Factor Analysis** dialog box. We present this also in Figure 12b.2. The **Rotation** dialog box consists of three sections: **Method, Display**, and **Maximum Iterations for Convergence**.

The **Method** section provides the researcher with a variety of factor rotation methods, including **Varimax**, **Direct Oblimin**, **Quartimax**, **Equamax**, and **Promax**. For this example, we have chosen the **Varimax** procedure. The **Display** section enables researchers to obtain the **Rotated solution** and the **Loading plot(s)** of the first two or three factors. We wish to take a look at the rotated solution but will bypass the loading plots.

Investigators can control the **Maximum Iterations for Convergence** (steps) needed for SPSS to perform the rotation. The default is set at 25 and we have left it at that.

Clicking the **Options** pushbutton of the **Factor Analysis** dialog box produces the **Factor Analysis**: **Options** dialog box also shown in Figure 12b.2. The **Options** dialog box has two sections: **Missing Values** and **Coefficient Display Format**.

The **Missing Values** section allows researchers to **Exclude cases listwise** (the default), **Exclude cases pairwise**, or **Replace with mean** of the particular variable. We have selected listwise deletion of cases.

The **Coefficient Display Format** section allows the investigator to sort the factor weightings by size and to suppress weightings with absolute values less than a specified value. Sorting coefficients by size usually makes it easier for researchers to comprehend the results, and we have chosen this form of display.

One other pushbutton (**Scores**) is available from the **Factor Analysis** dialog box. Clicking **Scores** produces a **Factor Analysis**: **Factor Scores** dialog box. This box allows researchers to create a new variable for each factor (component) derived from the analysis. Although this approach is both valid and legitimate, most researchers compute scale scores by taking the mean (or the sum) of the items that are "loaded" or relatively highly correlated with the factor. In the former procedure, each factor score is composed of all the variables; the factors are differentiated by the different weights assigned to each variable. In the latter procedure, variables received equal (unitary) weights regardless of their factor weights; each factor is ordinarily represented by a different and independent set of variables.

The Output From a Principal
Components Analysis With a Varimax Rotation

We have now set up the parameters to run a principal components analysis with SPSS using data based on the self-reported cultural competency of 1,244 California mental health practitioners. Let's see what the analyses suggest.

Assume that prior to running our principal components analysis (i.e., during our data screening phase) we examined our descriptive statistics and our interitem correlations, and checked for assumption violations. Further assume that we noted during this initial assessment that our variables were all measured on a quantitative scale, that each pair of variables appeared to be bivariate normally distributed, and that each respondent or case was independent of one another. Assume that we also noted that the large sample size indicates that our variables-to-cases ratio is optimal. We are therefore now ready to look at the principal components output.

The first output table of Figure 12b.3 shows the results of the KMO and Bartlett's test of sphericity assessments by means of a **KMO and Bartlett's test** table. The results from both tests look good. A KMO coefficient in the high .8s suggests that the data are suitable for principal components analysis. Likewise, a significant Bartlett's test enables us to reject the null hypothesis of lack of sufficient correlation between the variables. These two results give us confidence to proceed with the analysis.

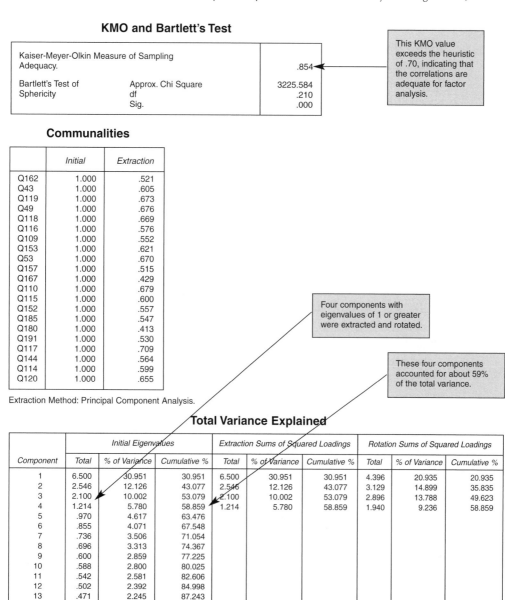

KMO and Bartlett's Test

Kaiser-Meyer-Olkin Measure of Sampling Adequacy.		.854
Bartlett's Test of Sphericity	Approx. Chi Square	3225.584
	df	.210
	Sig.	.000

> This KMO value exceeds the heuristic of .70, indicating that the correlations are adequate for factor analysis.

Communalities

	Initial	Extraction
Q162	1.000	.521
Q43	1.000	.605
Q119	1.000	.673
Q49	1.000	.676
Q118	1.000	.669
Q116	1.000	.576
Q109	1.000	.552
Q153	1.000	.621
Q53	1.000	.670
Q157	1.000	.515
Q167	1.000	.429
Q110	1.000	.679
Q115	1.000	.600
Q152	1.000	.557
Q185	1.000	.547
Q180	1.000	.413
Q191	1.000	.530
Q117	1.000	.709
Q144	1.000	.564
Q114	1.000	.599
Q120	1.000	.655

Extraction Method: Principal Component Analysis.

> Four components with eigenvalues of 1 or greater were extracted and rotated.

> These four components accounted for about 59% of the total variance.

Total Variance Explained

Component	Initial Eigenvalues			Extraction Sums of Squared Loadings			Rotation Sums of Squared Loadings		
	Total	% of Variance	Cumulative %	Total	% of Variance	Cumulative %	Total	% of Variance	Cumulative %
1	6.500	30.951	30.951	6.500	30.951	30.951	4.396	20.935	20.935
2	2.546	12.126	43.077	2.546	12.126	43.077	3.129	14.899	35.835
3	2.100	10.002	53.079	2.100	10.002	53.079	2.896	13.788	49.623
4	1.214	5.780	58.859	1.214	5.780	58.859	1.940	9.236	58.859
5	.970	4.617	63.476						
6	.855	4.071	67.548						
7	.736	3.506	71.054						
8	.696	3.313	74.367						
9	.600	2.859	77.225						
10	.588	2.800	80.025						
11	.542	2.581	82.606						
12	.502	2.392	84.998						
13	.471	2.245	87.243						
14	.447	2.130	89.373						
15	.434	2.069	91.441						
16	.407	1.939	93.380						
17	.359	1.709	95.090						
18	.346	1.646	96.736						
19	.314	1.495	98.230						
20	.242	1.155	99.385						
21	.129	.615	100.000						

Extraction Method: Principal Component Analysis.

Figure 12b.3 Selected Output Tables From the Principal Components Analysis

The next output table provides the communalities for the **Initial** and **Extraction** (i.e., final) principal components solution. As can be seen, in a principal components solution, the initial communalities are equal to 1.00. This means that all the variance is accounted for by each variable because principal components will create as many components as there are variables. Another way to think of this is to say that each variable is fully (1.00 or 100%) involved in the solution (because the solution goes to completion).

The **Extraction** (final) solution produces communalities that are less than 1.00 because the final solution retains only components that have eigenvalues greater than 1.00 (the SPSS default). Thus, less than the total amount of variance within the original items is captured. These communalities, sometimes symbolized as h^2, are based on the factor matrix (component matrix in this present analysis) that we discussed in Chapter 12A and will cover here in a moment. They are computed by summing the squared factor weights across each row of the matrix. Communalities at this stage of the analysis indicate the degree to which each variable is participating or contributing to (is captured by) the component solution. Researchers should inspect the **Extraction** communalities for any variables that appear to be particularly low. Such items may be candidates for removal from the analysis. After inspection of this table, we conclude that no such items are present, and proceed with the analysis.

The third output table of Figure 12b.3 summarizes the amount of variance accounted for by each component after the **Initial** part of the analysis, the **Extraction** phase of the analysis, and the **Rotation** phase of the analysis. Each row provides information on a component given the other components that have already been extracted. The left portion of the table labeled **Initial Eigenvalues** represents the solution having gone to completion. Thus, 21 components were extracted, accounting for 100% of the variance.

The default for SPSS, which we allowed to be in effect for this analysis, was to take seriously only those components with eigenvalues of 1.00 or greater. As can be seen in the portion labeled as **Extraction Sums of Squares Loadings,** only four factors reached this default criterion. The first component in an unrotated solution always accounts for the most variance—in this case, about 31%, followed by the second component, which accounted for about 12%, and so on. The total amount of variance accounted for by the first four principal components solution was about 59%. In practice, a robust solution should account for at least 50% of the variance (Tabachnick & Fidell, 2001b). The extraction and rotated cumulative percentage of variances accounted for (shown in the left portion of

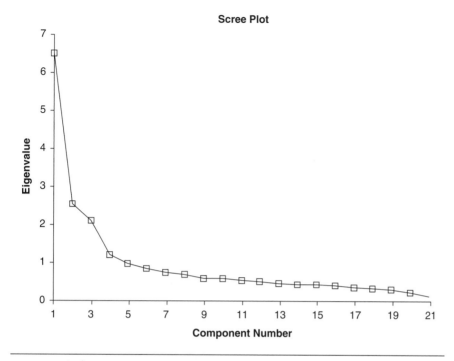

Figure 12b.4   Scree Plot of the Eigenvalues for the Principal Components Analysis

Figure 12b.3) will always be the same value. However, the rotated solution spreads the variability more evenly across the four components (factors).

Figure 12b.4 shows the **Scree Plot** for the initial (complete) solution. It is a graphical way of helping researchers determine how many components or factors to include in the solution that they will ultimately accept. This figure contains the eigenvalues on the Y (horizontal) axis and the component number on the X (vertical) axis. Researchers look to see where the curve turns or "flattens out" across the components. The scree plot takes its name from the debris that piles up on the sides of a volcano or a mountain. The turning point, in this case at Component 4, indicates a transition point between components with high and low eigenvalues. This plot confirms our previous observation derived from the **Total Variance Explained** table (Figure 12b.3) that four components best describes our principal components solution.

The **Unrotated Component Matrix** is shown in Figure 12b.5. Values in the array are correlations between the variables and the components. Thus, Variable **Q120** is correlated .774 with Component 1, −.186 with Component 2, and so on. This output is also the source of the communality results we showed in Figure 12b.3. For example, the communality of **Q162**

Component Matrix[a]

	Component			
	1	2	3	4
Q120	.774	−.186	−.077	−.124
Q114	.711	−.066	−.276	−.113
Q115	.703	−.213	−.225	−.101
Q119	.669	−.448	−.143	−.070
Q117	.663	−.454	−.238	−.088
Q118	.659	−.388	−.284	−.053
Q116	.641	−.302	−.249	−.112
Q180	.553	.242	−.022	−.218
Q152	.541	.489	.042	−.150
Q167	.540	.343	−.054	−.129
Q162	.371	.618	.005	−.036
Q153	.442	.586	.064	−.280
Q157	.360	.563	.040	−.257
Q110	.478	−.219	.598	.210
Q191	.443	−.061	.573	.045
Q185	.465	−.082	.569	.013
Q144	.520	−.026	.540	−.035
Q109	.447	−.212	.516	.203
Q53	.485	.128	−.307	.570
Q49	.490	.386	−.134	.519
Q43	.477	.294	−.238	.483

Extraction Method: Principal Component Analysis.

a. 4 components extracted.

Rotated Component Matrix[a]

	Component			
	1	2	3	4
Q117	.826	−.023	.146	.074
Q118	.801	.010	.099	.135
Q119	.783	−.021	.233	.067
Q116	.741	.096	.095	.092
Q115	.727	.189	.128	.141
Q120	.707	.257	.278	.112
Q114	.680	.312	.057	.189
Q153	.047	.780	.087	.052
Q157	.005	.715	.040	.045
Q152	.147	.694	.152	.174
Q162	−.052	.669	.042	.264
Q167	.257	.568	.098	.177
Q180	.326	.533	.135	.066
Q110	.157	−.026	.801	.108
Q109	.167	−.034	.714	.117
Q185	.133	.158	.710	−.019
Q191	.098	.151	.705	.007
Q144	.167	.247	.689	−.019
Q53	.276	.072	.020	.767
Q49	.085	.303	.114	.751
Q43	.175	.238	.030	.719

We have highlighted the items that correlate most strongly with their respected factor.

Extraction Method: Principal Component Analysis.
Rotation Method: Varimax with Kaiser Normalization.

a. Rotation converged in 5 iterations.

Figure 12b.5 Component Matrix Summarizing the Extraction Phase and Varimax Rotated Component Matrix

is shown in Figure 12b.3 as .521. That value is equal to the sum of the squared correlations (unrotated weightings) shown in Table 12b.5. Examining the row representing **Q162** confirms this ($.371^2 + .618^2 + .005^2 + -.036^2 = .520886$, which rounds to .521).

Notice that the correlations for the first component are generally moderately high. The highest weighting is seen for **Q120** (it is .774), but there are only two more in the .7s. At the same time, the weakest weights are still in the .3s. This illustrates the "one solution fits all" strategy when the least squares solution is applied.

Although there are some moderately high weightings for some variables on other components, there are not that many and they are not all that high. We see, for example, that the highest weighting on **Component 2** is for **Q162** with a correlation of .618 and only two variables (**Q162** and **Q157**) are weighted as high as the .5s. **Component 4** has only three variables showing any weighting of worth, and these are not especially strong.

The **Rotated Component Matrix**, also presented in Figure 12b.5, provides the "heart" of our SPSS principal components output. Some investigators prefer to suppress the printing of component weightings below a certain magnitude (e.g., .30) to simplify the presentation. We have chosen to display all the coefficients. The "sorting by size" format that we checked in the **Options** dialog box, although operative in the previous table, can be best seen here. Variables are ordered by correlations within each of the components starting with **Component 1**. We see that **Q117** had the highest and **Q114** had the lowest correlation on the first component and so appear in order at the top of the list. **Q153** was the highest correlated variable on **Component 2** and so appears directly under **Q114**. A casual inspection of this rotated component matrix shows that the solution has moved in the direction of simple structure. Not only has the first component been somewhat "deflated," correlations on all components have been "sharpened" in that they are either relatively high or relatively low.

It is with respect to Figure 12b.5 that the science of objectively evaluating the dispersion of each variable's correlation on each component occurs. Conversely, the art of principal components (or factor) analysis occurs when researchers creatively decide the essence of each component by creating an identifying component name. Selecting a component name is typically driven by the nature of the most highly weighted items (e.g., items in the .7s or .8s) of the component. This information is found by inspecting each variable's correlation on each respective component. Ideally, investigators hope to find that each variable will have a relatively high correlation on one component (or factor) and relatively low correlations on the remaining components.

Careful inspection of Figure 12b.5 suggests that this is the case. For example, Variables **Q117** through **Q114** all have high correlations on **Component 1** and low correlations on **Components 2, 3,** and **4**. The researcher can then scrutinize these seven items to determine their underlying commonality or essential nature.

The content of the items are shown in Table 12b.1 toward the end of this chapter, ordered in the same way as the rotated components matrix. Interpretation of components or factors is based on item content. Researchers study what the items of a factor relate to and attempt to determine what they have in common—that is, what the underlying theme or dimension may be that ties them together. This theme is the label given to the variate (the component or factor).

The first seven items were found to correlate to the first component. From the item wording shown in Table 12b.1, these items all seem to be related to mental health practitioners' understanding of issues relating to sexuality, gender, aging, social class, and disability; thus, we refer to this component as non-ethnic ability. Variables **Q153** through **Q180** all correlate relatively highly and exclusively on **Component 2**. These six items deal with mental health practitioner multicultural awareness. The next five items (**Q110–Q144**) appear to be related to practitioners' multicultural knowledge. The last three items (**Q53, Q49,** and **Q43**) all have high correlations on **Component 4**. These last items encompass practitioner multicultural sensitivity to mental health consumers.

Our task was simplified (for presentation purposes) by the small number of variables (21) entered into the principal components analysis. In practice, researchers routinely factor analyze large numbers of variables (e.g., 30, 50, 100, or more) simultaneously. With large arrays of items, investigators should be deliberate in their inspection of the rotated component matrix. We encourage the adoption of this simple process. Line up a ruler underneath the first variable in the **Rotated Component Matrix**—in the present example, **Q117**. Using a highlight marker, underscore the highest weighting for that variable. If there happens to be more than one relatively high weighting, then highlight all of them for that variable. Repeat this process for each variable in turn. Through this process, the underlying structure should begin to emerge and then the more creative process of imposing meanings by labeling components (factors) can begin.

We have now achieved our goal of data reduction by reducing an array of 21 multicultural mental health practitioner statements into four orthogonal (uncorrelated) principal components. At this point, we can begin to use these components as "analytical devices" or composite variables where we average an individual respondent's scores on the items that compose each of the four components. These new composite variables can then be used as dependent variables in subsequent statistical analyses.

Principal Axis Factoring With an Oblique Rotation

Using the same multicultural self-report data as before, we will now demonstrate how to conduct a factor analysis using a popular extraction technique called *principal axis* factoring. We will pair this with an oblique rotation technique called *oblimin*.

The process to now run the second analysis is very similar to the first. Only two of the dialog boxes need to be changed to accomplish this next analysis. In the **Factor Analysis**: **Extraction** dialog box, pull down the **Method** menu and select **Principal axis factoring**. Again, we request a **Correlation matrix**, an **Unrotated factor solution**, and a **Scree plot**. We will also ask for extraction of those factors whose **Eigenvalues** exceed 1.00. This is shown in Figure 12b.6.

Click the **Rotation** pushbutton to arrive at the **Factor Analysis**: **Rotation** dialog box (shown also in Figure 12b.6). Enter the **Method** section and click **Direct Oblimin.** Leave the **Delta** setting at **0** (the default). The delta setting is the way SPSS sets the limits on the degree of correlation it permits the factors to achieve. A delta value of 0 allows for a fair amount of correlation and can usually serve the purposes of most researchers most of the time. In the **Display** section of the **Rotation** dialog box we click the **Rotated solution** option.

The extraction phase is summarized in the **Total Variance Explained** table shown in Figure 12b.7. A quick inspection of this table is similar but not identical to what we found in our previous principal components analysis. The results labeled **Initial Eigenvalues** are the same as they were for the last analysis because in principal axis factoring, a principal components analysis is done initially. But then, as we have seen in Chapter 12A, the focus changed. Unlike principal components analysis, which analyzes the total variance, factor analysis deals with only the common variance. Principal axis factoring (also called principal factors analysis) substitutes commonalities for 1s on the diagonal of the correlation matrix and then extracts factors to account for the shared variance.

In its focus on the common variance, principal factors identified only three factors with eigenvalues over 1.00. These three factors cumulatively accounted for about 49% of the shared or common variance with this extraction method. This may be compared with the 59% of explained variance accounted for by the principal components analysis. Such a drop in explained variance occurs because variance not shared among the variables

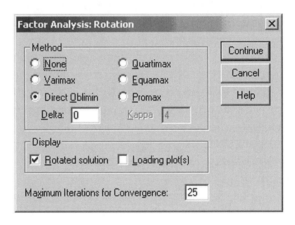

Figure 12b.6 Dialog Boxes for Extraction and Rotation From the Factor Analysis Main Dialog Box

is automatically not possible to be accounted for by the factor analysis procedures. Thus, principal axis (or any of the factor analyses) will therefore explain less variance than will be attributed to principal components.

The four-factor unrotated factor matrix is presented in Figure 12b.8 even though only three factors achieved eigenvalues over 1.00. We have done this for two reasons: (a) This allows us to contrast this outcome with the prior one, and (b) the three-factor solution was not nearly as interpretable as the four-component solution (that was ultimately selected by the researchers). Inspection of Figure 12b.8 suggests a pattern of results roughly similar to that found with the principal components solution. The first factor once again has relatively high to moderate correlations for all the variables, and

Total Variance Explained

Factor	Initial Eigenvalues			Extraction Sums of Squared Loadings			Rotation
	Total	% of Variance	Cumulative %	Total	% of Variance	Cumulative %	Total
1	6.500	30.951	30.951	6.019	28.664	28.664	4.985
2	2.546	12.126	43.077	2.046	9.745	38.408	3.324
3	2.100	10.002	53.079	1.591	7.578	45.987	3.038
4	1.214	5.780	58.859	.705	3.356	49.343	3.436
5	.970	4.617	63.476				
6	.855	4.071	67.548				
7	.736	3.506	71.054				
8	.696	3.313	74.367				
9	.600	2.859	77.225				
10	.588	2.800	80.025				
11	.542	2.581	82.606				
12	.502	2.392	84.998				
13	.471	2.245	87.243				
14	.447	2.130	89.373				
15	.434	2.069	91.441				
16	.407	1.939	93.380				
17	.359	1.709	95.090				
18	.346	1.646	96.736				
19	.314	1.495	98.230				
20	.242	1.155	99.385				
21	.129	.615	100.000				

Extraction Method: Principal Axis Factoring.

a. When factors are correlated, sums of squared loadings cannot be added to obtain a total variance.

The four factor principle axis solution accounted for about 49% of the common variance.

Figure 12b.7 Eigenvalues and Variance Accounted for by the Principal Axis Factoring

the correlations on the other factors are not very high. Notice that only three correlations on **Factor 4** are greater than .30 and that no variable showed its highest correlation on that factor. Such a result is not surprising given that the fourth factor did not reach an eigenvalue of 1.00.

Unlike orthogonal rotations such as varimax that produce one rotated solution matrix, oblique rotations such as oblimin produce two matrices: the **Pattern Matrix** and the **Structure Matrix** (both shown in Figure 12b.9). As we indicated previously, there has been a fair amount of discussion within the multivariate statistics literature as to which matrix to use. In practice, both often provide fairly comparable results; the main difference is that the pattern matrix reports the weightings in standardized

Factor Matrix[a]

	Factor			
	1	2	3	4
Q120	.759	−.159	−.054	−.107
Q114	.688	−.054	−.238	−.086
Q115	.681	−.185	−.183	−.082
Q117	.658	−.435	−.202	−.063
Q119	.658	−.413	−.106	−.049
Q118	.649	−.367	−.245	−.028
Q116	.616	−.261	−.193	−.076
Q152	.515	.450	.019	−.131
Q180	.513	.209	−.022	−.126
Q167	.502	.296	−.055	−.076
Q144	.495	.007	.467	−.030
Q49	.471	.365	−.131	.418
Q53	.464	.119	−.263	.442
Q43	.450	.261	−.203	.328
Q153	.423	.547	.033	−.251
Q162	.346	.536	−.018	−.034
Q157	.335	.481	.010	−.189
Q110	.467	−.171	.579	.176
Q185	.439	−.042	.481	.005
Q191	.417	−.022	.477	.025
Q109	.424	−.154	.451	.133

Extraction Method: Principal Axis Factoring.

a. 4 factors extracted. 7 iterations required.

Figure 12b.8 Factor Matrix for the Four-Factor Principal Axis Extraction

form (analogous to beta weights in multiple regression), whereas the structure matrix provides the structure coefficients representing the correlations of the variables to the factors.

As can be seen in both the **Pattern** and **Structure matrices**, fairly comparable correlations are found between the two. Generally, the pattern matrix produces slightly higher correlations for the more highly correlated items, and the structure matrix produces slightly higher correlations for the more weakly correlated items within each factor. This factor solution based on principal factors extraction and oblique rotation, although differing in the amount of explained variance and showing slightly different numerical correlations from the one derived based on principal components extraction and varimax rotation, nonetheless yielded very similar interpretations of the underlying structure of the variables. That is, exactly the same variables in virtually the same order correlated on the same factors. The only

Pattern Matrix[a]

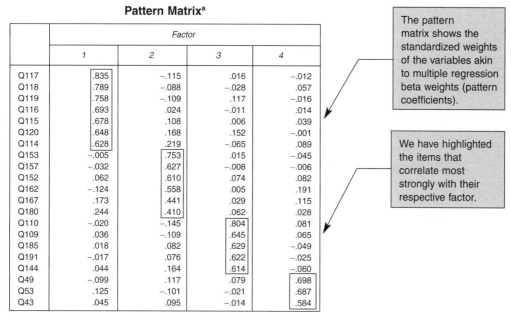

	Factor			
	1	2	3	4
Q117	.835	−.115	.016	−.012
Q118	.789	−.088	−.028	.057
Q119	.758	−.109	.117	−.016
Q116	.693	.024	−.011	.014
Q115	.678	.108	.006	.039
Q120	.648	.168	.152	−.001
Q114	.628	.219	−.065	.089
Q153	−.005	.753	.015	−.045
Q157	−.032	.627	−.008	−.006
Q152	.062	.610	.074	.082
Q162	−.124	.558	.005	.191
Q167	.173	.441	.029	.115
Q180	.244	.410	.062	.028
Q110	−.020	−.145	.804	.081
Q109	.036	−.109	.645	.065
Q185	.018	.082	.629	−.049
Q191	−.017	.076	.622	−.025
Q144	.044	.164	.614	−.060
Q49	−.099	.117	.079	.698
Q53	.125	−.101	−.021	.687
Q43	.045	.095	−.014	.584

The pattern matrix shows the standardized weights of the variables akin to multiple regression beta weights (pattern coefficients).

We have highlighted the items that correlate most strongly with their respective factor.

Extraction Method: Principal Axis Factoring.
Rotation Method: Oblimin with Kaiser Normalization.
a. Rotation converged in 5 iterations.

Structure Matrix

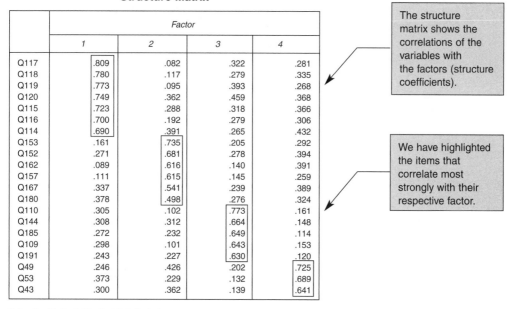

	Factor			
	1	2	3	4
Q117	.809	.082	.322	.281
Q118	.780	.117	.279	.335
Q119	.773	.095	.393	.268
Q120	.749	.362	.459	.368
Q115	.723	.288	.318	.366
Q116	.700	.192	.279	.306
Q114	.690	.391	.265	.432
Q153	.161	.735	.205	.292
Q152	.271	.681	.278	.394
Q162	.089	.616	.140	.391
Q157	.111	.615	.145	.259
Q167	.337	.541	.239	.389
Q180	.378	.498	.276	.324
Q110	.305	.102	.773	.161
Q144	.308	.312	.664	.148
Q185	.272	.232	.649	.114
Q109	.298	.101	.643	.153
Q191	.243	.227	.630	.120
Q49	.246	.426	.202	.725
Q53	.373	.229	.132	.689
Q43	.300	.362	.139	.641

The structure matrix shows the correlations of the variables with the factors (structure coefficients).

We have highlighted the items that correlate most strongly with their respective factor.

Extraction Method: Principal Axis Factoring.
Rotation Method: Oblimin with Kaiser Normalization.

Figure 12b.9 Pattern Matrix and Structure Matrix for the Principal Axis Solution With an Oblique Rotation

exception can be seen on **Factor 4** where here **Q49** correlated more strongly than **Q53,** whereas the reverse was true on **Component 4**; however, the correlations are so close in both cases that the reordering is trivial. In the present example, the **Structure Matrix** also produced a pattern of moderate correlations on **Factor 3** and **Factor 4** that are not present in the **Pattern Matrix**. These correlations make the interpretation more ambiguous with the **Structure Matrix** and thus, we would encourage the use of the **Pattern Matrix** for this example.

As a conclusion to this analysis, consider Figure 12b.10, which depicts the **Factor Correlation Matrix** for this oblique rotation. As can be seen, all the factors show low to moderate correlations between factor pairs. Specifically, **Factor 1** seems to be moderately correlated with **Factor 3** and **Factor 4,** whereas **Factor 2** has a moderate correlation with **Factor 4** and low correlations with **Factor 1** and **Factor 3**.

Factor Correlation Matrix

Factor	1	2	3	4
1	1.000	.238	.406	.409
2	.238	1.000	.267	.447
3	.406	.267	1.000	.189
4	.409	.447	.189	1.000

Extraction Method: Principal Axis Factoring.
Rotation Method: Oblimin with Kaiser
   Normalization.

Figure 12b.10   Correlations of the Principal Axis Factors

Results

An exploratory factor analysis using a principal component extraction method and a varimax rotation of 21 self-report cultural competence items was conducted on a random sample (n = 415) of 1,244 California mental health providers. Prior to running the analysis with SPSS, the data were screened by examining descriptive statistics on each item, interitem correlations, and possible univariate and multivariate assumption violations. From this initial assessment, all variables were found to be interval-like, variable pairs appeared to be bivariate normally distributed, and all cases were independent of one another. Because of the large sample size, the variables-to-cases ratio was deemed adequate. The Kaiser-Meyer-Olkin measure of sampling adequacy was .85, indicating that the present data were suitable for principal components analysis. Similarly, Bartlett's test of sphericity was significant ($p < .001$), indicating sufficient correlation between the variables to proceed with the analysis.

Using the Kaiser-Guttman retention criterion of eigenvalues greater than 1.0, a four-factor solution provided the clearest extraction. These four factors accounted for 59% of the total variance. Table 12b.1 presents the 21 items, the original scale and subscale they came from, their factor correlations, communality estimates, and item-total correlations. Communalities were fairly high for each of the 21 items, with a range of .51 to .71.

Factor 1: Non-Ethnic Ability (eigenvalue = 6.50) accounted for 31% of the variance and had seven items; Factor 2: Awareness of Cultural Barriers (eigenvalue = 2.55) and accounted for 12.1% of the variance and had six items; Factor 3: Multicultural Knowledge (eigenvalue = 2.10) accounted for 10% of the variance and had five items; and Factor 4: Sensitivity to Consumers (eigenvalue = 1.21) accounted for 5.8% of the variance and had three items. Corrected item-total correlation ranged from .33 to .70, and Cronbach's coefficient alpha ranged from .75 to .90 among the four factors, indicating good subscale reliability.

The rationale used in naming these four factors was guided in part by the recommendations of Comrey and Lee (1992) and Rummel (1970) in which sorted factor weights in excess of .65 were used to "drive" the process of labeling and interpreting each factor. The present four-factor model was deemed the best solution because of its conceptual clarity and ease of interpretability.

Table 12b.1 Summary of Items and Factor Loadings From Principal Components Analysis
With Varimax Rotation ($N = 415$)*

Variable	Scale Origin	Original Subscale Item Name	Component Loading				Communality	Corrected Item-Total Correlation
			1	2	3	4		
Q117	MAKSS	I have an excellent ability to assess accurately the mental health needs of gay men.	**.83**	−.02	.15	−.07	.71	.55
Q118	MAKSS	I have an excellent ability to assess accurately the mental health needs of lesbians.	**.80**	**−.01**	−.09	.14	.67	.55
Q119	MAKSS	I have an excellent ability to assess accurately the mental health needs of persons with disabilities.	**.78**	−.02	.23	−.06	.67	.56
Q116	MAKSS	I have an excellent ability to assess accurately the mental health needs of older adults.	**.74**	.09	.09	.09	.58	.53
Q115	MAKSS	I have an excellent ability to assess accurately the mental health needs of men.	**.73**	.19	.13	.14	.60	.61
Q120	MAKSS	I have an excellent ability to assess accurately the mental health needs of persons who come from very poor socioeconomic backgrounds.	**.71**	.26	.28	.11	.66	.70

Variable	Scale Origin	Original Subscale Item Name	Component Loading				Communality	Corrected Item-Total Correlation
			1	2	3	4		
Q114	MAKSS	I have an excellent ability to assess accurately the mental health needs of women.	**.68**	.31	.06	.19	.60	.62
Q153	MCA-SB	I am aware that counselors frequently impose their own cultural values upon minority clients.	.05	**.78**	.09	.05	.62	.41
Q157	MCA-SB	I am aware that being born a White person in this society carries with it certain advantages.	.01	**.72**	.04	.05	.52	.33
Q152	MCA-SB	I am aware of institutional barriers that may inhibit minorities from using mental health services.	.15	**.69**	.15	.17	.56	.50
Q162	MCA-SB	I am aware that being born a minority in this society brings with it certain challenges that White people do not have to face.	.–05	**.67**	.04	.26	.52	.35
Q167	MCCTS	I am aware of how much my cultural background and experiences have influenced my attitudes about psychological processes.	.26	**.57**	.09	.18	.43	.48

(Continued)

Table 12b.1 (Continued)

Variable	Scale Origin	Original Subscale Item Name	Component Loading				Communality	Corrected Item-Total Correlation
			1	2	3	4		
Q180	MCCTS	I can identify my reactions that are based on stereo-typical beliefs about different ethnic groups	.33	**.53**	.14	.07	.41	.49
Q110	MAKSS	I have an excellent ability to critique multi-cultural research.	.16	−.03	**.80**	.11	.68	.45
Q109	MAKSS	I have an excellent ability to identify the strengths and weaknesses of psychological tests in terms of their use with persons of different cultural/racial/ethnic backgrounds.	.17	−.03	**.71**	−.12	.55	.41
Q185	MCCTS	I can discuss within-group differences among ethnic groups (e.g., low socio-economic status (SES) Puerto Rican client vs. high SES Puerto Rican client).	.13	.16	**.71**	.02	.55	.43
Q191	MCCTS	I can discuss research regarding mental health issues and culturally different populations.	.09	.15	**.71**	.01	.53	.41

Variable	Scale Origin	Original Subscale Item Name	Component Loading				Communality	Corrected Item-Total Correlation
			1	2	3	4		
Q144	MCAS-B	I am knowledgeable of acculturation models for various ethnic minority groups.	.17	.25	**.69**	−.02	.56	.49
Q53	CCCI-R	My communication is appropriate for my clients.	.27	.07	.02	**.77**	.67	.41
Q49	CCCI-R	I am aware of institutional barriers that affect the client.	.09	.30	.11	**.75**	.68	.44
Q43	CCCI-R	I am aware of how my own values might affect my client.	.18	.24	.03	**.72**	.61	.42
Eigenvalues			6.50	2.55	2.10	1.21		
% of Variance			30.95	12.13	10.00	5.78		
Coefficient Alpha			.90	.78	.80	.75		

Notes. The variable names in the first column would not be part of the table placed into the manuscript; we included them here so that you may clearly see the inventory item that matches up with the variable names that were used in the analysis. Boldface indicates highest factor loadings. Component 1 = Non-Ethnic Ability, Component 2 = Multicultural Awareness, Component 3 = Multicultural Knowledge, Component 4 = Multicultural Sensitivity to Consumers. Corrected item-total correlations show the Pearson rs between the item and its subscale (the subscale score is "corrected" by excluding the particular item in computing the total score for the subscale).

12B Exercises

"The Course Questionnaire" (Clark, 1993) is designed to predict academic achievement.

1. Not at all true   2. Barely true   3. Moderately true   4. Exactly true

COURSE QUESTIONNAIRE

Please indicate which scale value best describes you:

1. If someone opposes me, I can find means and ways to get what I want.

2. It is easy for me to stick to my aims and accomplish my goals.

3. I remain calm when facing difficulties because I can rely on my coping abilities.

4. When I am confronted with a problem I usually find several solutions.

5. Often I don't succeed to take the time necessary to study for this course in a thorough way.

6. No matter what comes my way, I'm usually able to handle it.

7. Often I must rely on luck and chance during a quiz or exam in this course.

8. Often I do not invest the time necessary to do the best studying possible for this course.

9. I am often unable to muster up the patience necessary to accomplish my study goals for this course

Using the SPSS data file for Chapter 12B (located on the Web-based study site—http://www.sagepub.com/amrStudy), perform a principal components analysis with varimax rotation on all the items.

1. How many factors emerged using the Kaiser rule (i.e., eigenvalues greater than 1)?

2. What do you glean from the scree plot?

3. How much of the variance was explained by the factors?

4. Did the factors demonstrate simple structure (i.e., no item cross load at .3 or greater).

5. What is the relationship between the two factors?

6. Which rotation would be preferred? Defend your answer.

7. Write a results section for this study.

Confirmatory
Factor Analysis

Exploratory Versus Confirmatory Strategies

The previous chapter devoted to principal components and factor analysis represented an approach that is generically labeled *exploratory factor analysis*. It is exploratory in the sense that researchers adopt the inductive strategy of determining the factor structure empirically. Simply put, researchers allow the statistical procedure to examine the correlations between the variables and to generate a factor structure based on those relationships. From the perspective of the researchers at the start of the analysis, any variable may be associated with any component or factor. Confirmatory factor analysis, by contrast, requires researchers to use a deductive strategy. Within this strategy, the factors and the variables that are held to represent them are postulated at the beginning of the procedure rather than emerging from the analysis. The statistical procedure is then performed to determine how well this hypothesized theoretical structure fits the empirical data.

The Transition From Exploratory to Confirmatory Analysis

The transition that we are about to make between exploratory and confirmatory analysis is a fairly substantial one. The topics we have covered thus far, including exploratory factor analysis, are based on the general linear model. In this model, the solution to many of the statistical procedures we have studied involves determining the weights that a set of variables will be assigned when we form them into a linear composite or variate. One example is the multiple regression equation, a weighted linear composite of the predictor (independent variables) that best predicts the criterion (dependent) variable. A second example can be drawn from our discussion of MANOVA (multivariate analysis of variance) where a composite variable is computed as a vector representing the weighted sum of the dependent variables. And a third example is principal components analysis in which the component is a weighted linear composite of the variables in the analysis.

Understanding the nature of the variate is a primary goal of the general linear model. Accordingly, the general linear model determines the weights of the variables in the linear combination that produces the variate. As an alternative, you could potentially deduce from a theory or hypothesize from a less developed theory the weights that the variables should take on well in advance of the statistical analysis. You could use the general linear model to confirm or validate the weights for you because you would have determined them for yourself before you engaged in the statistical analysis. Specifically, the general linear model evaluates how well your hypothesized structure fits the data. This is the objective of structural equation modeling.

Confirmatory factor analysis is a specialized case of structural equation modeling. This statistical procedure allows (requires) researchers to hypothesize a particular model or factor structure that they believe underlies the variables measured in the study. Confirmatory factor analysis will then estimate the value of the parameters that tie the variables together (e.g., the pattern/structure coefficients), thus completing the description of the model, and will provide indexes that assess the quality of the fit between the model and the data.

A Structural Approach to Exploratory and Confirmatory Factor Analysis

A useful way to transition to confirmatory factor analysis is to use a structural or path analysis framework to characterize the exploratory approach because this is the framework within which we need to understand the confirmatory strategy. This has the advantage that we can also talk about the differences between principal components and factor analysis within the general domain of exploratory factor analysis. We will start with a quick overview of structural models; a more detailed account will be given in Chapter 14A "Causal Modeling: Path Analysis and Structural Equation Modeling." Once we can see the general structure of such a model, we will discuss principal components analysis. Then we will talk about factor analysis using principle axis factoring as our exemplar and contrast it with principal components analysis. Finally, we will present the confirmatory approach and contrast it with principle axis factoring.

Very Brief Overview of Structural Models

Many readers are somewhat familiar with these sorts of models. They are presented in the form of "flow" diagrams and are commonly published in the research literature in the context of path analysis. Path analysis and confirmatory factor analysis can be thought of as two applications of the more general approach known as structural equation modeling (Hoyle, 1995). The remaining chapters in the book, including this one, are designed to tie these types of designs together.

At a global level, causal models have three kinds of elements: text inside geometric shapes, lines with arrows pointing to or away from these shapes, and coefficients on the lines. The lines with arrows show the direction of hypothesized cause or inference, and we may refer to them occasionally as paths (in the sense of inferential flow and not to suggest that we are performing a path analysis per se). For example, an arrow pointing from *X* to *Y* can have several related interpretations, depending on the context. Among the ways to verbalize the meaning conveyed by the arrow are the following:

- ▶ *X* is hypothesized to cause *Y*
- ▶ *Y* follows (in some sense or context) from *X*
- ▶ One way that *X* can be made apparent is by measuring *Y*
- ▶ *X* in combination with other *X*s combine to form or define *Y*

The geometric shapes enclosing text represent variables of some kind. Rounded geometric shapes—that is, circles and ovals—represent latent variables. These are variables that are not directly measured in the study but are either constructed by the statistical procedure or hypothesized by the researchers (and specified in the model). The components in a principal components analysis and the factors in a factor analysis are examples of latent variables.

The other types of geometric shapes used in these sorts of models are rectangles or squares. Such squared-off shapes are used to denote measured variables—that is, variables that have been directly observed in the study, such as items on an inventory. These variables are also called *observed variables* (Raykov & Marcoulides, 2000).

The Structure of Principal Components Analysis

We have presented a portion of a principal components analysis in a structural equation model format in Figure 13a.1. To keep the figure simple enough to use for this discussion, we show only one component and only two measured variables associated with that component. We will

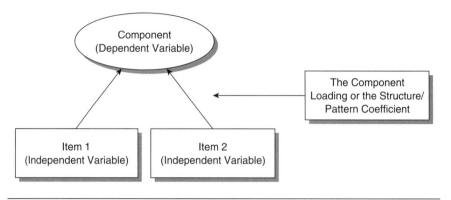

Figure 13a.1 Diagram of a Principle Component

show more of this analysis in a moment, but certain features of this model are noteworthy.

The principle component is contained in a circle, telling us that it is a latent variable. The inventory items are contained in squares, telling us that they are measured variables in the study. But now we have an additional ingredient. The arrows or paths point from the items toward the component, telling us that the causal or inferential flow is inductive. This treatment is in accord with Pedhazur and Schmelkin (1991) who state that "components in *PCA* [principal components analysis] may be conceived of as dependent variables whose values are obtained by differentially weighting the indicators, which are treated as the independent variables" (p. 598). Within this framework, the items, taken together, cause or define the factor. Recall that variables have weights (or correlations) with the factors quantified by pattern or structure coefficients. If we were to include these coefficients, they would be placed on the connectors between the measured variables and the latent variable. This model makes clear the inductive nature of principal components analysis.

The flow of causal inference also defines the roles that these variables play in the analysis. Independent variables cause, predict, or infer dependent variables. Because the causal inference flows from the measured variables, the measured variables are the independent variables, whereas the component is the dependent variable (Hauser, 1972). The measured variables are called different names by different authors: "formative indicators" by Pedhazur and Schmelkin (1991), "producers" by Costner (1969), and "caused indicators" by Blalock (1971). We will tend to refer to them as *indicators* or *indicator variables*. Because the causal inference flows to the component, it is considered to be the dependent variable in the model.

A more complete but still simplified model of a principal components model is shown in Figure 13a.2. In this figure, we show three components drawn within circles to represent the idea that they are latent variables, and six indicators (measured variables or inventory items). Recall from the previous chapter that the factor matrix shows the weights for all indicator variables on all components. Thus, we have drawn arrows from each indicator to each component.

We also hope or expect that some indicators will correlate more strongly with one component and other indicators will correlate more strongly with another component. In Figure 13a.2, we have placed Items 1 and 2 under **Component 1**, Items 3 and 4 under **Component 2**, and Items 5 and 6 under **Component 3** to show which items are best indicators of each component. The interpretation of the components would be based on what items were most strongly associated with them. For example, **Component 1** would be interpreted as whatever Items 1 and 2 had in common.

In this more complete model, we have included curved double-pointed arrows between pairs of components. In structural equation models, double-pointed lined arrows depict the notion that we are addressing the issue of correlations. In principal components analysis, your rotation strategy is going to be either varimax (which keeps factors uncorrelated) or oblique (which allows factors to be correlated). This specification, which we took for granted in the last chapter, clearly applies to all the components. That is, in a varimax rotation, all the components remain uncorrelated, and in an oblique rotation, all the factors are allowed a certain amount of correlation. We have visually represented this situation by using the double curved-arrow lines between all possible pairs of components.

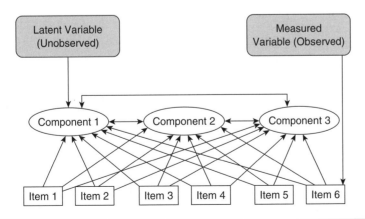

Figure 13a.2 A Principal Component Model

The Structure of Principal Axis Factor Analysis

We can contrast principal components analysis with principle axis factor analysis, one of the more popular factor analytic techniques. We have presented a portion of a principle axis analysis in a structural model format in Figure 13a.3. Again to keep the figure simple enough to use for this discussion, we show only one factor and only two measured variables associated with that component.

Figure 13a.3 is analogous to our model for a principal components analysis but there are some very important differences between that one and this one. Here, the factor, still a latent variable as shown by the circle in which it is drawn, is conceived of as the independent variable, and the indicator variables are the dependent variables. Note that the direction of the causal flow is from the latent variable or factor to the measured variables. This is one of the major differences between principal components and factor analysis. In factor analysis, the factor is seen as the focus point, and the measured variables are some of the ways that aspects of the factor can be measured. The term *indicator variable* is very descriptive of how the measured variables are viewed in the analysis; they are the filter through which the factor is known to us.

A more complete but still simplified factor model is drawn in Figure 13a.4. Again, there are six indicators and three factors pictured in a structure similar to what we did with the principal components analysis. Inference still flows from the latent factors to the indicators, and double arrow lines connect each pair of factors for the same reason: Factors will all be uncorrelated (by means of a varimax rotation) or will all be allowed some correlation (by means of an oblique rotation). And again, each factor shows six

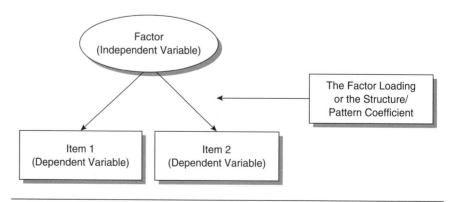

Figure 13a.3 Diagram of a Principal Axis Factor

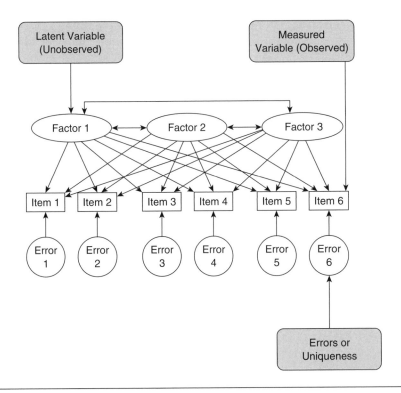

Figure 13a.4 A Principal Axis Factor Model

paths leading from it—one to each indicator—because each indicator will receive a certain weight (ideally, most small and two higher) for each factor. The model also depicts the higher weights of certain variables with certain factors (e.g., Items 1 and 2 are more strongly correlated with Factor 1).

One major difference between the models for principal components and principle axis, besides the direction of the arrows and the reversal of independent and dependent variable roles, is the presence here of error elements associated with the indicators. Essentially, this means that principle axis factoring explicitly recognizes that not all the variance of the indicators will be associated with the factors. Recall from our discussion of the difference between principal components and factor analysis in Chapter 12A that principal components attempts to account for the total variance of the measured variables but that factor analysis attempts to account for only the variance common to the factors.

Variance that is not common or shared is said to be unique to each measured variable, and this unique variance is called *error, residual,* or *unique variance* in the structural model (Maruyama, 1998). The unique variance is usually some combination of systematic variance (e.g., another construct may actually be represented to a certain extent) and unsystematic (measurement error). Calling this whole term "error variance" just means that it is not part of the variance common to the set of variables in the analysis and therefore unsystematic with respect to that common variance; it does not mean that all that variance is, in any absolute sense, completely unsystematic.

The errors terms are enclosed in circles because they, too, are latent. The causal flow is from the error to the indicator, telling us what is probably obvious to most researchers: Our measurement of the indicators contains some variance not captured in the factor structure.

Note that there are no double arrow lines connecting the error variables. That is because these error terms are assumed to be uncorrelated in principle axis factoring. There is some real risk, however, that such an assumption may not hold in all situations. The assumption that the errors are uncorrelated is certainly one restriction or limitation we face when using exploratory factor analysis. In addition to this restriction is the requirement that the factors must be presumed either to all be uncorrelated or to all be correlated. Add to that the atheoretical nature of exploratory analysis in general and you have the seeds of concern that have led some writers (e.g., Long, 1983) to urge great caution in using exploratory procedures lest we wind up with a "garbage in–garbage out" model.

The Structure of Confirmatory Factor Analysis

We display the more complete model for confirmatory factor analysis in Figure 13a.5. Two features of this model may be quickly apparent: (a) It is more similar to principle axis than to principal components, but (b) it is also simpler than the principle axis model because instead of having each measured variable relating to every factor, the researchers now clearly specify which measured variable "belongs" to which factor. Let's treat each in turn.

The similarity between principle axis factor analysis and confirmatory factor analysis occurs because—this may seem pretty obvious—they are both addressing factor analysis. Therefore, the causal flow is from the factors to the observed variables, and one thinks of these latter variables as indicators of the factors. Furthermore, there are error terms associated with each measured variable because factor analysis, whether in its exploratory or confirmatory form, partitions the variance of the indicators into common variance and unique variance. The analysis attempts to account for the common variance but treats the unique variance as residual or error variance.

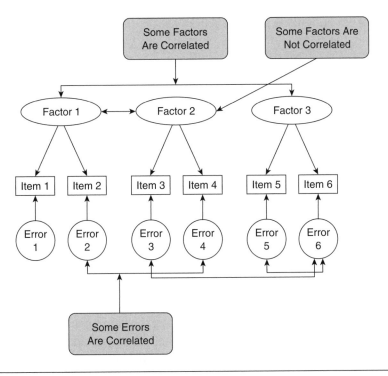

Figure 13a.5   An Example of a Confirmatory Factor Analysis (CFA)

The differences between the principle axis and confirmatory structures can be seen in the positioning of the arrows connecting (a) the factors to the indicators, (b) the factors to the factors, and (c) the errors to the errors. The first of these may be the most striking because the structure looks a lot simpler here than in principle axis factoring. In principle axis factoring, each factor is connected to all the indicators. This is done because the factors are a weighted composite of all the measured variables. Each factor is represented by a different set of weights, but all the indicators are in the equation. For Factor 1, for instance, observed Variables 1 and 2 should have, according to what the model shows, much greater weights than observed Variables 3 through 6. However, for Factor 2, Indicators 3 and 4 would have the greatest weights.

Another difference between the principle axis and confirmatory structures is the connections between pairs of factors. Exploratory analysis decrees that what will be true for one pair will be true for all pairs. If we invoke a varimax rotation, we decree that all factors will be uncorrelated; if we invoke an oblique rotation, we decree that all factors will be correlated.

That restriction is lifted in confirmatory factor analysis. Researchers are able to specify the relationships they believe holds between any two factors. In Figure 13a.5, we have specified that Factor 1 is correlated with Factors 2 and 3 but that Factors 2 and 3 are uncorrelated.

In an analogous manner, researchers can also specify the associations between pairs of error terms. Because these error terms reflect unique variance, the possibility exists that this variance may be systematic and thus interpretable. It may challenge the theoretical structure from which these hypotheses are derived (or the creativity or insightfulness of the researchers), but if the theory or researchers are up to the task, it may be possible to hypothesize that some pairs of unique variance are related. In Figure 13a.5, we have specified that Errors 2 and 4, Errors 3 and 6, and Errors 5 and 6 are correlated.

Confirmatory Analysis Is Theory Based

Exploratory factor analysis represents an inductive approach in that researchers employ a bottom-up strategy by developing a conclusion from specific observations. This conclusion is the interpretation of the factor based on those measured variables most strongly associated with it. These measured variables thus become indicators of the factor as a result of the statistical analysis. Although this strategy does appear to be empirically (inductively) based, research is not conducted in a vacuum, and researchers always have some ideas about the underlying structure of the variables that they have placed together in advance. For example, researchers interested in studying a particular construct will not select items haphazardly to write for their new inventory; rather, they will guide the content of the items to conform to what they know (or believe they know) about the construct. In this sense, no exploratory analysis is devoid of some researcher-based rationale (Gorsuch, 2003; Thompson, 2004).

Confirmatory factor analysis represents a deductive approach in that researchers employ a top-down approach by predicting an outcome from a theoretical framework. This outcome is the specification in advance of the statistical analysis of which measured variables are indicators of the factor. Further specification regarding the relationships between the factors and relationships between the error terms must also be forwarded by the researchers.

We have talked about the theoretical framework within which one engages in confirmatory analysis and the atheoretical environment where one must of necessity engage in exploratory analysis as though the two were easily distinguishable and compartmentalized. Statistical tests that analyze exploratory research are known as "first-generation" procedures, whereas statistical tests designed to confirm a theory are known as "second-generation" procedures (Fornell, 1987). Reality, however, has a way of complicating the decisions that researchers need to make regarding which procedure is to be used in a given situation.

Theory development in the social and behavioral sciences is an ongoing process, and very little research is conducted completely outside a theoretical context (Chin, 1998). The issue of contention is usually about the degree to which a theory has been articulated rather than whether or not there is one underlying the research. Sometimes it is not clear if an exploratory or confirmatory approach is more appropriate given that a particular theory may still be in the formative stage (Chin, Marcolin, & Newsted, 1996).

Furthermore, it is possible and often productive to make use of exploratory analysis as one of the theory-generating techniques open to researchers (Stevens, 2002). Thus, researchers having conducted a principal components analysis and interpreted the factors may be able to formulate some notions regarding the general construct that they were studying and begin to hypothesize what should occur under certain experimental or observational conditions. If they are able to fill in some of the details of their speculation, they may be ready to engage in confirmatory analysis the next time around.

Overview of Confirmatory Factor Analysis

The major objective in confirmatory factor analysis is determining if the relationships between the variables in the hypothesized model resemble the relationships between the variables in the observed data set. More formally expressed, the analysis determines the extent to which the proposed covariance matches the observed covariance.

Once a model is proposed (i.e., relationships between the variables have been hypothesized), a correlation/covariance matrix is created. The development and evaluation of a confirmatory analysis typically involves five steps (Bollen & Long, 1993): (a) model specification, (b) model identification, (c) model estimation, (d) model evaluation, and (e) model respecification.

We will illustrate these steps using a scale developed by Gamst et al. (2004) in a study designed to assess the degree to which mental health practitioners demonstrated the ability to work with and understand clients from a diverse set of cultural backgrounds. They labeled the construct as Multicultural Competence and called their scale the California Brief Multicultural Competence Scale (CBMCS). These researchers also had identified four indicator variables of sensitivity to consumers, non-ethnic ability, awareness of cultural barriers, and multicultural knowledge. For the sake of keeping this example manageable, these indicators will be treated as though they are measured variables by placing them within rectangles in the structural model. As the study was conducted, the inventory was composed of 21 items, each measured on a 4-point summative response scale. These indicators, then, are really themselves latent variables (variates) computed by averaging the scores on a subset of inventory items.

We will apply confirmatory factor analysis by following the above five steps to assess the construct validity of the model. Construct validity refers to the degree to which a measure actually assesses the theoretical construct it is supposed to assess and is often assessed through confirmatory factor analysis. Evidence for construct validity is achieved if the model is a good fit of the data.

Model Specification

The hypothesized model is diagrammed in Figure 13a.6. The researchers have specified their model (i.e., the four measured variables are hypothesized to be indicators of one factor). This model is an explanation of why these four variables relate. In the Bentler-Weeks method (Bentler & Weeks, 1980) of model specification, all variables (latent or measured) are assigned the role of either independent variables or dependent variables. Independent variables have arrows pointing away from the variable, whereas dependent variables have arrows pointing to the variable. In Figure 13a.6, there are five independent variables, the latent variable of multicultural competence and the four error or unique terms. The dependent variables are the four measured variables.

In this proposed model, the researchers are hypothesizing that multicultural competence causes sensitivity to consumers, non-ethnic ability, awareness of cultural barriers, and multicultural knowledge. Also, the researchers are specifying that there are other influences on the indicator variables besides multicultural competence. These other influences are represented as the error or unique-variance terms.

Model Identification

To assess whether the proposed model fits the data, a necessary but not sufficient condition must be met: The model must be identified (Bollen, 1989). Model identification has to do with the difference between, at a very general level, the number of variables in the analysis, and the number of parameters that need to be estimated by the model. These parameters, or at

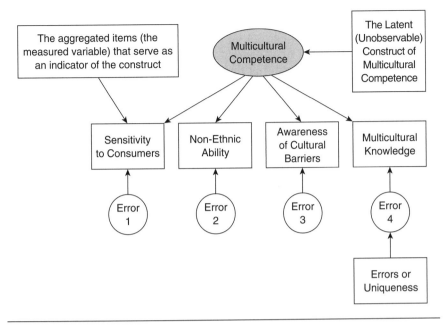

Figure 13a.6 The Hypothesized Model for Multicultural Competence

least estimates of them, are what the structural equation model is designed to generate and are therefore unknown at the start of the analysis. The parameters in the model are the pattern or structure coefficients relating the independent to the dependent variables, correlation coefficients relating the independent variables to each other, and the variance of the independent variables. If we subtract the number of unknown parameters from the number of known or nonredundant elements, we obtain the degrees of freedom for the analysis:

$$df = \text{number of nonredundant elements} - \text{number of unknown parameters}$$

The situation that must be met in the model identification stage is to have more known information elements than unknown parameters (Bentler & Chou, 1987). If there are more unknown elements than known ones, the value for the degrees of freedom is negative. The model is then said to be *underidentified* and cannot be processed meaningfully in the analysis. If the numbers of known and unknown elements are equal, the model is said to be saturated or *just-defined*. It will perfectly but, unfortunately, artificially fit the data, and again no meaningful solution will be obtained by running the analysis. Only when the degrees of freedom are positive (we have more known than unknown elements) can a meaningful analysis be performed. We then say that the model is *identified* (technically, positive values for degrees of freedom indicate that the model is overidentified) and that it is therefore ready to be processed.

The task in this model identification stage is to count the number of known and unknown elements and, if the initial count is insufficient, to do whatever is necessary to make sure that we wind up with more of the former than the latter. So the obvious question that can be asked at this juncture concerns what kind of elements can be counted. The answer is (a) entries in a covariance or correlation matrix for the measured (dependent) variables and (b) variances and coefficients of various sorts (correlation coefficients, pattern coefficients, structure coefficients) for the paths of the independent variables.

The number of known elements is equal to the number of unique or nonredundant entries (allowing the pairing of the variable with itself) in a matrix that represents the covariances or correlations of the indicator variables. Consider a set of three variables labeled A, B, and C. How many unique entries are there in the matrix? There are six: AA, BB, CC, AB, AC, and BC. If you imagine a square matrix and count the entries in its upper half plus the diagonal, you can see the six positions. Anything in the lower half is a redundancy.

Rather than physically counting this every time we start a confirmatory analysis, we can apply a simple formula to obtain the count of nonredundant elements (Raykov & Marcoulides, 2000). The formula is as follows:

$$\text{Number of nonredundant elements} = V\,(V + 1)\,/\,2$$

where V is the number of the measured variables in the study. If V is equal to 3 in our above illustration, then we have $3 \times (3 + 1)$ or 12 divided by 2, which gives us 6.

We can now return to our multicultural competence example shown in Figure 13a.6. The means and standard deviations of the four measured variables are shown in Table 13a.1, and the correlations between the measured variables are shown in Table 13a.2.

Counting the nonredundant elements in this study is done as follows. There are four indicator variables. Plugging that value into our simple formula gives us $4 \times (4 + 1)$ divided by 2 or 10 pieces of nonredundant or known information. This value of 10 is immutable—we cannot increase this number. If there turn out to be more than 10 unknown parameters, thus yielding a negative value for degrees of freedom, we must take some action to reduce that count of unknowns because we cannot raise the number of nonredundant elements.

Table 13a.1 Means and Standard Deviations of the Four Measured Variables

	N	*M*	*SD*
Sensitivity to consumers	80	53.97	6.910
Non-ethnic ability	80	52.22	7.323
Awareness	80	47.94	9.168
Multicultural knowledge	80	53.79	4.890

Table 13a.2 Correlations Among the Four Measured Variables

	2	*3*	*4*
1. Sensitivity to consumers	.462*	.244	.546*
2. Non-ethnic ability	—	.400*	.525*
3. Awareness		—	.261
4. Multicultural knowledge			—

*$p < .01$.

Model identification involves one other piece of business: The latent variable needs to be scaled. That is, to conduct the analysis, the latent variable must be assigned a metric of some kind. Now, we already pretty much know how we would be doing this if we had to—provided that the model is viable. We would compute a multicultural competence score in a way analogous to the way in which we computed the four indicator scores—namely, by averaging the scores on all the inventory items or averaging the scores on the four indicators themselves. Either way we did it, multicultural competence would then be assessed on the same 4-point scale that we used for the items and the indicators.

Now, in the empirical world of the researchers, if their model is workable, they would be working with the four factors and not with the more complex larger construct (that really is the whole point of factor analysis). But the mathematical world of statistics requires that the scale of the latent variable be specified in the model or the analysis is a no-go, so we very much want to specify the construct's metric.

Note that the indicators are already measured in the course of conducting the study and so have a measurement scale already tied to them. However, in structural equation modeling where we have specified, for example, factors, each of these (unobserved) latent variables must explicitly be assigned a metric within the context of the analysis. This is normally done by constraining one of the paths from the latent variable to one of its indicator (reference) variables, such as assigning the value of 1.0 to the pattern/structure coefficient for this path. Given this constraint, the remaining paths can then be estimated. The indicator selected to be constrained to 1.0 is called the *reference item.* Typically, we select as the reference item the one that in factor analysis loads most heavily on the dimension represented by the latent variable, thereby allowing it to anchor the meaning of that dimension. Alternatively, one may set the factor variances to 1, thereby effectively obtaining a standardized solution, or one may select the path associated with the indicator having the best reliability (because we are tying down the measurement of the construct).

Here, we will set the coefficient to a value of 1 (actually, any positive value will suffice) on the selected path. Such an act informs AMOS, the statistical software we use for structural equation modeling, that the construct is to be assessed on the same metric as that indicator. In Figure 13a.7, we have identified sensitivity to consumers as the indicator to which we will initially scale multicultural competence.

Here is why our action might seem a bit strange. One of the goals of the statistical analysis is to estimate parameters that were left unspecified by the model. The pattern or structure coefficients linking the construct and the indicators are among those parameters. But we have just filled in

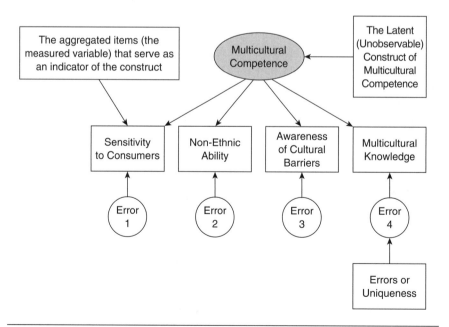

Figure 13a.7   Scaling Sensitivity to Consumers by Constraining It to a Value of 1

one of them, which sounds as though it might defeat the purpose of performing the analysis. The bad news here is that we had to make this specification in order to run the analysis in the first place. But the good news is that structural equation modeling uses a maximum likelihood procedure that iterates its solution until it reaches a stable result. The upshot of this is that even though we have specified a value of 1 as the coefficient, the statistical procedure will use that only as a starting place and will eventually produce its own estimate. There is even more good news. Yes, we specified the coefficient leading to one of the indicators, but if we had chosen a different indicator, our solution would still be essentially the same.

Having done our preparation work, we now need to determine how many unknowns there are. These unknown elements will be the parameters estimated by the statistical procedure. In this model, we will need to estimate (a) the variance of the multicultural competence latent factor, (b) the variances of the four unique error terms, (c) the remaining three pattern/structure coefficients relating the latent variable to the measured variables whose coefficients are not yet specified (we have already removed from the realm of the unknown one parameter by scaling the latent factor), and (d) the four pattern/structure coefficients relating the unique variables (the error terms) to the measured variables. This gives us a total of 13 parameters (1 + 4 + 3 + 4) that we are asking the model to estimate.

A quick calculation to figure out if this model is identified tells us that we are (temporarily only) in a bit of trouble. Subtracting the unknowns (13) from the known elements (10) yields −3 degrees of freedom. Thus, the model is not yet identified, and we are not ready to go forward into the analysis.

The portions of the model most susceptible to specification are the paths leading from the error terms to the indicator variables. What we do here is assign them an initial value of 1 as shown in Figure 13a.8, recognizing that they will be estimated in the solution. This removes these four parameters from the list of unknowns. It also serves the added advantage of scaling these latent error terms to their respective measured variables. Because the error variables represent unique variance, the model will actually have an easy job filling in these values. Once we learn of the correlation between the indicators and the latent factor (the common variance), these values may be calculated as the residual or what remains of the total variance once the common variance is accounted for.

Changing the status of these parameters from unknown to known in the model now puts us in the positive range for degrees of freedom. The known elements still count to 10. The unknown parameters after all our work are (a) the variance of the latent factor, (b) the variances of the four latent error variables, and (c) the remaining three pattern/structure coefficients. That

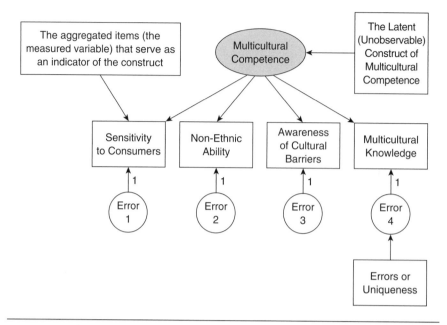

Figure 13a.8   Constraining the Error Variables

gives us a total of 8. By subtracting the number of unknown parameters from the number of known elements (10 − 8 = 2), we now have positive degrees of freedom. This model is *overidentified* (which is what we wanted to happen) and can thus be meaningfully solved.

Model Estimation

Once we have completed the identification stage, we are then ready to conduct the statistical analysis. This involves mathematically building the model and estimating the relationships between the variables in the model. We calculate these estimates using the maximum likelihood estimation (MLE) procedure, one of several methods available to researchers through the AMOS program. Maximum likelihood attempts to estimate the values of the parameters that would result in the highest likelihood of the actual data matching with the proposed model. These methods always require iterative solutions.

We will present the results of the data analysis shortly because to really justify examining and interpreting the outcome of the analysis, it is a good idea to determine how well the model is able to fit the data. As part of the procedure of running a confirmatory factor analysis, we will want to evaluate the model by evaluating these fit indexes.

Model Evaluation

The proposed or hypothesized model is assessed by producing estimates of the unknown parameters. These findings are then compared with the relationships (the correlation/covariance matrices) existent in the actual or observed data. Confirmatory factor analysis assesses how well the predicted interrelationships between the variables match the interrelationships between the actual or observed interrelationships. If the two matrices (the proposed and the actual) are consistent with one another, then the model can be considered a credible explanation for the hypothesized relationships.

Stevens (2002) divides the assessment of a model into two categories: "those that measure the overall fit of the model and those that are concerned with individual model parameters" (pp. 402–403). All the fit measures are analogous to the omnibus test in ANOVA in that they provide an overall assessment of the model. As in the ANOVA, post hoc tests need to be conducted to provide further interpretation of the analysis. Similarly, in confirmatory factor analysis, the overall fit of a model to the data may appear acceptable, yet some relationships in the model may not be supported by the data (Bollen, 1990).

The chi-square statistic is used to test the difference between the predicted and the observed relationships (correlations/covariances). Because the researcher is predicting a close fit, a nonsignificant chi square is desired. In the multicultural competence example, the chi-square value was 3.44. At two degrees of freedom, the probability of that value occurring by chance was .179 (it was greater than our default alpha value of .05 and is therefore not statistically significant), indicating an acceptable match between the proposed model and the observed data.

Jöreskog and Sörbom (1989) and Bentler (1990), however, advised against the sole use of the chi-square value in judging the overall fit of the model because of the sensitivity of the chi square to sample size. As sample size increases, power increases. Therefore, the chi-square test can detect small discrepancies between the observed and predicted covariances and suggest that the model does not fit the data. A good-fitting model could be rejected because of trivial but statistically significant differences between the observed and predicted values. Because of these limitations, many other fit indexes were developed as alternatives or supplements to chi square.

Assessing Fit of Hypothesized Models

How to assess the fit between the hypothesized model and the observed data continues to develop. Over the past 20 years, at least 24 fit indexes have been proposed (Klem, 2000). All of these fit indexes were developed to diminish the Type II error (i.e., concluding that the data do not support the proposed model when in fact they do). For the 24 fit measures available through statistical software programs, there is presently no general agreement on which measures are preferred (Maruyama, 1998). As Hair Anderson, Tatham, and Black (1998) state, "SEM [structural equation modeling] has no single statistical test that best describes the 'strength' of the model's predictions" (p. 653). None of the measures has a related statistical test, except for the chi-square test. The confusing consequence of these competing fit indexes is that different research studies report different fit indexes.

Complicating this matter of competing fit indexes is the lack of consensus among structural equation modeling writers as to how we may categorize or organize this array of fit indexes, although most agree that some organizational schema is necessary (because then we might be able to report fit indexes from each category). Further complicating the decision of what fit index to report, there is disagreement about which individual fit measures might best be classified together.

Researchers have proposed various classification schemas to organize the fit indexes. For example, Arbuckle (1999) devised an eight-category scheme (parsimony, sample discrepancy, population discrepancy, information-theoretic, baseline model, parsimony adjusted, goodness of fit, and miscellaneous), whereas Tabachnick and Fidell (2001b) suggest a five-category system (comparative, absolute, proportion of variance, parsimony, and residual based). Other authors (e.g., Hair et al., 1998; Jaccard & Wan, 1996) promote a three-group scheme (absolute, relative, and parsimonious). And finally, Maruyama (1998) adopts Hu and Bentler's (1999a) two-type scheme (absolute and relative but with the latter divided into four subtypes). The most cited organization system appears to be the three-classification scheme (absolute, relative, and parsimonious). Brief descriptions of the three classification schemes with their respective fit measures are presented below and summarized in Table 13a.3.

Absolute Fit Measures

Absolute fit measures indicate how well the proposed interrelationships between the variables match the interrelationships between the actual or observed interrelationships. This means how well the correlation/covariance of the hypothesized model fits the correlation/covariance of the actual or observed data. The four most common absolute fit measures assessing this general feature are the chi square, the goodness-of-fit index (GFI), the root mean square residual (RMSR), and the root mean square error of approximation (RMSEA). Because the researcher is predicting a close fit, a nonsignificant chi square is preferred. As we indicated, the chi-square test is too

Table 13a.3 Absolute, Relative, and Parsimonious Fit Measures

Fit Measures					
Absolute		*Relative*		*Parsimonious*	
Test	*Value*	*Test*	*Value*	*Test*	*Value*
χ^2	p >.05	CFI	>.95	PNFI	>.50
GFI	>.90	NFI>	>.90	PCFI >	>.50
RMSR	<.05	IFI	>.90		
RMSEA	<.10	RFI	>.90		

Note: χ^2 = Chi-square test; GFI = Goodness of Fit Index; RMSEA = Root Mean Square Error of Approximation; 2/df = Chi square divided by degrees of freedom test; PGFI = Parsimony Goodness of Fit Index, AGFI = Adjusted Goodness of Fit Index; CFI = Comparative Fit Index; NFI = Normed Fit Index; IFI = Incremental Fit Index; RFI = Relative Fit Index; PNFI = Parsimony Normed Fit Index; PCFI = Parsimony Comparative Fit Index.

powerful. As sample size increases, power increases, and the chi-square test can return a statistically significant outcome even when the model fits the data reasonably well.

The GFI is conceptually similar to the R^2 in multiple regression (Kline, 1998). It is the proportion of variance in the sample correlation/covariance accounted for by the predicted model, with values ranging from 0 (no fit) to 1 (a perfect fit). Although the GFI can vary from 0 to 1, theoretically, it can yield meaningless negative values. By convention, GFI should be equal to or greater than .90 as indicative of an acceptable model.

The RMSR is a measure of the average size of the residuals between actual covariance and the proposed model covariance. The smaller the RMSR, the better the fit (e.g., < .05). The RMSEA is the average of the residuals between the observed correlation/covariance from the sample and the expected model estimated for the population. Byrne (1998) states that the RMSEA "has only recently been recognized as one of the most informative criteria in covariance structure modeling" (p. 112). Values less than .08 are deemed acceptable, whereas values greater than .10 are generally unacceptable.

Relative Fit Measures

Relative fit measures are also known as comparisons with baseline measures or incremental fit measures. These are measures of fit relative to the independence model, which assumes that there are no relationships in the data (thus a poor fit) and the saturated model, which assumes a perfect fit. The incremental fit measures indicate the relative position on this continuum between worst fit to perfect fit, with values greater than .90 suggesting an acceptable fit between the model and the data. Incremental fit measures are also referred to as comparisons with baseline measures or relative fit measures.

Byrne (1998) suggests that the comparative fit index (CFI) should be the fit statistic of choice in structural equation modeling research. Knight, Virdin, Ocampo, and Roosa (1994) have suggested the following guidelines to evaluate the CFI: good fit > .90; adequate but marginal fit = .80 to .89; poor fit = .60 to .79; very poor fit < .60. Hu and Bentler (1999a, 1999b) revised the value representing a good fit to .95. Other common incremental fit measures are the normed fit index (NFI), non-normed fit index (NNFI), incremental fit index (IFI), and the relative fit index (RFI), with values between .90 and .95 indicating an acceptable fit.

Parsimonious Fit Measures

Parsimonious fit measures are sometimes called adjusted fit measures. These fit statistics are similar to the adjusted R^2 in multiple regression analysis; the parsimonious fit statistics penalize larger models with more estimated parameters. Here is why: Recall that MLE maximizes the likelihood that the data will support the proposed model. The more paths a researcher is estimating, the more likely the fit will be acceptable no matter how nonsensical the model may be. Researchers could "stack the deck" in their favor (unintentionally, of course) by increasing the complexity of their model. However, one of the goals of research is to develop more parsimonious models. These parsimonious fit measures can be used to compare models with differing number of parameters to determine the impact of adding additional parameters to the model.

Common parsimonious fit measures are the parsimonious adjusted goodness of fit (AGFI) and the parsimonious goodness of fit (PGFI). The AGFI corresponds to the GFI in replacing the total sum of squares by the mean sum of squares. PGFI adjusts for degrees of freedom in the baseline model. It is a variant of GFI that penalizes GFI by multiplying it by the ratio formed by the degrees of freedom in the tested model and degrees of freedom in the independence model. Ideally, values greater than .90 indicate an acceptable model; however, typically, parsimony-based measures have lower acceptable values (e.g., .50 or greater is deemed acceptable; Mulaik et al., 1989).

Where We Stand Now

The goal of researchers who use structural equation modeling techniques is to evaluate the plausibility of their hypothesized model (i.e., the relationships between the variables). The proposed model is either guided through prior research or based on some theoretical framework. The model is then compared with the actual or observed data. If the model and observed data resemble each other, then the model is said to fit the data.

Historically, chi square was used to assess the fit of the model, with the expectation that the *p* value would be nonsignificant. Because a chi square assesses the difference between expected values and observed results, a nonsignificant value would indicate a close fit. For models with relatively small cases (75 to 200), chi square is an adequate measure of fit (Kenny, 2003). However, for models with more cases, chi square will usually be statistically significant, suggesting a poor fit when there really are only trivial differences between the model and the data. Chi square is also affected by the size of the correlations in the model; larger correlations generally cause a poorer fit (Kenny, 2003). Because of these problems with chi square, alternative measures of fit are constantly being developed and studied.

Over the past 20 years, at least 24 fit indexes have been proposed (Klem, 2000). All these fit indexes were developed to diminish the chances of committing a Type II error (i.e., concluding that the data does not support the proposed model when in fact it does). One of the problems with chi-square tests was that with large samples, the results would suggest rejecting a model when, in fact, the model supported the data. Some of the alternative fit measures, however, have suffered the same fate as some technologies in the music industry: What was once considered "leading edge" is now considered inadequate and obsolete. What emerged with the development of alternative fit measures is the realization that no single fit index is powerful enough to assess the adequacy of the model. According to Maruyama (1998), "The different fit indexes differ with respect to dimensions such as susceptibility to sample size differences, variability in the range of fit possible for any particular data set, and valuing simplicity of model specification needed to attain an improved fit" (p. 239). Until recently, most texts on structural equation modeling presented a three-classification scheme: absolute, relative, and parsimonious.

Absolute fit measures judge how well the proposed interrelationships between the variables match the interrelationships between the actual or observed interrelationships. This means how well the correlation/covariance of the hypothesized model fits the correlation/covariance of the actual or observed data.

Relative fit measures are also known as comparisons to baseline measures or incremental fit measures. These are measures of fit relative to the independence model, which assumes that there are no relationships in the data (thus a poor fit) and the saturated model, which assumes a perfect fit.

The incremental fit measures indicate the relative position on this continuum between worst fit to perfect fit, with values greater than .90 suggesting an acceptable fit between the model and the data.

Both the absolute and the relative measures will report better fit measures if the models being evaluated have more parameter estimations. This is one of the by-products of the maximum likelihood method employed to estimate the parameters. Recall that the maximum likelihood method is an iterative process that compares the parameter estimates at each phase of the estimation procedure and reports the estimates that provide the best fit. With more parameters available to estimate, the greater the likelihood of developing a better fit.

To adjust for this inflated fit bias, the third classification, known as parsimonious fit measures, was developed. These fit measures adjust for the number of estimations by penalizing models with greater parameter estimations. Kelloway (1998) warns that unlike the absolute or relative fit measures that have conventional values of .90 or .95 as acceptable models, parsimonious fit measure have no generally acceptable cutoff. Parsimonious fit measures are recommended to compare two competing models, with the model with the higher fit measure as superior.

Which Fit Measures to Report?

There is disagreement among structural equation modeling researchers on just which fit indexes to report. One often-cited recommendation is from Jaccard and Wan (1996) who suggests reporting at least three fit tests—one absolute, one relative, and one parsimonious—to reflect diverse criteria. Recently, with the advances of more realistic simulation studies, Kline (2005) and Thompson (2004) recommend fit measures without reference to their classification. We suggest reporting chi square, the NFK, the CFI, and the RMSEA as fit measures. Although chi square is less informative as an assessment of a single model, it is useful in comparing nested models (i.e., where one model is a subset of another model). The model with the lower chi-square value is considered to be the preferable model. Both the NFI and the CFI should achieve a value of .95 for the model to be deemed acceptable. The RMSEA is the average of the residuals between the observed correlation/covariance from the sample and the expected model estimated from the population. Byrne (1994) stated, "[RMSEA] has only recently been recognized as one of the most informative criteria in covariance structure modeling" (p. 112). Loehlin (2004) proposes the following criteria for evaluating this index: (a) less than .08 indicates good fit, (b) .08 to .1 indicates a moderate fit, (c) greater than .1 indicates poor fit.

Model Estimation: Assessing Pattern/Structure Coefficients

The next step in assessing the model is to see if the factor pattern/structure coefficients are statistically significant and meaningful. Figure 13a.9 presents the pattern/structure coefficients of the four measured variables (indicators) to the factor Multicultural Competence.

All the factor pattern/structure coefficients achieved statistical significance at an a priori alpha level of $p < .05$. The statistically significant pattern/structure coefficients indicate that Multicultural Competence is composed of the four measured variables named in the model. The pattern/structure coefficients also achieved meaningful (practical) significance with coefficients greater than .3, although the inference strength from the latent factor to awareness of cultural barriers is a bit more tenuous than the inferences to the other three indicators. Have the researchers proven their model? The answer is no. Confirmatory factor analysis is not an arena for proof, but it can be a source of support for a model and can supply enough information to researchers to cause them to reject a model if it does not fit the data very well. Even in this latter case, researchers may be motivated to modify their existing model rather than completely discarding it if they can determine what might need to be remedied so that the model may be improved.

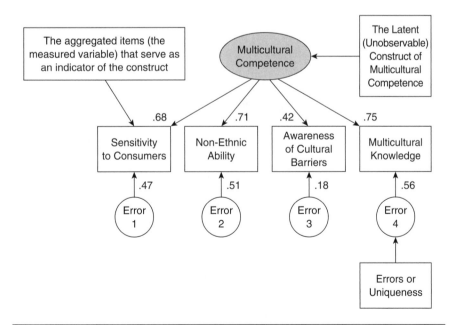

Figure 13a.9 The Model With the Estimated Coefficients

Model Respecification

It is not uncommon that the initial proposed model fails to achieve an adequate fit and that the researchers consider modifying the model (i.e., respecifying). In respecifying the model, the researchers may delete the non-significant coefficients in an attempt to trim their models. Researchers could also add coefficients between factors and indicator variables that were previously ignored as an approach to develop their models. In either situation, the analyses are now exploratory rather than confirmatory. Byrne (2001) explains:

> In other words, once an hypothesized CFA model, for example, has been rejected, this spells the end of the confirmatory factor-analytic approach, in its truest sense. Although CFA procedures continue to be used in any respecification and reestimation of the model, these analyses are exploratory in the sense that they focus on the detection of misfitting parameters in the originally hypothesized model. (p. 91)

The researchers need to consider if the respecification is theoretically justifiable. If deleting or adding a coefficient lacks any theoretical justification, the researchers need to avoid this temptation in an attempt to improve the model fit. Steiger (1990) warns researchers of their ability to justify new parameters when he stated, "What percentage of researchers would find themselves unable to think up a 'theoretical justification' for freeing a parameter? . . . I assume that the answer . . . is near zero" (p. 175).

If a model is respecified and achieves acceptable fit with the data, this new model needs to be retested on an independent sample. This new independent sample can either be a holdout sample from the original study (provided that the sample is large enough, perhaps 400 or more) or a new sample.

To illustrate an example of a respecified model, the following heuristic will be used. Researchers are assessing the construct validity of a new instrument used to determine aptitude for graduate school. They have proposed two latent factors, Verbal Ability and Math Ability. Each factor has three measured (indicator) variables. The verbal factor is composed of scores from three subscales: spelling, grammar, and comprehension. The math factor is composed of scores from three subscales: word problems, calculations, and conceptual understanding. The model is presented in Figure 13a.10.

The results of this hypothetical study are shown in Figure 13a.11. We display the pattern coefficients and the correlation between the two latent variables. As can be seen, the pattern coefficients are not especially high, although they are statistically significant and certainly meaningful (i.e., they do exceed .3).

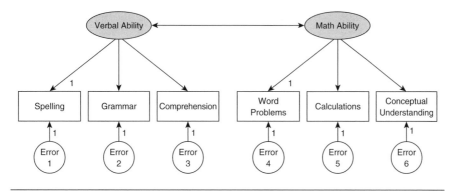

Figure 13a.10   Proposed Two-Factor Model With Six Indicator Variables

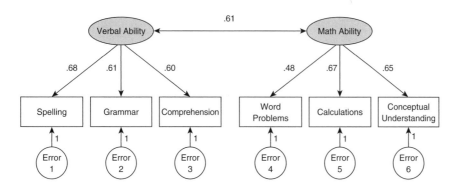

Figure 13a.11   Pattern Coefficients of the Six Indicator Variables for the Two Factors

The results of the overall model, however, indicated a moderate fit between the proposed model and the observed data. The chi square was statistically significant, indicating a lack of fit. Although the absolute fit measure of the GFI indicated a good fit (.975), the RMSEA indicated a marginal fit with .085. The incremental measure, the CFI, was also marginal (.944) because it did not quite meet the .95 criterion.

Perhaps a respecified model may better account for the observed data. As will be illustrated in Chapter 13B, confirmatory factor analysis output will provide modification indexes. These modification indexes are suggestions to improve the fit of a model. Recall that the researchers need to consider if the respecification is theoretically justifiable. Because all the coefficients achieved both statistical and practical significance, deleting any of the coefficients would be counterproductive.

However, it is possible to suggest additions to the model that may enhance its fit to the data. One plausible addition is adding a path (coefficient) from Verbal Ability to Word Problems. This path makes theoretical sense because verbal ability is necessary to comprehend math word problems. Another modification suggestion is that Math Ability could be assessed by the verbal indicator variable Comprehension. Cognitive psychologists can make the case that proficient mathematical ability aids in verbal comprehension. Thus, these "cross-loadings" make theoretical sense. Such a revised model is drawn in Figure 13a.12.

The results of the new model are shown in Figure 13a.13. Note that the correlation between Verbal Ability and Math Ability has decreased from .61 to .44. This drop occurred because some of the variance that was "exclusive" to Verbal Ability has been "released" to the math side of the model; that is, Verbal Ability now has a path to Word Problems. At the same time, some of the variance that was exclusive to Math Ability is now reassigned to the verbal side of the model; that is, Math Ability now has a path to Comprehension.

In terms of the pattern/structure coefficients, we see some gains here as well. The paths from the original model now show values that are a bit higher. For example, Spelling now "loads" on Verbal Ability at .71 compared with its prior value of .68, and Calculations now has a coefficient of .69 compared with its prior value of .67. The new coefficients, the ones that are cross loading, although not large in an absolute sense, do add explanatory power. Thus, by permitting word problems to be an indicator of verbal ability in addition to indicating math ability, and by permitting comprehension to be an indicator

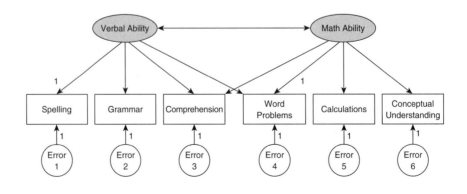

Figure 13a.12 A Respecified Model

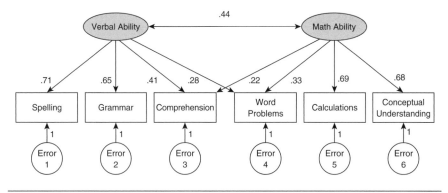

Figure 13a.13 The Results of the Respecified Model

of math ability in addition to indicating verbal ability, we have apparently reached a better understanding of the dynamics underlying these variables.

In terms of the statistical results, all the coefficients achieved statistical significance ($p < .05$). The chi-square value of .334 is nonsignificant, indicating a fit between the model and data. Improvements in the other fit indexes were also obtained. The absolute fit measure of the GFI increased to .996 and the RMSEA attenuated to .017. The incremental measure, CFI, increased to .998.

General Considerations

Structural equation modeling is able to accommodate some departures from normality. The AMOS program also performs state-of-the-art estimation of missing data by full information maximum likelihood instead of relying on ad hoc methods such as listwise or pairwise deletion or mean imputation.

Sample size is also something that researchers should take into consideration when performing confirmatory factor analysis or structural equation modeling in general. In the literature, sample sizes for these sorts of studies commonly run in the 200 to 400 range for models with 10 to 15 indicators. Loehlin (1992) recommends at least 100 cases and preferably 200. With more than 10 variables, sample sizes under 200 generally cause parameter estimates to be unstable and the tests of statistical significance tests lack a bit of power. One rule of thumb is that sample size should be at least 50 more than 8 times the number of variables in the model. Another rule of thumb, based on Stevens (2002), is to have at least 15 cases per measured variable or indicator. Bentler and Chou (1987) recommend at least 5 cases per parameter estimate (including error terms as well as path coefficients).

Recommended Readings

Fan, X., Thompson, B., & Wang, L. (1999). Effects of sample size, estimation method, and model specification on structural equation modeling fit indexes. *Structural Equation Modeling, 6,* 56–83.

Hu, L., & Bentler, P. M. (1999). Cutoff criteria for fit indexes in covariance structure analysis: Conventional criteria versus new alternatives. *Structural Equation Modeling, 6,* 1–55.

Jöreskog, K. G. (1969). A general approach to confirmatory maximum likelihood factor analysis. *Psychometrika, 34,* 183–202.

Muliak, S. (1972). *The foundations of factor analysis.* New York: McGraw-Hill.

Muliak, S. A., James, L. R., Van Alstine, J., Bennett, N., Lind, S., & Stilwill, C. D. (1989). Evaluation of goodness-of-fit indices for structural equation models. *Psychological Bulletin, 105,* 430–445.

Reilly, T. (1995). A necessary and sufficient condition for identification of confirmatory factor analysis models of complexity one. *Sociological Methods & Research, 23,* 421–441.

Steiger, J. H. (1998). A note on multisample extensions of the RMSEA fit index. *Structural Equation Modeling, 5,* 411–419.

Thompson, B. (2000). Ten commandments of structural equation modeling. In L. G. Grimm & P. R. Yarnold (Eds.), *Reading and understanding more multivariate statistics* (pp. 261–283). Washington, DC: American Psychological Association.

Thompson, B. (2004). *Exploratory and confirmatory factor analysis: Understanding concepts and applications.* Washington, DC: American Psychological Association.

Confirmatory Factor Analysis Using AMOS

W̲e begin our example of a confirmatory factor analysis by demonstrating how to construct a single factor model using the AMOS Graphics program, Version 5.0 (Arbuckle, 2004). AMOS is an acronym for "A̲nalysis of MO̲ment S̲tructures." AMOS Graphics allows researchers to simply instruct the program to draw their hypothesized model for evaluation. We will demonstrate how to use the AMOS Graphics program to produce a hypothesized model and navigate you through the extensive results output (with annotations) so you can understand the output. All these procedures are described in some detail. We then present a situation when researchers may need to assess if the model is invariant (i.e., equally applicable) across different groups or times. We conclude with a final demonstration of how the **Modification Indexes** can be employed to respecify a model if the initial model fails to achieve a satisfactory fit.

Preparing to Run a Confirmatory Factor Analysis

We will continue to use the example of multicultural competence of mental health providers that served as our example in Chapter 13A. Recall that Gamst et al. (2004) concluded that Multicultural Competence comprises four domains (factors): sensitivity to consumers, non-ethnic ability, awareness of cultural barriers, and multicultural knowledge. The researchers then developed the California Brief Multicultural Competence Scale to assess each of these domains. Thus, their research on multicultural competence evolved from a theory-generating procedure to a theory-testing procedure (Stevens, 2002). A large sample of mental health providers completed their inventory in a study to assess the construct validity of this instrument. Recall that construct validity refers to the degree that a measure actually assesses the theoretical construct it is supposed to assess and is often evaluated through confirmatory factor analysis. As previously noted, we have simplified the model for the sake of our presentation.

Begin by entering SPSS and open your SPSS data by clicking **File →Open → Data** and selecting the SPSS data file you wish to analyze.

Getting to Confirmatory Factor Analysis

To begin our analyses, we click **Analyze → Amos 5** (the last choice is Version 5 of the Amos program and assumes that you have obtained and separately loaded this application once SPSS has been loaded on your computer).

Constructing the Model

This action produces the AMOS screen shown in Figure 13b.1. In this AMOS screen, select **Diagram → Draw Indicator Variable.**

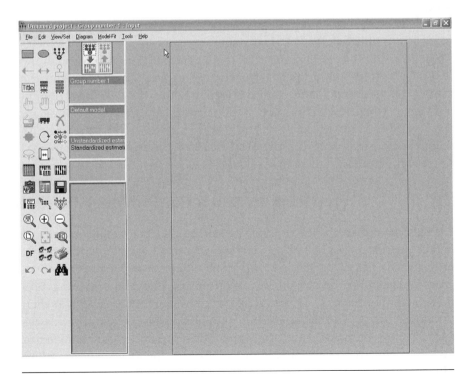

Figure 13b.1   The Initial Screen in AMOS

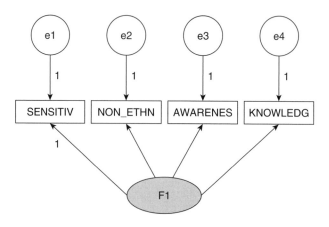

Figure 13b.2   The Model With the Latent Variables Named

Depress the left mouse button and draw a circle (or oval), then click the left mouse button four times. Notice that AMOS automatically selected the first indicator variable as the scaling base for the latent factor and has automatically set in place an initial value for the pattern/structure coefficient of 1. It has also assigned a value to all the paths from the error variables to the measured variables.

Click the right mouse button to disengage the Draw function. Then select **View/Set** and select **Variables in Dataset** (drag the appropriate names to the variables). After dragging the variables to the square indicator boxes, the model should be partly filled in.

We next must name the latent construct and the error terms. From the **Tools** menu, select **Tools → Macro → Name Unobserved Variables.** After that, select **Name Unobserved Variables.** AMOS automatically names the error variables and the latent variable. The completed diagram should look like Figure 13b.2.

Requesting Output From AMOS

We are now ready to tell AMOS what sort of output we want it to produce. To do this, we proceed to the following menu sequence: **View/Set →** **Analysis Properties.** The dialog box for **Analysis Properties** will appear. The box opens on the page keyed to the **Estimation** tab at the top. This page specifies, among other properties, the method that will be used to calculate the coefficients. **Maximum likelihood** is the AMOS default and the one that we will be using. Now select the tab representing **Output.** The dialog box shown in Figure 13b.3 will appear. The default selection on this page is the

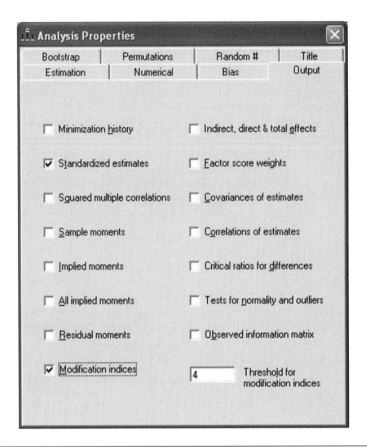

Figure 13b.3   The Output Tab on the Analysis Properties Dialog Box

first box that presents information on the number of iterations and so on that the calculations entailed. Remove that check mark by clicking the checkbox. Then, select the two checkboxes labeled **Standardized estimates** and **Modification indexes.** The first box lets us acquire the beta weights, and the second box provides us with suggestions for improving the model if the model is deficient in some way.

Examining the Output From a Confirmatory Factor Analysis

When you have completed selecting these properties, close the dialog box by clicking on the **X** icon in the upper right corner of the box. This action brings you back to the diagram of the model. Select from the task bar **Model-Fit → Calculate Estimates.**

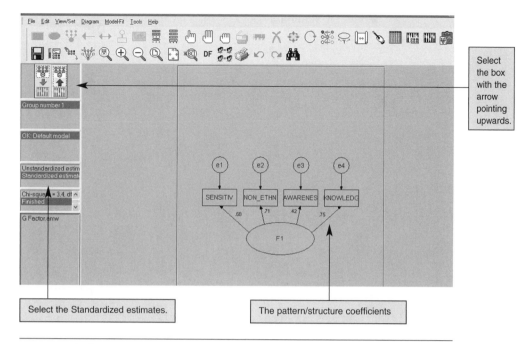

Figure 13b.4   The Model With the Standardized Coefficients Presented

As soon as you have selected **Calculate Estimates,** the screen will display the diagram and will now activate the little box in the upper left corner. By selecting (clicking on) the upward pointing red arrow, the path coefficients appear. The default in the AMOS program displays the unstandardized estimated coefficients. We ordinarily are more interested in the standardized ones. To obtain these instead, just click on **Standardized estimates** three boxes down from the red arrows. The standardized estimates of the coefficients are shown in Figure 13b.4.

We are now ready to examine the statistical results of the analysis. Select **View/Set → Text Output.** This will present the AMOS **Output** window (not shown). On the far left column, select **Model Fit** (second from bottom). This output presents the 24 fit measures arranged by classification. These can be seen in Figure 13b.5.

Overall Fit Indexes

In the **Model Fit Summary** output that AMOS provides, there are several tables, each presenting one or more model fit indexes. We have simplified this output by presenting only five of these tables. Notice that for each of the tables listed in the **Model Fit Summary** shown in Figure 13b.5, there are

Model Fit Summary

CMIN

Model	NPAR	CMIN	DF	P	CMIN/DF
Default model	8	3.445	2	.179	1.722
Saturated model	10	.000	0		
Independence model	4	72.658	6	.000	12.110

> This is identical to chi square. This value is not significant, indicating that the model fits the data.

RMR, GFI

Model	RMR	GFI	AGFI	PGFI
Default model	2.457	.978	.889	.196
Saturated model	.000	1.000		
Independence model	15.100	.651	.418	.390

> Values ≥ .95 reflects good match of model to data.

Baseline Comparisons

Model	NFI Delta1	RFI rho1	IFI Delta2	TLI rho2	CFI
Default model	.953	.858	.980	.935	.978
Saturated model	1.000		1.000		1.000
Independence model	.000	.000	.000	.000	.000

Parsimony-Adjusted Measures

Model	PRATIO	PNFI	PCFI
Default model	.333	.318	.326
Saturated model	.000	.000	.000
Independence model	1.000	.000	.000

> These will be used in Chapters 15A and 15B when we compare groups.

RMSEA

Model	RMSEA	LO 90	HI 90	PCLOSE
Default model	.096	.000	.262	.238
Independence model	.375	.301	.455	.000

> < .08 reflects good fit, .08 to .1 reflects moderate fit, and > .1 reflects poor fit.

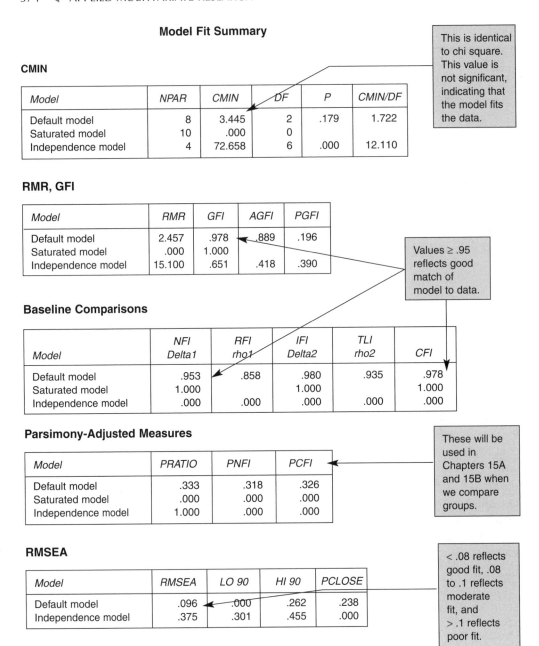

Figure 13b.5   A Variety of Model Fit Indexes Produced by AMOS

three models being assessed: (a) the default model (i.e., the proposed or hypothesized model), (b) the saturated model in which it is presumed that there is a perfect fit between the latent factor and indicator variables, and (c) the independence model in which it is presumed that the indicator variables are not at all related to the latent factor.

Various strategies have been suggested for assessing the results of these goodness-of-fit indexes. Byrne (2001), for example, has argued for examining only the default model. Recently, with the advances of more realistic simulation studies, Kline (2005) and Thompson (2004) recommend fit measures without reference to their classification. We suggest reporting chi square, the normed fit index (NFI), the comparative fit index (CFI), and root mean square error of approximation (RMSEA) as fit measures.

Minimum Discrepancy (Chi Square)

Directly below the title **Model Fit Summary** is the **CMIN** table. **CMIN** stands for "minimum discrepancy"; this generally refers to a comparison between the observed covariance to the hypothesized or predicted covariance. This is identical to the chi-square test of model fit, and we will interpret it as a chi square. The computed value of the chi-square statistic is 3.445. With 2 degrees of freedom, the p value tells us that the chi square is not significant ($p = .179$). Remember that the chi-square test assesses the relationship between expected and observed values. If the expected and the observed values are close, then no statistical significance would be detected. What we are comparing is the expected (proposed model) and the observed (actual) data. If the model represents the data as we hope, then the chi square will be nonsignificant.

Recall that Jöreskog and Sörbom (1996) and Bentler (1990) advised against the sole use of the chi-square value in judging the overall fit of the model because of the sensitivity of the chi square to sample size. As sample size increases, power increases. Therefore, the chi-square test can detect small discrepancies between the observed and predicted covariances and suggest that the model does not fit the data. A good-fitting model could therefore be rejected because of trivial but statistically significant differences between the observed and predicted values. Thompson (2004) suggests that the chi square has limited utility in assessing the fit of a single model, although he does believe that it can be productively used in comparing models (as we will see in Chapter 15A). Because of the limitations of chi square, other fit indexes have been developed as alternatives.

In the third table in the AMOS output labeled as **Baseline Comparisons**, we have the **CFI** and the **NFI**. These measures assess the fit of the proposed model relative to the independence model, which assumes that there are no relationships in the data. From the standpoint of the researchers, the independence model is the worst possible model. These measures indicate the improvement of the hypothesized model compared with the baseline, which assumes that there are no relationships in the data. The values of these measures can range between 0 and 1. Values of .95 or greater are deemed as an acceptable fit of the model to the data. The values of the **CFI** and the **NFI** are .978 and .953, respectively.

The **RMSEA** is located in the last table shown in Figure 13b.5. The **RMSEA** is the average of the residuals between the observed correlation/covariance from the sample and the expected model estimated from the population. Byrne (1994) stated, "(RMSEA) has only recently been recognized as one of the most informative criteria in covariance structure modeling" (p. 112). Loehlin (2004) proposes the following criteria for evaluating this index: (a) Less than .08 indicates good fit, (b) .08 to .1 indicates a moderate fit, and (c) greater than .1 indicates poor fit. In this example, the **RMSEA** is .096, indicating moderate fit.

Estimate Values for the Model

Next, from the far left-hand column on the **Amos Output** window select **Estimates** (the item directly above **Model-Fit**). This output window is shown in Figure 13b.6 and provides three tables: (a) the unstandardized **Regression Weights**, (b) the **Standardized Regression Weights**, and (c) the **Variances** of the five exogenous variables—the latent variable of Multicultural Competence and the four error (or unique) variables.

In the first table of Figure 13b.6, notice that the initial value for the unstandardized regression weights (called simply **Regression Weights** in the title of the table) between F1 (Multicultural Competence) and sensitivity (**SENSITIV**) is 1. This means that for every unit increase in Multicultural Competence, sensitivity increases by 1 unit. This coefficient was constrained at the initial stage in the analysis in order to scale the latent construct. The effect of this scaling on the analysis was to "lock in" this value of 1 as the unstandardized regression weight (the b weight) for that particular indicator variable. Because this weight has now been artificially associated with the measured variable, its statistical significance cannot (and should not) be estimated.

The next entry is non-ethnic ability (**NON_ETHN**) with an unstandardized regression weight of 1.109. This means that for every unit increase in Multicultural Competence, non-ethnic ability increases by 1.109. Thus, if Multicultural Competence increases from 2 to 3, then non-ethnic ability would increase from 2 to 3.109.

The standard error (**SE**) for this coefficient is .234. The **C.R.** stands for critical ratio, which is derived by dividing the unstandardized regression

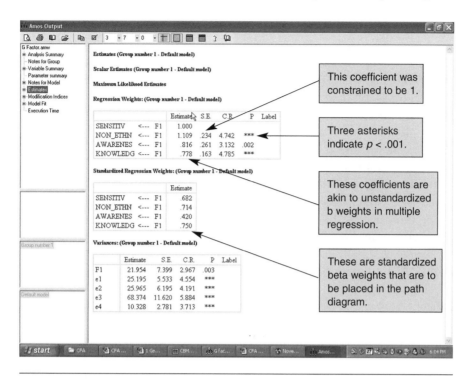

Figure 13b.6   Regression Weights and Exogenous Variables' Variance Estimates

weight (1.109) by the standard error (.234), a value that computes to 4.742. This value is interpreted as a *z* score, with values greater than 1.96, indicating statistical significance. In this example, the regression weight estimate is 4.742 standard errors above zero. In AMOS 5.0, any probability less than .001 is signified by an array of three asterisks. Given the output, we can see that the remaining three indicator variables did achieve statistical significance.

In the second table in Figure 13b.6, the standardized coefficients are presented. To determine whether these coefficients are statistically different from zero, we must consult the table above, where their significance was already calculated using the unstandardized values. Because the sensitivity variable was used as the basis for scaling the latent factor, even in its standardized form, we cannot determine whether or not it is statistically significant. Although it is probably common practice to not really be concerned with its statistical significance, it is probably worthwhile to repeat the analysis by dragging a different indicator into the first empty box at the start of the analysis. This will provide the statistical significance of the sensitivity indicator (with the significance of some other indicator remaining indeterminate this time).

The standardized coefficient can be individually interpreted as we would interpret a beta weight from a multiple regression analysis. For example, the coefficient between Multicultural Competence and sensitivity (**SENSITIV**) is .682. This means for every 1 standard deviation increase in Multicultural Competence, sensitivity increases by .682 standard deviations. These standardized coefficients are the pattern/structure coefficients that we would place in the path diagram.

We can also use these values, just as we use beta weights, to compare the relative influences of the latent factor on the indicator variables. Thus, in the example, we can say that the latent factor of Multicultural Competency is not as well indicated or assessed by awareness as it is by the other three whose beta weights (pattern/structure coefficients) are relatively greater and reasonably similar to each other. Be aware that, because we are dealing with beta weights, all the liabilities associated with them as discussed in Chapter 5A apply here as well.

The third table in Figure 13b.6 presents the variances of the five exogenous variables (the latent variable of Multicultural Competence and the four error variables). These values have no real value in our interpretation of the model.

Model Respecification

Our last AMOS example demonstrates the use of the **Modification Indices** to respecify a model. Recall that it is not uncommon that the initial proposed model fails to achieve an adequate fit and researchers need to consider modifying the model (i.e., respecifying). In respecifying the model, the researchers may delete the nonsignificant coefficients in an attempt to trim their models or add coefficients between factor and indicator variables that were previously ignored as an approach to develop their models. Researchers need to consider if the respecification is theoretically justifiable. If deleting or adding a coefficient lacks any theoretical justification, the researchers need to avoid this temptation in an attempt to improve the model fit.

To provide an example of a respecified model, we will consider a different and somewhat more complicated model. Assume that some researchers are assessing the construct validity of a new instrument used to determine aptitude for graduate school. The researchers proposed two latent factors (Verbal Ability and Math Ability). Each factor has three measured (indicator) variables. The Verbal Ability factor is composed of scores from three subscales: spelling, grammar, and comprehension. The Math Ability factor is composed of scores from three subscales: word problems, calculations, and conceptual understanding. This model is illustrated in Figure 13b.7.

After constructing the model, select **View/Set → Analysis Properties → Output** and check the **Modification indices** checkbox as well as the

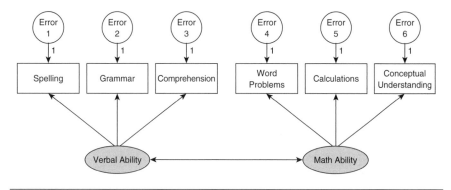

Figure 13b.7   Model of Verbal and Math Ability

Standardized estimates checkbox. Select **Model-Fit → Calculate Estimates** from the output check sheet.

The results of the overall model, which are not shown here, indicated a moderate fit between the proposed model and the observed data. The chi square was statistically significant, indicating a lack of fit. Both the **CFI** and **NFI** indicate a marginal fit with .944 and .931, respectively, because both values are below the recommended .95. The **RMSEA** indicates a moderate fit with .085.

The coefficients relating the latent factors to the indicator variables indicate that most of the values are in the .6 range, although the tie between Math Ability and word problems is only .48. The values of these coefficients are well above the generally accepted lower bound of .3 and so would ordinarily be acceptable, but because the fit indexes suggest that the model is less than a good fit to the data, some researchers would not be inclined to close the book on the model just yet.

Because the fit of the model to the data was not all that impressive, it is possible for the researchers to speculate that a respecified model (one that is a modified version of the original) may better account for the observed data. Although this respecified model would be evaluated through confirmatory factor analysis, the approach is substantially less confirmatory and substantially more exploratory because of its post hoc nature. However, it may be productive to explore an alternative model if it is theoretically reasonable. Researchers may then plan to evaluate it with a new sample in the future.

To modify the existing model, select **View/Set → Text Output → Modification Indexes** from the main menu. The corresponding output is shown in Figure 13b.8. Under the column labeled **MI** are the values of the modification index. Larger values indicate that the corresponding modification would create a more substantial impact in bettering the fit. The top table focuses on specifying correlations between the latent error variables and the other latent variables in the model. The largest **MI** value concerns the tie between **Error 3** (the error variable associated with comprehension) and the Math Ability factor. Creating a path between them would provide the largest increase to the fit. The only issue is that it does not make much theoretical sense to accomplish such a change, and this theoretical rationale must play a major role in any modification decisions in order to justify the act of modifying a model.

The second table of Figure 13b.8 focuses on specifying additional pattern/structure coefficient paths from the latent factors to the indicator variables and from some indicator variables to other indicator variables. At least two of the modification suggestions made by AMOS as shown in Figure 13b.8 actually make theoretical sense. These are the two modification indexes suggesting that adding a path (coefficient) from Verbal Ability to Word Problems (**MATH1**) and from Math Ability to Comprehension (**VERB3**) would improve the fit of a model. These particular paths make a certain amount of theoretical sense because verbal ability may be necessary to comprehend math word problems and math ability could be at least partially indicated by comprehension of verbal material.

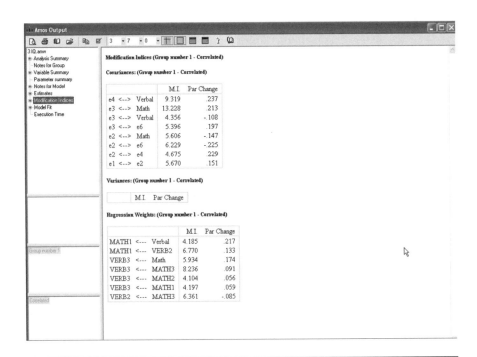

Figure 13b.8   Modification Suggestions Supplied by AMOS

To generate the new set of results that are applicable with this new model, we need to select **Model-Fit → Calculate Estimates.** A portion of the outcome of the new model is shown in Figure 13b.9. The fit indexes, although not shown here, suggest a better fit between the proposed model and the observed data. We show only the estimated factor coefficients and the correlations between the two latent variables. The chi square is

Regression Weights: (Group number 1—Default model)

			Estimate	S.E.	C.R.	P	Label
VERB1	<---	Verbal	1.000				
VERB2	<---	Verbal	1.082	.123	8.790	***	
VERB3	<---	Verbal	.638	.106	6.004	***	
MATH1	<---	Math	1.000				
MATH2	<---	Math	1.158	.135	8.587	***	
MATH3	<---	Math	.543	.109	4.982	***	
VERB3	<---	Math	.339	.076	4.450	***	
MATH3	<---	Verbal	.463	.134	3.446	***	

Standardized Regression Weights: (Group number 1—Default model)

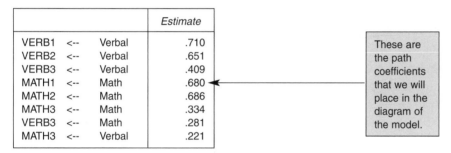

			Estimate
VERB1	<--	Verbal	.710
VERB2	<--	Verbal	.651
VERB3	<--	Verbal	.409
MATH1	<--	Math	.680
MATH2	<--	Math	.686
MATH3	<--	Math	.334
VERB3	<--	Math	.281
MATH3	<--	Verbal	.221

These are the path coefficients that we will place in the diagram of the model.

Covariances: (Group number 1—Default model)

			Estimate	S.E.	C.R.	P	Label
Verbal	<-->	Math	.493	.088	5.588	***	

Correlations: (Group number 1—Default model)

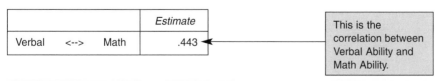

			Estimate
Verbal	<-->	Math	.443

This is the correlation between Verbal Ability and Math Ability.

Figure 13b.9 Path Coefficients Showing the Factor Weightings and the Correlations Between the Two Factors

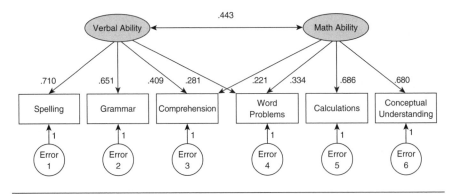

Figure 13b.10   The Pattern Coefficients Relating the Latent Factor to the
Indicators

nonsignificant, indicating a fit between the model and data. Improvements in the other fit indexes were also obtained. Both the **CFI** and **NFI** increased to .998 and .987, respectively, indicating an excellent fit (both values are above the recommended .95). The **RMSEA** decreased to .017, also indicating a good fit.

The path coefficients are shown in Figure 13b.10 and generally tend to be a bit higher than we saw for the prior model. For example, Spelling changed from .68 to .71, and Calculations changed from .67 to .69. But as discussed in Chapter 13A, the new "cross-loading" (e.g., a verbal ability indicator loading on the math ability factor) coefficients, although not large in an absolute sense, do add explanatory power. By specifying word problems to be an indicator of verbal ability and by specifying comprehension to be an indicator of math ability, we have apparently gained additional explanatory power.

It is possible to statistically compare the two models. We can do so using the chi-square difference test, something that we will talk more about in Chapter 15A. For now, all we need to say is that the comparison involves subtracting the smaller chi-square value from the larger value. The difference in the chi squares here, which is itself a chi square, is 30.78. With 2 degrees of freedom, this resulting chi square is statistically significant and supports the notion that the second model is superior to the first.

Results

This study examined the indicator variables that made up the California Brief Multicultural Competence Scale (CBMCS). This scale was developed to assess multicultural competence for mental health providers. The hypothesized model was assessed by AMOS version 5.0 maximum likelihood factor analysis (Arbuckle, 2004). The model was evaluated by four fit measures: (a) the chi square, (b) the normed fit index (NFI), (c) the comparative fit index (CFI), and (d) the root mean square error of approximation (RMSEA). Results of all four fit indexes support the proposed model. The chi square had a value of 3.445 (2, N = 351), p = .179, indicating an acceptable match between the proposed model and the observed data. The CFI and the NFI are measures of relative fit comparing the hypothesized model with the null model with acceptable values of .95 (Hu & Bentler, 1999a, 1999b). Both the CFI and NFI yielded values of .978 and .953, respectively, indicating an excellent fit of the model. The RMSEA measures the discrepancy between the sample coefficients and the population coefficients with values closer to zero indicative of a well-fitting model. The RMSEA was .096, indicating a moderate fit (Loehlin, 2004).

13B Exercises

Verbal/Math IQ Test

An educational psychologist hypothesizes that math and verbal abilities are separate cognitive functions. To test this theory, a confirmatory factor analysis (CFA) was performed on two latent variables with six measured variables. The Verbal factor is composed of scores from three subscales: "verb1" (spelling), "verb2" (grammar), and "verb3" (comprehension). The Math factor is made up of scores from three subscales: "math1" (word problems), "math2" (calculations), and "math3" (conceptual).

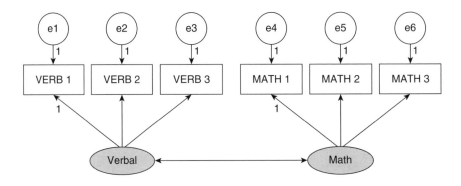

Figure 13.b11

Using the SPSS data file for Chapter 13B (located on the Web-based study site— http://www.sagepub.com/amrStudy), answer the following questions.

1. Report the chi square, *p* value, CFI, NFI, and the RMSEA.

2. Did all items "load" on their respective factors?

3. What is the correlation between "self-directed" and "other-directed"? Is it significant?

4. How would you interpret the correlation between the two factors?

5. Write a results section for this project.

Causal Modeling

Path Analysis and Structural Equation Modeling

Recall from Chapter 12A that the term *factor analysis* is often used as an umbrella label that includes a variety of statistical techniques (e.g., principal axis factoring, principal components analysis). Similarly, the term *path analysis* is often used as a general term to describe a causal model. These models always contain a set of measured variables because some data must have been collected before we can actually process the model. The issue is whether the model also encompasses latent variables as well. Traditionally, the label path analysis is used to describe a causal model with only measured variables, whereas the label "structural equation modeling" is used to describe a causal model with latent variables. We will conform to this distinction in this chapter. Structural equation modeling is usually referred to by its abbreviation of SEM, and we will use this abbreviation here as well.

We begin our discussion of causal modeling with path analysis. Path analysis was developed to assess the direct and indirect effects of some variables that were theorized to be causes of other variables. Presently, path analysis is viewed by some researchers as less interesting than SEM because of its use of only a single measure for each of the constructs in the model (Kline, 1998). However, understanding path analysis is important because (a) many studies published in the professional literature employ path analysis and (b) the principles of path analysis can be extrapolated to SEM.

Principles of Path Analysis

Path analysis was first introduced by Wright (1921) as an application of multiple regression analysis, and has gained in popularity in recent years. Today we also have the option to perform a path analysis in model-fitting programs as well as through regression. By using path analysis, researchers are able to evaluate explicitly hypothesized and often relatively complex causal (predictive) relationships between the variables represented in their data (Klem, 1995). In essence, the steps taken by researchers in conducting a path analysis are as follows:

- ▶ Draw out the interrelationships of the variables in the form of a diagram.
- ▶ Indicate the hypothesized strength (e.g., relatively strong, moderate, modest, weak) and direction (direct or inverse) of each variable's presumed effect on each other in each of the "paths."
- ▶ Perform the analyses yielding the path coefficients for each path.
- ▶ Compare the obtained path coefficients with the hypothesized path strengths and directions.
- ▶ Evaluate how well the causal (predictive) model fits the data based on the results of the analysis.

From the standpoint of multiple regression, you would think that path analysis would be associated with the label *predictive modeling* rather than with the more commonly used term *causal modeling* because path coefficients are beta weights from the prediction equation. Maybe invoking the term *cause* has added some extra interest in the procedure (and perhaps some controversy as well); explicating the cause of an event might suggest, to some, greater explanatory power than indicating how much we are able to predict an event.

Causal modeling in the context of path analysis really just results from synthesizing the outcome of several prediction analyses. Nonetheless, understanding the uses and limitations of path analysis is intimately related to the way in which causality is tied to the scientific method itself. Most scientists rarely make observations for their own sake. Instead, observation (data collection) serves as a means for scientists to organize or explain the phenomena they see in the empirical world or as a way of testing their theoretical formulations. Organizing or explaining efforts very often involves theorizing about the causal principles underlying the relationships between the variables on which they have collected data. We will therefore briefly examine the concept of causality as a foundation for our discussion of path analysis.

Causality and Path Analysis

Most of the data to which path analysis is applied have been collected using a correlational procedure. That is, the data on most or all the variables have been collected at the same time and under the same conditions for all participants. In such a situation, the research method would not support drawing causal inferences from the study.

So how do we get from "the research method would not support drawing causal inferences" to a statistical procedure that allows researchers to evaluate a causal model? The answer is indirectly, at best, via the following logic.

Causality Is an Inference

We start with the principle that causality is not present in the actual observations (and is therefore not present in the data) of any piece of research. That is, we cannot measure causality itself. When you direct your hand to the computer's mouse on the desk and move it, an observer may know that it was your effort that caused the mouse to move. But what the observer sees (i.e., what is in the province of one's actual experience) is essentially two events: your touching the mouse and its subsequent movement.

David Hume, the eminent British philosopher, made this case eloquently. Basically, he argued that all we see is co-occurrence, what we now call *correlation* or *covariation*. We see you touch the mouse (A) and then see it move (B). The former we call the cause; the latter we call the effect.

Experiencing such sequences repeatedly throughout our lives provides us with the necessary condition for causality: Present A and B occurs. This is one of the two pieces of information we use in our attribution of causality. In addition to necessity, Hume suggested, we also need a condition known as *sufficiency*. We say that A is sufficient for B if its absence is also associated with the absence of B. The mouse had better not move if you do not touch it.

Over a considerable history of experiencing A followed by B together with not-A followed by not-B, we build up a repertoire of the necessary and sufficient conditions associated with correlated events. Hume suggested that we represent this history when we assert that A is the cause of B. From Hume's analysis, we do not directly experience causality per se—all we have is a long series of correlations, which we have summarized within a causal structure.

Causality and Research Methods

Hume's analysis in many ways captures the logic of the scientific method. Take the conceptually simplest experiment consisting of an experimental group and a control group. A treatment is presented to those in the experimental group and not presented to those in the control group, with all other conditions comparable. Any difference between the two groups can therefore be attributed to the treatment effect; that is, we draw the inference that the treatment caused the two groups to be different.

This is a living example of Hume's analysis. The experimental group represents the necessary condition—presents the treatment (A) and obtains a certain effect (B). The control condition represents the sufficient condition—withhold the treatment (not-A) and do not observe the effect (not-B). By establishing the necessary and sufficient conditions, we are in a relatively strong position to draw the inference that the treatment causes such and such effect.

A correlation design does not permit us to observe behavior under the necessary and sufficient conditions. We are not able to systematically present and withhold a particular treatment. Cause and effect, even if they are present in the variables captured in the analysis, are inextricably woven together in such a design. At best, all we can see are some As followed by Bs and some not-As followed by not-Bs.

What we actually see in correlation data is covariation to a certain quantifiable extent. A and B, together with many other variables, can be quantitatively related to each other in terms of correlation. We can assess the degree to which each pair of variables covaries. Although we are a long way from drawing a causal inference based on an experimental manipulation, covariation presents us with a rich data source. Path analysis takes advantage of this richness.

The professional discussion concerning correlation and causality is far from over. Consider the following argument presented by Meehl and Waller (2002):

> One hears the objection "Correlation does not prove causality." If *prove* means *deduce,* of course it cannot in any empirical domain—courts of law, business, common life, or sciences. However, causal inference can be strongly corroborated—*proved,* in the usual sense of the term—by correlation. (p. 284)

Research Methods Versus Statistical Analysis

One of the more useful distinctions students can make is between the research methods used to collect the data and the statistical technique used to analyze the data. The research method sets the limits on the strength of your causal inferences. A well-controlled experimental study provides a strong base for such inferences, a quasi-experimental study will provide a much weaker base for causal inferences, and a correlation study will provide little or no basis for causal inferences.

Once the data have been collected, the die is cast in terms of the strength of causal inferences that can be drawn from the study. But the statistical analysis is yet to be done. From a statistical standpoint, we have data to be analyzed regardless of the manner by which the data have been collected. For example, suppose that we had a dichotomous variable based on whether or not individuals watched the third and final movie of *The Lord of the Rings* trilogy (coded 0 for "no" and 1 for "yes") and a quantitative measure of the degree to which they read fantasy literature.

We could use at least two different procedures to analyze these data. We could compute the Pearson *r* to assess the correlation between viewing the third and final movie of *The Lord of the Rings* trilogy and the amount of fantasy literature people read. Or, we could compute an independent groups *t* test (equivalent to a one-way between-subjects ANOVA) to assess differences between those who saw the final movie and those who did not on the amount of fantasy literature they read.

Because the data set is the same, these analyses would of necessity produce the same outcome, although we might use slightly different language (covariation or mean differences) to express the outcome. The point is that whether these data were collected through a correlation procedure (survey enough people who did and did not see the movie and ask them about their reading preferences) or an experimental procedure (near the time that the movie became available, randomly assign half the participants to watch the movie and have the others to do some other task after which you would ask them about their reading preferences), you could legitimately perform either of these analyses.

"Causal" Analysis of Correlation Data

We are now ready to answer the question of how one can evaluate a hypothesized causal model based on correlation data. The short answer is, "Data are data," and we can do any analysis that is consistent with the underlying assumptions, provided that we can make sense of the outcome. Setting up the model in the form of a path diagram is an articulation of the hypotheses that are to be tested. The relationships between the variables are contained in the data set. All that a causal analysis does is map one to the other.

Causal analysis is not designed to replace the experimental approach. But at the same time, correlation is embedded in causality (causality implies correlation). And correlation data are rich in information, which can be extracted and applied in a variety of ways. One very interesting application is to set up a prediction model interrelating three or more variables and then to test the viability of that model. This is exactly what path analysis does.

The Concept of a Causal Model

The Path Diagram

Causal analysis starts with researchers constructing a path diagram. As mentioned in Chapter 13A, variables are connected to other variables by arrows representing hypothesized causal linkages. Multiple regression or model-fitting analyses are then computed to determine the path coefficients. These path coefficients are no more than the standardized regression coefficients (beta weights) gleaned from the appropriate analysis; we are not focused on the raw score coefficients in path analysis. One then examines the magnitudes of these coefficients to decide if the hypothesized causal model has any statistical viability (usually at .3 or greater).

We have illustrated a relatively simple causal model as the path analysis shown in Figure 14a.1. We know that this is a path analysis because the variables are all measured variables (boxes are used for such variables). This particular model shows the hypothesized interrelationship between the observed variables A, B, and C. It proposes a relatively weak causal relationship (predictive path) from A to C, a relatively strong connection between A and B, and another relatively strong connection between B and C. In conceptual and causal terms, this path model proposes that A has an effect on C primarily because it "causes" or acts through B rather than having a strong effect on C directly. We can say that A is hypothesized to exert a strong indirect effect on C through the mediation role of B.

The variables encompassed in a path model are all measured variables. They are called by other names as well, such as *observed variables* and

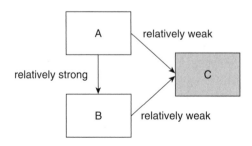

Figure 14a.1 A Simple Path Model

manifest variables. These measured variables can be classified in a couple of different ways. Variables can be either *endogenous* or *exogenous,* and they can also be thought of as playing the roles of *dependent variables* and *independent variables.* These classification schemas often overlap with each other. Paying attention to whether or not a variable is associated with an arrow pointing to it or away from it is the key to properly labeling it.

Endogenous and Exogenous Variables

Some variables are hypothesized in the model as being explained (having their variance accounted for) by other variables. The variables being explained are the endogenous variables. You can recognize such variables because they have arrows pointing toward them. In the model shown in Figure 14a.1, B and C are pointed to by arrows and are therefore classified as endogenous variables.

Some variables are not presumed to be explained by other variables in the model. Rather, they are simply taken as given in the model, presumably explained by some other factors beyond the scope of the model. These "not explained" variables are the exogenous variables. They can be recognized because there is no arrow pointing toward them. Variable A in Figure 14a.1 is an exogenous variable.

Dependent and Independent Variables

We talked in previous chapters about the possibility of treating a variable as either a dependent variable or as an independent variable in particular statistical analyses. This possibility can be even more forcefully made here. We will use multiple regression analysis as our example statistical technique for performing a path analysis to carry this discussion. Model fitting does something similar but is a bit more complicated. If we use multiple regression to perform a path analysis, we would run enough regression analyses (one multiple regression analysis for each endogenous variable) to obtain all the path coefficients in the model. In any one of the multiple regression analyses, the criterion variable is the dependent (endogenous) variable, and the predictors are the independent variables that are hypothesized to cause it. The independent variables in the analysis are those whose arrows point to the dependent variable.

Using conceptual language, independent variables predict or cause dependent variables. This sort of a relationship is reflected in the direction of arrows in the model. A variable will be treated as a dependent variable when it has one or more arrows pointing toward it. Variables will be treated as independent variables when those variables are "doing the pointing."

Examine the model shown in Figure 14a.1. Variable B has an arrow pointing to it from A. Thus, in one regression analysis, A will be the predictor (independent variable) and B will be the criterion (dependent variable). Variable C also has arrows pointing to it and will therefore serve as the dependent variable in another analysis. Those arrows emerge from both A and B, and so we know that these two variables will function as the independent variables in that analysis. Because we have covered all the endogenous variables, we have covered all the regression analyses that need to be performed.

Relating the Two Classification Schemas

Exogenous variables—those taken as a given in the model—do not have any arrows pointing to them. Therefore, they always serve as independent variables and cannot serve as dependent variables. Endogenous variables—those explained by the model—will always have arrows pointing toward them. Therefore, they will always function as dependent variables in a subset of the regression analyses. It is also true, as we have seen in the example model, that some of these endogenous variables can also be the source of arrows; it is thus possible that some of these endogenous variables may be used as independent variables in other regression analyses.

Preparing for a Path Analysis

The Assumptions of Path Analysis

Pedhazur (1997) provides five assumptions underlying the application of path analysis when multiple regression is used to perform the analysis. Kline (1998) discusses the assumptions for path analysis using model-fitting programs. These assumptions are summarized here (with a minor variation or two):

1. Relations between variables in the model are linear and causal. The relations are not curvilinear, and interaction relations are excluded. Linearity can and should be examined before the analysis is run, as described in Chapters 3A and 3B and through the curve estimation procedure in **Regression** in SPSS. This assumption applies to both approaches.

2. The errors associated with the endogenous variables are not correlated with the variables that are predicting that variable. This assumption applies to both approaches.

3. There is only a one-way causal flow in the model. Such a model is called a recursive model. This assumption applies only to multiple regression. A double causal flow (where we see two separate straight arrows between variables A and B, one pointing from A to B and the other pointing from B to A) is permitted in model-fitting programs.

4. The variables are measured on at least an interval or near-interval (e.g., summative response) scale. This assumption applies to both approaches.

5. The variables are measured without error; that is, the reliability of the measured variables is perfect. This assumption is unrealistic in behavioral science, but the analytic procedures presume that this is the case. This assumption applies to both approaches.

In addition, there is the general assumption that we have described in our multiple regression chapter that the set of variables selected for the analysis makes up the universe of all relevant variables. This is essentially the issue of specifying the model. Pedhazur (1997) states it well: "Examples of specification errors are: omitting relevant variables from the regression equation, including irrelevant variables in the regression equation, and postulating a linear model when a nonlinear model is more appropriate" (p. 288).

This admonition also applies to path analysis. If we are going to hypothesize a causal model and then evaluate how well it fits the data, it could be an exercise in futility if we had not included an important cause in it, and it could be more work for no purpose if we included variables that were irrelevant to the predictions we were making.

Missing Values in Path Analysis

In performing an analysis of a particular path model, it is important that the different analyses (in multiple regression) are performed on exactly the same group of cases in the data file (in model fitting, the analysis is done at one time on all the cases, so only one analysis is needed). To the extent that the sets of participants differ across regression analyses, it becomes increasingly difficult to argue that the path coefficients written into the path diagram can be compared with each other because some of them may have been based on different sets of subjects. Thus, some procedure to deal with missing values is usually done just prior to running the set of multiple regression analyses. Model-fitting programs differ to a certain extent in how they arrive at this same point, but all require that all the cases have valid values on the variables used in the analysis.

One way to make sure that all variables are represented by the same participants is to use the **Mean Substitution** specification on the **Missing** command in the regression analysis. This operation replaces all missing values with the mean value of the variable based on all the valid values. The upside of using this mean substitution strategy is that it allows us to use all our participants. However, adding the mean into the data set for subjects who do not have an original valid value on the variable reduces the variance associated with the variable (remember that variance reflects the difference between a score and the mean and that this replacement value is precisely at the mean). With enough subjects getting such a replacement value, it is possible to seriously shrink the variance conceivably to the point where the correlations between the variables, and hence the regression analysis, could be adversely affected.

In AMOS, the model-fitting program we discuss here, the issue of missing data is handled by a full-information maximum likelihood procedure (Anderson, 1957). This is a particular type of imputation procedure (see Chapter 3A) where the missing value is a dependent variable in a regression formula using all the other variables as predictors. An imputation procedure can also be used prior to multiple regression analysis.

Structuring the Path Analyses

There are two ways to analyze path models: (a) multiple regression analysis or (b) estimation with a model-fitting program (Kline, 1998). The multiple regression option employs the ordinary least squares method, whereas model-fitting programs typically use maximum likelihood (discussed in Chapter 6A) to calculate the path coefficients. These two options generally produce similar but not necessarily identical results. Later, we will discuss some of the additional benefits of using a model-fitting program.

The Multiple Regression Approach to Path Analysis

The multiple regression strategy to computing a path analysis employs the ordinary least squares method to calculate the path coefficients. In this approach, the path coefficients are the beta weights associated with the predictor variables in the regression equation. It is common for several multiple regression analyses to be used on different subsets of the variables before all the path coefficients are obtained.

Multiple regression was discussed in detail in Chapter 5A, but even there we held back a bit of the complexity involved. It's now time to tap into some of that complexity. Part of the language used in multiple regression

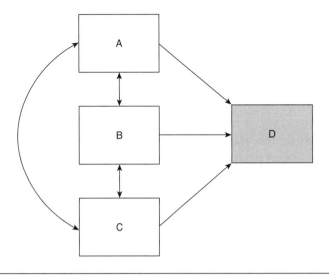

Figure 14a.2   A Single-Stage Model

refers to the "model," which we had identified as the multiple regression equation. Although that is still true, there is more to the model than just that. You can think of what is examined in regression as a single-stage model (Pedhazur & Schmelkin, 1991) or as a single-stage causal model.

A single-stage causal model contains a single endogenous variable that is the dependent variable in the regression analysis. This model also contains any number of exogenous or predictor variables presumed to be directly related to the dependent variable. We have drawn a single-stage model using three predictors and one criterion variable in Figure 14a.2. This shows a model with three predictors and one criterion variable. Although it is too simple for most researchers to take seriously as a causal model, its underlying structure is technically subsumed under causal modeling. Because there is only one endogenous variable (a variable that can serve as a dependent variable), only one multiple regression analysis needs to be performed. The beta weights from that analysis will be placed on the paths and will be called *path coefficients.*

A single-stage model can be differentiated from a multistage model (Pedhazur & Schmelkin, 1991). The *multi* in "multistage model" indicates that more than one endogenous variable has been identified. That is, more than one variable has arrows pointing to it. Multistage causal models are what most researchers have in mind when they speak about path analysis. In multistage models, we must perform more than one regression analysis. In fact, we perform as many multiple regression analyses as there are endogenous variables.

The causal model shown earlier in Figure 14a.1 is an example of a multistage model. Variables B and C are both at the receiving end of the arrows and are thus endogenous variables; they are presumed to be predicted from or caused by other variables in the model. There are thus two regression analyses needed here, one for each of these two variables to which the arrows point.

We perform one regression analysis for each endogenous variable in the causal model. Each endogenous variable becomes the dependent or criterion variable in that particular analysis. Any and all variables that are presumably causing it (i.e., any variables "pointing" to that endogenous variable) take the role of independent or predictor variables in that analysis. Remember, however, that a variable serving as a criterion (dependent) variable in one analysis could very well be one of the predictor variables in another analysis. The general rule governing the nature and number of regression analyses needed to address a path model is as follows:

> Each endogenous variable involves a separate regression analysis for which it will be the dependent variable. For each analysis, all the variables pointing to that endogenous variable will serve as independent variables.

The model in Figure 14a.1 proposes that there is a relatively strong link between A and B (that A is a relatively strong predictor or cause of B). This represents one regression analysis where the values of B are predicted from a knowledge of the corresponding values of A; that is, B will be the dependent variable and A will be the independent variable. The model also has two arrows pointing toward C, one from A and another from B. This represents the other regression analysis where C is predicted from both A and B; that is, C is the dependent variable and A and B are the independent variables.

In running each of the regression analyses, it is mandatory that we use the standard (simultaneous) method where all the predictor variables for that particular regression analysis are placed into the equation at the same time. As you recall, the beta weights (which will be the path coefficients) are assigned under the standard equation-building method by assuming that each variable is the last one to enter the model. Thus, variables are entered only after controlling for the influence of all the other predictors. We use the standard regression method because we need to generate the beta weights of all predictor variables. Here, low values of some beta weights (e.g., < .2) are potentially as informative as high values (e.g., > .3) of others if we are evaluating hypotheses of weaker as well as stronger causal influences in the model.

The Model-Fitting Approach to Path Analysis

The model-fitting program typically uses maximum likelihood to calculate the path coefficients. Maximum likelihood procedures attempt to estimate the values of the parameters that would result in the highest likelihood of obtaining the actual data based on the proposed model. These methods often require iterative solutions.

Kline (1998) encourages researchers to use a model-fitting program because these programs provide the following: (a) an overall fit of the model, (b) the indirect and total effects of the predictors' variables, and (c) estimates of the path coefficients for latent variables models (as opposed to measured or observed variables). We will discuss each in turn.

Overall Fit

The overall fit of the model is how well the model explains the data, an outcome not available in multiple regression. The best a researcher can do in regression analysis is to compare the observed correlation with the hypothesized correlations. If the two correlation matrixes are within .05 of the observed correlation matrix, then the researcher has some evidence of a proper fit (Agresti & Finlay, 1997). If multiple models are used, then the model that most closely resembles the observed model is considered "best."

Indirect and Total Effects

Indirect effects involve mediator variable(s). In our example, A is hypothesized to have a direct effect on C and an indirect effect on C mediated by B. This indirect effect is calculated by multiplying the path coefficient between A and B by the path coefficient between B and C. The total effect is calculated by adding the direct effect and the indirect effect. One can do this as well in multiple regression; model-fitting programs often perform this calculation for you.

Working With Latent Variables

Kline's (1998) third reason to encourage researchers to use model fitting as their causal analysis method is that the statistical programs enabling us to do this are also perfectly at home performing SEM—that is, including latent variables in the models that are assessed. By definition, using multiple regression precludes this option because the variables in the analysis must be represented one-for-one in the data file; that is, multiple regression must be performed on observed variables.

Comparing Multiple
Regression and Model-Fitting Approaches

As we have previously noted, multiple regression employs the ordinary least squares method to calculate the path coefficients; model-fitting approaches typically use maximum likelihood to calculate the path coefficients. The ordinary least squares estimation in multiple regression is known as a partial-information technique, whereas the maximum likelihood estimation in the model-fitting program is known as a full-information technique (Kelloway, 1998).

The differences between the partial- and the full-information techniques revolve around two interrelated features of the multiple regression and model-fitting procedures: (a) using some or all the information in any single analysis and (b) the iteration feature. We will discuss these features separately based on Kelloway's (1998) presentation. To keep things as simple as we can, we will focus on the path model in Figure 14a.1 as our illustration.

Using Some or All of the Information

Recall that the multiple regression approach in our example required us to run two separate regression solutions; one involved A predicting B, and the other involved A and B predicting C. Thus, in any single regression solution we are using, the information is only a subset of the data set. In some sense, any information concerning C's relationship to either A or B is irrelevant in the first regression solution. This can be contrasted with the model-fitting approach.

In model fitting, all the information concerning the interrelationships between all the variables is brought to bear simultaneously. The maximum likelihood procedure attempts to simultaneously generate the coefficients for all the variables with the goal of providing the best match to the data. Thus, when the model is estimating the coefficient that will work best to relate A and B, it is not doing the estimation in isolation. It is also very much involved with how C fits into all this because it is simultaneously working on the prediction of C from A and B. The coefficient it produces for the A-B path will therefore take into consideration how this solution relates to the one it is generating for C. The process is in some ways a gestalt; each part affects every other part, and it is the configuration of the parts into the whole that is paramount. In model fitting, it is the model as a whole that is fit to the data, not just a subset of the paths that the model contains. Selecting a value for one path intimately affects the values of the other paths; ultimately, the model stands or falls as a single entity rather than as a collection of separate and unrelated paths.

The Iteration Process

Not only does multiple regression use only a subset of the information contained in the data set to derive the values for the coefficients, it does so in a single evaluation of the data. For example, when the procedure is predicting C from A and B, it first controls for one variable and then controls for the other. These two processes—entering the variables into the equation after the other is controlled—are done independently of each other in two single assessments. The results are then summarized in the regression equation.

Model fitting typically uses an iterative maximum likelihood procedure. Not only does the procedure make use of all the information concerning the relationships between the variables simultaneously, it does not stop with its first best guess about the value of the coefficients for all the paths. Through a process of iteration as described in Chapter 12A, it uses its previous approximations to refine its estimates. Its target is to match the data, given the structure of the model, and we expect it to get closer and closer to that coveted match with successive attempts. At some juncture, it reaches the point of diminishing returns, and the mathematical criterion defining how much it is bettering its last attempt essentially says, "Okay, we're not making sufficient gains to keep this iterative process going. I'm going to issue the order to stop now."

Current Status

Partly as a result of using all the information simultaneously and partly as a result of engaging in an iterative estimation process, the model-fitting approach seems to us to be gaining acceptance in the behavioral and life sciences. Regression analysis can certainly be used to perform path analysis, but it is our impression that more researchers are gravitating to model-fitting programs such as AMOS. For those who do not have access to or do not have sufficient skill to use these latter types of programs, however, we should note that the path analysis results produced by the two approaches are very often similar.

A Path Analysis Example

In this example, researchers are investigating the causes or predictors of academic achievement in college. They are particularly interested in the influences of three independent variables, academic self-doubt, socioeconomic status (SES), and motivation, on the dependent variable of academic achievement. The correlation between the two exogenous variables (academic self-doubt and SES) is represented by the curved double arrow connecting them.

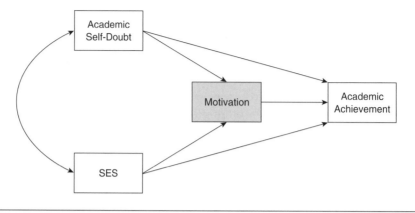

Figure 14a.3   Example of a Multistage Causal Model

This model is presented in Figure 14a.3. It contains two endogenous variables (motivation and academic achievement) and is considered to be a multistage causal model. Thus, two equations underlie this model in which the endogenous variables are being separately predicted.

In the model, the researcher is assessing what is called a saturated model in the sense that every variable is hypothesized to be related to every other variable. This model allows the researcher to examine the direct effects of academic self-doubt and SES on academic achievement. But it also allows us to examine some indirect effects as well. Not only are academic self-doubt and SES said to directly affect achievement, they are also hypothesized to exert an effect through the motivation variable. For example, students with less academic self-doubt may be more motivated to succeed, which in turn may yield greater academic achievement. Motivation takes on a "mediator" role in this model, and we would say that some of the causal influence of academic self-doubt and SES on academic achievement is mediated through motivation. Thus, academic self-doubt and SES are said to influence academic achievement in two ways: (a) by exerting a direct effect on academic achievement and (b) by exerting an indirect effect on academic achievement by affecting motivation.

The Multiple Regression Strategy to Perform a Path Analysis

The Analysis of the Model

This model, shown in Figure 14a.3, contains two exogenous variables and two endogenous variables. For every endogenous variable, a multiple regression analysis needs to be calculated. Therefore, in this example, two multiple regressions need to be conducted.

In the first regression analysis, we will focus on the academic achievement variable. Because the arrows are pointing to it—because causality is acting on it from the other variables—it is the dependent variable in the analysis. There are three variables identified as causes of academic achievement in the model: academic self-doubt, SES, and motivation. The first two are direct effects, and motivation represents a mediated effect.

In the second regression analysis, we will focus on motivation. It, too, is an endogenous variable and will be the dependent variable in this second analysis. Here, there are only two variables hypothesized as causally related to it—academic self-doubt and SES—and these will serve as the independent or predictor variables in the regression analysis.

The beta weights (i.e., the standardized regression weights) are assigned to the appropriate paths from each analysis. Thus, we learn the values for the path coefficients in a rather piecemeal fashion. The path coefficients leading to academic achievement are drawn from one regression analysis, and the path coefficients leading to motivation are drawn from the other analysis. You can now see why it so important to deal with missing values as we indicated earlier. Because beta weights from two separate analyses are being placed in the same model, it is necessary that the very same cases are captured in both.

We show the beta weights from these analyses as well as the correlation between the two exogenous variables in Figure 14a.4. Self-doubt and SES are both significant predictors of motivation. Because they exceed the .3 criterion, we would also treat them as having achieved practical significance as well. We see that the beta weight leading from academic self-doubt is negative, telling us that it is inversely related to motivation (e.g., higher levels of academic self-doubt are associated with lower motivational levels). The positive beta weight for SES informs us that higher status on the socioeconomic continuum predicts more motivation. Self-doubt in combination with SES predicted 36% of the variance of motivation (this is the R^2 value).

Only one of the three predictors of academic achievement yielded a significant beta weight. Motivation, with a beta weight of .48, accounted for 34% of the variance. Neither academic self-doubt nor SES produced any significant direct effect on achievement. Their effect, as we can now see, was indirect; their tie to academic achievement was accomplished through the mediator variable of motivation.

Respecifying the Model

We have seen that the originally proposed model, although not doing all that badly, was a bit off the mark. Two of the direct effects in the original did

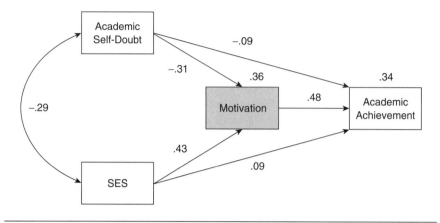

Figure 14a.4   Summary of Causal Effects for the Hypothesized Model of Academic Achievement From the Multiple Regression Analysis

not statistically materialize. In model-fitting approaches, we would respecify the model and use various fit indexes to base a judgment of whether or not our respecified model was a better fit to the data. But this is multiple regression, and those tools are not part of the program. The best we can do within this approach is to respecify the model and run the necessary multiple regression analyses again. Then we can at least place the beta weights from these new analyses on the paths.

The respecified model is shown in Figure 14a.5. The only difference here is that we have removed the two nonsignificant paths. Again, two multiple regressions will be calculated. In the first structural equation, the independent variable will be motivation, and the dependent variable will be academic achievement. In the second structural equation, the independent variables are academic self-doubt and SES; the dependent variable is motivation.

The results of this model, also shown in Figure 14a.6, indicate that all the path coefficients achieved both practical and statistical significance. This model may be considered as explaining the phenomenon more accurately. That is, academic self-doubt and SES are important variables in explaining academic achievement through the indirect effects they have on motivation.

The Model-Fitting Strategy to Perform a Path Analysis With Only Measured Variables

The model fitting approach was described in Chapter 13A in the context of confirmatory factor analysis. These procedures can also be used to perform

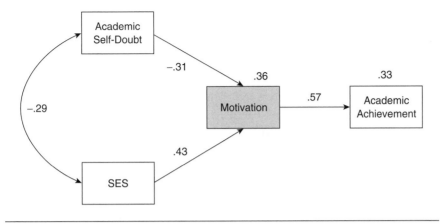

Figure 14a.5 Summary of Causal Effects for the Modified Model of Academic Achievement

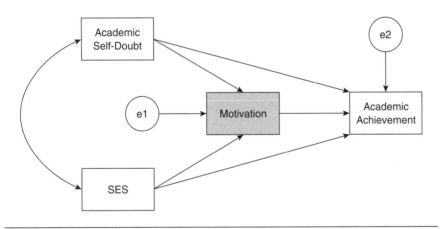

Figure 14a.6 The Hyphothesized Path Model

path analysis and are probably to be preferred over multiple regression if you are deciding between them. In the domain of model fitting, we can distinguish between two possible sets of variables. In one set, all the variables in the model are measured or observed variables. The causal model that ties them together is evaluated through path analysis. In the other set, the variables include both latent variables and observed or manifest variables. The causal model that relates these variables together is evaluated through SEM. We discuss path analysis in this section and SEM in the following section.

Resemblance of Regression and Structural Equations

We have discussed the differences between regression and model-fitting analyses. Among the differences are the following:

▶ Multiple regression is solved by ordinary least squares, whereas model-fitting programs estimate the parameters through the maximum likelihood technique.

▶ Least squares achieves the solution in one shot, whereas maximum likelihood uses an iterative strategy.

▶ Multiple regression solves the regression equation for each endogenous variable independently, whereas model-fitting procedures simultaneously assess all the paths of the entire model.

Nonetheless, there is a certain feature that these two approaches have in common. Just as separate equations are generated to predict the endogenous variables in multiple regression, so, too, are separate equations used to predict the endogenous variables in model-fitting programs. There are two differences that we note here: First, in multiple regression, these equations are dealt with separately. Model-fitting techniques also derive a separate equation for each endogenous variable. However, in this latter analysis, the equations are worked simultaneously.

Second, the form of the equation is a bit different. The standardized multiple regression equation is a weighted linear composite of the predictor variables. Each variable is weighted with respect to all the other predictors and the weights are designated as beta weights. The equation is designed to predict the dependent variable; that is, the weighted composite on one side of the equation equals the predicted value of the criterion variable on the other side of the equation. How well it predicts is told to us by R^2, which is the proportion of variance in the measured dependent variable that is predicted by the regression equation.

The model-fitting tradition takes a somewhat wider view, although it is not in conflict with what we have said about regression. As you have already seen in our discussion of confirmatory factor analysis, the model-fitting approach explicitly notes the error variance associated with variables in the model. More specifically, model-fitting programs assign an error component to every endogenous variable.

Because these endogenous variables will serve as the dependent variables in a prediction equation, we can think of what is predicted in model-fitting methods as the combination of the predicted value of the criterion variable and its error component (what is not able to be predicted). That is, what is predicted in such an equation is as follows:

predicted variance of the dependent variable + residual or error variance of the dependent variable

Conceptually, the combination of what we can and cannot predict of the dependent variable makes up all of it. Thus, the equation is designed to yield the actual or measured variable, which includes the part of it that is predictable and the part of it that is not. Because the error is explicitly included in the equation and we thus predict the full dependent variable, it is often referred to as a structural equation. The general form of the equation is as follows:

$$Y = \beta_1 X_1 + \beta_2 X_2 + \ldots + \beta_n X_n + \text{error}_Y$$

In this equation, Y is the measured dependent variable. This differs from the multiple regression equation where the target of the equation was the *predicted value* of Y, not the actual value. Here, the equation yields Y and not Y_{pred} because we have included the unaccounted for variance—the error_Y term—in the equation.

The difference between the forms of the equation in multiple regression and model fitting represents the emphasis they have and not necessarily a fundamentally different entity. Multiple regression simply focuses on generating the equation of the regression line that is the predicted value of the criterion variable. Thus, it makes sense for the multiple regression equation to yield Y_{pred}, the predicted value of the dependent variable. Model fitting is working hard to reproduce the original (observed or measured) data. Thus, it makes sense for the structural equation to yield Y, the observed value of the dependent variable. Both approaches to path analysis result in beta weights being used as the path coefficients; the difference is that these path coefficients have been derived using different analytic techniques.

The Analysis of the Model

Model-fitting programs typically use maximum likelihood to calculate the path coefficients, although other parameter estimation methods are available. Maximum likelihood attempts to estimate the values of the parameters of the model that would result in the highest likelihood of reproducing the actual data. These methods often require iterative solutions. Recall that in contrast to the multiple regression approach, which requires separate analyses for each endogenous variable, maximum likelihood estimates all the path coefficients simultaneously.

Model-fitting programs provide indexes so that you can gauge the overall fit of the model to the data. The overall fit of the model tells us how well the model explains the data. Stevens (2002) describes the assessment of a model as being analogous to the omnibus test in ANOVA in that even though the overall fit of a model to the data may appear acceptable, some relations (paths) in the model may not be supported by the data. An acceptable fit could be obtained simply because some paths have extremely high path coefficients, whereas other path coefficients are not significantly different from zero.

It is therefore important to distinguish between the overall fit of the model to the data. Fit indexes are overall assessments of the match between the model and the data. This aspect of the solution can be distinguished from the accuracy of prediction in the structural equations. Accuracy of the predictions is assessed by comparing the actual values of the endogenous variables with their predicted values, usually in terms of proportion of variance accounted for (R^2).

An Example Model

We will revisit the model used earlier in the multiple regression section where we are predicting academic achievement. This model is presented in Figure 14a.6 from the model-fitting perspective. Note that the difference between the models shown in Figure 14a.5 and Figure 14a.6 is the presence of the error terms in Figure 14a.6. This model includes the error or unique influences on the two endogenous variables (motivation and academic achievement). These error or unique influences are designated by the circles e1 and e2 and represent all the other influences that may affect the endogenous variables besides those specified in the model. In the model, the error terms already have been assigned values of 1 as the unstandardized path coefficients in order to define its metric (to provide it with a scale of measurement). The analysis will reestimate the value for the standardized coefficient.

Recall from Chapter 13A that to assess whether the proposed model fits the data, a necessary but not sufficient condition is that the model must be identified. As we described in Chapter 13A, to achieve model identification, we must have more known information elements than estimations of unknown parameters. The number of known elements can be determined in two ways if you wish to make the count by hand:

▶ Count the number of unique or nonredundant entries (allowing the pairing of the variable with itself) in a matrix that represents the covariances or correlations of the indicator variables. This was described in Chapter 13A.

▶ Count the number of variances there are in the model. This will correspond to the number of variables, but because information is the focus here and because variance is the entity that carries information, we count variances. Then add to that count the number of correlations there are in the correlation or covariance matrix (allowing the pairing of the variable with itself).

If all else fails, you may also use the following formula:

$$V (V + 1) / 2$$

where V is the number of the measured variables in this study.

In the present example we have $(4 \times 5) / 2$, or 10 nonredundant elements. These are the four variances associated with the four measured variables and the six pairs of correlations between the measured variables. However, we are estimating 10 parameters (i.e., the 5 path coefficients, 1 correlation, and variances of the 4 exogenous variables of academic self-doubt, SES, error 1, and error 2) for a total of 10 estimations. Recall that there has to be more known elements than unknown parameters. For a model to be identified, it must have a positive number for the degrees of freedom. In this case, the number of known elements and unknown parameters is equal and the degrees of freedom compute to zero.

To have degrees of freedom in the positive range, we are going to have to constrain another parameter. It is recommended that the path to be constrained is the one your theory would predict to have the largest coefficient. Assume that our theory does not address the magnitudes of the hypothesized causal influences. We will therefore select the path that communicates something new to you. From the model, we expect that greater levels of academic self-doubt produce decreased motivation. This is an inverse relationship and, if we constrain this path, we should do so using a value of −1 to reflect the presumed negative correlation of these two variables. The model that is now identified as a result of the single constraint we added is shown in Figure 14a.7. We now have one degree of freedom and can run the analysis on this identified model.

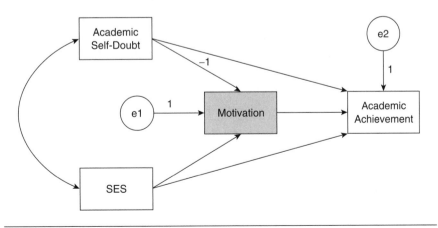

Figure 14a.7 Constraints Added to the Model to Allow the Model to Be Identified

The Model Results

As recommended by Thompson (2004), we would examine selected overall fit measures of the chi square, the normed fit index (NFI), the comparative fit index (CFI), and the root mean square error of approximation (RMSEA). The chi-square statistic is used to test the difference between the predicted and the observed relationships (correlations/covariances). Because the researchers are predicting a close fit, a nonsignificant chi square is desired. In this example the chi-square value was significant, indicating a poor match between the proposed model and the observed data.

We have already mentioned the suggestion that chi square should be supplemented with other fit measures (e.g., Bentler, 1992; Jöreskog & Sörbom, 1978) in judging how well the model fits the data. The CFI and the NFI are measures assessing the fit of the proposed model relative to the independence model, which assumes that there are no relationships in the data. These measures indicate the improvement of the hypothesized model compared with that baseline. Values of these indexes can range from 0 to 1, and values of .95 or greater are deemed acceptable. Because the values of the CFI and the NFI were .877 and .876, respectively, these measures do not support the model. To simplify this and later discussions, we do not show any tables representing the fit measures output; these tables will appear in Chapter 14B.

The RMSEA is the average of the residuals between the observed correlation/covariance from the sample and the expected model estimated from the population. A value of .08 indicates good fit. In this example the RMSEA was .336, indicating a poor fit. Thus, all four fit indexes failed to support the proposed model.

The path coefficients for the model are illustrated in Figure 14a.8. Comparing them with the results from the multiple regression analysis (Figure 14a.4) reveals them to be similar. The beta weight from academic self-doubt to motivation increased from −.31 to −.45, the beta weight from SES to motivation decreased from .43 to .35, and the beta weight from motivation to academic achievement increased from .48 to .51. The two direct paths from self-doubt and SES to achievement were virtually unchanged and still were not significant.

Because the model fell short of a good fit to the data, we could consider a respecification of it to see if the fit can be improved. Once again, it should be borne in mind that "retrofitting" a model is more on the exploratory side than on the confirmatory or theory-testing side of the continuum. Furthermore, we do not want to go on a "fishing expedition," trying one modification after another until the best respecification possible is found by trial and error. On the other hand, we might learn something useful if a

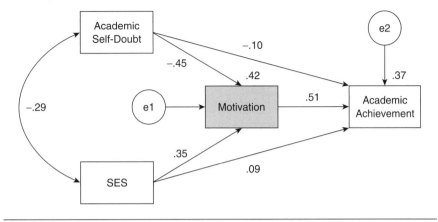

Figure 14a.8 Path Coefficients Produced by the Model-Fitting Technique

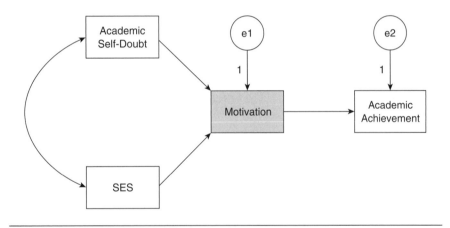

Figure 14a.9 The Respecified Model

single exploratory respecification were attempted. We will keep the changes simple here by proposing a revised model devoid of the paths that did not reach statistical significance in the original. The respecified model is shown in Figure 14a.9.

Notice that in this revised model no constraints are necessary because there are now more nonredundant elements than estimated parameters. Specifically, we still have the same 10 known elements because the number of variables is the same. But the number of estimated parameters has decreased because we are not including the direct paths from self-doubt and SES to academic achievement. Thus, we are now estimating three path coefficients, one correlation, and the variances of the four exogenous variables for a total of eight. Subtracting this value from the number of non-redundant elements results in the model having two degrees of freedom. This model is more parsimonious than the original but with two degrees of freedom; the chi-square statistic has a bit more power.

Respecified Model Results

Despite the increase in power, the chi square was not significant this time, indicating an acceptable fit between the proposed model and the observed data. The CFI and the NFI yielded values of .985 and .977, respectively, and appear to support the model. The RMSEA was .083, just missing the .08 rule of thumb for a good fit. The path coefficients for the respecified model are illustrated in Figure 14a.10.

Examining the coefficients, we see that all the path coefficients achieved practical significance (the beta weights are above .3) and statistical significance. The beta weights shown in this revised model are very close to the results obtained under multiple regression. The largest difference can be seen in the coefficient tying motivation to academic achievement. In the multiple regression solution, it was .48 but it turned out to be .57 in the model-fitting solution. The telling difference between the multiple regression and model-fitting analyses, however, is that we were able to acquire fit indexes in model fitting in addition to R^2 values to give us a sense of how well the model fit the data, whereas we have only the prediction accuracy information of the R^2 from regression to indicate how well we did.

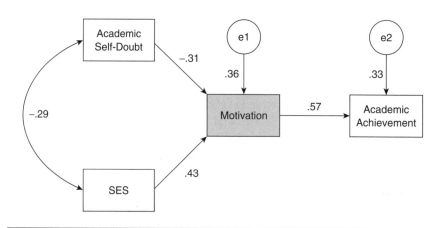

Figure 14a.10 Respecified Model With Path Coefficients

Structural Equation Modeling

Reliability and the Use of Multiple Indicators

In our presentation of the assumptions underlying path analysis, we indicated (with very little fanfare) that the observed variables are presumed to be measured without error (Pedhazur, 1997). Maruyama (1998) assesses how well such an assumption is usually met: "Within the social sciences, assumptions about perfect reliability must be viewed as generally unrealistic. What social scientist ever has had models in which there is no measurement error?" (p. 30).

With less than perfect reliability in the measurement of our variables, some error is introduced into the analysis (Chen et al., 2001). If the dependent variables are less than perfectly reliable, the standard error estimate increases, which in turn weakens significance tests (Pedhazur, 1997). However, "measurement errors in the independent variable lead to underestimation of the regression coefficient" (Pedhazur, 1997, p. 34).

The issue of perfect reliability plays itself out to the advantage of the researcher in SEM. How this is the case is a story with a twist. Let's look at the story briefly and then get to the twist.

The story has to do with the difference between SEM and path analysis and the impact this has on model identification. In SEM, we involve latent variables in the model. Remember from our treatment of confirmatory factor analysis that latent variables are by definition not measured—we have not collected data on them. They therefore do not have variances, and they do not appear in the correlation matrix; thus, their attributes do not count toward the number of nonredundant elements when we are determining the degrees of freedom of the model. Yet introduction of latent variables adds to the number of parameters we need to have the model estimate. As you can see, adding these parameters to those of the observed variables we already had in the model means that we are subtracting a larger value in the calculation of degrees of freedom.

This increase in the number of parameters we must estimate resulting from the introduction of latent variables affects model identification. To compute degrees of freedom, we subtract the number of unknown parameters from the number of nonredundant elements. Model identification is achieved when the value for degrees of freedom is positive. With latent variables in the model, we have more unknown parameters to estimate than before, which therefore gives us a negative value to the degrees of freedom. As a result, the model is no longer identified. The basic solution to this dilemma is that we must now include additional measured variables in the model to raise the number of known elements (the variances and correlation entries) so that when we subtract the former from the latter we arrive at a positive number.

Now for the twist in the story. Increasing the number of measured variables turns out to be a terrific strategy for another reason as well: It relates to the reliability issue introduced at the start of this section. In SEM we use at least two measured variables as indicators of the latent variable. You can think of this as a smaller version of confirmatory factor analysis. By using two indicators for each latent variable, we are able to produce an estimate of the measurement error (the "unreliability" of the measurement operations). We do this by focusing on the variance that is common to the indicators (the common variance) and treating the variance that is unique to them as error variance.

Consider academic self-doubt as our hypothetical example. As we have treated it in the multiple regression and in the model-fitting approaches to path analysis, it has been (it had to be) a measured variable. This variable had a certain amount of variance associated with it. Some of this variance we believed was "true score variance." But we (as the humans conducting the research) also reluctantly accept the idea that some of the variance of self-doubt was "error variance." The computer, however, not burdened with human frailties, could not distinguish one kind of variance from another. As far as it was concerned, it was all measured variance. So the computer program simply assumed, however naively, that it was all true score variance—that the measurement was perfectly reliable or error free.

SEM relieves the analytic procedure of the need to assume that all the variance it sees in the data file is true score variance. In SEM, we now transform the status of academic self-doubt to that of latent variable and use a set of two or more variables as indicators of the construct. For example, we can propose that academic self-doubt is indicated by concerns about one's writing ability, worries about time management, anxiety about orally presenting material in class, and so on. We can then decide to measure, for the sake of simplicity in our example, two of these indicators.

We now have two indicator variables associated with academic self-doubt. Think of self-doubt as the factor and these indicators as variables correlated with or weighted on the factor. To the extent that these variables are both indicators of the factor, they will share variance. If we know their total variance (which we do know because we have data for these variables) and if we know how much of that total variance is shared or common (which the procedure calculates), presumably representing academic self-doubt, then we are also able to determine how much variance is left over. This residual variance is variance unique to each indicator and can serve as an estimate of error variance. Thus, we (the analytic procedures) no longer have to assume that the reliabilities of the measured variables are perfect as we did in path analysis. Because these measured variables are now treated as indicators, and because we must have two or more indicators for each latent construct, we can actually estimate how far from perfection our measures have strayed.

From a research design perspective, the effort to change a path analysis design into a structural equation model means a potential gain in the precision of the research. That gain incurs a cost (is there nothing free in this world?). The researchers are now going to collect more data because some of the measured variables in the path analysis are now scheduled to be latent variables, and for each latent variable that is hypothesized, they will need at least two measured variables to be introduced. Furthermore, as another part of that cost, the researchers are going to have to determine how to assess the indicators. Sometimes they can obtain a published inventory that meets their needs, but sometimes they will be obliged to build that measurement on their own.

Researchers will have to decide for themselves, given the context in which they are working, whether or not they are inclined to think about designing a structural equation model when they have drawn out their path model. In many instances, we believe that the extra cost in time and resources will be judged by the researchers to be worthwhile.

The Structural Equation Models

SEM can be thought of as the union of confirmatory factor analysis and path analysis. This is because in SEM there are really two types of models: a measurement model and a structural model. Although the model as a whole is evaluated by a variety of goodness-of-fit indexes, SEM also evaluates the measurement and the structural model separately because it is possible that they may differentially fit the data.

The measurement model represents the degree to which the indicator variables capture the essence of the latent factor. It is basically confirmatory factor analysis for each latent variable. We call it a measurement model because the indicator variables are measured variables used to give us some access to or indication of the intangible, unmeasured latent factor.

The structural model is akin to path analysis in that we are looking at the causal relationships between the major variables of interest in the theory. Note, for example, that the indicators of self-doubt are not hypothesized as having a causal connection to motivation; they are mere indicators of the variable of interest—namely, academic self-doubt itself. The variables thought of by researchers as being the important or central variables are the latent variables. Therefore, causal connections are drawn between the latent variable of self-doubt and the latent variable of motivation. This is analogous to what was taken for granted in path analysis where we took the measured variables at face value (e.g., academic self-doubt), treating them with the reverence we usually reserve for latent constructs.

The structural equation model can be decomposed into the structural model and the measurement model. The structural model assesses the relationships between the latent variables, which in the example we have been using are the previous measured variables of academic self-doubt, SES, motivation, and academic achievement. The model purports that both academic self-doubt and SES influence academic achievement directly and influence it indirectly via motivation. These latent constructs are usually defined by two to five measured variables. Using multiple indicators or measures (the measurement model) allows the researcher to control more effectively for the inevitable measurement errors of any construct.

Once a model is proposed (i.e., relationships between the variables have been hypothesized), a correlation/covariance matrix is created. The estimates of the relationships between the variables in the model are calculated using the maximum likelihood estimation procedure just as was done in the path analysis example using a model-fitting program. The model is then compared with the relationships (the correlation/covariances matrix) of the actual or observed data. SEM assesses how well the predicted interrelationships between the variables match the interrelationships between the actual or observed variables. It has the capability to assess both the measurement model (how well the measured variables define their respective construct) and the structural model (how well the latent constructs relate to each other) simultaneously. If the two matrices (the one based on the hypothesized model and the one derived from the actual data) are consistent with one another, then the structural equation model can be considered a credible explanation for the hypothesized relationships. As was provided by the model-fitting programs, we obtain indexes informing us of the overall fit of the model to the data.

Structural Equation Model Example

The proposed structural equation model that we will use as our example is presented in Figure 14a.11. Note that the measured variables of the previous examples are now latent variables. We have used the minimum of two indicators for each. Each endogenous variable has an associated error term designated e1 through e9, but neither of the two exogenous variables (academic self-doubt and SES) are assigned errors. Each error term is scaled to its respective endogenous variable by assigning values of 1 to those paths.

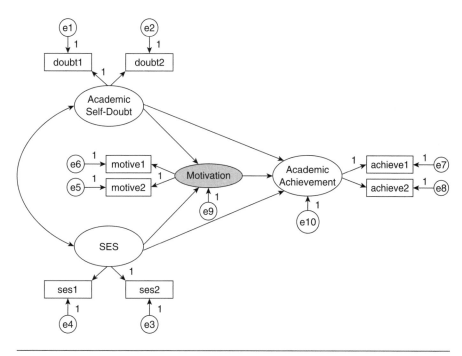

Figure 14a.11 Proposed Structural Equation Model

These error terms represent the residual variance remaining after the prediction work has been done. For example, e9 is the variance that is not accounted for by the combination of academic self-doubt and SES.

Recall from confirmatory factor analysis (Chapter 13A) that researchers must scale the latent factor. This can be accomplished by selecting one of the path coefficients from the latent variable to a measured variable and fix (constrain) that coefficient to the value to 1 (or −1 if there is an inverse relationship between the two).

In SEM, all the structural coefficients and all the measurement coefficients are simultaneously estimated. Fit measures need to be even more cautiously interpreted. In SEM, the overall fit of a model to the data may appear acceptable, yet some relations in the model may not be supported by the data. For example, an acceptable fit index could be achieved because of the strong measurement model, although the structural model is fairly weak. Alternatively, the structural model may be impressive, but the measurement model may be quite weak, making the interpretation meaningless.

The results of the SEM applied to our example are as follows. The chi square was significant, indicating an unacceptable fit between the proposed

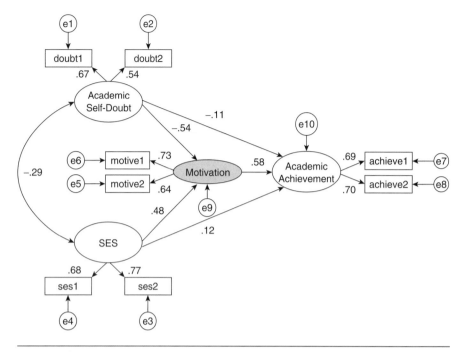

Figure 14a.12 Structure and Measure Coefficients in the SEM

model and the observed data. Because the chi square is sensitive to sample size and model complexity, we want to also use alternative fit measures to evaluate the plausibility of the proposed model. The CFI and the NFI yielded values of .983 and .962, respectively; this tends to support the model. The RMSEA was .063, indicating a good fit.

The path coefficients for the model are illustrated in Figure 14a.12. All the measured variables correlated with their respective factors at a reasonably strong level. However, three of the five structural paths failed to achieve statistical significance.

This study illustrates that even though the overall fit of a model to the data appears acceptable, some paths were not supported by the data. This acceptable fit was obtained simply because the measured paths had extremely high coefficients. To assess the accuracy of the prediction in the structural equations, we examine the proportion of variance accounted for (R^2). In this model, a weak effect size was reported for motivation (.07), and a moderate effect size was found for achievement (.15). Is this a good model? It depends. If prior research reported greater explained variance for the endogenous variables, then this model may not contribute much to the literature. However, if the results of this model exceed what the research has thus far shown, then this model may make a significant contribution to the literature. Because results are often domain specific, it is difficult if not impossible to provide absolute standards of acceptable model fit (Jaccard & Choi, 1996).

Recommended Readings

Anderson, J. C., & Gerbing, D. W. (1988). Structural equation modeling in practice: A review and recommended two-step approach. *Psychological Bulletin, 103,* 411–423.

Chambers, W. V. (2000). Causation and corresponding correlations. *Journal of Mind and Behavior, 21,* 437–460.

Cliff, N. (1983). Some cautions concerning the application of causal modeling methods. *Multivariate Behavioral Research, 18,* 81–105.

Duncan, O. D. (1966). Path analysis: Sociological examples. *American Journal of Sociology, 72,* 219–316.

Everitt, B. S. (1984). *An introduction to latent variable models.* New York: Chapman & Hall.

Green, S. B., Thompson, M. S., & Babyak, M. A. (1998). A Monte Carlo investigation of methods for controlling Type I errors with specification searches in structural equation modeling. *Multivariate Behavioral Research, 33,* 365–383.

Hoyle, R. H. (Ed.). (1995). *Structural equation modeling: Concepts, issues, and applications.* Thousand Oaks, CA: Sage.

Kelloway, E. K. (1995). Structural equation modeling in perspective. *Journal of Organizational Behavior, 16,* 215–224.

Kelloway, E. K. (1998). *Using LISREL for structural equation modeling: A researcher's guide.* Thousand Oaks, CA: Sage.

Leidy, N. K. (1990). A structural model of stress, psychosocial resources, and symptomatic experience in chronic physical illness. *Nursing Research, 39,* 230–236.

Maassen, G. H., & Bakker, A. B. (2001). Suppressor variables in path models: Definitions and interpretations. *Sociological Methods and Research, 30,* 241–270.

Magura, S., & Rosenblum, A. (2000). Modulating effect of alcohol use on cocaine use. *Addictive Behaviors, 25,* 117–122.

McDonald, R. P. (1996). Path analysis with composite variables. *Multivariate Behavioral Research, 31,* 239–270.

Mueller, R. O. (1997). Structural equation modeling: Back to basics. *Structural Equation Modeling, 4,* 353–369.

Rigdon, E. E. (1995). A necessary and sufficient identification rule for structural models estimated in practice. *Multivariate Behavioral Research, 30,* 359–383.

Tremblay, P. F., & Gardner, R. C. (1996). On the growth of structural equation modeling in psychological journals. *Structural Equation Modeling, 3,* 93–104.

CHAPTER **14B**

Path Analysis Using SPSS and AMOS

This chapter describes two approaches for conducting a path analysis and how to interpret the output from these approaches. Recall from Chapter 14A that there are two options to analyzing path models: (a) multiple regression analyses or (b) estimation with a model-fitting program. The multiple regression approach is conducted through SPSS, which employs the ordinary least squares method to calculate the path coefficients. The model-fitting program we will demonstrate is AMOS (Analysis of MOment Structures). The AMOS approach typically uses maximum likelihood to calculate all the path coefficients simultaneously. The SPSS approach uses separate multiple regression equations for each endogenous variable; this approach is referred to as a partial information technique. The AMOS approach solves for all the coefficients simultaneously. This simultaneous approach is referred to as a full-information model technique. These two options generally produce similar results for the path coefficients. Later, we will discuss some of the additional benefits of using the AMOS program.

For purposes of continuity, we will continue our analysis of the influences of academic self-doubt, socioeconomic status (SES), and motivation on academic achievement with college students. The model is illustrated in Figure 14b.1.

As noted in Chapters 3A and 3B, all statistical analyses are typically preceded by data screening activities (i.e., code cleaning and assessing missing values, outliers, and assumption violations) with SPSS programs such as **Frequencies**, **Explore**, **Scatter**, **MVA**, and so on. We will assume that these procedures have been completed and that the data are ready for the analysis.

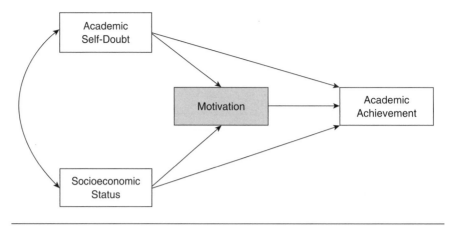

Figure 14b.1   Illustration of the Proposed Model

Multiple Regression Analysis

To assess a path analysis through SPSS, a separate standard (simultaneous) multiple regression has to be conducted for each endogenous variable. Endogenous variables are easily identified because they have a straight arrow pointing to them. In this example, the two endogenous variables are motivation and academic achievement. Thus, we will need to perform two separate standard (simultaneous) multiple regressions. In the first multiple regression, academic achievement will be regressed on academic self-doubt, SES, and motivation. The second multiple regression will require motivation to be regressed on academic self-doubt and SES. We refer you to Chapter 5B to run the regression procedure and will not repeat that here.

Interpreting the First Regression Equation Output

The output of the first structural equation includes the following edited tables: **Model Summary, ANOVA,** and **Coefficients.** The **Model Summary** table is presented at the top of Figure 14b.2. For path analysis the interest is with the R^2 coefficient (.343), which is the amount of variance in academic achievement accounted for by the three predictor variables (academic self-doubt, SES, and motivation). The **ANOVA** table provides a summary of the analysis of variance for regression. The F value is as follows: $F(3, 240) = 41.68, p < .001, R^2 = .343$. This means that the variance explained in this equation (34.3%) is greater than zero and extremely unlikely to have occurred by chance (less than 1 of 1,000).

Model Summary

Model	R	R Square	Adjusted R Square	Std. Error of the Estimate
1	.585[a]	.343	.334	3.647

a. Predictors: (Constant), Motivation, Academic
   Self-Doubt, Socioeconomic Status

ANOVA[b]

Model		Sum of Squares	df	Mean Square	F	Sig.
1	Regression	1663.187	3	554.396	41.684	.000[a]
	Residual	3192.026	240	13.300		
	Total	4855.213	243			

a. Predictors: (Constant), Motivation, Academic Self-Doubt, Socioeconomic Status
b. Dependent Variable: Academic Achievement

Coefficients[a]

Model		Unstandardized Coefficients		Standardized Coefficients		
		B	Std. Error	Beta	t	Sig.
1	(Constant)	3.773	2.131		1.770	.078
	Academic Self-Doubt	−.073	.044	−.097	−1.675	.095
	Socioeconomic Status	.236	1.164	.089	7.433	.151
	Motivation	.175	.023	.485	7.433	.000

a. Dependent Variable: Academic Achievement

Figure 14b.2 Selected Output From the First Regression Analysis

The **Coefficients** table presents the regression weights produced by the analysis. This portion of the output provides both the unstandardized b coefficients (shown by SPSS as an uppercase B) and the standardized beta coefficients with their respective t tests and significance levels for each independent variable. The **Coefficients** table describes the relative importance of each independent variable in the multiple regression equation or model.

Start the examination of the **Coefficients** table by inspecting the outcome of the t test for each predictor's regression weight. These t tests and significance levels allow researchers to assess each variable's unique contribution to the prediction of the dependent variable. In the present example, only motivation provides a statistically significant unique contribution to the prediction of academic achievement based on an alpha level of .05. However, neither academic self-doubt nor SES adds any statistically significant unique contribution to academic achievement.

Recall that unstandardized regression coefficients (bs) reflect each independent variable in its original metric (unit of measurement) and are therefore potentially difficult to compare with each other. For example, the b for SES (.236) is the largest of the bs, but that does not necessarily mean that it is the most important variable (in fact, we know that this weight is not significantly different from zero). This problem is at least partly solved with the standardized regression coefficients (beta weights). The betas or beta weights allow such comparisons because they are based on z scores with a mean of 0 and a standard deviation of 1. Note that the beta weight for SES is the lowest of the three. Recall the discussion in Chapter 4A warning against the sole use of beta weights to assess the relative importance of the variables. Nonetheless, motivation appears to be more heavily weighted in the model as a predictor of academic achievement than either of the other two predictors and is the only one that is statistically significant.

Generally in path analysis, the betas (as opposed to the b weights) are assigned to their respective paths because this allows for direct comparisons between the path coefficients. The beta coefficient for academic self-doubt of −.097 indicates that a 1-standard deviation increase in academic self-doubt is associated with a decrease of .097 standard deviations in academic achievement while statistically controlling or holding constant SES and motivation (these variables are covariates in this portion of the analysis).

The beta coefficient for SES is .089, indicating that a 1-standard deviation increase in SES is associated with an increase of .089 standard deviations in academic achievement while controlling or holding constant for both academic self-doubt and motivation. The beta coefficient for motivation is .485, indicating that a 1-standard deviation increase in motivation is associated with an increase of .485 standard deviations in academic achievement while controlling or holding constant for both academic self-doubt and SES.

Interpreting the Second Regression Equation Output

For the second regression equation, we will proceed directly to the **Model Summary** table presented in Figure 14b.3. The relevant information here is that the R^2 value was .356. The **ANOVA** table indicates a statistically significant F value, $F(2, 241) = 66.49$, $p < .001$. This means that the variance explained in this equation (35.6%) is greater than zero and extremely unlikely to have occurred by chance (less than 1 of 1,000).

Model Summary

Model	R	R-Square	Adjusted R-Square	Std. Error of the Estimate
1	.596ᵃ	.356	.350	9.999

> This R^2 value is placed adjacent to Motivation in the respecified model (see Figure14b.6).

a. Predictors: (Constant), Socioeconomic Status, Academic Self-Doubt

ANOVAᵇ

Model		Sum of Squares	df	Mean Square	F	Sig.
1	Regression	13297.080	2	6648.540	66.496	.000ᵃ
	Residual	24096.231	241	99.984		
	Total	37393.311	243			

a. Predictors: (Constant), Socioeconomic Status, Academic Self-Doubt
b. Dependent Variable: Motivation

Coefficientsᵃ

Model		Unstandardized Coefficients		Standardized Coefficients		
		B	Std. Error	Beta	t	Sig.
1	(Constant)	61.251	4.311		14.208	.000
	Academic Self-Doubt	−.634	.112	−.306	−5.657	.000
	Socioeconomic Status	3.187	.399	.431	7.979	.000

a. Dependent Variable: Motivation

> These are the path coefficients shown in the respecified model (see Figure 14b.6).

Figure 14b.3   Selected Output From the Linear Regression Analysis

The **Coefficients** table indicates that both regression weights achieved statistical significance ($p < .001$). The beta coefficient for academic self-doubt of −.306 indicates that a 1-standard deviation increase in academic self-doubt is associated with a decrease of .306 standard deviations in motivation while controlling or holding constant SES. The beta coefficient for SES is .431, indicating that a 1-standard deviation increase in SES is associated with an increase of .431 standard deviations in motivation while controlling or holding constant academic self-doubt.

The Correlation Between the Exogenous Variables

The correlation between the two exogenous variables (academic self-doubt and SES) was calculated using the Pearson correlation. In this example, the correlation between academic self-doubt and SES is −.29 (a moderate correlation coefficient).

Model Trimming in Regression

Recall that the paths from academic self-doubt to academic achievement and from SES to academic achievement failed to achieve practical significance (i.e., beta < .3) and statistical significance. These results indicate that neither academic self-doubt nor SES has a direct effect on academic achievement and suggest that perhaps these two paths should be removed from the model so that the model can be trimmed. In the second regression equation, academic self-doubt and SES explain 36% of the variance in motivation. Both path coefficients achieved practical and statistical significance and so have earned a place in any respecified model.

Given the two nonsignificant paths, a modified (respecified) model will now be evaluated. In this model, which can be seen in Figure 14b.4, the direct paths from academic self-doubt and SES to academic achievement have been removed.

The analysis of the respecified model begins by generating the two regression equations again, but this time without including the paths from academic self-doubt and SES to academic achievement.

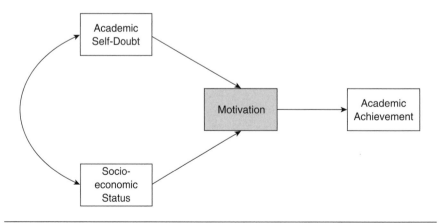

Figure 14b.4 Respecified Model Without the Two Nonsignificant Paths

First Regression Equation (Respecified) Output

The **Model Summary** table is presented in Figure 14b.5. The R^2 coefficient is .328, indexing the amount of variance in academic achievement accounted for by motivation. The **ANOVA** table shown also in Figure 14b.5 indicates a statistically significant F value, $F(1, 242) = 118.08, p < .001$. This means that the variance explained in this equation (32.8%) is greater than zero and extremely unlikely to have occurred by chance (less than 1 of a 1,000).

Model Summary

Model	R	R Square	Adjusted R Square	Std. Error of the Estimate
1	.573[a]	.328	.325	3.672

This R^2 value is placed adjacent to Academic Achievement (see Figure 14b.6).

a. Predictors: (Constant), Motivation

ANOVA[b]

Model		Sum of Squares	df	Mean Square	F	Sig.
1	Regression	1592.228	1	1592.228	118.088	.000[a]
	Residual	3262.985	242	13.483		
	Total	4855.213	243			

a. Predictors: (Constant), Motivation
b. Dependent Variable: Academic Achievement

Coefficients[a]

Model		Unstandardized Coefficients		Standardized Coefficients	t	Sig.
		B	Std. Error	Beta		
1	Constant	.898	1 115		.806	.421
	Motivation	.206	.019	.573	10.867	.000

a. Dependent Variable: Academic Achievement

This is the path coefficient shown in the respecified model (see Figure 14b.6).

Figure 14b.5 Selected Output From the First Regression Analysis of the Respecified Model

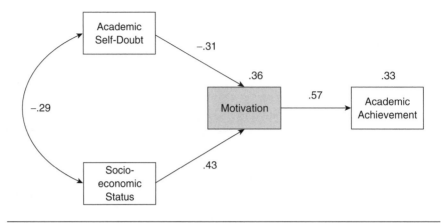

Figure 14b.6 Respecified Model With the Path Coefficients Filled In

The **Coefficients** table indicates that the motivation regression weight achieved statistical significance ($p < .001$). The beta coefficient for motivation of .573 indicates that a 1-standard deviation increase in motivation is associated with an increase of .573 standard deviation in academic achievement. The respecified model with the path coefficients is presented in Figure 14b.6.

The Model-Fitting Program Approach

The second way to analyze a path model is through a model-fitting program such as AMOS. AMOS typically uses maximum likelihood to calculate the path coefficients. Maximum likelihood attempts to estimate the values of the parameters that would result in the highest likelihood of the actual data being reproduced by the proposed model. This method often requires iterative solutions.

Recall that in contrast to the multiple regression approach, which requires separate analyses for each endogenous variable, maximum likelihood estimates all the path coefficient simultaneously. As is true for other model-fitting programs, AMOS provides (a) an overall fit of the model and (b) the indirect and total effects of the predictors variables. Recall that the overall fit of the model is how well the model explains the data. Stevens (2002) describes the assessment of a model as analogous to the omnibus test in ANOVAs. Yet even though the overall fit of a model to the data may appear acceptable, some relations (paths) in the model may not be supported by the data. An acceptable fit could be obtained simply because some paths have extremely high path coefficients, whereas other path coefficients are negligible. This means that fit indexes are not related to the accuracy of prediction in the structural equations. Accuracy of the predictions is assessed by comparing the actual values of the endogenous variables with their predicted values, usually in terms of proportion of variance accounted for (R^2).

The indirect effect in this example involves the mediator variable, motivation. Specifically, although academic self-doubt and SES have direct effects on academic achievement, academic self-doubt and SES also have indirect effects on academic achievement mediated by motivation. The total effect is simply the addition of the direct effect and the indirect effect. We are now going to demonstrate how to construct the hypothesized model using AMOS (the same model illustrated in the SPSS multiple regression approach).

Using the Model-Fitting Method With AMOS

From the **SPSS** task bar, select **Analyze → AMOS**. Using the task bar from **AMOS**, select **Diagram → Draw Observed.** You will then be in drawing mode. You will quickly see how to place and drag the mouse to produce boxes—the only shape that you can generate here because observed variables are always represented by squares or rectangles. Draw four boxes positioned as pictured in Figure 14b.1.

With the boxes for the observed variables in place, we now can draw the paths. From the **AMOS** task bar, select **Diagram → Draw Path**. Use the mouse to draw in the paths. Start at the beginning of the path and drag the mouse to the appropriate box. When you make contact, the arrow head will appear.

With the model now drawn, it is time to place the variable names in the boxes. From the **AMOS** task bar, select **View/Set → Select Variables in Dataset** to display the variables. Drag the variables to the appropriate variable box. Be aware that AMOS has a preference for variable labels and will deposit that item in the box; only if there is no label will it take the name.

We now need to draw the correlation between the two exogenous variables. From the **AMOS** task bar, select **Diagram → Draw Covariances** and connect academic self-doubt with SES.

The next step is to draw the error components associated with each of the endogenous variables. AMOS calls these "unique" variables and represents them by circles because they are not directly observed (they are latent variables and such variables are depicted as circles). From the **AMOS** task bar, select **Diagram → Draw Unique variable**. Use the mouse to draw these circles in the same fashion as you drew the boxes, and then draw the paths as described above. AMOS will automatically place 1s on the paths of these unique variables.

Finally, we need to name the error variables. From the **AMOS** task bar, select **Tools → Select Macro → Select Name Unobserved Variables**. AMOS will give the unique variables generic names with a lowercase "**e**" followed by a number. These error or unique influences are designated by the circles **e1** and **e2** and represent all the other influences that may affect the endogenous variables besides those specified in the model. The model is now fully drawn and will be similar to the model in Figure 14b.1.

Identifying the Model

Recall from the confirmatory factor analysis chapter that to assess whether the proposed model fits the data, a necessary but not sufficient condition is that the model must be identified; that is, it must have a positive value for its degrees of freedom, computed by subtracting the number of estimated parameters from the number of known elements. Thus, to achieve model identification, more information or known elements than estimations is necessary. The number of known elements can be computed by the following formula:

$$V(V + 1)/2$$

In this formula, V is the number of the measured variables in this study. With four measured variables, we have $4 \times 5/2$, or 10 pieces of information. The known elements are the four variances of the measured variables and the six pairs of correlations between the measured variables.

In this model we are estimating 10 parameters (i.e., the 5 path coefficients, 1 correlation, and variances of the 4 exogenous variables of academic self-doubt, SES, and **e1** and **e2**) for a total of 10 estimations. With 10 of each, the model has zero degrees of freedom. Because the 10 known elements are fixed, we are going to have to constrain another parameter to reduce the number of estimated parameters down to 9 to achieve 1 degree of freedom. It is recommended that the path to be constrained is the one your theory would predict to have the largest coefficient. When there are a number of plausible strong relationships, then the choice can be arbitrary. We elected to constrain the path from academic self-doubt to motivation; this is accomplished by double clicking on its path. The dialog box illustrated in Figure 14b.7 will appear with an empty **Regression weight** window. Enter the number **−1** into that window. We used a negative because there is an inverse relationship between these two variables.

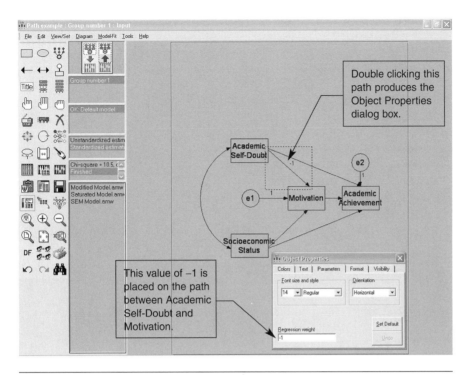

Figure 14b.7 Researcher Assigning a Parameter on the Path From Self-Doubt to Motivation to Constrain One Parameter and Have Positive Degrees of Freedom

Performing the Analysis

Performing the analysis entails asking AMOS to produce certain output. To accomplish this, from the **AMOS** task bar, select **View/Set → Select Analysis Properties** as shown in Figure 14b.8. Select the **Output** tab and check the following: **Standardized estimates, Squared multiple correlations, Modification indexes,** and **Indirect, direct, & total effects.** This is shown in Figure 14b.8.

We also want AMOS to compute the values for the estimated parameters. We ask it to do this by selecting from the task bar **Model-Fit → Calculate Estimates.** Completing this selection produces a "**Save As**" window; save your output to any location that makes sense for your work.

Examining the Results of the Model

We are now ready to take a look at the results. AMOS will display an output column to the right of the toolbar. In the top segment of that column

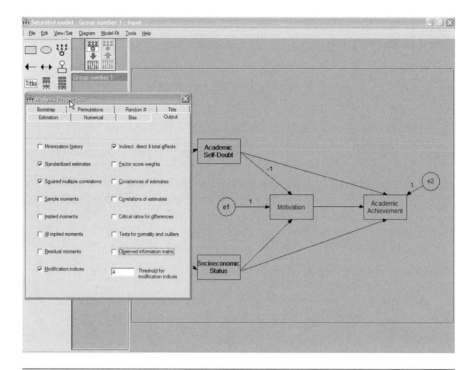

Figure 14b.8   Output Tab of the Analysis Properties Dialog Box

are arrows. Select the area above the red arrow to view the path diagram with its estimated parameters; the path coefficients and the correlation of the exogenous variables appear. By each endogenous variable, you will also see the R^2 value from the analyses. This model is shown in Figure 14b.9.

This output allows the researchers to quickly review the results of the initial model, but it can be at best a surface review because the significance testing and fit indexes need to be studied before we make too much of what we see. Nonetheless, one is always curious to learn what the coefficients are. Generally, the results are, as we expect, similar to those of the multiple regression analysis. The direct effects of academic self-doubt and SES on academic achievement are quite low and are probably not significant; these two variables seem to affect academic achievement indirectly by influencing the mediating variable of motivation. The values above the upper right portion of the boxes for the endogenous variables are the R^2 values for that portion of the model. These values indicate that 42% of the variance of motivation was explained by academic self-doubt and 37% of academic achievement was explained by the predictors of academic self-doubt, SES, and motivation.

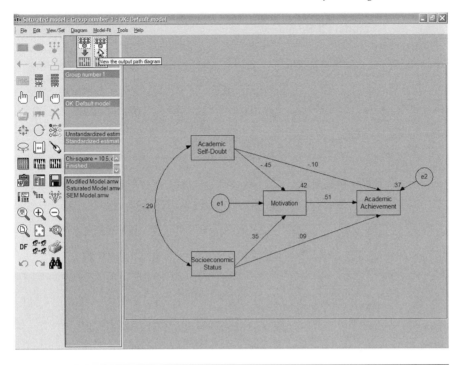

Figure 14b.9   Results of the Model Fitting

To view the text output resulting from the analysis, select **View/Set →
Text Output** from the **AMOS** task bar. That brings us to the **AMOS output**
window. The left column lists what may be viewed; we select **Model Fit.**
The model fit summary is then displayed, and we have reproduced part of
that in Figure 14b.10. As recommended by Thompson (2004), we will examine a subset of these overall fit measures: chi square, the normed fit index
(NFI), the comparative fit index (CFI), and the root mean square error of
approximation (RMSEA).

The chi-square statistic is used to test the difference between the predicted and the observed relationships (correlations/covariances), and
because the researchers are ordinarily predicting a close fit, a nonsignificant
chi square is desired. The chi square can be found in the first group labeled
CMIN on the default model row. Its value of 10.49 evaluated at 1 degree
of freedom is significant, indicating a poor match between the proposed
model and the observed data. Jöreskog and Sörbom (1978) and Bentler
(1992), however, advised against the sole use of the chi-square value in
judging the overall fit of the model because of the sensitivity of the chi
square to sample size. As sample size increases, power increases. Therefore,

Model Fit Summary

CMIN

Model	NPAR	CMIN	DF	P	CMIN/DF
Default model	9	10.487	1	.001	10.487
Saturated model	10	.000	0		
Independence model	4	230.007	6	.000	38.334

> This test result is significant, indicating poor model fit.

RMR, GFI

Model	RMR	GFI	AGFI	PGFI
Default model	8.603	.979	−.793	.098
Saturated model	.000	1.000		
Independence model	14.901	.642	.404	.385

Baseline Comparisons

Model	NFI Delta1	RFI rho1	IFI Delta2	TLI rho2	CFI
Default model	.954	.726	.959	.776	.958
Saturated model	1.000		1.000		1.000
Independence model	.000	.000	.000	.000	.000

> This value indicates a poor fit of the model.

RMSEA

Model	RMSEA	LO 90	HI 90	PCLOSE
Default model	.198	.102	.313	.007
Independence model	.392	.350	.436	.000

Figure 14b.10 Model Fit Summary Information Containing the Various Fit Indexes Calculated by AMOS

the chi-square test can detect small discrepancies between the observed and predicted covariances and suggest that the model does not fit the data. A good-fitting model could be rejected because of trivial differences between the observed and predicted values. Because of these limitations, other fit indexes were developed as alternatives to the chi square.

The CFI and the NFI are measures assessing the fit of the proposed model relative to the independence model, which assumes that there are no

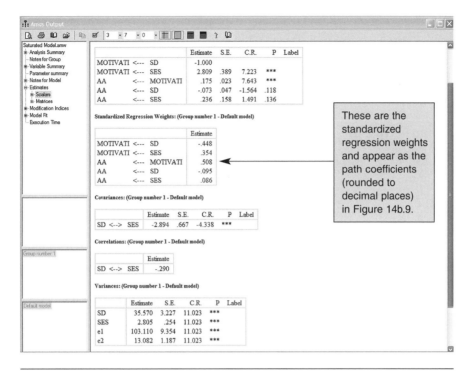

Figure 14b.11   Output Showing Model Coefficients

relationships in the data. The independence model is the worst possible model. These measures indicate the improvement of the hypothesized model compared with this independence model baseline, which assumes that there are no relationships in the data. Values of these fit indexes can range from 0 to 1. Values of .95 or greater are deemed acceptable. The obtained values can be seen in the third set of indexes on the output under **Baseline Comparisons;** the **CFI** and the **NFI** are in the last and first columns, respectively, and their values are .958 and .954, respectively. Based on the .95 or greater criterion, these measures support the model.

The RMSEA is the average of the residuals between the observed correlation/covariance from the sample and the expected model estimated from the population. Loehlin (2004) proposes the following classification: (a) less than .08 indicates good fit, (b) .08 to .1 indicates a moderate fit, (c) greater than .1 indicates poor fit. In this example the **RMSEA** is .198, indicating a poor fit.

Next we should examine the coefficients. Selecting **Estimates** from the left column presents us with the output shown in Figure 14b.11. The first set of results presents the unstandardized path coefficients with their respective probability level. Examining the coefficients, we see that the paths from academic self-doubt to academic achievement and from SES to academic achievement failed to achieve statistical significance. The standardized regression weights are shown below that. These are the path coefficients that were placed in the path diagram we initially viewed in Figure 14b.9.

Constructing the Respecified Model

AMOS also supplies suggestions as to what may be changed if the researchers have an interest in respecifying the model. As you might expect, these suggestions are based entirely on statistical considerations and have nothing to do with theoretical consistency or with common sense. Hence, these suggestions often need to be taken with more than a grain of salt. Although this table suggested eliminating academic self-doubt to motivation, there is no theoretical justification to do so. However, recall from the **Estimates** output that neither academic self-doubt nor SES achieves statistical significance to academic achievement. Thus, we will chart our own waters and eliminate these two paths in the respecified model.

We now erase the two nonsignificant paths. From the **AMOS** task bar, select **Edit → Erase.** This produces an erase icon that, when pointed onto the path and clicked, will erase the path. The new respecified model should look like Figure 14b.12. Notice that in this model no constraints are necessary because there are more knowns ($4 \times 5 / 2 = 10$) than estimations (unknowns; the 3 path coefficients, 1 correlation, and the variances of the 4 exogenous variables, which equals 8). This model has two degrees of freedom.

Examining the Results of the Respecified Model

To tell AMOS to assess the respecified model, from the **AMOS** task bar, select **Model-Fit → Calculate Estimates.** To examine the results, select **View/Set → Text Output → Model Fit.** We learn from this that the chi square is 5.34; with two degrees of freedom, it is not significant, indicating an acceptable fit between the proposed model and the observed data. Although we do not show the output here, we can tell you that the **CFI** and the **NFI** of .985 and .977, respectively, support the model. The **RMSEA** is .083, indicating a moderate fit. All four fit indexes thus support the proposed model. The path coefficients for the respecified model are illustrated in Figure 14b.13. Examining the coefficients, we see that all the path coefficients achieved practical significance and statistical significance.

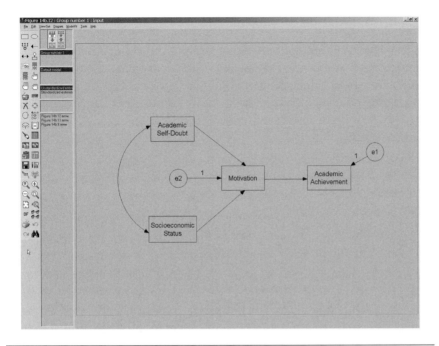

Figure 14b.12   The Respecified Model

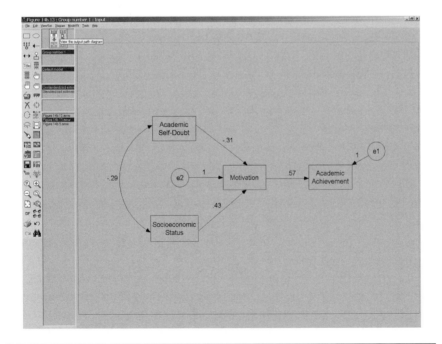

Figure 14b.13   Outcome of the Respecified Model

Structural Equation Modeling

Recall that one assumption in path analysis is that the observed variables are measured without error (Pedhazur, 1997). Maruyama (1998) asserts that "within the social sciences, assumptions about perfect reliability must be viewed as generally unrealistic. What social scientist ever has had models in which there is no measurement error?" (p. 30).

Thus a major limitation of path analysis is the use of a single measure for a construct in the proposed model because any single measure will inevitably have measurement error. Using more than a single measure for a construct is the most common method to reduce the effect of the measurement error of a single indicator. Also recall that the multiple regression procedure is incapable of assessing models, with latent variables necessitating the implication of model-fitting programs such as AMOS.

Structural equation modeling (SEM) overcomes this limitation of measurement errors associated with single measures by implementing multiple indicators. This makes SEM a more powerful alternative to the traditional path analysis because measurement errors can now be assessed and controlled. The full structural model can be decomposed into the structural model and the measurement model. The structural model assesses the relationships between the latent construct variables, which in this example are academic self-doubt, SES, motivation, and academic achievement. The model purports that both academic self-doubt and SES influence academic achievement directly and indirectly via motivation. These latent constructs are usually defined by two to five measured variables. These multiple measures (the measurement model) allow the researcher, as previously stated, to control more effectively for the inevitable measurement errors of any construct. By controlling for measurement error, unbiased estimates of the relationships between the latent constructs are possible. Once a model is proposed (i.e., relationships between the variables have been hypothesized), a correlation/covariance matrix is created. The estimates of the relationships between the variables in the model are calculated using the maximum likelihood estimation procedure just as in the path analysis example using a model-fitting program. Maximum likelihood attempts to estimate the values of the parameters that would result in the highest likelihood of the actual data to the proposed model. These methods often require iterative solutions.

The model is then compared with the relationships (the correlation/covariances matrix) of the actual or observed data. SEM assesses how well the predicted interrelationships between the variables match the interrelationships between the actual or observed interrelationships. SEM assesses

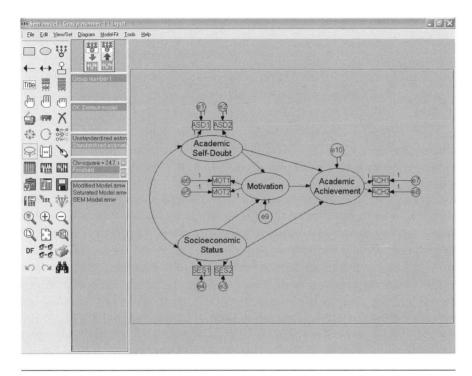

Figure 14b.14 A Structure Equation Model

the measurement model (how well the measured variables define their respective construct) and the structural model (how well the latent constructs relate to each other) simultaneously. If the two matrices (the proposed and the actual or data) are consistent with one another, then the structural equation model can be considered a credible explanation for the hypothesized relationships. Just like assessing models in path analysis with model-fitting programs, the results provide an overall fit of the model. These overall model fit measures need to be interpreted with greater caution because an impressive fit index could reflect that the measured component was acceptable but that the relationships between latent variables lacked both statistical and practical significance. Or the structural component was acceptable, but the measurement component was not.

The proposed structural equation model is presented in Figure 14b.14. We build this model as we have built the confirmatory and path models already discussed because SEM is really a combination of the two. Thus, everything that we have already discussed in using AMOS is applicable here.

Note that all the indicator variables in the previous path analysis have now been conceptualized as latent variables. Each must be associated with at least two indicator variables to have data to test the relationships between the latent variables. We have supplied generic names for these indicators in the figure. The model therefore simultaneously assesses both the structural and the measurement components of the model.

For heuristic purposes, each latent variable has two indicator variables. Recall from the confirmatory factor analysis chapter (13A) that researchers must scale the latent factor. This can be accomplished by selecting one of the path coefficients from the latent variable to a measured variable and fix (constrain) that coefficient to the value to 1 (often referred to as unity). Notice that the coefficients from the errors (unique terms) to the measured variables are constrained to 1. Constraining the coefficients linking the latent unique variables to the measured (indicator) variables provides the latent variables with the metric (scale) of their respective indicator variables. Thus, SEM is the union of confirmatory factor analysis and path analysis. In SEM, all the structural coefficients and the measured coefficients are simultaneously estimated. Fit measures need to be even more cautiously interpreted. It is therefore possible in SEM that we may have an acceptable fit of a model to the data based on the overall fit but still find that some of the relationships posited by the model are not supported.

For example, an acceptable fit index could be achieved because of the strong measurement model although the structural model is fairly weak. Alternatively, the structural model may be impressive, but the measurement model may be quite weak, making the interpretation meaningless.

The results of the SEM are as follows. The chi square was significant, indicating an unacceptable fit between the proposed model and the observed data. Because the chi square is sensitive to sample size and model complexity, we want to also use alternative fit measures to evaluate the plausibility of the proposed model. The **CFI** and the **NFI** yielded values of .983 and .962, respectively; this tends to support the model. The **RMSEA** was .063, indicating a good fit. The path coefficients for the respecified model are illustrated in Figure 14b.15. All the measured variables correlated with their respective factors at a reasonably strong level. However, three of the five structural paths failed to achieve statistical significance.

This study illustrates that even though the overall fit of a model to the data appears acceptable, some paths were not supported by the data. This acceptable fit was obtained simply because the measured paths had extremely high coefficients. To assess the accuracy of the prediction in the structural equations, we examine the proportion of variance accounted

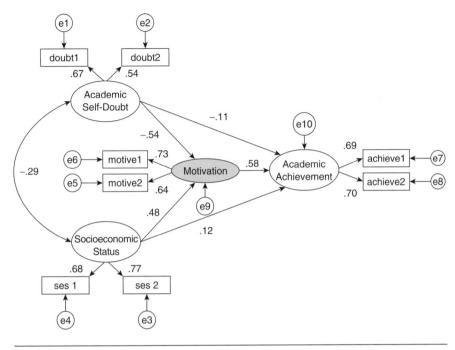

Figure 14b.15   Results of the SEM Procedure

for (R^2). Although not shown in the figure, in this model, a weak effect size was reported for motivation (.07) and a moderate effect size was found for academic achievement (.15). Is this a good model? It depends. If prior research reported greater explained variance for the endogenous variables, then this model may not contribute much to the literature. However, if the results of this model exceed what the research has thus far shown, then this model may make a significant contribution to the literature. Because results are often domain specific, it is difficult if not impossible to provide absolute standards of acceptable model fit.

Results (SPSS Version)

A path analysis, an application of multiple regression analysis in conjunction with causal theory, was used to analyze the causal models in this inquiry (see Figure 14b.1). To assess the significance of the relationships stated in the hypotheses, simultaneous regression equations were employed. A comparison of the path coefficients examined the relative importance that the exogenous and endogenous variables had on the dependent variable in the theoretical models.

Academic Achievement. The first equation in the structural model included the effects of the two exogenous variables (academic self-doubt and socioeconomic status) and one endogenous variable (motivation) on academic achievement. The results of this structural equation yielded a significant R^2 of .585, $F(3, 240) = 41.68$, $p <.001$. Only the path from motivation achieved a significant relationship with academic achievement, supporting the hypothesis that higher levels of motivation are correlated with greater academic achievement ($t = 7.43$, $p < .001$). However, both academic self-doubt and socioeconomic status failed to achieve a statistically significant relationship with academic achievement with t values of -1.67 and 1.44, respectively.

Motivation. The second structural equation assessed the effects of academic self-doubt and socioeconomic status on motivation. The squared multiple correlation for this structural equation was .356, a significant finding, $F(2, 243) = 66.49$ $p < .001$). A comparison of the standardized coefficients revealed that socioeconomic status was positively correlated with motivation ($t = 7.97$, $p < .01$) whereas academic self-doubt ($t = -5.65$, $p < .01$) had a negative effect on motivation.

Because both academic self-doubt and socioeconomic status failed to achieve statistically significant path coefficients with academic achievement in the first structural equation, a second model was proposed that deleted these paths (see Figure 14b.2). Results of this trimmed model indicated that motivation explained .328 of the variance in academic achievement, a statistically significant finding, $F(1, 243) = 13.48$ $p < .001$.

The results of this path analysis suggest that academic self-doubt and socioeconomic status influence academic achievement indirectly. Both academic self-doubt and socioeconomic status are mediated by motivation, which directly correlates with academic achievement. Neither academic self-doubt nor socioeconomic status affects academic achievement directly.

Results (AMOS Version)

The hypothesized model (see Figure 14b.12) was evaluated via AMOS 5.0 (Arbuckle, 2004) using the following indexes, the chi-square test, the comparative fit index (CFI), the normed fit index (NFI), and the root mean square error of approximation (RMSEA). In addition, the path coefficients were assessed for statistical significance at $p < .05$.

Although the chi-square test was significant, $\chi^2 (9, N = 245) = 10.47$, $p < .001$, the results yielded acceptably high goodness-of-fit indexes, indicating that the hypothesized model fit the observed data. The CFI and the NFI yielded impressive indexes of .958 and .954, respectively, whereas the RMSEA reported a value of .198, indicating a relatively poor fit of the model. All the path coefficients demonstrated both statistical significance ($p < .05$) and practical significance ($\beta > .3$). The endogenous variables of motivation and academic achievement both demonstrated strong amounts of variances explained with .36 and .23, respectively (not shown).

The results of this study support the theory that academic self-doubt and socioeconomic status influence academic achievement indirectly. Both academic self-doubt and socioeconomic status are mediated by motivation, which directly correlates with academic achievement. Neither academic self-doubt nor socioeconomic status effect academic achievement directly. Specifically, as motivation increases 1 standard deviation, the expected increase in academic achievement is .57 standard deviation. As socioeconomic status increases by 1 standard deviation, motivation increases by .43 standard deviation. However, as academic self-doubt increases by 1 standard deviation, motivation decreases by .31 standard deviation.

Results (SEM Version)

A two-step structural equation modeling strategy via AMOS 5.0 (Arbuckle, 2004) was employed in estimating parameters. This strategy involves the separate estimation of the measurement model prior to the simultaneous estimation of the measurement and structural submodels. Although the measurement model provides a confirmatory assessment of convergent validity and discriminant validity, the measurement model in conjunction with the structural model enables a comprehensive, confirmatory assessment of construct validity.

A series of four confirmatory factor analyses was conducted to assess construct validity of the latent variables (academic self-doubt, socioeconomic status, motivation, and academic achievement), with each latent variable measured by two observed variables. The chi square, the comparative fit index (CFI), the normed fit index (NFI), the root mean square error approximation (RMSEA), and statistical significance of the loadings were employed to assess model fit, with all four models achieving excellent fits.

The results of the full structural model are as follows: Although the chi-square test was significant, indicating an unacceptable fit between the proposed model and the observed data, the CFI and the NFI yielded values of .983 and .962, respectively, supporting the model. The RMSEA was .063, indicating a good fit. The path coefficients for the model are illustrated in Figure 14b.15. All the measured variables correlated with their respective factors at a reasonably strong level. However, three of the five structural paths failed to achieve statistical significance.

This study illustrates that even though the overall fit of a model to the data appears acceptable, some paths were not supported by the data. This acceptable fit was obtained simply because the measured paths had extremely high coefficients. To assess the accuracy of the prediction in the structural equations, we examine the proportion of variance accounted for (R^2). In this model, a weak effect size was reported for motivation (.07), and a moderate effect size was found for achievement (.15).

14B Exercises

Optimism and Longevity

This example was first introduced in the exercises for Chapter 5B. In this exercise, the cancer specialist developed the following saturated model (every variable is linked to every other variable). Perform a path analysis using SPSS.

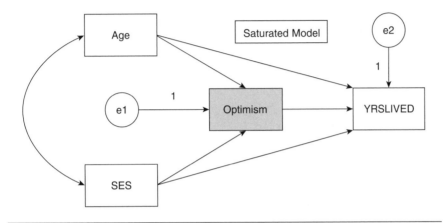

Figure 14b.16

Using the SPSS data file for Chapter 14B (located on the Web-based study site— http://www.sagepub.com/amrStudy), answer the following questions.

1. Name the exogenous variable(s).
2. Name the endogenous variable(s).
3. Name the mediating variable(s).
4. What is the beta coefficient for the direct effect of years lived and age? Is it statistically and practically significant?
5. How many indirect effects does age have on years lived? Is it statistically and practically significant?
6. Why are standardized weights rather than nonstandardized weights used?
7. What does this model tell the researcher?
8. Write a results section for this research.

Applying a Model to Different Groups

In Chapter 13 ("Confirmatory Factor Analysis") and Chapter 14 ("Causal Modeling"), the examples were analyzed on a single sample or group. When a model does not fit the data satisfactorily, we saw that it was possible to respecify it in an effort to produce a better fit. Such a strategy illustrates the more general situation in which multiple versions of the model are being evaluated. Another example of testing different variations of a model is when, in a confirmatory factor analytic study, one of two (or perhaps three) alternative factor structures may be generated from the theoretical formulation. Testing which of the alternatives fit the data better can be accomplished in exactly the same way as we compare a respecified model with the original one.

In contrast, there are other situations when the researchers may need to determine if the model is invariant (i.e., equivalent) across two or more groups. The groups could represent different genders, different ethnic identities, different ages, different sets of cohorts, and so on. When we examine such group differences, we are determining if the model demonstrates the property of invariance—that is, if the model was as good a fit for the data of one group as it was for another. The dimensions along which we might want to evaluate such group differences include the following:

▶ We can assess for group invariance across the items of a factor structure. For this confirmatory factor analysis application, researchers are interested in determining if the items of an instrument correlate (load) similarly across different groups.

▶ We could assess for group invariance across causal models. For this application, researchers want to determine if the individual paths in a causal model are equivalent across different groups or if the path coefficients vary among groups.

We will present examples of each of these in this chapter.

The General Strategy Used to Compare Groups

Overview

Comparing two or more groups to determine if a common model can be used to fit the data was initially developed by Jöreskog (1971). It involves, at a global level, two phases in the analysis that are somewhat analogous to what we use in ANOVA (analysis of variance). In the first phase, we perform what amounts to an omnibus comparison to determine if there is an overall difference between the groups. This is assessed by the chi-square goodness-of-fit index. If the chi square is statistically significant, we judge that a difference between the groups appears to exist, and that permits us to engage in the second phase of the analysis. This second phase is analogous to the post hoc tests or tests of simple effects in ANOVA. Here, we determine which of the paths are associated with coefficients that differ from group to group.

The First Phase

The first phase of the process is more complicated to explicate than the second, because several issues are being addressed by the analysis. Let's take it one step at a time and assume for ease of presentation that we have (a) only two groups—women and men, and (b) a model (path or factor) with only three coefficients to estimate. We will treat the steps involved here as though they are happening in sequence, recognizing that this is a simplification.

Permitting Coefficients to Freely Load

The first part of this process works with the two groups separately by estimating the weighting or path coefficients separately for the two groups (women and men in this example). The coefficients within each group (e.g., women), of course, are estimated simultaneously as we described in the earlier chapters, but the estimation process for the women in the sample is done independently of the estimation process for the men. At the end of this process, we have two sets of coefficients, one for women and another for men. These pairs of coefficients represent the "unconstrained" model.

Constraining the Coefficient Loadings

The second part of this process creates a "null" model in which the corresponding coefficients for the two groups are presumed to be equal. This presumption is the constraint that is superimposed on the model. The model then estimates all six path coefficients simultaneously under this constraint. For example, consider the first path. There are two coefficients it needs to estimate—the one for women and the one for men. But under this null model, these two coefficients are presumed to be equal and the computer program will make every effort to get the two values as close as it can. At the same time, however, it is estimating the women's and men's coefficients for the second and third paths and must balance all the information simultaneously to get each coefficient pair as close in value as it can. At the end of this process, we have a null model with coefficients for women and men under the constraint that each pair of coefficients is supposed to be the same.

Comparing the Free and Constrained Models

We obtain a chi-square fit measure telling us how well the unconstrained model fits the data (the model where the model independently was fit to the data for women and men). We also obtain a chi-square fit measure for how well the constrained model fits the data. The last step in this process is to make a comparison of these two models in terms of overall fit to the data.

In this last step, we use a final chi-square goodness-of-fit test to determine if there is a significant difference between the fit measures for the two models. We thus compare the two chi-square values, the one for the unconstrained model and the one for the constrained model, by using a chi-square test on these values. We do this by subtracting the chi-square value for one model from the chi-square value for the other; this yields an omnibus chi square whose statistical significance is then evaluated.

If this omnibus chi square is not statistically significant, we conclude that the same model can be applied to both groups. We would then probably run a model-fitting procedure on the combined set of women and men to obtain the "final" estimates of the coefficients. If the chi square is statistically significant, we conclude that there are differences between the two groups on at least one of the pairs of corresponding coefficients. To determine which corresponding coefficients differ between the groups, we would next conduct the second stage of the comparison process.

The Second Stage

We enter the second stage of the analysis knowing that the groups differ in some way. In this second stage of the model-fitting process, our job is to locate where those differences lie. To reach this goal, we examine each pair of coefficients that have been estimated for each path. For example, for the first path, we determine whether the estimated coefficient for women differs significantly from the estimated coefficient for men. We then make a similar determination for the second and third paths. At the end of this phase, we essentially have two different models, one for women and another for men. These models will have at least one set of corresponding coefficients that are of significantly different magnitudes. Examination of the similarities and differences between the two models would then be related back to the theoretical framework from which the general model was drawn.

Testing for Invariance: Confirmatory Factor Analysis

The Example We Use

The Multicultural Competence Study previously described in Chapter 13A will be used to illustrate how to assess model invariance for a confirmatory factor analysis. The model is presented in Figure 15a.1 and is based on the scale developed by Gamst et al. (2004) to assess the degree to which mental health practitioners demonstrated the ability to work with and understand clients from a diverse set of cultural backgrounds. They labeled the construct as Multicultural Competence and called their scale the California Brief Multicultural Competence Scale (CBMCS). These researchers also identified the four indicator variables of sensitivity to consumers, non-ethnic ability, awareness of cultural barriers, and multicultural knowledge. To keep this example relatively simple, we will treat these indicator variables as though they are measured variables.

In 1973, the American Psychological Association endorsed multicultural training of clinical psychologists. On the basis of that shift of program structure, we will base our hypothetical group comparison example on this change. Thus, one group will be made up of those clinicians who received their doctoral degree either in or prior to 1973 (pre-1974), the other group will represent those clinicians who received their doctoral degree after 1973 (post-1973).

Identifying the Unconstrained Model

Recall from the description of this example model in Chapter 13A that it contained 10 known elements: the variances of the four measured variables and their six covariances. In this first step of the first phase of the analysis, we are dealing separately with women and men. Each contributes 10 known

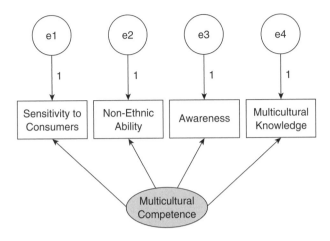

Figure 15a.1   The Hypothesized Factor Structure for Multicultural Competence

elements to the total count. Thus, the unconstrained model contains 20 known elements.

The model also attempts to estimate 8 parameters for women and 8 parameters for men. These parameters are the variances of the four error variables, the variance of the latent variable Multicultural Competence, and the three factor coefficients (one was constrained to 1 to scale the latent variable). Adding the parameters for women and men together gives us a total of 16. Subtracting the number of estimated parameters (16) from the number of known elements (20) yields 4 degrees of freedom. Thus, the unconstrained model is identified.

Identifying the Constrained Model

The constrained model actually has more degrees of freedom than the unconstrained model. There are still 20 known elements (10 from each group) but only 13 unknowns: the variances of the two latent factors (one from each group), the variances of the 8 unique or error variables (four from each group), but only three factor loadings because the factor loadings for each group are now considered to be the same. There are therefore 20 minus 13, or 7 degrees of freedom associated with the constrained model.

Outcome

The chi-square test for differences is used to assess if the items are invariant across both groups. The chi square for the first model (items are assessed

Table 15a.1   Structure/Pattern Coefficients for Both Groups

	Pre-1974 Group	Post-1973 Group	Sig. Dif.
Indicator Variable			
SENSITIVE	.43	.47	N/A
NON-ETHNIC	.38	.67	Yes
AWARENESS	.52	.57	N/A
KNOWLEDGE	.29	.84	Yes

Note: SENSITIVE = Sensitivity to Consumers, NON-ETHNIC = Non-Ethnic Ability, AWARENESS = Awareness of Cultural Barriers, and KNOWLEDGE = Multicultural Knowledge. Sig. Dif. = Statistically Significant Difference, $p < .05$.

independently) was 27.82, and the chi square for the second model (item are assessed as equal) was 81.570. To calculate the chi-square difference, simply subtract the smaller value from the larger value. In this example, the difference between the two chi squares is 53.75 and is tested at the degrees of freedom achieved by subtracting the degrees of freedom from one model from that of the other. In this case, there are 7 minus 4, or 3 degrees of freedom associated with the omnibus or difference chi square of 53.75. This is a large enough value to be statistically significant, indicating that at least one factor loading is different for the two groups. This chi-square test is analogous to the omnibus test in ANOVA. To detect which items are different for the two groups, each group's four coefficients are compared and assessed for statistical significance at the a priori alpha of .05. As we will see in Chapter 15B, significance tests between the coefficients are provided as part of the output. The factor loadings are presented in Table 15a.1.

The specific coefficient differences are non-ethnic ability and multicultural knowledge, with the post-1973 group showing greater importance of these indicators on multicultural competence. There was no statistically significant difference between the two groups on awareness of cultural barriers. Because the sensitivity-to-consumers indicator was initially constrained to 1 to provide the latent variable (Multicultural Competence), its metric (scale), statistical significance could not be calculated. If determining the sensitivity to consumers indicator was an important item to assess for differences, then the researchers could simply reanalyze the models by constraining one of the other three indicators to identify the model, thus allowing the sensitivity to consumers indicator to be assessed for statistical significance. The results of this study suggest that multicultural training increased competence, particularly with non-ethnic ability and multicultural knowledge.

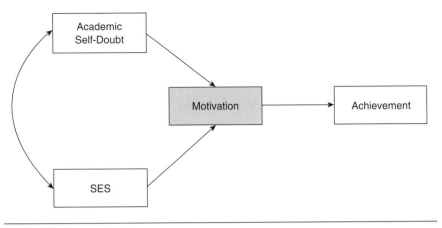

Figure 15a.2   The Hypothesized Path Diagram for Academic Achievement

Testing for Invariance: Path Analysis

The Example We Use

The path example described in Chapter 14A will be used to illustrate how to assess group invariance for a causal model. Recall from that example that the researchers were investigating the causes or predictors of academic achievement. In the model shown in Figure 15a.2, the researchers were assessing the direct effects of academic self-doubt and socioeconomic status on motivation and the direct effect of motivation on academic achievement. The model also investigated the indirect effects of academic self-doubt and socioeconomic status on academic achievement mediated through motivation. For example, students with less academic self-doubt may be more motivated to succeed, which in turn may yield greater academic achievement.

The researchers could be interested if the path coefficients are comparable for a sample of students attending an urban school compared with a matched set of students attending a rural school. To determine if the three path coefficients—(a) academic self-doubt to motivation, (b) socioeconomic status to motivation, and (c) motivation to academic achievement—operate equivalently across the two groups (urban or rural), we will compare the two models for the two groups simultaneously. Specifically, the researchers will test the null hypothesis (H_o) that there are no differences between the respective path coefficients for the two groups.

Similar to the confirmatory factor analysis invariance procedure, the testing of the null hypothesis is accomplished by comparing one model (which allows the public and private groups' paths to freely correlate on their respective variables) with a second model (where the public and private groups' paths are constrained to be equal to each other). If there is no difference between the two models (i.e., the null hypothesis is not rejected), this is evidence of invariance (i.e., the groups are equivalent). However, if there are differences between the two models, then one can conclude the groups are variant (different).

Identifying the Models

We will compare both groups (urban or rural) simultaneously. The first model has 20 knowns (10 from each group) and 14 unknowns (7 from each group). The 7 unknowns for each group are (a) the variance of the four exogenous variables (academic self-doubt, socioeconomic status, and the two error variables for motivation and academic achievement) and (b) the three paths of academic self-doubt to motivation, socioeconomic status to motivation, and motivation to academic achievement. The degrees of freedom for the combined groups are 6 ($20 - 14 = 6$). The second model (where the paths are constrained to be equal to each other) has 7 degrees of freedom. This is because there are now only three path coefficients being estimated because the pairs of path coefficients have been constrained to be equal to each other. There are still 20 knowns (10 from each group) but only 11 unknowns—the eight exogenous variables (four from each group) and the three path coefficients (three for both groups because they are considered to be the same). There are 9 degrees of freedom for the second model ($20 - 11 = 9$).

Outcome

The chi-square test for differences is again used to determine if the paths are invariant across both groups. The chi square for the first model (paths are assessed independently) was 38.82 and the chi square for the second model (items are assessed as equal) was 92.570. Recall that to calculate the chi-square difference and the degrees of freedom, simply subtract the smaller value from the larger value. In this example, the chi square was 63.75. Because the chi-square difference test was statistically significant at 3 degrees of freedom, we have learned that at least one path coefficient pair is different for the two groups.

To detect which paths are different for the two groups, each group's three path coefficients are compared and assessed for statistical significance at the a priori alpha of .05. As we will see later in Chapter 15B, statistically significant differences between the coefficients are provided. The path coefficients are presented in Table 15a.2.

Table 15a.2 Summary of Causal Effects for the Academic Achievement
Hypothesized Model

Outcome	Determinant	Direct Effect		Sig. Dif.
		Urban	*Rural*	
Achievement	Motivation	.34	.33	No
Motivation	Self-Doubt	.13	.56	Yes
	SES	.42	.21	Yes

Note: Achievement = Academic Achievement, Self-Doubt = Academic Self-Doubt, SES = Socioeconomic Status, Sig. Dif. = Statistically Significant Difference, $p < .05$.

The results of this study indicate that for urban students, the path coefficient between socioeconomic status and motivation is statistically significantly greater than for the rural students. However, for rural students the path coefficient between academic self-doubt and motivation is statistically significantly greater than for the urban students. There was no statistically significant difference between the two groups for the path coefficient between motivation and academic achievement.

Recommended Readings

Byrne, B. M., & Shavelson, R. J. (1987). Adolescent self-concept: Testing the assumption of equivalent structure across gender. *American Educational Research Association, 24,* 365–385.

Cheung, G. W., & Rensvold, R. B. (1999). Testing factorial invariance across groups: A reconceptualization and proposed new method. *Journal of Management, 25,* 1–27.

Hofer, S. M., Horn, J. L., & Eber, H. W. (1997). A robust five-factor structure of the 16PF: Evidence from independent rotation and confirmatory factorial invariance procedures. *Personality and Individual Differences, 23,* 247–269.

Horn, J. L., & McArdle, J. J. (1992). A practical and theoretical guide to measurement invariance in aging research. *Experimental Aging Research, 18,* 117–144.

Lievens, F., & Anseel, F. (2004). Confirmatory factor analysis and invariance of an organizational citizenship behaviour measure across samples in a Dutch-speaking context. *Journal of Occupational and Organizational Psychology, 77,* 299–306.

MacCallum, R. C., Wegener, D. T., Uchino, B. N., & Fabrigar, L. R. (1993). The problem of equivalent models in applications of covariance structure analysis. *Psychological Bulletin, 114,* 185–199.

Meredith, W. (1993). Measurement invariance, factor analysis and factorial invariance. *Psychometrika, 58,* 525–543.

Meredith, W., & Horn, J. L. (2001). The role of factorial invariance in modeling growth and change. In L. M. Collins & A. G. Sayer (Eds.), *New methods for the analysis of change* (pp. 204–240). Washington, DC: American Psychological Association.

Steenkamp, J-B. E. M., & Baumgartner, H. (1998). Assessing measurement invariance in cross-national consumer research. *Journal of Consumer Research, 25,* 78–90.

Vandenberg, R. J., & Lance, C. E. (2000). A review and synthesis of the measurement invariance literature: Suggestions, practices, and recommendations for organizational research. *Organizational Research Methods, 3,* 4–69.

Assessing Model Invariance Between Groups Using AMOS

Confirmatory Factor Analysis and Path Analysis

Recall from Chapter 15A that there are circumstances when researchers may need to determine if a model is invariant (i.e., equivalent) across two or more groups. In this chapter, we will describe how to use the AMOS (Analysis of MOment Structures) 5.0 Graphics program (Arbuckle, 2004) to assess group invariance using the examples from Chapter 15A. Those two examples were assessing (a) item invariance between two groups of mental health practitioners on the California Brief Multicultural Competence Scale (CBMCS) and (b) path invariance between samples of students attending an urban school compared with students attending a rural school. We will then navigate you through the extensive results output (with annotations) so you can comprehend the output.

Testing for Invariance: Confirmatory Factor Analysis

Recall from Chapter 13A that we discussed the California Brief Multicultural Competence Scale (CBMCS). The CBMCS was developed to assess the degree to which mental health practitioners demonstrated the ability to work with and understand clients from a diverse set of cultural backgrounds. The CBMCS comprises four indicator variables: (a) sensitivity to consumers, (b) non-ethnic ability, (c) awareness of cultural barriers, and

(d) multicultural knowledge. We concluded that the items demonstrated construct validity (i.e., these variables purport to measure the construct of Multicultural Competence). In Chapter 15A, we discussed conceptually if the items making up the CBMCS perform equivalently across two groups of practitioners: (a) those who received their degrees prior to 1974 (pre) and (b) those who received their degree after 1973 (post). We will now describe how to use the AMOS program to assess group invariance on the items of the CBMCS.

To compare groups for invariance, AMOS requires that the groups are separated in some electronic manner. Although it is possible to create a group membership variable in the larger data file (Arbuckle & Wothke, 1999), it is far easier to create separate data files representing the separate groups. We will assume that this has been done in our example. Thus, one data file will contain the therapists obtaining their degrees prior to 1973 and in another file, those obtaining their degrees after that date.

Constructing the Models for Comparison

To begin our analyses, we click **Analyze → Amos 5** (the last choice is Version 5 of the AMOS program and assumes that you have obtained and separately loaded this application once SPSS has been loaded on your computer) as shown in Figure 15b.1. The screen shows that we have selected the **Draw Indicator Variable** from **Diagram** on the main menu. We are selecting this in preparation for drawing the model.

To draw the model consisting of one latent variable and four indicator variables, depress the left mouse button and draw a circle (or oval), then click the left mouse button 4 times. This is shown in Figure 15b.2. The smaller circles depicting the error variables were inserted by AMOS automatically. Click the right mouse button to disengage the draw function.

In this group comparison process, we need to first create one model that will be applied to the two separate groups. We therefore need to indicate what the two groups are that will be compared. Our goal is to reach the **Manage Groups** dialog box. Select **Model-Fit → Manage Groups.** The **Manage Groups** dialog box will appear with **Group number 1** as the default name. This is shown in Figure 15b.3.

Place the cursor in the box and type over the **Group number 1** with **Pre** to indicate those practitioners who received their degrees before 1973. Then check the pushbutton **New**. The box will now appear with **Group number 2** as the default name. Place the cursor in the box and type over the **Group number 2** with **Post** to indicate those mental health practitioners who received their degrees after 1973. Then check the pushbutton **Close**.

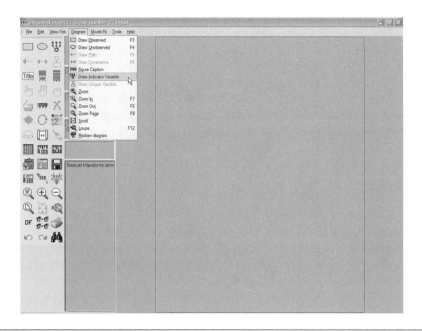

Figure 15b.1 Main AMOS 5.0 Screen With Diagram and Draw Indicator Variable Task Bars Presented

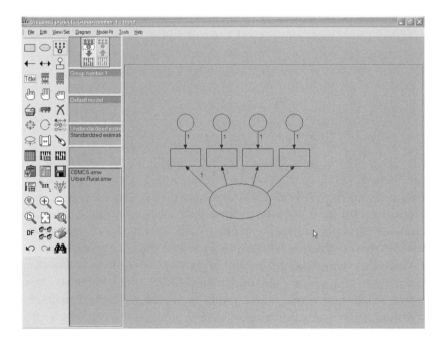

Figure 15b.2 Completed Diagram for the Model

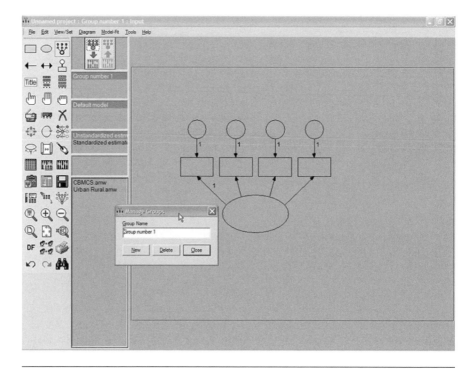

Figure 15b.3   Manage Groups Dialog Box

Now it is time to open the files. Select **File → Data Files.** The **Data Files** dialog box will appear with **Pre <working>** and **Post <working>** as the default names. This is shown in Figure 15b.4. Note that AMOS picked up our group labels. The expression **<working>** means that no data file has been selected yet. This is the next step for us to take. To retrieve each data file, highlight the appropriate row and click on **File Name** as shown in Figure 15b.4.

After clicking on **File Name,** we are presented with the **Open** dialog box, which allows us to navigate to the location of the data files; this also indicates to AMOS which data file is associated with which group.

The next step is to label the indicator variables by dragging their names to the boxes as described in Chapter 13B. Briefly, select **View/Set → Variables in Dataset,** which displays the variables in the data file. Drag the variable names to the boxes. Following that, label the factor by double clicking on it and typing your designation for it under **Variable Name.** To name all the error terms, select **Tools → Macro → Name Unobserved Variables**; AMOS will automatically assign names to the error terms using **e** with numerical counters. The model will now resemble the one presented in Figure 15b.5.

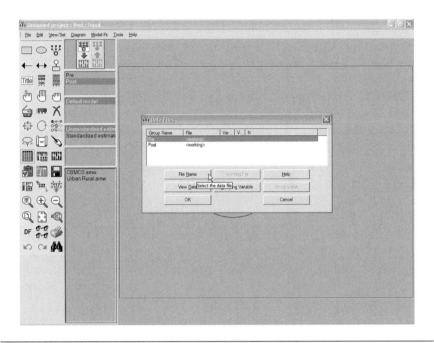

Figure 15b.4 Data File Dialog Box

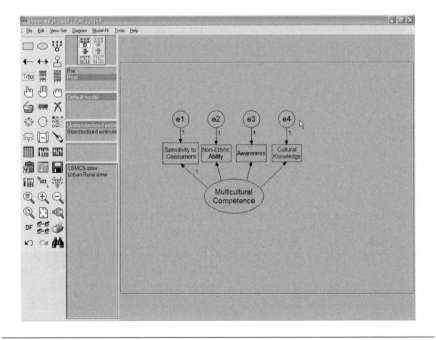

Figure 15b.5 Model With All Variable Names Filled In

To determine if the four aggregated items (sensitivity to consumers, nonethnic ability, awareness of cultural barriers, and multicultural knowledge) operate equivalently across the two groups (pre- 1974 and post-1973 degree recipients), we will compare two models simultaneously. Now, these two "models" are more complex than the model displayed in Figure 15b.5. The model in the figure is really only half of one of the models; it represents only one of the groups. The other half of the model, which is identical to what is drawn in Figure 15b.5, represents the other group. In this case, one of these models represents the pre-1974 group, and the other represents the post-1973 group. These two diagrams—together—make up one of the models that we will be comparing. The other model that we will be comparing is identical to what we just described.

So what are we going to compare? Although the models may look the same, they may very well have different values for their coefficients. The issue that we will deal with directly is whether or not there is a statistically significant difference between the corresponding coefficients of model for the two groups.

The two models that will be compared are based on different strategies for specifying the coefficients. One model, called the *free model,* allows the coefficients based on each group to be estimated independently of each other. In the other model, called the *constrained model,* the coefficients representing the two groups are set to be equal to each other. The reality, of course, is that the solution will not likely yield exactly the same values, but the statistical procedure tries its best to get them as close in value to each other as it is mathematically possible to do. This second model, conceptually, represents the null hypothesis that the coefficients for the two groups are not statistically different. This is our baseline. We will then compare the free model with this null model by using a chi-square difference test.

Recall that statistical tests concerned with detecting differences between groups assume that the groups are equal (i.e., researchers test the null hypothesis, H_0). If there is no difference between the two models (i.e., the null hypothesis is not rejected), this is evidence of invariance (i.e., the groups are equivalent). However, if there are differences between the two models, then one can conclude the groups are variant (different). This lack of measurement invariance suggests that the interpretation of the latent construct is not the same across the groups. This "interpretational confounding" occurs because the factor loadings are used to derive the meaning of the latent variables (factors). If the loadings differ substantially across groups, then the meaning of the factors will vary even though the factor keeps the same label (Garson, 2000).

The first model we will construct is the constrained model, that is, we will specify that the respective group coefficients are equal. To enable this specification, we must label the causal paths. To accomplish this labeling (naming the parameters), select **Tools → Macro → Name Parameters.** This produces the dialog box shown in Figure 15b.6. Check the **Regression weights** box (AMOS's term for the path coefficients or factor loadings) and retype over the **W** (the AMOS default for the **Prefix** corresponding to **Regression weights**) with *Pre.* This will indicate that these coefficients are from the pre-1974 group. Then click the **OK** pushbutton and you will see the labels **Pre1, Pre2,** and **Pre3** placed on three of the paths in the diagram.

In the left narrow column toward the top of the AMOS screen, you will find the group names. We will click on the second group (post-1973) to make it active. Then select **Tools → Macro → Name Parameters.** Check the **Regression weights** box and retype over the **W** with *Pst.* This will indicate that these coefficients are from the post-1973 group. Then click the **OK** pushbutton.

Having set the stage, we can now define the constrained model. Select **Model-Fit → Manage Models.** This will produce the **Manage Models** dialog box. Type **Equal** in the **Model Name** box. This label indicates that in

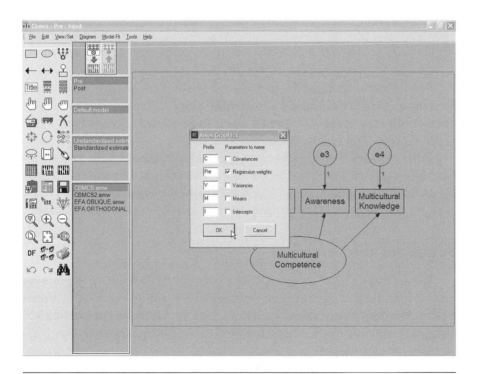

Figure 15b.6 Dialog Box for Labeling the Factor Loadings

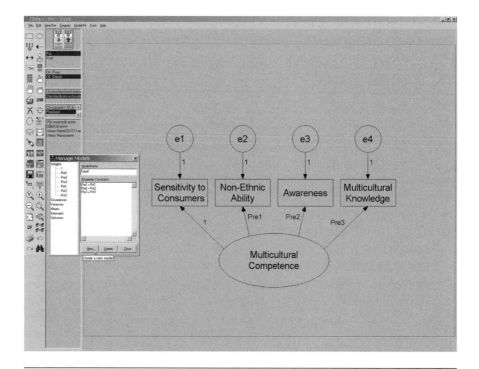

Figure 15b.7   Constraining the Parameters

this model the respective factor loadings are constrained to be equal for each group. In the **Parameter Constraints,** type the parameters that need to be considered equal (i.e., **Pre1 = Pst1**, **Pre2 = Pst2**, **Pre3 = Pst3**). This is presented in Figure 15b.7. Then click **New**.

In the **Model Name** box, type over **Default Model** with **Free.** This label indicates that in this model the factor loadings are free to be calculated for each group independently. Leave the **Parameter Constraints** area blank because we will place no constraints on the parameters. Then click **Close.**

Structuring the Analysis

We are now ready to tell AMOS what sort of output we want it to produce. To do this, we proceed on the following menu sequence: **View/ Set → Analysis Properties.** The dialog box for **Analysis Properties** will appear. The box opens on the page keyed to the **Estimation** tab. This page specifies, among other properties, the method that will be used to calculate the coefficients. **Maximum likelihood** is the AMOS default and the one that we will be using.

After viewing this page, we need to select the tab representing **Output.** Remove all checkmarks and then select the two boxes labeled **Standardized estimates** and **Critical ratios for differences.** The **Standardized estimates** box will produce the regression weights. Because we are comparing two models, AMOS will automatically calculate a chi-square difference test. If the resulting chi square is statistically significant, then it would be appropriate to determine which pairs of coefficients are different and which are not akin to a post hoc test in ANOVA. The **Critical ratios for differences** box will do this for us; it will report the *p* value for each pair of parameter estimates. Close the dialog box and select from the task bar **Model-Fit → Calculate Estimates** to perform the computations.

Examining the Output From a Model Comparison Analysis

To view the output, select **View/Set → Text Output → Model Comparison.** You will see a small but very important table showing you the resulting chi-square difference test. If it is not significant, stop there because you cannot reject the null hypothesis. In the present case, the value of the statistic was 53.75. With 3 degrees of freedom, it was statistically significant. That tells us that the free model is a better fit than the constrained model (the constrained model could never be a better fit—the most extreme case is that there is no difference).

Because this omnibus chi-square difference test was significant, we can examine the pairs of regression weights (factor loadings). Choose the **Free** model in the lower left box on the output page and then select **Pairwise Parameter Comparisons** (note that if you select **Pairwise Parameter Comparisons** while in the **Equal** model, there will be no output for the comparisons between the pre and post respective loadings). This is displayed in Figure 15b.8. AMOS in this instance gives us more information than many of us want. Basically, we want to compare the associated factor loadings (e.g., **pre1** with **post1**), but AMOS makes all possible comparisons and thus presents a great deal of information that you have to sort through. Your best bet with just a few paths is to either highlight the differences on a hard copy or write down the comparisons of interest longhand on paper.

The values in Figure 15b.8 are *z* scores representing the difference between the two factor loadings. AMOS subtracts the coefficient of the first group that we entered first on the **Manage Groups** dialog box (which in this case was pre) from the coefficient of the second group (which was post); that is, the difference is post minus pre. Values greater than ±1.96 are indicative of significant differences.

Examine the number **2.078** located in the first column, the fourth number down. This is the comparison between **pre1** and **post1** (non-ethnic

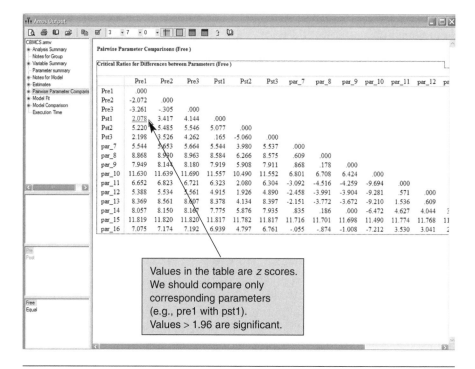

Figure 15b.8   Pairwise Parameter Comparisons

ability). Because it is positive and greater than 1.96, we know that the post coefficient is significantly larger than the pre coefficient. The other two critical ratios for awareness of cultural barriers and multicultural knowledge are also both positive and significant. The results of this study suggest that practitioners trained before 1973 view the construct of Multicultural Competence somewhat differently than do those trained after 1973. Specifically, the factor loading for non-ethnic ability increased for the post group, whereas the pre group demonstrated greater loadings for awareness of cultural barriers and multicultural knowledge. The estimated factor loadings have also been computed by AMOS. They can be found in the output table **Estimates**. Estimates are provided for each group separately, and you must click on the group name to see its parameters.

Because the sensitivity to consumers indicator was initially constrained to 1 to provide the latent variable (Multicultural Competence) its metric (scale), statistical significance could not be calculated for this path. If determining the sensitivity to consumers indicator was an important item to assess for differences, then the researchers could simply reanalyze the models by constraining one of the other three indicators to identify the model, thus allowing the sensitivity to consumers indicator to be assessed for statistical significance.

We now know that the free model is a better fit of the data and that all three of the factor loadings that were testable showed a significant difference. But "better" does not mean that the free model was a "good" fit—just that it did better than the null model. To determine how well the free model does fit the data, we need to examine the fit indexes. Select **Model Fit** to view them; we show our results in Figure 15b.9.

This window provides all the different classifications of the model fit measures. Recall there are 10 tables, each presenting one or more model fit indexes. We have simplified this output by presenting only three of these tables. Notice, however, that now for each of the tables there are four models being assessed: (a) the free model (i.e., the model designed to allow the

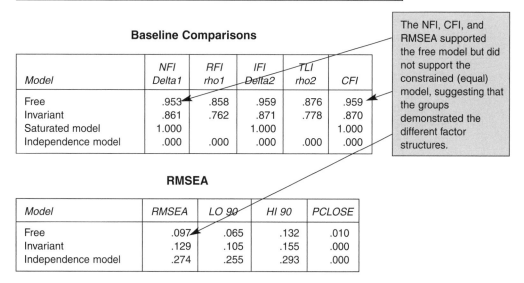

Model Fit Summary

CMIN

Model	NPAR	CMIN	DF	P	CMIN/DF
Free	16	27.819	4	.000	6.955
Invariant	13	81.567	7	.000	11.652
Saturated model	20	.000	0		
Independence model	8	586.782	12	.000	48.898

Baseline Comparisons

Model	NFI Delta1	RFI rho1	IFI Delta2	TLI rho2	CFI
Free	.953	.858	.959	.876	.959
Invariant	.861	.762	.871	.778	.870
Saturated model	1.000		1.000		1.000
Independence model	.000	.000	.000	.000	.000

> The NFI, CFI, and RMSEA supported the free model but did not support the constrained (equal) model, suggesting that the groups demonstrated the different factor structures.

RMSEA

Model	RMSEA	LO 90	HI 90	PCLOSE
Free	.097	.065	.132	.010
Invariant	.129	.105	.155	.000
Independence model	.274	.255	.293	.000

Figure 15b.9 Fit Indexes for the Models

666 ◀ APPLIED MULTIVARIATE RESEARCH

factor loadings to be computed independently for each group), (b) the equal (constrained) model where the loadings for the pairs of respective measured variables were constrained to be equal to each other, and two other models that are inconsequential for a multimodel comparison study, (c) the saturated model, and (d) the independence model.

We will concentrate on those fit measures identified by Thompson (2004) as the four most frequently used fit measures used by researchers: the chi square (labeled as **CMIN** in AMOS), comparative fit measure (CFI), the normed fit index (NFI), and the root mean square error of approximation (RMSEA).

The chi-square test is used to compare the observed covariance matrix with the hypothesized or predicted covariance matrix. If the two matrices are similar, then the chi square will not be statistically significant at the a priori level of .05. Although the chi-square test is statistically significant for both groups, the free group model achieved a statistically significant smaller chi square than did the equal model (smaller chi squares suggest a better fit). But as we know from previous discussions, chi square is sensitive to sample size; we therefore should supplement chi square with other fit indexes. The other three measures suggested by Thompson—NFI, CFI, and RMSEA— supported the free model but failed to support the constrained model. This is further evidence to suggest that the groups demonstrated fundamentally different factor structures for the construct of multicultural competence.

What Paths Are Constrained?

In this example, we presented a unidimensional scale where the measured indicators of the two groups were constrained to be equal to each other. However, not all parameters need to be constrained. Researchers decide, based on theoretical considerations, how restrictive the null model needs to be. For example, a researcher could be assessing invariance between two groups on a scale (or instrument) with two factors (instead of the single factor in our original example). In this example, researchers may be interested only in testing invariance of the correlation between the two factors and not the factor loadings or the invariance of only some of the factor loadings. Confirmatory factor analysis could be appropriately applied to these interests as well.

Testing for Invariance: Path Analysis

Although measurement invariance between groups is more common, researchers can also test for structural invariance across groups as well. Assessing for structural invariance determines whether the path coefficients have the same magnitude for each group in the analysis. This structural or path invariance procedure is conceptually identical to testing for measurement invariance.

The path example described in the previous chapter will illustrate how to assess group invariance for a causal model. In that model, the researchers were assessing the direct effects of academic self-doubt and socioeconomic status on motivation and the direct effect of motivation on academic achievement. The model also hypothesized indirect effects of academic self-doubt and socioeconomic status on academic achievement mediated through motivation. For example, students with less academic self-doubt may be more motivated to succeed, which in turn may yield greater academic achievement.

The researchers are now investigating if the three path coefficients—(a) academic self-doubt to motivation, (b) socioeconomic status to motivation, and (c) motivation to academic achievement—operate equivalently across the two groups (urban or rural). Specifically, the researchers will test the null hypothesis (H_0) that there is no difference between the respective path coefficients for the two groups. We test the null model by comparing two models. The first is the free model, which allows the urban and rural groups' path coefficients to be estimated independently; the second is the constrained model (called the equal model by AMOS) in which the path coefficients are constrained to be equal to each other. If there is no difference between the two models (i.e., the null hypothesis is not rejected), this is evidence of invariance (i.e., the groups are equivalent). However, if there are differences between the two models, then one can conclude the groups are not invariant (they are different).

We have covered the AMOS steps to construct path models in Chapter 14B and to compare models in the section above. A summary of that process is provided below:

1. **Diagram → Draw Observe Variable**
2. **Diagram → Draw Path**
3. **Diagram → Draw Covariance**
4. **Model-Fit → Manage Groups** (name the groups urban and rural)
5. **File → Data Files** (select the data files for the two groups)
6. **View/Set → Variables in Dataset** (drag each variable to the appropriate box)
7. **Tools → Macro → Name Unobserved Variables** (name all the error terms)
8. **Tools → Macro → Name Parameters** (check regression weights and covariances)

9. **Model-Fit → Manage Models → Model Name** (name the models free and equal)

10. **Model Name → Equal Model Parameter Constraints** (type the path names to be equal)

11. **View/Set → Analysis Properties → Output** (select standardized estimates and critical ratios for differences)

12. **Model-Fit → Calculate Estimates**

As soon as you have selected **Calculate Estimates,** the screen will display the path diagram and will now activate the little box in the upper left corner. At this point, select **View/Set → Text Output,** then select **Model Comparison** and the table that will be displayed provides the result of the chi-square difference test. In the present instance, this statistic was significant. We therefore conclude that one or more of the pairs of coefficients are significantly different.

Highlight the **Free** model in the lower left box on the output page and then select **Pairwise Parameter Comparisons.** This table shows the differences in z score units between the pairs of path coefficients. In this case, we did not need to constrain a path equal to 1 in order to identify the model. Thus, we were able to evaluate all the paths rather than all but one of them. When we examined the z scores, we found that the path coefficients for both motivation to academic achievement and socioeconomic status to motivation are statistically different for the two groups. The urban group demonstrated a stronger path coefficient from motivation to academic achievement (the difference was computed by subtracting rural from urban). However, the rural group demonstrated a stronger path coefficient from socioeconomic status to motivation. Now select **Estimates** to examine the path coefficients for the two groups. These provide the values of the regression weights for each group for each path.

Finally, select **Model-Fit.** This window provides all the different classifications of the model fit measures. Recall that there are 10 tables, each presenting one or more model fit indexes. These tables show that there are four models being assessed: (a) the free model (i.e., the model designed to allow the path coefficients to be computed independently for each group), (b) the equal model where the path coefficients were constrained to be equal to each other, and two other models that are inconsequential for a multimodel comparison study, (c) the saturated model and (d) the independence model. The **NFI**, **CFI**, and **RMSEA** indicated that the free model is superior to the equal model. This is further evidence that the groups demonstrated fundamentally different path coefficients for the hypothesized model of academic achievement.

Results (Factor Invariance)

To assess if the factor structure of the California Brief Multicultural Competence Scale (CBMCS) operates equivalently across the two groups of mental health practitioners—(a) those who received their degrees prior to 1974 and (b) those who received their degree after 1973, the pattern/structure coefficients were constrained to be equal to each other. The chi-square test for differences revealed that the factor structure was not invariant between the two groups, χ^2 (3, $N = 386$) = 53.74, $p < .001$, indicating that the interpretation of the latent construct is not the same between the groups. Specifically, those who received their degree after 1973 demonstrated statistically significantly greater values of the pattern/structure coefficients on non-ethnic ability, awareness of cultural barriers, and multicultural knowledge. The pattern/structure coefficients for the two groups are provided in Table 15b.1.

Table 15b.1 Comparing the Structure/Pattern Coefficients of the CBMCS for Both Groups

Indicator Variable	Pre-1974 Group	Post-1973 Group	Sig. Dif.
Sensitivity to Consumers	.43	.47	N/A
Non-Ethnic Ability	.38	.67	Yes
Awareness of Cultural Barriers	.42	.57	Yes
Multicultural Knowledge	.29	.84	Yes

Note: Sig. Dif. = Statistically Significant Difference ($p < .05$); N/A = not applicable.

Results (Path Invariance)

To assess if the hypothesized model operates equivalently across the two groups (urban or rural), the path coefficients were constrained to be equal to each other. The chi-square test for differences revealed that the hypothesized model was not invariant between the two groups, χ^2 (3, N = 240) = 53.74, p < .001. Whereas the urban group demonstrated a stronger path coefficient from motivation to academic achievement, the rural group demonstrated a stronger path coefficient from socioeconomic status to motivation. There were no statistically significant differences between the two groups on the path coefficient from socioeconomic status and motivation. The path coefficients for the two groups are provided in Table 15b.2.

Table 15b.2 Comparing the Path Coefficients of the Proposed Model for Both Groups

Outcome	Urban Group		Rural Group		Sig. Dif.
	Predictor	Direct	Predictor	Direct	
Academic Achievement	Motivation	−.57	Motivation	.38	Yes
	Academic Self-Doubt	−.38	Academic Self-Doubt	−.64	Yes
Motivation	Socioeconomic Status	.43	Socioeconomic Status	.42	Constrained to be equal

15B Exercises

Invariance

In this study, a researcher is investigating if a sample of males and females differs on optimism and life satisfaction. Both factors are measured by three items each. Using the SPSS data files for Chapter 15B (located on the Web-based study site—http:// www .sagepub.com/amrStudy) and AMOS 5.0, conduct a model invariance analysis.

1. Are the two models invariant? Explain your answer.

2. Do the items load on their respective factors for both groups?

3. Report the CFI, NFI, and RMSEA for both groups.

4. What is the correlation coefficient between the factors for both groups?

5. Write a results section for this analysis.

Appendix

Critical Values of Chi Square

Selected Critical Values of Chi-Square Distribution With Degrees of Freedom

df	*Probability of exceeding the critical value*				
	0.10	*0.05*	*0.025*	*0.01*	*0.001*
1	2.706	3.841	5.024	6.635	10.828
2	4.605	5.991	7.378	9.210	13.816
3	6.251	7.815	9.348	11.345	16.266
4	7.779	9.488	11.143	13.277	18.467
5	9.236	11.070	12.833	15.086	20.515
6	10.645	12.592	14.449	16.812	22.458
7	12.017	14.067	16.013	18.475	24.322
8	13.362	15.507	17.535	20.090	26.125
9	14.684	16.919	19.023	21.666	27.877
10	15.987	18.307	20.483	23.209	29.588
11	17.275	19.675	21.920	24.725	31.264
12	18.549	21.026	23.337	26.217	32.910
13	19.812	22.362	24.736	27.688	34.528
14	21.064	23.685	26.119	29.141	36.123
15	22.307	24.996	27.488	30.578	37.697
16	23.542	26.296	28.845	32.000	39.252
17	24.769	27.587	30.191	33.409	40.790
18	25.989	28.869	31.526	34.805	42.312
19	27.204	30.144	32.852	36.191	43.820
20	28.412	31.410	34.170	37.566	45.315
21	29.615	32.671	35.479	38.932	46.797
22	30.813	33.924	36.781	40.289	48.268
23	32.007	35.172	38.076	41.638	49.728
24	33.196	36.415	39.364	42.980	51.179
25	34.382	37.652	40.646	44.314	52.620
26	35.563	38.885	41.923	45.642	54.052

(Continued)

27	36.741	40.113	43.195	46.963	55.476
28	37.916	41.337	44.461	48.278	56.892
29	39.087	42.557	45.722	49.588	58.301
30	40.256	43.773	46.979	50.892	59.703
31	41.422	44.985	48.232	52.191	61.098
32	42.585	46.194	49.480	53.486	62.487
33	43.745	47.400	50.725	54.776	63.870
34	44.903	48.602	51.966	56.061	65.247
35	46.059	49.802	53.203	57.342	66.619
36	47.212	50.998	54.437	58.619	67.985
37	48.363	52.192	55.668	59.893	69.347
38	49.513	53.384	56.896	61.162	70.703
39	50.660	54.572	58.120	62.428	72.055
40	51.805	55.758	59.342	63.691	73.402
41	52.949	56.942	60.561	64.950	74.745
42	54.090	58.124	61.777	66.206	76.084
43	55.230	59.304	62.990	67.459	77.419
44	56.369	60.481	64.201	68.710	78.750
45	57.505	61.656	65.410	69.957	80.077
46	58.641	62.830	66.617	71.201	81.400
47	59.774	64.001	67.821	72.443	82.720
48	60.907	65.171	69.023	73.683	84.037
49	62.038	66.339	70.222	74.919	85.351
50	63.167	67.505	71.420	76.154	86.661
51	64.295	68.669	72.616	77.386	87.968
52	65.422	69.832	73.810	78.616	89.272
53	66.548	70.993	75.002	79.843	90.573
54	67.673	72.153	76.192	81.069	91.872
55	68.796	73.311	77.380	82.292	93.168
56	69.919	74.468	78.567	83.513	94.461
57	71.040	75.624	79.752	84.733	95.751
58	72.160	76.778	80.936	85.950	97.039
59	73.279	77.931	82.117	87.166	98.324
60	74.397	79.082	83.298	88.379	99.607
61	75.514	80.232	84.476	89.591	100.888
62	76.630	81.381	85.654	90.802	102.166
63	77.745	82.529	86.830	92.010	103.442
64	78.860	83.675	88.004	93.217	104.716
65	79.973	84.821	89.177	94.422	105.988
66	81.085	85.965	90.349	95.626	107.258
67	82.197	87.108	91.519	96.828	108.526
68	83.308	88.250	92.689	98.028	109.791
69	84.418	89.391	93.856	99.228	111.055

(Continued)

70	85.527	90.531	95.023	100.425	112.317
71	86.635	91.670	96.189	101.621	113.577
72	87.743	92.808	97.353	102.816	114.835
73	88.850	93.945	98.516	104.010	116.092
74	89.956	95.081	99.678	105.202	117.346
75	91.061	96.217	100.839	106.393	118.599
76	92.166	97.351	101.999	107.583	119.850
77	93.270	98.484	103.158	108.771	121.100
78	94.374	99.617	104.316	109.958	122.348
79	95.476	100.749	105.473	111.144	123.594
80	96.578	101.879	106.629	112.329	124.839
81	97.680	103.010	107.783	113.512	126.083
82	98.780	104.139	108.937	114.695	127.324
83	99.880	105.267	110.090	115.876	128.565
84	100.980	106.395	111.242	117.057	129.804
85	102.079	107.522	112.393	118.236	131.041
86	103.177	108.648	113.544	119.414	132.277
87	104.275	109.773	114.693	120.591	133.512
88	105.372	110.898	115.841	121.767	134.746
89	106.469	112.022	116.989	122.942	135.978
90	107.565	113.145	118.136	124.116	137.208
91	108.661	114.268	119.282	125.289	138.438
92	109.756	115.390	120.427	126.462	139.666
93	110.850	116.511	121.571	127.633	140.893
94	111.944	117.632	122.715	128.803	142.119
95	113.038	118.752	123.858	129.973	143.344
96	114.131	119.871	125.000	131.141	144.567
97	115.223	120.990	126.141	132.309	145.789
98	116.315	122.108	127.282	133.476	147.010
99	117.407	123.225	128.422	134.642	148.230
100	118.498	124.342	129.561	135.807	149.449

SOURCE: National Institute of Standards and Technology. *The NIST/SEMATECH Engineering Statistics Handbook.* A Web-based statistics handbook, developed as a joint partnership between the Statistical Engineering Division of NIST and the Statistical Methods Group of SEMATECH. (www.itl.nist.gov/div898/handbook/eda/section3/eda3674.htm). For the complete handbook, see www.itl.nist.gov/div898/handbook/.

References

Agresti, A. (1996). *An introduction to categorical data analysis.* New York: Wiley.

Agresti, A., & Finlay, B. (1997). *Statistical methods for the social sciences* (3rd ed.). Upper Saddle River, NJ: Prentice Hall.

Aiken, L. (2005, April). *Interaction in multiple regression.* Workshop presented at the annual meeting of the Western Psychological Association, Portland, OR.

Aiken, L. S., & West, S. G. (1991). *Multiple regression: Testing and interpreting interactions.* Newbury Park, CA: Sage.

Aiken, L. S., West, S. G., Sechrest, L., & Reno, R. R. (1990). Graduate training in statistics, methodology, and measurement in psychology: A survey of PhD programs in North America. *American Psychologist, 45,* 721–734.

Allen, M. J., & Yen, W. M. (1979). *Introduction to measurement theory.* Prospect Heights, IL: Waveland Press.

Allison, P. D. (1990). Change scores as dependent variables in regression analysis. In C. C. Clogg (Ed.), *Sociological methodology* (pp. 93–114). Washington, DC: American Sociological Association.

Allison, P. D. (1999a). Comparing logit and probit coefficients across groups. *Sociological Methods and Research, 28,* 186–208.

Allison, P. D. (1999b). *Multiple regression: A primer.* Thousand Oaks, CA: Pine Forge Press.

Allison, P. D. (2002). *Missing data.* Thousand Oaks, CA: Sage.

American Psychiatric Association. (2000). *Diagnostic and statistical manual of mental disorders.* (4th ed., Text Revision). Washington, DC: Author.

American Psychological Association. (2001). *Publication manual* (5th ed.). Washington, DC: Author.

Anastasi, A., & Urbana, S. (1997). *Psychological testing* (7th ed.). Upper Saddle River, NJ: Prentice-Hall.

Anderson, J. C., & Gerbing, D. W. (1988). Structural equation modeling in practice: A review and recommended two-step approach. *Psychological Bulletin, 103,* 411–423.

Anderson, T. W. (1957). Maximum likelihood estimates for a multivariate normal distribution when some observations are missing. *Journal of the American Statistical Association, 52,* 200–203.

Arbuckle, J. L. (1999). *Amos 4.0 user's guide.* Chicago: SmallWaters.

Arbuckle, J. L. (2004). Amos 5.0 [Computer software]. Chicago: SPSS.

Arbuckle, J. L., & Wothke, W. (1999). Amos 4.0 *user's guide.* Chicago: Smallwaters.

Barnett, V., & Lewis, T. (1978). *Outliers in statistical data.* New York: Wiley.

Belsley, D. A., Kuh, E., & Welsch, R. E. (1980). *Regression diagnostics: Identifying influential data and sources of collinearity.* New York: Wiley.

Bentler, P. M. (1990). Comparative fit indexes in structural models. *Psychological Bulletin, 107,* 238–246.

Bentler, P. M. (1992). On the fit of models to covariances and methodology to the Bulletin. *Psychological Bulletin, 112,* 400–404.

Bentler, P. M., & Chou, C. P. (1987). Practical issues in structural modeling. *Sociological Methods & Research, 16,* 78–117.

Bentler, P. M., & Weeks, D. G. (1980). Linear structural equations with latent variables. *Psychometrika, 45,* 289–308.

Benton, R. (1991). Statistical power considerations in ANOVA. In B. Thompson (Ed.), *Advances in educational research: Substantive findings, methodological developments* (Vol. 1, pp. 119–132). Greenwich, CT: JAI Press.

Berk, R. A. (2003). *Regression analysis: A constructive critique.* Thousand Oaks, CA: Sage.

Berry, W. D. (1993). *Understanding regression assumptions: Vol. 92. Quantitative applications in the social sciences.* Newbury Park, CA: Sage.

Bird, K. D., & Hadzi-Pavlovic, D. (1983). Simultaneous test procedures and the choice of a test statistic in MANOVA. *Psychological Bulletin, 93,* 167–178.

Blalock, H. M. (1971). Causal models involving unmeasured variables in stimulus-response situations. In H. M. Blalock (Ed.), *Causal models in the social sciences* (pp. 335–347). Chicago: Aldine.

Bochner, A. P., & Fitzpatrick, M. A. (1980). Multivariate analysis of variance: Techniques, models, and applications in communication research. In P. R. Monge & J. N. Cappella (Eds.), *Multivariate techniques in human communication research* (pp. 143–174). New York: Academic Press.

Bollen, K. A. (1989). *Structural equations with latent variables.* New York: Wiley.

Bollen, K. A. (1990). Overall fit in covariance structure models: Two types of sample size effects. *Psychological Bulletin, 107,* 256–259.

Bollen, K. A., & Long, J. S. (Eds.). (1993). *Testing structural equation models.* Newbury Park, CA: Sage.

Borenstein, M. (1994). The case for confidence intervals in controlled clinical trials. *Controlled Clinical Trials, 15,* 411–428.

Box, G. E. P., & Cox, D. R. (1964). An analysis of transformations. *Journal of the Royal Statistical Society, 26*(Series B), 211–243.

Box, G. E. P., Hunter, W. P., & Hunter, J. S. (1978). *Statistics for experimenters.* New York: Wiley.

Box, J. F. (1978). *R. A. Fisher, the life of a scientist.* New York: Wiley.

Bray, J. H., & Maxwell, S. E. (1985). *Multivariate analysis of variance.* Beverly Hills, CA: Sage.

Bryant, F. B., & Yarnold, P. R. (1995). Principal components analysis and exploratory and confirmatory factor analysis. In L. G. Grimm & P. R. Yarnold (Eds.), *Reading and understanding multivariate statistics* (pp. 99–136). Washington, DC: American Psychological Association.

Byrne, B. M. (1994). *Structural equation modeling with EQS and EQS/Windows: Basic concepts, applications, and programming.* Thousand Oaks, CA: Sage.

Byrne, B. M. (1998). *Structural equation modeling with LISREL, PRELIS, and SIM-PLIS: Basic concepts, applications, and programming.* Hillsdale, NJ: Erlbaum.

Byrne, B. M. (2001). *Structural equation modeling with AMOS: Basic concepts, applications and programming.* Mahwah, NJ: Erlbaum.

Byrne, B. M., & Shavelson, R. J. (1987). Adolescent self-concept: Testing the assumption of equivalent structure across gender. *American Educational Research Association, 24,* 365–385.

Carmer, S. G., & Swanson, M. R. (1973). An evaluation of ten pairwise multiple comparison procedures by Monte Carlo methods. *Journal of the American Statistical Association, 68,* 66–74.

Carroll, J. B. (1953). An analytical solution for approximating simple structure in factor analysis. *Psychometrika, 18,* 23–38.

Cattell, R. B. (1966). The scree test for the number of factors. *Multivariate Behavioral Research, 1,* 245–276.

Chambers, W. V. (2000). Causation and corresponding correlations. *Journal of Mind and Behavior, 21,* 437–460.

Chen, F., Bollen, K. A., Paxton, P. M., Curran, P., & Kirby, J. (2001). Improper solutions in structural equation models. *Sociological Methods & Research, 29,* 468–508.

Chen, P. Y., & Popovich, P. M. (2002). *Correlation: Parametric and nonparametric measures.* Thousand Oaks, CA: Sage.

Cheung, G. W., & Rensvold, R. B. (1999). Testing factorial invariance across groups: A reconceptualization and proposed new method. *Journal of Management, 25,* 1–27.

Chin, W. W. (1998). Issues and opinion on structural equation modeling. *MIS Quarterly, 21,* 7–16.

Chin, W. W., Marcolin, B. L., & Newsted, P. R. (1996). A partial least squares latent variable modeling approach for measuring interaction effects: Results from a Monte Carlo simulation study and voice mail emotion/adoption study. In J. I. DeGross, S. Jarvenpaa, & A. Srinivasan (Eds.), *Proceedings of the Seventeenth International Conference on Information Systems* (pp. 21–41). Cleveland, OH.

Clark, R. E. (1993). *The course questionnaire.* Unpublished manuscript.

Cliff, N. (1983). Some cautions concerning the application of causal modeling methods. *Multivariate Behavioral Research, 18,* 81–105.

Cohen, B. H. (1996). *Explaining psychological statistics.* Pacific Grove, CA: Brooks/Cole.

Cohen, J. (1968). Multiple regression as a general data analytic system. *Psychological Bulletin, 70,* 426–443.

Cohen, J. (1969). *Statistical power analysis for the behavioral sciences.* New York: Academic Press.

Cohen, J. (1977). *Statistical power analysis for the behavioral sciences* (rev. ed.). New York: Academic Press.

Cohen, J. (1988). *Statistical power analysis for the behavioral sciences* (2nd ed.). Hillsdale, NJ: Erlbaum.

Cohen, J. (1994). The earth is round ($p < .05$). *American Psychologist, 49,* 997–1003.

Cohen, J., Cohen, P., West, S. G., & Aiken, L. (2003). *Applied multiple regression/correlation analysis for the behavioral sciences* (3rd ed.). Hillsdale, NJ: Erlbaum.

Cole, D. A., Maxwell, S. E., Avery, R., & Salas, E. (1994). How the power of MANOVA can both increase and decrease as a function of the intercorrelations among dependent variables. *Psychological Bulletin, 115,* 465–474.

Comrey, A. L., & Lee, H. B. (1992). *A first course in factor analysis* (2nd ed.). Hillsdale, NJ: Erlbaum.

Conger, A. J., & Jackson, D. N. (1972). Suppressor variables, prediction, and the interpretation of psychological relationships. *Educational and Psychological Measurement, 32,* 579–599.

Conway, J. M., & Huffcutt, A. I. (2004). A review and evaluation of exploratory factor analysis practices in organizational research. *Organizational Research Methods, 6,* 147–168.

Cook, T. D., & Campell, D. T. (1979). *Quasi-experimentation: Design and analysis issues for field settings.* Boston: Houghton Mifflin.

Cooley, W. W., & Lohnes, P. R. (1971). *Multivariate data analysis.* New York: Wiley.

Cooley, W. W., & Lohnes, P. R. (1976). *Evaluation research in education.* New York: Irvington.

Coopersmith, S. (1981). *Self-esteem inventories.* Palo Alto, CA: Consulting Psychologists Press.

Costa, P. T., Jr., & McCrae, R. R. (1992). *The NEO PI-R professional manual.* Odessa, FL: Psychological Assessment Resources.

Costner, H. L. (1969). Theory, deduction, and rules of correspondence. *American Journal of Sociology, 75,* 245–263.

Courville, T., & Thompson, B. (2001). Use of structure coefficients in published multiple regression articles: Beta is not enough. *Educational and Psychological Measurement, 61,* 229–248.

Cowles, M. (1989). *Statistics in psychology: An historical perspective.* Hillsdale, NJ: Erlbaum.

Cowles, M., & Davis, C. (1982). On the origins of the .05 level of statistical significance. *American Psychologist, 37,* 553–558.

Cox, D. R. (1972). Regression models and life-tables. *Journal of the Royal Statistical Society, Series B, 34,* 187–202.

Cox, D. R., & Snell, E. J. (1989). *Analysis of binary data* (2nd ed.). London: Chapman & Hall.

Cronbach, L. J. (1970). *Essentials of psychological testing* (3rd ed.). New York: Harper & Row.

Cronbach, L. J., & Furby, L. (1970). How should we measure change? Or should we? *Psychological Bulletin, 74,* 68–80.

D'Andrea, M., Daniels, J., & Heck, R. (1991). Evaluating the impact of multicultural counselor training. *Journal of Counseling and Development, 70,* 143–150.

Darlington, R. B. (1990). *Regression and linear models.* New York: McGraw-Hill.

DeMaris, A. (1992). *Logit modeling: Practical applications.* Thousand Oaks, CA: Sage.

Diekhoff, G. (1992). *Statistics for the social and behavioral sciences: Univariate, bivariate, multivariate.* Dubuque, IA: Wm. C. Brown.

Diggle, P., Heagerty, P., Liang, K. Y., & Zeger, S. (2002). *Analysis of longitudinal data* (2nd ed.). Oxford, UK: Oxford University Press.

Draper, N. R., Guttman, I., & Lapczak, L. (1979). Actual rejection levels in a certain stepwise test. *Communications in Statistics, A8,* 99–105.

Duarte Silva, A. P., & Stam, A. (1995). Discriminant analysis. In L. G. Grimm & P. R. Yarnold (Eds.), *Reading and understanding multivariate statistics* (pp. 277–318). Washington, DC: American Psychological Association.

Duncan, O. D. (1966). Path analysis: Sociological examples. *American Journal of Sociology, 72,* 219–316.

Duncan, T. E., Duncan, S. C., & Li, F. (1998). A comparison of model- and multiple imputation-based approaches to longitudinal analyses with partial missingness. *Structural Equation Modeling, 5,* 1–21.

Dunlap, W. P., & Landis, R. S. (1998). Interpretations of multiple regression borrowed from factor analysis and canonical correlation. *Journal of General Psychology, 125,* 397–407.

Edwards, A. L. (1957). *Techniques of attitude scale construction.* New York: Appleton-Century-Crofts.

Efron, B. (1975). The efficiency of logistic regression compared to normal discriminant analysis. *Journal of the American Statistical Association, 70,* 892–898.

Ellis, M. V. (1999). Repeated measures designs. *Counseling Psychologist, 27,* 552–578.

Enders, C. K. (2001a). The impact of nonnormality on full information maximum-likelihood estimation for structural equation models with missing data. *Psychological Methods, 6,* 352–370.

Enders, C. K. (2001b). A primer on maximum likelihood algorithms available for use with missing data. *Structural Equation Modeling, 8,* 128–141.

Estrella, A. (1998). A new measure of fit for equations with dichotomous dependent variables. *Journal of Business and Economic Statistics, 16,* 198–205.

Everitt, B. S. (1979). A Monte Carlo investigation of the robustness of Hotelling's one and two sample T2 tests. *Journal of the American Statistical Association, 74,* 48–51.

Everitt, B. S. (1984). *An introduction to latent variable models.* New York: Chapman & Hall.

Eysenck, H. J. (1952). The uses and abuses of factor analysis. *Applied Statistics, 1,* 45–49.

Fabrigar, L. R., Wegener, D. T., MacCallum, R. C., & Strahan, E. J. (1999). Evaluating the use of exploratory factor analysis in psychological research. *Psychological Methods, 4,* 272–299.

Fan, X., Thompson, B., & Wang, L. (1999). Effects of sample size, estimation method, and model specification on structural equation modeling fit indexes. *Structural Equation Modeling, 6,* 56–83.

Ferguson, G. A. (1954). The concept of parsimony in factor analysis. *Psychometrika, 19,* 281–290.

Ferguson, G. A., & Takane, Y. (1989). *Statistical analysis in psychology and education* (6th ed.). New York: McGraw-Hill.

Finkel, S. E. (1995). *Causal analysis with panel data.* Thousand Oaks, CA: Sage.

Fisher, R. A. (1925). *Statistical methods for research workers.* London: Oliver & Boyd.

Fornell, C. (1987). A second generation of multivariate analysis: Classification of methods and implications for marketing research. In M. J. Houston (Ed.), *Review of marketing* (pp. 407–450). Chicago: American Marketing Association.

Fox, J. (1991). *Regression diagnostics.* Newbury Park, CA: Sage.

Fox, J. (2000). *Multiple and generalized nonparametric regression.* Thousand Oaks, CA: Sage.

Freud, S. (1938). The interpretation of dreams. In A. A. Brill (Ed. & Trans.), *The basic writings of Sigmund Freud* (3rd ed., pp. 183–539). New York: Modern Library.

Gabriel, K. R. (1969). A comparison of some methods of simultaneous inference in manova. In P. R. Krishnaiah (Ed.), *Multivariate analysis-II* (pp. 67–86). New York: Academic Press.

Galton, F. A. (1886). Regression towards mediocrity in hereditary stature. *Journal of the Anthropological Institute, 15,* 246–263.

Galton, F. A. (1888). Co-relations and their measurement, chiefly from anthropometric data. *Proceedings of the Royal Society of London, 40,* 42–73.

Gamst, G. (1985). Survival analysis: A new way to predict subscription order retention. *Newspaper Research Journal, 6,* Spring, 1–12.

Gamst, G., Aguilar-Kitibutr, A., Herdina, A., Hibbs, S., Krishtal, E., Lee, R., Roberg, R., Ryan, E., Stephens, H., & Martenson, L. (2003). Effects of racial match on Asian American mental health consumer satisfaction. *Mental Health Services Research, 5,* 197–208.

Gamst, G., Dana, R. H., Der-Karabetian, A., Aragon, M., Arellano, L., Morrow, G., & Martenson, L. (2004). Cultural competency revised: The California Brief Multicultural Competence Scale. *Measurement and Evaluation in Counseling and Development, 37,* 163–183.

Gamst, G., Dana, R. H., Der-Karabetian, A., & Kramer, T. (2001). Asian American mental health clients: Effects of ethnic match and age on global assessment and visitation. *Journal of Mental Health Counseling, 23,* 57–71.

Garnett, J. C. M. (1919). On certain independent factors in mental measurement. *Proceedings of the Royal Society of London, Series A, 96,* 91–111.

Garson, G. D. (2000). *PA 765 Statnotes: An online textbook.* Retrieved May 4, 2005, from www2.chass.ncsu.edu/garson/pa765/structur.htm

George, D., & Mallery, P. (2003). *SPSS for Windows step by step: A simple guide and reference 11.0 update* (4th ed.). Boston: Allyn & Bacon.

Ghiselli, E. E., Campbell, J. P., & Zedeck, S. (1981). *Measurement theory for the behavioral sciences.* San Francisco: W. H. Freeman.

Glenn, N. D. (2004). *Cohort analysis* (2nd ed.). Thousand Oaks, CA: Sage.

Gold, M. S., & Bentler, P. M. (2000). Treatments of missing data: A Monte Carlo comparison of RBHDI, iterative stochastic regression imputation, and expectation-maximization. *Structural Equation Modeling, 7,* 319–355.

Gorsuch, R. L. (1983). *Factor analysis* (2nd ed.). Hillsdale, NJ: Erlbaum.

Gorsuch, R. L. (1990). Common factor analysis versus component analysis: Some well and little known facts. *Multivariate Behavioral Research, 25,* 33–39.

Gorsuch, R. L. (2003). Factor analysis. In J. A. Schinka & W. F. Velicer (Eds.), *Handbook of psychology: Vol. 2. Research methods in psychology* (pp. 143–164). Hoboken, NJ: Wiley.

Graham, J. W., Cumsille, P. E., & Elek-Fisk, E. (2003). Methods for handling missing data. In W. F. Velicer & J. A. Schinka (Eds.), *Handbook of psychology: Research methods in psychology* (Vol. 2, pp. 87–114). New York: Wiley.

Green, S. A. (1991). How many subjects does it take to do a multiple regression analysis? *Multivariate Behavioral Research, 26,* 499–510.

Green, S. B., Thompson, M. S., & Babyak, M. A. (1998). A Monte Carlo investigation of methods for controlling Type I errors with specification searches in structural equation modeling. *Multivariate Behavioral Research, 33,* 365–383.

Grimm, L. G., & Yarnold, P. R. (2000). Introduction to multivariate statistics. In L. G. Grimm & P. R. Yarnold (Eds.), *Reading and understanding more multivariate statistics* (pp. 3-21). Washington, DC: American Psychological Association.

Guilford, J. P. (1954). *Psychometric methods.* New York: McGraw-Hill.

Guilford, J. P., & Fruchter, B. (1978). *Fundamental statistics in psychology and education* (6th ed.). New York: McGraw-Hill.

Guyatt, G., Jaeschke, R., Heddle, N., Cook, D., Shannon, H., & Walter, S. (1995). Interpreting study results: Confidence intervals. *Canadian Medical Association Journal, 152,* 169–173.

Hair, J. F., Anderson, R. E., Tatham, R. L., & Black, W. C. (1998). *Multivariate data analysis* (5th ed.). Upper Saddle River, NJ: Prentice Hall.

Hakstian, A. R., Roed, J. C., & Lind, J. C. (1979). Two-sample T2 procedure and the assumption of homogeneous covariance matrices. *Psychological Bulletin, 56,* 1255–1263.

Hand, D. J., & Crowder, M. (1996). *Practical longitudinal data analysis.* New York: Chapman & Hall.

Hand, D. J., & Taylor, C. C. (1987). *Multivariate analysis of variance and repeated measures.* London: Chapman & Hall.

Hardy, M. A. (1993). *Regression with dummy variables.* Thousand Oaks, CA: Sage.

Harmon, H. H. (1960). *Modern factor analysis.* Chicago: University of Chicago Press.

Harmon, H. H. (1967). *Modern factor analysis* (2nd ed.). Chicago: University of Chicago Press.

Harris, R. J. (1993). Multivariate analysis of variance. In L. K. Edwards (Ed.), *Applied analysis of variance in behavioral science* (pp. 255–296). New York: Marcel Dekker.

Harris, R. J. (2001). *A primer of multivariate analysis* (3rd ed.). Mahwah, NJ: Erlbaum.

Hauser, R. M. (1972). Disaggregating a social-psychological model of educational attainment. *Social Science Research, 1,* 159–188.

Hayton, J. C., Allen, D. G., & Scarpello, V. (2004). Factor retention decisions in exploratory factor analysis: A tutorial on parallel analysis. *Organizational Research Methods, 7,* 191–205.

Hill, M. A. (1997). *SPSS missing value analysis 7.5.* Chicago, IL: SPSS.

Himmelfarb. S. (1975). What do you do when the control group doesn't fit into the factorial design? *Psychological Bulletin, 82,* 363–368.

Hofer, S. M., Horn, J. L., & Eber, H. W. (1997). A robust five-factor structure of the 16PF: Evidence from independent rotation and confirmatory factorial invariance procedures. *Personality and Individual Differences, 23,* 247–269.

Holcomb-McCoy, C. C. (2000). Multicultural counseling competencies: An exploratory factor analysis. *Journal of Multicultural Counseling and Development, 28,* 83–97.

Holloway, L. N., & Dunn, O. J. (1967). The robustness of Hotelling's T2. *Journal of the American Statistical Association, 62,* 124–136.

Horn, J. L., & McArdle, J. J. (1992). A practical and theoretical guide to measurement invariance in aging research. *Experimental Aging Research, 18,* 117–144.

Hosmer, D. W., Jr., & Lemeshow, S. (2000). *Applied logistic regression* (2nd ed.). New York: Wiley.

Hosmer, D. W., Jr., & Lemeshow, S. (2002). *Applied survival analysis: Regression modeling of time to event data, textbook and solutions manual.* New York: Wiley.

Hotelling, H. (1931). The generalization of Student's ratio. *Annals of Mathematical Statistics, 2,* 360–378.

Hox, J. J. (2000). Multilevel analyses of grouped and longitudinal data. In T. D. Little, K. U. Schnabel, & J. Baumert (Eds.), *Modeling longitudinal and multilevel data* (pp. 15–32). Mahwah, NJ: Erlbaum.

Hoyle, R. H. (Ed.). (1995). *Structural equation modeling: Concepts, issues, and applications.* Thousand Oaks, CA: Sage.

Hu, L., & Bentler, P. M. (1999a). Cutoff criteria for fit indexes in covariance structure analysis: Conventional criteria versus new alternatives. *Structural Equation Modeling, 6,* 1–55.

Hu, L., & Bentler, P. M. (1999b). Evaluating model fit. In R. H. Hoyle (Ed.), *Structural equation modeling: Concepts, issues, and applications* (pp. 76–99). Thousand Oaks, CA: Sage.

Huberty, C. J. (1984). Issues in the use and interpretation of discriminant analysis. *Psychological Bulletin, 95,* 156–171.

Huberty, C. J. (1989). Multivariate analysis versus multiple univariate analyses. *Psychological Bulletin, 105,* 302–308.

Huberty, C. J. (1994). *Applied discriminant analysis.* New York: Wiley.

Huberty, C. J., & Barton, R. M. (1989). An introduction to discriminant analysis. *Measurement and Evaluation in Counseling and Development, 22,* 158–168.

Huberty, C. J., & Morris, J. D. (1989). Multivariate analysis versus multiple univariate analyses. *Psychological Bulletin, 105,* 302–308.

Huberty, C. J., Wisenbaker, J. M., & Smith, J. C. (1987). Assessing predictive accuracy in discriminant analysis. *Multivariate Behavioral Research, 22,* 307–329.

Huck, S. W. (2004). *Reading statistics and research* (4th ed.). New York: Pearson Education.

Hummel, T. J., & Sligo, J. (1971). Empirical comparison of univariate and multivariate analysis of variance procedures. *Psychological Bulletin, 76,* 49–57.

Hutcheson, G., & Sofroniou, N. (1999). *The multivariate social scientist: Introductory statistics using generalized linear models.* Thousand Oaks, CA: Sage.

Jaccard, J., & Becker, R. A. (1990). *Statistics for the behavioral sciences* (2nd ed.). Belmont, CA: Wadsworth.

Jaccard, J., & Choi, K. W. (1996). *LISREL approaches to interaction effects in multiple regression.* Thousand Oaks, CA: Sage.

Jaccard, J., & Wan, C. K. (1995). Measurement error in the analysis of interaction effects between continuous predictors using multiple regression: Multiple indicator and structural equation approaches. *Psychological Bulletin, 117,* 348–357.

Jaccard, J., & Wan, C. K. (1996). *LISREL approaches to interaction effects in multiple regression.* Thousand Oaks, CA: Sage.

Joachimsthaler, E. A., & Stam, A. (1990). Mathematical programming approaches for the classification problem in two-group discriminant analysis. *Multivariate Behavioral Research, 25,* 427–454.

Johnson, R. A., & Wichern, D. W. (1998). *Applied multivariate statistical analysis* (4th ed.). Upper Saddle River, NJ: Prentice Hall.

Jöreskog, K. G. (1969). A general approach to confirmatory maximum likelihood factor analysis. *Psychometrika, 34,* 183–202.

Jöreskog, K. G. (1971). Simultaneous factor analysis in several populations. *Psychometrika, 36,* 409–426.

Jöreskog, K. G., & Sörbom, D. (1978). *LISREL IV users guide.* Chicago: National Educational Resources.

Jöreskog, K. G., & Sörbom, D. (1989). *LISREL 7: A guide to the program and applications* (2nd ed.). Chicago: Scientific Software.

Jöreskog, K. G., & Sörbom, D. (1996). *LISREL 8 user's reference guide.* Chicago: Scientific Software International.

Judd, C. M., McClelland, G. H., & Culhane, S. E. (1995). Data analysis: Continuing issues in the everyday analysis of psychological data. *Annual Review of Psychology, 46,* 433–465.

Kachigan, S. K. (1986). *Statistical analysis: An interdisciplinary introduction to univariate & multivariate methods.* New York: Radius Press.

Kahane, L. H. (2001). *Regression basics.* Thousand Oaks, CA: Sage.

Kaiser, H. F. (1958). The varimax criterion for analytic rotation in factor analysis. *Psychometrika, 23,* 187–200.

Kaiser, H. F. (1970). A second-generation Little Jiffy. *Psychometrika, 35,* 401–415.

Kaiser, H. F. (1974). An index of factorial simplicity. *Psychometrika, 39,* 31–36.

Kazelskis, R. (1978). A correction for loading bias in a principal components analysis. *Educational and Psychological Measurement, 38,* 253–257.

Kelloway, E. K. (1995). Structural equation modeling in perspective. *Journal of Organizational Behavior, 16,* 215–224.

Kelloway, E. K. (1998). *Using LISREL for structural equation modeling: A researcher's guide.* Thousand Oaks, CA: Sage.

Kelley, T. L. (1935). An unbiased correlation ratio measure. *Proceedings of the National Academy of Sciences, 21,* 554–559.

Kenny, D. A. (2003). *Measuring model fit.* Retrieved May 4, 2004, from http://davidakenny.net/cm/fit.htm

Kenny, D. A., Bolger, N., & Kashy, D. A. (2002). Traditional methods for estimating multilevel models. In D. S. Moskowitz & S. L. Hershberger (Eds.), *Modeling intra-individual variability with repeated measures data: Methods and applications* (pp. 1–24). Mahwah, NJ: Erlbaum.

Keppel, G. (1991). *Design and analysis: A researcher's handbook* (3rd ed.). Englewood Cliffs, NJ: Prentice Hall.

Keppel, G., Saufley, W. H., Jr., & Tokunaga, H. (1992). *Introduction to design and analysis: A student's handbook* (2nd ed.). New York: W. H. Freeman.

Keppel, G., & Wickens, T. D. (2004). *Design and analysis: A researcher's handbook* (4th ed.). Upper Saddle River, NJ: Pearson Prentice Hall.

Keppel, G., & Zedeck, S. (1989). *Data analysis for research designs: Analysis of variance and multiple regression/correlation approaches.* New York: W. H. Freeman.

Kessler, R. C., & Greenberg, D. F. (1981). *Linear panel analysis: Models of quantitative change.* New York: Academic Press.

Kinnear, P. R., & Gray, C. D. (2000). *SPSS made simple: Release 10.* Hove, East Sussex, UK: Psychology Press.

Kirk, R. E. (1995). *Experimental design: Procedures for the behavioral sciences* (3rd ed.). Pacific Grove, CA: Brooks/Cole.

Kirk, R. E. (1996). Practical significance: A concept whose time has come. *Educational and Psychological Measurement, 56,* 746–759.

Klecka, W. R. (1980). *Discriminant analysis.* Beverly Hills, CA: Sage.

Klem, L. (1995). Path analysis. In L. G. Grimm & P. R. Yarnold (Eds.), *Reading and understanding multivariate statistics* (pp. 65–98). Washington, DC: American Psychological Association.

Klem, L. (2000). Structural equation modeling. In L. G. Grimm & P. R. Yarnold (Eds.), *Reading and understanding more multivariate statistics* (pp. 227–260). Washington, DC: American Psychological Association.

Kline, P. (1994). *An easy guide to factor analysis.* New York: Routledge.

Kline, R. B. (1998). *Principles and practice of structural equation modeling* New York: Guilford Press.

Kline, R. B. (2004). *Beyond significance testing.* Washington, DC: American Psychological Association.

Kline, R. B. (2005). *Principles and practice of structural equation modeling* (2nd ed.). New York: Guilford Press.

Klockars, A. J., & Sax, G. (1986). *Multiple comparisons.* Beverly Hills, CA: Sage.

Knight, G. P., Virdin, L. M., Ocampo, K. A., & Roosa, M. (1994). An examination of the cross-ethnic equivalence of measures of negative life events and the mental health among Hispanic and Anglo American children. *American Journal of Community Psychology, 22,* 767–783.

Konishi, S., & Honda, M. (1990). Comparison procedures for estimation of error rates in discriminant analysis under non-normal populations. *Journal of Statistical Computing and Simulation, 36,* 105–115.

Kromrey, J. D., & Foster-Johnson, L. (1998). Mean centering in moderated multiple regression: Much ado about nothing. *Educational and Psychological Measurement, 58,* 42–67.

Lachenbruch, P. A. (1975). *Discriminant analysis.* New York: Hafner Press.

LaFromboise, T. D., Coleman, H. L. K., & Hernandez, A. (1991). Development and factor structure of the Cross-Cultural Counseling Inventory-Revised. *Professional Psychology: Research and Practice, 22,* 380–388.

Lane, C. J., & Zelinski, E. M. (2003). Longitudinal hierarchical linear models of the Memory Functioning Questionnaire. *Psychology and Aging, 18,* 38–53.

Larsen, D. L., Attkisson, C. C., Hargreaves, W. A., & Nguyen, T. D. (1979). Assessment of client/patient satisfaction: Development of a general scale. *Evaluation and Program Planning, 2,* 197–207.

Lauter, J. (1978). Sample size requirements for the T2 test of MANOVA (tables for one-way classification). *Biometrical Journal, 20,* 389–406.

Lee, E. T., & Wang, J. W. (2003). *Statistical methods for survival data analysis* (3rd ed.). New York: Wiley.

Lehman, A. F. (1988). A quality of life interview for the chronically mentally ill. *Evaluation and Program Planning, 11,* 51–62.

Leidy, N. K. (1990). A structural model of stress, psychosocial resources, and symptomatic experience in chronic physical illness. *Nursing Research, 39,* 230–236.

Lievens, F., & Anseel, F. (2004). Confirmatory factor analysis and invariance of an organizational citizenship behaviour measure across samples in a Dutch-speaking context. *Journal of Occupational and Organizational Psychology, 77,* 299–306.

Likert, R. (1932). A technique for the measurement of attitudes. *Archives of Psychology, 140,* 5–53.

Likert, R., Roslow, S., & Murphy, G. (1934). A simple and reliable method of scoring the Thurstone attitude scales. *Journal of Social Psychology, 5,* 228–238.

Little, R. J., & Rubin, D. B. (2002). *Statistical analysis with missing data* (2nd ed.). Hoboken, NJ: Wiley.

Lix, L. M., & Keselman, H. J. (2004). Multivariate tests of means in independent groups designs: Effects of covariance heterogeneity and nonnormality. *Evaluation & the Health Professions, 27,* 45–69.

Loehlin, J. C. (1992). *Latent variable models: An introduction to factor, path, and structural analysis* (2nd ed.). Hillsdale, NJ: Erlbaum.

Loehlin, J. C. (2004). *Latent variable models: An introduction to factor, path, and structural analysis* (4th ed.). Mahwah, NJ: Erlbaum.

Long, J. S. (1983). *Confirmatory factor analysis.* Newbury Park, CA: Sage.

Lorenz, F. O. (1987). Teaching about influence in simple regression. *Teaching Sociology, 15,* 173–177.

Lovie, A. D. (1979). The analysis of variance in experimental psychology: 1934–1945. *British Journal of Mathematical and Statistical Psychology, 32,* 151–178.

Lutz, J. G., & Eckert, T. L. (1994). The relationship between canonical correlation analysis and multivariate multiple regression. *Educational & Psychological Measurement, 54,* 666–675.

Maassen, G. H., & Bakker, A. B. (2001). Suppressor variables in path models: Definitions and interpretations. *Sociological Methods and Research, 30,* 241–270.

MacCallum, R. C., Kim, C., Malarkey, W. B., & Kiecolt-Glaser, J. K. (1997). Studying multivariate change using multilevel models and latent curve models. *Multivariate Behavioral Research, 32,* 215–253.

MacCallum, R. C., Wegener, D. T., Uchino, B. N., & Fabrigar, L. R. (1993). The problem of equivalent models in applications of covariance structure analysis. *Psychological Bulletin, 114,* 185–199.

Magura, S., & Rosenblum, A. (2000). Modulating effect of alcohol use on cocaine use. *Addictive Behaviors 25,* 117–122.

Maruyama, G. M. (1998). *Basics of structural equation modeling.* Thousand Oaks, CA: Sage.

Mason, W. M., & Fineberg, S. E. (Eds.). (1985). *Cohort analysis in social research: Beyond the identification problem.* New York: Springer-Verlag.

Mason, W. M., & Wolfinger, N. H. (2001). Cohort analysis. In N. J. Smelser & P. B. Baltes (Eds.), *International encyclopedia of social and behavioral sciences* (pp. 2189–2194). Amsterdam: Elsevier Science.

Maxwell, S. E., & Delaney, H. D. (2000). *Designing experiments and analyzing data.* Mahwah, NJ: Erlbaum.

Mauchly, J. W. (1940). Significance test for sphericity of n-variate normal populations. *Mathematical Statistics, 11,* 37–53.

McClelland, G. H. (1993). Statistical difficulties of detecting interactions and moderator effects. *Psychological Bulletin, 114,* 376–390.

McDonald, R. A., Seifert, C. F., Lorenzet, S. J., Givens, S., & Jaccard, J. (2002). The effectiveness of methods for analyzing multivariate factorial data. *Organizational Research Methods, 5,* 255–274.

McDonald, R. P. (1996). Path analysis with composite variables. *Multivariate Behavioral Research, 31,* 239–270.

McLachlan, G. J. (1992). *Discriminant analysis and statistical pattern recognition.* New York: Wiley.

McLaughlin, M. L. (1980). Discriminant analysis. In P. Monge & J. Cappella (Eds.), *Multivariate techniques in human communication research* (pp. 175–204). New York: Academic Press.

Meehl, P. E., & Waller, N. G. (2002). The path analysis controversy: A new statistical approach to strong appraisal of verisimilitude. *Psychological Methods, 7,* 283–300.

Menard, S. (1991). *Longitudinal research.* Newbury Park, CA: Sage.

Menard, S. (2002). *Applied logistic regression analysis* (2nd ed.). Thousand Oaks, CA: Sage.

Meredith, W. (1993). Measurement invariance, factor analysis and factorial invariance. *Psychometrika, 58,* 525–543.

Meredith, W., & Horn, J. L. (2001). The role of factorial invariance in modeling growth and change. In L. M. Collins & A. G. Sayer (Eds.), *New methods for the analysis of change* (pp. 204–240). Washington, DC: American Psychological Association.

Mertler, C. A., & Vannatta, R. A. (2001). *Advanced and multivariate statistical methods: Practical application and interpretation.* Los Angeles: Pyrczak.

Mittag, K. C., & Thompson, B. (2000). A national survey of AERA members' perceptions of statistical significance tests and other statistical issues. *Educational Researcher, 29,* 14–20.

Morgan, G. A., Griego, O. V., & Gloeckner, G. W. (2001). *SPSS for Windows: An introduction to use and interpretation in research.* Mahwah, NJ: Erlbaum.

Mosteller, F., & Tukey, J. W. (1977). *Data analysis and regression.* Reading, MA: Addison-Wesley.

Mudholkar, G. S., & Subbaiah, P. (1980). MANOVA multiple comparisons associated with finite intersection tests. In P. R. Krishnaiah (Ed.), *Multivariate analysis V* (pp. 467–482). Amsterdam: North-Holland.

Mueller, R. O. (1997). Structural equation modeling: Back to basics. *Structural Equation Modeling, 4,* 353–369.

Muliak, S. (1972). *The foundations of factor analysis.* New York: McGraw-Hill.

Mulaik, S. A., James, L. R., Van Alstine, J., Bennett, N., Lind, S., & Stilwell, C. D. (1989). Evaluation of goodness-of-fit indices for structural equation models. *Psychological Bulletin, 105,* 430–445.

Murphy, G., & Likert, R. (1937). *Public opinion and the individual.* New York: Harper.

Myers, R. (1990). *Classical and modern regression with applications* (2nd ed.). Boston: Duxbury Press.

Neuhaus, J. O., & Wrigley, C. (1954). The quartimax method: An analytical approach to orthogonal simple structure. *British Journal of Statistical Psychology, 7,* 81–91.

Nicol, A. A. M., & Pexman, P. M. (2003). *Displaying our findings: A practical guide for creating figures, posters, and presentations.* Washington, DC: American Psychological Association.

Norusis, M. J. (1990). *SPSS advanced statistics user's guide.* Chicago: SPSS.

Nunnally, J. (1978). *Psychometric theory* (2nd ed.). New York: McGraw-Hill.

O'Brien, R. G., & Kaiser, M. K. (1985). MANOVA method for analyzing repeated measures designs: An extensive primer. *Psychological Bulletin, 97,* 316–333.

O'Connell, A. A., & McCoach, D. B. (2004). Applications of hierarchical linear models for evaluations of health interventions: Demystifying the methods and interpretations of multilevel models. *Evaluation & the Health Professions, 27,* 119–151.

Olejnik, S., & Algina, J. (2000). Measures of effect size for comparative studies: Applications, interpretations, and limitations. *Contemporary Educational Psychology, 25,* 241–286.

Olson, C. L. (1974). Comparative robustness of six tests in multivariate analysis of variance. *Journal of the American Statistical Association, 69,* 894–908.

Olson, C. L. (1976). On choosing a test statistic in MANOVA. *Psychological Bulletin, 83,* 579–586.

Olson, C. L. (1979). Practical considerations in choosing a MANOVA test statistic: A rejoinder to Stevens. *Psychological Bulletin, 86,* 1350–1352.

Pagano, R. R. (1986). *Understanding statistics in the behavioral sciences* (2nd ed.). New York: West.

Page, M. C., Braver, S. L., & MacKinnon, D. P. (2003). *Levine's guide to SPSS for analysis of variance* (2nd ed.). Mahwah, NJ: Erlbaum.

Pampel, F. C. (2000). *Logistic regression: A primer.* Thousand Oaks, CA: Sage.

Panel on Discriminant Analysis, Classification and Clustering. (1989). Discriminant analysis and clustering. *Statistical Science, 4,* 34–69.

Park, C., & Dudycha, A. (1974). A cross-validation approach to sample size determination. *Journal of the American Statistical Association, 69,* 214–218.

Pearson, K. (1901). On lines and planes of closest fit to systems of points in space. *Philosophical Magazine, 2,* 559–572.

Pedhazur, E. J. (1982). *Multiple regression in behavioral research: Explanation and prediction* (2nd ed.). New York: Holt, Rinehart and Winston.

Pedhazur, E. J. (1997). *Multiple regression in behavioral research: Explanation and prediction* (3rd ed.). Orlando, FL: Harcourt Brace.

Pedhazur, E. J., & Schmelkin, L. P. (1991). *Measurement, design, and analysis: An integrated approach* (student ed.). Hillsdale, NJ: Erlbaum.

Pett, M. A., Lackey, N. R., & Sullivan, J. L. (2003). *Making sense of factor analysis: The use of factor analysis for instrument development in health care research.* Thousand Oaks, CA: Sage.

Ponterotto, J. G., & Alexander, C. M. (1996). Assessing the multicultural competence of counselors and clinicians. In L. A. Suzuki, P. J. Meller, & J. G. Ponterotto (Eds.), *Handbook of multicultural assessment: Clinical, psychological, and educational applications* (2nd ed., pp. 651–672). San Francisco: Jossey-Bass.

Press, S. J., & Wilson, S. (1978). Choosing between logistic regression and discriminant analysis. *Journal of the American Statistical Association, 73,* 699–705.

Purvis, K., & Higgins, J. (1998). *Pilot to evaluate alternative quality of life instruments.* Research and Performance Outcome Development Unit, California State Department of Mental Health.

Ragsdale, C. T., & Stam, A. (1992). Introducing discriminant analysis to the business statistics curriculum. *Decision Sciences, 23,* 724–745.

Raudenbush, S. W. (2001). Toward a coherent framework for comparing trajectories of individual change. In L. M. Collins & A. G. Sayer (Eds.), *New methods for the analysis of change* (pp. 35–64). Washington, DC: American Psychological Association.

Raudenbush, S. W., & Bryk, A. S. (2002). *Hierarchical linear models: Applications and data analysis methods* (2nd ed.). Thousand Oaks, CA: Sage.

Raykov, T., & Marcoulides, G. A. (2000). *A first course in structural equation modeling.* Mahwah, NJ: Erlbaum.

Reilly, T. (1995). A necessary and sufficient condition for identification of confirmatory factor analysis models of complexity one. *Sociological Methods & Research, 23,* 421–441.

Rice, J. C. (1994). Logistic regression: An introduction. In B. Thompson (Ed.), *Advances in social science methodology* (Vol. 3, pp. 191–245). Greenwich, CT: JAI Press.

Rigdon, E. E. (1995). A necessary and sufficient identification rule for structural models estimated in practice. *Multivariate Behavioral Research, 30,* 359–383.

Rodgers, W. L. (1982). Estimable functions of age, period, and cohort effects. *American Sociological Review, 47,* 774–787.

Rosenthal, R. (1991). *Meta-analytic procedures for social research* (rev. ed.). Newbury Park, CA: Sage.

Rosenthal, R. (1994). Parametric measures of effect size. In H. Cooper & L. V. Hedges (Eds.), *The handbook of research synthesis* (pp. 231–244). New York: Russell Sage.

Rosenthal, R., & Rosnow, R. L. (1991). *Essentials of behavioral research: Methods and data analysis* (2nd ed.). New York: McGraw-Hill.

Roth, P. L. (1994). Missing data: A conceptual review from applied psychologists. *Personnel Psychology, 47,* 537–560.

Rousseeuw, P. J., & van Zomeren, B. C. (1990). Unmasking multivariate outliers and leverage points. *Journal of the American Statistical Association, 85,* 633–639.

Rubin, D. B. (1996). Multiple imputation after 18+ years. *Journal of the American Statistical Association, 91,* 473–489.

Rummel, R. J. (1970). *Applied factor analysis.* Evanston, IL: Northwestern University Press.

Runyon, R. P., Coleman, K. A., & Pittenger, D. J. (2000). *Fundamentals of behavioral statistics* (9th ed.). Boston: McGraw-Hill.

Salsburg. D. B. (2001). *The lady tasting tea.* New York: W. H. Freeman.

Schafer, J. L. (1997). *The analysis of incomplete multivariate data.* New York: Chapman & Hall (CRC).

Schafer, J. L., & Graham, J. W. (2002). Missing data: Our view of the state of the art. *Psychological Methods, 7,* 147–177.

Schafer, W. D. (1991a). Reporting hierarchical regression results. *Measurement and Evaluation in Counseling and Development, 24,* 98–100.

Schafer, W. D. (1991b). Reporting nonhierarchical regression results. *Measurement and Evaluation in Counseling and Development, 24,* 146–149.

Schmidt, F. (1996). Statistical significance testing and cumulative knowledge in psychology: Implications for the training of researchers. *Psychological Methods, 1,* 115–129.

Schroeder, L. D., Sjoquist, D. L., & Stephan, P. E. (1986). *Understanding regression analysis: An introductory guide.* Newbury Park, CA: Sage.

Schumacker, R. E., & Lomax, R. G. (1996). *A beginner's guide to structural equation modeling.* Mahwah, NJ: Erlbaum.

Seaman, M. A., Levin, J. R., & Serlin, R. C. (1991). New developments in pairwise multiple comparisons: Some powerful and practicable procedures. *Psychological Bulletin, 110,* 577–586.

Shaffer, J. P., & Gillo, M. W. (1974). A multivariate extension of the correlation ratio. *Educational and Psychological Measurement, 34,* 521–524.

Sherry, A., & Henson, R. K. (2005). Conducting and interpreting canonical correlation analysis in personality research: A user-friendly primer. *Journal of Personality Assessment, 84*(1), 37–48.

Singer, J. D., & Willett, J. B. (1991). Modeling the days of our lives: Using survival analysis when designing and analyzing longitudinal studies of duration and the timing of events. *Psychological Bulletin, 110,* 268–290.

Singer, J. D., & Willett, J. B. (2003). *Applied longitudinal data analysis: Modeling change and event occurrence.* Oxford, UK: Oxford University Press.

Snyder, P., & Lawson, S. (1993). Evaluating results using corrected and uncorrected effect size estimates. *Journal of Experimental Education, 61,* 334–349.

Spearman, C. (1904). "General intelligence," objectively determined and measured. *American Journal of Psychology, 15,* 201–293.

Spector, P. E. (1976). Choosing response categories for summated rating scales. *Journal of Applied Psychology, 61,* 374–375.

Spector, P. E. (1977). What to do with significant multivariate effects in multivariate analyses of variance. *Journal of Applied Psychology, 62,* 158–163.

Spicer, J. (2005). *Making sense of multivariate data analysis.* Thousand Oaks, CA: Sage.

Steenkamp, J-B. E. M., & Baumgartner, H. (1998). Assessing measurement invariance in cross-national consumer research. *Journal of Consumer Research, 25,* 78–90.

Steiger, J. H. (1990). Structural model evaluation and modification: An interval estimation approach. *Multivariate Behavioral Research, 25,* 173–180.

Steiger, J. H. (1998). A note on multisample extensions of the RMSEA fit index. *Structural Equation Modeling, 5,* 411–419.

Stevens, J. P. (1972). Four methods of analyzing between variation for the *k* group MANOVA problem. *Multivariate Behavioral Research, 7,* 499–522.

Stevens, J. P. (1980). Power of the multivariate analysis of variance tests. *Psychological Bulletin, 88,* 728–737.

Stevens, J. P. (1984). Outliers and influential data points in regression analysis. *Psychological Bulletin, 95,* 334–344.

Stevens, J. P. (2002). *Applied multivariate statistics for the social sciences* (4th ed.). Hillsdale, NJ: Erlbaum.

Stevens, S. S. (1946). On the theory of scales of measurement. *Science, 103,* 677–680.

Stevens, S. S. (1951). Mathematics, measurement, and psychophysics. In S. S. Stevens (Ed.), *Handbook of experimental psychology* (pp. 1–49). New York: Wiley.

Stigler, S. M. (1989). Francis Galton's account of the invention of correlation. *Statistical Science, 4,* 73–86.

Stigler, S. M. (1999). *Statistics on the table: The history of statistical concepts and methods.* Cambridge, MA: Harvard University Press.

Tabachnick, B. G., & Fidell, L. S. (2001a). *Computer-assisted research design and analysis.* Boston: Allyn & Bacon.

Tabachnick, B. G., & Fidell, L. S. (2001b). *Using multivariate statistics* (4th ed.). Needham Heights, MA: Allyn & Bacon.

Tellegen, A. (1982). *Brief manual for the Multidimensional Personality Questionnaire.* Unpublished, Department of Psychology, University of Minnesota, Minneapolis.

Thomas, D. (1992). Interpreting discriminant functions: A data analytic approach. *Multivariate Behavioral Research, 27,* 335–362.

Thompson, B. (1984). *Canonical correlation analysis: Uses and interpretation.* Beverly Hills, CA: Sage.

Thompson, B. (1989). Why won't stepwise methods die? *Measurement and Evaluation in Counseling and Development, 21,* 146–148.

Thompson, B. (1991). A primer on the logic and use of canonical correlation analysis. *Measurement and Evaluation in Counseling and Development, 24,* 80–95.

Thompson, B. (1994). Guidelines for authors. *Educational and Psychological Measurement, 54,* 837–847.

Thompson, B. (1996). AERA editorial policies regarding statistical significance testing: Three suggested reforms. *Educational Researcher, 25*(2), 26–30.

Thompson, B. (2000). Ten commandments of structural equation modeling. In L. G. Grimm & P. R. Yarnold (Eds.), *Reading and understanding more multivariate statistics* (pp. 261–283). Washington, DC: American Psychological Association.

Thompson, B. (2002). "Statistical," "practical," and "clinical": How many kinds of significance do counselors need to consider? *Journal of Counseling and Development, 80,* 64–71.

Thompson, B. (2004). *Exploratory and confirmatory factor analysis: Understanding concepts and applications.* Washington, DC: American Psychological Association.

Thompson, B., & Borrello, G. M. (1985). The importance of structure coefficients in regression research. *Educational and Psychological Measurement, 45,* 203–209.

Thurstone, L. L. (1927). A law of comparative judgment. *Psychological Review, 34,* 273–286.

Thurstone, L. L. (1928). Attitudes can be measured. *American Journal of Sociology, 33,* 529–554.

Thurstone, L. L. (1929). Theory of attitude measurement. *Psychological Review, 36,* 222–241.

Thurstone, L. L. (1947). *Multiple factor analysis.* Chicago: University of Chicago Press.

Thurstone, L. L., & Chave, E. J. (1929). *The measurement of attitude.* Chicago: University of Chicago Press.

Tolman, E. C. (1932). *Purposive behavior in animals and men.* New York: Appleton-Century-Crofts.

Toothaker, L. E. (1991). *Multiple comparisons for researchers.* Newbury Park, CA: Sage.

Tremblay, P. F., & Gardner, R. C. (1996). On the growth of structural equation modeling in psychological journals. *Structural Equation Modeling, 3,* 93–104.

Trusty, J., Thompson, B., & Petrocelli, J. V. (2004). Practical guide for reporting effect size in quantitative research in the Journal of Counseling & Development. *Journal of Counseling & Development, 82,* 107–110.

Tucker, L. R. (1955). The objective definition of simple structure in linear factor analysis. *Psychometrika, 20,* 209–225.

Tukey, J. W. (1977). *Exploratory data analysis.* Reading, MA: Addison-Wesley.

Turner, J. R. (2001). *Introduction to analysis of variance: Design, analysis, and interpretation.* Thousand Oaks, CA: Sage.

Vacha-Haase, T. (2001). Statistical significance should not be considered one of life's guarantees: Effect sizes are needed. *Educational and Psychological Measurement, 61,* 219–244.

Vandenberg, R. J., & Lance, C. E. (2000). A review and synthesis of the measurement invariance literature: Suggestions, practices, and recommendations for organizational research. *Organizational Research Methods, 3,* 4–69.

Weinfurt, K. P. (1995). Multivariate analysis of variance. In L. G. Grimm & P. R. Yarnold (Eds.), *Reading and understanding multivariate statistics* (pp. 245–276). Washington, DC: American Psychological Association.

Weinfurt, K. P. (2000). Repeated measures analysis: ANOVA, MANOVA, and HLM. In L. G. Grimm & P. R. Yarnold (Eds.), *Reading and understanding more multivariate statistics* (pp. 317–361). Washington, DC: American Psychological Association.

Weiss, D. J. (1972). Canonical correlation analysis in counseling psychology research. *Journal of Counseling Psychology, 19,* 241–252.

West, S. G., Enders, C. K., & Taylor, A. B. (2005, April). *Modern approaches to missing data: An introduction.* Workshop presented at the annual meeting of the Western Psychological Association, Portland, OR.

Wilkinson, L. (1975). Response variable hypotheses in the multivariate analysis of variance. *Psychological Bulletin, 82,* 408–412.

Wilkinson, L., & Task Force on Statistical Inference. (1999). Statistical methods in psychology journals: Guidelines and explanations. *American Psychologist, 54,* 594–604.

Wood, J. M., Tataryn, D. J., & Gorsuch, R. L. (1996). Effects of under- and over-extraction on principal axis factor analysis with varimax rotation. *Psychological Methods, 1,* 254–365.

Wright, R. E. (1995). Logistic regression. In L. G. Grimm & P. R. Yarnold (Eds.), *Reading and understanding multivariate statistics* (pp. 217–244). Washington, DC: American Psychological Association.

Wright, R. E. (2000). Survival analysis. In L. G. Grimm & P. R. Yarnold (Eds.), *Reading and understanding more multivariate statistics* (pp. 363–407). Washington, DC: American Psychological Association.

Wright, S. (1921). Correlation and causation. *Journal of Agricultural Research, 20,* 557–585.

Zwick, R. (1986). Rank and normal scores alternatives to Hotelling's T2. *Multivariate Behavioral Research, 21,* 169–186.

Zwick, W. R., & Velicer, W. F. (1986). Comparison of five rules for determining the number of components to retain. *Psychological Bulletin, 99,* 432–442.

Name Index

Subject Index

About the Authors

Glenn Gamst is Professor and Chair of the Psychology Department at the University of La Verne, where he teaches the doctoral advanced statistics sequence. He received his PhD from the University of Arkansas in experimental psychology. His research interests include the effects of multicultural variables such as client-therapist ethnic match, client acculturation status and ethnic identity, and therapist cultural competence on clinical outcomes. Additional research interests focus on conversation memory and discourse processing. He is an avid St. Louis Rams fan and classic Chevy aficionado.

A. J. Guarino is on the faculty at Auburn University, teaching the statistics sequence of ANOVA, multiple regression, MANOVA, and structural equation modeling (SEM) in the College of Education. In addition, he provides research consultation to faculty and students and supervises graduate students on their theses. His career includes over 25 years as a college instructor in psychology and education, and he has published over 40 research articles in a variety of fields, including education, psychology, nutrition, veterinary medicine, assessment, and statistics. He is a frequent presenter at the annual meetings of the American Psychological Association (APA), American Educational Research Association (AERA), American Psychological Society (APS), and the Western Psychological Association (WPA) and was recently elected president of the Louisiana Education Research Association (LERA). He is an evaluator for the Alabama State Office of School Readiness, investigating the effectiveness of the Head Start Projects, and is the statistical consultant to the Louisiana State University (LSU) Lab School, researching teachers' intent to remain in the teaching profession and assessing elementary and middle school student achievement as part of the No Child Left Behind (NCLB) Act. He also conducts workshops on structural equation modeling and confirmatory factor analysis. He received his bachelor's degree from the University of California, Berkeley. He earned a doctorate in statistics and research methodologies from the University of Southern California through the Department of Educational Psychology.

Lawrence S. Meyers is Professor of psychology at Sacramento State University. He teaches undergraduate and graduate courses in research design, data analysis, data interpretation, testing and measurement, and history and systems of psychology. He was coauthor of a textbook on research methods in the 1970s and has over three dozen publications; some of his relatively recent work has been in areas such as measurement and testing and positive psychology. He has also offered expert consulting in test validation, evaluation, and development; employment promotion and selection procedures; adverse impact analysis; and organizational and consumer survey design and analysis. He received his doctorate from Adelphi University and worked on a National Science Foundation Postdoctoral Fellowship at the University of Texas, Austin, and Purdue University.